THE MENTAL REPRESENTATION OF GRAMMATICAL RELATIONS

MIT Press Series on Cognitive Theory and Mental Representation
Joan Bresnan, Lila Gleitman, Samuel Jay Keyser, editors

THE MENTAL REPRESENTATION OF GRAMMATICAL RELATIONS

edited by
Joan Bresnan

The MIT Press
Cambridge, Massachusetts
London, England

This book was set in VIP Times Roman by Village Typographers, Inc., and printed and bound by The Murray Printing Company in the United States of America.

Library of Congress Cataloging in Publication Data

Main entry under title:

The Mental representation of grammatical relations.

  (MIT Press series on cognitive theory and mental representation)
  Bibliography: p.
  Includes index.
  1. Relational grammar—Addresses, essays, lectures.
2. Psycholinguistics—Addresses, essays, lectures.
I. Bresnan, Joan. II. Series.
P158.6.M46 1982 415 82–10071
ISBN 0–262–02158–7

To my parents, Wanda and Robert Bresnan

Contents

Contents

Part II
SYNTACTIC REPRESENTATION

Contents

Part III
COGNITIVE PROCESSING OF GRAMMATICAL REPRESENTATIONS

List of Contributors

Avery D. Andrews
Australian National University
Canberra, Australia

Joan Bresnan
Massachusetts Institute of
Technology
Cambridge, Massachusetts

Marilyn Ford
Massachusetts Institute of
Technology
Cambridge, Massachusetts

Jane Grimshaw
Brandeis University
Waltham, Massachusetts

Ronald M. Kaplan
Xerox Corporation Palo Alto
Research Center
Palo Alto, California

Lori S. Levin
Massachusetts Institute of
Technology
Cambridge, Massachusetts

K. P. Mohanan
Massachusetts Institute of
Technology
Cambridge, Massachusetts

Carol Neidle
Massachusetts Institute of
Technology
Cambridge, Massachusetts

Steven Pinker
Massachusetts Institute of
Technology
Cambridge, Massachusetts

Series Foreword

The major focus of this series is on theories of mental representation of natural language. The editors hope to provide a forum for—and thereby to encourage—the exciting collaborative work now taking place among linguists, computer scientists, philosophers, and psycholinguists leading toward new cognitive theories of mental representation.

We will publish original works of book and monograph length as well as unified collections of original articles that emerge from psycholinguistics. Special attention will be given to studies focusing on the formal aspects of mental representation.

Joan Bresnan
Lila Gleitman
Samuel Jay Keyser

Acknowledgments

The preparation of this volume, more than most, involved sustained teamwork. Special thanks are due to Douglas Pulleyblank, K. P. Mohanan, and Tara Mohanan for producing the detailed and conceptually informed index, and to Anne Mark for editing the entire volume and gallantly compiling the complete bibliography under difficult conditions. Thanks also to the members of The MIT Press who coped gracefully with innumerable production delays beyond their control.

Introduction: Grammars
as Mental Representations
of Language

Joan Bresnan
and
Ronald M. Kaplan

1. The Problem of the Psychological Reality of Grammars

A longstanding hope of research in theoretical linguistics has been that linguistic characterizations of formal grammar would shed light on the speaker's mental representation of language. One of the best-known expressions of this hope is Chomsky's *competence hypothesis:* "... a reasonable model of language use will incorporate, as a basic component, the generative grammar that expresses the speaker–hearer's knowledge of the language . . ." (Chomsky 1965:9). Despite many similar expressions of hope by linguists, and despite intensive efforts by psycholinguists, it remains true that generative–transformational grammars have not yet been successfully incorporated in psychologically realistic models of language use (Fodor, Bever, and Garrett 1974).

In discussing grammars as mental representations, it is essential to understand that the terms *grammar* and *theory* are both used on two entirely different levels of description. On the lower level of description, we speak of the grammar of a particular language such as Navajo. At this level, a grammar is a set of rules within a formal system. The grammar generates the language that it is a grammar of and, on analogy with the technical usage in other formal systems, the grammar is sometimes called a "theory" of the language that it generates. On the higher level of description, we speak of a theory of grammars. This is a set of primitives, axioms, and rules of inference (often unformalized) that characterizes the class of possible grammars of particular languages. A theory of grammar is sometimes referred to as a *Universal Grammar*.

These dual concepts of *grammar* and *theory* play very different roles in discussions of the mental representation of language. To learn to speak Navajo, one must acquire specific, if tacit, knowledge of the sentence patterns and pronunciation of Navajo. A grammar of Navajo, in that it provides specific rules for the construction of Navajo sentences, represents the kind of knowledge of that language that one must have to speak it. It is such grammars, grammars on the lower level, that we assume will represent the stored knowledge in competence-based models of linguistic performance. Grammar on the higher level, the Universal Grammar that is a theory of grammars, is not necessarily represented in such models in the same way. For example, principles of Universal Grammar might characterize aspects of the structure of the language-using device.

In response to the fact that generative–transformational grammars (on the lower level) have not been successfully incorporated in realistic models of language acquisition, comprehension, or production, many psycholinguists have come to the view that it is a mistake to adopt Chomsky's competence hypothesis; there need not be *any* transparent mapping between linguistically motivated formal grammars and psychological models of language use (for example, the language user may employ agrammatical heuristic strategies as knowledge representations (Fodor, Bever, and Garrett 1974)). If this is so, the knowledge representations actually used in language acquisition, production, and comprehension will not satisfy the postulates of Universal Grammar, which makes quite specific claims about the form, organization, and interpretation of rules of (lower-level) grammars. But then what mental structures is Universal Grammar a theory of?

In response, Chomsky has taken the view that it is a mistake to regard "psychological reality" as anything other than whatever linguistic theory is about: "Challenged to show that the constructions postulated in that theory have 'psychological reality,' we can do no more than repeat the evidence and the proposed explanations that involve these constructions" (Chomsky 1980b:191). Comparing the linguist to an astronomer studying thermonuclear reactions within the sun, Chomsky argues, "[I]n essence . . . the question of psychological reality is no more and no less sensible in principle than the question of the physical reality of the physicist's theoretical constructions" (Chomsky 1980b:192). However, neither Chomsky's response nor the response of those who have abandoned the competence hypothesis is satisfactory.

Consider first the view that rejects the competence hypothesis. In rejecting the hypothesis, proponents of this view do not also reject the notion that some form of stored linguistic knowledge is employed in all forms of language behavior. For example, it is generally acknowledged that models of linguistic comprehension must include a set of previously learned phonological and syntactic patterns for the language (English, Chinese, or Navajo) being comprehended. Similarly, models of linguistic production require stored information about the syntactic and phonological structure of the language being spoken, in order to convert the input (the speaker's message) into the form of speech. Likewise, models of language acquisition assume that the learner constructs and stores linguistic knowledge structures, forming an "internal grammar" on the basis of the primary data in the linguistic environment and a set of built-in constraints on the induction process. Each state of the learning process can be represented by a distinct internal grammar; but the sequence of these internal grammars must converge, in the final state of the learning process, on a "target" grammar which represents mature knowledge of linguistic structure. Finally, the formal grammars of linguistics are themselves abstract models of mature knowledge of language, as reflected in linguistic judgments and the other adult verbal behavior studied by linguists.

If it is uncontroversial that stored knowledge structures underlie all forms of verbal behavior,[1] the question arises of how these different components of linguistic knowledge are related. To reject the competence hypothesis is to adopt the theoretical alternative that a different body of knowledge of one's language is required for every type of verbal behavior. While this state of affairs is certainly a logical possibility, it is the weakest hypothesis that one could entertain, since it postulates multiple stores of linguistic knowledge that have no necessary connection. In contrast, the competence hypothesis postulates an isomorphic relationship between the different knowledge components and is thus the strongest and simplest hypothesis that one could adopt. On methodological grounds, it should be given priority over weaker alternatives: it enables us to unify our theories of the mental representation of language, to construct our processing models on the basis of a theoretical understanding of the structure of the knowledge domain, and to bring mutually constraining sources of evidence to bear on studies of process and of structure.

Granting that the competence hypothesis is desirable in principle, though, is it tenable in fact? In particular, if we do maintain the competence hypothesis, how can we then explain the conflict between psycholinguistic studies and linguistic theories of the mental representation of language? This is the scientific challenge posed by work on the "psychological reality" of grammars, as presented by Fodor, Bever, and Garrett 1974, Levelt 1974, and others. In response to this challenge, Bresnan 1978 pointed out that these psycholinguistic studies presupposed a transformational characterization of linguistic knowledge which could simply be wrong, a possibility that had also been suggested in the ATN-based work of Wanner, Kaplan, and others (Wanner and Maratsos 1978, Kaplan 1972). Wanner's and Kaplan's studies showed that a psycholinguistic model of syntactic processing based on a competence grammar can be computationally implemented and used to generate detailed and experimentally testable predictions. Bresnan argued that a more radical decomposition of competence grammars into an expanded lexical and contracted syntactic component promises to have far greater explanatory power than the current versions of transformational grammar, permitting a unification of linguistic and psycholinguistic research. Subsequent collaborative research by Bresnan, Kaplan, Ford, Grimshaw, Halvorsen, Pinker, and others has begun to bear this out, as the studies in this volume demonstrate. This work shows that the competence hypothesis is indeed tenable.

Consider next Chomsky's view, that psychological reality is whatever linguistic theory is about. Recalling the quotation cited earlier, we see that Chomsky construes the problem of psychological reality as an *ontological* problem: "[I]n essence . . . the question of psychological reality is no more and no less sensible in principle than the question of the physical reality of the physicist's theoretical constructions." In other words, he takes the question to be whether the rules and other constructs of linguistic theory "have reality," whether they describe real mental entities and processes. While Chomsky's answer to this question is surely a reasonable one, this is the wrong *question*. The cognitive psychologists, computer scientists, and linguists who have questioned the psychological reality of grammars have not doubted that a speaker's knowledge of language is mentally represented in the form of stored knowledge structures of some kind. All theories of the mental representation of language presuppose this. What has been doubted is that these internal knowledge structures are adequately characterized by transformational grammars—or indeed, by any grammars that are motivated solely by intuitions about the well-formedness of sentences. The challenge to Chomsky's theory is not the philosophical question that he addresses (whether theoretical constructs correspond to real mental entities and processes), but the scientific question (whether these theoretical constructs can unify the results of linguistic and psycholinguistic research on mental representation and processing). To the latter question, Chomsky's response is plainly inadequate: "Challenged to show that the constructions postulated in that theory have 'psychological reality,' we can do no more than repeat the evidence and the proposed explanations that involve these constructions" (Chomsky 1980b:191).

On Chomsky's view, then, a grammar is psychologically real if it contributes to the explanation of linguistic judgments and the other verbal behavior studied by linguists, and nothing more need be said. This, however, is a much weaker conception of psychological reality than we would like. (The following examples are taken from *The American Heritage Dictionary* and particularly the appendix "Indo-European Roots.") For example, the English words *baritone* and *grieve* both derive from an Indo-European root *gwer-* 'heavy'. Historically, the word *baritone* came into English from Italian (ultimately from Greek), while *grieve* came into Middle English from Old French (ultimately from Latin). Latin and Greek, of course, emerged historically from distinct ancient dialects of the common Indo-European mother tongue. Now it is possible to construct a formal system of morphophonemic rules and abstract representations that deductively account for these historical relations. By such rules one can formally derive English words from their Indo-European roots. Thus, the labiovelar *gw* is the source of both the initial labial *b* in *baritone* and the initial velar *g* in *grieve*. The same relationship appears in *bar* and *gravid,* as well as many other examples. Would such a formal rule system be psychologically real? With Chomsky's conception of psychological reality, we could answer affirmatively. The rule system might well contribute in some ways to an explanation of English speakers' linguistic judgments of what are well-formed sentences of their language. It could even be argued that the rules and representations of the system do characterize the *competence* of an idealized speaker–hearer, abstracting away from "performance" limitations of memory or perhaps education.

Given the stronger conception of psychological reality that we would like to maintain, this conclusion is absurd. It is most implausible that the remote historical derivations of the English lexicon are part of contemporary English speakers' mental representations of their language. Although this illustration slightly exaggerates the practice of some linguists, it serves to make two important points. First, linguistically motivated descriptions of a language need not bear any resemblance to the speaker's internal description of the language. Therefore, one cannot justifiably claim "psychological reality" for a grammar (in any interesting sense) merely because the grammar has some linguistic motivation. Second, the concept of *competence* has often been abused; in the above argument, for example, it now appears to mean that a linguistic rule system need not play *any* role in *any* model of performance. But the true import of the competence hypothesis is exactly the opposite: it requires that we take responsibility not only for characterizing the abstract structure of the linguistic knowledge domain, but also for explaining how the formal properties of our proposed linguistic representations are related to the nature of the cognitive processes that derive and interpret them in actual language use and acquisition. Chomsky's current conception of psychological reality represents a retreat from this more ambitious, and scientifically far more interesting, goal.

One might think that abuses of the above kind could be ruled out by appealing to theoretical simplicity: perhaps the rules deriving English words from Indo-European roots would not fit in elegantly with the simplest grammar for English. But simplicity is itself a theory-bound notion; as Chomsky 1970 has argued, the choice of a simplicity metric is made on the same empirical grounds as the choice of a theory. Moreover, it is easy to imagine even highly elegant and deductively satisfying rule systems that lack psychological reality in the sense we would like. There is evidence, for example, that the standard mathematical axiomatization of arithmetic differs from the system of conceptual competence that children display in counting (Greeno, Riley, and Gelman to appear). Although the two rule systems may be extensionally equivalent, it appears that they are built up from different sets of basic concepts and procedures. If this is so, we would *not* want to say that the standard mathematical axiomatic system is "psychologically real"; for while it does describe the conceptual structure of the knowledge domain, it appears to differ in essential ways from our internalized characterization of that knowledge.

Another response to our example would be to deny that there is anything absurd about it. The rules and representations of a linguistic system characterize the competence of an *ideal* speaker-hearer, who interprets his or her knowledge fully and faithfully, is immune to distraction, has no memory limitations, does not make errors, etc. The on-line behavior of real native speakers, to which a formal linguistic system may have no discernible relation, is jointly determined by that system *and* these other performance factors, and the latter are the source of any processing discrepancy. For this reason, processing considerations can have no direct bearing on grammatical theory.

As Chomsky (1980 and elsewhere) has pointed out, idealization has been a crucial ingredient for progress in the so-called mature sciences. Science progresses by abstracting away from the flux of experience to reveal underlying and invariant relationships. Likewise, linguistics and cognitive science will not make scientific progress unless we identify and focus on crucial idealizations, such as the ideal native speaker. There is nevertheless something suspicious about this appeal to idealization. It is used mainly to restrict the kind of evidence that may be brought to bear on representational issues. Thus, it appears to be a way of insulating linguistic theory from the other cognitive sciences.

This is not the role that idealization should play in science. The lawful relations that are constructed around such concepts as ideal gases, frictionless planes, infinitesimal masses, or infinite distances become scientifically interesting only when it can be shown that the behavior of real gases, planes, and particles can be made to come arbitrarily close to the postulated ideal as extraneous sources of variation are identified and controlled. In other words, there is a scientific responsibility to show that the real *does* asymptotically approach the ideal under appropriate circumstances. If this responsibility is taken seriously, there are more, not fewer, ways in which processing results might bear on representational issues, contrary to what Chomsky's appeal to idealization suggests. In particular, we must discover ways of showing that the actual behavior of real native speakers converges on the ideal behavior predicted by our grammatical theory, as interfering performance factors are reduced. Developing methods of reducing such interferences is of course a very hard scientific problem, but analogous problems had to be solved in the other sciences as a precondition for their major advances. Only as we make progress toward this goal will we be justified in speaking of a grammar as a model of the ideal native speaker's knowledge.

In attributing psychological reality to a grammar, then, we require more than that it provide us with a description of the abstract structure of the linguistic knowledge domain; we require evidence that the grammar corresponds to the speaker's *internal* description of that domain. Since we cannot directly observe this "internal grammar," we must infer its properties indirectly from the evidence available to us (such as linguistic judgments, performance of verbal tasks in controlled experimental conditions, observation of the linguistic development of children, and the like). The data of linguistics are no more or less privileged for this inquiry than any other data. The formal representations of linguistic theory, however, when joined with the information-processing approach of computer science and with the experimental methods of psycholinguistics, provide us with powerful tools for investigating the nature of this internal grammar and the processes that construct and interpret it. The methods and results of these different approaches can mutually constrain the form of a competence-based model of linguistic performance. In what follows we suggest that constraints on knowledge representation derived from considerations in theoretical linguistics may serve to limit the class of compatible information-processing models and, likewise, that computational considerations may have direct implications for the form in which linguistic representations must be cast.

2. Theoretical Constraints on Knowledge Representation

Theoretical constraints on representations of knowledge affect the classes of computations that can construct or interpret those representations. Thus, the choice of grammars can limit the choice of process models. A grammar may prove to be unrealizable in explanatory models of language processing because of the basic representational assumptions that it embodies. To amplify this point, let us compare the representational assumptions of two very different theories of grammar: the transformational theory and the lexical–functional theory. We will focus on the representation of grammatical relations; these are the associations between the semantic predicate argument structures (or thematic role structures) of sentences and their surface constituent structures. The term *grammatical relations* is thus used here in a theory-neutral sense, to be distinguished from *grammatical functions* such as SUBJ(ect) and OBJ(ect).

Let us consider first a simple, concrete example illustrating the different representational assumptions of the two theories. The basic motivation for syntactic transformations during the early days of generative grammar was the systematic relationship exhibited by pairs of sentences like *Mary kissed John* and *John was kissed by Mary*. In the first (active) sentence, the noun phrase preceding the verb has the agent or "kisser" role; in the second (passive) sentence, it has the theme or "kissed" role. If there were no transformational rules that moved the noun phrase following the verb to the position in front of the verb (so it was argued), we would have to postulate two different lexical entries for *kiss* — one with an agent subject which appears in the active form, and one with a theme subject in the passive form. The postulation of syntactic transformations removes this redundancy and expresses the regularity that systematically relates active sentences to passive sentences.

Given the original assumptions of transformational grammar (which lacked any mechanisms for representing grammatical relations other than transformations of phrase structures), the above argument was certainly persuasive. At a time when the lexicon was considered to be simply a collection of idiosyncratic properties of morphemes, it seemed obvious that a single lexical entry is better than two. When a richer theory of lexical rules and representations becomes available, though, the argument loses its persuasiveness. Lexical entries can represent semantic predicate argument structures independently of phrase structure forms, and lexical rules can capture the redundant relationship between the two lexical entries for *kiss*. For the two sentences given, we need to know only that in one, the subject is the agent and the object is the patient, and in the other, the subject is the patient and the *by*-object is the agent. In the lexical–functional theory, we represent this information in the lexical entries for the active and passive verbs, as in (1) and (2). (In (2) we have designated the English *by*-object by the more general function name OBL(ique)$_{AG(ent)}$.)

(1)
kiss: kiss⟨ (SUBJ)   (OBJ) ⟩
             AGENT PATIENT

(2)
kissed: kiss⟨(OBL$_{AG}$)   (SUBJ) ⟩
               AGENT PATIENT

Note that both lexical entries (1) and (2) have the same lexical predicate argument structure: kiss⟨AGENT PATIENT⟩. They differ in the grammatical functions that express the agent and patient arguments. The grammatical functions SUBJ, OBJ, and OBL$_{AG}$ are universal, but their phrase structure realizations vary from language to language, just as the surface forms of particular languages vary. Thus, in English the SUBJ is realized as an NP preceding the verb; the OBJ is realized as an NP following the verb; and the OBL$_{AG}$ is realized as a prepositional phrase marked with *by*. Finally, in order to capture the systematic relationship between the two lexical entries, we may propose a lexical rule that changes SUBJ to an optional OBL$_{AG}$ and OBJ to SUBJ:

(3)
(SUBJ) $\rightarrow$ (OBL$_{AG}$) / ϕ
(OBJ) $\rightarrow$ (SUBJ)

By such a rule, the passive lexical form (2) can be derived from the active form (1). Chapter 1 of this volume gives a detailed analysis of passive constructions in these terms. In general, systematic relations between lexical forms can be expressed by means of lexical rules or principles for associating grammatical functions with predicate arguments.

With this example of the active–passive relation in mind, let us now consider the underlying representational assumptions that result in these particular analyses. Despite continually changing theoretical assertions, the basic representational assumptions of transformational grammar have remained surprisingly constant since at least the "standard theory" (Chomsky 1965). The first assumption is that there is a one-to-one correspondence between the semantic predicate argument structure of a sentence and a set of ("deep") grammatical functions, such as "(logical) subject," "(logical) object," etc. The second assumption is that these grammatical functions can be reduced to a set of canonical phrase structure configurations: for example, the "logical subject" becomes the NP immediately dominated by S in the deep phrase structure representation of the sentence, and the "logical object" becomes the NP immediately dominated by VP. These two assumptions permit semantic predicate argument structures to be represented by canonical, or deep, syntactic phrase structures. Because the surface forms of sentences are also represented as syntactic phrase structures, the mapping between semantic arguments and surface form (which constitutes the grammatical relations of a sentence) must be expressed through operations on phrase structures. This naturally gives rise to the third representational assumption, that there is a set of structure-dependent operations, or syntactic transformations, which map between the deep phrase structure (representing semantic predicate argument structure) and the surface phrase structure. Analogues of these assumptions underlie current versions of transformational theory. For example, in Chomsky's 1981 government and binding theory, the one-to-one correspondence between predicate argument structures (thematic structures) and deep phrase structures (D-structures) appears as the *Theta Criterion*. The mapping between D-structures and surface phrase structures is accomplished in two steps: first, syntactic transformations (restricted to the form "Move α") map D-structures onto S-structures (abstract surface structures which contain indexed empty categories); second, a component of "stylistic" transformations, deletion rules, and morphophonological rules maps S-structures onto surface forms.

Under these assumptions, the grammatical relations of the sentence *John was kissed by Mary* must be represented in a particular way. First, by the assumption that there is a one-to-one correspondence between semantic predicate argument structure and deep grammatical functions, the surface subject of the passive sentence must have the same deep function as the surface object of the active sentence *Mary kissed John*, for these two NPs have the same thematic role of patient. Second, by the assumption that such deep functions reduce to a canonical set of underlying phrase structure configurations, *John* must be represented in the same deep structure position in both the active and the passive sentence. Third, by the assumption that the mapping between thematic role structure and surface form is effected by syntactic transformations, *John* must be moved from its deep structure position to its surface structure position. Thus, these basic assumptions about the representation of grammatical relations require that one of the constructions in question be formed by the movement of an NP from an underlying phrase structure position (as the logical object, for instance) to a surface phrase structure position (as the surface subject).

In sum, the guiding representational idea of transformational theories of syntax is that semantic predicate argument structure must be characterized in the vocabulary of constituent structure representation and must, in fact, be directly reflected in the forms of phrase structures. This is the meaning of Chomsky's Theta Criterion. As we have seen, this immediately leads to a theory in which the grammatical relations of sentences are encoded by phrase-structural computations (such as the transformational derivation).

In contrast, the theory of lexical–functional grammar (LFG) maintains a very different set of representational assumptions. First, on this theory, there is *no* one-to-one correspondence between semantic predicate argument structure and grammatical functions; the "theta criterion" of transformational theories is rejected. Instead, a single predicate argument structure may have several alternative lexical assignments of grammatical functions, governed by universal principles of function–argument association (see chapters 2, 3, and 5, M. Rappaport 1980, M. Baker 1982). This is illustrated by the active and passive lexical forms of the verb *kiss* in (1) and (2). Second, on the lexical–functional theory, grammatical functions are *not* reducible to canonical phrase structure configurations; on the contrary, the phrase structure categories themselves appear reducible to functional primitives (Jackendoff 1977 and chapter 5 of this volume), and the relation between structural configurations and grammatical functions is clearly many-to-many, varying across language types and even within languages (chapters 5 and 8, Simpson and Bresnan 1982). Since this theory requires no "normalized" phrase structure representation to express predicate argument relations, the structural component of the grammar can be vastly simplified, the entire transformational derivation being replaced by a single level of phrase structure representing the surface form of a language, the *constituent structure* (c-structure) (see chapters 4 and 5 of this volume). Third, in the lexical–functional theory, the mapping between thematic role structure and surface form is *not* effected by syntactic transformations (or equivalent structural computations). Rather, it is effected by correlating the grammatical functions that are assigned to lexical predicate argument structures with the grammatical functions that are syntactically associated with c-structure forms; *functional structures* (f-structures) formally represent these correlations. (See figure 1 for a simple illustration.) F-structures represent grammatical relations in an invariant universal format which is independent of language-particular differences in surface form. The f-structures are semantically interpreted (Halvorsen 1982), while the c-structures are phonologically interpreted.

Thus, in the lexical–functional theory, unlike the transformational theory, phrase structure computations play only a very restricted and superficial role in the mapping from predicate argument structure to surface form; the greater part of this mapping is lexically encoded independently of phrase structure form by the assignment of universal grammatical functions to lexical predicate argument structures. The guiding idea of the LFG theory is that *only* lexical rules can alter these function–argument associations. Syntactic rules must therefore preserve function–argument correspondences. This is called *the principle of direct syntactic encoding* (chapters 1 and 4 of this volume). One consequence of this principle is that active and passive verbs, because

c-structure

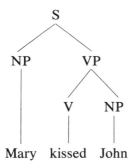

f-structure

$$\begin{bmatrix} \text{SUBJ} & \begin{bmatrix} \text{PRED} & \text{`MARY'} \end{bmatrix} \\ \text{TENSE} & \text{PAST} \\ \text{PRED} & \text{`KISS}\langle(\text{SUBJ})(\text{OBJ})\rangle\text{'} \\ \text{OBJ} & \begin{bmatrix} \text{PRED} & \text{`JOHN'} \end{bmatrix} \end{bmatrix}$$

Figure 1

they induce different grammatical relations, must have different lexical entries. Another consequence is that there can be no NP-movement transformations like the Passive transformation.

Because the various function–argument correspondences are already encoded in lexical entries, no phrase structure manipulations are needed to express the grammatical relations of sentences. Instead, active and passive lexical items are lexically inserted directly into surface constituent structures (c-structures). The syntactic instantiations of the grammatical functions can be read off from functional annotations to these surface structures, as described in chapter 4 of this volume. A phrase structure satisfying the active verb *kiss* must have both an object and a subject; a phrase structure satisfying the passivized form of the verb must have a subject, but no object. How the phrase structure subject is interpreted—whether as "the kisser" or "the one kissed"— depends on which lexical form of the verb is satisfied by the phrase structure tree.

This theory of grammatical representation explains why passivization in English appears to involve NP movement (and why other grammatical-relation-changing rules of English do so as well). The lexical rule of Passivization shown in (3) refers only to the grammatical functions SUBJ, OBJ, and OBL$_{AG}$, and not to the phrase structures in which these functions are syntactically expressed. In English, the SUBJ and OBJ functions are structurally expressed by different positions in the phrase structure: the subject NP appears before the verb and is immediately dominated by the S node, while the object NP appears after the verb and is immediately dominated by the VP node. It follows that when an active verb like *kiss* is lexically inserted into a structure, its patient argument, which has been lexically assigned the OBJ function (as in (1)), will be structurally expressed by a postverbal NP; and when a passivized verb like (*be*) *kissed* is lexically inserted into a structure, this same patient argument, which has now been lexically assigned the SUBJ function (as in (2)), will be structurally expressed by a preverbal NP. The lexical change in these function–argument correspondences will therefore induce a change in the phrase structure positions that express these arguments. Thus, the syntactic effects of Passivization in English will appear to involve the "movement" of an NP from one phrase structure position to another.

But this apparent NP movement is only an illusion, an effect arising from the way that these universal grammatical functions happen to be syntactically encoded in the surface forms of English. In other languages, the SUBJ, OBJ, and OBL$_{AG}$ functions are syntactically expressed through morphological case markings and not through distinctive positions in phrase structure. In such languages, predictably, the syntactic effects of Passivization involve, not the apparent movement of an NP, but an apparent change in morphological case (chapter 8). The syntactic mechanisms of LFG successfully generalize across radically different language types. For detailed analyses of varying language types within LFG, see Fassi Fehri 1981, Neidle 1982, Simpson in preparation, Simpson and Bresnan 1982, Klavans 1982, Bresnan, Kaplan, Peters, and Zaenen 1982, and Levin, Rappaport, and Zaenen to appear, in addition to the chapters in this volume. In contrast, syntactic transformations do not generalize across these language types and therefore fail to provide a universal mechanism for representing grammatical relations. Recognizing this, transformational theories, including the government and binding theory (Chomsky 1981), simply make the unsatisfying assumption that language types may differ in their fundamental syntactic mechanisms.

Other explanatory advantages of the LFG theory are discussed in Bresnan 1978 and elsewhere in this volume. They include explanations for the boundedness and structure-preserving properties of relation-changing rules and the fact that rule interactions follow from the basic organization of the grammar rather than from stipulated conditions on rules or representations.

3. Implications for Process Models

Let us now consider the implications of these representational theories for process models. To establish a clear basis of comparison, we will make explicit several definitions and assumptions. First, for the reasons given in section 1, we assume that there is a *competence grammar* that represents native speakers' tacit knowledge of their language. Next, suppose that we are given an information-processing model of language use that includes a processor and a component of stored linguistic knowledge K. As a minimum, we assume that K prescribes certain operations that the processor is to perform on linguistic representations, such as manipulating phrases or assigning grammatical functions. K may also include other kinds of information as well. For example, it could contain indexing information that helps the processor quickly determine which representational operations it should perform in a given situation, frequency information to aid in making heuristic decisions, and so forth. We call the subpart of K that prescribes representational operations the *representational basis* of the processing model. (The representational basis is the "internal grammar" of the model.) Since not all components of the internal grammar are necessarily utilized in every linguistic behavior, we do not require all information in the representational basis to be interpreted by every processing model. However, we do require that every rule of the representational basis be interpreted in a model of *some* behavior; thus, the internal grammar cannot contain completely otiose rules. We can now say that a model satisfies the *strong competence hypothesis* if and only if its representational basis is isomorphic to the competence grammar.

We are now in a position to see how the choice of grammatical theories can affect the choice of process models. Natural languages frequently require highly intricate feeding relations among rules. This is as true of phonological and morphological rules as it is of the rules that determine syntactic relations. Examples are easy to construct. Consider (4).

(4)

a.   Someone is giving too many gifts to politicians. (active)

b.   Someone is giving politicians too many gifts. (active–Dative)

c.   Politicians are being given too many gifts. (active–Dative–Passive)

d.   Too many gifts are being given to politicians. (active–Passive)

e. %Too many gifts are being given politicians. (active–Passive–Dative)

f.   There is someone giving too many gifts to politicians. (active–*There* Insertion)

g.   There is someone giving politicians too many gifts. (active–Dative–*There* Insertion or active–*There* Insertion–Dative)

h.   There are politicians being given too many gifts. (active–Dative–Passive–*There* Insertion)

i.   There are too many gifts being given to politicians. (active–Passive–*There* Insertion)

j. %There are too many gifts being given politicians. (active–Passive–Dative–*There* Insertion or active–Passive–*There* Insertion–Dative)

In these examples, the mappings between the surface subjects and objects and their semantic arguments depend upon the feeding relations of the rules. If the Dative rule feeds the Passive rule, for example, the subject will correspond to a different argument of the verb *give* than if it does not or if the reverse is the case, and if any rule feeds *There* Insertion, the subject will correspond to no argument of *give*. Similar intricacies appear elsewhere in English and in other languages.

In transformational theories of syntactic representation, as we have seen, the predicate argument structure to surface form mapping is performed by phrase structure computations. In such theories, grammatical relations which are encoded by intricate feeding relations must be represented by an ordered sequence of structural computations which is the transformational derivation.[2]

In the lexical–functional theory, in contrast, the predicate argument structure to surface form mapping is performed by lexical operations and surface function annotations. The feeding relations are expressed by the composition of operations that derive lexical entries. Thus, given the LFG representations, no special phrase structure computations are required to decode the grammatical relations which arise from these intricate feeding relations. As pointed out in Bresnan 1978, even the lexical computations are not required in generating sentences, since such lexical rules, as long as they have a finite output, can always be interpreted as *redundancy rules,* and in fact there is some independent motivation for doing so (Jackendoff 1975, C. L. Baker 1979). As such, the rules could be applied to enter new lexical forms into the mental lexicon, and the derived lexical forms could subsequently simply be retrieved for lexical insertion rather than being rederived (Miller 1978). The search space for any lexical form is bounded, since only a finite number of these lexical rules can be defined in the theory (chapter 10).

Consider now how we might model the process of decoding the grammatical relations of natural language sentences. Let us suppose that the model derives a representation of the predicate argument structure of a sentence from a representation of its surface form together with a store of linguistic knowledge structures represented by a grammar—the "internal grammar" of the model. Let us further suppose that the model satisfies the strong competence hypothesis. If the linguistic knowledge that is required in this process is represented by a transformational grammar, grammatical relations which are encoded by intricate feeding relations must be decoded by an ordered sequence of phrase structure computations (corresponding to the sequence of transformations in a transformational derivation of a sentence). The complexity of the decoding process is then a direct function of the length of the transformational derivation, a hypothesis known to psychologists as the *derivational theory of complexity.*[3] Despite important early work in its support (Miller 1962, Miller and McKean 1964), psychologists now appear to be universally agreed that this theory is false (Fodor, Bever, and Garrett 1974).

If the linguistic knowledge that is required in decoding grammatical relations is represented by an LFG, however, a range of possible models with very different complexity metrics can be obtained. The intricate syntactic feeding relations that can change grammatical relations will now be represented by sequences of *lexical,* not syntactic, rules. If these lexical rules are interpreted as redundancy rules, then all of the possible function–argument correspondences will already be expressed in the lexicon by finite sets of lexical forms. Thus, the lexical entry of a verb like *give* will include passive and dative lexical forms, which were derived by the lexical operations when the active form of the verb *give* was first entered in the lexicon. Because the outputs of these lexical redundancy rules already exist in the stored knowledge component of the model, the processor need not perform the operations specified by these rules as the model decodes the grammatical relations of a sentence. If we further assume that all lexical forms are accessed in parallel, then in this model the complexity of syntactic computations will not reflect the complexity of the lexically encoded feeding relations, but only the complexity of the analysis of the surface phrase structure tree. In this model, then, the relative complexity of active, active–Passive, active–Dative–Passive, and other sentences of (4) will depend only on the relative complexity of their surface structure analyses. Let us refer to this as *Model I.*

We can derive an interesting variant of Model I if we further suppose that semantic interpretation is interleaved with the syntactic analysis— an assumption compatible with LFG grammars because of their order-free composition property (see section 4 and Halvorsen 1982). Assume that the arguments of lexical forms can be accessed both by the *functions* they select (SUBJ or OBJ, etc.) and by their *semantic properties*. Then the process of extracting the grammatical relations of a sentence could be facilitated by semantic information that differentiated the arguments of a lexical form. For example, if we are analyzing a sentence like *The kite was admired by the girl,* and we know that *the kite* denotes an inanimate object, then we can use that semantic information to match *the kite* to the correct (theme) argument of *admire* (since kites can be admired but cannot admire). But if we are analyzing a sentence like *The woman was admired by the girl,* this semantic accessing of the lexical predicate argument structure would not facilitate the analysis (since women can both admire and be admired). In this model, *Model II,* the complexity of syntactic analysis could be reduced by asymmetries in the semantic structure of the predicates. Thus, Model II would produce "nonreversability" effects like those reported by Slobin 1966.

A *Model III* could be designed to accord with the derivational theory of complexity. Such a model can be obtained by using the lexical rules on-line to generate forms for lexical insertion. In other words, the processor performs the operations specified by the lexical rules as the model decodes the grammatical relations of a sentence. Thus, in order to analyze an example like (4c), *Politicians are being given too many gifts,* the Dative and Passive lexical rules would be applied to the active lexical form *give* and the outputs matched with the syntactic analysis. Thus, Model III would make the same complexity predictions as a transformational grammar-based processing model satisfying the strong competence hypothesis.

Could a transformational grammar-based model make the same complexity predictions as the LFG-based Models I and II? In LFG, the lexicon can store the finitely many lexical forms which are the outputs of the lexical redundancy rules. But in transformational grammars, there is no store of the infinitely many phrase structure trees which are the outputs of syntactic transformations. (This is clear if one notes that the passivized object NP itself can be of arbitrary depth, since NPs are recursive phrase structure categories.) Therefore, in order to decode the grammatical relations of sentences in a transformational grammar-based model that satisfies the strong competence hypothesis, the processor must perform the operations on phrase structure trees that the transformational rules specify. Because of the feeding relations among transformations, derivational complexity effects will result.

Is there any way to get around this problem? One way of doing so would be to use transformations, not to transform the infinitely many phrase structure trees that the phrase structure rules generate, but to transform the finitely many subcategorization frames of lexical entries. The Dative, Passive, and other structure-preserving transformations would be eliminated from the syntactic component, and corresponding lexical rules would be added to the lexical component. This approach substitutes for the transformational grammar knowledge structures an alternative representation of linguistic competence, one whose empirical divergences from the transformational theory were originally explored in Bresnan's 1976a, 1978 extended lexical grammars. Thus, to adopt this approach is to drop transformational grammars as the competence theory in favor of a precursor to the LFG theory.[4]

Another way of achieving the complexity predictions of an LFG-based processing model using a transformational grammar knowledge representation has been proposed by Berwick and Weinberg to appear. They argue that if one changes the underlying computational architecture of the transformational grammar-based model, the derivational theory of complexity no longer holds. What they actually show is that by using a finite amount of parallel processing, permitting parsing actions to be executed simultaneously, the analysis of a simple passive structure can take the same amount of time as the recognition of the corresponding active structure. In other words, the elementary operations of Passivization—the NP movement and the attachment of the passive verb to the analysis tree—can be accomplished simultaneously in unit time. To successfully mimic the results of the LFG-based model, however, they would have to demonstrate that the operations specified by *all* of the sequences of standard transformational operations—Dative, Dative–Passive, Dative–Passive–*There* Insertion, etc.—can be executed in unit time. But because these operations are in true feeding relationships, in which the necessary input of one operation is created by the output of another, it is simply not possible to execute them in parallel.

For every finite feeding sequence of transformations $t_1, ..., t_n$, it is possible to construct a new composite operation T_{1-n} that takes structures from the input form specified by t_1 directly to the output form specified by t_n. As long as there are only finitely many of the original transformations and as long as they are cyclic, bounded rules, this kind of recoding is possible. In this way the complexity effects of the LFG-based Models I and II may be simulated. But *the resulting model no longer satisfies the strong competence hypothesis;* that is, it is no longer true that the transformational grammar specifies the only operations that the processor can perform on linguistic representations. For example, the Dative transformation, which formerly played a role in the derivations of sentences like (4b,c,e,h,j), no longer exists in the model, and the same is true for the Passive transformation, along with all of the other cyclic transformations. Instead there is a new set of transformations, $T_1, T_2, ..., T_{1-2}, T_{2-1}, ...,$ etc., which have been motivated solely on the grounds of reducing computational complexity in this model. The composition procedure loses information in the sense that, given the output of composite rules, it is in general not possible to identify what the original rules were.

It might be suggested that the grammar of composite operations, which does reduce comprehension complexity, is in fact the better grammar, the one that more accurately models the native speaker's competence. It is difficult to support this conclusion, however, since this grammar trades simplicity of comprehension for complexity of linguistic descriptions: sentences exhibiting complex grammatical relations can no longer be classified into simple syntactic types solely on the basis of their derivations. For example, the passive morphology of English could formerly be correlated with a characteristic component of the mapping that encodes grammatical relations (namely, movement from object position to subject position). In the new grammar, this correlation disappears, and passive morphology is associated with an arbitrary set of NP movements. For these reasons, the new grammar could actually increase the complexity of language acquisition.

We see, then, that a transformational grammar-based process model cannot achieve the results of the LFG-based Models I and II without relinquishing the strong competence hypothesis. This is because the basic representational assumptions of transformational grammar require that complex grammatical relations be encoded by complex transformational derivations. Grammatical relations cannot be pre-stored in any component of the competence grammar, since it is a finite knowledge representation and the syntactic transformation is an operation on infinite sets of syntactic phrase structure representations. Nor can grammatical relations be computed in parallel, because of the feeding relationships that grammatical-relation-mapping rules enter into. Thus, the derivational theory of complexity is implicit in the fundamental representational assumptions of transformational grammar. To the extent that there is evidence against the derivational theory of complexity, this can be taken as evidence against the psychological reality of transformational grammars.

These conclusions do not mean that we must weaken the strong competence hypothesis or give up the goal of a unified theory of the mental representation of language. There are systems based on very different representational assumptions, such as LFG, which are realizable in more explanatory models of language processing, satisfying both the strong competence hypothesis and the substantive constraints of a theory of Universal Grammar.

4. Theoretical Constraints on Knowledge Processing

Just as theoretical constraints on knowledge representations affect the classes of computations that can construct and interpret those representations, so also the converse is true: theoretically motivated constraints on knowledge processing can affect the choice of knowledge representations. In this way, assumptions underlying models of how linguistic knowledge is processed can determine the choice of grammars.

In this section we discuss an abstract computational theory of syntactic processing which provides a conceptual framework for constructing models of various linguistic behaviors. Since all such behaviors (beyond the word-level ones) involve a mapping between strings and grammatical relations (the so-called syntactic mapping), we will proceed by postulating various properties that such a mapping might have. These assumptions imply certain conditions that the representational basis of a processing model must satisfy, and thus, if the strong competence hypothesis is to be maintained, they limit the formalisms that are suitable for linguistic theory.

The *syntactic mapping problem* is the problem of computing, for any human language, the grammatical relations of any string of words of that language.[5] This is an extremely difficult problem—first, because of the complex, many-to-many relation between the sentences of any natural language and their grammatical relations, and second, because of the radical variations in surface form across languages. Yet we know that the human brain instantiates a general solution to this problem, for despite the exotic variety of the world's languages, any normal child is capable of mastering any language. To solve the problem in a general way, we will therefore introduce theoretical assumptions about the nature of the computation which will serve to constrain the set of admissible solutions. These mapping constraints are motivated by general properties of the computational problem that linguistic knowledge processes must solve, by properties that are intuitively true of the human mind (the one entity that we know is capable of executing those processes), or by properties that we believe a satisfying scientific theory of these phenomena must possess. As is true of the basic assumptions in any scientific theory, the validity of these postulates is not susceptible to direct empirical evaluation. Rather, they stand at the center of a rich deductive system which has testable consequences at its empirical frontier. These central theoretical constraints will be accepted to the extent that the remote empirical predictions of models that embody them are confirmed. The last chapters of this volume describe actual processing models that do embody these theoretical assumptions and whose specific predictions are the subject of ongoing experimental investigations.

As general conditions on the syntactic mapping problem, each grammatical string must be paired with a phonological interpretation and the representation of its grammatical relations must be paired with a semantic interpretation; a string is syntactically unambiguous if and only if the mapping assigns it a unique representation of grammatical relations; and a string is ungrammatical if and only if the mapping assigns it no well-formed representation of grammatical relations. The essential properties of all generative grammars reflect certain theoretical constraints on the set of possible processes that compute solutions to the syntactic mapping problem. The constraints are *creativity* (the domain and range of the mapping are theoretically infinite), *finite capacity* (there is only a finite capacity for the knowledge representations used in the mapping), and, though not all generative grammars have turned out to satisfy this constraint, *reliability* (the mapping provides an effectively computable characteristic function for each natural language). Let us briefly review these constraints in turn.

Creativity

Prior to generative grammatical theory, most American structuralist linguists considered the aim of linguistics to be to establish procedures for discovering the grammatical structure of a given corpus of linguistic utterances as presented in fieldwork transcriptions. This would be equivalent to taking the domain and range of the syntactic mapping to be finite. However, Chomsky 1957, 1964, emphasizing the creativity of language use, argued that the most revealing way of looking at the problem is to take the domain and range of the mapping to be infinite sets of data and grammatical structures. While it is true that the entire body of language that any language user produces or comprehends in a lifetime is finite, the finiteness of the linguistic corpus appears to be an arbitrary restriction from the point of view of linguistic structure. The problem to be explained is how the language user can construct mental representations of grammatical relations for endless numbers of *novel* sentences. In principle—idealizing away from all limitations on lifespan, memory, and performance—the language user can identify the infinite set of grammatical sentences of the language. This is the justification for the *creativity constraint,* which requires the domain of the syntactic mapping to include all strings over the lexical vocabulary of the language, the range to include infinitely many representations as well, and the mapping to characterize the infinite set of grammatical sentences of the language; that is, a string is a member of the language if and only if the syntactic mapping assigns it a well-formed representation of grammatical relations.

Finite Capacity

The second constraint, *finite capacity,* was also proposed by Chomsky 1965. While the possible data and representations in the domain and range of the mapping are infinite, each language has only finite sets of elementary words and relations and there is only a finite capacity for representing and storing knowledge mentally. Given this constraint, the mapping must consist of the recursive composition of finitely many operations that can project a finite store of knowledge of a particular language onto infinite sets of data. Any mapping defined to be the recursive composition of finite elementary operations can be represented as a pair consisting of the specification in some formal language of the composition rules of those elementaries and a procedure which interprets those composition rules. For the syntactic processing case, the rules of composition are called *the grammar,* and we will use the notation m_G to name the procedure which applies to the rules. Thus, we can assume that the syntactic mapping decomposes into a grammar G of the particular language (which includes, for example, a set of syntactic patterns, or rules, of the language) and a procedure m_G which recursively matches the patterns, or applies the rules, of G to construct infinite sets of representations that relate surface strings of words to semantic predicate argument structures.

Reliability
The creativity constraint implies that our computation must characterize the infinitely many sentences of any natural language. The finite capacity constraint implies that this computation must decompose into a finite grammar G and a recursive procedure m_G for projecting G onto the infinitely many sentences of a language. These constraints are based upon the abilities of an ideal speaker of the language, abstracting away from the actual performance limitations of real language users. The same is true of the third constraint, reliability. Under the same idealization, a speaker of a language is regarded as a reliable arbiter of the sentences of his or her language. It is plausible to suppose that the ideal speaker can decide grammaticality by evaluating whether a candidate string is assigned (well-formed) grammatical relations or not. The syntactic mapping can thus be thought of as reliably computing whether or not any string is a well-formed sentence of a natural language. This motivates the *reliability constraint* that the syntactic mapping must provide an effectively computable characteristic function for each natural language.

The reliability constraint implies that the subset of data in the domain of the mapping for which there are well-formed grammatical relations is a recursive set (for the mapping must effectively compute whether an arbitrary string is grammatically well formed or not). Arguments for the recursiveness of natural language were first given by Putnam 1961:41, who concluded:

[T]he self-containedness of language [i.e., the classifiability of sentences out of context], the usability of nonsense sentences, and the relative universality of grammar intuitions within a dialect group, taken together support the model of the [human] classifier as a Turing machine who is processing each new sentence with which he is provided according to some mechanical program.

In other words, independently of knowledge of specific context, even independently of meaningfulness, speakers can reliably classify sentences as grammatical or ungrammatical, and they do so with a high degree of consistency across individuals within a dialect group. This convergent behavior suggests that classification of strings as grammatical or ungrammatical is based on an automatic procedure. Even though actual speakers may hesitate or conflict in their judgments of grammaticality, it is hypothesized that if extraneous and confusing sources of variation are controlled and if the speakers are given more time and memory, their judgments will approach the behavior of the ideal classifier in the limit.

Putnam also pointed out the consequent need to constrain transformational grammars if they were to be taken as characterizations of the mentally represented linguistic knowledge that is used to classify sentences. Although Chomsky 1965:208, note 37, assumed that constraints on transformational grammars such as the recoverability of deletions restricted the generative capacity of transformational grammars to recursive languages, Peters and Ritchie 1973 disproved this conjecture. Chomsky has increasingly downgraded the importance of constraints on generative capacity, relying on the idea of an evaluation metric to limit the class of available grammars in a learning model (Chomsky 1977b) or on an analogy between language acquisition and biological maturation (Chomsky 1980b). Despite this deemphasizing of grammatical processing in favor of grammatical acquisition, it nevertheless appears to be a precondition for any satisfying computational theory of syntactic processing that it account for the capability of the ideal speaker to classify natural language sentences. Peters and Ritchie 1973 pointed out that the actual generative transformational grammars that had been written for natural languages were in fact recursive, and subsequently both Peters 1973 and Wasow 1978 discovered properties that would constrain standard transformational grammars to generate only recursive sets.

Psychologically-based arguments for the recursiveness of natural language—including Putnam's—have been criticized on the grounds of English speakers' reactions to well-known "garden path" sentences like (5) and (6).

(5)
The canoe floated down the river sank.

(6)
The editor the authors the newspaper hired liked laughed.

For example, Matthews 1979:212 claims that the classification of examples (5) and (6) as grammatical or ungrammatical can be predictably affected by their position in a list with sentences such as (7) and (8).

(7)
The man (that was) thrown down the stairs died.

(8)
The editor (whom) the authors the newspaper hired liked laughed.

Sentences (5) and (6), he asserts, will typically be classified as ungrammatical if they precede sentences similar to (7) and (8), but grammatical if they follow them. He claims that this fact is inexplicable in terms of memory and other performance limitations on an idealized effective procedure for classifying sentences. Matthews 1979:217 argues that the same evidence also counts against the view that real native speakers instantiate an effective procedure when pairing sentences with their underlying structural descriptions during comprehension. Following Fodor, Bever, and Garrett 1974, he assumes that these phenomena are to be explained by postulating a collection of agrammatical heuristic strategies that directly pair certain simple types of sentences with their structural descriptions; but then, he concludes, there is no need to assume that the language user instantiates an effective procedure in comprehending or classifying the grammatical sentences of the language.

   In fact, however, we can draw precisely the opposite conclusion from such examples. Recent work on syntactic perception (reported in chapter 11 of this volume) has argued that the heuristic strategies approach fails to explain the ability of speakers to *recover* from garden paths. In general, if speakers are given sufficient time and resources (such as pencil and paper), they are able to recover all of the grammatical analyses provided by the competence grammar. The competence-based model of syntactic processing given in chapter 11 can explain both the ideal behavior (the recovery of all of the grammatical analyses) and the actual behavior (the experience of conscious garden paths) in terms of resource limitations on a recursive procedure for constructing grammatical relations.

In particular, note that examples (5) and (6) are locally ambiguous in their initial segments; with respect to the competence grammar of English, (5) permits a local initial analysis either as a simple sentence (*The canoe floated down the river*) or as a reduced relative (*The canoe* [*which was*] *floated* . . .), and (6) permits a local initial analysis either as a sequence of conjoined NPs (*The editor, the authors, the newspaper,* [*and*] . . .) or as a center-embedded relative clause like (8). General principles of local ambiguity resolution which are incorporated into an effective procedure for analyzing all and only the grammatical sentences of natural language can easily explain the initial false analyses assigned to these sentences (see chapter 11). The observed performance difficulties that many speakers have in recovering the true analyses without contextual clues can be explained by limitations on working memory and other computational resources during the grammatical analysis procedure.[6]

We see, then, that speakers' reactions to examples like (5)–(8) would actually follow from specific performance limitations on an idealized effective procedure for analyzing or classifying sentences. Although Matthews 1979 repeats the well-known arguments due to Fodor, Bever, and Garrett 1974 that a psycholinguistic theory of comprehension cannot plausibly incorporate a transformational grammar as the mental representation of linguistic knowledge, we have already observed that these arguments do not impugn the competence hypothesis, and hence they do not undermine the motivation for imposing the reliability constraint on the syntactic mapping.

A very different source of arguments against the recursiveness of natural language can be found in considerations of semantic interpretation. The most ingenious such argument is due to Hintikka 1974, 1979. Hintikka found that the acceptability of an infinite set of natural language sentences involving the quantifiers *any* and *ever* depends upon their semantic equivalence to other sentences. He argued that there is no effective procedure for determining the acceptability of these sentences, because (assuming that the semantic equivalence of natural language sentences is adequately modeled by logical equivalence) there is no effective procedure for testing the logical equivalence of even first order quantification sentences. This conclusion implies that the set of acceptable sentences is not only nonrecursive, but not even recursively enumerable, and hence well beyond the power of any generative grammar or Turing machine to specify.[7]

Such arguments for the nonrecursiveness of natural language enforce an important point. The automatic mental construction of grammatical relations must *not* require an evaluation of truth in the world, or logical truth conditions. The grammatical relations of the unacceptable sentences cited by Hintikka are in fact as easily perceived as those of other sentences. For example, his unacceptable *Louise ever kisses me* can be assigned perfectly well-formed grammatical relations, which specify that *Louise* and *me* are the subject and object arguments of a dyadic tensed active verb *kiss,* modified by a temporal quantifying adverb *ever.* This fact is unsurprising, since well-formed grammatical relations can be assigned even to nonsensical sentences like *Louise pilsely grisps a blawn neddle.* If such examples are judged "unacceptable" or "incorrect," this must then be attributed to some property of their nonsyntactic interpretation—whether it be the non-effectively-computable semantic property formulated by Hintikka or another, as yet undiscovered, property. If Hintikka's argument is correct, then semantics must diverge from syntax in a fundamental way, as he observes. The method of recursively characterizing the structure of natural language by means of a generative grammar may in fact be incapable of characterizing the semantics of quantification.

We can conclude that the reliability constraint on the syntactic mapping problem introduces no incoherence: "grammaticality" can be a recursive concept so long as it is not a function of truth in the world.

The above constraints—creativity, finite capacity, and reliability—are familiar from early work in generative grammar. Note that none of them is logically necessary for purposes of grammatical description. Their motivation comes rather from an abstract computational theory of syntactic processing. Exactly the same is true of two further constraints that we will now add: *order-free composition,* requiring that the grammatical relations that the mapping derives from an arbitrary segment of a sentence be directly included in the grammatical relations that the mapping derives from the entire sentence, independently of operations on prior or subsequent segments, and *universality,* requiring that the mapping incorporate a universal procedure for constructing representations of grammatical relations.

Order-free Composition

The constraint of *order-free composition* is motivated by the fact that complete representations of local grammatical relations are effortlessly, fluently, and reliably constructed for arbitrary segments of sentences. For example, the sentence fragments in (9) are immediately associated with grammatical representations which provide the same kinds of information as those of complete sentences.

(9)
a. There seemed to . . .
b. . . . not told that . . .
c. . . . too difficult to attempt to . . .
d. . . . struck him as crazy . . .
e. What did he . . .

In (9a) *there* is a grammatical but not a "logical" subject of *seemed* and is grammatically related to an infinitival complement of *seemed*. In (9b) the unexpressed subject of *told* can be the passivized indirect object of the verb, and *that* can be the complementizer of an unexpressed sentential complement corresponding to the "logical" object; other grammatical interpretations arise as well. The fragment in (9c) is syntactically ambiguous in the same way as the full sentence *It was too difficult to attempt to understand,* where the subject of *difficult* can be identified either with the clause *to attempt to understand (something)* or with an object within the clause (such as the object of *understand*). In (9d) *him* is the grammatical and the "logical" object of *struck,* and *crazy* is the predicative complement of the unexpressed subject of *struck.* The fragment in (9e) is interpreted as part of a question in which *what* is grammatically related to an unexpressed clause of which *he* is the grammatical subject. In each case, the grammatical relations for the fragment are complete in the sense that they express information that can be directly incorporated without change into the grammatical relations of some full sentence.

It is a fact, then, that given a sentence fragment one can always pick, entirely out of context, a *possible* reading from the finite set of grammatical alternatives, while *impossible* readings are excluded. It is no more possible to interpret the fragment . . . *easy to justify* . . . so that the subject of *easy* is also the subject of *justify* than it is possible to interpret *John's actions* as the subject of both *easy* and *justify* in the ungrammatical sentence **John's actions are easy to justify yours.* In contrast, the fragment . . . *unlikely to justify* . . . allows just this possibility, exactly as in the grammatical sentence *John's actions are un-likely to justify yours*. This fact suggests a very strong natural constraint on the syntactic mapping problem: the composition of operations as performed by m_G in the syntactic mapping must be order-free, in the sense that from an arbitrary sentence fragment, the mapping must de-rive—independently of operations on prior or subsequent segments—a set of possible grammatical relations, any of which can be directly included in the grammatical relations that the mapping derives from some sentence containing the segment. In other words, we have the following *order-free composition constraint* (referred to as *bounded context parsability* in Bresnan 1979a):

(10)
Order-free Composition Constraint
Under any valid interpretation of a string *xsy* consisting of adjacent segments *x,s,y,* the grammatical relations in $m_G(s)$ must be included in $m_G(xsy)$.

Note that this constraint allows for the fact that, in general, segments of a sentence—viewed as strings of words—have more possible gram-matical relations in isolation than within the sentence. Example (11) illustrates this point:

(11)
a. . . . her candy killed Mother See.
b. A man who hated her candy killed Mother See.

The string of words in (11a) can be interpreted so that *her candy* is the subject of *killed* and *Mother See* is the object of *killed;* but the subject – verb relation between *her candy* and *killed* is not included in the gram-matical relations of the whole sentence (11b). However, (11a) can also be interpreted as a sequence of two unrelated subsegments, *her candy* and *killed Mother See,* both of whose local grammatical relations are then directly contained in the grammatical relations of the entire sen-tence (11b). Note that in the limiting case, all of the words in a certain segment may be unrelated, as in (12a):

(12)
a. . . . to by for . . .
b. The one that he should be spoken to by for God's sake is his supervisor.

In this limiting case, the representation of grammatical relations of the segment can simply be identified with the lexical representations of the unrelated words. In sum, the order-free composition constraint asserts that sentential context may determine the *choice* of one of a set of locally computed grammatical relations for a segment, but the computation of grammatical relations for a segment may not involve the computation of the grammatical relations of the context. In other words, this postulate severely constrains the role of context-sensitive operations in the syntactic mapping.

The order-free composition property is equivalent to requiring that the mapping m_G be *monotonic*.[8] In other words, the mapping m_G from segments to sets of grammatical relations must preserve inclusion: under any valid interpretation, if one string of words (s_1) is contained in another (s_2), then the (compatible) grammatical relations of the one $(m_G(s_1))$ must be included in those of the other $(m_G(s_2))$. Intuitively, monotonic functions are incremental. Thus, the monotonicity constraint requires the operations of m_G to add increments of local information from the string to the global representation of information and not subtract from the global representation.

Universality

The fifth assumption that we shall adopt to constrain the syntactic mapping problem is the *universality* of the mapping procedure. It is plausible to assume that the procedure for grammatical interpretation, m_G, is the same for all natural language grammars G; that is, there is a universal m_U such that for any G, $m_G = m_U$. This constraint is motivated by the universality of the system for mentally representing natural language. We assume that the grammar G representing mature knowledge of a particular language is induced by a universal learning function. As in chapter 10 of this volume, we assume that data for the learning function are sets of pairs (s, r), where s is the perceived surface string of words and r is the mental representation of meaningful grammatical relations of s; the learning function maps these data onto hypothesized grammars. To test a hypothesized grammar G^*, there must be some universal effective procedure for constructing the mental representations r of lexical strings s given G^*; call it m_U. While it is conceivable that this universal procedure is different from the one that the language learner normally uses in comprehending language (m_G), the simplest, strongest, and most plausible assumption is that the procedures are the same. If so, the acquisition process must depend just as much upon the ability to comprehend language as the growing comprehension of language depends upon the acquisition process. The interaction of these two information-processing systems, linguistic acquisition and linguistic comprehension, motivates the universality constraint that $m_G = m_U$ for all G.

5. Implications for Syntactic Knowledge Representation

These processing constraints on the syntactic mapping problem—*creativity, finite capacity, reliability, order-free composition,* and *universality*—impose important limitations on the possible forms of syntactic knowledge representation, ruling out many possible systems of grammar—even apparently descriptively adequate ones—as systems of the mental representation of language. The creativity and finite capacity constraints require knowledge representations consisting of finite systems of explicit rules that are capable of characterizing infinite sets of natural language sentences. The reliabilty constraint further requires that these rule systems specify languages within the class of recursive sets, thereby ruling out unrestricted rewriting systems (Chomsky 1963), arbitrary augmented transition networks (Woods 1970), and arbitrary standard transformational grammars (Peters and Ritchie 1973) as representations of linguistic competence. The remaining two constraints impose still stronger conditions on possible grammatical theories.

Because of these constraints, the syntactic mapping decomposes into a finite grammar G which generates the language and a finite set of operations m_G which recursively apply the rules of G to extract the meaningful grammatical relations of the language. In general, it is the syntactic (as opposed to the lexical) rules of generative grammars which specify infinite sets of structures; hence, it is these rules that m_G must recursively apply in extracting the grammatical relations of a string. Recall that the order-free composition constraint states that under any valid interpretation of a string xsy consisting of adjacent segments x,s,y, the grammatical relations in $m_G(s)$ must be included in $m_G(xsy)$. Clearly, grammars whose syntactic rule components consist only of context-free phrase structure rules satisfy this requirement; in such grammars, a noun phrase is a noun phrase regardless of its external context. For these grammars, the order in which the segments are analyzed in the mapping from the data to the representation will therefore be irrelevant. However, non-context-free syntactic rules do not in general have this property; such rules may alter the analysis of the grammatical relations of a phrase according to the analysis of its context, and the resulting representation may therefore depend upon the order of application of these "context-sensitive" rules to different segments. Consequently, if m_G has the order-free composition property, the grammar G must be such that information about the surface-to-predicate argument structure associations given as the output of m_G is independent of the order in which any "context-sensitive" nonlexical grammatical rules are applied in the derivation of the representation from the data.[9] For reasons we have already seen (section 3), transformational grammars do not have this property. Transformational grammars explicitly operate by changing the grammatical relations for each region of the string. It is of course possible to modify transformational grammars so that local grammatical relations in the transformational derivation are always preserved in surface forms, and this formal effect is partially achieved by the Projection Principle (note 2). However, for reasons already discussed in note 2, transformational grammars with this provision still do not possess the order-free composition property: the order dependencies merely migrate to other components of the mapping onto surface forms. Augmented transition networks also lack the order-free composition property, for they enable register reassignments to modify previously determined grammatical relations.

The universality constraint implies that grammatical relations must be encoded in a form which allows a universal decoding process for all natural languages. One might think that one of the various well-known algorithms for context-free phrase structure parsing might provide just such a universal decoding process for natural languages, but recent work in theoretical linguistics forces us to reject this possibility. Bresnan, Kaplan, Peters, and Zaenen 1982 have shown that there is no context-free phrase structure grammar that can correctly characterize the parse trees of Dutch. The problem lies in Dutch cross-serial constructions, in which the verbs are discontinuous from the verb phrases that contain their arguments. The phenomenon of "discontinuous constituents"—that is, noncontiguous constituents defining single functional units—is pervasive in natural language, occurring in its most extreme forms in Australian aboriginal languages (Hale 1979, Pullum 1982). The results of Bresnan, Kaplan, Peters, and Zaenen 1982 show that context-free grammars cannot provide a *universal* means of representing these phenomena.

The processing constraints on the representation of syntactic knowledge may now seem too strong. On the one hand, G must have the order-free composition property of context-free phrase structure grammars, but on the other hand, G cannot be a context-free phrase structure grammar because context-free grammars cannot universally characterize the correct surface constituent structures of natural languages. Nevertheless, a solution to the syntactic mapping problem does exist. For any language L, where S is the set of strings over the lexical vocabulary of L, let us take G to be a *lexical–functional grammar* for L, and R (the representations of grammatical relations) to be the set of *functional structures* of the language as defined by G. Then a map $m:(S,G) \rightarrow R$ exists which satisfies all of the given constraints. This result is based on the mathematical characterization of lexical–functional grammars in chapter 4 of this volume. It provides the foundations of a computational theory for investigating the mental processes that construct representations of grammatical relations.

6. Conclusion: An Introduction

The work in this volume represents a new approach to the study of the mental representation of grammatical relations, based on the cognitive theory outlined above. The universality of the LFG theory of grammatical representation is supported by the chapters on grammatical relations in English, French, Russian, Icelandic, and Malayalam (a Dravidian language). The order-free composition property is illustrated by the f-structure solution algorithm given in chapter 4. Finally, the suitability of the LFG theory for modeling syntactic processes is shown in the last three chapters, which are psychological studies of competence-based models of language acquisition, comprehension, and production.

Notes

This material is based on work supported in part by the National Science Foundation under Grant No. BNS 80–14730 and in part by the Cognitive and Instructional Sciences Group, Xerox Corporation Palo Alto Research Center.

1. Some philosophers consider this controversial. Matthews 1982, for example, argues against this view as a form of "computational reductionism." However, he overlooks the fact that the attribution of an internal representation to a computational device may itself involve intensional descriptions. To take an example due to Brian Smith, the description of a machine as running LISP

cannot be reduced to purely extensional terms, because what counts as an instance of the LISP language depends on the functioning of the program and not on any particular electronic or mechanical configuration that realizes it.

2. This holds for true feeding relations—relations in which the output provided by each operation creates the necessary input for the next operation in a "cascade." If all syntactic rules could be applied simultaneously, there would be no true syntactic feeding relations. Chomsky 1981 has attempted to maintain a new representational principle, the *Projection Principle,* which—by making the transformational derivation "transparent" in S-structure—would in effect permit simultaneous application of syntactic transformations. However, there are grammatical phenomena which seem to force a structuralist theory into cascades, at one level of representation if not another. For even if the Projection Principle could be maintained for the mapping between D-structure and S-structure, the mapping from S-structure to surface form will itself fail to satisfy the principle of simultaneous applicability of rules; this problem is particularly obvious in the case of radically nonconfigurational languages (Klavans 1982, Simpson and Bresnan 1982), where the mapping from configurational to nonconfigurational form would involve operations of "scrambling," constituent breakup, and deletion, which produce different surface forms depending on their order of application. Thus, the Projection Principle does not eliminate feeding relations among transformational operations in the derivation of surface forms.

It is interesting to note that combining the Projection Principle with other assumptions in current transformational theory leads to empirically wrong results. First, as Chomsky notes, it is inconsistent with many analyses within his own framework, which remain to be reconciled with it. Second, that framework lacks any well-motivated analysis of a number of constructions that appear inconsistent with the Projection Principle, such as dative-alternation constructions and noncompositional idiom constructions (on the latter, see chapter 1 of this volume and Rothstein 1981). Third, recent work on "raising" constructions (chapter 5), derived nominals (M. Rappaport 1980), subcategorization (Grimshaw 1981), and small clauses (Williams 1982, Bresnan 1982, Neidle 1982) has brought forth evidence that optimal grammars for these phenomena will violate the Projection Principle.

3. There is a slight subtlety here. The statement that such a model will have computational complexity in proportion to the length of the derivation is a fact about that kind of model. The derivational theory of complexity involves another small step, the claim that complexity of the decoding process in the model will correspond to actual experienced cognitive load under some straightforward assumptions about psychological costs.

4. There are certain differences between a lexical–transformational theory and the LFG theory. For example, in the former the transformations will operate on structural categories—NP, V, PP, etc.—in the strict subcategorization frames, rather than on the functions SUBJ, OBJ, etc., of the LFG theory. This difference is in fact a disadvantage for the former theory; in recent work, Grimshaw 1981 has given linguistic evidence that lexical items subcategorize for *grammatical functions,* not for phrase structure categories.

5. Recall that the term *grammatical relations* is used here in a theory-neutral way to refer to the associations between the surface constituents and the semantic predicate argument structure of a sentence. Thus, the grammatical relations of a sentence can be represented by a (semantically interpreted) constituent structure tree in phrase structure grammars, by a pair of deep and surface phrase structure trees in transformational grammar, by a pair of initial and final relational strata in relational grammar, and by an f-structure in LFG.

6. Specifically, according to the perceptual theory of chapter 11, the true analysis of (5) would require morphosyntactic reanalysis of *floated* from a past tense verb to a passive participle after the grammatical analysis of the initial hypothesized sentence that contains it has been completed; the difficulty of recovering the correct analysis can therefore be explained by limitations on memory for morphosyntactic categorizations during the syntactic analysis of sentences. Similarly, the true analysis of (6) requires recognition of a center-embedded syntactic structure, which could impose an excessive burden on working memory during the grammatical analysis of a sentence, as Church 1980 argues.

7. See Hintikka 1979, 1980 for counterarguments to various objections to his argument that have been raised in the literature, such as Chomsky's 1980b proposal that a constraint on "Logical Form" accounts for Hintikka's generalization in an effectively checkable way.

8. Recall that a function $f:X \rightarrow Y$ is called *monotonic* if X and Y are ordered sets and $X_1 < X_2$ implies that $f(X_1) \leq f(X_2)$.

9. This "order-free" restriction does not refer to the absence of an "extrinsic" ordering on these rules (as in Chomsky and Lasnik 1977), but rather to the stronger requirement that the order of application of these rules in the derivation of the representation of grammatical relations from the data cannot alter that representation.

Part I

LEXICAL
REPRESENTATION

Chapter 1

The Passive in Lexical Theory

Joan Bresnan

This chapter will present and justify a lexical theory of passivization. A number of researchers have previously proposed lexical analyses of this construction (Shopen 1972, Freidin 1974, 1975, Brame 1976, 1978, Bresnan 1976a, 1978, Wasow 1978, 1980, Hoehle 1978). But passivization is so inextricably connected to the central grammatical systems of complementation in many languages that it poses major challenges for any lexical analysis. First, can a lexical analysis of passivization be incorporated within an explicit, coherent, and universal theory of syntax? Second, can compelling evidence be found that the lexical theory is superior to alternative transformational, or structuralist, theories of passivization? And third, can the lexical theory explain evidence which seems to support a transformational analysis of passivization? It must be admitted that few if any lexical analyses of passivization that have been proposed in the past have answered all three of these challenges satisfactorily.

The first two sections of this chapter address the first two questions. Section 1.1 presents fundamentals of the lexical theory of syntax that will be elaborated in subsequent chapters of this volume. It is argued that this is a more explanatory theory of linguistic competence than proposed alternatives in that it permits a unification of theories of the mental representation of language; and it is a more explanatory theory of linguistic universals in that it explains both the universal semantic effects of rules like Passivization and their variable syntactic manifestations across languages. Section 1.2 presents clear evidence from English that Passivization must be a lexical rule, shows that passivized verbs undergo word-formation processes in the lexicon, and derives and verifies a semantic consequence of the lexical analysis of passivization. Finally, section 1.3 responds to a battery of arguments that have been given for a Passive transformation by showing in each case how the phenomena in question are explained as well or better by the lexical theory.

It must be added that the evidence to be given favors the lexical theory of passivization over the broadest class of transformational theories of this process, including NP-movement theories, base-generated trace theories, and case theories. In all of these theories, the grammatical relations of the passive verb are defined by syntactic phrase structure representations, which undergo movement rules or structural indexing rules, in order to relate the "deep" grammatical relations to the surface forms of sentences. In what follows, the term *Passive transformation* applies, mutatis mutandis, to all such rules.

1.1 Fundamentals of the Lexical Theory

The lexical theory of grammar provides a formally explicit and coherent theory of how surface structures are related to representations of meaningful grammatical relations. Rules of grammar defined in the formal system of grammatical representation provide each sentence of a language with dual representations consisting of a *constituent structure* (*c-structure*) and a *functional structure* (*f-structure*) (see chapter 4 of this volume). The constituent structure represents the superficial constituency of the sentence (which is phonologically interpreted), and the functional structure is the representation of its meaningful grammatical relations (which is semantically interpreted). Given a grammar G and a lexicon L, there is an algorithm for constructing the c- and f-structures of any string S of lexical words in L and for determining whether S is grammatical in G (see chapters 4 and 11). The interpretation of functional structures is rendered extremely simple by the fact that the grammatical relations of each predicate have already been lexically encoded.

The Lexical Encoding of Grammatical Relations

Grammatical relations are lexically encoded by assigning grammatical functions to the predicate argument structures of lexical items. The predicate argument structure positions may be identified with thematic roles such as "agent," "theme," "instrument," etc.; the grammatical function assignment then associates these thematic roles with grammatical functions (SUBJECT, OBJECT, etc.). Grammatical functions are universals of the lexical theory.

The possible mappings from thematic roles to grammatical functions are limited by universal grammar: in particular, *function–argument biuniqueness* (cf. chapter 3) implies that all such mappings must assign a unique function to each thematic role (or predicate argument) and a unique thematic role (or predicate argument) to each function which is associated with a predicate argument. Grammatical functions and thematic roles are not in one-to-one correspondence, however, because there are nonthematic grammatical functions (for example, the "raised" subjects and idiomatic objects to be discussed below in section 1.3). Further, the thematic roles of the grammatical functions associated with a predicate may be changed by lexical rules, such as Passivization.

The Syntactic Encoding of Grammatical Functions
In the lexical theory, grammatical functions have no intrinsic semantic significance; they merely provide the mapping between surface syntactic structures and predicate argument structure. The grammar of each language must characterize which syntactic constituents in that language can be mapped onto predicate arguments. The characterizations differ from language to language, but the functions remain the same: all languages have subjects, objects, oblique or prepositional or postpositional objects, and complements of various types, which can be mapped onto the predicate arguments of verbs and other lexical categories.

Because the universal grammatical functions are encoded in the syntactic categories of particular languages in various ways, each grammar must specify a language-particular mapping from the categories of c-structure or morphological case, to grammatical functions. In *configurational languages* such as English (chapter 5 of this volume) and French (chapter 2), grammatical functions are assigned to c-structure positions. In *nonconfigurational languages* such as Malayalam (see chapter 8), grammatical functions are assigned to morphological case features.

In a particular grammar, the correspondence between grammatical functions and either the c-structure positions or the case features in which the functions are encoded need not be one-to-one. The same function can be realized by distinct c-structure configurations (e.g., the clitic and nonclitic objects in French) or by distinct case features (e.g., the nominative and dative subjects in Malayalam). Conversely, different functions can be realized by the same c-structure configuration

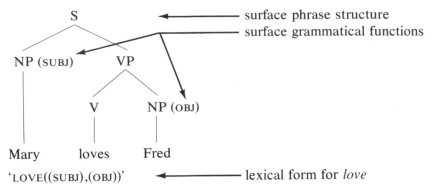

'LOVE((SUBJ),(OBJ))' ◄─────────── lexical form for *love*

Lexical encoding of grammatical relations for the active verb *love*

(SUBJ) (OBJ)
  | | ◄─ lexical assignment of grammatical functions
'LOVE(arg 1 , arg 2)'◄─ predicate argument structure
  (agent) (theme)

Figure 1.1
Syntactic encoding of grammatical functions in surface structure

(e.g., the OBJ2 and NCOMP in English) or by the same case features (e.g., the nominative object or subject in Malayalam).

The theory of universal grammar limits the possible mappings from syntactic categories to grammatical functions. All grammars definable in the formal theory observe the principle of *direct syntactic encoding,* which requires that every nonlexical rule of grammar preserve function assignments. The principle of direct syntactic encoding prevents rules of syntax from replacing one function with another, and so guarantees that the syntactic encoding of grammatical functions in a language applies directly to surface structures without the mediation of a syntactic or functional derivation. See figures 1.1 and 1.2.

A Unified Theory of Language
To express linguistically significant generalizations, the direct encoding principle depends crucially on the lexical encoding of alternative grammatical relations for each verb. Transformational derivations are eliminated from the syntactic component of the grammar by means of the expanded lexical component. Two types of "transformational" (that is, structure-dependent) relations remain: a class of unbounded movement or deletion rules (Bresnan 1978) and a class of bounded rules

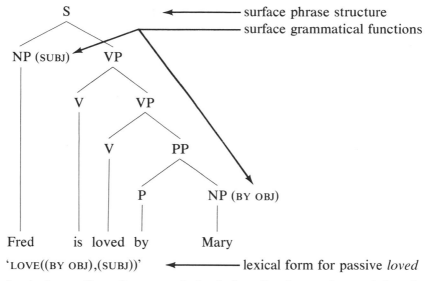

Figure 1.2
Syntactic encoding of grammatical functions in surface structure

that change the order but not the function of constituents ("scrambling" rules). The former are eliminated by the theory of syntactic binding (see chapter 4 of this volume). The latter are analyzed as operations on c-structure rules; an example is the Verb Scrambling rule in Malayalam (discussed in chapter 8).

As argued in Bresnan 1978, the resulting trade-off between syntactic and lexical components provides a more explanatory theory of linguistic competence. First, because the direct encoding principle provides a direct relation between surface structures and functional structures, the class of grammars defined by the lexical theory can be directly incorporated in more realistic models of sentence perception (chapter 11) and production (chapter 12).

The Augmented Transition Network (ATN) grammars used by Wanner and Maratsos 1978 and Kaplan 1972, 1975 in modeling sentence comprehension did not employ the direct encoding principle. Passive sentences were analyzed by replacing the initial assignment *John* = SUBJECT in *John was kissed by Mary* with the revised assignment *John* = OBJECT as soon as the passive morphology on the verb was encountered. But, as Kaplan 1978 subsequently noted, the surface assignment of grammatical functions is required for interpreting many natural language constructions, such as tag questions: in both the active *Mary will kiss John, won't she/*he?* and the passive *John will be kissed by Mary, won't *she/he?*, the tag pronoun *she* or *he* refers to the surface subject. Given the direct encoding principle and the expanded lexical component, only the surface function assignments need be maintained in the nondeterministic search space of the parser, and the multiple actions and predicates of the earlier ATN parsers can be reduced to a simple "additive" operation without complicating the grammar (Kaplan 1978). Thus, the lexical theory contributes to linguistically more adequate and computationally simpler models of language processing.

A second way in which the trade-off between lexical and syntactic components in the lexical theory leads to a more explanatory theory of linguistic competence is that it appears to permit a psychologically more realistic model of language acquisition (chapter 10 of this volume). Third, as the next subsection will demonstrate, the lexical theory permits a much deeper theory of linguistic universals. In short, it offers a *unified* theory of the mental representations that support the acquisition and use of language.

The Universal Character of Passivization

It is evident from the principle of direct syntactic encoding that any rule of grammar which changes the grammatical functions of constituents must be a lexical rule. Moreover, any such rule will have a universal characterization which reveals its invariant form across languages. This follows because grammatical functions are independent of language-particular realizations in terms of syntactic structure or morphological case.

Passivization can be universally characterized as shown in (1) (cf. Perlmutter and Postal 1977).[1]

(1)
Passivization in Universal Grammar
(SUBJ) $\mapsto$ ϕ / (OBL)
(OBJ) $\mapsto$ (SUBJ)

The functions SUBJ, OBJ, OBL belong to the inventory of universal functions that includes SUBJ(ect), OBJ(ect), OBJ(ect)2(second), POSS(essor), OBL(ique), COMP(lement), and ADJUNCT. The last three grammatical functions have multiple subtypes, which are distinguished within particular grammars by a finite class of categorial or morphological features. For example, the multiple types of oblique objects in English are marked by the closed class of prepositions, and include BY OBJ, TO OBJ, FOR OBJ; the oblique objects in other languages are marked by postpositions or by case (e.g., INSTRUMENTAL, GENITIVE, ABLATIVE); various types of COMP function (e.g., NCOMP, ACOMP, PCOMP, VCOMP) can be marked by categorial features. The oblique objects are characteristically linked to individuating semantic, or thematic, roles.

As illustrated in (2), Passivization changes a transitive lexical form whose subject is agent and whose object is theme to a grammatically intransitive lexical form (that is, one lacking an OBJ function).

(2)

Effect of Passivization on a Lexical Form

a. L((SUBJ), (OBJ)) →
        agent theme
b. L((OBL)/ϕ, (SUBJ))
        agent   theme

In the passivized lexical form (2b), the subject function is now correlated with the theme role of L, and the optional oblique function is correlated with the agent role.

Language-particular instantiations of the universal Passivization rule will differ in the specification of the particular OBL function that expresses the agent role and in the verbal morphology that registers the application of the rule to verbs. As illustrations, the Passivization rules of English and Malayalam (a Dravidian language spoken in southern India) are given in (3) and (4). See chapter 8 of this volume for justification of the formulation of Passivization in Malayalam; the motivation for the form of the English rule will be given in the sections to follow.

(3)

Passivization in English

Functional change: (SUBJ) → ϕ / (BY OBJ)
                       (OBJ) → (SUBJ)
Morphological change: V → V$_{[Part]}$

(4)

Passivization in Malayalam

Functional change: (SUBJ) → φ / (INSTR)

                       (OBJ) → (SUBJ)

Morphological change: V → V + appeṭ-

As shown in (3), the morphological effect of Passivization in English is to alter the base verb to a participle. Since participles are tenseless in English, this change implies that in tensed constructions, passivized verbs will occur only with tense-bearing verbs that can take participial complements, such as *get* (*John just got handed a can of worms*), *have* (*We had the agents sent phony passports*), *keep* (*She keeps the library painted a dark burgundy*), or *be* (*John was handed a book*). In tenseless constructions, such as relative adjuncts (*Anyone handed a can of worms should . . .*) or clausal adjuncts (*Handed a can of worms, John . . .*), the participle predictably appears without an auxiliary. In contrast, the morphological effect of Passivization in Malayalam, shown in (4), is to affix the verb base with *appeṭ-*, which itself takes further inflection for tense. As a result, no "auxiliary" verb is utilized in the passive constructions of Malayalam.

The syntactic effects of Passivization in a particular language will follow from the syntactic encoding of the SUBJ, OBJ, and OBL functions in that language. This is a fundamental explanatory advantage of this theory of passivization over transformational theories.[2] This advantage is strikingly demonstrated by Mohanan's revealing study of Malayalam, which appears in full in chapter 8 of this volume. As Mohanan shows, Malayalam is a nonconfigurational language with respect to its clause structure. The basic rule of clause structure and the syntactic encoding of subject, object, and the oblique instrumental are given in simplified form in (5a,b).

(5)

Partial Syntactic Encoding (Malayalam)

a.   S → NP* V

b.   i.   (↓CASE) = NOM   ii.   (↓CASE) = ACC

           (↑SUBJ) = ↓   (↓ANIM) = +

                                         (↑OBJ) = ↓

     iii. (↓CASE) = NOM   iv.   (↓CASE) = INSTR

           (↓ANIM) = −   (↑INSTR) = ↓

           (↑OBJ) = ↓

Rule (5a) specifies that a simple sentence consists of a sequence of NPs in any order followed by a verb. The sets of equations in (5b) are assigned arbitrarily to the constituents of S: they specify that (i) if a phrase is nominative, it may be interpreted as the subject of the S; if a phrase is (ii) accusative and animate or (iii) nominative and inanimate, it may be interpreted as the object; and (iv) if a phrase is instrumental, it may be interpreted as the oblique function INSTR(umental). General conditions of functional completeness, coherence, and consistency ensure that the correct grammatical options are taken.

In contrast, English is a configurational language: the subject and object functions are assigned to specific c-structure configurations, shown in simplified form in (6) (see also chapter 4).

(6)

Partial Syntactic Encoding (English)

a.   S $\rightarrow$ NP   VP   VP $\rightarrow$ V   (NP)   (PP)

b.   ($\uparrow$SUBJ)=$\downarrow$ ($\uparrow$OBJ)=$\downarrow$ ($\downarrow$PCASE)=BY

($\uparrow$BY OBJ)=$\downarrow$

The rules in (6a) give the c-structure of the simple English sentence. The sets of equations in (6b) are assigned to c-structure positions as indicated by the vertical lines. Thus, they specify that the subject of a simple S is the NP immediately dominated by S and preceding the VP; that the optional postverbal NP immediately dominated by VP is the object; and that a PP whose preposition is *by* may be the oblique BY OBJ.

It follows from the syntactic encoding functions (5) and (6) that passivization in Malayalam entails case changes but no position changes, while passivization in English entails position changes (since the subject and object functions are realized by different c-structure positions) (see the discussion in chapter 8). These consequences are illustrated in figures 1.3 and 1.4. The order of NPs in the Malayalam sentences of figure 1.3 is freely interchangeable: only the case marking of the NPs and the suffixation of -*appeṭ* to the verb mark the passive construction. In the simple English examples of figure 1.4, the order of NPs in the c-structures is fixed, as it serves to identify the syntactic subject and object. The treatment of the auxiliary verb *was* in figure 1.4 follows chapter 4 of this volume and requires a rule VP $\rightarrow$ V   VP

($\uparrow$VCOMP)=$\downarrow$

c-structure

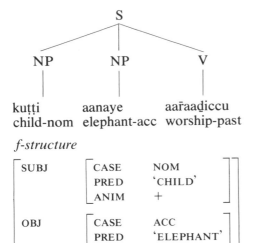

kuṭṭi   aanaye   aaṛaaḍiccu
child-nom   elephant-acc worship-past

f-structure

$$
\begin{bmatrix}
\text{SUBJ} & \begin{bmatrix} \text{CASE} & \text{NOM} \\ \text{PRED} & \text{`CHILD'} \\ \text{ANIM} & + \end{bmatrix} \\
\\
\text{OBJ} & \begin{bmatrix} \text{CASE} & \text{ACC} \\ \text{PRED} & \text{`ELEPHANT'} \\ \text{ANIM} & + \end{bmatrix} \\
\\
\text{TENSE} & \text{PAST} \\
\\
\text{PRED} & \text{`WORSHIP((SUBJ),(OBJ))'} \\
& \qquad\quad \text{agent theme}
\end{bmatrix}
$$

Figure 1.3a
Representation of *The child worshipped the elephant* in Malayalam

in addition to those given in (6). Other analyses are possible within the theory, but the choice among them is not relevant to the issues here.

To interpret the functional structures of figures 1.3 and 1.4, the grammatical functions of each f-structure are matched with the grammatical functions assigned to its predicate (PRED). Interpretation of the f-structure is strictly local in that all grammatical arguments required by each predicate must be elements of the immediate f-structure of the predicate (see chapter 4). As a result of interpreting the f-structures in figures 1.3 and 1.4, *the child* and *the elephant* will be respectively interpreted as the agent and the theme of *worship* in all four examples.

The illusion that passivization involves the "movement" of an NP in a sentence from the postverbal object position to the preverbal subject position thus arises from the syntactic encoding function particular to English. The apparent "movement" of the NP in configurational lan-

c-structure

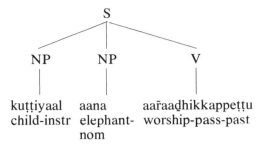

f-structure

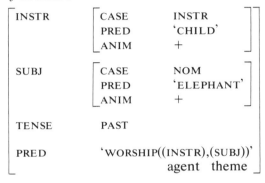

Figure 1.3b
Representation of *The elephant was worshipped by the child* in Malayalam

guages like English has been the basis for transformational analyses of passivization from the beginning to the present. These analyses are formulated in terms of structure-dependent operations—for example, "move NP"—which are defined on the relatively superficial syntactic structures of particular languages. But such operations are no more a universal feature of passivization than the auxiliary *be*, the verb phrase, or the morphology of the English passive participle (Perlmutter and Postal 1977). The structural primitives of transformational theory are simply insufficiently abstract to characterize the universal attributes of function-dependent rules like Passivization. In contrast, the functional primitives of the lexical theory are independent of language-particular c-structure configurations and hence are sufficiently abstract to permit a universal theory of function-dependent rules.

c-structure

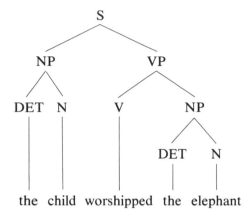

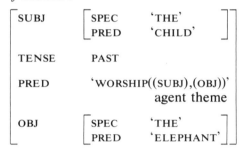

f-structure

$$\begin{bmatrix} \text{SUBJ} & \begin{bmatrix} \text{SPEC} & \text{`THE'} \\ \text{PRED} & \text{`CHILD'} \end{bmatrix} \\ \\ \text{TENSE} & \text{PAST} \\ \\ \text{PRED} & \text{`WORSHIP((SUBJ),(OBJ))'} \\ & \qquad\quad \text{agent theme} \\ \\ \text{OBJ} & \begin{bmatrix} \text{SPEC} & \text{`THE'} \\ \text{PRED} & \text{`ELEPHANT'} \end{bmatrix} \end{bmatrix}$$

Figure 1.4a
Representation of *The child worshipped the elephant* in English

c-structure

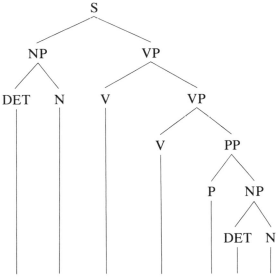

the elephant was worshipped by the child

f-structure

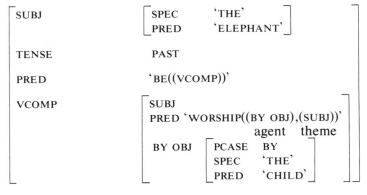

Figure 1.4b
Representation of *The elephant was worshipped by the child* in English

In sum, in the lexical theory of passivization, grammatical functions are universal primitives which must be both lexically and syntactically encoded in each language. The lexical encodings map the grammatical functions onto thematic roles, or semantic predicate arguments, while the syntactic encodings map the grammatical functions onto surface syntactic and morphological structures. By formulating Passivization as a rule that changes the lexical encoding of universal grammatical functions, the lexical theory explains both its universal semantic effects (including its interactions with rules of control, anaphoric binding, and other lexical rules) and its variable syntactic manifestations (which follow from the syntactic encoding functions of each grammar); see below and chapters 5, 6, 7, and 8. For these reasons, the lexical theory provides a more explanatory account of linguistic universals than structuralist theories such as transformational grammar.

1.2 Passivization as a Lexical Rule

As we have just seen, small changes in the lexical encoding of grammatical relations can have striking syntactic effects in configurational languages. The attempt to characterize structural effects of passivization in such languages seems to have diverted the attention of linguists from the more subtle phenomena which reveal that it is a fundamentally lexical process. But when examined carefully, this evidence is compelling.

In this section I will show that Passivization is a lexical rule. First I will examine how the morphology of English passive verbs is lexically represented, basing the discussion on the valuable work of Lieber 1980. This outline provides the background for interpreting the data in the second subsection. There, I will present evidence from English that passivized verbs undergo word-formation processes which, by the lexicalist hypothesis of Chomsky 1970, Aronoff 1976, and virtually all generative grammarians currently working on morphology, are agreed to be lexical rules. Since it is assumed that the rule systems of natural language are decomposed into components of lexical rules, syntactic rules, phonological rules, and so on, which are subject to autonomous sets of constraints, this constitutes the strongest possible kind of evidence that Passivization is a lexical rule. Finally, in the last part of the section, I will derive and verify a semantic consequence of the hypothesis that Passivization is a lexical rule.

Lexical Representation of the Morphology of Passive Verbs in English
The morphological effect of Passivization is to convert the active verb
V to its passive participle. The passive participle is morphologically
identical to the perfect participle, as illustrated in (7)–(11). The (a)
examples are passives; the (b) examples are perfects.

(7)
a. Fred is *loved* by Mary.
b. Fred has *loved* Mary.

(8)
a. Our team was *beaten* by their team.
b. Our team had *beaten* their team.

(9)
a. The picture was *hung* on the wall.
b. The picture had *hung* on the wall.

(10)
a. The rock was *broken* by the sledgehammer.
b. The rock had *broken* the sledgehammer.

(11)
a. The block was *split* by the stick.
b. The block had *split* the stick.

In (7), the passive and perfect forms are related to the root *love* by *-ed*
suffixation. In (8), they are related to the root *beat* by *-en* suffixation. In
(9), they are related to the root *hang* by vocalic ablaut. In (10), they are
related to the root *break* by vocalic ablaut and *-en* suffixation. And in
(11), they are identical to the root *split*.

Because the forms of verbs signal various grammatical properties of
the surface syntactic constructions in which the verbs occur, transformational accounts of verbal morphology have assumed that transformations themselves may add or alter morphological features (see, for
example, Chomsky 1965:174f). But in the lexical theory, verbs directly
encode the surface grammatical relations of the syntactic constructions
in which they occur, and syntactic constructions automatically inherit
the grammatical features of their lexical heads (see, for example,
chapters 2 and 4 of this volume). As a result, the lexical theory of
syntax permits a far more restrictive theory of inflectional morphology,
in which no syntactic feature-changing rules of any type are needed.
Drawing freely on Lieber's 1980 lexical theory of inflectional morphol-

ogy, I will illustrate how the morphology of passive and perfect verbs in English can be lexically represented.

Let us assume that the lexical entry of a verb gives morphological information only about the root and stem forms of the verb, designated V and V_s, respectively. The finite verbal inflections -s and -ed will be given by the lexical affixation rules in (12) and (13).

(12)

-s: $[V \underline{\quad}]_{V[Finite]}$, TENSE = PRES

SUBJ PERS = 3

SUBJ NUM = SG

(13)

-ed: $[V \underline{\quad}]_{V[Finite]}$, TENSE = PAST

(12) specifies that -s is suffixed to a root V to form a finite verb having the features of present tense, third person subject, singular number subject. (13) specifies that -ed is suffixed to a root V to form a finite verb having the features of past tense. The features of these affixes are added to the features of the verbs to which they are attached. A root V can also serve by itself as a finite verb having the feature values given by the rule in (14).

(14)

V: $[\underline{\quad}]_{V[Finite]}$, TENSE = PRES

SUBJ PERS $\neq$ 3 or SUBJ NUM $\neq$ SG

If exceptional finite forms are lexically listed, they will serve to block the production of regular forms by lexical rules such as (12)–(14). For example, the occurrence of $[is]_{V[Finite]}$ as the third person, singular, present tense form of *be* will block the application of rule (12) to form $*[be\text{-}s]_{V[Finite]}$.[3]

Participles are nonfinite verbs; hence, the features [Part] and [Finite] must be mutually exclusive. Passive and perfect participles can be formed, as in (7) above, by lexically suffixing -ed to a verbal root:

(15)

-ed: $[V \underline{\quad}]_{V[Part]}$

Suffixation of -ed is the regular and productive means of forming these participles. -en suffixation applies to a restricted class V_n of roots like *beat* and stems V_s like *brok*- (cf. examples (9) and (10) above):

(16)

-en: $[V_{(s)} \quad]_{V[Part]}$, where $V_{(s)} \in V_n$

Still more restricted classes of strong roots undergo allomorphic processes such as vocalic ablaut (e.g., *hang → hung, break → brok-*); the ablaut stem may undergo rule (16) or it may itself form the participle. As before, the unproductive forms serve to block application of the productive rule (15).

With these rules for forming participles, the following partial lexical entries can be given for the verbs in (7)–(11).

(17)

love: V, 'LOVE((SUBJ),(OBJ))'

(18)

beat: V, V $\in$ V$_n$, 'BEAT((SUBJ),(OBJ))'
        [—]$_{V[Finite]}$, TENSE = PAST

(19)

hang: V, 'HANG((SUBJ),(PCOMP))'
              'HANG$_{caus}$((SUBJ),(OBJ),(PCOMP))'[4]

hung: V$_s$, [—]$_{V[Part]}$
        [—]$_{V[Finite]}$, TENSE = PAST

(20)

break: V, 'BREAK((SUBJ))'
              'BREAK$_{caus}$((SUBJ),(OBJ))'

broke: V$_s$, V$_s$ $\in$ V$_n$
        [—]$_{V[Finite]}$, TENSE = PAST

(21)

split: V, [—]$_{V[Part]}$, 'SPLIT((SUBJ))'
                    'SPLIT$_{caus}$((SUBJ),(OBJ))'
        [—]$_{V[Finite]}$, TENSE = PAST

Partial lexical entries provide unpredicted morphological information, which includes properties of roots and stems, and unpredicted grammatical information, which includes the basic lexical forms of verbs. Lexical rules like (12)–(16) fill out these morphological specifications. The basic lexical forms are expanded by rules like Passivization and by universal conditions on grammatical function assignments and relations (see chapter 3).

Passivization is now stated in (22).

(22)

Passivization

Operation on lexical form: (SUBJ) $\mapsto \phi$ / (BY OBJ)

$\qquad\qquad\qquad\qquad\quad$ (OBJ) $\mapsto$ (SUBJ)

Morphological change: $\qquad$ V $\mapsto$ V$_{[Part]}$

By means of the morphological change specified in the rule, a passivized verb will acquire the morphology of the participle of that verb. Thus, from the lexical entries (17)–(21), Passivization produces (23)–(27).

(23)

$$[\text{lov-ed}]_{V[Part]}, \text{'LOVE}(\left\{ \begin{matrix} (\text{BY OBJ}) \\ \phi \end{matrix} \right\}, (\text{SUBJ})))'$$

(24)

$$[\text{beat-en}]_{V[Part]}, \text{'BEAT}(\left\{ \begin{matrix} (\text{BY OBJ}) \\ \phi \end{matrix} \right\}, (\text{SUBJ})))'$$

(25)

$$[\text{hung}]_{V[Part]}, \text{'HANG}(\left\{ \begin{matrix} (\text{BY OBJ}) \\ \phi \end{matrix} \right\}, (\text{SUBJ})))'$$

(26)

$$[\text{brok-en}]_{V[Part]}, \text{'BREAK}(\left\{ \begin{matrix} (\text{BY OBJ}) \\ \phi \end{matrix} \right\}, (\text{SUBJ})))'$$

(27)

$$[\text{split}]_{V[Part]}, \text{'SPLIT}(\left\{ \begin{matrix} (\text{BY OBJ}) \\ \phi \end{matrix} \right\}, (\text{SUBJ})))'$$

Note that Passivization has applied only to the transitive lexical forms (that is, those which contain (OBJ) in their grammatical function assignment).

Unlike passive participles, perfect participles have the active lexical form of the verb. In addition, perfect participles require the auxiliary *have*, while the auxiliary *be* may occur with the passive participle.[5] The rule of Perfect Formation given in (28) associates the syntactic features of the perfect with V$_{[Part]}$.

(28)

Perfect Formation

V $\mapsto$ V$_{[Part]}$; PERF = +

Perfect Formation preserves the lexical forms of the verbs it applies to. Since both Perfect Formation and Passivization apply to root verbs, the two rules will be mutually exclusive; hence, the perfect features will always be associated with the active lexical forms of the verb.

The Formation of Adjectives from Passive Participles
Passivized lexical entries like (23)–(27) are available to lexical word-formation processes. In this section we will see that passivized verbs are the input to two types of lexical rules that form adjectives: Participle–Adjective Conversion and verbal compounding, discussed in the next two subsections. If passive constructions were derived by syntactic processes, such as transformations or surface-interpretive rules of structural indexing (which are equivalent to transformations), then they could not undergo lexical word-formation processes such as these.

Participle–Adjective Conversion   Adjectival passives are identical in form to verbal passives, but belong to the category adjective rather than the category verb. Contrasting pairs of verbal and adjectival passives occur in (29)–(31).

(29)
a.   The jacket was *unzipped* by someone wearing fingernail polish.
b.   The jacket was *untouched* by human hands.

(30)
a.   Margaret's statement was *considered* profound.
b.   That was a very *considered* statement.

(31)
a.   The prisoners were *spared* execution.
b.   The *spared* prisoners were freed.

Although adjectival passives resemble verbal passives, a number of studies demonstrate that they are categorially distinct (Siegel 1973, 1974, Wasow 1977, 1978, 1980, Bresnan 1978, Hust 1977, 1978). I will enumerate here some of the categorial differences between the verbal and adjectival passives in these examples; for a more detailed discussion of the evidence, see the references just cited.

Example (29a) contains a verbal passive based on the verb to *unzip;* prefixed to a verb, *un-* forms a verb that denotes the reversal of the action denoted by the base verb, as in *zip/unzip, tie/untie, do/undo,* etc. (29b) contains an adjective based on the adjectival passive *touched;*

prefixed to an adjective A, *un-* forms an adjective that means 'not-A', as in *happy/unhappy, clear/unclear, appetizing/unappetizing, breakable/ unbreakable*, etc. The adjectival prefix *un-* does not attach to verbs; for example, there is no verb **to untouch*. But this prefix does attach to adjectival passives (*untouched, unloved, uninhabited*), a fact that can be explained if adjectival passives are adjectives, not verbs.

Example (30a) shows the passive verb *considered* with an adjectival complement; verbs but not adjectives can take these complements in English (Wasow 1977:357–358, footnote 10). (30b) shows the adjectival passive *considered* in the prenominal position of an adjective and modified by *very*. Adjectives but not verbs can be modified by *very*; compare (30b) with **Margaret's statement was very considered profound*.

Example (31a) contains the passive verb *spared* followed by its second object NP. English adjectives do not take NP objects (cf. Wasow 1977:357–358, footnote 10, Bresnan 1978:7, and Maling 1980). But the *spared* in (31b) is an adjectival passive occurring in prenominal position.

Previous morphological analyses of adjectival passives (such as those of Siegel 1974 and Allen 1978) have assumed that they are formed by an affixation rule such as (32), which is analogous to A → [A + ness]$_N$ (deriving *happiness* from *happy*) and A → [un + A]$_A$ (deriving *unhappy* from *happy*).

(32)
V → [V + ed]$_A$

But Lieber 1979, 1980 observes that the rule forming adjectival passives is crucially unlike these affixation rules: in fact, the rule cannot be stated as a rule affixing *-ed* to a verb to derive an adjective, because adjectival participles exhibit a high degree of allomorphy. Lieber gives examples like those in (33) to illustrate this point.

(33)

Verb	Participle	Adjectival Passive
sing	sung	an unsung hero
fight	fought	hard-fought battles
write	written	a well-written novel
give	given	a recently given talk
consider	considered	an unconsidered action
inhabit	inhabited	an uninhabited island
break	broken	my broken heart
split	split	split wood

The adjectival passives of some verbs are formed by vocalic ablaut, others by *-en* suffixation, others by both; still others are identical to the root verb. Moreover, as Lieber notes, this allomorphy is not phonologically conditioned, so the word-formation rule (32) would have to be augmented with further rules such as those in (34).

(34)
a. $V \rightarrow [V + ed]_A$
b. $V \rightarrow [V + en]_A$
c. $V \rightarrow [V_s]_A$, where V_s is an ablaut form of V
d. $V \rightarrow [V]_A$

The obvious defect of this analysis is that it misses the generalization that the form of the adjectival passive of a verb is based on the form of the passive participle of that verb. On this account there is no reason why the adjectival form should resemble the participle: it is only an accident that we have *an unsung hero* or *my broken heart* or *split wood* and not *an unsinged hero* or *my breaked heart* or *splitted wood*. Lieber proposes to capture this generalization by making the passive participle the input to the rule of Adjective Formation, as in (35).[6]

(35)
$V_{[Part]} \rightarrow [V_{[Part]}]_A$

Given that it is the passive form of the verb that is the input to the rule and that rules of category conversion only relabel their input, the identity of form between verbal and adjectival passives follows. But not only is the passive participle the input to Adjective Formation, the passive lexical form must be as well: after all, *the eaten dog* means 'the dog that was eaten' and not 'the dog that has eaten', and in fact all of the adjectival passives cited above have a meaning based on the passive rather than the active verb (hence the name "adjectival *passive*"). Thus, the rule will be formulated as in (36).

(36)
Participle – Adjective Conversion

Morphological change:	$V_{[Part]} \mapsto [V_{[Part]}]_A$
Operation on lexical form:	P(...(SUBJ)...) $\mapsto$ STATE-OF P(...(SUBJ)...)
Condition:	SUBJ = theme of P

Rule (36) takes the passive participle and the passive lexical form as its input. The verbal predicate P is made into an adjectival predicate STATE-OF P, the latter term being intended to cover the subtle difference in meaning between the verbal passive and the adjectival passive. The conversion is restricted by the condition that the subject of the participle must be a theme. The theme argument in a predicate is that argument which undergoes the motion or change in state denoted by the predicate (Gruber 1965, Jackendoff 1976, S. Anderson 1977, Wasow 1980); in the unmarked case it corresponds to the object of a transitive verb and the subject of an intransitive verb (S. Anderson 1977). While there are obvious difficulties in providing a consistent thematic analysis of nonmotional and nonlocational verbs, nevertheless, *some* appropriate semantic restriction on the subject argument of (36) is required, as will be seen. Finally, as this formulation implies, adjectival passives do occur with *by*-object agents; compare example (29b) and *That claim is unsupported by data, Antarctica is uninhabited by humans, One fact is unexplained by this formulation.* This analysis leaves unexplained the fact that *by*-objects are more restricted with adjectival passives (**That statement was very considered by everyone*) than with verbal passives (*That statement was considered profound by everyone*), but it may ultimately follow from properties of the predicate change. The fact that the rule refers to the relation between grammatical functions and the thematic roles of predicate argument structures supports the theory of lexical representation sketched in section 1.1.

The subject of a passivized verb is normally the theme argument, for, in replacing the object with the subject, Passivization preserves the predicate argument structure and hence the original thematic relations of the verb to which it applies. Thus, if OBJ is assigned to a theme argument in the active lexical form, SUBJ is assigned to the theme argument in the passive lexical form. Now consider the active and passive lexical forms for the verb *eat,* given in (37a,b,c). (On the lexical rule of Intransitivization which derives (37b), see chapter 3.)

(37)

a. 'EAT((SUBJ),(OBJ))'   [active transitive lexical form:
                                          Fido will eat something]

b. 'EAT((SUBJ),ϕ)'   [active intransitivized lexical form:
                                          Fido will eat]

c. 'EAT(ϕ,(SUBJ))'   [passivized lexical form:
                                          Fido will be eaten]

If the predicate argument structure *eat*(1,2) has argument 1 as agent (the eater) and argument 2 as theme (the eaten thing), only the lexical form in (37c) is eligible for Participle–Adjective Conversion. In the active transitive (37a), the subject corresponds to the agent and the object to the theme; hence, this lexical form cannot undergo rule (36). In the active intransitive (37b), the subject still corresponds to the agent; as a result, this lexical form is also ineligible for Adjective Conversion. But in the passivized lexical form (37c), the subject corresponds to the theme and rule (36) can apply. It follows that *the eaten dog* can mean only 'the dog that was eaten' and not 'the dog that has eaten'.

Not all passivized verbs have subject themes, as examples of the *to*-dative alternation will show. In both (38) and (39) *a present* is the theme, *Louise* is the source, and *the child* is the goal.

(38)
Louise gave a present to the child.

(39)
Louise gave the child a present.

Assuming for *give* a predicate argument structure *give*(1,2,3) in which argument 1 is the source, argument 2 the theme, and argument 3 the goal, the lexical forms for examples (38) and (39) are as shown in (40) and (41).

(40)
'GIVE((SUBJ),(OBJ),(TO OBJ))'

(41)
'GIVE((SUBJ),(OBJ2),(OBJ))'

The grammatical interpretation of these lexical forms is illustrated in figures 1.5 and 1.6. For an explicit discussion of the grammatical interpretation of the PP in such examples, see chapter 4 of this volume.

To the extent that it is systematic, the *to*-dative alternation can be formulated as an operation on lexical forms, replacing (OBJ) by (OBJ2) and (TO OBJ) by (OBJ) as in (42).

(42)
To-*Dative*
(OBJ) $\mapsto$ (OBJ2)
(TO OBJ) $\mapsto$ (OBJ)

Rule (42) will derive the lexical form (41) from (40). As a lexical operation, the rule of *To*-Dative can be used to simplify or abbreviate the multiple lexical forms for verbs exhibiting the *to*-dative alternation.[7]

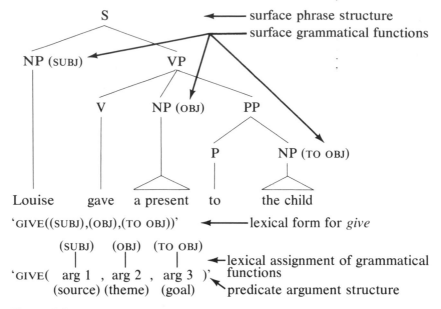

Figure 1.5

Evidence for a lexical analysis of *To*-Dative has been given by Oehrle 1976, Dowty 1978, and Baker 1979. In the present theory, *To*-Dative must be a lexical rule—first, because it changes the types of grammatical arguments of the verbs it applies to (and so affects their polyadicity), and second, because it produces lexical forms which undergo the lexical rule of Passivization. Dative constructions which have been passivized are shown in (43a,b).

(43)
a.   A present was given to the child by Louise.
b.   The child was given a present by Louise.

Passivization derives (44a) from (40) and (44b) from (41), as the reader can easily verify.

(44)

a.   'GIVE($\left\{\begin{matrix}(\text{BY OBJ})\\ \phi\end{matrix}\right\}$,(SUBJ),(TO OBJ))'

b.   'GIVE($\left\{\begin{matrix}(\text{BY OBJ})\\ \phi\end{matrix}\right\}$,(OBJ2),(SUBJ))'

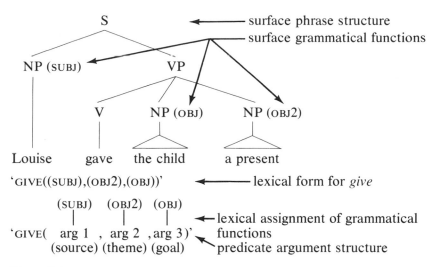

Figure 1.6

The grammatical interpretation of these lexical forms is illustrated in figures 1.7 and 1.8.

Although there are two verbal passives based on the dative, there is only one adjectival passive, as (45) indicates.

(45)
a.   a frequently given present   [*present* = theme]
b.   *a frequently given child   [*child* = goal]

The contrast follows from the condition on Adjective Conversion (36): in (44a), the SUBJ function is assigned to argument 2, the theme argument; in (44b), the SUBJ function is assigned to argument 3, the goal argument. Thus, Adjective Conversion can apply only to the first lexical form (44a). This explanation holds for the following contrast as well.[8]

(46)
a.   an unsent letter   [*letter* = theme]
b.   *an unsent mother   [*mother* = goal]

These dative passive examples illustrate clearly how the lexical theory of passivization explains differences in the productivity and semantic restrictedness of verbal and adjectival passives. Such differences follow not from the distinction between transformational and lexical rules, as transformationalists have previously argued (Chomsky

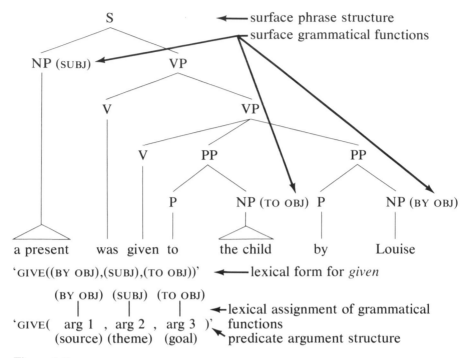

Figure 1.7

1970, Wasow 1977), but from the characteristics of different types of lexical rules. In particular, Adjective Conversion (36) changes both the syntactic category and the predicate argument structure of the participles to which it applies, while Passivization (22) preserves both. Wasow 1978, 1980 hypothesizes that in general "major" lexical rules which analyze grammatical function assignments are more productive than "minor" lexical rules which analyze thematic relations. This hypothesis suggests many intriguing questions for further research.[9]

The requirement that the subject be a theme is essential to the rule of Participle–Adjective Conversion (36). Previous formulations of Adjective Formation, such as Wasow's 1977, 1978, 1980, have taken an *active* verb with its active lexical entry as input. The active root must be converted to a participle and assigned to the category adjective. As part of the word-formation process, the rule changes the OBJ of the verb to the SUBJ of the derived adjective, specifying that the OBJ of the (active) verbal base be a theme or "logical" object.

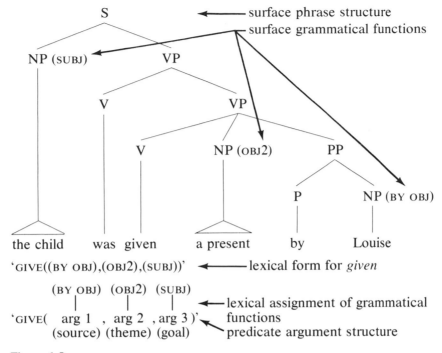

Figure 1.8

The rule given here (36) is both simpler and more general than these previous formulations. By taking the passivized verb as its input, it obviates duplication of the effects of Passivization. It is more general because, where previous formulations are applicable only to transitive verbs whose objects are themes, this rule is applicable to all intransitive verbs whose subjects are themes. These verbs include both passivized verbs (which are intransitive because they lack grammatical objects) and other intransitive verbs.

Where the previous analyses claim that adjectival participles are based only on transitive verbs, rule (36) claims that adjectival participles are based on the intransitive participles of verbs. Thus, unlike previous formulations, (36) predicts that intransitive verbs other than passives may undergo Adjective Conversion (but only if their subjects are themes). This prediction is borne out by the existence of examples like (47a–j), observed in Bresnan 1978:8:

(47)

a. elapsed time   [time that has elapsed]
b. a fallen leaf   [a leaf that has fallen]
c. a widely travelled man   [a man who has travelled widely]
d. an undescended testicle   [a testicle that has not descended (into the scrotum)]
e. a risen Christ   [a Christ that has risen (from the dead)]
f. a stuck window   [a window that has stuck]
g. the drifted snow   [the snow that has drifted]
h. a lapsed Catholic   [a Catholic who has lapsed]
i. a collapsed lung   [a lung that has collapsed]
j. a failed writer   [a writer who has failed]

The subjects of the intransitive verbs in (47) are all themes which undergo the motion or change of state specified by the verb. In short, the simpler and more general rule (36) is the correct one.

It has now been established that Adjective Conversion applies to intransitive participles having subject themes. These include perfect participles as in (47) and passive participles as in (33). This result is extremely important, because it implies that Passivization is a lexical rule. Structures which are analyzed by lexical rules (such as word-formation rules) must be lexical structures, and cannot be transformationally derived (Chomsky 1970, Wasow 1977, Bresnan 1978; see also chapter 3). Adjective Conversion is a lexical rule because the structures it produces undergo established lexical rules of word formation, such as un- Prefixation and -ness Suffixation (Allen 1978). The lexical rule of Adjective Conversion applies to verbs which are passive both in form and in meaning; hence, both the form and the meaning of passive verbs must be lexically and not transformationally derived.

Two remarks must be made about this conclusion. First, it might be thought that the thematic condition on Participle–Adjective Conversion is predictable from a surface interpretive rule such as S. Anderson's (1977) Theme Rule. The Theme Rule asserts that transitive objects and intransitive subjects are interpreted as themes. Because it applies after Passivization (a transformational rule for Anderson), Anderson's Theme Rule must apply to transformationally derived syntactic structures. From this it would follow that all adjective phrases, being syntactically intransitive, are interpreted as having subject themes. In particular, all deverbal adjectives based on transitive verbs would have a "passive" interpretation simply by virtue of their being syntactic adjectives (S. Anderson 1977:367–368, 370–371, 374). But this is clearly false, as many examples like (48) and (49) show.

(48)

a. That argument is unconvincing.   (active interpretation: That argument doesn't convince me.)
b. That audience is unconvinced.   (passive interpretation: That audience is not convinced.)

(49)

a. That novel is very boring.   (active interpretation)
b. That person is very bored.   (passive interpretation)

Thus, even if it is granted that the subjects of adjectives are interpreted as themes in some sense, the Theme Rule cannot account for the thematic conditions on the verbal bases of lexically derived adjectives.

Second, it might be thought that the requirement that the theme argument be the *subject* of the participle undergoing conversion can be dispensed with. Could the rule not be stated as an operation on predicate argument structure alone, without distinguishing the passive's subject argument? Evidence bearing on this question can be sought in pairs of verbs which express similar thematic roles in their predicate argument structures, but by means of different grammatical functions. A possible example is the pair of verbs *like* and *please,* as in *Mary likes piano music* and *Piano music pleases Mary.* Both verbs express a relation between an "experiencer" and an "experienced," but the experiencer is the SUBJECT of *like* and the OBJECT of *please.* Despite this similarity in their thematic structures, we find that the adjectival passives of the two verbs differ in meaning: *(very) pleased* (cf. *displeased*) refers to the experiencer (the SUBJECT of the passive verb *pleased*) and *liked* (cf. *disliked*) refers to the experienced (the SUBJECT of the passive verb *liked*). For a thematic analysis of these verbs in terms of theme, goal, etc., we may say that the experienced is a theme of *like* on the evidence of *His music is universally likeable.* (Recall (footnote 8) that *-able* suffixation results in the subject being the theme.) As for the experiencer, we could either analyze it as a "conscious theme," on the grounds that the experiencer undergoes a change of emotional state as a result of the experience, or we could extend the thematic condition on Adjective Conversion (36) to both themes and experiencers. Whichever decision is made, it remains that the *subject* argument of the passivized verb undergoing Adjective Conversion must be distinguished from the others. Further evidence that the theme argument of the passivized participle must be lexically associated with the subject function comes from the lexical rules of verbal compounding studied by Roeper and Siegel 1978. This is discussed in the next subsection.

Verbal Compounds   Nouns in English can be compounded with verbal participles to form derived adjectives. In a compound of the form [$_A$ N V-ing], the noun N can be interpreted as the direct object of the base verb V if V is transitive.

(50)
a.   a *dish-washing* machine (a machine that washes dishes)
b.   a *book-chewing* dog (a dog that chews books)

If the base verb of the compound is intransitive, the noun can be interpreted as the verb's prepositional object:

(51)
a.   *cave-dwelling* people (people who dwell in caves)
b.   a *sea-going* man (a man who goes to sea)

However, a noun cannot be interpreted as an agentive *by*-object of the verb:

(52)
gourmet-frying tomatoes (tomatoes that fry gourmets; *not* tomatoes that are fried by gourmets)

Roeper and Siegel 1978 show that these restrictions follow from the *first sister principle*, which says, in effect, that a compound of the form [$_A$ X V-ing] receives the same interpretation as [$_{VP}$ V (P) XP...], where V is the base verb of V-*ing*, *XP* is the phrasal category of X, and *P* is an optional preposition. In other words, the compounded element X on the left of V-*ing* is interpreted as the first grammatical argument XP to the right of the base verb V. Thus, for a transitive verb like *wash* in *dish-washing*, the noun *dish* will be interpreted as the first NP argument to the right of V, which is the direct object (*wash dishes*). For an intransitive verb like *dwell* in *cave-dwelling*, the noun *cave* will be interpreted as the first NP argument to the right of V, which must be a prepositional object (*dwell in caves*). And because active verbs never take agentive *by*-objects, a noun compounded with V-*ing* into an adjective will not be interpreted as a *by*-object of V; hence, *gourmet-frying* does not mean *'fry by gourmets'.

The first sister principle explains not only the interpretations of the nouns in the compounds of (50)–(52), but also restrictions on the interpretations of other compounded elements. For example, the manner adverb *slow(ly)* is the first argument to the right of the intransitive verb *grow* in (53a), but it is not the first argument to the right of the transitive verb *grow* in (53b), because the direct object intervenes in the latter case.

(53)
a.   *slow-growing* wheat (wheat that grows slowly)
b.   *slow-growing farmers (farmers that grow something slowly)

Similarly, *red* is the first argument to the right of the intransitive verb *look* (54a) but not of the transitive verb *color* (54b).

(54)
a.   *a red-looking paint* (a paint that looks red)
b.   **a red-coloring paint* (a paint that colors something red)

And finally, the first sister principle explains why a compounded noun cannot be interpreted as the *subject* argument of the base verb, because the subject NP cannot be the first sister of the base verb:

(55)
a.   a *dog-chewing* book (a book that chews dogs; *not* a book that dogs chew)
b.   *man-eating* flesh (flesh that eats men; *not* flesh that men eat)

(The examples in (55) have another possible interpretation as compounded *nouns* — 'a book for dog-chewing', 'flesh for man-eating' — but these nominal compounds are not relevant here. The irrelevant structures have the form $[_N$ N V-ing] N and can be distinguished by their characteristic primary stress on the leftmost noun; the structures considered here have the form $[_A$ N V-ing] N and characteristically permit nuclear stress on the rightmost noun.) Thus, the first sister principle entails that the subject argument of a participle must remain "open" under compounding: no noun that occurs compounded with a participle can be interpreted as the subject of that participle.

When we turn to an examination of noun compounding with passive participles, somewhat different restrictions appear. First, in a compound of the form $[_A$ N V-ed], the noun N can never be interpreted as the direct object of the base verb V. This is in direct contrast to (50):

(56)

a. *dish-washed (cf. machine-washed)
b. *book-chewed (cf. dog-chewed)
c. *fish-fried (cf. pan-fried)

If we take the active verb as the base for compounding, this is a coun-terexample to the first sister principle, since the first NP argument to the right of the active base verb V *would* be its direct object. Second, a noun compounded with a passive participle can be interpreted as the *second* NP argument to the right of the active base verb V. Thus, (57a–e) contrast with (53b) and (54b) and provide a second type of counterexample to the first sister principle.

(57)

a. pan-fried (fry something in a pan)
b. home-grown (grow something at home)
c. land-based (base something on land)
d. leaf-strewn (strew something with leaves)
e. snow-covered (cover something with snow)

Third, a noun compounded with a passive participle can be interpreted as an agentive *by*-object. Thus, (58) contrasts with (52) and constitutes a third type of counterexample to the first sister principle.

(58)

a. rat-bitten (*bite something by rats)
b. wolf-reared (*rear something by wolves)
c. moth-eaten (*eat something by moths)
d. horse-drawn (*draw something by horses)

(If we interpret the nouns in (58) as subjects rather than *by*-objects, they still remain counterexamples to the first sister principle.) Fourth, when elements other than nouns are compounded with passive partici-ples, they are interpreted as the *second* element to the right of the active base verb, again contradicting the first sister principle:

(59)

a. oft-heard (hear something often; cf. *oft-hearing)
b. widely-noticed (notice something widely; cf. *widely-noticing)
c. much-imitated (imitate something much; cf. *much-imitating)

The seemingly exceptional facts in (56)–(59) led Roeper and Siegel to formulate a special "readjustment rule" to delete the direct object in the subcategorization frame of the active verb which is to undergo compounding. But if the passivized verb is the base for compounding, the pattern of facts in (56)–(59) is precisely what is predicted by the first sister principle. To see this, one need only compare (56)–(59) with (56′)–(59′).

(56′)
a.   *dish-washed ((something was) *washed dishes)
b.   *book-chewed ((something was) *chewed books)
c.   *fish-fried ((something was) *fried fish)

(57′)
a.   pan-fried ((something was) fried in a pan)
b.   home-grown ((something was) grown at home)
c.   land-based ((something was) based on land)
d.   leaf-strewn ((something was) strewn with leaves)
e.   snow-covered ((something was) covered with snow)

(58′)
a.   rat-bitten ((something was) bitten by rats)
b.   wolf-reared ((something was) reared by wolves)
c.   moth-eaten ((something was) eaten by moths)
d.   horse-drawn ((something was) drawn by horses)

(59′)
a.   oft-heard ((something was) heard oft(en))
b.   widely-noticed ((something was) noticed widely)
c.   much-imitated ((something was) imitated much)

What appeared to be irregularities in verbal compounding are explained by the lexical theory of passivization.

The contrasting restrictions on the active (-ing) and passive (-en) verbal compounds simply follow from the fact that the passivized verb is *lexically* represented as intransitive. Thus, in the compound *rat-biting, rat* is interpreted as the first grammatical argument NP to the right of the active participle *biting*—namely, the direct object. And in the compound *rat-bitten, rat* is interpreted as the first grammatical argument NP to the right of the passive participle *bitten*—namely, the agentive *by*-object.

It also follows from this theory that nouns compounded with the active perfect participles such as *fallen* and *collapsed* should be uninterpretable either as subjects or as agentive *by*-objects. This explains the contrasts given in (60)–(61).

(60)
a.   moth-eaten
b.   *snow-fallen (cf. new-fallen)

(61)
a.   wolf-reared
b.   *lung-collapsed (cf. half-collapsed)

Even the exceptional participle *read* falls into place. *Read* is exceptional because it has two interpretations in adjectival compounds, as in (a) *a well-read book* and (b) *a well-read man*. Interpretation (a) is based on the passive participle of the transitive verb *read* (*The book was read many times*). Interpretation (b) is based on the active perfect participle of an intransitive sense of *read* (*The man has read* (*in many areas, about many things*)). From this analysis it is predicted that only the (a)-type participle would permit a compounded noun to be interpreted as its agent. And indeed we find that the possible compound *president-read books* is well-formed in comparison with *book-read presidents*.

In sum, the intransitivity of the passivized verb must be represented in the lexicon. This conclusion follows from the basic assumptions of our theory. First, *near-decomposition:* the rule systems of natural language are organized into components in such a way as to maximize the interactions of rules within components and to minimize the interactions of rules across components. Thus, syntactic rules will not be interspersed among lexical rules and vice versa. Consequently, structures which are analyzed by lexical rules must be lexical structures and cannot be syntactically derived. Second, *the lexicalist hypothesis:* derivational rules of word formation are lexical rules, as proposed by Chomsky 1970, Siegel 1974, Aronoff 1976, Allen 1978, Wasow 1977, Bresnan 1978, Roeper and Siegel 1978, and others. Now as Roeper and Siegel 1978 show, verbal compounding, like Adjective Conversion, is indisputably a lexical process of word formation in English. Verbal compounding changes the lexical category of the derived words (from X + V to A); its constituents are lexical rather than phrasal categories; it applies only to elements that can be lexically subcategorized by the verbal base; and the words it produces can undergo other lexical processes, such as derivational suffixation (e.g., *well-formedness, soft-spokenness*). Since we have seen clear evidence that passivized verbs undergo the lexical processes of verbal compounding and Adjective

Conversion, we conclude that passivized verbs are represented in the lexicon.

An interesting question arises from this conclusion. The first sister principle appears to relate compounded words to syntactic contexts over which adjacency is definable. To express this fact, Roeper and Siegel assume that compounding operates on the strict subcategorization frames of verbs. But because the lexical theory has no other need for strict subcategorization frames (cf. chapter 2 of this volume and section 1.3 below), this raises the question of the exact status of the first sister principle in this theory. In fact, there is evidence that adjacency is independent of strict subcategorization features.

There exist adjective–noun compounds of the form [$_A$ A N-ed], meaning 'having an A N': *hairy-chested* ('having a hairy chest'), *full-bosomed* ('having a full bosom'), *tight-fisted* ('having a tight fist'), *broken-hearted, weak-kneed,* etc. The adjective and noun must be interpretable as adjacent sisters in a noun phrase, for adjectives that cannot occur in prenominal position cannot be compounded in this way. For example, the predicate adjective *asleep* (as in *My foot is asleep*) cannot occur in prenominal position (**an asleep foot*), and neither can it undergo A–N compounding: **asleep-footed.* Moreover, where the prenominal adjectives differ in meaning from predicate adjectives, the A N compound bears the prenominal meaning. For example, *a heavy hand* refers to a nonliteral quality of clumsiness or severity, while *The hand is heavy* refers more literally to weight; and the compound *heavy-handed* has the nonliteral interpretation. But in general, neither adjectives nor nouns are strictly subcategorized for one another.

These facts suggest that syntactic adjacency may be a general condition on the morphological incorporation of independent lexical categories into single words. It is unlikely that this "global" condition is a formal condition of grammar. Rather, it may be the formal reflection in grammars of causal factors that affect the perception and lexicalization of words. Thus, since all lexical categories dominate strings of adjacent morphemes, it may be that only adjacent words can be perceived as belonging to a single lexical category. Similarly, recent work suggests that certain semantic (Grimshaw in press) and phonological (Kiparsky in preparation) generalizations over grammars may reflect causal factors in language acquisition and language change that cannot and should not be stated as formal conditions of grammar.

Lexical Quantification of Predicate Arguments

As shown in chapter 3, the organization of the grammar imposes an intrinsic ordering on lexical rules and sentence interpretive rules: in particular, rules for the semantic interpretation of sentences may be ordered after but not before the rules that operate on lexical forms. The intrinsic ordering of lexical rules before sentence interpretive rules affects the order of interpretation of quantifiers so that the lexical quantification of predicate arguments has narrow scope with respect to the syntactic quantification of sentences. Examples (62) and (63) are given to illustrate this point. Example (63) contains the active intransitivized lexical form 'READ((SUBJ),ϕ)', which is derived from 'READ((SUBJ),(OBJ))' by the substitution (OBJ) $\mapsto \phi$. The predicate argument to which ϕ is assigned is existentially interpreted.

(62)
Everyone was reading something.

(63)
Everyone was reading.

Example (62) can be ambiguously interpreted with respect to the scope of the quantifiers *everyone* and *someone*. The sentence may have either the '$\exists\forall$' interpretation 'There was something such that everyone was reading it' or the '$\forall\exists$' interpretation 'For every person, there was something such that that person was reading it'.[10] But (63) is unambiguous: the lexically introduced quantification of *read*'s second argument can have only narrow scope with respect to the syntactically introduced quantifier *everyone;* thus, the sentence has only the '$\forall\exists$' interpretation 'For every person, there was something such that that person was reading it'. Therefore, the relative scope of lexical and syntactic quantifiers reflects their order of interpretation.

Because Passivization (22) includes the substitution (SUBJ) $\mapsto \phi$, the predicate argument to which the subject corresponds in the active can be existentially interpreted in the passive. It follows from the lexical theory of passivization that the quantifier of this predicate argument must have narrow scope with respect to syntactic quantifiers. As examples (64) and (65) show, this predicted consequence holds true.

(64)
Everything was read by someone.

(65)
Everything was read.

Example (64) is ambiguous with respect to the scope of the syntactic quantifiers *everything* and *someone:* it may have either the '∃∀' interpretation 'There was someone such that everything was read by that person' or the '∀∃' interpretation 'For everything, there was someone who read it'. But example (65) has only the '∀∃' interpretation 'For everything, there was someone who read it'. (See again footnote 10.)

This result confirms the conclusions of the previous section: although it has striking structural effects in configurational languages, passivization is a fundamentally lexical process.

1.3 Pseudoarguments for a Passive Transformation

The previous sections have shown the lexical theory of passivization to be far more explanatory than transformational theories. What then of the familiar arguments for a Passive transformation? In this part, it is shown that, in every case, the lexical theory explains the phenomena at least as well as the transformational theory; in most cases, the lexical explanation is better.

Selectional Generalizations

It is often argued that a transformational analysis of passivization is advantageous because the selectional restrictions of individual predicates need be defined only once, on the deep structure configurations of sentences. Base generation of the passive is thought to needlessly multiply statements of selectional restrictions, requiring one statement for the active configuration and another for the passive configuration. But in fact, the lexical theory provides a superior account of selectional generalizations.

In the lexical theory assumed here, selectional restrictions are replaced by the semantic compatibility requirements of predicate argument structures. Each predicate argument structure represents a semantic function of n grammatically interpretable arguments, and to each predicate argument a grammatical function is assigned by the lexical form. When a grammatical function such as SUBJ (or OBJ) is assigned to a predicate argument, the functional subject (or object) of the predicate in a sentence will be bound to that argument (see chapter 4). The semantic function represented by a predicate must be compatible with the semantic interpretations of all of the subjects, objects, and other grammatical arguments that are bound to the arguments of that predicate.

To illustrate, the dyadic predicate argument structure *admire*(1,2) represents a semantic function that is compatible with ordered pairs of admirers and admired things. The active lexical form 'ADMIRE((SUBJ),(OBJ))' imposes the requirements that the subject of the active verb *admire* be interpretable as an admirer (argument 1), and that the object be interpretable as an admired thing (argument 2). Abstract attributes such as sincerity can be objects of admiration, but cannot be admirers; consequently, *John admires sincerity* meets the compatibility requirements of *admire*(1,2) but #*Sincerity admires John* does not. The rule of passivization gives us the passive lexical form 'ADMIRE((BY OBJ),(SUBJ))', which imposes the requirements that the passive subject be interpretable as an admired thing (argument 2), and that the *by*-object be interpretable as an admirer (argument 1). Consequently, *Sincerity is admired by John* meets the compatibility requirements of *admire*(1,2) but #*John is admired by sincerity* does not.

The lexical rule of Passivization preserves the predicate argument structure and hence the "selectional restrictions" of the active verb. In changing the grammatical function assignments of the active lexical form to the passive lexical form, Passivization reassociates the predicate arguments with different grammatical functions, and thus the "selectional restrictions" appear to change. But in fact there is no change in the semantic compatibility requirements of the predicate argument structure, and thus no need for multiple statements of "selectional restrictions."

The lexical theory attributes selectional restrictions to the semantics of predicate argument structures, while the transformational theory (Chomsky 1965) postulates a finite set of grammatical features ([abstract], [animate], etc.) in terms of which all selectional restrictions are to be formulated. But there exist verbs whose selectional restrictions cannot plausibly be decomposed into such a feature set. An example is the verb *crane,* analyzed in chapter 3 of this volume, which means 'to stretch one's neck for a better view'. The object of *crane* is severely restricted, as (66) indicates.

(66)
a.   John craned his neck.
b.   *John craned my neck.
c.   *John craned his leg.

But what set of grammatical features correctly characterizes this restriction? Those that might be postulated ([+neck]?; [+body part],

[+between head and shoulders]?; etc.) are hardly well motivated as grammatical features.

Moreover, examples like (67) and (68) show that the restriction must be semantic.

(67)
The Hydra yawned and craned a neck.

(68)
a. John injured *his neck* when he craned *it* (as Mary entered the room).
b. *John injured *my neck* when he craned *it* (as Mary entered the room).
c. *John injured *his leg* when he craned *it* (as Mary entered the room).

(67) shows that the possessive pronoun modifying the object of *crane* is not required if the object is appropriately interpretable. (68) shows that even the object head noun *neck* is not required, so long as the object is appropriately interpretable. It should also be noticed that the pronoun *it* does not bear any of the previously postulated selectional features ([+neck], etc.).

The semantic compatibility requirements of 'CRANE((SUBJ),(OBJ))' are that its first argument be interpretable as an agent and its second argument as the agent's (inalienably possessed) neck. This accounts for examples (66)–(68), and for the passivized examples (69a–c).

(69)
a. Not a neck/*leg was craned when I entered the room.
b. Anyone's neck/*leg can be injured if it is craned too far.
c. Your neck/*leg can be injured by being craned too far.

Moreover, it easily accounts for ungrammatical examples like *His neck was craned by John,* given the condition on bound anaphora proposed in chapter 3. In sum, the lexical theory of semantic compatibility appears superior to the transformational theory of selectional restrictions.

Simplicity of Strict Subcategorization

The transformational analysis is thought to have the advantage of simplifying the strict subcategorization of verbs. The grammatical status of examples like (70a) and (70b) follows from the grammatical status of their transformational sources, represented by (71a) and (71b), respectively.

(70)
a.   John was bitten by Fred.
b.   *John was bitten Mary by Fred.

(71)
a.   Fred bit John.
b.   *Fred bit John Mary.

Specifically, the strict subcategorization frame of the active verb *bite* permits it to be lexically inserted into transitive deep structure configurations corresponding to (71a) but not into the ditransitive configuration corresponding to (71b); consequently, the Passive transformation can derive (70a) but not (70b). Without the Passive transformation, it is often argued, separate subcategorization frames would have to be formulated for active and passive verbs, losing the generalization that relates (70) to (71).

In the lexical theory assumed here, strict subcategorization is not required, because its effects follow from general conditions on the interpretation of lexical forms. *Functional completeness* requires that *every predicate argument be bound to a functional argument of the type specified by the lexical form*. Thus, the example *John admired is functionally incomplete because there is no object bound to the second predicate argument in 'ADMIRE((SUBJ),(OBJ))'.[11] *Functional coherence* requires that *every meaningful functional argument of the type specifiable by a lexical form must be bound to a predicate argument*.[12] Thus, the example *Fred bit John Mary is functionally incoherent because there is a second object *Mary* which cannot be bound to a predicate argument in the lexical form 'BITE((SUBJ),(OBJ))'. In contrast, the example *Fred sent John Mary* is functionally coherent because all three functional arguments, the subject *Fred,* the object *John,* and the second object *Mary,* can be bound to predicate arguments in the lexical form 'SEND((SUBJ),(OBJ2),(OBJ))'. Given a grammar together with the general conditions of functional completeness and functional coherence, each lexical form for a verb defines a set of grammatical contexts in which the verb can be lexically inserted.

It is true that in the lexical theory there are separate lexical forms for active and passive verbs. These permit both active and passive sentences to be base-generated and eliminate any need for the multiple constituent structure representations of a sentence that constitute its transformational derivation. But the generalization that relates (70) to (71) is not thereby lost. The lexical rule of Passivization captures it by deriving the passive lexical form 'BITE((BY OBJ),(SUBJ))' from the active lexical form 'BITE((SUBJ),(OBJ))'. Given this passive lexical form, example (70a) *John was bitten by Fred* is functionally complete and coherent, but example (70b) **John was bitten Mary by Fred* is functionally incoherent, having an extra object *Mary* that cannot be bound to a predicate argument. Since there is no active lexical form corresponding to (71b) **Fred bit John Mary,* Passivization cannot derive another lexical form which will make (70b) functionally coherent. It is evident that a Passive transformation has no advantage over the lexical rule of Passivization in capturing these subcategorizational generalizations.

Wasow 1977:341 makes a related argument for a Passive transformation when he points out that in a transformational analysis, the grammatical status of examples (72) and (73) follows from that of (74) and (75), respectively.

(72)
a.   *The United Fund was given.
b.   The United Fund was given ten dollars.

(73)
a.   Ten dollars was given.
b.   Ten dollars was given to the United Fund.

(74)
a.   *Someone gave the United Fund.
b.   Someone gave the United Fund ten dollars.

(75)
a.   Someone gave ten dollars.
b.   Someone gave ten dollars to the United Fund.

Wasow remarks,

In order to account for [these facts] with [only] the standard machinery of selection and strict subcategorization, it would be necessary to make the obligatoriness of the presence of an NP-complement to *given* dependent on the selectional features of its subject. If, instead, these examples are derived transformationally, [(72) and (73) follow respectively from (74) and (75)], which can be captured quite straightforwardly with the standard machinery.

In the lexical theory assumed here, examples (72) and (73) also follow straightforwardly from (74) and (75). The lexical forms for *give* in (75) are shown in (76).

(76)

$$\text{`GIVE}((\text{SUBJ}),(\text{OBJ}),\left\{\begin{array}{c}(\text{TO OBJ})\\ \phi\end{array}\right\})\text{'}$$

From (76), the rule of *To*-Dative (42) derives the lexical form in (77).

(77)
`GIVE((SUBJ),(OBJ2),(OBJ))'

(77) corresponds to (74b); but no lexical form can be derived for (74a). (The lexical form for (74a) would have to be `GIVE((SUBJ),ϕ,(OBJ)))', but this lexical form cannot be derived either by *To*-Dative (42) or by Intransitivization ((OBJ) $\mapsto \phi$).) From (76) and (77), Passivization derives (78) and (79).

(78)

$$\text{`GIVE}(\left\{\begin{array}{c}(\text{BY OBJ})\\ \phi\end{array}\right\},(\text{SUBJ}),\left\{\begin{array}{c}(\text{TO OBJ})\\ \phi\end{array}\right\})\text{'}$$

(79)

$$\text{`GIVE}(\left\{\begin{array}{c}(\text{BY OBJ})\\ \phi\end{array}\right\},(\text{OBJ2}),(\text{SUBJ}))\text{'}$$

(78) provides lexical forms for (73a,b). (79) provides the lexical form for (72b). There is no lexical form for (72a), and none can be derived by Passivization. Again it is evident that a Passive transformation has no advantage over the lexical rule of Passivization in capturing these subcategorizational generalizations.[13]

In summary, the transformational theory simplifies strict subcategorization by permitting lexical insertion into only one, canonical, structure which is then transformed into other structures. The lexical theory simplifies strict subcategorization by "transforming" the subcategorizational properties of verbs in the lexicon and then inserting the lexically transformed verbs into syntactic structures. The lexical theory accounts for subcategorizational regularities just as well as the transformational theory. Moreover, the lexical theory of subcategorization has an explanatory advantage over the transformational theory. In the lexical theory, Passivization and *To*-Dative are operations on lexical forms; as such, they derive lexical forms from lexical forms. Given a grammar together with the functional completeness and functional coherence conditions, each lexical form derived by these rules defines a set of grammatical contexts into which a passive or dative verb can be lexically inserted. For this set of grammatical contexts to be usable, the derived lexical form must be satisfiable by the same grammar as the basic lexical form. For example, suppose that a grammar for English allowed only a single object NP following a verb: VP → V (NP) (PP). This grammar satisfies the basic lexical form for *give*, (76), but because it generates no grammatical contexts in which two objects occur, it does not satisfy the derived lexical form produced by the rule of *To*-Dative, (77). As a result, verbs that have undergone *To*-Dative could not be lexically inserted in this grammar. In fact, the real grammar of English allows two object NPs following a verb: VP → V (NP) (NP) (PP). This is shown by the existence of ditransitive constructions like *Please spare me your sarcasm, I envy John his good looks, That remark just cost you your job,* in which a basic lexical form requires two NP objects. The same is true of passives: the grammatical contexts required by passive lexical forms are already generated by the grammar for active lexical forms. Compare, for example, *The picture was hung on the wall by the guard* and *The picture has hung on the wall by the guard.* Given the autonomy of the lexical and phrase structure components of the grammar, the lexical theory explains this "structure-preserving" property of Passivization, *To*-Dative, and all rules that affect the polyadicity of natural language predicates. In transformational theory, the structure-preserving property of certain transformations has been extensively studied (Emonds 1976) or simply assumed (Chomsky 1977b), but not explained. In fact, Grimshaw in chapter 2 of this volume shows that transformational conceptions of structure preservation fail to explain a range of facts that follow from the lexical theory that grammatical functions are assigned to lexical predicates.

Idiom Chunks

Another familiar argument for a Passive transformation is based on the distribution of idiomatic NPs. It is argued that certain idiomatic NPs can be base-generated as the objects of only a single verb. The NP *tabs* in the idiom *keep tabs on* is an example of this.

(80)

The FBI kept tabs on Jane Fonda.

(81)

*The FBI extended tabs to Jane Fonda.

(82)

*The FBI uses tabs.

These idiomatic NPs may also appear as passivized subjects of the same verb:

(83)

Tabs were kept on Jane Fonda by the FBI.

(84)

*Tabs were extended to Jane Fonda by the FBI.

(85)

*Tabs are used by the FBI.

It is argued that if passives are base-generated, the restriction on idiomatic objects must be stated twice, once for the active (e.g., *tabs* occurs as the object only of *keep*) and once for the passive (e.g., *tabs* occurs as the subject only of *be kept*). But if passives are transformationally derived from active configurations, the restriction need be stated only once, on the deep structure source of the passive construction. Thus, nontransformational analyses of passives appear to fail to capture generalization in describing the distribution of idiom chunks.

This argument is a variant of the argument from selectional generalizations, but here nonsemantic selection is involved. *Tabs* is a grammatical object that is not a "logical object": it does not correspond to an argument in predicate argument structure. In the lexical theory assumed here, predicate argument structure is independent from grammatical function assignments (see chapter 3), and so the idiom *keep tabs on* can be represented by the (partial) lexical entry given in (86a). In (86b), *the FBI* is the subject, *Jane Fonda* is the *on*-object, and *tabs* is the object; the semantic relation *keep-tabs-on* holds between the subject and the *on*-object.

(86)

a. keep: V, 'KEEP-TABS-ON((SUBJ),(ON OBJ))'

$$(\text{OBJ FORM}) =_c \text{TABS}^{[14]}$$

b. The FBI kept tabs on Jane Fonda.

The lexical rule of Passivization converts (86a) to (87a).

(87)

a.   kept: $V_{[Part]}$, 'KEEP-TABS-ON($\left\{\begin{matrix}\text{(BY OBJ)}\\ \phi\end{matrix}\right\}$,(ON OBJ))'

(SUBJ FORM) $=_c$ TABS

b.   Tabs were kept on Jane Fonda by the FBI.

In (87b), *the FBI* is the *by*-object, *Jane Fonda* is again the *on*-object, and *tabs* is the subject; the semantic relation *keep-tabs-on* holds between the *by*-object and the *on*-object.

To clarify exactly why the lexical form given in (87b) is the result of applying passivization to the lexical form given in (86a), I will describe briefly the notation for lexical forms introduced later in chapter 3. A lexical form is a predicate argument structure together with an assignment of grammatical functions. An assignment of grammatical functions to a predicate argument structure $P(1,...,m)$ is a list of grammatical function expressions $G = g_1,...,g_n$ such that the mapping from $1,...,m$ to G defined by $i \mapsto g_i$ is injective (one-to-one and into). A grammatical function expression is (a) a grammatical function name (such as SUBJ, OBJ, or TO OBJ) surrounded by one or two sets of parentheses, (b) the null grammatical function symbol ϕ, or (c) an equation specifying the value of a grammatical function name. In this notation, the lexical form given in (86a) appears as shown in (88).

(88)

a. $\langle$(SUBJ),(ON OBJ),(OBJ FORM) $=_c$ TABS$\rangle$ [assignment of grammatical functions]

b.   keep-tabs-on(1,2)   [predicate argument structure]

(88) indicates that (SUBJ) is assigned to argument 1 of *keep-tabs-on*, (ON OBJ) to argument 2, and (OBJ FORM) $=_c$ TABS to no predicate argument. The rule of Passivization changes an assignment of grammatical functions by making the substitutions (SUBJ) $\mapsto \phi$ or (SUBJ) $\mapsto$ (BY OBJ), and (OBJ) $\mapsto$ (SUBJ). By the left associativity of the functional notation, (OBJ FORM) $=_c$ TABS is equivalent to ((OBJ) FORM) $=_c$ TABS (see chapter 4). Passivization will substitute (SUBJ) for (OBJ) here, deriving ((SUBJ) FORM) $=_c$ TABS, which is equivalent to (SUBJ FORM) $=_c$ TABS. Thus, from (88), Passivization gives (89). The two passive grammatical function assignments in (89) indicate that either ϕ or (BY OBJ) is assigned to argument 1 of *keep-tabs-on*, (ON OBJ) to argument 2, and (SUBJ FORM) $=_c$ TABS to no predicate argument.

(89)

a. $\langle \phi, (\text{ON OBJ}), (\text{SUBJ FORM}) =_c \text{TABS} \rangle$
    $\langle (\text{BY OBJ}), (\text{ON OBJ}), (\text{SUBJ FORM}) =_c \text{TABS} \rangle$

b. keep-tabs-on(1,2)

In sum, given the basic lexical form of the idiomatic *keep-tabs-on,* the lexical rule of Passivization produces derived lexical forms which permit the occurrence of the idiom chunk *tabs* as the passivized subject of *be kept.* A Passive transformation is not necessary to predict the distribution of such idiom chunks.

A second example of the lexical analysis of idiom chunks is *to pull someone's leg,* which has the idiomatic meaning 'to play a joke on, or tease, someone'. The idiomatic meaning does not arise with verbs other than *pull,* or with objects other than [*possessor's*] *leg.*

(90)
Mary is pulling your leg.   [idiomatic or literal]

(91)
Mary is tugging your leg.   [only literal]

(92)
Mary is pulling your arm.   [only literal]

The lexical form for this idiom is given in (93). (93) represents *to pull someone's leg* as a semantic relation between the subject of *pull* and *pull*'s object's possessor, denoted by "(OBJ POSS)".

(93)
'PULL-LEG((SUBJ),(OBJ POSS))'
          (OBJ FORM) $=_c$ LEG

The lexical rule of Passivization derives from (93) the lexical form given in (94). Example (95) illustrates the passivized idiom; examples (96) and (97) predictably lack idiomatic meanings.

(94)

'PULL-LEG$\left(\left\{ \begin{matrix} (\text{BY OBJ}) \\ \phi \end{matrix} \right\},(\text{SUBJ POSS})\right)$'

          (SUBJ FORM) $=_c$ LEG

(95)
Your leg is being pulled.   [idiomatic or literal]

(96)
Your leg is being tugged.   [only literal]

(97)
Your arm is being pulled.   [only literal]

The distribution of idiom chunks like *tabs* and [*possessor's*] *leg* in passive constructions follows from their distribution in active constructions in the lexical theory just as in the transformational theory.

In distinguishing semantic selection from formal selection, the lexical theory has an interesting consequence. As shown in the first part of section 1.3, an extreme degree of semantic selection is exhibited by the verb *crane,* whose object must be interpretable as its subject's inalienably possessed neck: *John craned his neck/*my neck/*his leg.* But even with *crane,* the object can vary so long as the semantic requirements of the predicate argument structure are satisfied. Thus, examples like (68a) (repeated here) are grammatical, while (68b,c) are not.

(68)
a.   John injured *his neck* when he craned *it* (as Mary entered the room).
b.   *John injured *my neck* when he craned *it* (as Mary entered the room).
c.   *John injured *his leg* when he craned *it* (as Mary entered the room).

In contrast, the selection of idiom chunks (which have no intrinsic meaning) is formal, not semantic. Consequently, examples like (98) and (99) are ungrammatical (a consequence pointed out by Jane Grimshaw).

(98)
a.   *Although the FBI kept *tabs* on Jane Fonda, the CIA kept *them* on Vanessa Redgrave.
b.   *Tabs* were kept on Jane Fonda by the FBI, but *they* weren't kept on Vanessa Redgrave.

(99)
a.   John injured *his leg* when Mary pulled *it*.   [only literal]
b.   If you don't take care of *your leg,* it will be pulled.   [only literal]

Because of the autonomy of predicate argument structure from representations of syntactic context, the contrast between these two types of selection is naturally explained in the lexical theory.

Note finally that the existence of meaningful subparts of idiom chunks poses no problem for the lexical theory. A functional object can bear the FORM feature even when its functional parts are semantically interpreted, as the case of *pull* [*someone's*] *leg* illustrates. Similarly, examples like *keep close tabs on* meaning 'watch closely' can be easily accounted for, because the presence of a FORM feature does not preclude the generation of optional modifiers. Completely fixed idiom chunks can be given a complete functional specification, although many of them may be instances of morphological incorporation, as the next section will describe.

Prepositional Passives

Because syntactic transformations analyze constituent structure without reference to semantic or grammatical relations (Chomsky 1973, Bresnan 1976b), an argument for the Passive transformation is often based on the existence of prepositional passives like those in (100).

(100)
a. The fields look like they've been *marched through* by an army.
b. Everything is being *paid for* by the company.
c. Your books need to be *gone over* by an accountant.
d. He is *looked on* as selfish by everyone.
e. These things are *spoken of* by my family with reluctance.
f. My desk has obviously been *rummaged around in* by someone.

In these prepositional passives it appears as though an NP unrelated to the verb has been passivized, as one might expect if passivization were accomplished by a syntactic transformation. How can such passives be accounted for in the lexical theory?

In fact, of course, there is a lexical relation between the verb and its passivized subject: in each case the verb–preposition combination expresses a lexicalized dyadic relation. Thus, *marched through* means 'crossed', *paid for* means 'purchased', *gone over* means 'examined', *looked on* means 'regarded', *spoken of* means 'mentioned', *rummaged around in* means 'searched'. Prepositional objects which are not lexically related to a verb in this way cannot be passivized:

(101)

a. *No reason was left for.
    (They left for no reason.)

b. *A river is lived over by the miller.
    (The miller lives over a river.)

c. *The operation was died after.
    (The patient died after the operation.)

d. *The house was being moved around in by the burglars.
    (The burglars were moving around in the house.)

We will see that only the lexical theory offers an explanation for these facts.

It was originally proposed in Bresnan 1972 that *march through, pay for, go over, look on, speak of, rummage around in,* and the like, are complex lexical verbs having the morphological structure $[V + P]_V$. In the lexical theory, such verbs would be formed by a lexical rule of V–P Incorporation, which morphologically incorporates a verb and an adjacent preposition into a single complex verb that governs a direct object, as in (102).

(102)

V–P Incorporation

Operation on lexical form: (P OBJ) $\mapsto$ (OBJ)

Morphological change: V $\leftrightarrow$ [V P]$_V$

In the rule of V–P Incorporation, it is unnecessary to stipulate that the preposition P be adjacent to the verb with which it is incorporated, because syntactic adjacency is assumed to be a necessary condition not only for incorporation but also for other morphological processes such as compounding.[15] Nor is it necessary to stipulate that verbal inflections attach to the verbal base of the complex verb (*paid for* vs. *pay for-ed, gone over* vs. *go over-en,* etc.), for endocentric inflection is characteristic of English complex verbs. Whether a complex verb is formed by prefixation (*re-think, re-do; overeat, oversleep, overshoot; outdance, outtalk, outthink*), compounding (*backtrack, backslide*), or back-formation (*proof-read, babysit*), verbal inflections attach to the verbal base. Thus we have *re-did* vs. *re-do-ed, overshot* vs. *overshoot-ed, outthought* vs. *outthink-ed, backslid* vs. *backslided, proof-read* vs. *proof-read-ed, babysat* vs. *babysitted.* Endocentric inflection predictably fails to apply when morphologically complex

verbs are formed by conversion from compound nouns (*to snowshoe,
to pop fly*) and so lack a verbal base: *snowshoe-d* vs. **snowshod, pop
flied* vs. **pop flew*. But endocentric nominal inflection does appear
within compound nouns (*snow goose/snow geese* vs. **snow gooses*),
and adjectival inflection occurs within compound adjectives (*better-
informed = more well-informed*).

Rule (102) would apply to (103a) to derive (104a); (103a) is lexically
inserted into structures like (103b), while (104a) is lexically inserted
into structures like (104b).

(103)

a. [speak]$_V$, 'SPEAK-OF((SUBJ),(OF OBJ))'

b. [$_S$ we won't [$_{VP}$ speak [$_{PP}$ of [$_{NP}$ John]] here]]

(104)

a. [[speak]$_V$[of]$_P$]$_V$, 'SPEAK-OF((SUBJ),(OBJ))'

b. [$_S$ we won't [$_{VP}$[$_V$ speak of] [$_{NP}$ John] here]]

The lexical rule of Passivization cannot apply to (103a) (which lacks an
(OBJ)), but it can apply to (104a). The result is (105a), which is lexically
inserted into structures like (105b).

(105)

a. [[spoken]$_{V[Part]}$[of]$_P$]$_{V[Part]}$, 'SPEAK-OF($\left\{\begin{matrix}(BY\ OBJ)\\ \phi\end{matrix}\right\}$,(SUBJ))'

b. [$_S$[$_{NP}$ John] won't [$_{VP}$ be [$_{V[Part]}$ spoken of] here]]

A different analysis of prepositional passives was suggested in Bresnan 1978. This treatment eschewed V–P Incorporation in favor of
augmenting the rule of Passivization (22) with the optional substitution
(P OBJ) $\mapsto$ (SUBJ), where P is any preposition name. As an argument in
favor of this analysis, Bresnan 1978 noted that the preposition behaves
like a constituent of the PP in examples such as *It's John of whom I was
speaking*. However, such examples are also consistent with rule (102) if
that rule is taken to be optional. Most significantly, however, only the
incorporation analysis is compatible with the universal formulation of
transitive passivization given in (1). This leads us to look for further
evidence bearing on the choice of analyses.

In fact, there is striking evidence in favor of the incorporation analysis (102) (see chapter 5). First, the complex passive participles undergo
Adjective Conversion.

(106)
a. After the tornado, the fields had a *marched through* look.
b. Each *unpaid for* item will be returned.
c. You can ignore any recently *gone over* accounts.
d. His was not a *well-looked on* profession.
e. They shared an *unspoken of* passion for chocolates.
f. Filled with candy wrappers and crumpled bills, her bag always had a *rummaged around in* appearance.

This is an immediate consequence of rules (102) and (36), together with the convention for endocentric verbal inflection.

Notice that these converted prepositional passives provide strong confirmation for the conclusion reached in the previous section, that lexically passivized verbs undergo conversion to adjectives. For V–P combinations that cannot be passivized also cannot undergo conversion. For example, *look like* fails to passivize:

(107)
*The twin is looked like by his brother.

As a result, no adjective **looked-like* is possible:

(108)
*a looked-like twin

This is despite the fact that *like* is a strandable preposition:

(109)
What does this look like?

and can occur elsewhere in compounds (e.g., *like-minded*). Similarly, we find the pattern given in (110)–(112).

(110)
*No reason was left for.

(111)
*the left-for reason

(112)
What did he leave for?

The fact that exceptions to Passivization are also exceptions to the formation of adjectival passives is unexplained by transformational theories of passivization, but follows immediately from the lexical theory.

Next, adverbial phrases from the sentence cannot be interpolated into the prepositional passive between the verb and its adjoining preposition:

(113)

a. *The fields look like they've been *marched* so recently *through*.
b. *Everything was *paid* twice *for*.
c. *Your books were *gone* most thoroughly *over*.
d. *He is *looked* generally *on* as selfish.
e. *These things are *spoken* with reluctance *of*.
f. *Her bag was always being *rummaged around* so slowly *in*.

This follows from rule (102) together with the *lexical integrity hypothesis,* which prohibits syntactic reorderings into or out of lexical categories (such as V, N, etc.) (see chapter 5). Notice that adverbial phrases can much more easily be interpolated between an active verb and an adjacent preposition stranded by relativization:

(114)

a. ?Where are the fields that the army has marched so recently through?
b. That's something that I would have paid twice for.
c. These are the books that we have gone most thoroughly over.
d. ?There is nothing here that one should speak with reluctance of.
e. That's the bag that I saw her rummaging around so slowly in.

This too would follow from the incorporation analysis: while necessary for prepositional passives, incorporation is optional for actives.[16]

Finally, a subtle prediction can be drawn from the incorporation analysis. It will be shown in chapter 5 that before an adjectival complement only an incorporated verb–preposition complex can appear. The reason for this is that the expansion VP → V NP AP but not VP → V PP AP defines a normal sequence of categories in the English verb phrase, for complement APs. (Complement APs, or ACOMPs, must be distinguished from adjunct APs as well as *as*-prepositional phrases; see chapters 5 and 6). Thus, the analysis of sentence (115a) must be (115b), not (115c).

(115)

a. They look on John as selfish.
b. [$_S$ they [$_{VP}$[$_V$ look on] [$_{NP}$ John] [$_{AP}$ as selfish]]]
c. *[$_S$ they [$_{VP}$[$_V$ look] [$_{PP}$ on John] [$_{AP}$ as selfish]]]

Because the preposition *on* does not form a constituent PP with the NP in this context, the contrast between the cleft constructions (116a) and (116b) is predicted.

(116)
a.   It is John that they look on as selfish.
b.   *It is on John that they look as selfish.

Clefting can apply to NP and PP constituents, but not to nonconstituent P NP sequences (cf. *It is this bill that you must pay up, *It is up this bill that you must pay*). In contrast to (115a), (117a) has dual analyses, permitted by the two phrase structure expansions VP → V NP PP and VP → V PP PP.

(117)
a.   They look on John with pride.
b.   [$_S$ they [$_{VP}$[$_V$ look on] [$_{NP}$ John] [$_{PP}$ with pride]]]
c.   [$_S$ they [$_{VP}$[$_V$ look] [$_{PP}$ on John] [$_{PP}$ with pride]]]

As a result, the grammaticality of both cleft constructions in (118a) and (118b) is predicted.

(118)
a.   It is John that they look on with pride.
b.   It is on John that they look with pride.

In summary, the rule of V–P Incorporation (102) is a lexical process of transitivization that "feeds" the lexical Passivization rule. If a prepositional object is not represented in the lexical form of a verb, V–P Incorporation, and hence Passivization, is impossible. This explains the failure of Passivization in (101): the prepositional objects in these examples are *not* grammatical arguments of the verbs, but elements of prepositional adjuncts or complements (see chapter 5).

A second pseudoargument for a Passive transformation can be derived from prepositional passives. The argument notes that stress reduction on monosyllabic prepositions is blocked before the site of a transformational movement (trace):

(119)
a.   They paid for that.   [f'r]
b.   What did they pay for?   [for], *[f'r]

(120)
a. They slept in bed.   ['n]
b. What did they sleep in?   [in], *['n]

It is then observed that stress reduction is also blocked in prepositional passives, a fact that could be explained by assuming that the
transformation involved in passivization leaves a trace:

(121)
a. That was paid for.   [for], *[f'r]
b. That bed was slept in.   [in], *['n]

While it is true that stress reduction is generally blocked in prepositional passives, the hypothesized Passive transformation cannot be the
explanation for it, for adjectival passives show the same phenomenon:

(122)
a. That was unpaid for.   [for], *[f'r]
b. That bed looks unslept in.   [in], *['n]

Recall that syntactic transformations cannot move constituents into or
out of words (that is, elements dominated by lexical categories such as
the A in [A unpaid for], [A unslept in]); hence, they cannot leave traces
within words (lexical categories). Even if traces could appear within
words in violation of the lexical integrity hypothesis, they would fail to
be properly bound in many perfectly grammatical cases. For example,
in *horribly slept-in looking beds,* the hypothetical trace following *in*
would both precede and c-command its "antecedent" *beds.* Moreover,
in examples like *an uncared-for look, an undismayed air,* there is no
antecedent for a trace at all. The examples mean (at least under the
most natural interpretation) 'a look suggesting that one/something is
uncared for' (not: 'a look that has not been cared for') and 'an air which
suggests that one is undismayed' (not: 'an air which has not been dismayed').[17] A simple rule that would account for all these observations
(suggested by William Leben, personal communication) is that a
constituent-final preposition cannot undergo stress reduction. In (119b)
and (120b), the dangling prepositions are final in the PP ([PP P]); in
(121), the prepositions are final in the V ([V V P]); in (122), the prepositions are final in the A ([A V P]). Thus, the phenomena can be
accounted for more generally without recourse to transformational
derivations, and so the secondary argument for a Passive transformation should be rejected.

In connection with this discussion of prepositional passives, it should be added that not only prepositions, but also adverbs and nouns, can be incorporated into complex verbs in English. Examples like *think better of, make fun of, look askance at, catch sight of* abound. These all permit "external" passives, as in (123).

(123)
a.   We had a plan, but it was eventually *thought better of.*
b.   He's always being *made fun of* by his friends.
c.   That might be *looked askance at* in some circles.
d.   Mary was *caught sight of* in the crowd.

Like the idiomatic objects in *keep tabs on, pull someone's leg,* the internal nouns in (123) have noncompositional meanings: *to make fun of* means 'to ridicule', *to catch sight of* means 'to glimpse'. But unlike idiomatic objects, the internal nouns fail to passivize.

(124)
a.   *Sight was caught of Mary in the crowd.
b.   *Fun is being made of John by his friends.

The internal adverbs in (123) also differ from free syntactic adverbs. First, their meaning in combination with the verb is noncompositional: *to think better of* means 'to decide against', *to look askance at* means 'to doubt' or 'to disapprove of'. Second, these adverbs cannot be removed from their internal positions without a wrench in grammaticality or meaning: *Why was it eventually thought of better?, ?*People look at that kind of behavior askance.* (Under a compositional interpretation, *He is looking at me askance* is grammatical, but slightly archaic.) Third, the internal position of these adverbs differs from that of syntactic adverbs: cf. *That might be looked askance at* and **That might be looked obliquely at; It was thought better of* and **It was thought often of.*[18]

If we assume the partial lexical entries given in (125), the rules of V–P Incorporation (102) and Passivization (22) will derive the lexical forms that underlie the examples in (123).

(125)
a.   [think]$_V$[better]$_{Adv}$: V, 'THINK-BETTER-OF((SUBJ),(OF OBJ))'
b.   [make]$_V$[fun]$_N$: V, 'MAKE-FUN-OF((SUBJ),(OF OBJ))'
c.   [look]$_V$[askance]$_{Adv}$: V, 'LOOK-ASKANCE-AT((SUBJ),(AT OBJ))'
d.   [catch]$_V$[sight]$_N$: V, 'CATCH-SIGHT-OF((SUBJ),(OF OBJ))'

Thus, far from posing a problem for the lexical theory, prepositional passives receive a natural and well-motivated analysis.

In the lexical theory, Passivization is possible only when there is a lexical form that meets its functional specifications. For prepositional passives in English, this can happen only when there is a lexical form that can undergo V–P Incorporation—hence, only when there is a lexical relation between the prepositional object and the passivized verb. This is in sharp contrast to the transformational theory of passivization, in which transformations analyze constituent structure without reference to semantic or grammatical relations. But a constituent structure sequence of the form V (N) (ADV) P cannot in general be passivized. In addition to the examples given in (101), there are sentences like (126a–c).

(126)

a.   Mary *drove Barry over* a macadam road. →
      *A macadam road was *driven Barry over* by Mary.

b.   John *threw seed around in* a wide circle. →
      *A wide circle was *thrown seed around in* by John.

c.   I never *put clothes into* that closet. →
      *That closet was never *put clothes into* by me.

The transformational theory of passivization does not explain the contrasts between (126) and (123) and between (101) and (100). To rule out examples like (101) and (126), it has been proposed that when analyzed by the Passive transformation the sequence V (N) (ADV) P must be a "semantic unit" (Chomsky 1973), or that the passivized verb phrase must be semantically interpretable as a "property" (Fiengo 1974), as a "predicate" (Chomsky 1976), or as a "possible semantic word" (Hornstein and Weinberg to appear). (The representations of these notions have not been explicitly defined.) But why such stipulations must be applied at all is left unexplained.

For example, Hornstein and Weinberg to appear attempt to explain restrictions on prepositional passives by assuming that passivization involves NP movement, that the NPs of PPs dominated by VP can be extracted by movement rules, and that those of PPs immediately dominated by S cannot. Yet there are PPs in VP that do not permit stranding, as in *the skill that he worded this with*. The verb *word* is subcategorized for a manner phrase, which therefore is in the VP; nevertheless, the manner preposition cannot be stranded. Conversely, the purposive *for (He did that for fun)*, which is subcategorized by no verb, is dominated by S; it nevertheless strands (*What did he do that for?*). Moreover, Hornstein and Weinberg's account fails to explain contrasts like those between (127a) and (127b), (128a) and (128b).

(127)

a.   The house that the burglars were moving around so quietly in was boobytrapped.

b.   *The house was being moved around quietly in by the burglars.

(128)

a.   What did Harry talk to John about?

b.   *Something was talked to John about by Harry.

To describe such contrasts, Hornstein and Weinberg stipulate that the VP predicate containing the prepositional passive must be a "semantic word." To account for examples like (113) (e.g., *Everything was paid twice for*) they further stipulate that "semantic words" must correspond to contiguous syntactic strings. The first stipulation is ad hoc: there is no reason why the passive predicates and not the active predicates should be "semantic words." The second stipulation is simply false: there are many noncontiguous syntactic strings like *put . . . to shame* ('embarrass'), *take . . . to task* ('reprove'), *bring . . . to* ('revive') which are semantic units.

The observation that prepositional passives such as *paid for, made fun of*, and the like, are "semantic words" is certainly true. But this observation *follows* in the lexical theory from the fact that *paid for, made fun of* are morphologically complex words in the lexicon. The lexical theory of passivization explains the word-like properties of prepositional passives; the transformational theory does not.

Moreover, the transformational formulations of the semantic restrictions all appear to fail for passivized idiom chunks. The verb *kept* is precisely *not* a semantic unit in *Tabs were kept on Jane Fonda; pulled* is not a semantic unit in the idiomatic *Your leg is being pulled*. In what sense is being kept on Jane Fonda a property of tabs, or being pulled a property predicated of someone's leg (in the idiomatic example)? Although they are too vague to be evaluated systematically, all of these notions ("semantic unit," "property," "predicate," "possible semantic word") will clearly be inadequate without reference to *lexical* representations.

Double Passives

Yet another familiar argument for a Passive transformation is based on the existence of double passives in English. These are exemplified in (129)–(133).

(129)
a. No one took advantage of her talents.
b. Not much advantage was taken of her talents.
c. Her talents weren't taken advantage of.

(130)
a. The D.A. made much of your absence on the night of the murder.
b. Much was made of your absence on the night of the murder by the D.A.
c. Your absence on the night of the murder was made much of by the D.A.

(131)
a. We could make good use of a baritone like yourself in our chorale.
b. Good use could be made of a baritone like yourself in our chorale.
c. A baritone like yourself could be made good use of in our chorale.

(132)
a. No one could find fault with Inge's performance.
b. No fault could be found with Inge's performance.
c. Inge's performance couldn't be found fault with.

(133)
a. No one took any notice of Simone.
b. No notice was taken of Simone.
c. Simone was taken no notice of.

If passivization were restricted as it is in the lexical theory to subject–object relations—so the argument runs—then it could not possibly account for the examples in (129)–(133). For if *advantage* is the direct object of *take* in (129a), then *her talents* cannot be, and conversely; thus, if (129b) can be derived, then (129c) cannot be, and conversely. Similarly for (130)–(133). But if passivization is accomplished by a syntactic transformation (which must ignore grammatical relations), then both postverbal NPs are eligible for transformational movement (as in Bresnan 1976b, for example).

The lexical theory has a straightforward solution to the problem posed by double passives. The expressions *take advantage of, make much of, make use of, find fault with,* and the like, have double analyses. One analysis resembles the analysis of idiomatic objects like *keep tabs on;* the other resembles the analysis of incorporated nouns like *make fun of.* The two analyses of *take advantage of* are illustrated in (134).

(134)
a.   take: V, 'TAKE-ADVANTAGE-OF((SUBJ),(OF OBJ))'

$\qquad\qquad\qquad\qquad$ (OBJ FORM) $=_c$ ADVANTAGE

b.   [take]$_V$[advantage]$_N$: V, 'TAKE-ADVANTAGE-OF((SUBJ),(OF OBJ))'

These analyses account for the idiomatic meanings of doubly passivizing constructions: in the above examples, *take advantage of* means 'exploit', *make much of* means 'highlight', *make use of* means 'use', *find fault with* means 'criticize', and *take no notice of* means 'ignore'. The analyses would also account for the ungrammaticality of **Mary wanted the advantage, but she didn't take it of Bill* (cf. the earlier discussion of idiom chunks). Finally, they capture the fact that the incorporated verb has the same idiomatic meaning as the nonincorporated verb. In general, rules of incorporation preserve predicate argument structure and hence meaning (cf. (102)), although, like other lexical derivatives, incorporated verbs may undergo semantic drift.[19]

Passivization applies directly to (134a), which has a direct object; it can apply to (134b) only after V–P Incorporation has applied, converting the (OF OBJ) to (OBJ) and incorporating *of* with the verb [take advantage]$_V$. The results are shown in (135a) and (135b), respectively.

(135)
a.   [$_S$[$_{NP}$ advantage] [$_{VP}$ was [$_V$ taken] [$_{PP}$ of John]]]
b.   [$_S$[$_{NP}$ John] [$_{VP}$ was [$_V$[$_V$ taken advantage] of]]]

According to this analysis of the double passive constructions, the "external" object can passivize only when the "internal" noun has been incorporated with the verb. It follows from the lexical integrity hypothesis that when the external object is passivized, the internal noun cannot be moved from its position within the lexical category V; but when the internal object is passivized, nothing should prevent its movement. This prediction is correct.

(136)
a.   How much advantage was taken of John?
b.   *How much advantage was John taken of?

Parallel predictions for the other verbs are borne out; compare (137), for example.

(137)
a.   What use can be made of a baritone?
b.   *What use can a baritone be made of?

The optional or obligatory modifiers of the internal nouns that may appear in these doubly passivizing expressions (*take unfair advantage of, take terrible advantage of, make good use of,* etc.) can also be accounted for in a straightforward way, along the lines sketched in (138). (138) assigns to *take unfair advantage of* a predicate "unfairly-take-advantage-of".

(138)
[take]$_V$[A advantage]$_N$: V, 'A-LY(TAKE-ADVANTAGE-OF((SUBJ),(OF OBJ)))'

The fact that double passives are restricted to specific lexical items is a natural consequence of the lexical theory of passivization, but follows from nothing in transformational theories of passivization.

The *Away* Argument
Williams 1980 bases an interesting argument for a Passive transformation on the adverbial particle *away,* which adds a continuative or repetitive meaning to intransitive verbs, as in *John is eating away, The clock just ticks quietly away in the corner.* Williams observes that this continuative particle occurs only with intransitives:

(139)
a.   The dial is spinning away.
      cf. *John is spinning the dial away.
b.   John is hitting away at Bill.
      cf. *John is hitting Bill away.

Assuming that *away* may be lexically inserted only with intransitive verbs in deep structure, Williams observes that the contrast between (140a) and (140b) follows from the assumption that the object of *eat* in (140a) is lexically removed (before insertion of *away* into deep structure), while the object of *hit* in (140b) is transformationally removed (after insertion of *away* into deep structure).

(140)
a.   John is eating away.
b.   *Who is Bill hitting away?

From (141) Williams concludes that the object of a passivized verb must be transformationally removed:

(141)
*Bill was being hit away by Fred.

By the same reasoning, however, one would conclude that the objects of the middle verbs in (142) must be transformationally removed.

(142)
a.   *The hula-hoop is selling away from coast to coast.
     cf. The hula-hoop is selling (well) from coast to coast.
b.   *Front-wheel-drive cars really handle away in snow conditions.
     cf. Front-wheel-drive cars really handle (well) in snow conditions.

Yet as shown in chapter 3 of this volume, Middle Formation is a *lexical* intransitivization rule, which undergoes word-formation processes such as *Out-* Prefixation:

(143)
a.   The hula-hoop outsells rollerskates across the country.
b.   Front-wheel-drive cars outhandle all others in snow conditions.

Out- Prefixation applies only to verbs which are basically intransitive or lexically intransitivized, but not to transitive verbs such as *fell, find: *A big lumberjack can't always outfell a little one, *The Brownies outfound the Girl Scouts in the treasure hunt.* See chapter 3 for details of the argument and chapter 2 for evidence that Middle Formation is a lexical rule of intransitivization in French (*"se* moyen"). Therefore, if a verb fails to cooccur with *away,* as in (142) or (141), it need not be because the verb is transitive in deep structure; *away* does not provide a *necessary* condition for intransitivity.

What then is the explanation for the failure of *away* to occur with passives? Aspectual particles like continuative *away* and completive *up* alter the meaning of the verbs that select them. The alteration induced by *away* can be described by means of a lexical rule that converts a punctative verb (roughly: a verb directly modifiable by *once,* describing a single but repeatable activity or process) into a continuative verb (roughly: a verb not directly modifiable by *once,* describing a repetitive activity or process). Thus, we have *John eats once, #John eats away once* (in the continuative sense of *away*); *The clock ticks once, #The clock just ticks away once; The dial spins once, #The dial spins away once; John hits away at Bill, #John hits away once at Bill.* The middle verbs *sell, handle* are not punctative (*#The hula-hoop sells once from coast to coast, #Front-wheel-drive cars handle once in snow conditions*) and so do not permit modification by *away* (cf. (142)). The rule can be formulated as converting P (...) into CONTINUE (P (...)) for intransitive verb V whose predicates P are punctative. Note that in (122), as in section 1.2 before, *V* designates a verbal root.

(144)

V-Away *Formation*

Operation on lexical entry:

V, P (...(SUBJ)...) →

V, CONTINUE (P (...(SUBJ)...)), (PRT) = AWAY

Conditions: P is punctative and V is intransitive

Given (144) as a lexical rule, the failure of passives to undergo it simply indicates that it *precedes* the lexical rule of Passivization. This ordering is in fact already implied by the intrinsic formulation of the rules. The rule of V-*Away* Formation must apply to the root form of the verb, not to its progressive participle, for the progressive participle is not punctative, but its verbal root is. This explains the contrast between examples like *#John is eating once, #The clock is ticking once* and examples like *John is eating away, The clock is ticking away.* After the rule applies to the (punctative) root, the participle may be formed. Similarly, the rule cannot apply to passive participles, for passive participles are not roots and their roots are not intransitive. But after the rule applies to an intransitive root V, the passive participle may be formed, via V–P Incorporation (102) followed by Passivization. This is the origin of *The trees had been hacked away at.* As evidence that incorporation has taken place, consider *the hacked-away-at look of the wood,* which like *a lot of unwritten up data* contains an incorporated aspectual particle (cf. the earlier discussion of prepositional passives).

In conclusion, the lexical theory explains the cooccurrence properties of *away* by means of a lexical rule such as (144), which has independent motivation. The *away* argument for a Passive transformation turns out to be another pseudoargument.

Raising and Equi

Among the most compelling of the arguments for a Passive transformation are those based on the interactions of passivization, raising, and equi. Versions of the argument from raising have appeared in Wasow 1977 and S. Anderson 1977. The reasoning goes as follows.

If Passivization were a lexical rule, its domain of application would be restricted to the information available in a single lexical entry for a verb. The lexical entry for a verb may specify the categories strictly subcategorized by that verb, as well as the thematic relations of the verb, but this is essentially local information, pertaining to the sister constituents of the verb in the verb phrase and to the verb's subject. Yet there are cases where Passivization affects NPs that bear no grammatical relation at all to the passivizing verb. These are the *raising constructions*, illustrated in (145).

(145)
a.   Hot dogs are believed by John to cause cancer.
b.   Cancer is now thought to be unlikely to be caused by hot dogs.

In (145a) *hot dogs* is the deep subject of *to cause cancer* and bears no grammatical relation to the passivizing verb *believe* which occurs two clauses above it. Although the examples in (145) are superficially similar to those in (146), the latter are the fundamentally different constructions known as *equi constructions*.

(146)
a.   The dogs are instructed by John to attack intruders.
b.   Intruders are now forced to be prepared to be attacked by dogs.

In the equi constructions, the passivized NPs bear grammatical relations to the passivizing verb. For example, in (146a) *the dogs* is the deep object of *be instructed* and in (146b) *intruders* is the deep object of *be forced*. If Passivization were a lexical rule, and if passive verbs were lexically inserted into their surface configurations, the fundamental differences in the grammatical relations of (145) and (146) would be lost. Passivization must be a syntactic transformation, as assumed in virtually all transformational analyses of English predicate complement constructions (including Rosenbaum 1967, Bresnan 1972, Emonds 1976).

This argument assumes that the grammatical relations of sentences are represented in deep phrase structure configurations, which are mapped into surface structures by rules like Raising and Equi (discussed in the references to transformational analyses of complementation mentioned above). Given these assumptions, it is hard to see how Passivization could plausibly be analyzed as a lexical rule. But conversely, if Passivization is a lexical rule, Raising and Equi cannot be syntactic transformations, and the grammatical relations of sentences must be represented in some form different from deep structures. Since Passivization is in fact a lexical rule, what will be shown here is that the grammatical relations of raising and equi constructions are naturally represented without transformational derivations.

In the lexical theory, the key difference between raising and equi constructions lies in the lexical forms of their main verbs. Sentences like *John believes hot dogs to cause cancer* and *John instructs dogs to attack intruders* have identical syntactic structures, given in (147) and (148).

(147)

[$_S$[$_{NP}$ John] [$_{VP}$[$_V$ believes] [$_{NP}$ hot dogs] [$_{VP}$ to [$_V$ cause] [$_{NP}$ cancer]]]]

(148)

[$_S$[$_{NP}$ John] [$_{VP}$[$_V$ instructs] [$_{NP}$ dogs] [$_{VP}$ to [$_V$ attack] [$_{NP}$ intruders]]]]

In both (147) and (148), the NP directly following the main verb is the grammatical object of the verb.

The object of the verb *believe* is interpreted differently from the object of the verb *instruct* because the verbs have different lexical forms, as shown in the partial lexical entries (149) and (150).

(149)

believe: V, 'BELIEVE((SUBJ),(VCOMP))'

(OBJ) = (VCOMP SUBJ)

(150)

instruct: V, 'INSTRUCT((SUBJ),(OBJ),(VCOMP))'

(OBJ) = (VCOMP SUBJ)

As (149) shows, the object of *believe* is assigned to no predicate argument; it follows that this use of *believe* imposes no semantic selection upon its grammatical object. As represented in (150), *instruct* will impose semantic selection upon its grammatical object. In other words, the object of *believe* in (149) is a grammatical object but not a "logical object" of the verb; while the object of *instruct* in (150) is both a grammatical object and a "logical object" of the verb. (The notions of "logical subject" and "logical object" introduced in Chomsky 1965 have no theoretical significance in the lexical theory assumed here, and in fact represent a confusion of different levels of representation. They are used here to relate the lexical representation of grammatical relations to the familiar transformational conception.)

The relations between the grammatical objects of *believe* and *instruct* and the subjects of their verbal complements follow from the theory of grammatical control. All lexical forms containing the subjectless complements VCOMP, ACOMP, etc., are assigned lexical control equations. In the unmarked case the lexical controller of the complement's subject will be the object if there is one and the subject otherwise (see chapters 3 and 5). This is expressed by the predictable equation (OBJ) = (VCOMP SUBJ).

Passivization applies to the lexical forms in (149) and (150) in exactly the same way, producing (151) and (152).

(151)

$$[\text{believe-d}]_{\text{V[Part]}}, \text{`BELIEVE}(\left\{\begin{matrix}(\text{BY OBJ})\\\phi\end{matrix}\right\},(\text{VCOMP}))\text{'}$$

$$(\text{SUBJ}) = (\text{VCOMP SUBJ})$$

(152)

$$[\text{instruct-ed}]_{\text{V[Part]}}, \text{`INSTRUCT}(\left\{\begin{matrix}(\text{BY OBJ})\\\phi\end{matrix}\right\},(\text{SUBJ}),(\text{VCOMP}))\text{'}$$

$$(\text{SUBJ}) = (\text{VCOMP SUBJ})$$

These configurations correspond to *Hot dogs are believed by John to cause cancer* (= (145a)) and *The dogs are instructed by John to attack intruders* (= (146a)), respectively. In (151) passive *believed* has a grammatical subject which is not a predicate argument, while in (152) passive *instructed* has a grammatical subject which is also a predicate argument. The relations between the grammatical objects and the verbal complements of the passivized verbs are also predictable from the theory of grammatical control: because the passivized verbs have no objects, their subjects will be the lexical controllers of the complements' subjects. (Thus, these passivized verbs predictably have the grammatical control properties of intransitive verbs.) This accounts for the differences between (145a) and (146a).

In place of the transformational rules of Raising and Equi, it is possible to formulate lexical rules which derive lexical forms containing VCOMPs from those containing SCOMPs. Raising-to-Object, for example, could be formulated as the substitution (SCOMP) $\mapsto$ (VCOMP)(OBJ), which would replace (SCOMP) in a grammatical function assignment with the sequence of functions $\langle(\text{VCOMP}), (\text{OBJ})\rangle$. In the notation introduced in examples (88) and (89), the effect of the rule would be to derive (154) from (153).

(153)
a. ⟨(SUBJ),(SCOMP)⟩   [assignment of grammatical functions]
b. believe(1,2)   [predicate argument structure]
c. *John* believes *that hot dogs cause cancer.*   [example]

(154)
a. ⟨(SUBJ),(VCOMP),(OBJ)⟩   [assignment of grammatical functions]
b. believe(1,2)   [predicate argument structure]
c. *John* believes *hot dogs to cause cancer.*   [example]

The control equation (OBJ) = (VCOMP SUBJ) automatically follows from the representation (154).

A rule of Equi could be formulated to make the substitution (SCOMP) ↦ (VCOMP), thereby relating such examples as *John instructed me that I should arrive late* and *John instructed me to arrive late.*[20] This rule would derive (156) from (155).

(155)
a. ⟨(SUBJ),(OBJ),(SCOMP)⟩   [assignment of grammatical functions]
b. instruct(1,2)   [predicate argument structure]
c. *John* instructed *me that I should arrive late.*   [example]

(156)
a. ⟨(SUBJ),(OBJ),(VCOMP)⟩   [assignment of grammatical functions]
b. instruct(1,2)   [predicate argument structure]
c. *John* instructed *me to arrive late.*   [example]

Again, the control equation relation (OBJ) = (VCOMP SUBJ) automatically follows from the representation (156).

A lexical rule could also be given for raising-to-subject constructions, but as pointed out in Bresnan 1972, only a handful of raising-to-subject predicates occur with full sentential complements; the great majority of these verbs occur with no other complement type than the subjectless infinitival (VCOMP). For example, we have *Fred tends to ignore Mary, Louise is apt to lose her temper, The women are bound to win, John used to love hot dogs, There is going to be a movie made about us,* but **It tends that Fred ignores Mary, *It is apt for Louise to lose her temper, *It is bound that the women will win, *It used for John to love hot dogs, *It is going that there will be a movie made about us.* For discussion of the criteria for analyzing these as examples of raising, see Kajita 1968,

Bresnan 1972, and Pullum and Postal 1979. Thus, the lexical form for most subject-raising verbs will simply be given as shown in (157).

(157)
tend: V, 'TEND((VCOMP))'
        (SUBJ) = (VCOMP SUBJ)

The relation (SUBJ) = (VCOMP SUBJ) is predictable from the theory of control, because *tend* is an intransitive verb. By comparing (157) with (158), the contrast between a subject-to-subject raising predicate and a subject-controlled equi predicate can be seen.

(158)
try: V, 'TRY((SUBJ),(VCOMP))'
        (SUBJ) = (VCOMP SUBJ)

Again the relation (SUBJ) = (VCOMP SUBJ) predictably holds for (158), because *try* lacks a grammatical object. Where *try* differs from *tend* is in the assignment of its subject to a predicate argument; as a consequence, *try* but not *tend* will impose semantic selection on its subject. The same contrast exists between *seem* and *want,* between *be (un)likely* and *be (un)prepared,* and in general between subject-to-subject raising predicates and subject-controlled equi predicates.

Returning to examples (145b) and (146b), we can now see how their differing grammatical relations are represented. In (145b) *Cancer is now thought to be unlikely to be caused by hot dogs,* the passivized subject *cancer* is identified as the subject of the verbal complement *to be unlikely* . . . by the lexical control equation for the passive participle *thought,* (SUBJ) = (VCOMP SUBJ). Because *think* is a passivized subject-to-object raising predicate (cf. (151)), its surface subject does not correspond to any of its predicate arguments; thus, while *cancer* does bear a (surface) grammatical relation to *think,* it does not bear a logical or thematic relation to that verb. The lexical form for the subject-to-subject raising adjective *unlikely* also carries the information (SUBJ) = (VCOMP SUBJ), so *cancer* is interpreted as the subject of the verbal complement *to be caused by hot dogs.* Still it does not bear a logical or thematic relation to *unlikely,* whose lexical form resembles that of *tend* (cf. (157)). Finally, the lexical form of the passive participle *caused* associates the subject *cancer* with the second predicate argument (the "logical object" of *cause*), and the *by*-object *hot dogs* with its first predicate argument (the "logical subject" of *cause*). The result is that *cancer* does bear grammatical relations to all three predicates in (145)—

thought, unlikely, and *caused;* but it bears a predicate argument relation only to *caused.* By comparing *forced, prepared,* and *attacked* with *instructed* (152), *try* (158), and *caused,* respectively, the reader can see that in (146b) *Intruders are now forced to be prepared to be attacked by dogs,* the subject *intruders* bears both grammatical relations and predicate argument relations to all three predicates.

Thus, Passivization is a lexical rule whose domain of application is restricted to the information available in a single lexical entry for a verb. That lexical information can apply only to the functional subjects, objects, and complements that are immediately related to the predicate of the verb: it is strictly local in the *functional structure* that is derived by grammatically interpreting the sentence (see chapters 4 and 5 of this volume). The theory of control permits grammatical interpretation to link a functional subject or object with a subjectless complement through lexical control equations (SUBJ) = (VCOMP SUBJ), (OBJ) = (VCOMP SUBJ). Chains of these local links produce the seemingly nonlocal grammatical relations of examples like (145b). We see, then, that the arguments for a Passive transformation based on the interactions of passivization with raising and equi are illusory.

The distinctive properties of raising constructions are naturally captured in the lexical theory simply because of the independence of predicate argument structure from syntactic constituent structure representations. Like idiom chunks, "raised" objects are examples of grammatical objects that do not correspond to logical objects. It follows that the subjects of passivized raising predicates will bear no logical or thematic relations to these predicates either. An interesting consequence is that these participles should fail to undergo the rule of Adjective Conversion (36). This is in fact the case (as noted by Wasow 1978, 1980).

(159)
a.   John remained unpersuaded to quit smoking.
b.   *John remained unbelieved to have quit smoking.

(160)
a.   *How widely believed was Bill to have quit smoking? (Williams 1980) [cf. How widely believed was it that Bill quit smoking?]
b.   How thoroughly convinced was Bill to quit smoking? (Williams 1980)

The verbs *persuade* and *convince,* like *force* and *instruct,* are object-control equi predicates. Because their active objects are themes, their passive subjects meet the conditions for Participle – Adjective Conversion. *Unpersuaded* and *convinced* in (159a) and (160b) are adjectives derived by this rule; adjectives but not verbs permit *un-* prefixation, and adjectives but not verbs can be preposed by question formation. But the corresponding adjectival passives *unbelieved* and *believed* are ill-formed, a fact which is predicted by the lexical analysis of raising, passivization, and adjective conversion.[21] For the same reasons, the contrasts in examples like (161) and (162) are predicted.

(161)
a.   How well kept are secrets in your department?
b.   *How well kept are tabs on celebrities?

(162)
a.   The bills remained unpaid.
b.   *Heed remained unpaid to these problems.

The idiomatic subjects *tabs* and *heed* in examples like *Tabs are kept on celebrities, Heed was paid to these problems* are not thematic, and so the passive participles of the idioms fail to undergo Adjective Conversion, even when nonidiomatic uses of the verb successfully convert.

The lexical analysis of raising and equi constructions has further interesting consequences. In order for the functional coherence condition to be satisfied, every functional argument must be bound to a predicate argument. The object of an equi verb such as *persuade* or *force* will be bound to an argument of its matrix predicate, but the object of a raising verb such as *believe* or *expect* can be bound only to a predicate argument of some predicate within the verbal complement. It follows that if the verbal complement of an equi verb is omitted, the result will be functionally incomplete but coherent; while if the verbal complement of a raising verb is omitted, the result will be incoherent as well as incomplete. Where verbs permit their complements to be omitted, the phenomenon known as *null complement anaphora,* or complement ellipsis, arises (see chapter 3 and Grimshaw 1979a). (163a–c) are examples of complement ellipsis with equi verbs.

(163)
a.   John persuaded Bill.
b.   John promised Bill.
c.   John forced Bill.

But as Williams 1980 points out, there are no examples of complement ellipsis with true raising verbs. Thus, (164a–c) are all ill-formed in the relevant senses (where a verbal complement has been omitted).

(164)
a.   *John wanted Bill.
b.   *John believed Bill.
c.   *John expected Bill.

The lexical theory of raising predicts the contrast between (163) and (164): examples like (164) are functionally incoherent.[22]

There Insertion

Another familiar argument for a Passive transformation is based on *there* insertion in English. The expletive *there* appears in English under very restricted conditions which have been formulated in terms of an insertion transformation (see, for example, Emonds 1976). Yet in certain cases the rule that inserts *there* apparently must apply before Passivization. If Passivization were a lexical rule, this would be impossible, because under the lexicalist hypothesis lexical rules must apply to lexical structures and cannot apply to transformationally derived structures.

An example in which *There* Insertion appears to precede Passivization is given in (165).

(165)
a.   There is believed to be a reindeer on the roof.
b.   There is a reindeer believed to be on the roof.

According to the transformational analysis of *There* Insertion, *there* is inserted in the lowest transformational cycle on the deep structure underlying (165a). *There* is inserted into subject position in the lower clause, displacing the original subject *a reindeer* just to the right of the first verb *be* to the right of the subject position. On the next cycle, *there* is raised and passivized, becoming the derived subject of *believed*. If *there* had been inserted after the passivization of *believe,* then the insertion would have applied in the upper transformational cycle, and *a reindeer* would appear just to the right of *is,* as in (165b). Thus, Passivization cannot be a lexical rule, because the syntactic transformation of *There* Insertion can apply before it.

Because Passivization is in fact a lexical rule and passive constructions are base-generated, the above observations argue that *there-*

constructions must be base-generated as well. The partial lexical entries given in (166) account for *there* insertion in examples like *There is a pig in the yard, There is a pig running through the garden, There is a pig loose, There is going to be a pig roasted tonight.* These examples have an evocative reading which can be (crudely) paraphrased 'Behold: a pig is in the yard', 'Behold: a pig is running through the garden', etc. This 'behold' sense of *there is NP XP* is associated with the monadic predicate *there-be*(1), which holds of events or states of affairs.

(166)

a.   there: $NP_{[Pro]}$, (FORM) = THERE

b.   be: V, 'THERE-BE((XCOMP))', X = P, V, A
               (OBJ) = (XCOMP SUBJ)
               (SUBJ FORM) $=_c$ THERE
               (SUBJ NUM) = (OBJ NUM)

This sense of *there is NP XP* is not, and should not be, identified with an existential reading ('there exists NP such that it is XP'), for NP can be an idiom chunk. For example, (167) does not have the interpretation 'There exist tabs such that they were kept on Jane Fonda by the FBI' (which is senseless), but it can be interpreted as evoking a state of affairs: 'Behold: tabs were kept on Jane Fonda by the FBI'.

(167)
There were tabs kept on Jane Fonda by the FBI.

Figure 1.9 conveys how example (167) is grammatically interpreted. As the diagrams illustrate, in constituent structure the main verb *be* (*were*) has the subject *there,* the object *tabs,* and the verbal complement *kept on Jane Fonda by the FBI.* With respect to the verb *be,* the subject *there* is interpreted exactly like an idiom chunk (cf. the earlier discussion and footnote 14) and the object *tabs* is interpreted exactly like a "raised" object (cf. the preceding section). The lexical entry (166) specifies that the number feature of the object is identified with the number feature of the subject: this accounts for the plural form of the verb *be.*

As observed in Morgan 1972, there is a dialect of English in which the number of an object of *be,* if the object is a coordinated structure, is identified with the number of the first conjunct:

(168)
There was/*were a man and three women here.

c-structure

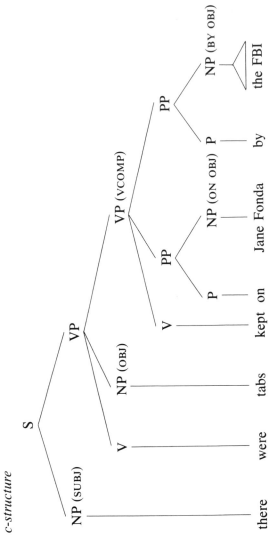

Figure 1.9a

f-structure

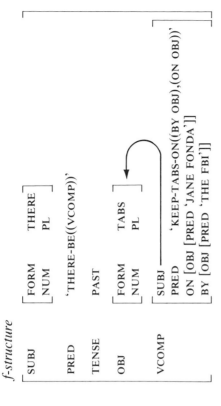

Figure 1.9b

The first conjunct induces the number of the entire NP only in object position, however: *A man and three women *was/were here, Three women and a man *was/were here*. Noncoordinated objects of *be* agree in number as in other dialects of English:

(169)
There *was/were three women here.

This dialect provides excellent evidence in favor of the base generation of *there*-constructions, for a transformation of *There* Insertion cannot be ordered with respect to Number Agreement in this dialect. (If Number Agreement preceded *There* Insertion, (169) but not (168) could be derived; if *There* Insertion preceded Number Agreement, (168) but not (169) could be derived.) But given that *there*-constructions are base-generated, the dialect can be correctly described by adding to the object NP in phrase structure the rule $(\downarrow\text{NUM}) = (\downarrow(\text{CONJ1})\ \text{NUM})$, where CONJ1 is optional in the rule. This rule assigns to the object NP the number of the first conjunct, if there is one, and has no effect otherwise. The number agreement part of the lexical entry for *there-be* will then merge the object NP number with the subject number. For a detailed explanation of the interpretation of these feature rules, see chapter 4.

The lexical analysis of *there* insertion immediately explains the contrasts in (170a,b), which are exactly parallel to (171a,b).

(170)
a. I believe there to have been tabs kept on Jane Fonda by secret agents.
b. *I instructed there to be tabs kept on Jane Fonda by secret agents.

(171)
a. I believe tabs to have been kept on Jane Fonda by secret agents.
b. *I instructed tabs to be kept on Jane Fonda by secret agents.

In both cases, the contrast follows because *believe* imposes no semantic satisfaction conditions on its grammatical objects, while *instruct* does, as we have seen. Lacking intrinsic meaning, both *there* and *tabs* fail to satisfy the predicate argument structure of *instruct*. In just the same way, the contrasts in (172a,b) are predicted to be parallel to those in (173a,b).

(172)

a.   There tended to be tabs kept on celebrities by the FBI.
b.   *There tried to be tabs kept on celebrities by the FBI.

(173)

a.   Tabs tended to be kept on celebrities by the FBI.
b.   *Tabs tried to be kept on celebrities by the FBI.

And finally, given the passivized lexical forms for *believe* (151) and *instruct* (152), (174a,b) are predicted as well.[23]

(174)

a.   There are believed to be tabs kept on celebrities by the FBI.
b.   *There are instructed to be tabs kept on celebrities by the FBI.

It should now be evident how examples like (165a) *There is believed to be a reindeer on the roof* are derived without a transformation of *There* Insertion. What may yet seem problematic for the lexical analysis proposed here is that in examples like (165b) *There is a reindeer believed to be on the roof,* as in (167) *There were tabs kept on Jane Fonda by the FBI,* the lexical theory requires base-generating an NP between the auxiliary *be* (*is, were*) and the passive participle *believed, kept.* Moreover, in examples like (175) the progressive auxiliary *be* will be separated from its *-ing* participle by a base-generated NP. What justification is there for this apparent wrenching of the syntactic structures in which auxiliaries are normally found?

(175)

a.   There is a pig running loose.
b.   There is a pig being roasted.

Justification for postulating the constituent structures presupposed by the lexical analysis of *there* insertion comes from the happenstance *have* construction discussed later in chapter 3. Examples of this construction and some of its properties are given in (176).

(176)

a.   We have a pig running loose in the garden.
b.   We had a window broken last night while we were away.
c.   We have a pig in the garden.
d.   We have a pig loose/*fat.
e.   We have John to consider.
f.   *We have a pig a pet.

As these examples show, the construction consists of a sequence NP V NP XP, where XP may be a progressive VP, a passive VP, a PP, an AP denoting a temporary property, or a *to*-infinitive, but not an NP. The construction means that the event or state of affairs described by NP XP happened or took place and affected the subject NP in some way. This "happenstance" meaning of the construction must be distinguished from the causative sense of *have,* discussed in chapter 3. Unlike the causative *have,* the happenstance *have* cannot occur in the progressive:

(177)
*We were having a window broken last night.   [happenstance sense]

All of these properties also hold of the *there-be*-construction analyzed above.

(178)
a.   There is a pig running loose in the garden.
b.   There was a window broken last night while we were away.
c.   There was a pig in the garden.
d.   There was a pig loose/*fat.
e.   There is John to consider.
f.   *There is a pig a pet.

(179)
*There was being a window broken last night.

In addition, the happenstance construction appears to be possible with an idiom chunk as the second NP:

(180)
We had tabs being kept on us by the FBI.

Finally, both constructions fail to be self-embeddable, except in the NP–*to*–VP case:

(181)
a.   *We had our having a pig loose.
b.   We had our having a pig loose to consider.

(182)
a.   *There was there being a pig loose.
b.   There was there being a pig loose to consider.

There are a few divergences in the two constructions: for example, we have *There is a knack to this*, but not **We have a knack to this;* conversely, there is *We had a man break into our house last night*, but not **There was a man break into our house last night*. Nevertheless, the appearance of *have*-constructions of the types given in (176), (177), and (180) provides extremely strong justification for the lexical analysis of *there*-constructions: because the *have*-constructions are base-generated, the structures in which *there* insertion is found have independent motivation in the base.

Like idiom chunks, *there* is meaningful only in combination with a verb that selects its form feature. Thus, the lexical analysis of *there* insertion immediately explains the following contrasts (on the assumption that there is no transformation of *to be* deletion).

(183)

a.   I consider there to be a great opportunity here.
     [cf. I consider that to be a great opportunity here.]

b.   *I consider there a great opportunity here.
     [cf. I consider that a great opportunity here.]

(184)

a.   There is considered to be a great opportunity here.
     [cf. That is considered to be a great opportunity here.]

b.   *There is considered a great opportunity here.
     [cf. That is considered a great opportunity here.]

Note that idiom chunks can appear as the objects of *consider* when it takes an NP or AP complement:

(185)

a.   Consider your leg pulled.   [idiomatic]

b.   Your leg, my friend, can be considered pulled.   [pompous, but idiomatic]

(186)

a.   Consider your goose cooked.   [idiomatic]

b.   Your goose can be considered cooked.   [idiomatic]

This shows that *consider* fails to impose semantic selection on its objects in these constructions. Consequently, the ungrammaticality of (183b) and (184b) can be attributed to the absence of the verb *be* which lexically encodes the idiomatic meaning of *there*. Note that the un-grammaticality of **I consider tabs kept on celebrities too often* simply follows from the fact that *keep tabs on* lacks an adjectival passive for the reasons noted in the discussion of example (161) above, together with the fact that noninfinitival complements to *consider* are APs or NPs. Finally, note that the lexical form of *pull [possessor's] leg* (93) will meet the thematic condition of Adjective Conversion (36), just as the appropriate lexical form for the idiom *Your goose is cooked* will.

These results follow naturally from the theory that grammatical relations, including those in *there* insertion constructions, are lexically encoded. Other verbs select *there* as subject, with slightly different meanings and syntactic properties. For example, there is an existential *there* in *There are infinitely many prime numbers* and a "presentational" *there* in *There arose a great clatter*. However, these constructions pose no problems of principle for the lexical theory.

Conclusion

As we have seen in section 1.3, the lexical theory explains the phenomena previously thought to support a transformational analysis of passivization. Surprisingly, perhaps, the lexical theory of passivization provides more convincing and revealing explanations of these phenomena than transformational theories. Moreover, as sections 1.1 and 1.2 showed, the major results of the lexical theory are unexplained by transformational theories of passivization. First, in the lexical theory passivization has a universal characterization which reveals its invariant form across languages. This result follows because the rule of Passivization changes the lexical assignments of grammatical functions to predicate argument structures and because grammatical functions are independent of language-particular realizations in terms of syntactic structure and morphological case. Second, passivized verbs undergo lexical processes of word formation (such as Adjective Conversion and compounding), which means that these verbs must be represented as passives in the lexicon. This result follows because only lexical structures can be analyzed by word-formation rules, given the lexicalist hypothesis and the near-decomposition of grammars into lexical, syntactic, and other components.

Transformational theories cannot account for these facts without abandoning the attempt to define the intransitivity of passives in structuralist terms. But even if this were done, the lexical theory remains the more explanatory account, for in the lexical theory Passivization could not be *other* than a lexical rule. The vast range of descriptive options available in transformational grammars is precluded from the lexical theory by the principle of direct syntactic encoding and by the other inherent restrictions in the formal system of grammatical representation (discussed in chapter 4 of this volume).

Through its greater restrictiveness, the lexical theory advances us further toward our ultimate goal of explaining how the rich and intricate representational structures of language can possibly be acquired and used by our species with such facility. This is so because, unlike transformational grammars, lexical grammars have proved to be recursive (chapter 4 of this volume), learnable (chapter 10), realistically parsable (chapter 11), and "producible" (chapter 12). They therefore provide a stronger basis than ever before for a psychologically realistic theory of grammar. With such a basis, it has become possible for psychology and linguistics to converge on a unified theory of language.

Notes

1. (1) gives the formulation of transitive Passivization. In many languages, intransitive verbs also passivize (Comrie 1977). Intransitive Passivization is expressed by the subrule (SUBJ) $\mapsto \phi$.

2. The universality of grammatical functions is an important contribution of the theory of relational grammar (Perlmutter and Postal 1977), which of course shares this explanatory advantage. However, relational grammar does not employ the direct syntactic encoding principle, and so differs from the lexical theory in the decomposition of grammars into lexical and syntactic rules. Some of the consequences of this decomposition have already been given, and further consequences will be pointed out below. See also Bell's 1980 comparison of the two theories.

3. Aronoff 1976 introduced blocking as a mechanism to prevent the application of a word-formation rule if it produced a form which would be identical in function to a form produced by another word-formation rule.

4. This is a causativized lexical form for the verb, as are *break*$_{caus}$ and *split*$_{caus}$ in (20) and (21).

5. Passive participles can (and often must) occur without the passive auxiliary *be*, but perfect participles never occur without *have*. For example, the italicized participles in (i) are passives, while those in (ii) are perfects:

(i)
a.   Anyone being *given* a forged ticket should report it at once.
b.   Anyone *given* a forged ticket should report it at once.

(ii)
a.   Anyone having *given* the doorman a forged ticket should report it at once.
b.   *Anyone *given* the doorman a forged ticket should report it at once.

To express this fact, the perfect participle in (28) must select the auxiliary *have*. This could be accomplished by interpreting "PERF = +" as a constraint equation ($\uparrow$PERF) $=_c$ + (see chapter 4) and adding the equation ($\uparrow$VCOMP PERF) = + to the lexical entry for the perfect auxiliary verb *have*.

6. Certain apparent exceptions to this generalization have a natural explanation noted by Lieber 1979:footnote 10. For example, the verb *prove* has two passive participles, *proved* and *proven*, but only one of them is adjectival (*an easily proven theorem*, *an easily proved theorem*). Lieber proposes the following explanation.

It is well known that for many centuries the remnants of the OE strong verbs have been going over to the class of regular verbs forming participles in *-ed*. In the case of *prove*, we might suppose that the *-en* verbal participle is the original one, from which the adjectival participle *proven* was formed. When the regular verbal participle in *-ed* was then formed, the rule of morphological conversion [rule (36) here] forming adjectival participles from verbal ones was blocked.

7. The lexical forms for nonalternating verbs like *donate* and *cost* can simply be listed:

(i)
a.   Louise donated her paintings to us.
b.   *Louise donated us her paintings.
c.   'DONATE((SUBJ),(OBJ),(TO OBJ))'

(ii)
a.   That remark just cost you your job.
b.   *That remark just cost your job to you.
c.   'COST((SUBJ),(OBJ2),(OBJ))'

8. The possibility of double adjectival forms like *untaught skills, untaught students* is explained by Wasow 1977. The verb *teach* has distinct thematic relations in *John teaches handicapped children manual skills* and *John teaches handicapped children*: in the former, *handicapped children* is a goal; in the latter, *handicapped children* is a theme. As evidence, Wasow cites examples like *the teaching of/*to handicapped children is important* and *The teaching of manual skills *of/to handicapped children is important*. In nominal constructions, *of* marks a theme and *to* a goal. As further evidence, Wasow points out that *-able* suffixation requires that the subject be a theme (*That story isn't tellable, *John isn't tellable*), and we have both *Manual skills are teachable* and *Handicapped children are teachable*.

9. Many language-particular differences in rules might be attributed to this difference. For example, Passivization in Semitic languages would seem to be a "minor" lexical rule, in that the passivized object must be a theme and the rule

is highly exceptional (M. Rappaport 1979, Borer 1978). It might also be asked whether adjectival passives could be produced by a "major" rule of Passivization (Williams 1980), but the fact that adjectives lack direct objects (Maling 1980) already suggests that the answer is negative.

10. The '$\forall\exists$' interpretation is entailed by the '$\exists\forall$' interpretation; thus, it will be true if the '$\exists\forall$' interpretation is true, but not conversely.

11. If the lexical form specifies the null grammatical function ϕ, as in 'READ((SUBJ),ϕ)', no functional argument can be bound to that predicate argument, which is already semantically interpreted. The example *John read* is thus functionally complete. If the lexical form specifies an omissible grammatical function, as in 'INQUIRE((SUBJ),((SCOMP)))', no functional argument need be bound to that predicate argument, but the predicate argument is not already semantically interpreted. The example *John inquired* is thus functionally complete but incompletely interpreted semantically. *John inquired* is an example of complement ellipsis; its semantic interpretation depends upon the discourse context (see Grimshaw 1979a and chapter 3 of this volume).

12. Idiomatic functional arguments, being meaningless, are not semantically compatible with predicate arguments; their analysis is discussed in the next subsection.

13. In later work (Wasow 1978, 1980), Wasow gives lexical formulations of *To*-Dative and Passive. Wasow's formulation of the *To*-Dative rule takes the double-NP form of the verb as basic and derives the NP PP form with an optional PP. In our notation it would be written as shown in (i):

(i)
(OBJ2) → (OBJ)
(OBJ) → (TO OBJ)/ϕ

An advantage of this formulation is that it accounts for the optionality of the indirect object with many dative verbs:

(ii)
a.   John sold two cars.
b.   John gave books.

Yet there are some verbs which do not allow the indirect object to be omitted.

(iii)
a.   *John promised the apple. (cf. John promised Mary the apple.)
b.   *Mary denied a chance. (cf. Mary denied John a chance.)
c.   *Susan handed the books. (cf. Susan handed us the books.)

Both versions of the rule have lexical exceptions (cf. footnote 7 and below), and both versions of the rule ((i) and (42)) are compatible with the lexical theory.

14. The formula (OBJ FORM) $=_c$ TABS is a *constraint equation*, which must be evaluated on the functional structure that results from the grammatical interpretation of the sentence (see chapter 4). Intuitively, it means that the object must have a form feature whose value is TABS. The lexical entry for *tabs* will

have the corresponding feature equation (FORM) = TABS, as well as feature equations such as (NUM) = PL. A lexical item bears the FORM feature only if it lacks intrinsic meaning, and many different items bear this feature, including the expletive *there* (see the later section on raising and equi constructions). Thus, a verb selects an idiomatic object by specifying the value of the form feature which that object must have. The completeness and formal coherence conditions guarantee that idiom chunks will appear only with idioms; again see chapter 4.

15. Adjacency accounts for the differences among the compounds *early riser* vs. **early molester, rapidly-acting* vs. **rapidly-making* (see the earlier discussion of verbal compounding). Adjacency also characterizes the examples of V–N incorporation in French idioms given in chapter 2 of this volume and the rule of V–V Incorporation in Italian studied by Rizzi 1978 within a transformational framework (cf. footnote 19 below).

16. Subtle alterations in emphasis can markedly alter the acceptability of these examples. Compare (114a) with the much worse (i).

(i)
?*The fields that the army marched recently through are ruined.

The explanation may be that the rules involved have discourse functions that come into conflict: the placement of an NP or PP after an adverb seems to highlight the new information content of the shifted phrase with respect to preceding phrases; but relativization of the prepositional object removes most of this content, causing unacceptable results like (i). However, the addition of *so* (*such*, or *most*) to the interpolated adverb diminishes its new information content by suggesting a presupposed context; and the faintly rhetorical cast of the question (114a) compared with the assertion (i) does likewise. The point here is that the stylistic inconsistencies of examples like (i) would account for their relative unacceptability compared with (114). Note that such alterations do not improve the passive examples given in (113). (On examples like *She is spoken highly of*, compare the discussion of adverb incorporation (examples (123)–(125) and footnote 18 below).)

17. On the conditions that ensure proper binding of traces, see Chomsky 1976, 1980 and Fiengo 1977. Fiengo's 1977:54–57 transformational analysis of adjectival passives fails to account for both their distribution and their interpretation in examples like those mentioned here. First, accounting for the compound adjectives (*slept-in looking, uncared-for appearing*) under Fiengo's analysis would require either deriving compound adjectives transformationally from sentential sources following passivization (in violation of the lexicalist theory of derivational morphology) or allowing transformations to move constituents out of lexical words (which is normally impossible: *It seems* [$_A$ *epoch-making*] → **What does it seem* [$_A$ *-making*]?; *Here the river grows* [$_A$ *swift-running*] → **How does the river grow* [$_A$ *-running*]?). Second, accounting for the adjectival passives without "antecedent" (*an uncared-for look, an undismayed air*) and other pronominal adjectival passives under this analysis would require an unmotivated proliferation of transformations to derive them from sentential pas-

sivized sources (e.g., *an air [which suggests]* [$_S$ *NP be dismayed* t]), to efface the sentential superstructure (for which there is no surface evidence), and then to reposition the derived adjectives into pronominal position (just where adjectives must be base-generated anyway: *an utter fool, a perfect angel,* etc.).

18. Some examples are structurally ambiguous: *She is spoken highly of, She is spoken of highly.* These have as respective sources (a) *speak highly of,* whose passive is derived via V–P Incorporation from the adverb-incorporated verb [$_V$[$_V$ speak] [$_{Adv}$ highly]], and (b) *speak of highly,* whose passive is derived from the preposition-incorporated verb [$_V$[$_V$ speak] [$_P$ of]] which is modified by the syntactic adverb *highly.* As evidence for these dual analyses, it can be noted that some speakers accept *She is spoken highly of* but reject *She is spoken of highly,* while others accept both; the former reject *How highly is she spoken of?,* while the latter accept it. This patterning of judgments follows if the former speakers have only (a) and the latter have both (a) and (b).

19. It has been argued that the homogeneity of meaning, preserved selectional properties, and productivity of some types of incorporated forms indicate that they should not be base-generated (Rizzi 1978). This is a misconception, as the evidence from V–P Incorporation in English shows. A more interesting argument (also due to Rizzi 1978:149–152) is that incorporated V–V forms in Italian cannot be base-generated because this incorporation is both preceded and followed by transformational rules. The transformational rules in question are Passive and (very marginally) *Wh* Movement with the interrogative verb *sapere* 'to know'. If Passivization is a lexical rule in Italian as in English, the lexical theory predicts the possibility of incorporated passives in Italian. As for interrogative *sapere,* incorporation provides evidence for the base generation of interrogative complements with preposed *wh*-phrases, as proposed in Brame 1978, Gazdar to appear, and chapter 4 of this volume. The existence of sluicing constructions provides some independent evidence for base generation of *wh*-preposed interrogatives in English; see Levin's analysis in chapter 9 of this volume.

20. In fact, verbs with infinitival complements almost always diverge in meaning from verbs with sentential complements. It appears that *to instruct to* has quite another meaning from *to instruct that:* in *John instructed the dogs to attack intruders,* John might have given nonverbal instruction to the dogs, while in *John instructed the dogs that they should attack intruders,* verbal instruction is strongly implied. Lexical rules of Raising and Equi are applicable only insofar as the functional and semantic relations between lexical forms are systematic and predictable; otherwise, the VCOMP forms will simply be listed.

21. Examples like (160) are mistakenly cited by Williams 1980 as evidence that Passivization must be a transformation and not a lexical rule: "In the lexical theory . . . no such difference [with respect to adjective conversion] between the *persuade* and the *believe* type verbs is expected, since they have identical complement structures." But in the lexical theory, they do *not* have identical complement structures: *believed* has the lexical form given in (149) and *persuaded* has one similar to (150).

22. Again Williams 1980 mistakenly argues that the evidence disconfirms the lexical theory of passivization: "This argument shows that the subcategorization of *believe* type verbs is wrong in the lexical theory, and, by the connections made in the section, that the lexical theory of passive is wrong." His argument fails to take into account the independence in the lexical theory of predicate argument structure from syntactic contextual features, which is strongly motivated by ellipsis phenomena (see chapter 3 of this volume).

23. The plural number of *are* in (174a) is a consequence of the number merger equation in (166b) [(SUBJ NUM) = (OBJ NUM)], since *there* is identified through the control equations as the subject of *be*, and the object *tabs* of *be* is plural. It is also a consequence that for the dialect mentioned above, we have *There is/*are believed to be a man and three women there*.

Chapter 2

On the Lexical Representation of Romance Reflexive Clitics

Jane Grimshaw

2.1 Introduction

The Romance "reflexive" clitics have a number of puzzling properties which have been quite intensively investigated in recent work. I will propose here an analysis of the French clitic *se* in its many functions: as an "intrinsic" clitic, as a reflexive/reciprocal clitic, and as a marker of the middle form. In this analysis, *se* is not a pronoun, and it is never an object or an indirect object. It is rather a grammatical marker which is the reflex of lexical rules of Inchoativization, Reflexivization, and Middle Formation.

I will argue that the rules governing NP Extraposition and causative complements must be stated in terms of grammatical functions (subject, object, indirect object, etc.) and not over structural configurations. The theory of grammatical functions developed in chapters 1 and 3 of this volume then explains why the rules distinguish between transitive and intransitive verbs.

Kayne 1975 has shown that verbs with reflexivized objects behave like intransitive verbs with respect to NP Extraposition and causative complements. The analysis of *se,* together with the theory of grammatical functions, provides a solution to this intriguing problem.

My proposal is based on the theory of lexical rules developed by Bresnan (in Bresnan 1978, chapters 1, 3, and 5 of this volume, and to appear), Kaplan and Bresnan in chapter 4, and Wasow 1977, 1978. Two central properties of the theory are the role assigned to grammatical functions in syntactic rules and the extension of lexical rules beyond the domain of derivational morphology to the statement of syntactic generalizations. I will argue that both of these properties are crucial in explaining the behavior of *se* and the intransitivity constraint on NP

Extraposition and the Causative Complement Rule. Thus, if my conclusions are correct, this investigation lends significant support to the theory of lexical rules.

2.2 A Sketch of the Grammar of French Clitics

It is not my intention here to give a comprehensive account of cliticization, but a rough analysis provides essential background for later material. I will give a basic analysis of cliticization, which I will use to provide an informal introduction to the theoretical concepts that will play a crucial role in later sections.

The standard transformational analysis of cliticization (most fully developed in Kayne 1975) is motivated by two fundamental considerations. First, clitics satisfy subcategorization requirements of verbs. Accusative clitics, for example, occur only with verbs which take direct object NPs and occur with verbs which absolutely require NPs. Second, clitics are in complementary distribution with the NP or PP complements to which they correspond; thus, accusative clitics are in complementary distribution with NP direct objects. These points are illustrated in (1) and (2):

(1)
a.   *Jean voit.
       'John sees.'
b.   *Jean lui voit.
       'John sees to him.'
c.   *Jean le voit l'homme.
       'John sees him the man.'

(2)
a.   Jean voit l'homme.
       'John sees the man.'
b.   Jean le voit.
       'John sees him.'

In a transformational analysis, pronominal complements are generated in the same position as the corresponding NPs or PPs and are then moved to preverbal position. Obviously, such an analysis will account automatically for these generalizations, and it is incumbent on anyone proposing a lexical analysis of cliticization to show how it can do the same. Base generation of clitics is proposed in Rivas 1977, Morin 1978, Wehrli 1978, and Lapointe 1978.

Let us assume the (considerably simplified) phrase structure (PS) rules in (3) (where V′ = $\overline{\text{V}}$):

(3)

a. S → NP VP

b. VP → V′ (NP) $\left(\left\{\begin{matrix}\text{NP}\\\text{AP}\end{matrix}\right\}\right)$ (PP)

c. PP → P   NP

The VP rule allows for two NP positions. The first is the position of direct object NPs, and the second that of predicate nominals. The two cooccur rather rarely in French, in examples like (4):

(4)

Nous avons élu Jean $\left\{\begin{matrix}\text{président}\\\text{premier président de la république}\end{matrix}\right\}$.

'We elected John president/first president of the republic.'

NP and AP can also cooccur in cases like (5), taken from Kayne 1975:fn. 63.

(5)

Marie a rendu Jean fou.

'Mary made John crazy.'

Each of the NP nodes in the PS rules is associated with a grammatical function: SUBJ(ECT), OBJ(ECT), NCOMP(LEMENT) (for predicate nominals), A OBJ(ECT) (for the indirect object—object of the preposition à). (I am ignoring PPs introduced by other prepositions and am using a greatly simplified version of the lexical analysis of PPs proposed in chapters 4 and 5 of this volume.) The AP is associated with the grammatical function ACOMP(LEMENT).

(6)

a. S →   NP   VP
          (↑SUBJ)=↓

b. VP →   V′   (NP) $\left(\left\{\begin{matrix}\text{NP}\\(↑\text{NCOMP})=↓\\\text{AP}\\(↑\text{ACOMP})=↓\end{matrix}\right\}\right)$ (PP)
               (↑OBJ)=↓

c. PP →   P   NP
               (↑A OBJ)=↓

The functional equations ($\uparrow$SUBJ)=$\downarrow$, etc., are used in constructing functional structures. I will explain how they are interpreted later in this section.

When clitics occur in combination, their order is fixed. The description in (7) is based on Perlmutter 1971 and Emonds 1975.

(7)

1.	2.	3.	4.	5.
1st & 2nd person, acc. and dat.	3rd person acc.	3rd person dat.	*y*	*en*
(*me,te,nous,vous*)	(*le,la,les*)	(*lui,leur*)		

I will assume the PS rule in (8) for V', ignoring *y* and *en*.[1] (The CL nodes are numbered for ease of reference only.)

(8)
V' $\rightarrow$ (CL)$_1$ (CL)$_2$ (CL)$_3$ (AUX) V

All clitics precede the first auxiliary verb if there is one. The CL nodes, just like the NP nodes, are assigned grammatical functions. Object clitics can occur in positions 1 and 2, indirect objects in 1 and 3. Thus, the rule for V' is (9), where the first position has two alternative grammatical function assignments.

(9)
$$V' \rightarrow \quad (CL)_1 \qquad (CL)_2 \qquad (CL)_3 \quad (AUX) \quad V$$
$$\begin{cases} (\uparrow OBJ)=\downarrow \\ (\uparrow A\ OBJ)=\downarrow \end{cases} (\uparrow OBJ)=\downarrow \quad (\uparrow A\ OBJ)=\downarrow$$

The restrictions on person are expressed by constraints on the value of the feature PERS(ON) associated with the nodes. Finally, constraints are required on CASE, which distinguishes *le, la* from *lui, les* from *leur*. All are third person and, unconstrained, all could occur indiscriminately in either CL$_2$ or CL$_3$. The CASE constraints ensure that only dative clitics can occur in CL$_3$ and accusatives in CL$_2$. The final version of the rule is given in (10); I will explain below how the various equations give the correct result.

(10)
$$V' \rightarrow \quad (CL)_1 \qquad (CL)_2 \qquad (CL)_3 \quad (AUX) \quad V$$
$$\begin{cases} (\uparrow OBJ)=\downarrow \\ (\uparrow A\ OBJ)=\downarrow \end{cases} (\uparrow OBJ)=\downarrow \quad (\uparrow A\ OBJ)=\downarrow$$
$$(\downarrow PERS)=1,2 \quad (\downarrow PERS)=3 \qquad (\downarrow PERS)=3$$
$$(\downarrow CASE)=ACC \quad (\downarrow CASE)=DAT$$

This concludes our look at the PS rules. A key point here is that PS configurations do not correspond one-to-one with grammatical functions. (If they did, there would be no need to have both.) The function OBJ, for example, is assigned in three different structural configurations: the first NP after V, CL_1, and CL_2. The same structural configuration can in turn correspond to more than one grammatical function: a clitic in CL_1 can function as an OBJ or as an A OBJ.

The second important component in the grammar is of course the lexicon. The lexical entry for a predicate contains a *lexical form,* which expresses the grammatically relevant argument structure associated with a predicate (the number of grammatically realizable logical arguments that the predicate takes). The lexical form also states which grammatical functions are associated with which of the predicate's logical arguments. Thus, the lexical form of *élire* 'elect' (see (4)) is 'ÉLIRE((SUBJ),(OBJ),(NCOMP))'. *Élire* is a triadic predicate and has SUBJ assigned to its first argument, OBJ to its second, and NCOMP to its third. *Rendre* (see (5)) is also triadic. SUBJ is assigned to its first argument, OBJ to its second, and ACOMP to its third: 'RENDRE((SUBJ),(OBJ),(ACOMP))'. Lexical forms are subject to certain general constraints, the one that will most concern us being that no single grammatical function can be assigned to more than one argument. The motivation for this is obvious. If SUBJ could be assigned to both the arguments of *see*— 'SEE((SUBJ),(SUBJ))' instead of 'SEE((SUBJ),(OBJ))'—then we would expect to find sentences like (11) with the interpretation of (12).

(11)
John saw.

(12)
John saw John.

This is ruled out in principle by the requirement of functional uniqueness (the function-argument biuniqueness of chapter 3).

Lexical entries for the verbs *voir* 'see', *élire* 'elect', and *rendre* 'make' are given in (13):[2]

(13)
voir: V, (↑PRED) = 'VOIR((SUBJ),(OBJ))'
élire: V, (↑PRED) = 'ÉLIRE((SUBJ),(OBJ),(NCOMP))'
rendre: V, (↑PRED) = 'RENDRE((SUBJ),(OBJ),(ACOMP))'

Entries for the clitics *le* and *lui* and the noun *Jean* are given in (14).

(14)

le:	CL, (↑PRED)	= 'PRO(NOUN)'
	(↑CASE)	= ACC
	(↑NUM)	= SG
	(↑PERS)	= 3
	(↑GEND)	= M
lui:	CL, (↑PRED)	= 'PRO'
	(↑CASE)	= DAT
	(↑NUM)	= SG
	(↑PERS)	= 3
Jean:	N, (↑PRED)	= 'JEAN'
	(↑NUM)	= SG
	(↑PERS)	= 3
	(↑GEND)	= M

The PRED (for PREDICATE) feature in lexical entries is the one that carries what can loosely be termed the "meaning" of the lexical item. (Not every grammatical argument has a PRED feature. See the discussion of *il* in section 2.4 and of idioms in section 2.5.)

Information from the lexicon and from the PS rules combines in the construction of *functional structures*. Functional structures express grammatical information in a form which can serve as the input to semantic interpretation rules. There is an algorithm for constructing functional structures (see chapter 4 of this volume), but intuitively it is clear what happens. (15) is the functional structure for (2a), *Jean voit l'homme*.

(15)

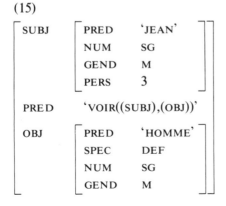

For (2b), *Jean le voit*, the functional structure is (16).

(16)

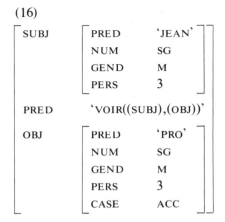

Both *le* and *l'homme* are in structural configurations associated with the function OBJ. In the functional structure their properties, lexically specified, are therefore attributed to the OBJ, and hence indirectly to the second argument of *voir*.

The functional structure (16) for (2b), *Jean le voit*, which will serve as our example, is constructed using the functional equations on the PS rules which generate the sentence and the functional equations in the lexical entries for *Jean, le,* and *voir*. The structure of (2b), with associated functional equations, is given in (17):

(17)

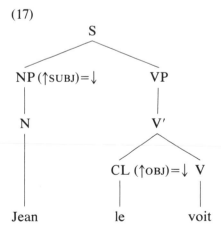

↑ is to be read as 'mother' everywhere it occurs, ↓ as 'ego'. *Ego* is the node to which the functional equation is assigned, *mother* is the immediately dominating node. Thus, (↑SUBJ) = ↓ is to be read as 'mother's SUBJ = ego', (↓CASE) = ACC as 'ego's CASE = ACC'.

$X = Y$ in these equations can be interpreted as 'information about Y is information about X'. Thus, $(\uparrow \text{SUBJ}) = \downarrow$ means that information about ego is information about ego's mother's SUBJ. All the properties of the NP *Jean* in (17) are therefore properties of the grammatical SUBJ of S.

In the unmarked case, heads of phrases are assigned the equation $\uparrow = \downarrow$. Information about ego is then information about its mother and is thus "passed up" to the dominating node. For example, in $[_{NP}[_N \text{ Jean}]]$, properties of the N node are passed up to NP.

Lexical equations work in the same way. The entry for *Jean* in (14) specifies that mother's PRED = 'JEAN', etc. Therefore, N's PRED = 'JEAN'. By $(\uparrow = \downarrow)$ NP's PRED = 'JEAN' and by $(\uparrow \text{SUBJ}) = \downarrow$ S's SUBJ's PRED = 'JEAN', and we arrive at the subpart of (16) given in (18):

(18)

$$
\text{SUBJ} \begin{bmatrix} \text{PRED} & \text{'JEAN'} \\ \text{NUM} & \text{SG} \\ \text{GEND} & \text{M} \\ \text{PERS} & 3 \end{bmatrix}
$$

For *voir* we know that $(\uparrow \text{PRED}) = \text{'VOIR((SUBJ),(OBJ))'}$, that is, that V's PRED = 'VOIR((SUBJ),(OBJ))'. By $(\uparrow = \downarrow)$ on V, V', and VP, we conclude eventually that S's PRED = 'VOIR((SUBJ),(OBJ))', which we can add to the functional structure:

(19)

$$
\begin{array}{ll}
\text{SUBJ} & \begin{bmatrix} \text{PRED} & \text{'JEAN'} \\ \text{NUM} & \text{SG} \\ \text{GEND} & \text{M} \\ \text{PERS} & 3 \end{bmatrix} \\
\text{PRED} & \text{'VOIR((SUBJ),(OBJ))'}
\end{array}
$$

The same is true for *le*. By the lexical entry for *le*, CL's PRED = 'PRO', CASE = ACC, PERS = 3, GEND = M, NUM = SG. By $(\uparrow \text{OBJ}) = \downarrow$ on CL$_2$, we know that V''s OBJ = CL. Therefore, V''s OBJ's PRED = 'PRO', CASE = ACC, PERS = 3, GEND = M, NUM = SG. Again by $(\uparrow = \downarrow)$ on V' and VP we derive that S's OBJ's PRED = 'PRO', S's OBJ's CASE = ACC, S's OBJ's PERS = 3, S's OBJ's GEND = M, and S's OBJ's NUM = SG. This gives us the complete functional structure (16).

An important question concerns the status of ↑ and ↓ in phrase structure rules and lexical entries: do they have to be learned, or are they predictable? A survey of the rules and entries proposed above reveals that they follow the generalizations in (i)–(iii):

(i)
In lexical entries, only ↑ occurs, since information about a word is always passed up to the node dominating it.

(ii)
In the phrase structure rules (6) and (10), equations on grammatical features (PERS, CASE, etc.) are of the form (↓ ____) = ____ . The equations specify that the word inserted in 'ego' must have particular grammatical properties.

(iii)
Equations on the grammatical functions (SUBJ, OBJ, NCOMP, etc.) are of the form (↑ ____) = ↓. That is, 'ego' bears a particular grammatical function with respect to the node dominating it.

Thus, we hypothesize that the information conveyed by ↑ and ↓ is redundant. (6), (10), and (14) can be replaced by (6′), (10′), and (14′), with ↑ and ↓ filled in by universal convention. Whether the convention is absolute, or whether it should be interpreted as expressing the unmarked interpretation of grammatical equations, remains an open question.

(6′)
a. S → NP VP
       SUBJ

b. VP → V′ (NP) $\left(\left\{ \begin{array}{c} \text{NP} \\ \text{NCOMP} \\ \text{AP} \\ \text{ACOMP} \end{array} \right\} \right)$ (PP)
         OBJ

c. PP → P NP
          A OBJ

(10′)
V′ → (CL)₁   (CL)₂   (CL)₃   (AUX) V
      $\begin{bmatrix} \text{OBJ} \\ \text{A OBJ} \end{bmatrix}$ OBJ   A OBJ

      PERS=1,2 PERS=3   PERS=3
                CASE=ACC   CASE=DAT

(14')
le: CL, PRED = 'PRO'
      CASE = ACC
      NUM = SG
      PERS = 3
      GEND = M
          etc.

The functional structures derived by this procedure are well-formed only if they obey certain constraints. The first of these is *consistency*, which is satisfied if every grammatical feature of each grammatical unit has a unique value.

Suppose, for example, that the clitic *lui* were inserted in CL_2 instead of *le,* in (17). The lexical entry for *lui* specifies that ($\uparrow$PRED) = 'PRO', ($\uparrow$PERS) = 3, ($\uparrow$NUM) = SG, ($\uparrow$CASE) = DAT. From the lexical entry, then, we derive the result that CL_2's CASE = DAT. But from the equations associated with CL_2, we derive the result that CL_2's CASE = ACC. According to the rules for constructing functional structures, properties of CL_2 are properties of the OBJ of the clause. Thus, **Jean lui voit,* with *lui* in CL_2, has the functional structure (20), which is inconsistent because the grammatical unit OBJ has two conflicting values for the feature CASE.

(20)

$$
\begin{bmatrix}
\text{SUBJ} & \begin{bmatrix} \text{PRED} & \text{'JEAN'} \\ & \text{etc.} \end{bmatrix} \\
\text{PRED} & \text{'VOIR((SUBJ),(OBJ))'} \\
\text{OBJ} & \begin{bmatrix} \text{PRED} & \text{'PRO'} \\ \text{CASE} & \text{ACC} \\ \text{CASE} & \text{DAT} \\ \text{NUM} & \text{SG} \\ \text{PERS} & 3 \end{bmatrix}
\end{bmatrix}
$$

So the equations on PERS and CASE in (10) guarantee that if the wrong clitic is inserted under a CL node, the sentence will be ill-formed, because its functional structure will be inconsistent.

The complementary distribution of clitics and corresponding NPs and PPs follows from the requirement of consistency. Consider (1c), **Jean le voit l'homme,* the functional structure of which is (21):

(21)

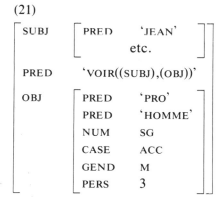

Here lexical information both about *le* and about *l'homme* has been attributed to the OBJ of the clause, since both are in configurations associated with the OBJ function. Again we have a clash in the value of a feature, and (1c) is ill-formed.

Even if both OBJs had the same PRED feature (if both were pronouns, for example), the functional structure would still be ill-formed. Grammatical features such as CASE or NUM can be merged when their values are identical. For example, an argument might be attributed masculine GEND both by virtue of the form of the definite article (*le* versus *la*) and by virtue of the lexical entry for the noun itself: in *le garçon* 'the boy', for example. Here the two values of GEND are simply merged, and the functional structure is well-formed. However, the values of the PRED feature, which carries meaning, can never be merged. So if an argument has two PRED features (whether identical or not), the functional structure is inconsistent. See chapter 4 of this volume for presentation of this analysis.

The other conditions on functional structure are *completeness* and *coherence*. *Completeness* is satisfied if, for every grammatical function assigned to an argument of the PRED of a clause, there is a corresponding grammatical argument in the clause.

Completeness explains why (1a), *Jean voit,* is ungrammatical:

(22)

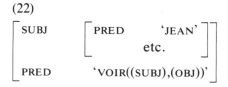

Here there is no grammatical OBJ to correspond to the second argument of *voir;* (22) has an argument "missing."

Coherence is satisfied if every meaningful grammatical argument occurs in a clause whose PRED has a matching grammatical function assigned to one of its arguments.

Coherence explains why (23) is ungrammatical:

(23)
*Jean voit l'homme à Paul.
 John sees the man to Paul

(24)

$$
\begin{bmatrix}
\text{SUBJ} & \begin{bmatrix} \text{PRED} & \text{`JEAN'} \\ & \cdot \\ & \cdot \end{bmatrix} \\
\text{PRED} & \text{`VOIR((SUBJ),(OBJ))'} \\
\text{OBJ} & \begin{bmatrix} \text{PRED} & \text{`HOMME'} \\ & \cdot \\ & \cdot \end{bmatrix} \\
\text{A OBJ} & \begin{bmatrix} \text{PRED} & \text{`PAUL'} \\ & \cdot \\ & \cdot \end{bmatrix}
\end{bmatrix}
$$

Here the A OBJ is "left over," that is, the sentence has too many grammatical arguments.

(1b), *Jean lui voit,* when *lui* is generated under CL_3, is both incoherent and incomplete. *Lui* can occur only under CL_3 (for the reasons given earlier), and CL_3 is associated with the grammatical function A OBJ. Thus, no grammatical argument will be assigned to the OBJ argument of *voir,* and the grammatical A OBJ will not be assigned to any argument of *voir.*

Given the analysis of clitics proposed here, the basic generalizations governing clitics follow from very general properties of the theory. Consistency explains why clitics are in complementary distribution with corresponding NPs and PPs. Coherence and completeness explain why clitics are subject to, and meet, the subcategorization requirements of verbs.

2.3 The Reflexive/Reciprocal and Intrinsic Clitics

A Pronominal Analysis of Reflexives and Reciprocals

One clitic series has been omitted from our description so far: the reflexive/reciprocal series (*me, te, se, nous, vous, se*) illustrated in (25):

(25)
a. Je me vois.
    'I see myself.'
b. Je me parle.
    'I speak to myself.'
c. Ils se voient.
    'They see themselves/each other.'
d. Ils se parlent.
    'They speak to themselves/each other.'

In most analyses r-clitics (= reflexive/reciprocal clitics) are treated just like the others. In transformational analyses (e.g., Kayne 1975) *se* is generated as a postverbal direct object NP or a postverbal PP and is placed on the verb by a transformation. Since all r-clitics precede all others and are in complementary distribution with the CL_1 clitics, we could simply extend our analysis by generating r-clitics as alternative realizations of CL_1 in (10). Like the other clitics, they would be assigned the grammatical function OBJ or A OBJ.

This kind of analysis seems a priori reasonably well-motivated. R-clitics seem to demonstrate the same basic behavior as the others: they meet the subcategorization of verbs requiring direct or indirect objects, and they are in complementary distribution with the corresponding NPs or PPs:

(26)
a. *Je me vois Jean.
    'I see myself John.'
b. *Je me parle à Jean.
    'I speak to myself to John.'
c. *Ils se voient les enfants.
    'They see $\left\{\begin{array}{l}\text{themselves}\\\text{each other}\end{array}\right\}$ the children.'
d. *Ils se parlent aux enfants.
    'They speak to $\left\{\begin{array}{l}\text{themselves}\\\text{each other}\end{array}\right\}$ to the children.'

Thus, it appears that the only difference between r-clitics and the others is that r-clitics happen to be bound anaphors, coreferential with the subject of the verb.

Intrinsic Clitics

The strength of this position is impugned, however, by the existence of what are often termed "intrinsic" or "inherent" clitics (Ruwet 1972, Gross 1968). These clitics are morphologically and structurally indistinguishable from r-clitics and show the same distributional characteristics. Yet they do not correspond to logical or grammatical arguments of the verb at all.[3] As an example, consider the verb *s'évanouir* (= *se* + *évanouir*) 'to vanish':

(27)

a.   Il s'évanouit.
      'He vanishes.'

b.   *Il évanouit.

c.   *Il évanouit $\begin{Bmatrix} \text{le verre} \\ \text{au verre} \end{Bmatrix}$.
      'He makes the glass vanish.'

d.   *Il s'évanouit $\begin{Bmatrix} \text{le verre} \\ \text{au verre} \end{Bmatrix}$.

Here *se* does not correspond to a dative or accusative argument: *évanouir* is monadic and takes neither. It appears rather to be an arbitrary grammatical marker which makes no direct contribution to the interpretation of the sentence.

   Many researchers have pointed out that the occurrence of these clitics is productive in one set of cases (see Ruwet 1972 for French, Napoli 1973 for Italian, and Pimenta-Bueno 1976 for Portuguese).

(28)

Causative	*Inchoative*
briser 'break'	se briser 'be/become broken'
endormir 'put to sleep'	s'endormir 'go to sleep'
coucher 'put to bed'	se coucher 'go to bed'

These verbs illustrate the (very productive) relationship between causative and inchoative forms. The causative forms are transitive, but the inchoative forms are intransitive:

(29)

a. Jean brisera le verre.
    'John will break the glass.'
b. *Jean brisera.
    'John will break.'
c. Le verre se brisera.
    'The glass will break.'
d. *$\begin{Bmatrix} \text{Jean} \\ \text{Le verre} \end{Bmatrix}$ se brisera la fenêtre. ·
    $\begin{Bmatrix} \text{John} \\ \text{The glass} \end{Bmatrix}$ will break the window.'

In other words, se appears to be in complementary distribution with NP objects and to meet the subcategorization of transitive verbs. But se is not an argument of the verb, so the explanation for its distribution cannot be the same as was suggested for the nonreflexive clitics in section 2.1. Rather, se functions as a marker of an intransitive inchoative verb form. The relationship between the two forms seems entirely comparable to that between causative and inchoative break, open, etc., in English.

In general the properties of intrinsic clitics parallel exactly those produced by well-established lexical rules, such as rules of derivational morphology. We find both productive cases (the inchoatives) and totally nonproductive arbitrary cases. S'évanouir lacks the anticipated base *évanouir 'to cause to vanish'. Se trouver 'to be, exist' has a candidate base trouver 'to find' but has undergone semantic drift. This is typical of derivational morphology (see, for example, Aronoff 1976) and is also common in cases like the English verb–particle construction. Here we find eke out, as in eke out a living, but no verb eke. We find strike out with no verb strike of the right meaning. Eckersley struck Jackson out and Eckersley struck out the side are both possible meaning something like 'Eckersley caused Jackson/each of the side to get three strikes against him'. Rice struck out with the bases loaded is possible, meaning something like 'Rice became out by getting three strikes against him'. Thus, we expect to find Eckersley struck him meaning 'Eckersley caused him to get a strike against him' and Rice struck in the ninth inning meaning 'Rice got a strike against him in the ninth inning'. But strike never occurs alone with the appropriate meaning.

These characteristics—accidental gaps, semantic drift, and so on— are all expected if intrinsic se is introduced by a lexical rule, which will parallel in many respects a rule of derivational morphology.

Lexical Analysis of Intrinsic Clitics

The intrinsic *se* is not a pronoun like the clitics discussed earlier, but simply a grammatical marker. In the case of inchoatives it is a reflex of the inchoativization of a verb; in the case of nonproductive intrinsics it is an arbitrary grammatical marker with no systematic semantic correlate. Intrinsic *se* is thus rather like an affix in character: the difference is just that it is not part of the verb. (Recall that *se*, like other clitics, can be separated from its verb by auxiliaries.)

We can postulate the lexical entries in (30) for (a representative sample of) intrinsic clitics:

(30)
$$\text{se: } \text{CL}, (\uparrow\text{REFL}) \quad = +$$
$$(\uparrow\text{SUBJ PERS}) = 3$$
$$\text{me: } \text{CL}, (\uparrow\text{REFL}) \quad = +$$
$$(\uparrow\text{SUBJ PERS}) = 1$$
$$(\uparrow\text{SUBJ NUM}) = \text{SG}$$

Here the equations on $(\uparrow\text{SUBJ PERS})$ and $(\uparrow\text{SUBJ NUM})$ guarantee that the clitics will agree with the SUBJ in person and number; otherwise, the functional structure will be inconsistent.[4] Intrinsic clitics are distinguished from nonreflexives by being [+Reflexive], represented by the equation $(\uparrow\text{REFL}) = +$. They have no PRED feature at all, as they are nonreferential and meaningless.

The PS rule (10) for V' must be modified to allow for intrinsic clitics in CL_1.

(31)
$$\text{V}' \rightarrow \quad (\text{CL})_1 \quad (\text{CL})_2 \dots \dots \text{V}$$
$$(\downarrow\text{REFL})= +$$

They will be generated as *alternative* CL_1 realizations to those discussed in section 2.1 and will be assigned no grammatical function. The equation on this expansion of CL_1 ensures that only clitics which have $(\uparrow\text{REFL}) = +$ in their lexical entries will occur in this expansion. The pronominal clitics analyzed in section 2.1 will have the value $-$ for the REFL feature: $(\uparrow\text{REFL}) = -$. They can never be inserted in this expansion of CL_1, and therefore they are always assigned a grammatical function by the PS rules. Intrinsic clitics can be inserted only in this expansion, so they will never be assigned a grammatical function.

The lexical rule of Inchoativization has the following effects. For any predicate with the semantic composition CAUSE (x, BECOME (PRED (y))), a new predicate is formed (called $Pred_{inch}$) with the semantic composition BECOME ($Pred$ (y)). Since lexical forms represent only the grammatically relevant structure of predicates, the lexical form of a causative predicate will be $Predicate_{cause}$ (,), with some assignment of grammatical functions to the arguments. That of an inchoative predicate will be $Predicate_{inch}$ ( ). By the unmarked assignment of grammatical functions to predicate argument structure, when a predicate has only one argument, the argument is assigned the grammatical function SUBJ.

The other effect of the rule is to add a constraint equation (↑REFL) $=_c$ + to the lexical form of the verb. Constraint equations, for which the notation "$=_c$" is used, express conditions that must be satisfied by a functional structure. Unlike functional equations, they are not used in constructing functional structures. The equation (↑REFL) $=_c$ + associated with a verb will be passed up through V, V', and VP to S and will thus be interpreted as 'S's REFL $=_c$ +'. S's REFL will be + only if an intrinsic clitic is present in CL_1. Only intrinsic clitics have the equation (↑REFL) = + in their lexical entries. If there is an intrinsic clitic, *se* for example, in CL_1, (↑REFL) = + will be passed up to CL_1, then to V', VP, and finally to S, satisfying the constraint equation. (All verb forms are assumed to be marked (↑REFL) $=_c$ − by a redundancy rule, to prevent intrinsic and r-clitics from occurring randomly with verbs. Thus, (32) and (37) below should in fact be viewed as changing the value of the feature REFL from − to +.) Effectively, then, an intrinsic clitic can cooccur with a verb only if the verb has undergone Inchoativization, and a verb which has undergone Inchoativization must cooccur with an intrinsic clitic.

The rule therefore has two parts: an operation on predicate argument structure (which has the indirect effect of intransitivizing the lexical form), and the addition of a morphosyntactic equation. (This analysis explains why selectional restrictions that hold of the grammatical object of the causative also hold of the grammatical subject of the inchoative. They are semantic restrictions on the second argument of the causative, to which OBJ is assigned. The related inchoative predicate has what was the second argument of the causative as its first argument. The SUBJ argument of the inchoative corresponds to the OBJ argument of the causative.)

(32)

Inchoativization

a. $Pred_{cause}$: CAUSE $(x,$ BECOME (Predicate $(y))) \rightarrow$
     $Pred_{inch}$: BECOME (Predicate (y))

b. $(\uparrow REFL) =_c +$

For *briser* the lexicon gives the base lexical form (33) and the derived lexical form in (34):

(33)

briser: V, $(\uparrow PRED) = $ 'BRISER$_{cause}$((SUBJ),(OBJ))'

(34)

$(\uparrow PRED) = $ 'BRISER$_{inch}$((SUBJ))'

$(\uparrow REFL) =_c +$

The grammar assigns to *Le verre se brise* 'The glass breaks' the functional structure in (35).

(35)

$$
\begin{bmatrix}
\text{SUBJ} & \begin{bmatrix} \text{PRED} & \text{'VERRE'} \\ \text{NUM} & \text{SG} \\ \text{PERS} & 3 \\ \text{SPEC} & \text{DEF} \end{bmatrix} \\
\text{PRED} & \text{'BRISER}_{inch}\text{((SUBJ))'} \\
\text{REFL} & +
\end{bmatrix}
$$

The constraint equation associated with *briser*$_{inch}$ is satisfied by (35), so *Le verre se brise* is well-formed in this respect. **Le verre brise* is ill-formed because the constraint equation is not satisfied.

In (35) there is no clash between the values for the SUBJ's NUM and PERS specified by the lexical entry for *se* and the values derived from the entry for *verre*, the grammatical SUBJ. (35) is therefore consistent. It is also complete and coherent; thus, *Le verre se brise* is grammatical.

If *me* appeared instead of *se* here, the functional structure would be inconsistent. The lexical entry for *me* (30) contains the equations $(\uparrow SUBJ\ NUM) = SG$ and $(\uparrow SUBJ\ PERS) = 1$. Thus, the value of S's SUBJ's PERS derived from *me* would clash with the value of S's SUBJ's PERS derived from *verre*, producing an inconsistency. In other words, intrinsic clitics will always agree with the SUBJ in number and person, and impossible examples like *Le verre me brise* with the interpretation 'The glass broke' will not be generated.

For the unpredictable cases of intrinsic *se,* we have the lexical entries in (36):[5]

(36)
évanouir: V, ($\uparrow$PRED) = 'ÉVANOUIR((SUBJ))'
              ($\uparrow$REFL) $=_c$ +
trouver: V, ($\uparrow$PRED) = 'TROUVER((SUBJ))'
              ($\uparrow$REFL) $=_c$ +

The key points of the analysis can be summarized as follows. *Se* in the inchoative cases resembles the accusative clitics *le,* etc., in occurring only with verbs which are generally transitive and in being in complementary distribution with direct object NPs. However, the explanation in the two cases is entirely different. *Le, la,* and *les* occur with verbs that require objects because they are themselves objects. Inchoative *se* occurs with verbs that are *otherwise* transitive because it is a reflex of a rule which takes as its input *dyadic transitive verbs. Le, la,* and *les* are in complementary distribution with direct object NPs again because they are themselves objects, and only one object can occur per predicate. Inchoative *se* is in complementary distribution with NP objects because it is introduced by Inchoativization, which has the consequence of intransitivizing a predicate. Either the predicate is inchoative and takes *se,* or it is causative and takes an NP object.

Thus, inchoative *se* in a sense gives the illusion of playing the role of an object, not because it is an object, but because of the properties of the rule which introduces it.

Lexical Analysis of Reflexive/Reciprocal *Se*

We return now to the question raised earlier in this section: should the r-clitics (reflexive/reciprocal *se* and its variants) be analyzed as grammatical arguments like accusative and dative pronouns? As we noted above, this would appear to explain their distribution in (25) and (26). But we have also seen that intrinsic *se* has the same distributional characteristics. The explanation in the case of intrinsic *se* lies in the nature of the lexical rule of Inchoativization and not in assigning pronominal, and hence argument, status to the intrinsic clitics.

This raises the interesting possibility that r-clitics might be, like intrinsic clitics, grammatical reflexes of a lexical rule, and not pronominal arguments at all. (Pimenta-Bueno 1976 suggests for Portuguese, for example, that both reflexives and inchoatives are derived by deletion of an NP from the subcategorization frame of a verb.) What would be involved in such an analysis? Since r-clitics are indistinguishable from intrinsic *se* in all the relevant respects (PS position, agreement with the subject NP, etc.), the rules and lexical entries already motivated for intrinsic *se* will provide the correct analysis for r-clitics. No special machinery need be added to the grammar if Reflexivization is lexical.

All we need add is the lexical rule itself. Like Inchoativization, Reflexivization is an operation on predicate argument structure, but its effect is to bind one argument to another. We can express the fact that the reflexive predicate has a logical argument that is unavailable for grammatical interpretation by means of the null grammatical function symbol ϕ. ϕ, rather than SUBJ, OBJ, etc., is assigned to a logical argument just in case that argument cannot receive any syntactic expression. ϕ cannot be assigned to an unbound argument, or the sentence will be ill-formed because one of the arguments of the predicate will be neither filled nor bound.

For any predicate argument structure *Predicate* (x,y,z), the rule forms a new *Predicate*$_{refl}$ derived from the nonreflexive predicate by binding one of its arguments to its first argument. Thus, from $P(x,y,z)$ we get $P_{refl}(x,x,z)$ or $P_{refl}(x,y,x)$. Thus, Reflexivization is a two-part rule: it involves binding in predicate argument structure and addition of the same constraint equation used by Inchoativization.

We do not need to stipulate as part of the rule that in the lexical form of the reflexive predicate, ϕ is assigned to the bound argument. Rather, we hypothesize that this change in lexical form is an automatic consequence of binding in predicate argument structure.

(37)
Reflexivization
Predicate $(x,.....,y,.....) \rightarrow$
Predicate$_{refl}$ $(x,.....,x,.....)$
$\quad$ $(\uparrow\text{REFL}) =_c +$

Two remarks are in order here: (a) It is impossible for a predicate to undergo Reflexivization more than once, for a number of reasons. First, ϕ is a grammatical function; therefore, if it is assigned to two arguments of a predicate, functional uniqueness will be violated (see sections 2.2 and 2.4). Second, Reflexivization makes a [−reflexive] predicate [+reflexive], so it could not reapply to its own output. (b) Both reflexives and reciprocals involve the same lexical rule. If the binding argument is plural, then both the reflexive and the reciprocal readings will be possible. I will use the terms *Reflexivization* and *reflexive* to refer to the lexical rule and its output without distinguishing between reflexives and reciprocals.

Reflexivization is illustrated by the lexical entries of *voir* 'see' and *parler* 'speak' given in (38) and (39).

(38)

voir: V, $(\uparrow \text{PRED}) = $ 'VOIR((SUBJ),(OBJ))'

$\qquad (\uparrow \text{PRED}) = $ 'VOIR$_{\text{refl}}$((SUBJ),ϕ)'

$\qquad\quad (\uparrow \text{REFL}) =_c +$

(39)

parler: V, $(\uparrow \text{PRED}) = $ 'PARLER((SUBJ),(A OBJ))'

$\qquad (\uparrow \text{PRED}) = $ 'PARLER$_{\text{refl}}$((SUBJ),ϕ)'

$\qquad\quad (\uparrow \text{REFL}) =_c +$

(40) shows the functional structure for *Jean se voit* 'John sees himself'.

(40)

$$
\begin{bmatrix}
\text{SUBJ} & \begin{bmatrix} \text{PRED} & \text{'JEAN'} \\ \text{NUM} & \text{SG} \\ \text{PERS} & 3 \\ \text{GEND} & \text{M} \end{bmatrix} \\
\text{PRED} & \text{'VOIR}_{\text{refl}}\text{((SUBJ)},\phi\text{)'} \\
\text{REFL} & +
\end{bmatrix}
$$

The constraint equation associated with *voir*$_{\text{refl}}$ is satisfied by (40), and (40) is consistent, complete, and coherent.

According to this analysis, then, r-clitics are never pronominal objects or indirect objects, but are reflexes of binding in predicate argument structure. They are simply morphemes required by the constraint equation associated with Reflexivization.

Reflexive *se* will appear to meet the subcategorization of (for example) a transitive verb, because in the reflexive verb form the second argument has been bound and is assigned ϕ, while in the nonreflexive verb form the second argument is assigned the function OBJ. The reflexive verb has one fewer grammatical arguments (and one fewer open semantic arguments) than its nonreflexive counterpart. This produces the illusion that the *se* is itself an argument of the verb. For the same reason, *se* will be in complementary distribution with a direct object NP when Reflexivization has bound the argument to which OBJ was assigned in the nonreflexive lexical form. *Se* will be in complementary distribution with an indirect object when the argument which was assigned the A OBJ function is bound to the subject.

Self- and *ta-:* Independent Evidence for Lexical Reflexivization and Inchoativization

An important question raised by this analysis is whether there is independent evidence to support the claim that rules which bind arguments in this fashion are among the battery of possible lexical rules. The answer is clearly affirmative; witness the existence of the word-formation rule of *Self-* Prefixation in English:

(41)

self-destructive, self-absorbed, self-indulgent, self-satisfied, self-conscious, self-confident, self-educated

Self- Prefixation closely resembles French Reflexivization, but it is a word-formation rule and is self-evidently lexical.[6] *Self-* Prefixation binds one argument to another in predicate argument structure and assigns ϕ to the bound argument, as well as, of course, prefixing *self-*.[7] *Satisfied* in *John is satisfied with his car* has the lexical form in (42):

(42)
'SATISFIED((SUBJ),(P OBJ))'

Self-satisfied has the lexical form in (43):

(43)
'SATISFIED$_{refl}$((SUBJ),ϕ)'

Thus, *satisfied* allows a grammatically expressed second argument, but *self-satisfied* does not.

(44)
a.   John is self-satisfied.
b.   *John is self-satisfied with his car.

This is quite general for *self-* adjectives:

(45)

$$
\text{Bill is} \left\{ \begin{array}{l} \text{self-confident} \\ \text{self-educated} \\ \text{confident of his abilities} \\ \text{educated by his school} \\ \text{*self-confident of his abilities} \\ \text{*self-educated by his school} \end{array} \right\}.
$$

Self- adjectives alternate with forms in which binding of the second argument is grammatically expressed:

(46)

a.   John is satisfied with himself.

b.   Bill was educated by himself.

This reflects the fact that in English (as in French) there is both lexical and nonlexical Reflexivization.

Self- (like *le* and *se*) is governed by the familiar distributional generalizations. It can be added only to dyadic predicates (*self-tall, *self-intelligent*), and it is in complementary distribution with the second argument of the adjective (see (44) and (45)). In fact, the (spurious) argument for analyzing *se* as a reflexive pronoun could be made with equal strength for *self-*. Its behavior would follow if it were analyzed as *being* the oblique object of the adjective. If, for example, it was generated as an oblique object in deep structure and then transformationally placed on the adjective, its distribution could be explained. But it has been convincingly argued that within a lexicalist theory, transformations cannot have access to, or in general modify, the internal structure of words (a position that was first articulated and defended in Chomsky 1972). Similarly, the lexical theory does not allow subparts of words to enter into grammatical relations with a predicate.

Happily, there is another solution available to us: *Self-* Prefixation is a lexical rule of derivational morphology. Reflexivization is therefore a possible lexical rule, and we conclude that the analysis of French reflexivization as a lexical process is entirely consistent with what we know independently about lexical rules. Furthermore, we confirm the position that the distributional generalizations governing r-clitics (essentially the same as those governing *self-*) do not *have* to be explained by hypothesizing that r-clitics are grammatical arguments, but can instead be explained by the lexical rule of Reflexivization.

Phenomena of this kind appear to be widespread. Hebrew and Arabic have morphological reflexivization and inchoativization, requiring rules that are exactly comparable to those proposed here for French except that the marker corresponding to *se* is a bound morpheme, like *self-*, added by a rule of morphology. The examples in (47) illustrate this for Modern Standard Arabic, where the morpheme *ta-* is prefixed or infixed (depending on the morphological class of the verb). The resulting verb may have a reflexive or an inchoative meaning or, like the French cases, it may be related to its apparent base in an unpredictable way. (I am indebted to John McCarthy for providing the examples in (47), which are from Wright 1971.)

(47)

a. xawwafa 'he frightened ____' (transitive)
b. *ta*xawwafa 'he was/became frightened' (intransitive)
c. qallada 'he adorned ____ with necklaces' (transitive)
d. *ta*qallada 'he adorned himself with necklaces' (intransitive)
e. masaka 'he grabbed ____' (transitive)
f. *ta*maasaka 'he held together, was interlocked, was firmly connected' (intransitive)
g. ramaa 'he threw ____' (transitive)
h. *ta*raamaa 'he threw himself down, prostrated himself' (intransitive)
i. daraba 'he beat ____' (transitive)
j. ʔid*ta*raba 'he was/became agitated' (intransitive)
k. ʕaðara 'he excused ____' (transitive)
l. ʔiʕ*ta*ðara 'he excused himself, apologized' (intransitive)

Given the lexical analysis of *se,* the essential difference between Arabic *ta-*, French r-clitics, and English *self-* lies in whether the rule that specifies the overt marker is morphological or grammatical. The operations on predicate argument structure are the same.

Predictions of Lexical Reflexivization

The lexical analysis of reflexivization has a number of desirable properties. It explains the distributional properties of r-clitics and relates them in an interesting way to properties of intrinsic *se*. It effects a significant unification of inchoative and r-clitics. They have exactly the same grammar; in fact, they are the same clitics. They are both introduced by lexical rules which are very similar in effect. It is hard to see how a similar unification can be achieved by other means. (We will see

in section 2.4 that *se moyen,* or "middle *se,*" can also be unified with
the other cases of *se.*) The lexical rules required are independently
motivated by *self-* and *ta-.*

However, more decisive evidence in favor of the analysis can be
found. There is one crucial difference between the analysis of reflexive
se as a pronominal object or indirect object and the lexical analysis in
which it is not a grammatical argument at all. According to the former
analysis, a verb is grammatically transitive when *se* corresponds to its
object, just as it is when a nonreflexive clitic does. There is no difference between *voir* in (48b) and (48c), other than that the pronoun in
(48c) happens to be a reflexive, coreferential with the subject NP.

(48)

a.   voir: V, (↑PRED) = 'VOIR((SUBJ),(OBJ))'

b.   Je vois l'homme.
     'I see the man.'

     Je le vois.
     'I see him.'

c.   Je me vois.
     'I see myself.'

However, according to the lexical theory, *voir* is grammatically intransitive in (48c). The lexical forms for (48b) and (48c) ((49a) and (49b),
respectively) differ crucially in that the grammatical function OBJ is not
assigned to any argument of *voir* in (49b).

(49)

a.   (↑PRED) = 'VOIR((SUBJ),(OBJ))'

b.   (↑PRED) = 'VOIR$_{\text{refl}}$((SUBJ),ϕ)'

Suppose then that we can find rules which are sensitive to grammatical transitivity, in the sense that a rule applies either only to grammatical transitives or only to grammatical intransitives. Then the two
theories will make entirely different predictions. The pronoun analysis
of reflexive *se* will predict that where *se* corresponds to (in the pronoun
analysis *is*) the object, a rule which applies only to transitive verbs will
apply, while one which applies only to intransitive verbs will not. Conversely, the lexical reflexivization analysis predicts that in this case the
verb will pattern with intransitives and not with transitives.

In the next section I will show that in fact reflexive verbs behave as
predicted by the lexical theory: as intransitives.

2.4 Syntactic Evidence for the Lexical Analysis of Intrinsic and Reflexive/Reciprocal Clitics

Evidence from NP Extraposition

The evidence from NP Extraposition is based on Kayne's research on *se* in this construction (Kayne 1975). The rule of NP Extraposition is responsible for sentences in which a (nonsentential) subject NP appears postverbally, *il* filling the subject position (Martin 1970, Kayne 1975, Postal 1979). (The following example is from Martin 1970:377.)

(50)
a.   Un train passe toutes les heures.
b.   Il passe un train toutes les heures.
      'A train goes by every hour.'

Transitive verbs are completely impossible in this construction, as the following examples (from Martin 1970:380 and Kayne 1975:330, 379, respectively) show:

(51)
a.   Un train conduira les voyageurs à Paris.
b.   *Il conduira un train les voyageurs à Paris.
c.   *Il conduira les voyageurs un train à Paris.
      'A train will take the travellers to Paris.'

(52)
a.   Trois filles mangeront cette tarte.
b.   *Il mangera cette tarte trois filles.
c.   *Il mangera trois filles cette tarte.
      'Three girls will eat that pie.'

(53)
a.   Trois mille hommes ont dénoncé la décision.
b.   *Il a dénoncé la décision trois mille hommes.
c.   *Il a dénoncé trois mille hommes la décision.
      'Three thousand men denounced the decision.'

As (54) shows, this prohibition extends to verbs with nonreflexive clitic pronoun objects. (The example is due to Kayne 1975:379.)

(54)
a.   *Il les conduira un train à Paris.
      'A train will take them to Paris.'

b. *Il la mangera trois filles.
    'Three girls will eat it.'

c. *Il l'a dénoncée trois mille hommes.
    'Three thousand men denounced it.'

Yet verbs with reflexive clitics corresponding to objects permit NP Extraposition.

(55)

Il $\begin{Bmatrix} \text{s'est dénoncé} \\ \text{se dénoncera} \end{Bmatrix}$ trois milles hommes ce mois-ci.

'Three thousand men $\begin{Bmatrix} \text{denounced} \\ \text{will denounce} \end{Bmatrix}$ themselves this month.'

(56)

Il $\begin{Bmatrix} \text{s'est offert} \\ \text{s'offrira} \end{Bmatrix}$ une femme pour mener le combat.

'A woman $\begin{Bmatrix} \text{offered} \\ \text{will offer} \end{Bmatrix}$ herself to lead the fighting.'

(57)

Il $\begin{Bmatrix} \text{s'est présenté} \\ \text{se présentera} \end{Bmatrix}$ beaucoup d'hommes pour cet emploi.

'Many men $\begin{Bmatrix} \text{presented} \\ \text{will present} \end{Bmatrix}$ themselves for this job.'

((55) and (56) are based on Kayne 1975:381 and Fauconnier 1974:213, respectively.) NP Extraposition is thus subject to an intransitivity constraint from which *se dénoncer, s'offrir,* and *se présenter* are exempted.

The displaced subject in NP Extraposition sentences is positioned just like a direct object NP: it precedes locative and temporal phrases. (50b) can be analyzed as shown in (58):

(58)

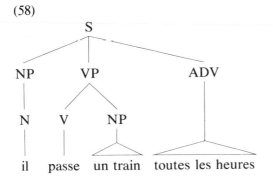

The syntactic generalization governing NP Extraposition can be captured by a lexical rule. The rule assigns the grammatical function OBJ to the argument which was formerly assigned SUBJ, and it adds a constraint equation to the effect that the form of the grammatical subject must be *il*.

(59)

NP Extraposition

(SUBJ) $\mapsto$ (OBJ)

($\uparrow$SUBJ FORM) $=_c$ IL

The lexical entry for *il* is given in (60):

(60) .

il: N, ($\uparrow$FORM) = IL
        ($\uparrow$NUM) = SG
        ($\uparrow$PERS) = 3

The *il* of NP Extraposition (as opposed to the personal pronoun *il* 'he') is simply a place filler, like English *it* and *there*. Since *il* has no semantic significance, it is assigned no PRED feature, but just a FORM feature. Grammatical arguments which have no PRED do not have to be assigned to the argument of any PRED; (63) is thus not incoherent. However, they can occur only if they are selected by an equation associated with a lexical form.

NP Extraposition will apply freely to intransitive verbs. It will apply to the lexical form of *passer* in (61), for example, giving the new lexical form in (62).

(61)

passer: V, ($\uparrow$PRED) = 'PASSER((SUBJ))'

(62)

          ($\uparrow$PRED) = 'PASSER((OBJ))'
          ($\uparrow$SUBJ FORM) $=_c$ IL

In (58) *un train* is assigned the grammatical function OBJ by virtue of the PS rules, and *il* is assigned the grammatical function SUBJ. The functional structure (simplified) of (58) is (63).

(63)

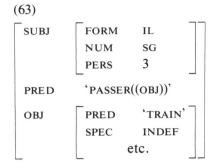

$$
\begin{bmatrix}
\text{SUBJ} & \begin{bmatrix} \text{FORM} & \text{IL} \\ \text{NUM} & \text{SG} \\ \text{PERS} & 3 \end{bmatrix} \\
\text{PRED} & \text{`PASSER((OBJ))'} \\
\text{OBJ} & \begin{bmatrix} \text{PRED} & \text{`TRAIN'} \\ \text{SPEC} & \text{INDEF} \\ & \text{etc.} \end{bmatrix}
\end{bmatrix}
$$

(63) is well-formed since the constraint equation associated with the new lexical form of *passer* is satisfied, and because *un train* is the grammatical OBJ it is assigned to the OBJ argument of *dormir*.

It is a consequence of this analysis and the theory of lexical forms that NP Extraposition can never apply to a transitive verb, because it would always yield a lexical form in which the same grammatical function is assigned to two different arguments. This is of course prohibited by the principle of functional uniqueness (see section 2.2 of this chapter; chapters 1, 3, and 5 of this volume; and Bresnan to appear). For example, were the rule to apply to *dénoncer,* the result would be the ill-formed (65):

(64)

dénoncer: V, ($\uparrow$PRED) = 'DÉNONCER((SUBJ),(OBJ))'

(65)

$\qquad$ ($\uparrow$PRED) = 'DÉNONCER((OBJ),(OBJ))'

$\qquad$ ($\uparrow$SUBJ FORM) $=_c$ IL

The crucial role of functional uniqueness is obscured in (51)–(53) by the (presumably accidental) fact that French phrase structure admits of only one NP OBJ position. As a result, the first postverbal NP in these examples will be an OBJ and the second an NCOMP; the sentences are incoherent because NCOMP is not selected by any predicate. (On the fate of verbs which do select NCOMP, see section 2.6.)

The examples in (54) with clitic objects are the key ones, because both the clitic and the postverbal NP can be assigned OBJ by the PS rules. Here we have two logical possibilities. The verb might select only one OBJ, in which case consistency will be violated, as established in section 2.1. Alternatively, the verb might select two OBJs, and the sentence would be consistent. It is this possibility, of course, which the principle of functional uniqueness prohibits.

But when a transitive verb has been made intransitive by the application of Reflexivization or Inchoativization, NP Extraposition can apply. Reflexivization of *dénoncer* gives (66), and NP Extraposition applied to the reflexive form gives (67).

(66)
$(\uparrow\text{PRED}) = \text{'DÉNONCER}_{\text{refl}}((\text{SUBJ}),\phi)\text{'}$
   $(\uparrow\text{REFL}) =_{c} +$

(67)
$(\uparrow\text{PRED}) = \text{'DÉNONCER}_{\text{refl}}((\text{OBJ}),\phi)\text{'}$
   $(\uparrow\text{SUBJ FORM}) =_{c} \text{IL}$
   $(\uparrow\text{REFL}) =_{c} +$

Thus, because Reflexivization intransitivizes the verb, reflexives behave like grammatical intransitives with respect to NP Extraposition. This is a consequence of the analysis of reflexivization presented earlier, together with the theory of lexical forms.

Of course, inchoatives also permit NP Extraposition, although their causative (transitive) bases do not:

(68)
Il se brisera beaucoup de verres.
'Many glasses will break.'

(69)
a.   *Il brisera beaucoup de verres les enfants.
b.   *Il brisera les enfants beaucoup de verres.
      'The children will break many glasses.'

Applying NP Extraposition to *briser*$_{\text{cause}}$, we get the familiar violation of functional uniqueness: OBJ assigned to more than one argument. But with *briser*$_{\text{inch}}$ the output is impeccable:

(70)
a. $\text{'BRISER}_{\text{cause}}((\text{SUBJ}),(\text{OBJ}))\text{'}$
b. $\text{'BRISER}_{\text{cause}}((\text{OBJ}),(\text{OBJ}))\text{'}$
      $(\uparrow\text{SUBJ FORM}) =_{c} \text{IL}$

(71)
a. $\text{'BRISER}_{\text{inch}}((\text{SUBJ}))\text{'}$
      $(\uparrow\text{REFL}) =_{c} +$

b. 'BRISER$_{inch}$((OBJ))'
   ($\uparrow$REFL) $=_c$ +
   ($\uparrow$SUBJ FORM) $=_c$ IL

So NP Extraposition provides us with crucial evidence to choose between lexical and nonlexical reflexivization. Verbs with reflexivized objects behave like grammatical intransitives, as the lexical theory predicts.

I should point out that the claim that the displaced subject NP occupies direct object position is not wholly uncontroversial, although Ruwet 1972, Kayne 1975, and Pollock 1978 make this suggestion. Kayne 1979 cites the examples in (72) and (73), attributing them to Hériau 1976.

(72)
Il prend corps dans ce pays une grande espérance.
'There is taking shape in this country a great hope.'

(73)
Il reste encore disponible bon nombre de places.
'There remain still available a good number of seats.'

Kayne observes that in (72) and (73) the displaced subject is not in the canonical object position: it follows a PP in (72) and an AP in (73).[8] Kayne concludes that NP Extraposition is not "structure-preserving" (Emonds 1970, 1976). (This is discussed further in section 2.6 below. Note also that (72) is doubly interesting since it involves an apparent violation of the generalization that NP Extraposition is impossible with transitive verbs. The violation is only apparent, however; see section 2.5.)

Such examples might seem problematic for my analysis of NP Extraposition, which requires that the displaced subject be generated in an NP position, and in an NP position assigned the function OBJ. But even under Kayne's assumptions, the PS configuration required for (72) and (73) must be available independently of NP Extraposition. Kayne 1979:713 argues that the *il y avoir* construction is base-generated; the postverbal NP in his *Il y a un livre sur la table* 'There is a book on the table' is an underlying object. But note that (74), in which a PP precedes the underlying object, is perfectly grammatical:

(74)
Il y a dans ce pays une grande espérance.
'There is in this country a great hope.'

It appears, then, that a certain amount of reordering of constituents is possible in French; the reordering cannot be reduced to the effects of NP Extraposition, since it has not applied in (74).

Reordering can be expressed in the lexical theory by rules which reorder the elements in phrase structure rules, preserving grammatical function assignments. (An alternative solution is proposed in Falk 1980.) For this case, (6b) is reordered to give (75):

(75)
VP → V' (PP)   (NP)
            (↑OBJ)=↓

Reordering of this kind is limited to sisters, since it is stated over the righthand side of PS rules.

Thus, Kayne's examples (72) and (73), as well as (74), can be generated by VP reordering of this kind. The reordering is obviously rather marked in French grammar and is governed by factors which are not yet fully understood—probably heaviness of the NP plays a role.

Intransitivity is, though necessary, not a sufficient condition for NP Extraposition. Martin 1970:379–380 demonstrates that the displaced subject must be indefinite:

(76)

Il passera
{
un train
beaucoup de trains
quelques trains
*le train
*ton train
*ce train
}
d'ici deux heures.

'A train/many trains/some trains/the train/your train/this train will go by two hours from now.'

There are also semantic constraints on the class of verbs which permit NP Extraposition (Martin 1970). Martin characterizes the class as verbs concerning unexpected occurrence, existence, or nonexistence,[9] giving the examples in (77) and (78) (1970:381, 382):

(77)
a. Il existe des ouvrages qui . . .
    'Some works exist which . . .'
b. Il restait un problème important que . . .
    'An important problem which . . . remained.'

c. Il dormait un chien dans la pièce.
   'A dog slept in the room.'
d. Il meurt un homme toutes les minutes.
   'A man dies every minute.'

(78)
*Il maigrissait la plupart des prisonniers.
'Most of the prisoners became thin.'

This restriction is reminiscent of the restriction on presentational *There* Insertion in English—sentences in which *there* occupies subject position despite the fact that *be* does not appear. (See Aissen 1975, Emonds, 1976, Guéron 1980, Stowell 1978.)

As a consequence of this factor, not all intransitives undergo the rule, and this extends, as we would expect, to intransitives derived by Inchoativization and Reflexivization. Martin gives the examples in (79).

(79)
a. *Il se battait des ennemis farouches.
   'Fierce enemies fought one another.'
b. *Il se fardait un acteur dans sa loge.
   'An actor made himself up in his dressing room.'

All in all, our prediction is that intransitive reflexive and inchoative verbs will permit NP Extraposition if they are compatible with the semantic requirements of the rule. This prediction is borne out.

One further point should be mentioned here: the analysis of NP Extraposition predicts that, other things being equal, an accusative clitic pronoun should be able to act as the subject of a sentence in which NP Extraposition has applied. This is because accusative clitics have the grammatical function OBJ, just like the "postposed" subject NPs in the earlier examples. Thus, we would expect to find examples like (80):

(80)
*Il le passera d'ici deux heures.
'It will go by two hours from now.'

But of course (80) will be excluded independently by the definiteness restriction on the displaced NP, which rules out personal pronouns of any kind.[10]

Thus, NP Extraposition provides crucial evidence for the lexical analysis of reflexivization. If *se* were a grammatical OBJ, we would expect verbs like *se dénoncer* to behave like transitives. The fact that they behave like intransitives follows from the lexical analysis of *se,* in which it is never a grammatical argument.

Evidence from Causative Complements
I will not present here a full analysis of the notorious *"faire* construction" (Bordelois 1974, Kayne 1975, Rouveret and Vergnaud 1980), although I hope to do so in a later paper. Rather, I want to focus on just one aspect of the construction: the behavior of the NP functioning as the subject of the lower verb. Again, the evidence I will present rests heavily on Kayne's results (Kayne 1975).

The *faire* construction is illustrated in (81) and (82):

(81)
J'ai laissé Jean partir.
'I let John leave.'

(82)
J'ai $\begin{Bmatrix} \text{fait} \\ \text{laissé} \end{Bmatrix}$ partir Jean.

'I $\begin{Bmatrix} \text{made} \\ \text{let} \end{Bmatrix}$ John leave.'

Laisser allows both variants, but with *faire* only the second form is possible. Here the NP which corresponds to the subject of *partir* follows the verb.

The examples in (83) (from Kayne 1975:203) show that the "postposed" subject precedes all PP complements to the verb:

(83)
a.   On fera parler Jean de son dernier voyage.
     'One will make John talk about his last journey.'
b.   Il faisait tirer les soldats sur les criminels.
     'He made the soldiers shoot at the criminals.'
c.   Elle fera rentrer son enfant dans sa chambre.
     'She will make her child go back into his bedroom.'

The simplest possible analysis of these sentences is thus that the postposed NP is in the position generally occupied by direct object NPs.[11,12]

(84)

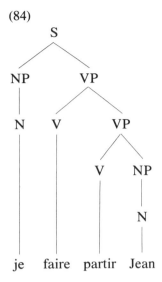

je   faire   partir Jean

For our purposes, the key fact about the *faire* construction is that when the verb in the causative complement is transitive, the subject appears after the verb and the direct object and *must* be in a PP introduced by *à*.[13] Kayne 1975:204 gives the following examples:

(85)

a.   Il fera boire un peu de vin à son enfant.
      'He will make his child drink a little wine.'

b.   Elle a fait visiter la ferme à ses parents.
      'She made her relatives visit the farm.'

(86)

a.   *Il fera boire un peu de vin son enfant.

b.   *Elle a fait visiter la ferme ses parents.

With intransitive verbs the postposed NP cannot appear in a PP:

(87)

a.   *J'ai laissé partir à Jean.

b.   *J'ai fait partir à Jean.

These basic generalizations about causative complements are captured by the lexical rule given in (88):[14]

(88)

Causative Complement Rule (CCR)

CCR(i)   (SUBJ) $\mapsto$ (OBJ)

CCR(ii)   (SUBJ) $\mapsto$ (A OBJ)

(88) applies to the lexical forms of *partir* and *boire* as shown in (89).

(89)

partir: V, ($\uparrow$PRED) = 'PARTIR((SUBJ))'

           ($\uparrow$PRED) = 'PARTIR((OBJ))'

boire: V, ($\uparrow$PRED) = 'BOIRE((SUBJ),(OBJ))'

         ($\uparrow$PRED) = 'BOIRE((A OBJ),(OBJ))'

Partir's grammatical OBJ is assigned to its sole logical argument in causative complements. *Boire*'s grammatical A OBJ is assigned to its first argument or "logical subject."

This analysis explains why the displaced subject of transitive verbs cannot occur in a bare NP form. No transitive verb could ever undergo CCR(i). If it did, the output would be a lexical form: *Predicate* ((OBJ),(OBJ)). This, like the result of applying NP Extraposition to a transitive verb, violates functional uniqueness.[15]

We have here, then, a second case of the crucial kind. The lexical analysis of *se* predicts that verbs with intrinsic *se* and verbs with reflexive *se,* even when *se* "corresponds to" a direct object NP, should pattern with *partir,* not with *boire.*

Consider, for example, the analysis of *s'endormir* 'to fall asleep'.

(90)

endormir: V, ($\uparrow$PRED) = 'ENDORMIR$_{cause}$((SUBJ),(OBJ))'

          ($\uparrow$PRED) = 'ENDORMIR$_{inch}$((SUBJ))'

            ($\uparrow$REFL) $=_c$ +

While CCR(i) cannot apply to the transitive causative form of *endormir,* it can apply to the inchoative form, giving the lexical form in (91):

(91)

'ENDORMIR$_{inch}$((OBJ))'

($\uparrow$REFL) $=_c$ +

Thus, we predict correctly that (92a) is grammatical and (92b) ungrammatical.

(92)
a.   J'ai fait s'endormir les enfants.
b.   *J'ai fait s'endormir aux enfants.
        'I made the children go to sleep.'

Exactly the same is true for reflexive/reciprocal *se*.[16] The lexical entry for *tuer* 'kill', given in (93), will serve as an illustration.

(93)
tuer: V, $(\uparrow PRED) = $ 'TUER((SUBJ),(OBJ))'
        $(\uparrow PRED) = $ 'TUER$_{refl}$((SUBJ),ϕ)'
        $(\uparrow REFL) =_c +$

Unlike the nonreflexive form, the reflexive form is intransitive, and it should therefore undergo CCR(i):

(94)
'TUER$_{refl}$((OBJ),ϕ)'
$(\uparrow REFL) =_c +$

(95) (from Kayne 1975:407) shows that this is in fact the case:

(95)
a.   La crainte du scandale a fait se tuer le frère du juge.
b.   *La crainte du scandale a fait se tuer au frère du juge.
        'Fear of scandal made the brother of the judge kill himself.'

It should perhaps be emphasized at this point that nonreflexive accusative clitics behave just like full NPs with respect to (88), although the picture is complicated by the fact that they appear cliticized to the causative verb and not to the lower verb (Kayne 1975):

(96)
a.   La crainte du scandale l'a fait tuer au juge.
b.   *La crainte du scandale l'a fait tuer le juge.
        'Fear of scandal made the judge kill him.'

So again the lexical analysis of *se* makes exactly the right predictions. It explains why reflexive verbs, but no transitive verbs, undergo CCR(i) and not CCR(ii).

Se Moyen
"*Se moyen*" or "Middle *se*" is illustrated in (97):

(97)

Beaucoup de livres se vendent dans cette ville.
'Many books *se* sell in this town.'

This use of *se* is an apparent anomaly: if *se* is a reflexive/reciprocal pronoun, how can it, and why should it, be employed for middle forms? (97) is not reflexive in meaning; rather, it is interpreted like an agentless passive: 'Many books are sold in this town'. Yet, given the lexical analysis, this use of *se* falls into place rather naturally.

First, the clitic of *se moyen* has the same syntax and the same lexical entry as the other uses of *se*, so nothing need be said about its grammar. *Se moyen* is of course not a pronoun, but instead a marker of the application of a lexical rule which creates middle verb forms.[17] The Middle Rule is almost identical to the rule for agentless passives.[18] It assigns the grammatical function ϕ to the former SUBJ argument, and SUBJ to the former OBJ argument. Assignment of ϕ in a lexical form has as an automatic consequence binding by an existential quantifier in predicate argument structure, as in Passivization (see chapters 1, 3, and 5 of this volume and Bresnan 1978, to appear).[19] The one difference between Passivization and the Middle Rule is that the latter adds the familiar constraint equation $(\uparrow\text{REFL}) =_c +$ to the derived lexical form.[20]

(98)

The Middle Rule

$(\text{SUBJ}) \mapsto \phi$

$(\text{OBJ}) \mapsto (\text{SUBJ})$

$(\uparrow\text{REFL}) =_c +$

For *vendre* 'sell' the rule applies as shown in (99) and (100).

(99)

vendre: V, $(\uparrow\text{PRED}) = \text{'VENDRE}((\text{SUBJ}),(\text{OBJ}))\text{'}$

(100)

$\qquad (\uparrow\text{PRED}) = \text{'VENDRE}(\phi,(\text{SUBJ}))\text{'}$

$\qquad (\uparrow\text{REFL}) =_c +$

This analysis of *se moyen* has several immediate consequences. *Se moyen* will appear only with transitive verbs, since the Middle Rule incorporates an operation on OBJ:

(101)

*Les enfants se $\begin{Bmatrix} \text{dorment} \\ \text{partent} \end{Bmatrix}$.

'The children *se* sleep/leave.'

The Middle Rule, like Passivization, will never apply to verbs with predicate nominals, because they are not OBJS:

(102)

*Un bon professeur se devient.

'One becomes a good teacher.'

Since verbs to which the Middle Rule has applied are grammatically intransitive, NP Extraposition should apply to them, and it does (Kayne 1975, Pollock 1978, Gross 1975). (The examples are from Kayne 1975:93, footnote 29 and 1975:330.)

(103)

Il se vend beaucoup de livres dans cette ville.

'Many books are sold in this city.'

(104)

Il se construit beaucoup d'immeubles dans cette ville.

'Many buildings are constructed in this town.'

NP Extraposition applies to (100) to give (105), which obeys functional uniqueness:

(105)

($\uparrow$PRED) = 'VENDRE(ϕ,(OBJ))'

($\uparrow$REFL) $=_c$ +

($\uparrow$SUBJ FORM) $=_c$ IL

Thus, *se moyen* fits into the lexical analysis of *se* in a straightforward way. In all cases, *se* is the reflex of a lexical rule: Reflexivization, Inchoativization, or the Middle Rule. Reflexivization *can* have the effect of intransitivization (if the former OBJ argument is bound); the other rules always do. From this follows the interaction of the appearance of *se* with the intransitivity constraint.

Alternative Solutions to the Problem of *Se*

The puzzling behavior of *se* with respect to NP Extraposition and causative complements was first observed and extensively discussed by Kayne, and I have drawn heavily on his results here. He argued (Kayne

1975) that reflexive verbs behave like intransitives in these constructions because a cyclic rule of *Se* Placement cliticizes *se* onto the verb
before NP Extraposition or *Faire* Infinitive (the rule which forms
causatives) applies. In this analysis, placement of nonreflexive clitics is
postcyclic. Thus, a nonreflexive clitic corresponding to a direct object
NP will still be in the VP when NP Extraposition and *Faire* Infinitive
apply, giving rise to the asymmetry between *se* and the nonreflexive
clitics.

Rouveret and Vergnaud 1980:140–143 suggest a rather different solution: "The reflexive clitic *se* is base-generated as an affix on the verb
(...) and is coindexed with an empty NP complement by a rule of
construal *Se* Agreement" (p. 140). The empty NP is later deleted.
Other clitics are generated as verbal complements and transformationally cliticized to the verb. As a result, when *se* is the clitic, the verb is
intransitive, and when a pronominal or full NP object is present, the
verb is transitive.

These solutions have one basic property in common. At the point in
the derivation where NP Extraposition and *À* Insertion in causative
complements apply, verbs with *se* corresponding to objects will be
structurally intransitive, while verbs with full NPs or other clitics as
objects will be structurally transitive. The same important questions
can be raised about both solutions.[21] Why are verbs with reflexive
objects intransitive? Why are verbs with nonreflexive objects transitive? Couldn't the facts be the other way around?

Kayne's solution could easily be adapted to this situation: Clitic
Placement would be a cyclic rule, *Se* Placement postcyclic. Rouveret
and Vergnaud's solution is similarly adaptable. Nonreflexive clitics
could be base-generated with empty NP positions in the VP, and
reflexive clitics could be underlyingly postverbal complements. Thus,
while these solutions are descriptively successful, they cannot be said
to explain the difference between reflexive and nonreflexive clitics.
The correlation between the semantic properties of *se* and its grammatical properties is treated as accidental. What is needed is a principled connection between inchoative or reflexive semantics and the
syntactic mechanisms of cyclic placement or base generation. (See
Kayne 1975:716, footnote 17 for some suggestions along these lines.)

In the lexical theory the correlation is inescapable. A transitive
predicate—one having OBJ assigned to one of its arguments—may be

mapped onto an intransitive predicate only if some semantic operation makes the argument assigned OBJ unavailable for grammatical interpretation. This can be effected in only two ways: by binding (of an argument to another argument, or of an argument to an existential quantifier; see the previous subsection, as well as section 2.6), or by a change in the internal semantic composition of a predicate. Recall that ϕ is assigned to an argument if and only if the argument is bound in predicate argument structure. Reflexivization is of course a case of binding, and Inchoativization is a case of change in semantic composition.

The pronominal clitics are simply freely referring items: verbs with pronominal objects do not fall into the same semantic categories as verbs with *se*. They could not be analyzed in terms of the semantic operations of binding or change in semantic composition.

The lexical theory is compatible with an analysis in which *se* is simply a pronoun and therefore can serve as an OBJ, as outlined in section 2.3. In that case, syntactic rules would treat any verb with a clitic object (reflexive or otherwise) as transitive. If French reflexive clitics are, as I have argued, lexically introduced morphemes, not pronouns, rules will treat verbs with *se* as intransitive and verbs with *le, la, les,* etc., as transitive. But under no circumstances could the language treat verbs with *se* as transitive and verbs with pronominal objects as intransitive.

Thus, the lexical theory explains the correlation between reflexivization/inchoativization and grammatical intransitivity.

2.5 A Note on Idioms

We have established that NP Extraposition and the CCR distinguish between grammatical transitives and intransitives. The general rule is that transitives never allow NP Extraposition or CCR(i). Yet there are a few examples like (106) and (107) which seem to cast doubt on the correctness of this generalization. ((106) is from Kayne 1976:716. (107) is a simplified version of (72), which is also from Kayne 1979.)

(106)
Il lui a traversé l'esprit une idée si extraordinaire que . . .
'Such an extraordinary idea crossed his mind that . . .'

(107)

Il prend corps une grande espérance.

'A great hope is taking shape.'

Here NP Extraposition has applied despite the presence of what are apparently direct object NPs: *l'esprit* and *corps*.

What are we to conclude in the face of these examples? Both NP Extraposition and CCR(i) replace SUBJ with OBJ, so if *l'esprit* and *corps* are OBJS, we predict that (106) and (107) are impossible. We could of course abandon this analysis, and with it the explanation for the intransitivity constraint observed in all the previously analyzed examples. But this would be the wrong conclusion, not only for the obvious reason—that we want to maintain our explanation for the intransitivity constraint—but also because it would offer no explanation for a further generalization. All the apparent exceptions to the intransitivity constraint are idiomatic or fixed expressions.

We can explain this generalization if we hypothesize (as Bresnan does for English in chapters 1 and 3 of this volume and in Bresnan to appear) that some fixed expressions may be reanalyzed as complex verbs. If *traverser l'esprit* and *prendre corps* are complex verbs in (106) and (107), then *l'esprit* and *corps* are not grammatical objects, but subparts of the verbs. There is, then, no reason why the verbs should not allow NP Extraposition:

(108)

a.   traverser l'esprit: V, ($\uparrow$PRED) = 'TRAVERSER-L'ESPRIT((SUBJ))'

b.   ($\uparrow$PRED) = 'TRAVERSER-L'ESPRIT((OBJ))'

    ($\uparrow$SUBJ FORM) $=_c$ IL

(109)

a.   prendre corps: V, ($\uparrow$PRED) = 'PRENDRE-CORPS((SUBJ))'

b.   ($\uparrow$PRED) = 'PRENDRE-CORPS((OBJ))'

    ($\uparrow$SUBJ FORM) $=_c$ IL

Of course, not all idiomatic expressions are analyzed as complex verbs, and not all of them allow NP Extraposition and CCR(i). Kayne 1975 gives several relevant examples: *faire son apparition* 'make one's appearance, appear' and *avoir lieu* 'take place, occur' do not allow NP Extraposition even though they seem to belong to the appropriate semantic class (examples from Kayne 1975:331):

(110)

a. *Il fera leur apparition trois nouvelles étoiles cette nuit.

b. *Il fera trois nouvelles étoiles leur apparition cette nuit.
   'Three new stars will appear tonight.'

(111)

a. *Il aura lieu des manifestations demain.

b. *Il aura des manifestations lieu demain.
   'Some demonstrations will take place tomorrow.'

For causative complements, Kayne 1975:209 gives the examples in
(112), with *entendre raison* 'listen to reason' and *lâcher prise* 'let go'

(112)

a. Elle fera entendre raison à Jean.
   'She will make John listen to reason.'

b. Il a fait lâcher prise à son chien.
   'He made his dog let go.'

These idioms resist NP Extraposition and require *â* before the displaced subject NP in causatives. This is evidence that these idioms are
not complex verbs, but rather grammatical transitives. *Avoir* in *avoir
lieu* has the lexical form in (113). It is monadic, but grammatically
transitive, and its grammatical OBJ must be *lieu*.

(113)

avoir: V, ($\uparrow$PRED) = 'AVOIR-LIEU((SUBJ))'
          ($\uparrow$OBJ FORM) =$_c$ LIEU

lieu: N, ($\uparrow$FORM) = LIEU

If NP Extraposition is applied to the lexical form of *avoir lieu*, the result
is (114):

(114)

($\uparrow$PRED) = 'AVOIR-LIEU((OBJ))'
($\uparrow$OBJ FORM) =$_c$ LIEU
($\uparrow$SUBJ FORM) = IL

However, no well-formed functional structure can be constructed for
Il aura lieu des manifestations using this lexical form. *Lieu* is an OBJ and
des manifestations an NCOMP, so the functional structure (115) is
incoherent.

(115)

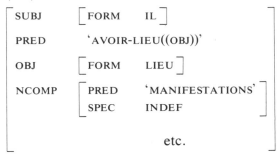

$$\begin{bmatrix} \text{SUBJ} & \begin{bmatrix} \text{FORM} & \text{IL} \end{bmatrix} \\ \text{PRED} & \text{`AVOIR-LIEU((OBJ))'} \\ \text{OBJ} & \begin{bmatrix} \text{FORM} & \text{LIEU} \end{bmatrix} \\ \text{NCOMP} & \begin{bmatrix} \text{PRED} & \text{`MANIFESTATIONS'} \\ \text{SPEC} & \text{INDEF} \end{bmatrix} \\ & \text{etc.} \end{bmatrix}$$

The basic claim, then, is that idioms of V NP form will be grammatically transitive unless they have been reanalyzed. This explains why idioms can apparently violate the intransitivity constraint. Further confirmatory evidence can be found for this claim, as well. For example, we expect that some fixed expressions will be ambiguously analyzed. This is the explanation for (116):

(116)

Jean a fait prendre corps $\begin{Bmatrix} \phi \\ \text{à} \end{Bmatrix}$ un enorme projet.

'John made an enormous project take shape.'

In its complex verb analysis, *prendre corps* permits NP Extraposition and CCR(i). In its grammatical transitive analysis, it permits CCR(ii). So the displaced subject in a causative complement can be realized as an OBJ or as an A OBJ. Recall that in general intransitive verbs do not allow CCR(ii), so we correctly predict that it is only idiomatic expressions that will display the two alternative forms in causative complements.

Similarly, note the intriguing examples provided by Rouveret and Vergnaud 1980:133 and footnote 31.

(117)
a.　Cela a fait changer tout le monde d'avis.

b.　Cela a fait changer d'avis à tout le monde.
　　'That made everyone change their minds.'

(118)
a.　Cela a fait changer tout le monde de chemise.

b.　*Cela a fait changer de chemise à tout le monde.
　　'That made everyone change their shirts.'

Here we find *changer d'avis* 'change one's mind' allowing both CCR(i) and CCR(ii), while *changer de chemise* 'change one's shirt' allows only CCR(i). Furthermore, there is a difference in constituent order between (117a) and (117b). In (117a) *d'avis* follows *tout le monde,* the displaced subject. In (117b) *d'avis* follows *changer* and precedes *tout le monde.*

We can give a simple account of these facts. *Changer* is a verb which selects a prepositional object: the object of *de,* in fact. It has the lexical form in (119).

(119)
changer: V, ($\uparrow$PRED) = 'CHANGER((SUBJ),(DE OBJ))'

It is a grammatical intransitive and undergoes CCR(i):

(120)
($\uparrow$PRED) = 'CHANGER((OBJ),(DE OBJ))'

But the fixed expression *changer d'avis* has a second analysis, as a grammatically transitive idiom. (Kayne 1975:210, footnote 9, suggests that some prepositional objects may trigger CCR(ii). I refer the reader to his discussion.)

(121)
changer: V, ($\uparrow$PRED) = 'CHANGER-D'AVIS((SUBJ))'
                ($\uparrow$OBJ FORM) $=_c$ AVIS
                ($\uparrow$OBJ SPEC) $=_c$ DE
avis: N, ($\uparrow$FORM) = AVIS

Here *d'avis* is an OBJ, so CCR(i) cannot apply and CCR(ii) must. Since *changer d'avis* has two analyses, both (117a) and (117b) are possible. *Changer de chemise* has only one analysis, and (118b) is ill-formed.

The order of the postverbal constituents in (117a,b) follows from this analysis and the PS rules given in section 2.2. The NP assigned OBJ precedes all PP complements. So where *d'avis* is an OBJ, it precedes the PP *à tout le monde;* where it is a DE OBJ, it follows the OBJ *tout le monde.*

Other consequences of the analysis could be pursued, but I think this is sufficient to show that the behavior of idioms is perfectly consistent with the intransitivity constraint. In fact, we can explain why only idiomatic expressions can *appear* to violate the constraint, and why they alone can be ambiguously analyzed by the CCR.

2.6 On the Grammatical Function OBJECT; or The Function of Functions

So far I have tried to justify the analysis of r-clitics by showing that two rules treat verbs with r-clitics corresponding to objects as intransitive. I have assumed that the transitive–intransitive distinction for these rules is correctly stated in terms of the grammatical function OBJ, and I have shown how, given this assumption, the behavior of the rules can be explained. A predicate is grammatically transitive iff the grammatical function OBJ is assigned to it. The claim embodied by this analysis is thus that there is a class of rules (NP Extraposition and the CCR among them) which makes crucial reference to grammatical functions, where grammatical functions map phrases in particular structural configurations onto the logical arguments of a predicate. In order to justify this claim, it is necessary to show that the properties of this class of rules could not instead be stated and explained in terms of phrase structure configurations or in terms of some aspect of logical predicate argument structure. Evidence of this kind would motivate grammatical functions by showing that they cannot be reduced to independently needed concepts of linguistic theory.

The Definition of *Transitive*
It is fairly straightforward to see what the alternative formulations of a notion *transitive* would have to be. A verb would be "structurally transitive" if it occurred in the context ____ NP.[22] (This definition will encompass verbs with clitic objects also, provided that they are transformationally derived and provided that Clitic Placement follows the rules which are sensitive to transitivity. Otherwise, the definition would have to be complicated. I will not speculate as to what the definition would have to be, since it is immaterial to my argument.) A verb would be "logically transitive" if it was (at least) dyadic and if its second argument was of a particular semantic type, including NPs like *John, a man, the man, every man,* and excluding adjectives.[23]

A glance backward at section 2.4 reveals that either of these definitions would be compatible with the data presented there. NP Extraposition could apparently equally well be restricted either to verbs with no following NP or to verbs with no second logical argument of the relevant type. The CCR could prohibit *à* in these conditions and require it elsewhere.

Thus, it appears that the three hypotheses are at least descriptively equivalent over this range of data. (It is not so obvious that they are explanatorily equivalent, a point which I will take up below.) The crucial evidence is available, however.

Let us first take up the hypothesis of "logical transitivity." To distinguish this from "grammatical transitivity," we need (A) verbs which are logically transitive but grammatically intransitive and/or (B) verbs which are logically intransitive but grammatically transitive.

A clear case of type A is provided by passives. Passive sentences permit NP Extraposition with almost total freedom (though see Kayne 1975, Postal 1979 on some interesting exceptions to this generalization). Kayne 1975:245 gives these examples:

(122)

a. Il a été mangé beaucoup de pommes hier soir.
   'Many apples were eaten last night.'

b. Il sera détruit une centaine d'habitations.
   'A hundred dwellings will be destroyed.'

Martin 1970:386 observes: "La présence de l'auxiliaire d'existence *être* prédispose la phrase passive à la T_{imp}." ('The presence of the auxiliary of existence *être* 'to be' predisposes passive sentences to T_{imp} [the Impersonal Transformation or NP Extraposition]'). Passives seem to meet the semantic requirement of NP Extraposition, as in English they permit *There* Insertion freely.

But the status of the logical arguments under Passivization is constant with respect to logical transitivity: passive predicates are no more logically intransitive than are their active counterparts. If the condition on NP Extraposition is a matter of logical arguments, passive predicates should never allow NP Extraposition.

Passives are, of course, grammatically intransitive. Bresnan's analysis of English passivization in chapter 1 of this volume can be applied naturally to French. Passivization is a lexical rule which changes the assignment of grammatical functions to logical arguments: it is a rule which applies to lexical forms. For full passives, the rule changes OBJ to SUBJ and SUBJ to PAR OBJ (the OBJ of the preposition *par*). For "agentless" passives, the SUBJ is replaced by the null grammatical function ϕ. (A consequence of assigning ϕ to an argument is that the argument is bound by an existential quantifier; see chapter 1 of this volume and the analysis of *se moyen* above.)

(123)
Passivization
(OBJ) ⟼ (SUBJ)

$(\text{SUBJ}) \mapsto \left\{ \begin{array}{c} (\text{PAR OBJ}) \\ \phi \end{array} \right\}$

(124) shows the base form for *manger* 'eat' and its passive forms.

(124)
manger: V, (↑PRED) = 'MANGER((SUBJ),(OBJ))'
              (↑PRED) = 'MANGER((PAR OBJ),(SUBJ))'
              (↑PRED) = 'MANGER(ϕ,(SUBJ))'

While NP Extraposition cannot apply to the active form, it can apply to the passive forms, giving the lexical forms in (125).

(125)
(↑PRED) = 'MANGER((PAR OBJ),(OBJ))'
  (↑SUBJ FORM) =$_c$ IL
(↑PRED) = 'MANGER(ϕ,(OBJ))'
  (↑SUBJ FORM) =$_c$ IL

The syntactic and functional structures of (126) are given in (127).

(126)
Il a été mangé beaucoup de pommes.
'Many apples were eaten.'

(127)

a.

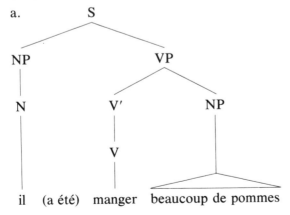

b.

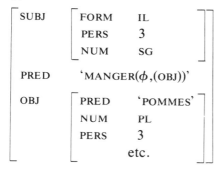

$$\begin{bmatrix} \text{SUBJ} & \begin{bmatrix} \text{FORM} & \text{IL} \\ \text{PERS} & 3 \\ \text{NUM} & \text{SG} \end{bmatrix} \\ \text{PRED} & \text{'MANGER}(\phi,(\text{OBJ}))\text{'} \\ \text{OBJ} & \begin{bmatrix} \text{PRED} & \text{'POMMES'} \\ \text{NUM} & \text{PL} \\ \text{PERS} & 3 \\ & \text{etc.} \end{bmatrix} \end{bmatrix}$$

Thus, the grammatical transitivity hypothesis correctly predicts that NP Extraposition will be possible with the passive version of a transitive verb, but not with its active version.

Similarly, "unspecified object" verbs (*manger* 'eat', *boire* 'drink', etc.) are grammatically intransitive, having the lexical forms shown in (128):

(128)
'MANGER((SUBJ),ϕ)'
'BOIRE((SUBJ),ϕ)'

In many analyses, however, these verbs are considered logically transitive, having a second argument bound by an existential quantifier. Thus, the logical argument hypothesis would predict that they should not undergo NP Extraposition and that they should trigger the presence of *à* in causative complements. The grammatical transitivity hypothesis predicts that they should be indistinguishable from intransitive verbs with respect to NP Extraposition and the CCR, since they have no grammatical object. The relevant lexical forms for *manger* are given in (129). (129a) is the transitive base form, (129b) the unspecified object form, (129c) the NP Extraposition form, and (129d) the causative complement form.

(129)
a. 'MANGER((SUBJ),(OBJ))'
b. 'MANGER((SUBJ),ϕ)'
c. 'MANGER((OBJ),ϕ)'
    ($\uparrow$SUBJ FORM) $=_c$ IL
d. 'MANGER((OBJ),ϕ)'

(130) illustrates the behavior of unspecified object verbs in causative complements, which is as the grammatical transitivity hypothesis predicts:

(130)
a.   J'ai fait manger Jean.
b.   *J'ai fait manger à Jean.
      'I made John eat.'

With respect to NP Extraposition, the situation is a little more complex. Recall that there is a semantic restriction on the class of predicates which permit NP Extraposition. Thus, the grammatical transitivity hypothesis predicts that NP Extraposition will be possible only if the unspecified object verbs fall into the appropriate semantic class. In fact, it appears that speakers vary in this respect. (Postal 1979 gives a different account of this variation.) Ruwet 1972:166, footnote 18 cites an observation made by J.-C. Milner to the effect that these verbs do not permit the rule, giving the example (131), among others.

(131)
a.   Quelqu'un a mangé.
b.   *Il a mangé quelqu'un.
      'Someone ate.'

But in Pollock 1978:94, comparable sentences are said to be well-formed:

(132)
a.   Beaucoup de linguistes mangent dans ce restaurant.
b.   Il mange beaucoup de linguistes dans ce restaurant.
      'Many linguists eat in this restaurant.'

The logical argument hypothesis wrongly predicts that no speakers could ever accept NP Extraposition with this class of verbs. Passives and unspecified object deletion verbs thus provide overwhelming evidence that the logical transitivity hypothesis makes the wrong predictions in cases of type A.

Some idioms are prime cases of type B. Many of the idioms analyzed in section 2.5 are grammatically transitive but logically intransitive. For example, *avoir lieu* means 'occur' and is monadic. *Faire leur apparition* means 'appear' and is also monadic. Yet as Kayne's examples (110)–(112) clearly show, idioms of this type do not allow CCR(i), nor do they permit NP Extraposition (although they do seem to have the appropriate meaning). So the logical transitivity hypothesis makes the wrong predictions for type B as well as for type A.

To distinguish the grammatical transitivity hypothesis from the structural transitivity hypothesis we need (C) verbs which are structurally transitive but grammatically intransitive and/or (D) verbs which are structurally intransitive but grammatically transitive.

I have been unable to find cases of type (D) (unless verbs with accusative clitics count as structurally intransitive, in which case structural transitivity makes the wrong prediction for them), but type (C) is sufficient to make the point. Predicate nominals are NPs, and verbs that directly precede them must therefore be structurally transitive. However, they are not grammatically transitive, since predicate nominals are associated with the grammatical function NCOMP, not with the grammatical function OBJ.[24]

For example, *devenir* 'become' has the lexical form shown in (133).

(133)
devenir: V, ($\uparrow$PRED) = 'DEVENIR((SUBJ),(NCOMP))'

(134)
Son fils deviendra un bon professeur.
'$\begin{Bmatrix} \text{His} \\ \text{Her} \end{Bmatrix}$ son will become a good teacher.'

The grammatical function NCOMP is associated with the second NP position in the French VP (see (6)). None of the arguments of *devenir* is assigned the grammatical function OBJ, so *devenir* is grammatically intransitive; its lexical form should undergo CCR(i), giving (135).

(135)
($\uparrow$PRED) = 'DEVENIR((OBJ),(NCOMP))'

Kayne 1975:208 gives the examples in (136) and (137), which show that this prediction is correct.[25]

(136)
Cela fera devenir son fils un bon professeur.
'That will make his/her son become a good teacher.'

(137)
*Cela fera devenir un bon professeur à son fils.

Note that the order of postverbal NPs in (136) is as we expect: the OBJ NP precedes the NCOMP NP, as (6) predicts.

If it were structural transitivity that determined the form of causative complements, *devenir un bon professeur* should be exactly like *boire un peu de vin,* since both are analyzed as V NP.

To sum up, the grammatical transitivity hypothesis predicts that passives, unspecified object deletion verbs, and verbs with predicate nominal complements will all behave like intransitives, while at least some idioms will behave like grammatical transitives. The intransitivity constraint on NP Extraposition and the CCR cannot be naturally described in terms of structural or logical transitivity.

On OBJECT and NCOMP

It might be objected that the intransitivity constraint is not really *explained* by functional uniqueness, because the account given here depends on the analysis of NP Extraposition and CCR(i) as rules which replace SUBJ with OBJ. Suppose that they were instead analyzed as replacing SUBJ with NCOMP; then they could apply to transitive verbs with no ill effects. The question is, then, whether or not this potential alternative is excluded for principled reasons. If so, we have arrived at an explanation for the constraint.

The answer hinges on a fundamental difference between grammatical functions like SUBJECT, OBJECT, PREPOSITIONAL OBJECT, etc., and functions like NCOMP, ACOMP, PCOMP, etc. (XCOMP in general). Thinking in terms of first-order logic, SUBJ and its fellows correspond simply to arguments of predicates, but the XCOMP functions correspond to predicates. For example, compare the role of the NCOMP *a fool* in *John is a fool* with the role of the OBJ *a book* in *We bought a book.*

(138)
fool (John)
buy (we, a book)

The NCOMP corresponds to a predicate 'fool', which takes John as its argument. The OBJ, on the other hand, corresponds merely to the second argument of the predicate *buy.* The same basic distinction is of course maintained in more complex examples. In *We give John a book, we, John,* and *a book,* are simply arguments of *give,* but in the syntactically parallel *We consider John a fool,* 'fool' is predicated of *John.*

Substituting an "argument function" for a "predicative function," or vice versa, therefore amounts to a muddling of logical types, which is hard to construe in any sensible fashion. It is easy to see that a restrictive theory of the semantic operations that lexical rules may perform could exclude this kind of mapping on general grounds. For example, Bresnan suggests that predicate deletion and addition (as in causativization and inchoativization), along with binding, are the only possibilities (Bresnan in preparation a).

With some such characterization of possible semantic operations, there is no need to stipulate in the theory of grammatical functions that no rule can replace SUBJ with NCOMP. The result follows, given the semantic correlates of the XCOMP grammatical functions.

This not only allows us to explain the intransitivity constraint, but also has further consequences. The theory now explains why no morphological rules interchange argument and predicative functions. For example, no rules of word formation take a transitive verb as base and give a verb which takes predicate nominals as output.

Furthermore, we can now explain why Passivization cannot apply to predicate nominals, although purely structure-dependent rules like *Wh* Fronting can. If Passivization is stated as replacing OBJ with SUBJ (see the previous subsection), then we have achieved descriptive success. NCOMPs will not undergo the rule. But why could there not be a second case of the rule—one that replaced NCOMP with SUBJ, deriving (140) from (139)?

(139)
'PREDICATE((SUBJ),(NCOMP))'

(140)
'PREDICATE(ϕ,(SUBJ))'

Clearly this is another case of mixing arguments and predicates. The second argument of the verb has a predicative function assigned to it, and the rule changes the predicative function to an argument function.

Thus, the hypothetical second case of Passivization would not merely represent a minor complication in the grammar; it would be fundamentally incompatible with the theory of lexical rules.

Functional Uniqueness and Structure Preservation

The principle of functional uniqueness explains the intransitivity constraint (IC), once NP Extraposition and CCR(i) are analyzed as operations on grammatical function assignments. Base generation of NP Extraposition and causative complement constructions explains why they appear to conform to Emonds's structure-preserving constraint (Emonds 1970, 1976). They must be isomorphic to some output of the PS rules, since they *are* an output of the PS rules.

Given this, it is striking that structure preservation is the most likely source of an alternative explanation for the IC, and that constraints like the IC appear to provide the most potent evidence for the structure-preserving hypothesis.

An explanation for the IC in terms of structure preservation would proceed as follows. The postposed subject must occupy an NP position. The NP position is empty in the case of an intransitive verb, so the subject can be moved into it. But with a transitive verb that position is filled, so the subject NP cannot be postposed without violating structure preservation.[26,27]

The theory of structure preservation predicts that the existence of an IC will correlate in a principled way with the number of NP positions available within the VP. If there are two positions in a VP, one could be occupied by a direct object and the other by the displaced subject. So structure preservation will explain an IC only if the constraint can be reduced to the number of NP positions available.

Examples like (141) (= (4)) and (142) (= (136)) demonstrate that French has NP NP constructions, albeit of a limited type.

(141)

Nous avons élu Jean $\begin{cases} \text{président} \\ \text{premier président de la république} \end{cases}$.

(142)
Cela fera devenir son fils un bon professeur.

These sentences motivate the PS rule VP → V NP NP for French. (This conclusion holds regardless of whether (142) is considered to be base-generated, as here, or derived by the application of a structure-preserving transformation.) But if there are two available NP positions, then structure preservation cannot explain the IC on NP Extraposition or CCR(i). One position could be occupied by the postposed subject, the other by the direct object.

The lexical theory, on the other hand, allows two possible sources for an IC. The first is trivial "structure preservation": if the PS rules allow for only one NP, then of course only one NP can be generated. The second is functional uniqueness, and the crucial property here is that there is no direct correlation between the existence of an IC and the number of NP positions permitted by the PS rules.[28] For example, suppose there are two NP positions within the VP, one assigned the function A and the other the function B. A rule making the subject an A will not apply if an A is already present as an argument of the verb, even though a second NP position is available. This last kind of IC cannot be reduced to the number of NP nodes generated by the base and is exactly what is needed for NP Extraposition and CCR(i). SUBJ cannot be replaced by OBJ if OBJ is already assigned to an argument, and this is completely independent of the phrase structure of VP.[29]

This conclusion suggests a reevaluation of the theory of structure preservation. Brame 1976, 1978 and Bresnan 1978 have pointed out that base generation provides a general explanation for the property of structure preservation. It now seems that restrictions like the IC should be explained in terms of grammatical functions. This raises the question of whether the theory can be successfully extended to other examples and types of "doubling" prohibitions, of the kind investigated in Emonds 1970, 1976. For example, in Grimshaw 1979b I examined the structure preservation account of the IC on Stylistic Inversion (Bowers 1976, Emonds 1976), concluding that the existence of NP NP constructions is inconsistent with this solution. Thus, English poses the same problem for structure preservation that French does. But if the NP displacement in Stylistic Inversion could be analyzed as an operation on the lexical form of predicates that substitutes OBJ for SUBJ, the IC for Stylistic Inversion would be explained in the same way as the French case. If such a program can be successfully carried out, base generation and the theory of grammatical functions would provide an explanation for the phenomena previously subsumed under structure preservation.

To sum up, the grammatical transitivity hypothesis and the theory of grammatical functions explain the IC, in terms of general constraints on grammatical functions and lexical forms. The alternatives do not seem to offer any explanation. If this conclusion is correct, we have very strong evidence for the claim that some grammatical rules cannot be properly stated in terms of structural configurations or in terms of predicate argument structure, but rather must be stated in terms of the grammatical functions which provide a mapping between them.

Notes

I would like to thank Joan Bresnan and Alan Prince for many helpful suggestions and for their comments on the chapter at various stages of development. Thanks also go to Denis Bouchard, Dominique Sportiche, and Nathalie Van Bockstaele for their aid. An earlier version of this chapter was presented at the Sloan Workshop on Lexical Representation at Stanford University in June 1979. Partial support for this research was provided by the Sloan Foundation, in the form of a Postdoctoral Fellowship in the Center for Cognitive Science at MIT.

1. (8) is not intended as a serious proposal for the analysis of the French auxiliary. It has been convincingly argued (e.g., by Kayne 1975) that clitics and the verb they precede form a constituent, contrary to the prediction of (8). Emonds 1975, 1976 proposes a left-branching structure for V'. His rule is (i):

(i)

$$V' \rightarrow \left\{ \begin{matrix} V' \\ (\text{PRO}) \quad (\text{CL}) \quad \text{TENSE} \end{matrix} \right\} V$$

According to this rule, PRO and/or CL + V is a constituent. I will continue to assume (8) for simplicity.

2. Entries for *rendre* and *élire* will also contain "control equations" (see chapters 1 and 3 of this volume) which indicate that the OBJ of the verb is the SUBJ of its NCOMP or ACOMP: for example, ($\uparrow$OBJ) = ($\uparrow$ACOMP SUBJ) for *rendre*. The control relations are quite general, and the equations can be assigned by lexical redundancy rules.

3. Certain cases of *y* and *en* also seem to be intrinsic in the sense that they do not alternate with *à NP* or *de NP* arguments: *il y avoir* 'there be', *s'en aller* 'go away', *en vouloir à* 'hold a grudge against', *en avoir marre de* 'be fed up with', etc. See Kayne 1975:433–436, Emonds 1975:9–10, Ruwet 1972, Gross 1968.

4. The fact that *se* and the subject NP match in number and person in this theory must be the result of an agreement rule. It cannot be due to coreference between *se* and the subject, because *se* is not a pronoun. The agreement rule required is similar to the one for subject–verb agreement: for example, a 3rd person singular verb could be assigned the equations ($\uparrow$SUBJ NUM) = SG, ($\uparrow$SUBJ PERS) = 3.

5. The nonproductive cases of intrinsic *se* are thus simply listed in the lexicon and are not the output of any lexical rule. It might seem that this represents the loss of a significant generalization, since the lexical entries for these cases closely resemble the (derived) entries for inchoatives. But this does not, I think, constitute evidence for positing (nonoccurring) base forms and deriving the nonproductive intrinsic forms by rule (although this is a possibility). Similar configurations are found in morphological analysis (see, for example, Aronoff 1976). Rather, one can hypothesize that lexical entries are relatively stable if they conform closely to the result of a regular process, even if they are not strictly speaking derived by that process. Note in addition that the correspon-

dence in the case of intrinsic *se* is less than perfect. All inchoatives are intransitives, but some unpredictable *se* verbs are transitives. For example, Kayne 1975:392 cites *s'imaginer* 'imagine', as in *Jean s'imagine Paul,* and analyzes *se* here as an inherent dative.

6. Chomsky 1972:55–58 discusses this rule and argues that it is lexical, not transformational. He observes examples like (i) and (ii).

(i)
This is clearly a self-inflicted wound.

(ii)
Self-addressed envelopes are barred by law from the mails.

In (i) and (ii) there is no antecedent for *self-* in the sentence at all. These cases still obey the basic generalizations governing *self-*. The base verbs are triadic: someone inflicts something on someone, someone addresses something to someone. In the *self-* forms, the third argument is bound to the first, which is unspecified and not syntactically expressed in (i) and (ii).

7. As Chomsky 1972 points out, *Self-* Prefixation is subject to what Aronoff 1976 has called *semantic drift.* For example, *self-important* does not mean 'important to self', but rather 'pompous'. *Self-evident* does not mean 'evident from self or to self', but 'obvious'.

8. Though Ruwet 1972:21 cites (i), which is structurally parallel to (73) and yet is apparently ill-formed.

(i)
*Il a été contente beaucoup de monde.
'Many people were happy.'

9. Martin's characterization seems to be too strict for many speakers; see (68), for example. The exact nature of the semantic condition on NP Extraposition remains somewhat mysterious.

10. Interestingly, Martin cites the following example, given by Damourette and Pichon (1911–1940):

(i)
Mme A – Il vient tes élèves, tantôt?
M P   – Il les vient.

In the first sentence a definite NP occurs in the extraposed position, and in the second the corresponding accusative personal pronoun appears cliticized to the verb and functions as its subject. Martin comments that this example seems to be completely atypical. Nevertheless, one can speculate that, were the condition on definiteness to be relaxed, as it is here, the subject NP could in fact occur as an accusative clitic on the verb, as the analysis predicts. Partitive *en* can occur in just this context, as shown by (ii) and (iii) (from Kayne 1975:382, 1979:712, respectively):

(ii)
Il en existe trois.
'Three of them exist.'

(iii)

Il en est arrivé trois.

'Three of them arrived.'

11. Kayne 1975 argues that in the surface structure of a causative complement, the subject NP is still directly dominated by S, and that the surface structure is the output of a rule of V' Raising, which fronts V and a direct object NP if there is one. The evidence for this derived structure is that the "postposed" subject NP still behaves like a subject with respect to the Specified Subject Condition (Chomsky 1973).

12. VP reordering of the kind discussed in the last subsection is also found in causative complements. Kayne 1975:210, footnote 9 cites (i), where the A OBJ precedes the OBJ.

(i)

Elle fera boire à Jean le vin qui se trouvait sur la table.

'She will make John drink the wine which was on the table.'

The same reordering occurs in (ii) (as Kayne observes), where the PP precedes the NP despite the fact that the *Faire*-Infinitive rule (Causative Complement Rule in our terms) has not applied.

(ii)

Elle offrira à Jean le vin qui se trouvait sur la table.

'She will offer to John the wine which was on the table.'

This is evidently the preferred order when the NP is heavy.

13. This is not strictly accurate. The PP can instead be introduced by the preposition *par*. Kayne 1975 gives a number of reasons for distinguishing *faire par* from *faire à*. My discussion here will ignore *faire par*.

14. There is no need to stipulate in (88) that only intransitives undergo case (i); this is entirely predictable, as shown below. However, the fact that (ii) cannot apply to intransitives cannot be explained in the same way. In effect, (88) is to be interpreted as "apply (i) if possible, otherwise apply (ii)." It is very likely that many of the properties of rules like NP Extraposition and the CCR need not be stipulated (i.e., learned) but might follow from the kind of principles proposed in relational grammar (see Perlmutter in press and references therein, also Cole and Sadock 1977). For example, suppose that grammatical functions are arranged in a kind of relational hierarchy: SUBJ – OBJ – P OBJ. Suppose further that "demotions" involve functions that are as closely connected on the hierarchy as possible. Then it would follow that CCR(ii) does not apply to intransitives, since the demotion in CCR(i) is possible, and it involves the functions SUBJ and OBJ which are more closely connected than SUBJ and A OBJ.

Assuming this, what would have to be learned about NP Extraposition and the CCR? The theory predicts that NP Extraposition and CCR(i) cannot apply to transitives and that CCR(ii) cannot apply to intransitives. Thus, the child has to learn that NP Extraposition has no case (ii); it does not allow the SUBJ to be replaced by an A OBJ. The scope of the negation is misleading here. More accurately, the child must *not* learn that NP Extraposition *does* have a case (ii);

the child does not hypothesize a case (ii) in the absence of evidence for it. The child must learn that the CCR does have a case (ii) and that the P OBJ concerned is an A OBJ. This can be learned from positive evidence. Thus, in the context of a more fully articulated theory of lexical rules, (59) and (88) will be very significantly simplified.

15. The grammatical function A OBJ is equally subject to functional uniqueness. Therefore, we expect that while *J'ai fait se donner des bonbons aux enfants* will be well-formed (see footnote 16), where the third argument of *donner* has not been reflexivized, CCR(ii) should not be able to apply:

(i)
'DONNER((SUBJ),(OBJ),(A OBJ))'

(ii)
'DONNER((A OBJ),(OBJ),(A OBJ))'

But the *faire* construction with two PPs introduced by *à* is not impossible, as these sentences from Kayne 1975:334 demonstrate:

(iii)
a.   ?Paul fera porter à son fils ces livres à ta femme.
        'Paul will make his son take these books to your wife.'
b.   Paul lui fera porter ces livres à ta femme.
        'Paul will make him take these books to your wife.'

Examples like these are presently rather problematic for my analysis. The crucial question is whether *à son fils* and *à ta femme* in (iiia) and *lui* and *à ta femme* in (iiib) both have the grammatical function A OBJ and are both arguments of the same verb. I have not yet investigated this matter in enough detail to draw any firm conclusions.

16. Of course, Reflexivization can also apply to an indirect object. *Donner* 'give' (*Je donnerai des bonbons aux enfants* 'I will give some candy to the children') has the lexical form in (i):

(i)
donner: V, ($\uparrow$PRED) = 'DONNER((SUBJ),(OBJ),(A OBJ))'

Reflexivization of the third argument gives (ii):

(ii)
($\uparrow$PRED) = 'DONNER$_{refl}$((SUBJ),(OBJ),ϕ)'
($\uparrow$REFL) =$_c$ +

(ii) is grammatically transitive and will undergo CCR(ii):

(iii)
'DONNER$_{refl}$((A OBJ),(OBJ),ϕ)'
($\uparrow$REFL) =$_c$ +

This is the source of sentences like (iv).

(iv)
J'ai fait se donner des bonbons aux enfants.
'I made the children give some candy to themselves/each other.'

17. Italian, Spanish, and Portuguese also use the morpheme corresponding to French *se* as an impersonal subject (Napoli 1973, Rizzi 1976, 1978, Pimenta-Bueno 1976, Pranka 1979). Unlike the reflexive clitics, this impersonal subject clitic does function as a pronominal grammatical argument; it participates in subject raising, for example.

18. Kayne 1975 discusses several similarities between the middle and passive constructions: for example, neither is possible in causative complements, and both require agreement between the subject NP and a past participle.

19. The exact interpretation of the bound argument seems to depend on semantic and/or pragmatic factors which I have not investigated in any depth. For example, (i) does not mean that there is someone who sells the houses easily, but that anyone trying to sell them would find it easy to do so.

(i)
Ces maisons se vendent bien.
'These houses *se* sell well.'

The same variation in interpretation is found in English passives: *These houses are easily sold* versus *Many books are sold*.

20. I am indebted to Yves-Charles Morin for informing me that the Middle Rule is not restricted to third person objs. The example in (i), which has a middle interpretation, is due to him:

(i)
Si tu étais une chemise, tu ne te vendrais pas pour trop cher.
'If you were a shirt, you wouldn't sell for too much.'

21. Kayne's and Rouveret and Vergnaud's proposals address a wider range of properties of the *faire* construction than I have considered here. In particular, both proposals offer solutions to the problem of why nonreflexive clitics must appear cliticized to *faire* and not to the embedded verb (cf. (96)), while reflexive clitics can occur on the embedded verb. In evaluating my criticism of their suggestions, the reader should bear in mind that its import cannot be fully assessed except in the context of a lexical analysis of the *faire* construction which covers the same range of phenomena as the Kayne and Rouveret–Vergnaud proposals. This said, I think the success of the lexical hypothesis within the smaller domain is indicative of great explanatory potential, which is not to be taken lightly.

22. Or, alternatively, if it subcategorized NP. The two definitions are equivalent for my argument, which hinges on predicate nominals. Predicate nominals are subcategorized: *turn foolish/*a fool, grow pretty/*a pretty woman,* versus *become foolish/a fool/pretty/a pretty woman.*

23. In terms of a model theoretic semantics, arguments would be of the relevant type if their semantic type was that of property sets of individuals. (My thanks to Kris Halvorsen.)

24. There is plenty of evidence that predicate nominals are not objs. They never passivize; that is, rules which apply to objs do not apply to them. They cooccur with objs, for example in (4) above and in the comparable English

examples. This would be impossible if they were OBJs, because of the requirement of functional uniqueness.

25. NP Extraposition does not apply to verbs with predicate nominal or predicate adjective complements:

(i)
*Il est devenu trois filles médecins.
'Three girls became doctors.'

(ii)
*Il est devenu trois filles complètement folles.
'Three girls became completely mad.'

((ii) is from Kayne 1975:332.) This property of NP Extraposition does not follow from my analysis; see Postal 1979 for a proposal concerning the ungrammaticality of (i).

26. This hypothesis has a decidedly checkered history. Kayne 1975:331–332, 379–382 raises the possibility that structure preservation is the explanation for the IC with respect to causative complements and NP Extraposition, rejecting the possibility for causative complements and leaving the question open for NP Extraposition. Ruwet 1972 and Pollock 1978 both propose that structure preservation is the explanation for the IC on NP Extraposition. Of course, if the transformations are not structure-preserving, then structure preservation cannot explain why they are governed by the IC.

27. The structure-preservation account of the IC would be consistent with the fact that passives and unspecified object deletion verbs allow NP Extraposition and CCR(i). See the beginning of this section.

28. There is of course a second significant difference between the two proposals. The structure-preservation account of the IC incorporates a structural definition of transitivity. It therefore predicts that predicate nominals and direct objects will behave uniformly, since both fill an NP node, making it unavailable for other material. This prediction is incorrect. See the beginning of this section for more discussion.

29. A similar result could probably be obtained in government/binding theory (Chomsky 1980 and lectures, Fall 1979) if the conditions governing NP Extraposition and the CCR were stated in terms of syntactic case, which in many ways corresponds closely to the notion of grammatical function. If each verb assigns a given case only once, then no verb can have two accusative arguments (cf. functional uniqueness). Reflexivization could be analyzed as a lexical rule which changes the subcategorization frame of a verb and hence its case-assigning properties. The basic idea would be that NP Extraposition and CCR(i) would not apply in the presence of a [+accusative] NP, because the former subject could not receive the appropriate accusative case. In fact, Rouveret and Vergnaud 1980 make use of the idea that these rules are sensitive to case marking. Their rule of *À* Insertion for causative complements applies to V NP NP sequences where the first NP is [+accusative] (p. 131). Predicate nominals are not marked accusative, so (136) and not (137) will be generated.

The crucial property that abstract case and grammatical functions have in common is of course that they cannot be reduced to structure: in the structural configuration V NP, NP may either be [+accusative] (i.e., an OBJ) or it may have a different case marking (whatever is assigned to predicate nominals). In both theories, the choice is determined by lexical properties of the verb.

Chapter 3

Polyadicity   Joan Bresnan

The theory of lexical representations to be presented here originated in Bresnan 1978 and has been further developed in the works that appear in this volume and in Wasow 1978, 1980. According to this theory, the predicate argument structures of lexical items are represented independently of their syntactic contextual features as functions of a fixed number of grammatically interpretable arguments. A mapping between predicate argument structure and syntactic constituent structure is specified by means of grammatical functions. These are assigned to surface phrase structure positions by syntactic rules and to predicate argument structure positions by lexical rules. A lexical predicate argument structure with grammatical functions specified is called a *lexical form*. How these terms apply to a simple English sentence is illustrated in figure 3.1.

In figure 3.1, the information above the dotted line is provided by the syntactic component of a generative grammar for English, and the information below the dotted line is provided by the lexical component. Thus, the lexical form for the verb *hand* has a triadic predicate argument structure whose three arguments are identified numerically. Arguments 1, 2, and 3 of this predicate argument structure have been assigned the respective grammatical functions (SUBJ) [subject], (OBJ) [object], and (TO OBJ) [*to*-object] by lexical rules. The syntactic component generates the surface phrase structure tree for *Fred handed a toy to the baby* and identifies the NPs dominating *Fred, a toy,* and *the baby* as (SUBJ), (OBJ), and (TO OBJ), respectively. The association between *handed* and its lexical form is effected by lexical insertion. (The role of inflection in the theory of grammar will be ignored here, but see Lieber 1980 and chapters 1 and 5 of this volume.)

In figure 3.2, the verb *hand* has a different lexical form, produced by assigning a different set of grammatical functions to the same predicate

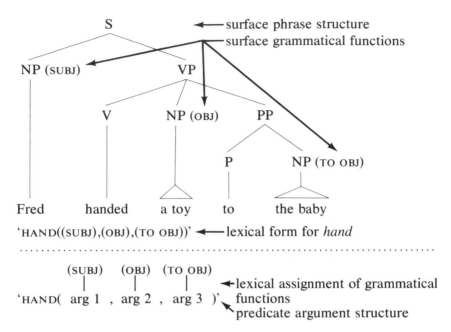

Figure 3.1

argument structure as before. As shown in figure 3.2, (OBJ) is now assigned to argument 3 and (OBJ2) [second object] is assigned to argument 2. The order of grammatical function symbols in a lexical form does not correspond to the left-to-right order of constituents in phrase structure, but rather to the numerical order of "logical" or thematic arguments in the predicate argument structure.

When the structural grammatical functions are matched with the lexical grammatical functions in figures 3.1 and 3.2, it is evident that *Fred, a toy,* and *the baby* correspond to the same "logical" arguments in the predicate argument structure of *hand.* Both syntactic structures can be base-generated, and the seeming transformational relationship between them can be expressed instead as a relationship between the lexical forms for *hand.*

My intent in this chapter is to explain and justify the basic elements of the lexical theory: the independence of predicate argument structure from representations of syntactic context, the polyadicity of predicates, universal conditions on the assignment of grammatical functions to predicate argument structures, and the treatment of "variable polyadicity" in the theory. In chapter 1 of this volume I have argued that

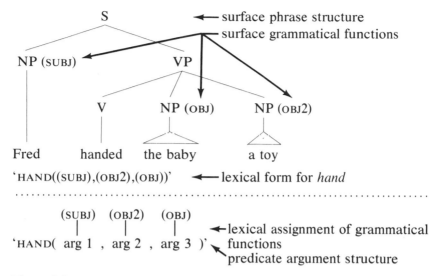

Figure 3.2

the rule of Passivization must be expressed by operations on lexical forms rather than operations on syntactic phrase structure representations. For the formal system of grammatical representation and a detailed analysis of English complementation within it, see chapters 4 and 5.

3.1 Predicate Argument Structure

A predicate argument structure is an abstract characterization of those arguments of a semantic predicate that are open to grammatical interpretation. According to the theory of lexical forms, the predicate argument structures of lexical items are represented independently of their syntactic contextual features as functions of a fixed number of grammatically interpretable arguments. The independence of predicate argument structure from syntactic constituent structure representations has been established very clearly in work by Grimshaw 1979, which I will briefly review here.

It is well known that verbs select their complement types, whether declarative (*that*-complements) or interrogative (*wh*-complements):

(1)
a.   Mary agreed *that Susan is living with strange people.*
b.   #Mary agreed *what kind of people Susan is living with.*

(2)

a.   #Mary inquired *that Susan is living with strange people*.

b.   Mary inquired *what kind of people Susan is living with*.

(3)

a.   Mary discovered *that Susan is living with strange people*.

b.   Mary discovered *what kind of people Susan is living with*.

(The symbol # marks an example as semantically anomalous.) The verb *agree* selects *that*-complements, *inquire* selects *wh*-complements, and *discover* selects both. Both complement types are syntactic Ss in English (Bresnan and Grimshaw 1978:332–334). But a proper subclass of verbs that select interrogative Ss is also found to occur with relative clause constructions that have the meaning of an interrogative complement. For example, the relative clause in (4) means the same as the *wh*-complement in (3b):

(4)

Mary discovered *the kind of people that Susan is living with*.

Example (4) can also be interpreted as containing an ordinary relative clause, the meaning of which is brought out in (5).

(5)

Mary is a great explorer. She discovered the Nether Islanders, who are the kind of people that Susan is living with.

Under either interpretation, however, the relative clause construction is syntactically an NP. Relative clauses having the meaning of indirect questions are termed *concealed questions* by Baker 1968. To explain the observation that concealed questions occur only with verbs that take interrogative complements, Baker suggests that concealed questions might be transforms of Ss.

   Grimshaw 1979 argues against such a transformational derivation of concealed questions by pointing out that verbs allow concealed questions if and only if they both select *wh*-complements and are also subcategorized for object NPs. For example, *discover* both selects *wh*-complements (example (3b)) and is also subcategorized for object NPs (example (5), second sentence); hence, it takes concealed questions (example (4)). In contrast, *inquire* selects *wh*-complements (example (2b)) but is not subcategorized for object NPs:

(6)

$$\text{*Mary inquired} \begin{Bmatrix} \text{the kind of people} \\ \text{the Nether Islanders} \end{Bmatrix}.$$

Hence, *inquire* fails to allow concealed questions:

(7)
*Mary inquired *the kind of people that Susan is living with.*

On the transformational account of concealed questions, this correlation is an accident.

To account for concealed questions, Grimshaw proposes, in effect, that predicate argument structure is an autonomous level of representation which cannot be put in one-to-one correspondence with representations of syntactic context. The verbs *discover* and *inquire* both have dyadic predicate argument structures in which there are arguments corresponding to an agent, x, and an interrogative, Q, as illustrated in (8a,b). (The variables x, Q, etc., in these and following examples are just glosses on the predicate argument structures and have no notational significance.)

(8)
a.   'DISCOVER(1,2)'
             $x \ Q$
b.   'INQUIRE(1,2)'
             $x \ Q$

But since *discover* takes NP-objects (OBJ) as well as S-complements (SCOMP), while *inquire* takes only S-complements, the verbs permit different grammatical functions to be associated with the semantic Q argument:

(9)
a. $\text{'DISCOVER((SUBJ)}, \begin{Bmatrix} \text{(SCOMP)} \\ \text{(OBJ)} \end{Bmatrix})\text{'}$
             $x \qquad\quad Q$
b.   'INQUIRE((SUBJ),(SCOMP))'
             $x \qquad Q$

Thus, a concealed question is merely a syntactic direct object interpreted as a semantic Q argument. A consequence of this analysis is that objects other than relative clauses can be concealed questions, as in (10):

(10)
a.   I never discovered *his name*.   [= what his name was]
b.   Can you tell me *the time?*   [= what the time is]

If predicate argument structure is represented independently of syntactic context, we should also expect that the same grammatical functions could be associated with different semantic arguments, which is of course the case. In (11), the sentential complement function (SCOMP) is associated with an interrogative (Q) argument and with a propositional (P) argument.

(11)
a.   'INQUIRE((SUBJ),(SCOMP))'
                    x   Q
b.   'AGREE((SUBJ),(SCOMP))'
                x   P

Further evidence of the independence of predicate argument structure from syntactic context can be obtained from the phenomenon of complement ellipsis, or *null complement anaphora,* also analyzed by Grimshaw 1979. Examples are given in (12) and (13).

(12)
A: Louise has a great soul.
B: I agree.

(13)
A: Do you know who's going to the party?
B: No, but I'll inquire.

In isolation or in initiating discourse, (12B) and (13B) would be semantically incomplete, but in the context of (12A) and (13A), they are completely interpretable. The verbs *agree* and *inquire* can be analyzed as having a semantically open argument in their predicate argument structures which corresponds to an optional grammatical function assignment. The open argument must be semantically interpreted; when the syntactic complement is missing, the argument must be interpreted from context. The optionality of the SCOMP is represented by parentheses in (14).

(14)
a. 'INQUIRE((SUBJ),((SCOMP)))'
             x   Q
b. 'AGREE((SUBJ),((SCOMP)))'
             x   P

As one would expect from the lexical representation of complement ellipsis given in (14), the phenomenon is lexically governed. Contrast (15) and (16) with (12) and (13).

(15)
A: Louise has a great soul.
B: *I admit.   [*Compare:* I admit that she has.]

(16)
A: Do you know who's going to the party?
B: *No, I couldn't discover.   [*Compare:* No, I couldn't discover who is.]

In contrast with *agree* and *inquire,* the verbs *admit* and *discover* do not allow optional omission of their sentential complements.

Thus, Grimshaw's hypothesis is that complement ellipsis can arise only when an open semantic argument in predicate argument structure corresponds to an omissible grammatical argument. The omissibility of grammatical arguments clearly presupposes an independent representation of predicate argument structure. As illustrated in (17), when an optional SCOMP is omitted, only the semantic argument remains.

(17)
'INQUIRE((SUBJ),2)'
             x   Q

In (17) there is no grammatical function in terms of which the open Q argument can be represented. A consequence of this representation is that verbs permitting complement ellipsis can impose semantic selection on the context of ellipsis, but not syntactic selection. Semantic selection of the context of ellipsis by the verb is illustrated by the contrasts shown in (18) and (19). (See Grimshaw 1979 for discussion of other factors affecting the context of ellipsis.)

(18)
A: Do you know who's coming to the party?
B: I'll inquire.   [*Compare:* I'll inquire who's coming to the party.]
     #I agree.   [*Compare:* #I agree who's coming to the party.]

(19)

A: Louise has a great soul.

B: I agree. [*Compare:* I agree that Louise has a great soul.]
        #I'll inquire. [*Compare:* #I'll inquire that Louise has a great
        soul.]

The absence of syntactic selection of the context of ellipsis by the verb
is illustrated by the lack of a contrast between (20) and (21).

(20)
Although he wanted to know what time it was, he was afraid to inquire.

(21)
Although he wanted to know the time, he was afraid to inquire.

Both (20) and (21) are grammatical, despite the fact that *inquire* cannot
have a grammatical argument of the kind that appears in the ellipsis
context (21); compare (22).

(22)
*Although he wanted to know *the time,* he was afraid to inquire *the
time*.

The difference between (21) and (22) follows from the autonomous
representation of predicate argument structure in the theory of lexical
forms. By contrast, in a theory in which predicate argument structure is
encoded in syntactic structure (for example, by annotating phrase
structure nodes with semantic or thematic role information), these facts
would be unexplained. The evidence from concealed questions and
complement ellipsis strongly supports the independence of predicate argument structure from representations of syntactic constituent
structure.

3.2 Polyadicity of Predicates

The *polyadicity* of a predicate is the number and kind of arguments it
has. In the theory of lexical forms, the predicate argument structures of
lexical items are represented as functions of a fixed number of grammatically interpretable arguments; that is, each predicate argument
structure has n arguments to which grammatical functions can be assigned. Semantic arguments which are not grammatically interpretable—purely "internal" semantic arguments—are not expressed at
this level of representation.

An example of a semantic argument which is not expressed in predicate argument structure is the "inherent object" in the verb *to homer,* which means 'to hit a home run'. On the basis of the meaning of this verb, one might postulate a dyadic predicate argument structure such as (23), where the second argument is filled by a semantic constant.

(23)
'HIT(1,HOME RUN)'

Nevertheless, as (24)–(25) illustrate, the verb *homer* never takes a grammatical argument that corresponds to this semantic argument; *homer* is always grammatically intransitive.

(24)
Fred homered in the ninth.

(25)
Fred has homered *a home run/*his last home run.

Thus, because the internal semantic argument HOME RUN is not assigned a *grammatical* function, it is not represented directly in the predicate argument structure of *homer,* which is given in (26).

(26)
'HOMER(1)'

The predicate argument structure does not express the internal semantic structure of a given predicate, but instead represents just those arguments of the predicate to which grammatical functions can be assigned. Those aspects of the meaning of *homer* which (23) was intended to express can be captured instead by a specification of the internal semantic structure of the predicate as informally expressed in (27a) or by a meaning postulate such as (27b) (Carnap 1952).

(27)
a.   'HOMER(1)' ≡ '1 hit a home run'
b. $(\forall x)((\text{homer}(x)) \Rightarrow (\text{hit-a-home-run}(x)))$

Internal semantic arguments are sometimes grammatically expressed. For example, the verb *crane* can be defined as 'to stretch one's neck for a better view'. The predicate argument structure of *crane* can be given as (28a), with the meaning restrictions specified in (28b) or (28c).

(28)

a.   'crane(1,2)'
b.   'crane(1,2)' $\equiv$ '1 stretch 2 for a better view, where 2 is 1's neck'
c. $(\forall x)(\forall y)((\text{crane}(x,y)) \Rightarrow (\text{stretch}(x,y)\&(y=x\text{'s neck})))$

The internal semantic argument '1's neck' is grammatically expressed as the direct object of the verb *crane*. As indicated in the lexical form (29), the object is assigned to the second argument position of *crane;* hence, it will be interpreted as 'x's neck', where x is the agent.

(29)

'CRANE((SUBJ),(OBJ))'

The semantic interpretation of the grammatical object is in fact restricted by the semantic specification of the second argument given in (28):

(30)

a.   John craned his neck.
b.   *John craned my neck.
c.   *John craned his umbrella.

Note that a possessive pronoun referring to the subject is not needed in the direct object: the direct object need only satisfy the predicate argument specifications in (28), which require that it be interpreted as (inalienably) possessed by the agent. Thus, sentence (31) is appropriately interpretable because the Hydra is a many-headed (and hence many-necked) creature:

(31)

The Hydra yawned and craned a neck.

Nor is the noun *neck* required, so long as the direct object of *crane* is appropriately interpretable. Compare (30) with (32):

(32)

a.   John injured *his neck* when he craned *it* (as Mary entered the room).
b.   *John injured *my neck* when he craned *it* (as Mary entered the room).
c.   *John broke *his umbrella* when he craned *it* (as Mary entered the room).

The fact that the grammatical form of the direct object may vary while the semantic interpretation remains fixed follows from the representations given in (28) and (29). Evidence that *neck* is indeed the direct object of *crane* can be found in the derived nominal construction, where objects are marked by the preposition *of*. Just as *sing songs* is nominalized as *the singing of songs,* so *crane necks* is nominalized as shown in (33).

(33)
Her entrance into the room was registered with *much craning of necks*.

The direct object of *crane* can also be passivized as in (34) and (35).

(34)
Not a neck was craned when I entered the room.

(35)
Anyone's neck can be injured $\begin{Bmatrix} \text{if } \textit{it is craned} \text{ too far} \\ \text{by } \textit{being craned} \text{ too far} \end{Bmatrix}$.

It can be concluded that the verb *crane* has an internal semantic argument '*x*'s neck' that is grammatically expressed as a direct object.

The representation proposed for verbs like *crane* has interesting implications. If the possessor ('*x*'s') is grammatically expressed, it must be interpretable as a bound variable, as in (28). In English only possessive pronouns can be so interpreted in this context, and then only if they are bound to the subject of their clause nucleus (a *clause nucleus* being a functional structure that contains both a subject and a predicate; see chapter 5 of this volume). Accordingly, we find (36)–(38).

(36)
a. *Someone craned *John*'s neck.
b. **John*'s neck was craned by someone.

(37)
a. *Someone craned *my* neck.
b. **My* neck was craned by someone.

(38)
a. *I* craned *my* neck.
b. **My* neck was craned by me.

(36a) and (36b) are ruled out because *John*'s cannot be interpreted as a bound variable, not being a possessive pronoun. (37a) and (37b) contain the possessive pronoun *my*, but in neither case is it bound to the subject of its clause nucleus; in (37b) in particular, it is part of the subject of its

clause nucleus. (38a) satisfies the conditions for grammatically expressing the possessor, but (38b) fails for the same reason as (37b).[1]

A further implication of the above analysis can be given. Consider
example (39).

(39)
John had his house painted.

(39) is three ways ambiguous. There is a *causative* sense ('John got
someone to paint his house'), a *completive* sense ('John completed
painting his house'), and a *happenstance* sense, in which the house's
being painted happens to affect John in some way—either adversely
('John had his house painted on him') or positively ('We all took paint
brushes over so John could have his house painted before he returned'). In the causative and happenstance senses, someone other
than John is the agent of *paint;* in the completive sense, John must be
the agent. All the senses of the *have* construction can occur with true
passive participles. In all of (40a,b,c), for example, *painted* is a passive
participle:

(40)
a. John had his house painted white (on him).   [happenstance]
b. John had his house painted white (by hiring a painter).   [causa-
    tive]
c. (By working every night,) John had his house painted white (in a
    week).   [completive]

Here *painted* must be the verbal passive participle because the deverbal adjective *painted* (which occurs in *the painted house* and in the
derived adjective *unpainted*) cannot take a predicate complement
white: compare **unpainted white* (Bresnan 1978:7). Now, unlike (39),
(41) lacks the happenstance and causative senses:

(41)
John had his neck craned.

Example (41) can have the completive sense brought out in (42):

(42)
When Mary entered the room, John had his neck craned in an instant.[2]

This fact follows immediately from the analysis of *crane* and the interpretation of bound possessive anaphors. Because of the predicate
argument structure given for *crane*, *his neck* in (41) must be interpreted

as 'x's neck', where x is the agent of *crane*. As a bound anaphor, *his* can be bound only to the subject of its clause nucleus. In example (41), *his* belongs to the clause nucleus of *have*, whose subject is *John* (because *his neck* is the direct object of *have*); hence, *his* will be bound to *John*. But *John* is the agent of *crane* under the completive interpretation of the *have* construction ('John completed craning his neck'). Thus, on the completive interpretation, the inalienable possessor of the neck is necessarily the agent of *crane*, and the predicate argument structure (28) is satisfied. In contrast, a causative interpretation of (41) is impossible: as before, *his* will be bound to *John*, but *John* is not the agent of *crane* under the causative interpretation (*'*John* got someone to crane *his* [John's] neck'). For the same reasons, the happenstance interpretation is ruled out as well (*'John had his neck craned on him').

In sum, an argument i is represented in predicate argument structure only if there is a grammatical function assignment that associates i with some grammatical argument (such as SUBJ or OBJ). By this condition, the inherent semantic object of a verb like *homer* is not represented as an argument in predicate argument structure, while the inherent semantic object of *crane* is so represented. Thus, the polyadicity of a predicate *as it is represented in predicate argument structure* depends upon the grammatical properties of the predicate and not solely upon its logical or semantic properties.

3.3 Universal Conditions on Grammatical Function Assignments

A *lexical form* is a predicate argument structure together with an assignment of grammatical functions. An assignment of grammatical functions to a predicate argument structure $P(1,...,m)$ can be represented as a list of *grammatical function expressions* $\langle g_1,...,g_n \rangle$ such that for every predicate argument i, there is a corresponding g_i. A grammatical function expression is (a) a grammatical function name (such as SUBJ, OBJ, or TO OBJ) surrounded by one or two sets of parentheses,[3] (b) the null grammatical function symbol ϕ, whose meaning is explained in the next section, or (c) an equation specifying the value of a grammatical function name. (Examples of (c) are given in chapter 1 of this volume.)

Examples of (a) and (b) are given in (43)–(45).

(43)

a. ⟨(SUBJ),((SCOMP))⟩   [grammatical function assignment]
b. 'INQUIRE(1,2)'   [predicate argument structure]
c. *Mary* inquired *who was*   [example sentence]
    coming.

(44)

a. ⟨(SUBJ),ϕ,(TO OBJ)⟩   [grammatical function assignment]
b. 'WRITE(1,2,3)'   [predicate argument structure]
c. *John* wrote *to Mary*.   [example sentence]

(45)

a. ⟨(SUBJ),(VCOMP),(OBJ)⟩   [grammatical function assignment]
b. 'BELIEVE(1,2)'   [predicate argument structure]
c. *Fred* believes *hot dogs to*   [example sentence]
    taste bad.

As these examples show, the number of predicate arguments m may be less than the number n of grammatical functions assigned to a predicate argument structure: this happens in (45), where *believe* is assigned a grammatical object that is not a "logical object" in that it does not correspond to a predicate argument. (Such grammatical functions correspond to so-called "raised" objects or subjects; see chapters 4 and 5.) On the other hand, for every predicate argument in these examples, there is some grammatical function expression assigned to it, if only a ϕ or an omissible grammatical function such as ((SCOMP)). For this reason lexical forms can be represented with a grammatical function expression occupying each predicate argument position (allowing $n-m$ grammatical function expressions to occur outside predicate argument structure).

The theory of lexical forms specifies universal conditions on the assignment of grammatical functions to predicate argument structures. For example, there are *unmarked assignments* of grammatical functions to predicates: the unmarked assignment to a monadic predicate argument structure is ⟨(SUBJ)⟩; to a dyadic predicate argument structure, it is ⟨(SUBJ),(OBJ)⟩. Given these unmarked assignments of grammatical functions to predicate argument structures as universals, it is unnecessary to stipulate for individual lexical items those grammatical function assignments that conform to the universal pattern. Similarly, there are *unmarked relations* between grammatical functions; for example, the theory of control specifies that the subject of a verbal complement to a matrix verb V is V's object if there is one, and V's subject otherwise (see chapter 5). Thus, in example (45c) it is predictable that the grammatical object of *believe* (namely, *hot dogs*) functions as the subject of *believe*'s verbal complement (*to taste bad*); and so the equation (↑OBJ) = (↑VCOMP SUBJ) is implicit in the lexical entry.

Conditions on grammatical function assignments and relations provide a universal characterization of the grammatical functions which are primitives in this theory. An important formal condition on possible grammatical function assignments is stated in (46).

(46)
Biuniqueness of Function–Argument Assignments
$G = g_1,...,g_n$ is a possible grammatical function assignment to $P(1,...,m)$ if and only if the mapping from $1,...,m$ to G defined by $i \mapsto g_i$ is injective (one-to-one and into).

(46) implies that the same grammatical function cannot be assigned to different predicate arguments and that different grammatical functions cannot be assigned to the same predicate argument. (46) does not rule out alternative grammatical function assignments to the same predicate argument structure (as in example (9a) above), but it does exclude the assignments illustrated in (47).

(47)
a.

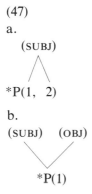

b.
(SUBJ)   (OBJ)

*P(1)

The biuniqueness condition strongly restricts the set of possible operations on lexical forms. For example, it would eliminate as a possible lexical rule the replacement of (OBJ) by (SUBJ) in all lexical forms (for that operation would produce impermissible assignments like (47a)). It follows in particular that rules of transitive passivization (which operate on transitive lexical forms to convert objects to subjects) must employ some means of eliminating the underlying subject; this consequence appears in fact to be a universal property of passive rules (cf.

Perlmutter and Postal 1977). More generally, the biuniqueness condition explains fundamental properties of grammars that have been attributed to the structure-preserving hypothesis; see chapter 2 of this volume for elucidation.

Because every predicate argument must be assigned a *unique* grammatical function, the biuniqueness condition rules out examples like (48), where the two BY OBJs are interpreted as the agent in the predicate argument structure of *admire*.[4]

(48)
*She was admired *by him by the President*.

Similarly, the biuniqueness condition rules out examples like (49), where the two objects OBJ and OBJ2 are interpreted as the patient in the predicate argument structure of *eat*.

(49)
*She ate *supper* quickly *every pizza*.

If grammatical functions are uniquely assigned to predicate arguments, we have a grammatical means of determining the polyadicity of predicate argument structures. This can be seen by first contrasting (48) with (50).

(50)
She was sitting *by him by the President*.

In (50) there are two *by*-phrases; by the biuniqueness condition they cannot be grammatical arguments of *sitting*. Unlike the *by*-phrases associated with the passive (as in (48)), these are both locative adjuncts. In contrast to the grammatical functions which are assigned to predicate arguments, multiple locative, temporal, and manner adjuncts can occur in a single clause:

(51)
Fred *deftly* [Manner] handed a toy to the baby *by reaching behind his back* [Manner] *over lunch* [Temp] *at noon* [Temp] *in a restaurant* [Loc] *last Sunday* [Temp] *in Back Bay* [Loc] *without interrupting the discussion* [Manner].

Such multiple temporal, locative, and manner phrases cannot be interpreted as grammatical arguments of the verb *hand* without violating either the biuniqueness condition on functional assignments or the finiteness of predicate argument structures. They are semantically interpreted as phrasal or clausal operators rather than as predicate arguments (see Halvorsen forthcoming).

In contrast, the biuniqueness condition admits many types of prepositional phrases as possible grammatical arguments of the verb. An example is the instrumental phrase in (52).

(52)

John escaped from prison *with dynamite*.   [= John used dynamite to escape from prison]

No more than one instrumental phrase can occur with a single verb:

(53)

*John escaped from prison *with dynamite with a machine gun*. [= John used dynamite and used a machine gun to escape from prison]

Given the biuniqueness condition, this fact can be explained by analyzing the instrumental phrase as a grammatical argument of the main verb. It is possible to define a lexical rule of *Instrumentalization* (analogous to lexical rules of *Causativization*) which converts an n-adic predicate argument structure P to an $n+1$-adic predicate argument structure *P-with* whose $n+1$st argument is assigned the grammatical function INSTR OBJ [instrumental object]. For motivation, note that Instrumentalization alters the inherent semantic properties of a predicate as illustrated in (54)–(55). See Bresnan in preparation a for a detailed explanation of this and other properties of Instrumentalization.

(54)

a.   John killed Harry.

b.   John killed Harry with dynamite.

(55)

a.   An explosion killed Harry.

b.   #An explosion killed Harry with dynamite.

In conclusion, conditions on the assignment of grammatical functions to predicate argument structures restrict the class of possible lexical forms and operations, universally characterize the grammatical functions, and provide a grammatical means of determining the polyadicity of predicate argument structures.

3.4 Variable Polyadicity and Scope

The *variable polyadicity* of English action verbs—the capacity of these verbs to occur with variable numbers of grammatical arguments—was noted by Kenny 1963:

(56)
a.   Fred reads Russian novels easily.
b.   Fred reads easily.
c.   Russian novels read easily.

The optional suppression of a grammatical argument in a lexical form is expressed by means of the null grammatical function symbol ϕ. For example, the lexical forms of *read* in (56a–c) can be expressed as (57a–c), respectively.

(57)
a.   'READ((SUBJ),(OBJ))'
b.   'READ((SUBJ),ϕ)'
c.   'READ(ϕ,(SUBJ))'

By means of ϕ, lexical rules of Intransitivization, Passivization, Impersonal Passivization (Comrie 1977), and Middle Formation (Grimshaw in chapter 2 of this volume) can be formulated straightforwardly. For example, the lexical rule of Intransitivization given in (58) operates on (57a) to produce (57b).

(58)
Intransitivization
(OBJ) $\mapsto \phi$

The assignment of the null function ϕ to an argument, as in (57b), indicates that the argument is semantically bound and that no grammatical function is assigned to it. As a result, *Fred reads easily* is semantically complete and nonelliptical and can be used to initiate discourse, in contrast to the cases of complement ellipsis discussed in section 3.1 above.

The *activo-passive*, or *middle*, use of *read* illustrated in (57c) can be derived by applying the lexical rule of Activo-Passivization shown in (59) to the lexical form given in (57a).[5]

(59)

Activo-Passivization (*Middle Formation*)

(SUBJ) $\mapsto \phi$

(OBJ) $\mapsto$ (SUBJ)

Where Intransitivization suppresses the grammatical object of *read,* Activo-Passivization suppresses the (underlying) grammatical subject and replaces the object with the subject. The effect of Activo-Passivization is to change the assignment of the SUBJ function from the agent to the patient argument of *read* and to eliminate the grammatical expression of the agent argument altogether. By altering the assignments of grammatical functions to predicate arguments in these ways, lexical rules produce the effects of variable polyadicity. While some lexical operations simply produce alternative assignments of grammatical functions to the same predicate argument structure, other lexical operations alter predicate argument structure by the addition or elimination of predicate arguments. Examples of the latter type are the Causativization and Instrumentalization rules referred to in the preceding section (Bresnan in preparation a) and lexical Reflexivization and Inchoativization (see chapter 2 of this volume).

The theory of lexical forms provides a *grammatical* means for determining the polyadicity of predicate argument structures and hence a principled answer to the question, How many predicate arguments does a predicate argument structure have? In contrast, when logical *entailment* is used as the means for determining the polyadicity of predicate argument structures, no principled solution appears possible (Kenny 1963). If John escaped from prison, then there is a time, a place, and a manner in which John escaped from prison. But, as we have already seen, temporal, locative, and manner adjuncts cannot be predicate arguments of ESCAPE-FROM without violating universal conditions on predicate argument structure. Thus, the entailments of a verb in simple sentences do not suffice for determining the number of arguments in its predicate argument structure. Nor are such entailments needed for the representation of arguments in predicate argument structure; we have already seen that instrumental objects may be the predicate arguments of instrumentalized verbs, but *John escaped from prison* does not entail that there was some *instrument* which John used to escape from prison *with* (he might simply have left one day, walking out the front door).

Entailments sometimes do give a correct indication of predicate argument structure. For example, if John reads easily, then there is something that John reads easily, while if John falls easily, there cannot be something that John "falls" easily. This difference in the entailments of *read* and *fall* corresponds to a difference in their predicate argument structures; while both verbs can be used intransitively, *read* has a dyadic predicate argument structure (cf. (57)), while *fall* has a monadic one. The independence of predicate argument structure from assignments of grammatical functions enables the theory of lexical forms to represent the difference naturally.[6]

(60)

a.   'READ((SUBJ),ϕ)'

b.   'FALL((SUBJ))'

If the variable polyadicity of natural language predicates is the effect of lexical rules, as proposed here, several results follow immediately. First, the rules that affect polyadicity will interact with other lexical rules. Second, the rules that affect polyadicity will fail to interact with nonlexical rules. These consequences follow from the hypothesis that the rule systems of natural language are organized into components of rules in such a way as to maximize the interactions of rules within components and to minimize the interactions of rules across components. Thus, rules for the grammatical and semantic interpretation of sentences will not be interspersed among rules of word formation (which are lexical rules), and vice versa; see Bresnan 1978:509 for further discussion. Consequently, structures which are analyzed by lexical rules must be lexical structures and cannot be syntactically derived.

By eliminating the OBJ function, both Intransitivization and Activo-Passivization create grammatically intransitive lexical forms. Certain lexical rules are known to be sensitive to the grammatical transitivity of the verbs they apply to. One such rule is *Out-* Prefixation, studied by Fraser 1974:29–30. When prefixed to grammatically intransitive verbs, *out-* serves to transitivize them. The meaning of A [$_\text{V}$ *out-V*]s B is approximately paraphrased as 'A surpasses B in V-ing' or 'A Vs to a greater extent than B'. Examples are given in (61).

(61)

a.   Mary *outlasted* John.

b.   The lamp *outshines* the candle.

c.   Few people *outgrin* the Cheshire cat.

While *last, shine,* and *grin* are intransitive verbs, *fell (trees), find,* and *like* arc transitive:

(62)

a.   *A big lumberjack can't always *outfell* a little one.

b.   *The Brownies *outfound* the Girl Scouts in the treasure hunt.

c.   *Extroverts *outlike* introverts.

But transitive verbs may be prefixed by *out-* if thcy are intransitivized. Thus, the intransitive *spend* (as in *Mary spends freely*), *guess* (as in *Mary guessed correctly*), and *throw* (as in *A centerfielder must throw well*) provide sources for the verbs in (63).

(63)

a.   Mary *outspent* John.

b.   The Brownies *outguessed* the Girl Scouts in the contest.

c.   Among ballplayers, the extroverts *outthrow* the introverts.

In particular, the intransitivized *read* can undergo *Out-* Prefixation:

(64)

At all ages, Russian children could outdraw, outspell, and *outread* their American counterparts.

Activo-passive verbs undergo *Out-* Prefixation as well:

(65)

a.   Rubber wears well.

b.   Rubber *outwears* leather when used for shoe soles. (Fraser 1974:29)

(66)

a.   Russian novels sell well.

b.   Russian novels *outsell* French novels across the country.

(67)

a.   Front-whccl-drive cars handle well.

b.   Front-wheel-drive cars *outhandle* all others in snow conditions.

Not all intransitive verbs allow *Out-* Prefixation, but only intransitives do.

   In summary, the rules of Intransitivization and Activo-Passivization produce forms that undergo the lexical rule of *Out-* Prefixation and so must themselves be lexical rules. Given the lexicalist theory of word formation (Chomsky 1970, Bresnan 1978), this fact is inconsistent with transformational analyses of these rules (e.g., Chomsky 1964:42, Lakoff 1970:127, Fiengo 1974:65). But the theory of lexical forms explains the fact that rules which alter the grammatical polyadicity of predicates may produce structures which are analyzed by (lexical) rules of word formation.

The theory of lexical forms has a second major consequence, mentioned above: the rules that affect polyadicity will not interact with nonlexical rules; in particular, sentence-interpretive rules will not be interspersed among operations on lexical forms. Now lexical forms define the possible contexts of lexical insertion, and lexical insertion is presupposed by rules for the semantic interpretation of sentences. Hence, these semantic rules may be ordered after but not before the rules that operate on lexical forms. In other words, the organization of the grammar imposes an intrinsic ordering on lexical rules and sentence-interpretive rules.

The intrinsic ordering of lexical rules before sentence-interpretive rules affects the order of interpretation of quantifiers: the lexical quantification of predicate arguments has narrow scope with respect to the syntactic quantification of sentences. This can be seen by comparing sentences like (68) and (69):

(68)
Everyone was reading something.

(69)
Everyone was reading.

Example (68) is ambiguous with respect to the scope of the quantifiers *everyone* and *something*. The sentence may mean either 'There was something such that everyone was reading it' or 'For every person, there was something such that that person was reading it'. But (69) is unambiguous: the lexically introduced quantification of *read*'s second argument can have only narrow scope with respect to the syntactically introduced quantifier *everyone*, and so the sentence has only the meaning 'For every person, there was something such that that person was reading it'. Thus, the relative scope of lexical and syntactic quantifiers reflects their order of interpretation.

In conclusion, the theory of lexical forms not only provides a solution to the problem of the variable polyadicity of natural language predicates, but also explains why rules that affect polyadicity interact with other lexical rules but not with the rules for interpreting syntactic quantifiers.[7]

Notes

I would like to thank Marilyn Ford, Jane Grimshaw, Per-Kristian Halvorsen, Ronald Kaplan, and Susan Rothstein for valuable suggestions. An earlier version of this chapter appeared in T. Hoekstra, H. van der Hulst, and M. Moortgat, eds., *Lexical Grammar*, Dordrecht: Foris Publications.

1. It should be noted that the requirement that the possessor of the neck (if grammatically expressed) be a bound anaphor holds for the verbal forms of *crane* but not the adjectival *craned*. This difference accounts for the contrast between (i) and (ii):

(i)

His neck was craned throughout the lecture.   [adjectival *craned*]

(ii)

*His neck was being craned throughout the lecture.   [verbal *craned*]

Unlike the adjectival *craned*, the verbal *crane* may occur in the progressive:

(iii)

John was craning his neck throughout the lecture.

Thus, *his* does not have to be bound to a subject in (i) but it does in (ii).

2. Note that the adjectival *craned* is ruled out in a sentence parallel to (42):

(i)

*When Mary entered the room, she had John's neck craned in an instant.

Cf. footnote 1.

3. In fact, the symbol "↑" precedes the grammatical function names, as explained in chapter 4 of this volume, but this detail is not important here.

4. The consistency condition (see chapter 4 of this volume) would rule out identical grammatical functions for these two *by*-phrases; but the problem remains of explaining why distinct grammatical functions (such as BY1 OBJ and BY2 OBJ) could still not be cointerpreted as the agent in the predicate argument structure.

5. Activo-Passivization also appears to affect temporal properties of the verb it applies to. Compare (i) and (ii):

(i)

Fred is reading Russian novels easily.

(ii)

*Russian novels are reading easily.

In general, lexical operations may affect not only the functional assignment, but also the semantic structure and the morphology of lexical items; however, operations of the latter types are not treated here. See chapter 1 of this volume and Bresnan in preparation a.

6. Fodor and Fodor 1980 incorrectly assume entailment as a criterion of the polyadicity of predicate argument structures in their criticism of Bresnan 1978. For a more detailed discussion of the issues they raise and a rebuttal of their critique, see Bresnan in preparation b.

7. Thus, the claim made by Fodor and Fodor 1980 that the lexical interpretive theory must "stipulate" the relative scope of quantifiers in examples like (68) is erroneous. They make an alternative proposal which induces an order on the application of meaning postulates and other rules of inference. Their proposal has empirical consequences which compare unfavorably with the analysis given here (Bresnan in preparation b).

Part II

SYNTACTIC REPRESENTATION

Chapter 4

Lexical-Functional Grammar: A Formal System for Grammatical Representation

Ronald M. Kaplan
Joan Bresnan

In learning their native language, children develop a remarkable set of capabilities. They acquire knowledge and skills that enable them to produce and comprehend an indefinite number of novel utterances and to make quite subtle judgments about certain of their properties. The major goal of psycholinguistic research is to devise an explanatory account of the mental operations that underlie these linguistic abilities.

In pursuing this goal, we have adopted what we call the *Competence Hypothesis* as a methodological principle. We assume that an explanatory model of human language performance will incorporate a theoretically justified representation of the native speaker's linguistic knowledge (a *grammar*) as a component separate both from the computational mechanisms that operate on it (a *processor*) and from other nongrammatical processing parameters that might influence the processor's behavior.[1] To a certain extent the various components that we postulate can be studied independently, guided where appropriate by the well-established methods and evaluation standards of linguistics, computer science, and experimental psychology. However, the requirement that the various components ultimately must fit together in a consistent and coherent model imposes even stronger constraints on their structure and operation.

This chapter presents a formalism for representing the native speaker's syntactic knowledge. In keeping with the Competence Hypothesis, this formalism, called *lexical-functional grammar* (LFG), has been designed to serve as a medium for expressing and explaining important generalizations about the syntax of human languages and thus to serve as a vehicle for independent linguistic research. Of equal significance, it is a restricted, mathematically tractable notation for which simple, psychologically plausible processing mechanisms can be defined. Lexical-functional grammar has evolved both from previous research within the transformational framework (e.g., Bresnan 1978) and from earlier computational and psycholinguistic investigations (Woods 1970, Kaplan 1972, 1973b, 1975b, Wanner and Maratsos 1978).

The fundamental problem for a theory of syntax is to characterize the mapping between semantic predicate-argument relationships and surface word and phrase configurations by which they are expressed. This mapping is sufficiently complex that it cannot be characterized in a simple, unadorned phrase structure formalism: a single set of predicate-argument relations can be realized in many different phrase structures (e.g., active and passive constructions), and a single phrase structure can express several different semantic relations, as in cases of ambiguity. In lexical-functional grammar, this correspondence is defined in two stages. Lexical entries specify a direct mapping between semantic arguments and configurations of surface grammatical functions. Syntactic rules then identify these surface functions with particular morphological and constituent structure configurations. Alternative realizations may result from alternative specifications at either stage of the correspondence. Moreover, grammatical specifications impose well-formedness conditions on both the functional and the constituent structures of sentences.

This chapter is concerned with the grammatical formalism itself; its linguistic, computational, and psychological motivation are dealt with in separate chapters and in other papers. In the next several sections we introduce the formal objects of our theory, discuss the relationships among them, and define the notation and operations for describing and manipulating them. Illustrations in these and later sections show possible LFG solutions to various problems of linguistic description. Section 4.5 considers the functional requirements that strings with valid constituent structures must satisfy. Section 4.6 summarizes arguments for the independence of the constituent, functional, and semantic levels of representation. In section 4.7 we introduce and discuss the formal apparatus for characterizing long-distance grammatical dependencies. We leave to the end the question of our system's generative power. We prove in section 4.8 that despite their linguistic expressiveness, lexical-functional grammars are *not* as powerful as unrestricted rewriting systems.

4.1 Constituent Structures and Functional Structures

A lexical-functional grammar assigns two levels of syntactic description to every sentence of a language. Phrase structure configurations are represented in a *constituent structure*. A constituent structure (or "c-structure") is a conventional phrase structure tree, a well-formed labeled bracketing that indicates the superficial arrangement of words and phrases in the sentence. This is the representation on which phonological interpretation operates to produce phonetic strings. Surface grammatical functions are represented explicitly at the other level of description, called *functional structure*. The functional structure ("f-structure") provides a precise characterization of such traditional syntactic notions as subject, "understood" subject, object, complement, and adjunct. The f-structure is the sole input to the semantic component, which may either translate the f-structure into the appropriate formulas in some logical language or provide an immediate model-theoretic interpretation for it.

Constituent structures are formally quite different from functional structures. C-structures are defined in terms of syntactic categories, terminal strings, and their dominance and precedence relationships, whereas f-structures are composed of grammatical function names, semantic forms, and feature symbols. F-structures (and c-structures) are also distinct from semantic translations and interpretations, in which, for example, quantifier-scope ambiguities are resolved. By formally distinguishing these levels of representation, our theory attempts to separate those grammatical phenomena that are purely syntactic (involving only c-structures and f-structures) from those that are purely lexical (involving lexical entries before they are inserted into c-structures and f-structures) or semantic (for example, involving logical inference). Our framework thus facilitates an empirically motivated division of labor among the lexical, syntactic, semantic, and phonological components of a grammar.

A c-structure is determined by a grammar that characterizes all possible surface structures for a language. This grammar is expressed in a slightly modified context-free formalism or a formally equivalent specification such as a recursive transition network (Woods 1970, Kaplan 1972). For example, the ordinary rewriting procedure for context-free grammars would assign the c-structure (3) to the sentence (2), given the rules in (1):

(1)
a. S   → NP VP
b. NP → DET N
c. VP → V NP NP

(2)
A girl handed the baby a toy.

(3)

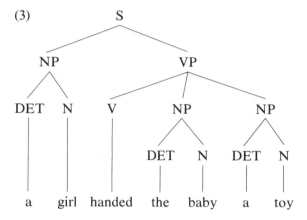

We emphasize that c-structure nodes can be derived only by phrase structure rules such as (1a–c). There are no deletion or movement operations which could, for example, form the double-NP sequence from a phrase structure with a *to* prepositional phrase. Such mechanisms are unnecessary in LFG because we do not map between semantically and phonologically interpretable levels of phrase structure. Semantic interpretation is defined on functional structure, not on the phrase structure representation that is the domain of phonological interpretation.

The functional structure for a sentence encodes its meaningful grammatical relations and provides sufficient information for the semantic component to determine the appropriate predicate-argument formulas. The f-structure for (2) would indicate that the *girl* NP is the grammatical subject, *handed* conveys the semantic predicate, the *baby* NP is the grammatical object, and *toy* serves as the second grammatical object. The f-structure represents this information as a set of ordered pairs each of which consists of an *attribute* and a specification of that attribute's *value* for this sentence. An attribute is the name of a grammatical function or feature (SUBJ, PRED, OBJ, NUM, CASE, etc.). There are three primitive types of values:

(4)

a. Simple *symbols*

b. *Semantic forms* that govern the process of semantic interpretation

c. Subsidiary *f-structures,* sets of ordered pairs representing complexes of internal functions

A fourth type of value, *sets* of symbols, semantic forms, or f-structures, is also permitted. We will discuss this type when we consider the grammatical treatment of adjuncts.

Given possibility (4c), an f-structure is in effect a hierarchy of attribute/value pairs. We write an f-structure by arranging its pairs vertically inside square brackets with the attribute and value of a single pair placed on a horizontal line. The following is a plausible f-structure for sentence (2):

(5)

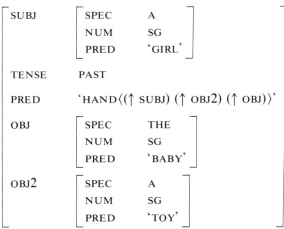

In this structure, the TENSE attribute has the simple symbol value PAST; pairs with this kind of value represent syntactic "features." Grammatical functions have subsidiary f-structure values, as illustrated by the subject function in this example:

(6)

$$\begin{bmatrix} \text{SPEC} & \text{A} \\ \text{NUM} & \text{SG} \\ \text{PRED} & \text{`GIRL'} \end{bmatrix}$$

The attributes SPEC (specifier) and NUM mark embedded features with the symbol values A and SG, respectively.

The quoted values of the PRED attributes are semantic forms. Semantic forms usually arise in the lexicon[2] and are carried along by the syntactic component as unanalyzable atomic elements, just like simple symbols. When the f-structure is semantically interpreted, these forms are treated as patterns for composing the logical formulas encoding the meaning of the sentence. Thus, the semantic interpretation for this sentence is obtained from the value of its PRED attribute, the semantic form in (7):

(7)

'HAND⟨(↑ SUBJ) (↑ OBJ2) (↑ OBJ)⟩'

This is a predicate-argument expression containing the semantic predicate name HAND followed by an argument list specification enclosed in angle brackets. (The angle brackets correspond to the parentheses in the logical language that would ordinarily be used to denote the application of a predicate to its arguments. We use angle brackets in order to distinguish the semantic parentheses from the parentheses of our syntactic formalism.) The argument list specification defines a mapping between the logical or thematic arguments of the three-place predicate HAND (e.g., agent, theme, and goal) and the grammatical functions of the f-structure. The parenthetic expressions signify that the first argument position of that predicate is filled by the formula that results from interpreting the SUBJ function of the sentence, the formula from the OBJ2 is substituted in the second argument position, and so on. The formula for the embedded SUBJ f-structure is determined by *its* PRED value, the semantic form 'GIRL'. GIRL does not have an argument list because it does not apply to arguments specified by other grammatical functions. It is a predicate on individuals in the logical universe of discourse quantified by information derived from the SPEC feature.[3]

There are very strong compatibility requirements between a semantic form and the f-structure in which it appears. Loosely speaking, all the functions mentioned in the semantic form must be included in the f-structure, and all functions with subsidiary f-structure values must be mentioned in the semantic form. A given semantic form is in effect compatible with only one set of grammatical functions (although these may be associated with several different c-structures). Thus, the semantic form in (8) is not compatible with the grammatical functions in

(5) because it does not mention the OBJ2 function but does specify
(↑ TO OBJ), the object of the preposition *to*.

(8)
'HAND⟨(↑ SUBJ) (↑ OBJ) (↑ TO OBJ)⟩'

This semantic form is compatible instead with the functions in the
f-structure (9):

(9)

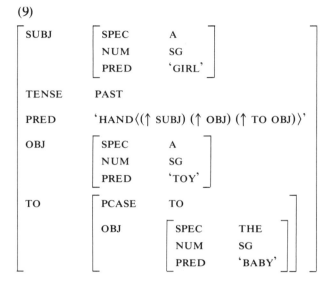

We show in section 4.4 how this f-structure is assigned to the
NP–*to*–NP sentence (10):

(10)
A girl handed a toy to the baby.

This f-structure, with (8) as its PRED value, defines *girl, baby,* and *toy* as
the agent, goal, and theme arguments of HAND, just as in (5). The native
speaker's paraphrase intuitions concerning (2) and (10) are thus accurately expressed. This account of the English dative alternation is possible because our grammatical functions SUBJ, OBJ, TO OBJ, etc., denote
surface grammatical relationships, not the underlying, logical relationships commonly represented in transformational deep structures.

The semantic forms (7) and (8) are found in alternative entries of the
lexical item *handed,* reflecting the fact that the predicate HAND permits
the alternative surface realizations (2) and (10), among others. Of
course, many other verbs in the lexicon are similar to *handed* in having

separate entries along the lines of (7) and (8). Our theory captures the systematic connection between NP–NP and NP–*to*–NP constructions by means of a lexical redundancy rule of the sort suggested by Bresnan (see Bresnan 1978 and chapter 1 of this volume). The semantic form (7) results from applying the "dativizing" lexical rule shown in (11) to the semantic form in (8).

(11)

$(\uparrow \text{OBJ}) \quad \mapsto (\uparrow \text{OBJ2})$

$(\uparrow \text{TO OBJ}) \mapsto (\uparrow \text{OBJ})$

According to this rule, a word with a lexical entry containing the specifications ($\uparrow$ OBJ) and ($\uparrow$ TO OBJ) may have another entry in which ($\uparrow$ OBJ2) appears in place of ($\uparrow$ OBJ) and ($\uparrow$ OBJ) appears in place of ($\uparrow$ TO OBJ).

It is important to note that these relation-changing rules are not applied in the syntactic derivation of individual sentences. They merely express patterns of redundancy that obtain among large but finite classes of lexical entries and presumably simplify the child's language acquisition task (see chapter 10 for discussion). Indeed, just as our formalism admits no rules for transforming c-structures, it embodies a similar prohibition against syntactic manipulations of function assignments and function/argument mappings:

(12)
Direct Syntactic Encoding
No rule of syntax may replace one function name by another.

This principle is an immediate consequence of the Uniqueness Condition, which is stated in the next section. The principle of direct syntactic encoding sharpens the distinction between two classes of rules: rules that change relations are lexical and range over finite sets, while syntactic rules that project onto an infinite set of sentences preserve grammatical relations.[4] Our restrictions on the expressive power of syntactic rules guarantee that a sentence's grammatical functions are "visible" directly in the surface structure and thus afford certain computational and psychological advantages.

4.2 Functional Descriptions

A string's constituent structure is generated by a context-free c-structure grammar. That grammar is augmented so that it also produces a finite collection of statements specifying various properties of the string's f-structure. The set of such statements, called the *functional description* ("f-description") of the string, serves as an intermediary between the c-structure and the f-structure.

The statements of an f-description can be used in two ways. They can be applied to a particular f-structure to decide whether or not it has all the properties required by the grammar. If so, the candidate f-structure may be taken as the f-structure that the grammar assigns to the string. The f-description may also be used in a constructive mode: the statements support a set of inferences by which an f-structure satisfying the grammar's requirements may be synthesized. The f-description is thus analogous to a set of simultaneous equations in elementary algebra that express properties of certain unknown numbers. Such equations may be used to validate a proposed solution, or they may be solved by means of arithmetic inference rules (canceling, substitution of equals for equals, etc.) to discover the particular numbers for which the equations are true. In line with this analogy, this section presents an algebraic formalism for representing an f-description.

The statements in an f-description and the inferences that may be drawn from them depend crucially on the following axiom:

(13)

Uniqueness

In a given f-structure, a particular attribute may have at most one value.

This condition makes it possible to describe an f-structure by specifying *the* (unique) values of the grammatical functions of which it is composed. Thus, if we let the variables f_1 and f_2 stand for unknown f-structures, the following statements have a clear interpretation:

(14)

a.   the SUBJ of $f_1 = f_2$
b.   the SPEC of $f_2 = $ A
c.   the NUM of $f_2 = $ SG
d.   the PRED of $f_2 = $ 'GIRL'

In fact, these statements are true if f_1 and f_2 are the f-structures (5) and (6), and the statements in (14) may thus be considered a part of the f-description of sentence (2).

We have defined a functional structure as a set of ordered pairs satisfying the Uniqueness Condition (13). We now observe that this is precisely the standard definition of a *mathematical* function. There is a systematic ambiguity in our use of the word *function:* an f-structure is a mathematical function that represents the *grammatical* functions of a sentence. This coincidence provides a more conventional terminology for formulating the statements of an f-description. For example, statement (14c) can be paraphrased as (15a), and this can be stated more formally using the familiar parenthesis notation to indicate the application of a function to an argument, as in (15b):

(15)
a.   The function f_2 is such that applying it to the argument NUM yields the value SG.
b. $f_2(\text{NUM}) = \text{SG}$

Thus, the statements of an f-description are simply equations that describe the values obtained by various function applications. Unlike the typical functions of elementary algebra, an f-structure is a function with a finite domain and range and thus can be defined by a finite table of arguments and values, as represented in our square bracket notation. Also, we do not draw a clear distinction between functions and their values. Algebraic equations commonly involve a known function that takes on a given value when applied to some unknown argument; the problem is to determine that argument. In (15b), however, the argument and the corresponding value are *both* known, and the problem is to find the function![5] Moreover, applying an f-structure to an argument may produce a function that may be applied in turn to another argument. If (16a) is true, then the stipulations in (15b) and (16b) are equivalent.

(16)
a. $f_1(\text{SUBJ}) = \begin{bmatrix} \text{SPEC} & \text{A} \\ \text{NUM} & \text{SG} \\ \text{PRED} & \text{`GIRL'} \end{bmatrix} = f_2$

b. $f_1(\text{SUBJ})(\text{NUM}) = \text{SG}$

The form of function composition illustrated in equation (16b) occurs quite often in f-descriptions. We have found that a slight adaptation of the traditional notation improves the readability of such specifications. Thus, we denote a function application by writing the function name *inside* the parentheses next to the argument instead of putting it in front. In our modified notation, the stipulation (15b) is written as (17a) and the composition (16b) appears as (17b).

(17)

a. $(f_2 \text{ NUM}) = \text{SG}$

b. $((f_1 \text{ SUBJ}) \text{ NUM}) = \text{SG}$

We make one further simplification: since all f-structures are functions of one argument, parenthetic expressions with more than two elements (a function and its argument) do not normally occur. Thus, we introduce no ambiguity by defining our parenthesis notation to be left-associative, by means of the identity (18):

(18)

$$((f \; \alpha) \; \beta) \equiv (f \; \alpha \; \beta)$$

This allows any leftmost pair of parentheses to be removed (or inserted) when convenient, so that (17b) may be simplified to (19):

(19)

$(f_1 \text{ SUBJ NUM}) = \text{SG}$

With this notation, there is a simple way of determining the value of a given function-application expression: we locate the f-structure denoted by the leftmost element in the expression and match the remaining elements from left to right against successive attributes in the f-structure hierarchy. Also, the English genitive construction provides a natural gloss for these expressions: (19) may be read as "f_1's SUBJ's NUM is SG."

4.3 From C-Structures to F-Descriptions

Having said what an f-description is, we now consider how the f-description for a string is produced from a grammar and lexicon. This is followed by a discussion of the inferences that lead from an f-description to the f-structure that it describes.

The statements in an f-description come from functional specifications that are associated with particular elements on the righthand sides of c-structure rules and with particular categories in lexical entries. These specifications consist of templates from which the f-description statements are derived. A template, or statement *schema,* has the form of the statement to be derived from it except that in place of f-structure variables it contains special *metavariables.* If a rule is applied to generate a c-structure node or a lexical item is inserted under a preterminal category, the associated schemata are *instantiated* by replacing the metavariables with actual variables $(f_1, f_2, \ldots)$. Which actual variables are used depends on which metavariables are in the schemata and what the node's relationship is to other nodes in the tree. The metavariables and grammatically significant tree relations are of just two types:

(20)

Immediate domination, with metavariables $\uparrow$ and $\downarrow$

Bounded domination, with metavariables $\Uparrow$ and $\Downarrow$

Statements based on nonimmediate but bounded tree relations are needed to characterize the "long-distance" dependencies found in relative clauses, questions, and other constructions. We postpone our discussion of bounded domination to section 4.7, since it is more complex than immediate domination.

Schemata involving immediate domination metavariables and relations yield f-description statements defining the local predicate-argument configurations of simple sentence patterns such as the dative. To illustrate, the c-structure rules (21a,b,c) are versions of (1a,b,c) with schemata written beneath the rule elements that they are associated with.

(21)

a. S   →   NP   VP
                  ($\uparrow$ SUBJ)=$\downarrow$ $\uparrow$=$\downarrow$

b. NP → DET N

c. VP → V   NP   NP
                  ($\uparrow$ OBJ)=$\downarrow$ ($\uparrow$ OBJ2)=$\downarrow$

According to the instantiation procedure described below, the SUBJ and OBJ schemata in this grammar indicate that the subject and object f-structures come from NPs immediately dominated by S and VP. While superficially similar to the standard transformational definitions of *subject* and *object* (Chomsky 1965), our specifications apply only to surface constituents and establish only a loose coupling between functions and phrase structure configurations. Given the OBJ2 schema, for example, an NP directly dominated by VP can also function as a second object. These schemata correspond more closely to the SETR operation of the augmented transition network (ATN) notation (Woods 1970): ($\uparrow$ SUBJ) = $\downarrow$ has roughly the same effect as the ATN action (SETR SUBJ *). The direct equality on the VP category in (21a) has no ATN (or transformational) equivalent, however. It is an *identification* schema indicating that a single f-structure is based on more than one constituent, and thus that the f-structure is somewhat "flatter" than the c-structure.

The syntactic features and semantic content of lexical items are determined by schemata in lexical entries. The entries for the vocabulary of sentence (2) are listed in (22). (This illustration ignores the morphological composition of lexical items, which makes a systematic contribution to the set of inflectional features represented in the schemata.)

(22)

a: DET, $(\uparrow$ SPEC$) =$ A
                $(\uparrow$ NUM$) =$ SG

girl: N, $(\uparrow$ NUM$) =$ SG
                $(\uparrow$ PRED$) =$ 'GIRL'

handed: V, $(\uparrow$ TENSE$) =$ PAST
                $(\uparrow$ PRED$) =$ 'HAND$\langle(\uparrow$ SUBJ$)$ $(\uparrow$ OBJ2$)$ $(\uparrow$ OBJ$)\rangle$'

the: DET, $(\uparrow$ SPEC$) =$ THE

baby: N, $(\uparrow$ NUM$) =$ SG
                $(\uparrow$ PRED$) =$ 'BABY'

toy: N, $(\uparrow$ NUM$) =$ SG
                $(\uparrow$ PRED$) =$ 'TOY'

A lexical entry in LFG includes a categorial specification indicating the preterminal category under which the lexical item may be inserted, and a set of schemata to be instantiated. As shown in (22), schemata originating in the lexicon are not formally distinct from those coming from c-structure rules, and they are treated uniformly by the instantiation procedure.

Instantiation is carried out in three phases. The schemata are first attached to appropriate nodes in the c-structure tree, actual variables are then introduced at certain nodes, and finally those actual variables are substituted for metavariables to form valid f-description statements. In the first phase, schemata associated with a c-structure rule element are attached to the nodes generated by that element. Lexical schemata are considered to be associated with a lexical entry's categorial specification and are thus attached to the nodes of that category that dominate the lexical item.[6] Attaching the grammatical and lexical schemata in (21) and (22) to the c-structure for sentence (2) produces the structure shown in (23). In this example we have written the schemata above the nodes they are attached to.

(23)

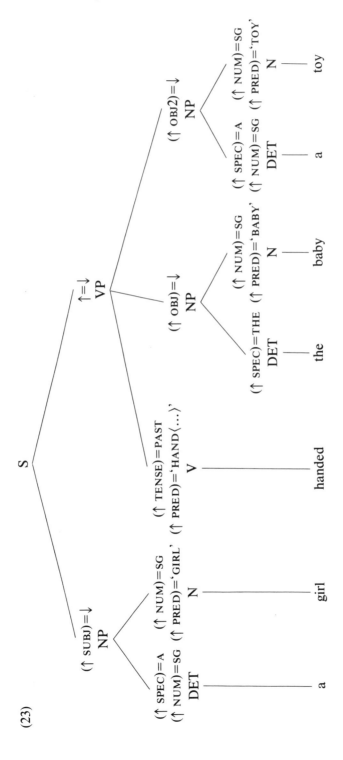

In the second phase of the instantiation procedure, a new actual variable is introduced for the root node of the tree and for each node where a schema contains the ↓ metavariable. Intuitively, the existence of ↓ at a node means that one component of the sentence's f-structure corresponds to that subconstituent. The new variable, called the ↓-*variable* of the node, is a device for describing the internal properties of that f-structure (called the node's ↓ *f-structure*) and its role in larger structures. In (24) we have associated ↓-variables with the nodes as required by the schemata in (23).

With the schemata and variables laid out on the tree in this way, the substitution phase of instantiation is quite simple. Fully instantiated statements are formed by substituting a node's ↓-variable first for all the ↓'s at that node and then for all the ↑'s attached to the nodes it immediately dominates. Thus, arrows pointing toward each other across one line in the tree are instantiated with the same variable.[7] The ↑ is called the "mother" metavariable, since it is replaced by the ↓-variable of its mother node. From the point of view of the S-dominated NP node, the schema (↑ SUBJ) = ↓ may be read as 'My mother's f-structure's SUBJ is my f-structure'.[8] In this case, the mother's variable is the root node's ↓-variable and so represents the f-structure of the sentence as a whole.

When we perform the substitutions for the schemata and variables in (24), the schemata attached to the S-dominated NP and VP nodes yield the equations in (25), and the daughters of the VP cause the equations in (26) to be included in the sentence's f-description:

(25)

a. $(f_1 \text{ SUBJ}) = f_2$

b. $f_1 = f_3$

(26)

a. $(f_3 \text{ OBJ}) = f_4$

b. $(f_3 \text{ OBJ2}) = f_5$

The equations in (25)–(26) taken together constitute the syntactically determined statements of the sentence's functional description. The other equations in the f-description are derived from the schemata on the preterminal nodes.

(24)

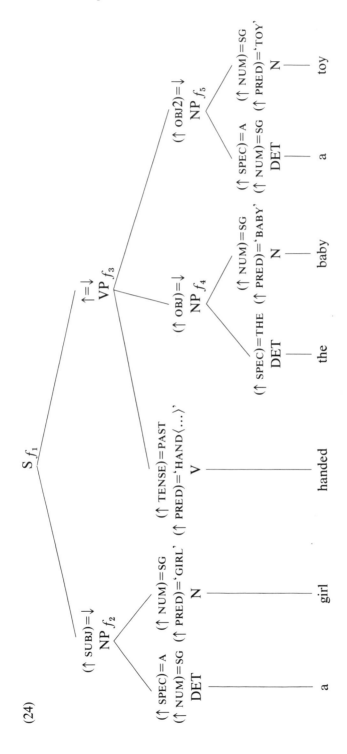

(27)

a. $(f_2 \text{ SPEC}) = \text{A}$ from *a*
b. $(f_2 \text{ NUM}) = \text{SG}$

c. $(f_2 \text{ NUM}) = \text{SG}$ from *girl*
d. $(f_2 \text{ PRED}) = \text{'GIRL'}$

e. $(f_3 \text{ TENSE}) = \text{PAST}$ from *handed*
f. $(f_3 \text{ PRED}) = \text{'HAND}\langle(\uparrow\text{SUBJ}) (\uparrow\text{OBJ2}) (\uparrow\text{OBJ})\rangle\text{'}$

g. $(f_4 \text{ SPEC}) = \text{THE}$ from *the*

h. $(f_4 \text{ NUM}) = \text{SG}$ from *baby*
i. $(f_4 \text{ PRED}) = \text{'BABY'}$

j. $(f_5 \text{ SPEC}) = \text{A}$ from *a*
k. $(f_5 \text{ NUM}) = \text{SG}$

l. $(f_5 \text{ NUM}) = \text{SG}$ from *toy*
m. $(f_5 \text{ PRED}) = \text{'TOY'}$

(For simplicity in this chapter, we do not instantiate the $\uparrow$ metavariable when it appears within semantic forms. This is permissible because the internal structure of semantic forms is not accessible to syntactic rules. However, the semantic translation or interpretation procedure may depend on a full instantiation.) Adding (27a–m) to the equations in (25)–(26) gives the complete f-description for sentence (2).

4.4 From F-Descriptions to F-Structures

Once an f-description has been produced for a given string, algebraic manipulations can be performed on its statements to make manifest certain implicit relationships that hold among the properties of that string's f-structure. These manipulations are justified by the left-associativity of the function-application notation (18) and by the substitution axiom for equality. To take an example, the value of the number feature of sentence (2)'s f-structure (that is, the value of $(f_1 \text{ OBJ NUM})$) can be inferred in the following steps:

(28)

$$
\begin{aligned}
(f_1 \text{ OBJ NUM}) &= (f_3 \text{ OBJ NUM}) & \text{Substitution using (25b)} \\
&= ((f_3 \text{ OBJ}) \text{ NUM}) & \text{Left-associativity} \\
&= (f_4 \text{ NUM}) & \text{Substitution using (26a)} \\
&= \text{SG} & \text{Substitution using (27h)}
\end{aligned}
$$

An f-description also supports a more important set of inferences: the equations can be "solved" by means of a construction algorithm that actually builds the f-structure they describe.

An f-structure solution may not exist for every f-description, however. If the f-description stipulates two distinct values for a particular attribute, or if it implies that an attribute name is an f-structure or semantic form instead of a symbol, then its statements are inconsistent with the basic axioms of our theory. In this case we classify the string as syntactically ill-formed, even though it has a valid c-structure. The functional well-formedness conditions of our theory thus account for many types of ungrammaticality. It is therefore essential that there be an algorithm for deciding whether or not an f-description is consistent, and for producing a consistent f-description's f-structure solution. Otherwise, our grammars would generate all but not *only* the sentences of a language.

Fortunately, f-descriptions are well-understood mathematical objects. The problem of determining whether or not a given f-description is satisfiable is equivalent to the decision problem of the quantifier-free theory of equality. Ackermann 1954 proved that this problem is solvable, and several efficient solution algorithms have been discovered (for example, the congruence closure algorithm of Oppen and Nelson 1977). In this section we outline a decision and construction algorithm whose operations are specially adapted to the linguistic representations of our theory.

We begin by giving a more precise interpretation for the formal expressions that appear in f-description statements. We imagine that there is a collection of entities (symbols, semantic forms, and f-structures) that an f-description characterizes, and that each of these entities has a variety of names, or *designators,* by which the f-description may refer to it. The character strings that we have used to represent symbols and semantic forms, the algebraic variables we introduce, and the function-application expressions are all designators. The entity denoted by a designator is called its *value.* The value of a symbol or semantic form character string is obviously the identified symbol or semantic form. The value of a variable designator is of course not obvious from the variable's spelling; it is defined by an assignment list of variable–entity pairs. A basic function-application expression is a parenthesized pair of designators, and its value is the entity, if any, obtained by applying the f-structure value of the left designator to the symbol value of the right designator.[9] This rule applies recursively if either expression is itself a function-application: to obtain the value of $((f_1 \text{ OBJ}) \text{ NUM})$, we must first obtain the value of $(f_1 \text{ OBJ})$ by applying the value of f_1 to the symbol OBJ.

Note that several different designators may refer to the same entity. The deduction in (28), for example, indicates that the designators $(f_1 \text{ OBJ NUM})$ and $(f_4 \text{ NUM})$ both have the same value, the symbol SG. Indeed, we interpret the equality relation between two designators as an explicit stipulation that those designators name the same entity. In processing an f-description, our algorithm attempts to find a way of associating with designators values that are consistent with the synonymy relation implied by the equality statements and with the procedure just outlined for obtaining the values of different types of designators.

The algorithm works by successive approximation.[10] It goes through a sequence of steps, one for each equation in the f-description. At the beginning of each step, it has a collection of symbols, semantic forms, and f-structures that satisfy all the equations considered at preceding steps, together with an assignment of tentative values for the variables occurring in those equations. The algorithm revises the collection of entities and value assignments to satisfy in addition the requirements of one more equation from the f-description. The entities after the last equation is processed thus satisfy the f-description as a whole and provide a final value for the ↓-variable of the c-structure tree's root node. This is the f-structure that the grammar assigns to the string.

The processing of a single equation is carried out by means of two operators. One operator, called *Locate,* obtains the value for a given designator. The entities in the collection might be augmented by the Locate operator to ensure that a value exists for that designator. When the values for the lefthand and righthand designators have been located, the second operator, *Merge,* checks to see whether those values are the same and hence already satisfy the equality relation. If not, it constructs a new entity by combining the properties of the distinct values, provided those properties are compatible. The collection is revised so that this entity becomes the common value of the two designators and also of all previously encountered synonyms of these designators. Stated in more formal terms, if d_1 and d_2 are the designators in an equation $d_1 = d_2$, and if brackets represent the application of an operator to its arguments, then that equation is processed by performing Merge[Locate[d_1], Locate[d_2]].

A technical definition of these operators is given in the appendix. In this section we present an intuitive description of the solution process, using as an example the f-description in (25)–(27). The final result does not depend on the order in which equations are considered, so we will simply take them as they appear above. We start with an empty collection of entities and consider equation (25a): $(f_1 \text{ SUBJ}) = f_2$. To locate the value of $(f_1 \text{ SUBJ})$, we must first obtain the value of f_1. There is as yet no assignment for that variable, so the Locate operator creates a value out of whole cloth: it adds a special "place-holder" entity to our collection and assigns it as the value of f_1. A representation for the new entity and variable assignment is shown in (29):

(29)

f_1 ———

A place-holder is represented by a blank line, indicating that it is an entity none of whose properties are known. The variable prefix signifies that whatever that entity is, it has been assigned as the tentative value of f_1. A place-holder is just a bookkeeping device for recording the relations between entities before we have discovered anything else about them.

With the value of f_1 in hand, we return to the larger designator $(f_1 \text{ SUBJ})$. This provides more specific information about the entity that the place-holder stands for: the value of f_1 must be an f-structure that has SUBJ as one of its attributes. We revise our collection again to take account of this new information:

(30)

$f_1 \left[\text{SUBJ} \qquad \text{———} \right]$

Knowing nothing about the value of SUBJ in the f_1 f-structure, we have represented it by another place-holder. This place-holder is the entity located for the designator $(f_1 \text{ SUBJ})$. We now turn to f_2, the second designator in the equation. This is a variable with no previous assignment, so our location procedure simply assigns it to another newly created place-holder:

(31)

f_2 ———

This completes the location phase of the algorithm's first step: the equation's designators now denote the place-holders in (30) and (31).

The Merge operator changes the collection once more, so that the two designators denote the same entity. The two place-holders are distinct, but neither has any properties. Thus, a common value, also a place-holder with no properties, can be constructed. This place-holder appears as the value of SUBJ in the f_1 f-structure, but it is also assigned as the value of f_2, as shown in (32):

(32)

$$f_1 \begin{bmatrix} \text{SUBJ} & f_2 \text{———} \end{bmatrix}$$

The structure (32) is now the only member of our entity collection. Notice that with this assignment of variables, the designators (f_1 SUBJ) and f_2 have the same value, so the equation (f_1 SUBJ) = f_2 is satisfied.

We move on to equation (25b), the identification $f_1 = f_3$. This means that the variables f_1 and f_3 are two different designators for a single entity. That entity will have all the properties ascribed via the designator f_1 and also all the properties ascribed to the synonymous f_3. The f-structure (32) is located as the value of f_1, and a new place-holder is assigned to f_3. Since the place-holder has no properties, the result of combining it with the f-structure is simply that f-structure again, with its variable prefixes modified to reflect the new equality. Thus, the result of the merge for the second equation is (33):

(33)

$$f_1\, f_3 \begin{bmatrix} \text{SUBJ} & f_2 \text{———} \end{bmatrix}$$

The variable assignments in (33) now satisfy the first two equations of the f-description.

The equation at the next step is (26a): (f_3 OBJ) = f_4. f_3 already has an f-structure value in (33), but it does not include OBJ as one of its attributes. This is remedied by adding an appropriate place-holder:

(34)

$$f_1\, f_3 \begin{bmatrix} \text{SUBJ} & f_2 \text{———} \\ \text{OBJ} & \text{———} \end{bmatrix}$$

This place-holder is merged with one created for the variable f_4, yielding (35):

(35)

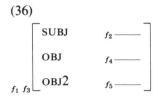

$$f_1\,f_3 \begin{bmatrix} \text{SUBJ} & f_2\,\rule{1cm}{0.4pt} \\ \text{OBJ} & f_4\,\rule{1cm}{0.4pt} \end{bmatrix}$$

Equation (26b) is handled in a similar fashion and results in (36):

(36)

$$f_1\,f_3 \begin{bmatrix} \text{SUBJ} & f_2\,\rule{1cm}{0.4pt} \\ \text{OBJ} & f_4\,\rule{1cm}{0.4pt} \\ \text{OBJ2} & f_5\,\rule{1cm}{0.4pt} \end{bmatrix}$$

After we have processed these equations, our collection of entities and variable assignments satisfies all the syntactically determined equations of the f-description.

The lexically derived equations are now taken into account. These have the effect of adding new features to the outer f-structure and filling in the internal properties of the place-holders. Locating the value of the lefthand designator in equation (27a), $(f_2 \text{ SPEC}) = \text{A}$, converts the SUBJ place-holder to an f-structure with a SPEC feature whose value is a new place-holder:

(37)

$$f_1\,f_3 \begin{bmatrix} \text{SUBJ} & f_2\begin{bmatrix} \text{SPEC} & \rule{1cm}{0.4pt} \end{bmatrix} \\ \text{OBJ} & f_4\,\rule{1cm}{0.4pt} \\ \text{OBJ2} & f_5\,\rule{1cm}{0.4pt} \end{bmatrix}$$

The value of the righthand designator is just the symbol A. Merging this with the new SPEC place-holder yields (38):

(38)

$$f_1\,f_3 \begin{bmatrix} \text{SUBJ} & f_2\begin{bmatrix} \text{SPEC} & \text{A} \end{bmatrix} \\ \text{OBJ} & f_4\,\rule{1cm}{0.4pt} \\ \text{OBJ2} & f_5\,\rule{1cm}{0.4pt} \end{bmatrix}$$

Note that this modification does not falsify any equations processed in previous steps.

Equation (27b) has the same form as (27a), and its effect is simply to add a SG-valued NUM feature to the SUBJ f-structure, alongside the SPEC:

(39)

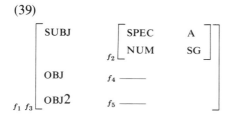

Though derived from different lexical items, equation (27c) is an exact duplicate of (27b). Processing this equation therefore has no visible effects.

The remaining equations are quite straightforward. Equation (27d) causes the PRED function to be added to the SUBJ f-structure, (27e)– (27f) yield the TENSE and PRED functions in the f_1–f_3 structure, and (27g)–(27m) complete the OBJ and OBJ2 place-holders. Equation (27l) is similar to (27c) in that it duplicates another equation in the f-description and hence does not have an independent effect on the final result. After considering all the equations in (27), we arrive at the final f-structure (40):

(40)

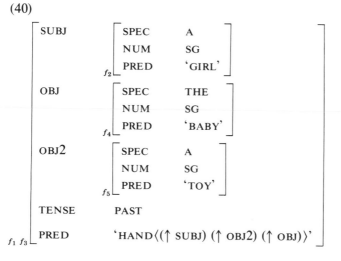

Since f_1 is the ↓-variable of the root node of the tree (24), the outer f-structure is what our simple grammar assigns to the string. This is just the structure in (5), if the variable prefixes and the order of pairs are ignored.

This example is special in that the argument positions of all the function-application designators are filled with symbol designators. Certain grammatical situations give rise to less restricted designators, where the argument position is filled with another function-application. This is possible because symbols have a dual status in our formalism: they can serve in an f-structure both as attributes and as values. These more general designators permit the grammatical relation assigned to the ↓ f-structure at a given node to be determined by internal features of that f-structure rather than by the position of that node in the c-structure. The arguments to a large number of English verbs, for instance, may appear as the objects of particular prepositions instead of as SUBJ, OBJ, or OBJ2 noun phrases. In our theory, the lexical entry for a "case-marking" preposition indicates that its object noun phrase may be treated as what has traditionally been called a verb's *oblique object*. The semantic form for the verb then specifies how to map that oblique object into the appropriate argument of the predicate.

The *to* alternative for the double-NP realization of *handed* provides a simple illustration. The contrasting sentence to our previous example (2) is (10), repeated here for convenience:

(41)
A girl handed a toy to the baby.

The c-structure for this sentence with a set of ↓-variables for the functionally relevant nodes is shown in (42). It includes a prepositional phrase following the object NP, as permitted by the new c-structure rules (43a,b). (We use the standard context-free abbreviation for optionality, parentheses that enclose categories and schemata. Thus, (43a) also derives intransitive and transitive verb phrases. Optionality parentheses should not be confused with the function-application parentheses within schemata. We also use braces in rules to indicate alternative c-structure expansions.)

(42)

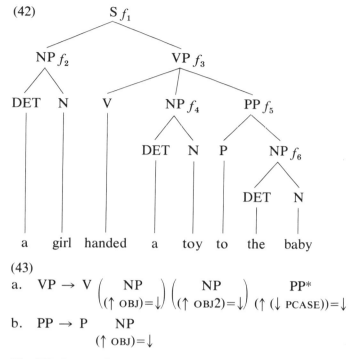

(43)

a. VP → V $\begin{pmatrix} NP \\ (\uparrow \text{OBJ})=\downarrow \end{pmatrix} \begin{pmatrix} NP \\ (\uparrow \text{OBJ2})=\downarrow \end{pmatrix} \begin{matrix} PP* \\ (\uparrow (\downarrow \text{PCASE}))=\downarrow \end{matrix}$

b. PP → P   NP
$\qquad\quad (\uparrow \text{OBJ})=\downarrow$

The PP element in (43a) exhibits two new rule features. The asterisk on the PP category symbol is the Kleene-star operator; it indicates that that rule element may be repeated any number of times, including none.[11] The schema on the PP specifies that the value of the PCASE attribute in the PP's f-structure determines the functional role assigned to that structure. Because the lexical schemata from *to* are attached to the P node, that feature percolates up to the f-structure at the PP node. Suppose that *to* has the case-marking lexical entry shown in (44a)[12] and that *handed* has the entry (44b) as an alternative to the one given in (22). Then the PP f-structure serves the TO function, as shown in (45).

(44)

a. to: P, $(\uparrow \text{PCASE}) = $ TO
b. handed: V, $(\uparrow \text{TENSE}) = $ PAST

$\qquad\qquad\quad (\uparrow \text{PRED}) = $ 'HAND⟨($\uparrow$ SUBJ) ($\uparrow$ OBJ) ($\uparrow$ TO OBJ)⟩'

(45)

$$
\begin{bmatrix}
\text{SUBJ} & \begin{bmatrix} \text{SPEC} & \text{A} \\ \text{NUM} & \text{SG} \\ \text{PRED} & \text{`GIRL'} \end{bmatrix} \\[2em]
\text{TENSE} & \text{PAST} \\[1em]
\text{PRED} & \text{`HAND}\langle(\uparrow \text{ SUBJ}) (\uparrow \text{ OBJ}) (\uparrow \text{ TO OBJ})\rangle\text{'} \\[1em]
\text{OBJ} & \begin{bmatrix} \text{SPEC} & \text{A} \\ \text{NUM} & \text{SG} \\ \text{PRED} & \text{`TOY'} \end{bmatrix} \\[2em]
\text{TO} & \begin{bmatrix} \text{PCASE} & \text{TO} \\ \text{OBJ} & \begin{bmatrix} \text{SPEC} & \text{THE} \\ \text{NUM} & \text{SG} \\ \text{PRED} & \text{`BABY'} \end{bmatrix} \end{bmatrix}
\end{bmatrix}
$$

The BABY f-structure is accessible as the TO OBJ, and it is correctly mapped onto the goal argument of HAND by the semantic form for *handed* in (44b) and (45). As mentioned earlier, this is systematically related to the semantic form in (22) by a dative lexical redundancy rule, so that the generalization marking sentences (2) and (41) as paraphrases is not lost.

Most of the statements in the f-description for (41) are either the same as or very similar to the statements in (25)–(27). The statements most relevant to the issue at hand are instantiated inside the prepositional phrase and at the PP node in the verb phrase:

(46)
a. $(f_3 (f_5 \text{ PCASE})) = f_5$ from PP in (43a)
b. $(f_5 \text{ PCASE}) = \text{TO}$ from *to*

The designator on the left side of (46a) is of course the crucial one. This is processed by first locating the values of f_3 and $(f_5 \text{ PCASE})$, and then applying the first of these values to the second. If (46b) is processed before (46a), then the value of $(f_5 \text{ PCASE})$ will be the symbol TO, and (46a) will thus receive the same treatment as the more restricted equations we considered above.

We cannot insist that the f-description be processed in this or any other order, however. Since equality is an equivalence relation, whether or not an f-structure is a solution to a given f-description is not a property of any ordering on the f-description statements. An order dependency in our algorithm would simply be an artifact of its operation. Unless we could prove that an acceptable order can be determined for any set of statements, we would run the risk of ordering paradoxes whereby our algorithm does not produce a solution even though satisfactory f-structures do exist. A potential order dependency arises only when one equation establishes relationships between entities that have not yet been defined. Place-holders serve in our algorithm as temporary surrogates for those unknown entities. Our examples above illustrate their use in representing simple relationships. Changing the order in which equations (46a,b) are processed demonstrates that the proper treatment of more complicated cooccurrence relationships does not depend on a particular sequence of statements.

Suppose that (46a) is processed before (46b). Then the value of $(f_5$ PCASE) will be a place-holder as shown in (47a), and f_3 will be assigned an f-structure with place-holders in both attribute and value positions, as in (47b):

(47)

a. $f_5\left[\begin{array}{cc} \text{PCASE} & \underline{\hspace{2cm}} \end{array}\right]$

b. $f_3\left[\begin{array}{cc} \underline{\hspace{1cm}} & \underline{\hspace{1.5cm}} \end{array}\right]$

The value of the larger designator $(f_3\ (f_5$ PCASE)) will thus be the second place-holder in (47b). When this is merged with the f-structure assigned to f_5, the result is (48):

(48)

$f_3\left[\begin{array}{cc} \underline{\hspace{1cm}} & f_5\left[\begin{array}{cc} \text{PCASE} & \underline{\hspace{2cm}} \end{array}\right] \end{array}\right]$

It is not clear from (48) that the two blank lines stand for the same place-holder. One way of indicating this fact is to annotate blank lines with an identifying index whenever they represent occurrences of the same place-holder in multiple contexts, as shown in (49). An alternative and perhaps more perspicuous way of marking the important formal relationships is to display the blank line in just one of the place-holder's positions and then draw connecting lines to its other occurrences, as in (50):

(49)

$$f_3\left[\quad\underline{\quad}_1 \qquad f_5\left[\text{PCASE} \qquad \underline{\quad}_1 \right]\right]$$

(50)

$$f_3\left[\quad\underline{\quad} \qquad f_5\left[\text{PCASE} \qquad \right]\right]$$

This problem of representation arises because our hierarchical f-structures are in fact directed graphs, not trees, so all the connections cannot easily be displayed in textual form. With the cooccurrences explicitly represented, processing equation (46b) causes the symbol TO to be substituted for the place-holder in both positions:

(51)

$$f_3\left[\text{TO} \qquad f_5\left[\text{PCASE} \qquad \text{TO} \right]\right]$$

The index or connecting line is no longer needed, because the common spelling of symbols in two positions suffices to indicate their formal identity. The structure (51) is combined with the result of processing the remaining equations in the f-description, yielding the final structure (45).

The Kleene-star operator on the PP in (43a) allows for sentences having more than one oblique object:

(52)
The toy was given to the baby by the girl.

The f-structure of this sentence will have both a TO OBJ and a BY OBJ.Because of the functional well-formedness conditions discussed in the next section, these grammatical relations are compatible only with a semantic form that results from the passive lexical rule:

(53)
'HAND⟨(↑ BY OBJ) (↑ SUBJ) (↑ TO OBJ)⟩'

Although the c-structure rule suggests that any number of oblique objects are possible, they are in fact strictly limited by semantic form specifications. Moreover, if two prepositional phrases have the same preposition and hence the same PCASE feature, the Uniqueness Condition implies that only one of them can serve as an argument. If the sentence is to be grammatical, the other must be interpreted as some sort of adjunct. In (54), either *the policeman* or *the boy* must be a nonargument locative:

(54)
The baby was found by the boy by the policeman.

Thus, the PP element in rule (43a) derives the PP nodes for dative *to*-phrases, agentive *by*-phrases, and other, more idiosyncratic English oblique objects. Schemata similar to the one on the PP will be much more common in languages that make extensive use of lexically as opposed to structurally induced grammatical relations (e.g., heavily case-marked, nonconfigurational languages).

We have illustrated how our algorithm builds the f-structure for two grammatical sentences. However, as indicated above, f-descriptions which contradict the Uniqueness Condition are not solvable, and our algorithm must also inform us of this inconsistency. Consistency checking is carried out by both the Locate and the Merge operators. The Locate operator, for example, cannot succeed if a statement specifies that a symbol or semantic form is to be applied as a function or if a function is to be applied to an f-structure or semantic form argument. The string is marked ungrammatical if this happens. Similarly, a merger cannot be completed if the two entities to be merged are incompatible, either because they are of different types (a symbol and an f-structure, for example) or because they are otherwise in conflict (two distinct symbols or semantic forms, or two f-structures that assign distinct values to the same argument). Again, this means that the f-description is inconsistent.

Our algorithm thus produces *one* solution for an arbitrary consistent f-description, but it is not the *only* solution. If an f-structure F is a solution for a given f-description, then any f-structure formed from F by adding values for attributes not already present will also satisfy the f-description. Since the f-description does not mention those attributes or values, they cannot conflict with any of its statements. For example, we could add the arbitrary pairs x–y and z–w to the SUBJ f-structure of (40) to form (55):

(55)

$$
\begin{bmatrix}
\text{SPEC} & \text{A} \\
\text{NUM} & \text{SG} \\
\text{PRED} & \text{`GIRL'} \\
\text{X} & \text{Y} \\
\text{Z} & \text{W}
\end{bmatrix}
$$

Substituting this for the original SUBJ value yields another solution for (25)–(27). This addition procedure, which defines a partial ordering on the set of f-structures, can be repeated indefinitely. In general, if an f-description has one solution, it has an infinite number of "larger" solutions.

Of course, there is something counterintuitive about these larger solutions. The extra features they contain cannot conflict with those specifically required by the f-description. In that sense they are grammatically irrelevant and should not really count as f-structures that the grammar assigns to sentences. This intuition, that we only countenance f-structures with relevant attributes and values, can be formalized in a technical refinement to our previous definitions that makes "*the* f-structure of a sentence" a well-defined notion.

Looking at the partial ordering from the opposite direction, an f-description may also have solutions smaller than a given one. These are formed by removing various combinations of its pairs (for example, removing the X–Y, Z–W pairs from (55) produces the smaller original solution in (40)). Some smaller f-structures are too small to be solutions of the f-description, in that they do not contain pairs that the f-description requires. For example, if the SPEC feature is removed from (55), the resulting structure will not satisfy equation (27a). We say that an f-structure F is a *minimal* solution for an f-description if it meets all of the f-description's requirements and if no smaller f-structure also meets those requirements.

A minimal solution exists for every consistent f-description. By definition, each has at least one solution. Either that one is minimal, or there is a smaller solution. If that one is also not minimal, there is another, still smaller, solution. Since an f-structure has only a finite number of pairs to begin with, there are only a finite number of smaller f-structures. This sequence will therefore stop at a minimal solution after a finite number of steps.

However, the minimal solution of an f-description is not necessarily unique. The fact that f-structures are partially but not totally ordered means that there can be two distinct solutions to an f-description both of which are minimal but neither of which is smaller than the other. This would be the case for an f-description that contained the equation (56), asserting that the subject and object have the same person, if other equations were not included to specify that common feature's value.

(56)

($\uparrow$ SUBJ PERSON) = ($\uparrow$ OBJ PERSON)

Any f-structure that is a minimal solution for all other equations of the f-description and contains any value at all for both the OBJ and SUBJ person features will also be a minimal solution for the larger f-description that includes (56). The values FIRST, SECOND, or THIRD, for instance, would all satisfy (56), but an f-structure without *some* person value would not be a solution. An f-description that does not have a unique minimal solution is called *indeterminate*. In effect, such an f-description does not have enough independent specifications for the number of unknown entities that it mentions.

We can now formulate a precise condition on the well-formedness of a string:

(57)

Condition on Grammaticality

A string is grammatical only if it has a valid c-structure with an associated f-description that is both consistent and determinate. The f-structure assigned to the string is the value in the f-description's unique minimal solution of the $\downarrow$-variable of the c-structure's root node. This condition is necessary but not sufficient for grammaticality; we later postulate additional requirements. As presented above, our solution algorithm decides whether or not the f-description is consistent and, if it is, constructs one solution for it. We observe that if no place-holders remain in that solution, it is the unique minimal solution: if any attribute or value is changed or removed, the resulting structure is not a solution since it no longer satisfies the equation the processing of which gave rise to that attribute or value. On the other hand, if there are residual place-holders in the f-structure produced by the algorithm, the f-description is indeterminate. Those place-holders can be replaced by any number of values to yield minimal solutions. Our algorithm is thus a decision procedure for all the functional conditions on grammaticality specified in (57).

4.5 Functional Well-formedness

The functional well-formedness conditions of our theory cause strings with otherwise valid c-structures to be marked ungrammatical. Our functional component thus acts as a filter on the output of the c-structure component, but in a sense that is very different from the way surface structure filtering has been used in transformational theory (e.g., Chomsky and Lasnik 1977). We do not allow arbitrary predicates to be applied to the c-structure output. Rather, we expect that a substantive linguistic theory will make available a universal set of grammatical functions and features and indicate how these may be assigned to particular lexical items and particular c-structure configurations. The most important of our well-formedness conditions, the Uniqueness Condition,[13] merely ensures that these assignments for a particular sentence are globally consistent so that its f-structure exists. Other general well-formedness conditions, the Completeness and Coherence Conditions, guarantee that grammatical functions and lexical predicates appear in mutually compatible f-structure configurations.

Consider the string (58), which is ungrammatical because the numbers of the final determiner and noun disagree:

(58)
*A girl handed the baby a toys.

The only f-description difference between this and our previous example is that the lexical entry for *toys* produces the equation (59) instead of (27l):

(59)
$(f_5 \text{ NUM}) = \text{PL}$

A conflict between the lexical specifications for *a* and *toys* arises because their schemata are attached to daughters of the same NP node. Some of the properties of that node's f-structure are specified by the determiner's lexical schemata and some by the noun's. According to the Uniqueness Condition, all properties attributed to it must be compatible if that f-structure is to exist. In the solution process for (58), f_5 will have the tentative value shown in (60) when equation (59) is encountered in place of (27l). The value of the lefthand designator is the symbol SG, which is incompatible with the PL value of the righthand designator. These two symbols cannot be merged.

(60)

$$f_5 \begin{bmatrix} \text{SPEC} & \text{A} \\ \text{NUM} & \text{SG} \end{bmatrix}$$

The consistency requirement is a general mechanism for enforcing grammatical compatibilities among lexical items widely separated in

the c-structure. The items and features that will enter into an agreement
are determined by both lexical and grammatical schemata. Number
agreement for English subjects and verbs illustrates a compatibility that
operates over a somewhat wider scope than agreement for determiners
and nouns. It accounts for the unacceptability of (61):

(61)
*The girls hands the baby a toy.

The grammar fragment in (21) needs no further elaboration in order to
reject this string. The identification on the VP in (21a) indicates that one
f-structure corresponds to both the S and the VP nodes. This implies
that any constraints imposed on a SUBJ function by the verb will in fact
apply to the SUBJ of the sentence as a whole, the f-structure corresponding to the first NP. Thus, the following lexical entry for *hands*
ensures that it will not cooccur with the plural subject *girls:*

(62)
hands: V, ($\uparrow$ TENSE) = PRESENT
$\quad\quad\quad\quad$ ($\uparrow$ SUBJ NUM) = SG
$\quad\quad\quad\quad$ ($\uparrow$ PRED) = 'HAND$\langle$($\uparrow$ SUBJ) ($\uparrow$ OBJ2) ($\uparrow$ OBJ)$\rangle$'

The middle schema, which is contributed by the present tense morpheme, specifies the number of the verb's subject. It is instantiated as
(63a), and this is inconsistent with (63b), which would be derived from
the lexical entry for *girls:*

(63)
a. $\quad$ (f_3 SUBJ NUM) = SG
b. $\quad$ (f_2 NUM) = PL

The conflict emerges because f_2 is the SUBJ of f_1, and f_1 is equal to f_3.

$\quad$ We rely on violations of the Uniqueness Condition to enforce many
cooccurrence restrictions besides those that are normally thought of as
agreements. For example, the restrictions among the elements in an
English auxiliary sequence can be handled in this way, even though the
matching of features does not at first seem to be involved. There is a
natural way of coding the lexical features of auxiliaries, participles, and
tensed verbs so that the "affix-hopping" phenomena follow as a consequence of the consistency requirement. Auxiliaries can be treated as
main verbs that take embedded VP' complements. We expand our
grammar as shown in (64) in order to derive the appropriate c-structures. (The optional *to* permitted by rule (64b), while necessary for

other types of VP complements, does not appear with most auxiliary heads. This restriction could be imposed by an additional schema.)

(64)

a.   VP → V $\begin{pmatrix} \text{NP} \\ (\uparrow \text{OBJ})=\downarrow \end{pmatrix} \begin{pmatrix} \text{NP} \\ (\uparrow \text{OBJ2})=\downarrow \end{pmatrix} \begin{matrix} \text{PP*} \\ (\uparrow (\downarrow \text{PCASE}))=\downarrow \end{matrix} \begin{pmatrix} \text{VP}' \\ (\uparrow \text{VCOMP})=\downarrow \end{pmatrix}$

b.   VP′ → (*to*)   VP
$\qquad\qquad\quad \uparrow=\downarrow$

Rule (64a) allows an optional VP′ following the other VP constituents. Of course, auxiliaries exclude all the VP possibilities except the VCOMP; this is enforced by general completeness and coherence conventions, as described below. For the moment, we focus on their affix cooccurrence restrictions, which are represented by schemata in the lexical entries for verbs. Each nonfinite verb will have a schema indicating that it is an infinitive or a participle of a particular type, and each auxiliary will have an equation stipulating the inflectional form of its VCOMP. (A small number of additional features are needed to account for the finer details of auxiliary ordering and for other cooccurrence restrictions, as noted for example by Akmajian, Steele, and Wasow 1979.) The lexical entries in (65)–(66) are for *handing* considered as a present participle (as opposed to a past tense or passive participle form) and for *is* as a progressive auxiliary:[14]

(65)

handing: V, (↑ PARTICIPLE) = PRESENT
$\qquad\qquad$ (↑ PRED) = 'HAND⟨(↑ SUBJ) (↑ OBJ2) (↑ OBJ)⟩'

(66)

is: V,$\qquad$ a. (↑ TENSE) = PRESENT
$\qquad\qquad$ b. (↑ SUBJ NUM) = SG
$\qquad\qquad$ c. (↑ PRED) = 'PROG⟨(↑ VCOMP)⟩'
$\qquad\qquad$ d. (↑ VCOMP PARTICIPLE) = PRESENT
$\qquad\qquad$ e. (↑ VCOMP SUBJ) = (↑ SUBJ)

Schema (66d) stipulates that the PARTICIPLE feature of the verb phrase complement must have the value PRESENT. The VCOMP is defined in (64a) as the ↓ f-structure of the VP′ node, and this is identified with the ↓ f-structure of the VP node by the schema in (64b). This means that the PARTICIPLE stipulations for *handing* and *is* both hold of the same f-structure. Hence, sentence (67a) is accepted but (67b) is rejected because *has* demands of its VCOMP a non-PRESENT participle:

(67)

a.   A girl is handing the baby a toy.

b.   *A girl has handing the baby a toy.

Schemata (66c,e) deserve special comment. The semantic form for *is* specifies that the logical formula derived by interpreting the VCOMP function is the single argument of a predicate for progressiveness. Even though the f-structure for (67a) will include a SUBJ function at the level of the PROG predicate, that function does not serve as an argument of PROG. Instead, it is asserted by (66e) to be equivalent to the SUBJ at the *handing* level. This would not otherwise exist, because there is no subject NP in the VP' expansion. The effect is that the *girl* is correctly interpreted as the first argument of HAND. (66e) is an example of a schema for *functional control,* which we will discuss more fully below.

These illustrations of the filtering effect of the Uniqueness Condition have glossed over an important conceptual distinction. A schema is often included in a lexical entry or grammatical rule in order to *define* the value of some feature. That is, instantiations of that schema provide sufficient grounds for inserting the feature–value pair into the appropriate f-structure (assuming of course that there is no conflict with the value defined by other equations). However, sometimes the purpose of a schema is only to *constrain* a feature whose value is expected to be defined by a separate specification. The feature remains valueless when the f-description lacks that specification. Intuitively, the constraint is not satisfied in that case and the string is to be excluded. Constraints of this sort thus impose stronger well-formedness requirements than the definitional inconsistency discussed above.

Let us reexamine the restriction that schema (66d) imposes on the participle of the VCOMP of *is.* We have seen how this schema conspires with the lexical entries for *handing* (65) and *has* to account for the facts in (67). Intuitively, it seems that the same present participle restriction ought to account for the unacceptability of (68):

(68)

*A girl is hands the baby a toy.

This string will not be rejected, however, if *hands* has the lexical entry in (62) and (66d) is interpreted as a defining schema. The PARTICIPLE feature has no natural value for the finite verb *hands,* and (62) therefore has no specification at all for this feature. This permits (66d) to define the value PRESENT for that feature without risk of inconsistency, and the final f-structure corresponding to the *hands* VP will actually contain a PARTICIPLE–PRESENT pair. We have concluded that *hands* is a present participle just because *is* would like it to be that way! If, on the other hand, we interpret (66d) as a constraining schema, we are prevented from making this implausible inference and the string is appropriately rejected. The constraining interpretation is clearly preferable.

Introducing a special interpretation for f-description statements is not strictly necessary to account for these facts. We could allow only the defining interpretation of equations and still obtain the right pattern of results by means of additional feature specifications. For example, we could insist that there be a PARTICIPLE feature for every verbal form, even finite forms that are notionally not participles at all. The value for tensed forms might be NONE, and this would be distinct from and thus conflict with PRESENT and all other real values. The lexical entry for *hands* would become (69), and (68) would be ruled out even with a defining interpretation for (66d):

(69)
hands: V, ($\uparrow$ PARTICIPLE) = NONE
            ($\uparrow$ TENSE) = PRESENT
            ($\uparrow$ SUBJ NUM) = SG
            ($\uparrow$ PRED) = 'HAND$\langle$($\uparrow$ SUBJ) ($\uparrow$ OBJ2) ($\uparrow$ OBJ)$\rangle$'

There are two objections to the presence of such otherwise unmotivated features: they make the formal system more cumbersome for linguists to work with and less plausible as a characterization of the linguistic generalizations that children acquire. Lexical redundancy rules in the form of marking conventions provide a partial answer to both objections. A redundancy rule, for example, could assign special no-value schemata to every lexical entry that is not already marked for certain syntactic features. Then the NONE schema would not appear in the entry for *hands* but would still be available for consistency checking.

Although we utilize lexical redundancy rules to express a variety of other generalizations, we have chosen an explicit notational device to highlight the conceptual distinction between definitions and constraints. The ordinary equal-sign that has appeared in all previous examples indicates that a schema is definitional, while an equal-sign with the letter *c* as a subscript indicates that a schema expresses a constraint. With this notation, the lexical entry for *is* can be formulated more properly as (70):

(70)
is: V, (↑ TENSE) = PRESENT
    (↑ SUBJ NUM) = SG
    (↑ PRED) = 'PROG⟨(↑ VCOMP)⟩'
    (↑ VCOMP PARTICIPLE) =$_c$ PRESENT
    (↑ VCOMP SUBJ) = (↑ SUBJ)

The notational distinction is preserved when the schemata are instantiated, so that the statements in an f-description are also divided into two classes. Defining equations are interpreted by our solution algorithm in the manner outlined above and thus provide evidence for actually constructing satisfactory structures. Constraining equations are simply not given to the solution algorithm. They are reserved until all defining equations have been processed and all variables have been assigned final f-structure values. At that point, the constraining equations are evaluated, and the string is accepted only if they all turn out to be true. This difference in interpretation accurately reflects the conceptual distinction represented by the two types of equations. It also gives the right result for string (68): since the revised VCOMP requirement in (70) will be false for the f-structure constructed from its defining equations, that string will be rejected without adding the special NONE value to *hands*.

Whether or not a particular cooccurrence restriction should be enforced by consistency among defining equations or the later evaluation of constraining equations depends on the meaning that is most naturally assigned to the absence of a feature specification. A constraining equation is appropriate if, as in the examples above, an unspecified value is intended to be in conflict with all of a feature's real values. On the other hand, a value specification may be omitted for some features as an indication of vagueness, and the restriction is then naturally stated in terms of a defining equation.[15] The case features of English nouns seem to fall into this second category: only pronouns have explicit nominative/accusative markings; all other nouns are intuitively unmarked, yet may appear in either subject or object positions. The new subject-NP schema in (71) defines the subject's case to be NOM. The NOM value will thus be included in the f-structure for any sentence with a nominative pronoun or nonpronoun subject. Only strings with accusative pronouns in subject position will have inconsistent f-descriptions and be excluded.

(71)

$$\text{S} \rightarrow \quad \begin{matrix} \text{NP} \\ (\uparrow \text{ SUBJ})=\downarrow \\ (\downarrow \text{ CASE})=\text{NOM} \end{matrix} \quad \begin{matrix} \text{VP} \\ \uparrow=\downarrow \\ (\uparrow \text{ TENSE}) \end{matrix}$$

Defining schemata always assert particular values for features and thus always take the form of equations. For constraints, two nonequational specification formats also make sense. The new TENSE schema in (71), for example, is just a designator not embedded in an equality. An instantiation of such a constraint is satisfied just in case the expression has *some* value in the final f-structure; these are called *existential* constraints. The TENSE schema thus expresses the requirement that S-clauses must have tensed verbs and rules out strings like (72):

(72)

*A girl handing the baby a toy.

As with equational constraints, it is possible to achieve the effect of an existential schema by introducing ad hoc feature values (e.g., one that discriminates tensed forms from all other verbals), but this special constraint format more directly represents the intuitive content of the requirement.

Finally, constraints may also be formed by adding a negation operator to an equational or existential constraint. The sentence is then acceptable only if the constraint without the negation turns out to be false. Such constraints fall quite naturally within our formal framework and may simplify a variety of grammatical descriptions. The negative existential constraint in (73), for example, is one way of stipulating that the VP after the particle *to* in a VP' is untensed:

(73)

$$\text{VP}' \rightarrow \quad \begin{pmatrix} to \\ \neg \, (\uparrow \text{ TENSE}) \end{pmatrix} \quad \begin{matrix} \text{VP} \\ \uparrow=\downarrow \end{matrix}$$

According to these well-formedness conditions, strings are rejected when an f-structure cannot be found that simultaneously satisfies all the explicit defining and constraining statements in the f-description. LFG also includes implicit conventions whose purpose is to make sure that f-structures contain mutually compatible combinations of lexical predicates and grammatical functions. These conventions are defined in terms of a proper subset of all the features and functions that may be represented in an f-structure. That subset consists of all functions whose values can serve as arguments to semantic predicates,[16] such as subject and various objects and complements. We refer to these as the *governable grammatical functions*. A given lexical entry mentions only a few of the governable functions, and we say that that entry *governs* the ones it mentions. (For a fuller discussion of government in lexical-functional theory, see chapter 5 of this volume.) Our conditions of functional compatibility simply require that an f-structure contain all of the governable functions that the lexical entry of its predicate actually governs, and that it contain no other governable functions.

This compatibility requirement gives a natural account for many types of ill-formedness. The English c-structure grammar, for example, must permit verbs not followed by NP arguments so that ordinary intransitive sentences can be generated. However, the necessary intransitive VP rule can then be applied with a verb that normally requires objects to yield a c-structure and f-structure for ill-formed strings such as (74):

(74)
*The girl handed.

The unacceptability of this string follows from the fact that the lexical entry for *handed* governs the grammatical functions OBJ and OBJ2 or TO OBJ, which do not appear in its f-structure. On the other hand, there is nothing to stop the c-structure rule that generates objects from applying in strings such as (75), where the verb is intransitive.

(75)
*The girl fell the apple the dog.

This string exhibits the opposite kind of incompatibility: the governable functions OBJ and OBJ2 do appear in its f-structure but are not governed by the intransitive verb *fell*.

Stated in more technical terms, string (74) is ungrammatical because its f-structure is not *complete,* while (75) fails because its f-structure is not *coherent.* These properties of f-structures are precisely defined as follows:

(76)
Definitions of Completeness and Coherence
a.   An f-structure is *locally complete* if and only if it contains all the governable grammatical functions that its predicate governs. An

f-structure is *complete* if and only if it and all its subsidiary f-structures are locally complete.

b. An f-structure is *locally coherent* if an only if all the governable grammatical functions that it contains are governed by a local predicate. An f-structure is *coherent* if and only if it and all its subsidiary f-structures are locally coherent.

Functional compatibility then enters into our notion of grammaticality by way of the following obvious condition:

(77)

Grammaticality Condition

A string is grammatical only if it is assigned a complete and coherent f-structure.

Since coherence and completeness are defined in terms of local configurations of functions, there are straightforward ways of formally verifying that these conditions are satisfied. For example, a set of constraints that encode these requirements can be added to all f-descriptions by a simple redundancy convention. We identify a set of *governable designators* corresponding to the governable grammatical functions and a set of *governed designators* corresponding to the functions governed by a particular lexical entry. The set of governable designators for a language is simply a list of every designator that appears as an argument in a semantic form for at least one entry in the lexicon. Thus, the set of governable designators for English includes ($\uparrow$ SUBJ), ($\uparrow$ OBJ), ($\uparrow$ BY OBJ), ($\uparrow$ VCOMP), etc. The set of governed designators for a particular lexical entry then contains only those members of the governable list that appear in that entry. If existential constraints for all the governed designators are instantiated along with the other schemata in the lexical entry, then the f-structure in which the lexical predicate appears will be locally complete if and only if it satisfies all those constraints. The f-structure will be locally coherent if and only if *negative* existential constraints for all the governable but ungoverned designators are also satisfied. Under this interpretation, example (74) above is incomplete because its f-structure does not satisfy the constraining schema ($\uparrow$ OBJ) and (75) is incoherent because $\neg$ ($\uparrow$ OBJ) is not satisfied.

It is important to observe that a designator is considered to be governed by an entry if it appears anywhere in the entry, not solely in the semantic form argument-list (though to be governable, it must appear as an argument in *some* lexical entry). In particular, the designator may appear only in a functional control schema or only in a schema defining or constraining some feature. Thus, the lexical entry for *is* in (66) above is considered to govern the designator (↑ SUBJ) because of its appearance in both the number-defining schema and the control schema for the VCOMP's SUBJ. (↑ SUBJ), however, is not assigned to an argument in the semantic form 'PROG⟨(↑ VCOMP)⟩'.

A grammatical function is also considered to be governed by an entry even when its value is constrained to be a semantically empty syntactic formative. Among these formatives are the expletives *there* and *it,* plus the components of various idiomatic expressions (e.g., the idiomatic sense of *tabs* in the expression *keep tabs on*). The lexicon marks such items as being in ordinary syntactic categories (pronoun or noun, for example), but their schemata specify a symbol value for a FORM attribute instead of a semantic form value for a PRED attribute:

(78)
tabs: N, (↑ FORM) = TABS
      (↑ NUM) = PL

A *tabs* NP may appear in any c-structure NP position and will be assigned the associated grammatical function. The Coherence Condition ensures that that function is governed by the lexical head of the f-structure; (79) is ruled out for the same reason that (75) is ill-formed:

(79)
*The girl fell tabs.

If the f-structure is coherent, then its lexical head makes some specification about the *tabs* function. For the acceptable sentence (80), the lexical entry for the idiomatic *kept* has a constraining schema for the necessary FORM value, as illustrated in (81):

(80)
The girl kept tabs on the baby.

(81)
kept: V, (↑ TENSE) = PAST
      (↑ PRED) = 'OBSERVE⟨(↑ SUBJ) (↑ ON OBJ)⟩'
      (↑ OBJ FORM) =$_c$ TABS

This constraining schema precludes the OBSERVE reading of *kept* with the nonidiomatic OBJ in (82a) and also rejects OBJS with the wrong formative feature (82b):

(82)

a.   *The girl kept the dog on a baby.

b.   *The girl kept there on a baby.

The ill-formedness of (83), however, is not predicted from the functional compatibility conditions we have presented:

(83)

*The girl handed there tabs.

In this example a governed function serving as an argument to the predicate HAND has a semantically empty value. A separate condition of semantic completeness could easily be added to our grammaticality requirements, but such a restriction would be imposed independently by a semantic translation procedure. A separate syntactic stipulation is therefore unnecessary.

   In this section we have described several mechanisms for rejecting as functionally deviant strings that have otherwise valid c-structure derivations. The Uniqueness Condition is the most basic well-formedness requirement, since an f-structure does not even exist if it is not satisfied. If an f-structure does exist, it must satisfy any constraining schemata and the Completeness and Coherence Conditions must hold. The combined effect of these conventions is to impose very strong restrictions among the components of a sentence's f-structure and c-structure, so that semantic forms and grammatical formatives can appear only in the appropriate functional and constituent environments. Because of these functional well-formedness conditions, there is no need for a separate notion of c-structure subcategorization to guarantee that lexical cooccurrence restrictions are satisfied. Indeed, Grimshaw in preparation and Maling 1980 suggest that an account of lexical cooccurrences based on functional compatibility is superior to one based on subcategorization.

   These mechanisms ensure that syntactic compatibility holds between a predicate and its arguments. A sentence may have other elements, however, that are syntactically related to the predicate but are not syntactically restricted by it. These are the adverbial and prepositional modifiers that serve as *adjuncts* of a predicate. Although adjuncts and predicates must be associated in an f-structure so that the correct semantic relationship can be determined, adjuncts are not within range of a predicate's syntactic schemata. A predicate imposes neither category nor feature restrictions on its adjuncts, semantic appropriateness being the only requirement that must be satisfied. As the temporal adjuncts in sentence (84) illustrate, adjuncts do not even obey the Uniqueness Condition.

(84)
The girl handed the baby a toy on Tuesday in the morning.

Since adjuncts do not serve as arguments to lexical predicates, they are not governable functions and are thus also immune to the Completeness and Coherence Conditions.

Given the formal devices we have so far presented, there is no f-structure representation of adjuncts that naturally accounts for these properties. If an individual adjunct is assigned as the value of an attribute (e.g., TEMP, LOC, or simply ADJUNCT), the Uniqueness Condition is immediately applicable and syntactic cooccurrence restrictions can in principle be stated. However, the shared properties of adjuncts do follow quite naturally from a simple extension to the notion of what a possible value is. Besides the individual f-structure values for the basic grammatical relations, we allow the value of an attribute to be a *set* of f-structures. Values of this type are specified by a new kind of schema in which the membership symbol $\in$ appears instead of a defining or constraining equal-sign.

The membership schema $\downarrow \in (\uparrow$ ADJUNCTS$)$ in the VP rule (85), for example, indicates that the value of ADJUNCTS is a set containing the PP's f-structure as one of its elements.

(85)
$$\text{VP} \rightarrow \text{V} \quad \text{NP} \qquad \text{NP} \qquad \text{PP*}$$
$$\qquad\qquad (\uparrow \text{OBJ})=\downarrow \ (\uparrow \text{OBJ2})=\downarrow \ \downarrow\in(\uparrow \text{ADJUNCTS})$$

The * permits any number of adjuncts to be generated, and the $\downarrow$ metavariable will be instantiated differently for each one. The f-description for sentence (84) will thus have two membership statements, one for the *on Tuesday* PP and one for *in the morning*. These statements will be true only of an f-structure in which ADJUNCTS has a set value containing one element that satisfies all other statements associated with *on Tuesday* and another element satisfying the other statements of *in the morning*. The outline of such an f-structure is shown in (86):

(86)

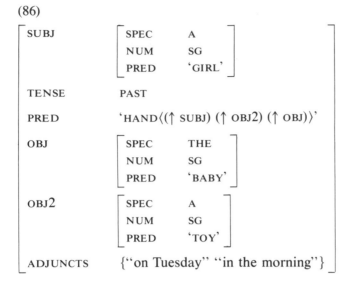

The braces in this representation surround the elements of the set value; they are distinct from the braces in c-structure rules that indicate alternative expansions. We have elided the adjuncts' internal functions since they are not immediately relevant to the issue at hand and are the topic of current syntactic and semantic research (e.g., chapter 6 of this volume and Halvorsen in preparation).

The peculiar properties of adjuncts now follow from the fact that they are treated syntactically as elements of sets. Membership statements define adjuncts to be elements of a predicate's adjunct "pool," but there is no requirement of mutual syntactic compatibility among the various elements. Hence, the Uniqueness Condition does not apply. Further, since there is no notation for subsequently referring to particular members of that set, there is no way that adjuncts can be restricted by lexical schemata associated with the predicate.[17] Adjuncts are susceptible only to conditions that can be stated on the rule elements that generate them. Their category can be specified, and feature requirements can be imposed by schemata involving the ↓ metavariable. Since reference to the adjunct via ↓ is not possible from other places in the string, our formal system makes adjuncts naturally context-free. (Conjoined elements are similar to adjuncts in some of these respects and might also be represented in an f-structure as sets.)

Although the PP in (85) appears in the same position as the oblique object PP category in our previous VP rule, the schemata on the two PP rule elements are quite different and apply to alternative lexical entries of the preposition. The oblique object requires the case-marking lexical entry (with the PCASE feature defined), while semantic translation of the adjunct requires the predicate alternative of the preposition. Adjuncts and oblique objects can both appear in the same sentence and in any order, as illustrated by (87a,b),[18] and sometimes a PP may be interpreted ambiguously as either an adjunct or an oblique object, as in (87c):

(87)
a.   The baby was handed the toy at five o'clock by the girl.
b.   The baby was handed the toy by the girl at five o'clock.
c.   The baby was handed the toy by the girl by the policeman.

To account for these facts, the adjunct possibility must be added as an alternative to the oblique object PP in our previous VP rule (64a). The star operator outside the braces in (88) means that the choice between the two PPs may be repeated arbitrarily.

(88)

$$\text{VP} \rightarrow \text{V} \begin{pmatrix} \text{NP} \\ (\uparrow \text{OBJ})=\downarrow \end{pmatrix} \begin{pmatrix} \text{NP} \\ (\uparrow \text{OBJ2})=\downarrow \end{pmatrix} \left\{ \begin{matrix} \text{PP} \\ (\uparrow (\downarrow \text{PCASE}))=\downarrow \\ \\ \text{PP} \\ \downarrow \in (\uparrow \text{ADJUNCTS}) \end{matrix} \right\}^* \begin{pmatrix} \text{VP}' \\ (\uparrow \text{VCOMP})=\downarrow \end{pmatrix}$$

An equivalent but more compact formulation of this rule is given in (89). We have factored the common elements of the two PP alternatives, moving the braces so that they enclose just the alternative schemata.

(89)

$$\text{VP} \rightarrow \text{V} \begin{pmatrix} \text{NP} \\ (\uparrow \text{OBJ})=\downarrow \end{pmatrix} \begin{pmatrix} \text{NP} \\ (\uparrow \text{OBJ2})=\downarrow \end{pmatrix} \text{PP}^* \left\{ \begin{matrix} (\uparrow (\downarrow \text{PCASE}))=\downarrow \\ \downarrow \in (\uparrow \text{ADJUNCTS}) \end{matrix} \right\} \begin{pmatrix} \text{VP}' \\ (\uparrow \text{VCOMP})=\downarrow \end{pmatrix}$$

A simple extension to our solution algorithm permits the correct interpretation of membership statements. We use a new operator *Include* for membership statements, just as we use *Merge* for equalities. If d_1 and d_2 are designators, a statement of the form $d_1 \in d_2$ is processed by performing Include[Locate[d_1], Locate[d_2]]. As formally defined in the appendix, the Include operator makes the value located for the first designator be an element of the set value located for the second designator; the f-description is marked inconsistent if that second value is known not to be a set. With this extension, our algorithm becomes a decision procedure for f-descriptions that contain both membership and equality statements.

4.6 Levels of Representation

We have now covered almost all the major structures and mechanisms of lexical-functional grammar, except for the bounded tree relations that govern long-distance grammatical dependencies. We postpone that discussion for still a few more pages in order to first review and reinforce some earlier claims.

We said at the outset that constituent structures and functional structures are formally quite different, and the descriptions of the preceding pages have amplified that point considerably. However, the mechanisms of our formal system—the immediate domination meta-variables and the various grammatical and lexical schemata—presuppose and also help to establish a very close, systematic connection between the two levels of representation. Our claim of formal distinctness would of course be meaningless if this close connection turned out to be an isomorphism, so it is worth describing and motivating some ways in which c-structures and f-structures for English diverge. We show that individual c-structure nodes are not isomorphic to subsidiary f-structures for particular sentences and, more generally, that there is no simple relationship between node configurations and grammatical functions.

We observe first that our instantiation procedure defines only a partial correspondence between c-structure nodes and subsidiary f-structures. There are both c-structure nodes with no corresponding f-structures and also f-structures that do not correspond to c-structure nodes. The former situation is illustrated in our previous examples by every c-structure node which is not assigned a ↓-variable and therefore has no ↓ f-structure. The English imperative construction gives a simple illustration of the latter case: the subsidiary f-structure representing 'YOU' as the "understood" subject is not associated with a c-structure node. Plausible c- and f-structures for the imperative sentence (90a) would be generated by the alternative expansion for S in (90b), assuming that the lexical entry for *hand* has a +-valued INF(initive) feature. (A more realistic example would specify an imperative mood marker and perhaps other features.)

(90)

a.   Hand the baby a toy.

b.   S $\rightarrow$ VP

$$\uparrow = \downarrow$$

$$(\uparrow \text{INF}) =_c +$$

$$(\uparrow \text{SUBJ PRED}) = \text{'YOU'}$$

With this rule, the c-structure contains no NP dominated by S, yet the $\downarrow$ f-structure of the S node has as its SUBJ another full-fledged f-structure, defined completely by grammatical schemata:

(91)

$$\begin{bmatrix} \text{SUBJ} & \begin{bmatrix} \text{PRED} & \text{'YOU'} \end{bmatrix} \\ \text{INF} & + \\ \text{PRED} & \text{'HAND}\langle(\uparrow \text{SUBJ})\,(\uparrow \text{OBJ2})\,(\uparrow \text{OBJ})\rangle\text{'} \\ \text{OBJ} & \begin{bmatrix} \text{SPEC} & \text{THE} \\ \text{NUM} & \text{SG} \\ \text{PRED} & \text{'BABY'} \end{bmatrix} \\ \text{OBJ2} & \begin{bmatrix} \text{SPEC} & \text{A} \\ \text{NUM} & \text{SG} \\ \text{PRED} & \text{'TOY'} \end{bmatrix} \end{bmatrix}$$

A standard transformational grammar provides a dummy NP as a deep structure subject so that the correct semantic interpretation can be constructed and the necessary cooccurrence restrictions enforced. Our functional subject is sufficient for these purposes; the dummy NP is without surface justification and therefore does not appear in the c-structure.

Second, when nodes and subsidiary f-structures do correspond, the correspondence is not necessarily one-to-one. An identification schema, for example, usually indicates that two distinct nodes are mapped onto a single f-structure. In (40) a single f-structure is assigned to the $\downarrow$-variables for both the S and VP nodes in the c-structure (24), in accordance with the identification equation (25b). The two distinct nodes exist in (24) to capture certain generalizations about phrase structure cooccurrences and phonological patterns. The identification has the effect of "promoting" the functional information associated with the VP so that it is at the same hierarchical level as the SUBJ. This brings the SUBJ within range of the PRED semantic form, simplifying the statement of the Completeness and Coherence Conditions and allowing a uniform treatment of subjects and objects. As noted above, this kind of promotion also permits lexical specification of certain contextual restrictions, such as subject–verb number agreements.

Let us now consider the relationship between configurations of c-structure nodes and grammatical functions. The imperative example shows that a single functional role can be filled from distinct node configurations. While it is true for English that an S-dominated NP always yields a SUBJ function, a SUBJ can come from other sources as well. The grammatical schema on the VP for the imperative actually defines the SUBJ's semantic form. For a large class of other examples, the understood subject (that is, not from an S–NP configuration) is supplied through a schema of *functional control*. Control schemata, which identify grammatical relations at two different levels in the f-structure hierarchy, offer a natural account for so-called "equi" and "raising" phenomena.[19]

Sentence (92) contains the equi-type verb *persuaded*. The intuitive interpretation of the *baby* NP in this sentence is as an argument of both PERSUADE and GO. This interpretation will be assigned if *persuaded* has the lexical entry (93), given our previous VP rule (88) and the new schemata in (94) for the VP''s optional *to*.

(92)
The girl persuaded the baby to go.

(93)
persuaded: V, $(\uparrow \text{TENSE}) = \text{PAST}$
$(\uparrow \text{PRED}) = \text{'PERSUADE}\langle(\uparrow \text{SUBJ}) (\uparrow \text{OBJ}) (\uparrow \text{VCOMP})\rangle\text{'}$
$(\uparrow \text{VCOMP TO}) =_c +$
$(\uparrow \text{VCOMP SUBJ}) = (\uparrow \text{OBJ})$

(94)
$$\text{VP}' \rightarrow \begin{pmatrix} to \\ (\uparrow \text{TO}) = + \\ (\uparrow \text{INF}) =_c + \end{pmatrix} \quad \begin{matrix} \text{VP} \\ \uparrow = \downarrow \end{matrix}$$

Our rules generate a c-structure in which *persuaded* is followed by an NP and a VP', where the VP' is expanded as a *to*-complement. This is shown in (95):

(95)

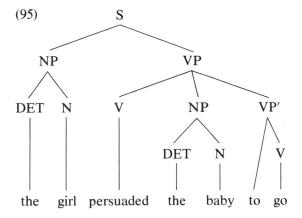

The f-structure for the *baby* NP becomes the OBJ of *persuaded* and the VP' provides the VCOMP. The control schema, the last one in (93), identifies the OBJ f-structure as being also the SUBJ of the VCOMP. That f-structure thus appears in two places in the functional hierarchy (96):

(96)

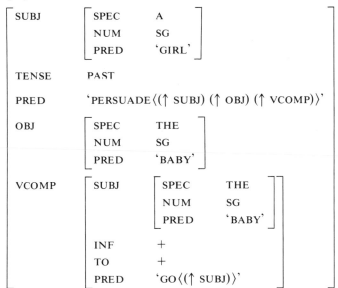

The complement in this f-structure has essentially the same grammatical relations that would be assigned to the *that*-complement sentence (97), even though the c-structure for the *that*-complement is quite different:

(97)
The girl persuaded the baby that the baby (should) go.

The contrast between oblique objects and adjuncts shows that similar c-structure configurations—a VP dominating a PP—can be mapped into distinct grammatical functions. A comparison of the equi verbs *persuaded* and *promised* provides another illustration of the same point. Sentence (98) is the result of substituting *promised* for *persuaded* in sentence (92):

(98)
The girl promised the baby to go.

This substitution does not change the c-structure configurations, but for (98) the *girl*, not the *baby*, is understood as an argument of both the matrix and complement predicates. This fact is easily accounted for if the control schema in the lexical entry for *promised* identifies the complement SUBJ with the matrix SUBJ instead of the matrix OBJ:

(99)
promised: V, ($\uparrow$ TENSE) = PAST
$\qquad$ ($\uparrow$ PRED) = 'PROMISE$\langle$($\uparrow$ SUBJ) ($\uparrow$ OBJ) ($\uparrow$ VCOMP)$\rangle$'
$\qquad$ ($\uparrow$ VCOMP TO) =$_c$ +
$\qquad$ ($\uparrow$ VCOMP SUBJ) = ($\uparrow$ SUBJ)

With this lexical entry, the f-structure for (98) correctly defines GIRL as the argument of GO in (100). The f-structure difference for the two types of equi verbs thus follows from the differing functional control schemata in their lexical entries, not from any c-structure difference.

(100)

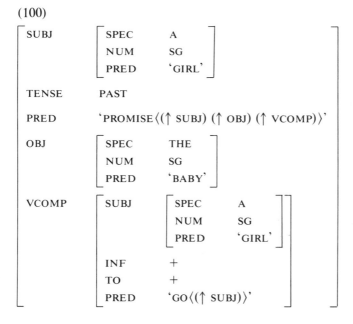

From a formal point of view, there is no restriction on which grammatical relations in the matrix and complement may be identified by a schema for functional control. Very strong limitations, however, are imposed by the substantive linguistic theory that is based on our lexical-functional formalism. As discussed in chapter 5, the functional control schemata of human languages universally identify the SUBJ of a complement with the SUBJ, OBJ, or OBJ2 of the matrix. (The TOPIC function in English relative clauses and in *tough*-movement constructions may also be functionally controlled, as described in section 4.7.) Control schemata for VP complements different from those above for *promised* and *persuaded* may not appear in the grammar or lexicon of any human language. This universal stipulation explains the familiar contrast in the passivization behavior of *persuade* and *promise:*

(101)

a.   The baby was persuaded to go by the girl.

b.   *The baby was promised to go by the girl.

In chapter 1 it was argued that the systematic relationship between actives and their corresponding passives can be expressed by a universal lexical rule. In simple terms, this rule asserts that for any language, if an active lexical entry for a stem mentions the SUBJ and OBJ functions, then there is a passive lexical entry based on the same stem in which SUBJ is replaced by an oblique-object function and OBJ is replaced by SUBJ. For English, the passive oblique object is marked by the preposition *by*, so the English instance of this universal rule is as follows. (See chapter 1 of this volume for a discussion of the morphological changes that go along with these functional replacements.)

(102)

$(\uparrow \text{SUBJ}) \mapsto (\uparrow \text{BY OBJ})$
$(\uparrow \text{OBJ}) \mapsto (\uparrow \text{SUBJ})$ $(\uparrow \text{PARTICIPLE}) = \text{PASSIVE}$

This rule indicates the replacements to be performed and also specifies that a PARTICIPLE schema appears in passive entries in addition to other schemata derived from the stem. Accordingly, the passive lexical entries based on the stems underlying the past tense forms *persuaded* and *promised* are as follows:

(103)

a.   persuaded: V, $(\uparrow \text{PARTICIPLE}) = \text{PASSIVE}$
          $(\uparrow \text{PRED}) = \text{`PERSUADE}\langle(\uparrow \text{BY OBJ})\ (\uparrow \text{SUBJ})\ (\uparrow \text{VCOMP})\rangle\text{'}$
          $(\uparrow \text{VCOMP TO}) = _c +$
          $(\uparrow \text{VCOMP SUBJ}) = (\uparrow \text{SUBJ})$

b.   promised: V, $(\uparrow \text{PARTICIPLE}) = \text{PASSIVE}$
          $(\uparrow \text{PRED}) = \text{`PROMISE}\langle(\uparrow \text{BY OBJ})\ (\uparrow \text{SUBJ})\ (\uparrow \text{VCOMP})\rangle\text{'}$
          $(\uparrow \text{VCOMP TO}) = _c +$
          $(\uparrow \text{VCOMP SUBJ}) = (\uparrow \text{BY OBJ})$

Notice that $(\uparrow \text{SUBJ})$ and $(\uparrow \text{OBJ})$, the lefthand designators in the lexical rule, are replaced inside semantic forms as well as in schemata. The control schema in (103a) conforms to the universal restriction on functional control, but the one in (103b) does not. Since (103b) is not a possible lexical entry, *promise* may not be passivized when it takes a VP complement.

We have argued that the *to*-complement and *that*-complement of *persuaded* have essentially the same internal functions. The sentences (92) and (97) in which those complements are embedded are not exact paraphrases, however. The *that*-complement sentence allows a reading in which two separate babies are being discussed, while for sentence (92) there is only one baby who is an argument of both PERSUADE and GO. This difference in interpretation is more obvious when quantifiers are involved: (104a) and (104b) are roughly synonymous, and neither is equivalent to (104c).

(104)
a. The girl persuaded every baby to go.
b. The girl persuaded every baby that he should go.
c. The girl persuaded every baby that every (other) baby should go.

Since semantic translation is defined on functional structure, f-structures must mark the difference between occurrences of similar subsidiary f-structures where semantic coreferentiality is implied, as in the *to*-complement, and occurrences where the similarity is only accidental.

The necessary f-structure distinction follows from a simple formal property of semantic forms that we now introduce. The semantic form representations that appear in schemata are treated as "meta" semantic forms, templates for an infinite number of distinct "actual" semantic forms. Just as an actual variable is substituted for a metavariable by the instantiation procedure, so a metaform is replaced by a unique actual form, identified by attaching an index to the predicate-argument specification. A given schema, say (105a), might be instantiated as (105b) at one node in the tree and (105c) at another:

(105)
a. $(\uparrow$ PRED$) = $ 'BABY'
b. $(f_4$ PRED$) = $ 'BABY'$_1$
c. $(f_6$ PRED$) = $ 'BABY'$_2$

F-description statements and f-structures thus contain recognizably distinct instances of the semantic forms in the grammar and lexicon. Each indexed actual form enters into predicate-argument relations as indicated by the metaform, but the different instances are not considered identical for the purposes of semantic translation or functional uniqueness.

Returning to the two complements of *persuaded,* we observe that only one schema with 'BABY' is involved in the derivation of the *to*-complement, while two such schemata are instantiated for the *that*-complement. The indices of the two occurrences of 'BABY' are therefore the same in the indexed version of the *to*-complement's f-structure (106) but different in the f-structure for the *that*-complement (107). ((107) ignores such details as the tense and mood of the *that*-complement.)

(106)

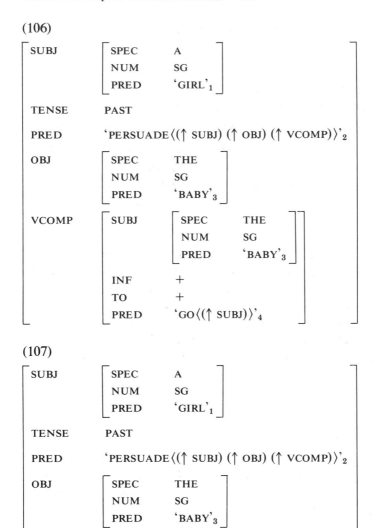

(107)

The semantic contrast between the two complement types is marked in these f-structures by the differing patterns of semantic form indexing.

It is technically correct to include indices with all semantic forms in f-descriptions and f-structures, but the nonidentity of two forms with dissimilar predicate-argument specifications is clear even without explicit indexing. We adopt the following convention to simplify our representations: two semantic form occurrences are assumed to be distinct unless they have the same predicate-argument specification and the same index. With this convention, only the indices on the BABY semantic forms are necessary in (106), and none of the indices are needed in (107). Control equations imply that entire substructures to which co-indexed semantic forms belong will appear redundantly in several positions in an enclosing f-structure. This suggests a stronger abbreviatory convention which also highlights the cases of f-structure identity. The internal properties of a multiply-appearing subsidiary f-structure are displayed at only one place in an enclosing f-structure. The fact that it is also the value of other attributes is then indicated by drawing lines from the location of those other attributes to the fully expanded value:

(108)

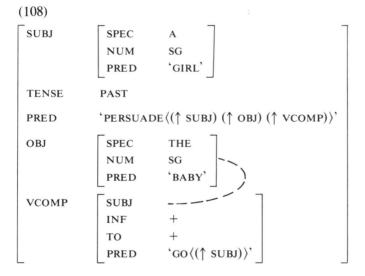

This graphical connection makes it clear even without explicit indices on 'BABY' that the object f-structure serves in several functional roles.

While a semantic form instance occurring in several positions indicates semantic coreferentiality, different instances are seen as both semantically and functionally distinct. This means that any attempt to equate different instances will violate the Uniqueness Condition, even if they have the same predicate-argument specification. This is an important consequence of the semantic form instantiation procedure. For

example, it rules out an analysis of string (109) in which both prepositional phrases are merged together as the BY OBJ, even though the PP
f-structures agree in all other features:

(109)
*The baby was given a toy by the girl by the girl.

As another example, the distinctness of semantic form instances permits a natural description of English subject–auxiliary inversion. As
shown in (110), the auxiliary can occur either before or after the subject, but it must appear in one and not both of those positions.

(110)
a.   A girl is handing the baby a toy.
b.   Is a girl handing the baby a toy?
c.   *A girl the baby a toy.
d.   *Is a girl is handing the baby a toy?

In transformational theories, facts of this sort are typically accounted
for by a rule that moves a single base-generated item from one position
to another. Since no transformational apparatus is included in LFG, we
must allow the c-structure grammar to optionally generate the auxiliary
in both positions, for example, by means of the following modified S
and VP rules:

(111)

a. $S \rightarrow \begin{pmatrix} V \\ (\downarrow AUX)=_c+ \end{pmatrix} \quad \begin{matrix} NP \\ (\uparrow SUBJ)=\downarrow \\ (\downarrow CASE)=NOM \end{matrix} \quad \begin{matrix} VP \\ \uparrow=\downarrow \\ (\uparrow TENSE) \end{matrix}$

b. $VP \rightarrow$
$(V) \begin{pmatrix} NP \\ (\uparrow OBJ)=\downarrow \end{pmatrix} \begin{pmatrix} NP \\ (\uparrow OBJ2)=\downarrow \end{pmatrix} \begin{matrix} PP^* \\ \left\{\begin{matrix} (\uparrow (\downarrow PCASE))=\downarrow \\ \downarrow\in(\uparrow ADJUNCTS) \end{matrix}\right\} \end{matrix} \begin{pmatrix} VP' \\ (\uparrow VCOMP)=\downarrow \end{pmatrix}$

These rules provide c-structure derivations for all the strings in (110).
However, (110c) is incoherent because there are no PREDs for the NP
arguments, and it also fails to satisfy the TENSE existential constraint.
The f-description for (110d) is inconsistent because the separately instantiated semantic forms for *is* are both assigned as its PRED. The AUX
constraint in (111a) permits only verbs marked with the AUX feature to
be fronted.

In section 4.5 we treated the auxiliary *is* as a main verb taking an
embedded VP complement with a control schema identifying the ma-

trix and embedded subjects (see (70)). *Is* is unlike *persuaded* and *promised* in that the f-structure serving two functional roles is not an argument of two predicates: SUBJ does not appear in the semantic form 'PROG⟨(↑ VCOMP)⟩'. The wider class of raising verbs differs from equi verbs in just this respect. Thus, the lexical entry for PERSUADE maps the *baby* f-structure in (108) into argument positions of both PERSUADE and GO. The OBJ of the raising verb *expected,* however, is an argument only of the complement's predicate, as stipulated in the lexical entry (112):

(112)
expected: V, (↑ TENSE) = PAST
    (↑ PRED) = 'EXPECT⟨(↑ SUBJ) (↑ VCOMP)⟩'
    (↑ VCOMP TO) =$_c$ +
    (↑ VCOMP SUBJ) = (↑ OBJ)

Except for the semantic form change, the f-structure for sentence (113a) is identical to (108). This minor change is sufficient to account for the well-known differences in the behavior of these two classes of verbs, as illustrated by (113b) and (113c) (see chapter 1 for a fuller discussion).

(113)
a. The girl expected the baby to go.
b. The girl expected there to be an earthquake.
c. *The girl persuaded there to be an earthquake.

The difference between the raising and equi semantic forms shows that the set of grammatical relations in an f-structure cannot be identified with argument positions in a semantic translation. This is evidence for our early claim that the functional level is also distinct from the semantic level of representation. A stronger justification for this distinction comes from considerations of quantifier scope ambiguities. The sentence (114a) has a single f-structure, yet it has two semantic translations or interpretations, corresponding to the readings (114b) and (114c):

(114)
a. Every man voted in an election.
b. 'There was an election such that every man voted in it.'
c. 'For every man there was an election such that he voted in it.'

The *election* quantifier has narrow scope in (114b) and wide scope in (114c). This ambiguity is not represented at the level of syntactic functions since no syntactic generalizations depend on it. Instead, the alternative readings are generated by the procedure that produces semantic translations or interpretations for f-structures. (This line of argumentation was suggested by P. K. Halvorsen (personal communication). Halvorsen 1980 and forthcoming gives a detailed description of a translation procedure with multiple outputs.)

The distinctions among c-structure, f-structure, and semantic structure are supported by another scope-related phenomenon. Sentence (115a) also has two readings, as indicated in (115b) and (115c):

(115)
a. Everybody has wisely selected their successors.
b. 'Wisely, everybody has selected their successors (i.e., it is wise of everybody to have selected their successors).'
c. 'Everybody selected their successors in a wise manner.'

The adverb has sentence scope in (115b) and so-called VP scope in (115c). The single f-structure for this sentence not only fails to represent the ambiguity but also fails even to preserve a VP unit to which the narrow scope might be attached. The f-structure is flattened to facilitate the statement of certain syntactic cooccurrence restrictions, to simplify the Completeness and Coherence Conditions, as mentioned above, and also to permit simple specifications of control relations. Independent motivation for our proposal that the scope of semantic operators is not tied to a VP c-structure node or an f-structure corresponding to it comes from Modern Irish, a VSO language that nonetheless exhibits this kind of ambiguity (McCloskey 1979).

We have shown that functional structure in LFG is an autonomous level of linguistic description. Functional structure contains a mixture of syntactically and semantically motivated information, but it is distinct from both constituent structure and semantic representation. Of course, we have not demonstrated the necessity of such an intermediate level for mapping between surface sequences and predicate-argument relations. Indeed, Gazdar to appear b argues that a much more direct mapping is possible. In Gazdar's approach, the semantic connection between a functional controller and controllee, for example, is established by semantic translation rules defined directly on c-structure configurations. The semantic representation for the embedded complement includes a logical variable that is bound to the controller in the semantic representation of the matrix. It seems, however, that there are language-particular and universal generalizations that have no natural expression without an f-structure-like intermediate level. For example, in addition to semantic connections, functional control linkages seem to transmit purely syntactic elements—expletives like *it* and *there,* syntactic case-marking features (chapter 7 of this volume and Andrews to appear), and semantically empty idiom chunks. Without an f-structure level, either a separate feature propagation mechanism must be introduced to handle this kind of dependency in the c-structure, or otherwise unmotivated semantic entities or types must be introduced so that semantic filtering mechanisms can be applied to the syntactic elements. As another example, it is argued in chapter 9 of this volume that a natural account of sluicing constructions requires the mixture of information found in f-structures. And finally, it is observed in chapters 1, 5, and 8 of this volume and in Mohanan to appear, that universal characterizations of lexical rules and rules of anaphora are stated more naturally in terms of grammatical functions than in terms of phrase structure configurations or properties of semantic representations. Further investigation should provide even stronger justification for functional structure as an essential and independent level of linguistic description.

4.7 Long-Distance Dependencies

We now turn to the formal mechanisms for characterizing the long-distance grammatical dependencies such as those that arise in English questions and relatives. As is well known, in these constructions an element at the front of a clause is understood as filling a particular grammatical role within the clause. Exactly which grammatical function it serves is determined primarily by the arrangement of c-structure nodes inside the clause. The *who* before the indirect question clause is understood as the subject of the question in (116a) but as the object in (116b):

(116)
a.   The girl wondered who ____ saw the baby.
b.   The girl wondered who the baby saw ____.
c.   *The girl wondered who ____ saw ____.
d.   *The girl wondered who the baby saw the toy.

In both cases, *who* is assigned the clause-internal function appropriate to the c-structure position marked by the blank, a position where an expected element is missing. Examples (116c,d) indicate that there must be one and only one missing element. Sentence (117), in which the *who* is understood as the object of a clause embedded inside the question, shows the long-distance nature of this kind of dependency:

(117)
The girl wondered who John believed that Mary claimed that the baby saw ___.

Sentence (118), however, demonstrates the well-known fact that the regions of the c-structure that such dependencies may cover are limited in some way, although not simply by distance:

(118)
*The girl wondered who John believed that Mary asked who ___ saw ___.

The dependencies illustrated in these sentences are examples of what we call *constituent control*. As with functional control, constituent control establishes a syntactic identity between elements that would otherwise be distinct. (The term *syntactic binding* is sometimes used as a synonym for *constituent control*.) In the case of functional control, the linkage is between the entities filling particular functional roles and, as described in section 4.6, is determined by lexical schemata that are very restricted substantively. Functional control schemata identify particular functions (such as SUBJ or OBJ) at one f-structure level with the SUBJ of a particular complement. Linkages over apparently longer distances, as in (119), are decomposed into several strictly local identifications, each of which links a higher function to the SUBJ one level down.

(119)
John persuaded the girl to be convinced to go.

The f-description for this example contains statements that equate the OBJ of *persuaded* with the SUBJ of *be,* the SUBJ of *be* with the SUBJ of *convinced,* and finally the SUBJ of *convinced* with the SUBJ of *go.* The fact that *girl* is understood as the subject of *go* then follows from the transitivity of the equality relation. However, it is characteristic of functional control that *girl* also bears grammatical relations to all the intermediate verbs, and that the intermediate verbs necessarily carry the required control schemata. A long-distance functional linkage can be made unacceptable by an intermediate lexical change that has no c-structure consequences:

(120)
a.   There was expected to be an earthquake.
b.   *There was persuaded to be an earthquake.

The f-structure becomes semantically incomplete when the equi verb *persuaded* is substituted for the intervening raising verb.

Constituent control differs from functional control in that constituent structure configurations, not functional relations, are the primary conditioning factors. As noted in (112), at one end of the linkage (called the *constituent controllee*), the clause-internal function may be determined by the position of a c-structure gap. The relative clause in (121) demonstrates that the c-structure environment alone can also define the other end of the linkage (called the *constituent controller*):

(121)
The toy the girl handed _____ to the baby was big.

This sentence has no special words to signal that *toy* must enter into a control relationship. Finally, the linked entity bears no grammatical relation to any of the predicates that the constituent dependency covers (e.g., *believed* and *claimed* in (117)), and there are no functional requirements on the material that may intervene between the controller and the controllee. Instead, the restrictions on possible linkages involve the configuration of nodes on the controller–controllee c-structure path: for example, the interrogative complement of *asked* on the controller–controllee path in (118) is the source of that string's ungrammaticality.

Decomposing these long-distance constituent dependencies into chains of functional identifications would require introducing otherwise unmotivated functions at intermediate f-structure levels. Such a decomposition therefore cannot be justified. A strategy for avoiding spurious functions is to specify these linkages by sets of alternative direct functional identifications. One alternative would link the *who* to the SUBJ of the clause for (116a), and a second alternative would link to the OBJ for (116b). Question clauses with one embedded sentential complement would require alternatives for the SCOMP SUBJ and SCOMP OBJ; the two embeddings in (117) would require SCOMP SCOMP OBJ; and so on. This strategy has an obvious difficulty: without a bound on the functional distance over which this kind of dependency can operate, the necessary alternative identifications cannot be finitely specified.[20] The functional apparatus of our theory thus does not permit an adequate account of these phenomena.

If a single constituent contains no more than one controllee, it is possible to encode enough information in the c-structure categories to ensure a correspondence between controllers and controllees, as suggested by Gazdar to appear b. This encoding obviously captures the fact that these dependencies are sensitive to constituent configurations. Gazdar also shows that appropriate semantic representations can be defined by translations associated with the phrase structure rules. Maling and Zaenen 1980 point out that this approach becomes considerably less attractive if a single constituent can contain more than one controllee, as in the familiar interaction of *tough*-movement and questions in English:

(122)
I wonder which violin the sonatas are easy to play ___ on ___.

Furthermore, no encoding into a finite number of categories is possible for languages such as Swedish and Norwegian, for which, according to Maling and Zaenen to appear and Engdahl 1980a,b, no natural limit can be set on the number of controllees in a single constituent.

Our problem, then, is to provide a formal mechanism for representing long-distance constituent dependencies that does not require unmotivated grammatical functions or features, allows for an unbounded number of controllees in a single constituent, and permits a succinct statement of the generalizations that govern grammatical phenomena of this sort. The necessary descriptive apparatus is found in the formal interpretation of *bounded domination metavariables*.

The bounded domination metavariables $\Uparrow$ and $\Downarrow$ are similar to the immediate domination variables $\uparrow$ and $\downarrow$ in that they appear in grammatical and lexical schemata but are instantiated with actual variables when the f-description is formed. The instantiation procedure for both kinds of variables has the effect of substituting the same actual variable for matched metavariables attached to different nodes in the c-structure. The difference is that for a matched $\uparrow$–$\downarrow$ pair, the schemata must be attached to nodes in a relationship of immediate domination, while matching $\Downarrow$ and $\Uparrow$ may be attached to nodes separated in the tree by a longer path. These are called "bounded domination metavariables" because that path is limited by the occurrence of certain "bounding" nodes. The ⇓ metavariable is attached to a node at the upper end of the path and represents the controller of a constituent control relationship. (Technically, the terms *controller* and *controllee* refer to the bounded domination metavariables and not to the nodes that they are attached to. In this respect, we depart from the way these terms have been used in other theoretical frameworks.) The matching ⇑ is lower in the tree and represents the controllee of the relationship. The instantiation procedure for these variables establishes the long-distance identification of the controller and controllee directly, without reliance on transitive chains of intervening equations.

We illustrate the general properties of our mechanism with a simple example, suppressing for the moment a number of formal and linguistic details. Consider the indirect question sentence (116b), repeated here for convenience:

(116)

b.   The girl wondered who the baby saw ____.

We assume that the predicate for *wondered* takes an interrogative complement argument, as indicated in the lexical entry (123):[21]

(123)
wondered: V, (↑ TENSE) = PAST
             (↑ PRED) = 'WONDER⟨(↑ SUBJ) (↑ SCOMP)⟩'

According to the rules in (124), SCOMPs are based on constituents in the category S', and S' expands as an NP followed by an S:

(124)
a.   VP → V   S'
                  (↑ SCOMP)=↓

b.   S' →   NP   S
              (↑ Q-FOCUS)=↓   ↑=↓
                   ↓=⇓

The schemata in (124b) mark the initial NP as the question's focus (Q-FOCUS) and also identify it with ⇓, the controller of a gap in the following S. The initial NP for our example is realized as the interrogative pronoun *who*, which has the following lexical entry:

(125)
who: N, (↑ PRED) = 'WHO'

The final rule for this example associates the controllee metavariable ⇑ with a gap position inside the clause. As shown in (126), we allow c-structure rules to expand a nonterminal category as the empty string, symbolized by *e*. This gives a formal representation for the intuition that an element of that category is missing.

(126)
$$NP \rightarrow \quad e$$
$$\uparrow = \Uparrow$$

The schema on the empty expansion introduces the controllee meta-variable.[22] This NP alternative must be utilized for the object of *saw* so that (116b) is assigned the c-structure (127):

(127)

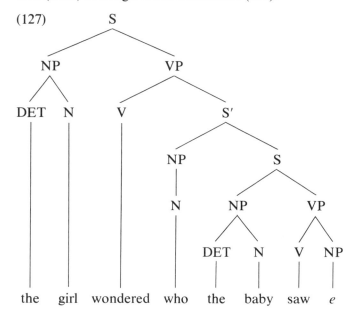

the   girl   wondered   who   the   baby   saw   *e*

The instantiation procedure for metavariables still has an attachment phase, a variable introduction phase, and a substitution phase, just as it was presented in section 4.3. Schemata are attached to appropriate c-structure nodes in the first phase without regard to the kinds of metavariables they contain. The attachments for nodes in the embed-ded S′ subtree are shown in (128). In the second phase, distinct actual variables are introduced for the root node and for every node where a schema contains a ↓ metavariable. This provides the ↓-variables for the nodes, as before. However, an additional variable is introduced for each node with a schema containing the controller metavariable ⇓, providing a ⇓-variable for that node. For this simple example, only the *who* NP node has a controller and receives the extra variable assign-

(128)

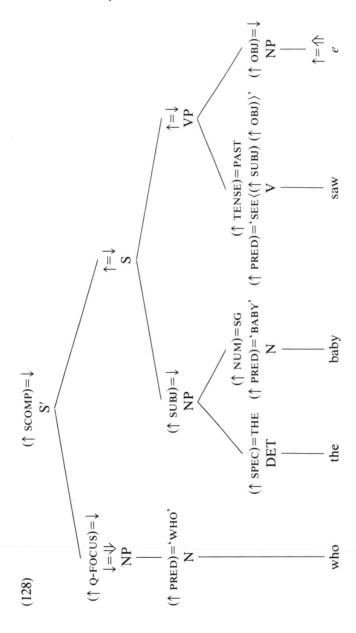

ment. The annotations $\downarrow:f_5$ and $\Downarrow:f_6$ on that node in (129) record the association between metavariables and actual variables. For immediate domination metavariables, the instantiation is completed by substituting a node's $\downarrow$-variable for all the $\downarrow$'s at that node and for all corresponding $\uparrow$'s, those in schemata attached to its daughter nodes. The treatment of bounded domination metavariables is similar in that the $\Downarrow$-variable of a node replaces all the $\Downarrow$'s at that node and all corresponding $\Uparrow$'s. The essential difference is that the nodes to which corresponding $\Uparrow$'s are attached may be further away in the c-structure.

The $\Uparrow$ corresponding to the $\Downarrow$ on the *who* NP in (129) is attached to the empty object of *saw*. The substitution phase of instantiation thus adds the following statements to the f-description:

(130)
a. $(f_4 \text{ Q-FOCUS}) = f_5$
b. $f_5 = f_6$
c. $(f_5 \text{ PRED}) = \text{'WHO'}$
d. $(f_9 \text{ OBJ}) = f_{10}$
e. $f_{10} = f_6$

Equation (130b) comes from the *who* NP node and (130e) comes from the empty NP expansion. Both equations contain the $\Downarrow$-variable f_6 and thereby establish the crucial linkage: the semantic form 'WHO' serves as the PRED in the object f-structure for *saw* and accounts for the fact that *who* is understood as the second argument of SEE. This is apparent in f-structure (131), the solution to sentence (116b)'s f-description:

(131)

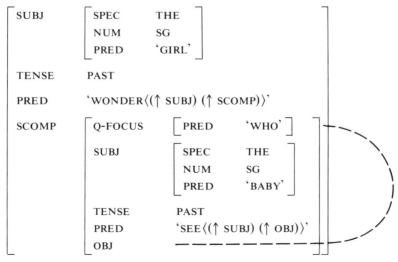

(129)

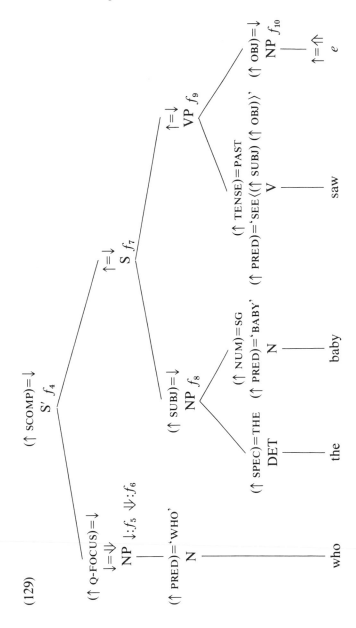

Thus, constituent control dependencies are handled in LFG by extending the instantiation procedure for mapping schemata on c-structure nodes into f-description statements. Because we do not rely on intermediate functional identifications, the statements in (130) are sufficient to establish the same connection over longer c-structure distances, for example, over the intervening *to*-complement in (132):

(132)
The girl wondered who the baby persuaded the boy to see _____.

Except for possibly a different choice of actual variables, the instantiation procedure would again produce the statements (130), correctly representing the constituent control relation. The f-structure for this sentence has both a functional control linkage and a constituent control linkage:

(133)

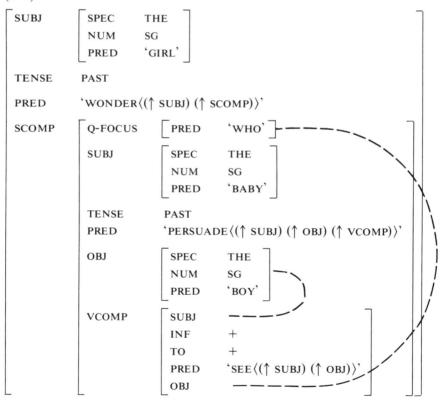

Note that there are no extraneous attributes or values to carry the constituent control linkage through the PERSUADE f-structure.

The instantiation procedure as described substitutes the same actual variable for a $\Downarrow$ and any "corresponding" $\Uparrow$'s. Beneath this vague notion of correspondence lies some additional notation and a rich set of definitions and restrictions that we now make precise. We observe first that corresponding $\Downarrow$'s and $\Uparrow$'s must meet certain category requirements. As examples (134a,b) indicate, the verb *grow* meaning 'become' may be followed by an adjective phrase but not an NP, while the verb *reach* meaning 'extend to' has just the opposite distribution. Example (134c) shows that a controller may be associated with an AP at the beginning of an indirect question, but its corresponding controllee must then be in an adjectival position. Example (134d) demonstrates that metavariables associated with NPs must also be compatible:

(134)
a.   She'll grow that tall/*height.
b.   She'll reach that *tall/height.
c.   *The girl wondered how tall she would grow/*reach ____.
d.   *The girl wondered what height she would *grow/reach ____.

We therefore allow bounded domination metavariables to carry specifications of c-structure categorial features. These specifications are written as subscripts on the metavariables, and we require that corresponding controllers and controllees have compatible subscripts. Thus, a $\Downarrow_{NP}$ may correspond to a $\Uparrow_{NP}$ but not to a $\Uparrow_{AP}$. The contrast in (134d) then follows from adding the subscript NP to the metavariables in our previous rules:

(135)
a.   S' →   NP   S
          ($\uparrow$ Q-FOCUS)=$\downarrow$ $\uparrow$=$\downarrow$
                   $\downarrow$=$\Downarrow_{NP}$

b.   NP →   e
          $\uparrow$=$\Uparrow_{NP}$

The rules for handling adjectival and prepositional dependencies have analogous categorial markings, and cross-categorial correspondences are thereby excluded.

For these examples, the categorial subscripts are redundant with the categories of the nodes that the metavariables are associated with, but this is not always the case. In (136a) the metavariable associated with the topicalized S' is matched with a controllee on an *e* in a c-structure NP position, a prepositional object. (136b) rules out the possibility that the S' is dominated by an NP. The contrast between (136c) and (136d) shows that a topicalized S' cannot control an S' c-structure position.

(136)
a.   That he might be wrong he didn't think of ___.
b.   *He didn't think of that he might be wrong.
c.   He didn't think that he might be wrong.
d.   *That he might be wrong he didn't think ___.

This pattern follows directly from associating a $\Downarrow_{NP}$ metavariable with the fronted S' node.

Another obvious property of acceptable correspondences is that certain tree relations must hold between the nodes to which corresponding controller and controllee metavariables are attached. The *e* corresponding to the *who* controller in (129) must be dominated by the adjacent S node. It cannot be located earlier or later in the main clause, nor inside a more complicated NP in the *who* position. To put it in more technical terms, we say that the S node in (129) is the root of a *control domain* for the *who* $\Downarrow_{NP}$. For a controller attached to a given node in the c-structure, a control domain consists of the nodes in a subtree that a corresponding controllee may be attached to. Our notion of corresponding metavariables thus turns on a rigorous characterization of what nodes can be roots of control domains and what nodes dominated by the root are contained in the domain.

A controller metavariable carries still another specification that determines what node may be its domain root. A closer examination of the indirect question construction shows why this is needed. Rule (135a) suggests that any NP may appear at the front of an indirect question, but this is of course not the case. The fronted phrase is restricted to contain an interrogative word of some sort. That word need not be at the top level of the NP as in (116b), but may rather be deeply embedded within it:

(137)
The girl wondered whose playmate's nurse the baby saw ___.

This sentence would be generated by the alternative NP rule (138), which allows for possessors with genitive case in prenominal position. (We assume that morphological rules correlate the genitive case marking with the *'s* suffix, and that *whose* is morphologically composed of *who* + *'s*.)

(138)

NP →   NP   N
       (↓ CASE)=$_c$ GEN
       (↑ POSS)=↓

A very natural way of guaranteeing the presence of a question word in the appropriate contexts is to specify a constituent control relation between the fronted NP of an indirect question and the interrogative embedded underneath it. This is possible because constituent control in our theory may affect not only null elements but also a designated set of lexical items which includes interrogative pronouns, determiners, and adverbs.

Even though interrogative elements differ in their major categorial features, we assume that they are distinguished from other lexical items by the appearance of a morphosyntactic feature [+wh] in their categorial feature matrices, and we use this feature as the metavariable subscript for the interrogative constituent control dependency. However, it is not sufficient to revise our previous S' rule simply by adding a [+wh] controller metavariable to the fronted NP:

(139)

S' →   NP   S
    (↑ Q)=⇓$_{[+wh]}$ ↑=↓
    (↑ FOCUS)=↓
      ↓=⇓$_{NP}$

When the schemata from this rule are attached to the nodes in sentence (137)'s c-structure, two different controllers, ⇓$_{NP}$ and ⇓$_{[+wh]}$, are associated with the fronted NP node. While we still intend the S to be the domain root for the ⇓$_{NP}$, we intend the root for ⇓$_{[+wh]}$ to be the fronted NP itself. In order to represent this distinction, we must explicitly mark the individual controllers with category symbols that determine their respective domain roots. The superscript S in the controller ⇓$_{NP}^{S}$ indicates that the corresponding ⇑$_{NP}$ must be found in an S-rooted control domain, while the [+wh] controllee for ⇓$_{[+wh]}^{NP}$ must be found beneath an NP node. Moreover, the domain roots must be either the nodes to which the controllers are attached or sisters of those nodes, as indicated in the following definition:

(140)

Root Node of a Constituent Control Domain

Suppose $\Downarrow_{\bar{c}}^{r}$ is a controller metavariable attached to a node N. Then a node R is the root node of a control domain for $\Downarrow_{\bar{c}}^{r}$ if and only if
a. R is a daughter of N's mother, and
b. R is labeled with category r.

Introducing root-category superscripts into the S' rule, we have:

(141)
$$S' \rightarrow \quad\quad NP \quad\quad\quad S$$
$$(\uparrow Q) = \Downarrow_{[+wh]}^{NP} \quad \uparrow = \downarrow$$
$$(\uparrow FOCUS) = \downarrow$$
$$\downarrow = \Downarrow_{NP}^{S}$$

The [+wh] controllee for the interrogative linkage is associated with a lexically realized N node, not with an empty string expansion, and the schema containing the controllee metavariable does not come from the grammar but rather from the lexical entry for *who:*

(142)
who: N, $(\uparrow PRED) = $ 'WHO'
$$\uparrow = \Uparrow_{[+wh]}$$

The lexical entry and our revised question rule yield the f-structure (143) for sentence (137).[23]

The root-node category specification provides one part of the characterization of what a control domain can be. To complete this characterization, we must define which nodes dominated by the domain root are contained in the domain. The *wh*-island in example (144) demonstrates that at least some nodes in the domain root's subtree do not belong to the domain:

(144)
*The girl wondered what the nurse asked who ____ saw ____.

Without some limitation on the extent of a domain, $\Uparrow_{NP}$'s at the gaps would be interpretable as the controllees for *who* and *what,* respectively. Limitations on what nodes may belong to a given control domain come from the fact that nodes in certain c-structure configurations are classified as *bounding nodes*. The path from a node in a domain to the domain root is then restricted as in (145).

(143)

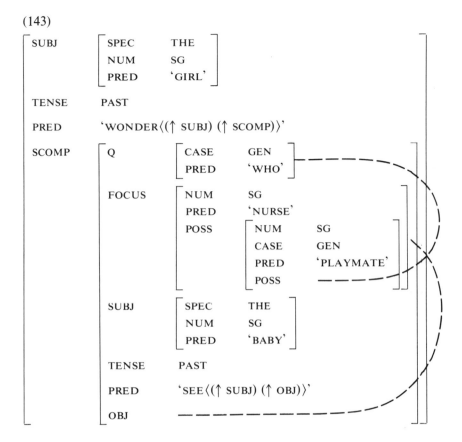

(145)

Bounding Convention

A node M belongs to a control domain with root node R if and only if R dominates M and there are no bounding nodes on the path from M up to but not including R.

The domain root thus carries a substantial theoretical burden as a c-structure intermediary between the nodes to which a controller metavariable and its corresponding controllees are attached. The categorial superscript on the controller metavariable is a direct and definite selector of its domain roots. However, the path from a root to a corresponding controllee's node, while restricted by the Bounding Convention, is not uniquely determined by the grammar.

It remains to extend our notion of grammaticality to take bounded domination metavariables explicitly into account. Intuitively, we require all controllers to have corresponding controllees and all controllees to have corresponding controllers, so that there are no uninstantiated metavariables in the f-description. We add the following to our previous list of grammaticality conditions:

(146)
Grammaticality Condition

A string is grammatical only if its f-description is *properly instantiated*.

The controller/controllee correspondence is one consequence of the formal definition of *proper instantiation:*

(147)
Definition of Proper Instantiation

The f-description from a c-structure with attached schemata is properly instantiated if and only if:
a. no node is a domain root for more than one controller,
b. every controller metavariable has at least one control domain,
c. every controller metavariable corresponds to one and only one controllee in each of its control domains,
d. every controllee metavariable corresponds to one and only one controller,
e. all metavariable correspondences are *nearly nested,* and
f. every domain root has a *lexical signature*.

For a properly instantiated f-description, there is a one-to-one mapping between controllees and domain roots, and each domain root is associated with one and only one controller. This establishes the necessary correspondence between metavariables. The definition of *nearly nested correspondences* and the consequences of the restriction (147e) are presented at the end of this section, where we discuss the possibility of a single constituent containing several controllees.

The lexical signature clause is motivated primarily by formal considerations. It establishes a connection between controlled *e*'s and actual lexical items that plays an important role in the recursiveness proof presented in section 4.8. For each domain root there must be a distinct word in the terminal string. This word is called the *lexical signature* of the domain root. The domain root must dominate its lexical signature. The effect of (147f) is that each domain root, and thus each control domain, must be reflected in the string in some unique way.[24] One possible interpretation of this formal condition is that a control domain must have a lexically realized "head." The head can be defined in terms of the X' category system. It can also be defined purely in functional terms: a lexical head is the lexical item that contributes the PRED semantic form to a constituent's $\downarrow$ f-structure.

According to (147), corresponding metavariables of a grammatical sentence must be in a c-structure configuration as outlined in (148):

(148)

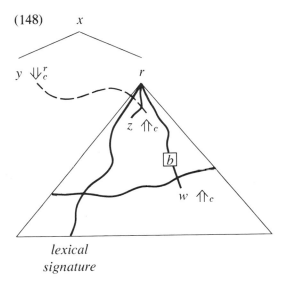

lexical
signature

In this c-structure and in the illustrations below, bounding nodes are enclosed in boxes. The dashed line passes by the domain root to connect the corresponding controller and controllee. The lower $\Uparrow_c$ in (148) cannot correspond to the controller because the bounding node b lies on the path to the root r.

Bounding nodes define "islands" of the c-structure that constituent control dependencies may not penetrate. They serve the same descriptive purpose as Ross's 1967 constraints on transformational variables and Chomsky's 1977b notion of cyclic or bounding categories. Those theories, however, have descriptive inadequacies. Ross hypothesized that constraints such as the Complex NP Constraint apply to all human languages, but this has proved not to be the case. All Scandinavian languages, for example, permit long-distance dependencies to cross the boundaries of indirect questions, and all except for Icelandic permit them to cross the boundaries of relative clauses as well (for illustrations, see Erteschik 1973, Allwood 1976, Engdahl 1980a,b, Maling and

Zaenen to appear). Moreover, although dependencies into English relative clauses (149a) are unacceptable, Ross himself noted that extractions from phrases within the lexically filled NPs in examples like (149b,c) are possible even in English:

(149)
a.   *I wonder who the man that ____ talked to ____ saw Mary.
b.   I wonder who John saw a picture of ____.
c.   Who was it that John denied the claim that he dated ____?

The restrictions on constituent control into English sentential complements and relative clauses seem to be governed by different generalizations; Godard forthcoming convincingly argues that a similar pattern holds for complements and relatives in French. In Chomsky's theory, the Subjacency Convention provides a general limitation on syntactic rules. The domains of rule application are thereby restricted by the occurrence of nodes in specified categories. Chomsky shows that many of the properties of English dependencies follow from the assumption that S' and NP (and possibly S) are bounding categories. One reasonable extension to Chomsky's theory defines bounding categories on a language-by-language basis: stipulating a smaller (or perhaps empty) set of bounding categories in the grammar of Swedish might give an account of the freer dependencies exhibited by that language. However, the English sentences (149b,c) have no natural description in Chomsky's system if *all* NPs in English are bounding nodes.[25]

Bounding node specifications in lexical-functional grammar acknowledge the fact that restrictions on long-distance dependencies may vary between languages and between different nodes of the same category in particular languages. This flexibility does not diminish the explanatory potential of our formal system. We expect that a substantive theory of human language based on our formalism will stipulate a small, principled set of c-structure configurations in which bounding nodes may appear. The grammars of particular languages must draw from this universal inventory of possible bounding nodes to identify the bounding categories in individual c-structure rules (see Zaenen 1980 for some partial proposals). Further work will of course be needed to formulate and justify a universal bounding node theory. Our goal at present is only to illustrate the notation and formal properties of our constituent control mechanisms. A simple notational device is used to indicate that constituent control is blocked by nodes in particular c-structure configurations: enclosing a category on the righthand side of a c-structure rule in a box specifies that the nodes derived by that rule element are bounding nodes.

We incorporate this notation into our treatment of indirect questions for the variety of English in which they form islands. The S in these constructions is a bounding node, as shown in the revised rule:

(150)

$$S' \rightarrow \quad NP \qquad \boxed{S}$$
$$(\uparrow Q) = \Downarrow_{[+wh]}^{NP} \quad \uparrow = \downarrow$$
$$(\uparrow FOCUS) = \downarrow$$
$$\downarrow = \Downarrow_{NP}^{S}$$

Notice first that the bounding node introduced by this rule does not block the simple indirect question sentence (116b). As shown in (151), this is because the S is the root node of the controller's control domain. Therefore, in accordance with the Bounding Convention (145), it does not interfere with the metavariable correspondence.

(151)

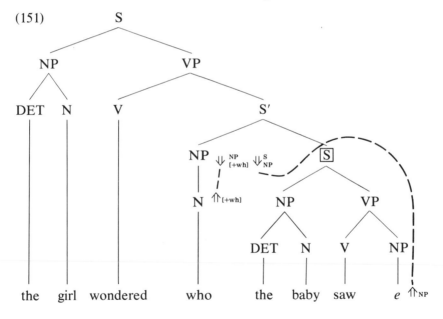

The dashed line in this illustration runs between the corresponding metavariables, not between the nodes they are attached to. The connected metavariables will be instantiated with the same actual variable.

The situation is different for the more complicated string (144). Neither of the gaps inside the *asked* question belongs to the control domain whose root node is the sister of *what*. This is because the *who* domain root is a bounding node on the path from each of the controllees to the root for the *what* $\Downarrow_{NP}^{S}$:

(152)

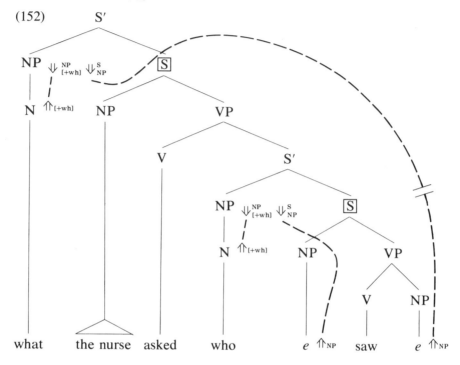

what   the nurse   asked   who   *e* $\Uparrow_{NP}$ saw   *e* $\Uparrow_{NP}$

Conditions (147c,d) are not satisfied, and the string is marked ungrammatical.

Our box notation also permits an account of the apparent difference in NP bounding properties illustrated in (149). The S′ in the relative clause expansion rule (153) is boxed, thus introducing a bounding node that separates both of the gaps in example (149a) from the *who* controller:

(153)

NP → NP $\boxed{S'}$

A proper instantiation for this example is therefore impossible. Constituent control into the other NP constructions in (149) is acceptable because they are derived by alternative rules which do not generate bounding nodes. This distribution of bounding nodes has a further consequence. Together with our hypothesis that the interrogative word inside a fronted NP is subject to constituent control, it explains certain restrictions on the location of the interrogative. Sentence (154a) shows that a fronted NP may contain a relative clause, but example (154b) demonstrates that the interrogative pronoun may not appear *inside* the relative. This is just what we would predict, since the relative clause bounding node that separates the NP metavariables in (154c) also blocks the [+wh] correspondence in (154b):

(154)

a.   The girl whose pictures of the man that called Mary I saw talked to John.

b.   *The girl the pictures of the man that called whom I saw talked to John.

c.   *The girl who I saw pictures of the man that called talked to John.

Though similar in these examples, there are English constructions in which NP and [+wh] metavariables do not have the same privileges of occurrence. We see in (155) and (156) that a controlled interrogative may, but a controlled *e* may not, be located in the possessive modifier of an NP:

(155)
The girl wondered whose nurse the baby saw ____.

(156)
*The girl wondered who the baby saw ____'s nurse.

The ungrammaticality of (156) follows from making the prenominal genitive NP be a bounding node, as in the revised NP rule (157):

(157)
$$\text{NP} \rightarrow \qquad \boxed{\text{NP}} \qquad \text{N}$$
$$(\downarrow \text{CASE})=_c \text{GEN}$$
$$(\uparrow \text{POSS})=\downarrow$$

The genitive bounding node also blocks a direct correspondence for the [+wh] metavariables in (155), but a simple schema can be added to rule (157) to circumvent the blocking effect just for interrogative dependencies. This schema, $\Uparrow_{[+wh]} = \Downarrow^{NP}_{[+wh]}$, splits what seems to be a single control domain into two separate domains, one embedded inside the other. It equates a [+wh] controllee for the upper domain with a [+wh] controller for a lower domain:

(158)

$$NP \rightarrow \qquad \boxed{NP} \qquad N$$

$$(\downarrow \text{ CASE})=_c \text{GEN}$$
$$(\uparrow \text{ POSS})=\downarrow$$
$$\Uparrow_{[+wh]}=\Downarrow^{NP}_{[+wh]}$$

Because this schema links only [+wh] metavariables, constituent control only for interrogatives is possible inside the genitive NP;[26] control for empty NPs is prohibited. The relevant c-structure relations for sentence (155) are illustrated in (159):

(159)

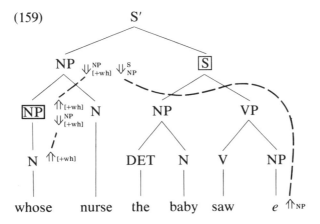

Special constraints have been proposed in transformational theory (e.g., Ross's 1967 Left Branch Condition) to account for the asymmetry in (155) and (156). The lexical-functional description of these facts is stated within the grammar for English, without postulating extragrammatical universal constraints. It thus predicts that this is an area of variation among languages.

In contrast to the nonuniform bounding characteristics of NPs, it can be argued that in languages like English, Icelandic, and French, all Ss are bounding nodes (see the discussions of verb inversion in control domains in Bresnan and Grimshaw 1978 and Zaenen 1980). If so, the Bounding Convention would also block the derivation of sentences such as (160), where the controllee is inside a VP *that*-complement:

(160)

The girl wondered who the nurse claimed that the baby saw ____.

The linking schema appearing in the alternative S' rule (161) will let the dependency go through in this case:

(161)

$$S' \rightarrow (that) \quad \boxed{S}$$
$$\uparrow = \downarrow$$
$$\Uparrow = \Downarrow^S$$

Neither of the metavariables in this linking schema has a categorial subscript. This is an abbreviation for a finite set of alternative schemata of the form $\Uparrow_c = \Downarrow_c^S$, where c is one of the types NP, [+wh], PP, etc. Thus, this schema will link metavariables of any type, passing on to the lower controller the compatibility requirement of the upper one. With this rule, the c-structure (162) is assigned to the sentential complement in (160). Observe that the *that* node belongs to the control domain of the *who* $\Downarrow_{NP}^S$ controller, since there is no bounding node on the path leading down to it. The $\Uparrow$ on the left of the linking schema is thus instantiated with the $\Downarrow_{NP}^S$-variable of the *who* node. A separate variable is introduced for the $\Downarrow^S$ on the right, and this is substituted for the $\Uparrow_{NP}$ of the empty NP, which belongs to the domain rooted in the complement S. The semantically appropriate connections for (160) are thus established.[27]

The definitions of our theory place controllees in a one-to-one correspondence with domain roots and hence with lexical signatures. Our definitions do not establish a correspondence between controllees and arbitrary constituents: there is nothing to prevent control domains from overlapping, and any constituent in several domains may contain several controllees.[28] Control domains will overlap whenever a domain root belonging to the domain of a higher controller is not marked as a bounding node. The potential for multiple dependencies into a single constituent is greater for languages whose grammars specify fewer bounding nodes. The hypothesis that Swedish has fewer bounding nodes than English would thus account for the less restrictive patterns of Swedish dependencies.

There are examples of multiple dependencies in English, however, which we will use to illustrate the operation of our formal mechanism. The recent literature contains many discussions of the interaction of *tough*-movement and questions (see Chomsky 1977b and Fodor 1978, for example, and the references cited therein):[29]

(163)
I wonder which violin the sonata is tough for her to play ＿＿ on ＿＿.

(162)

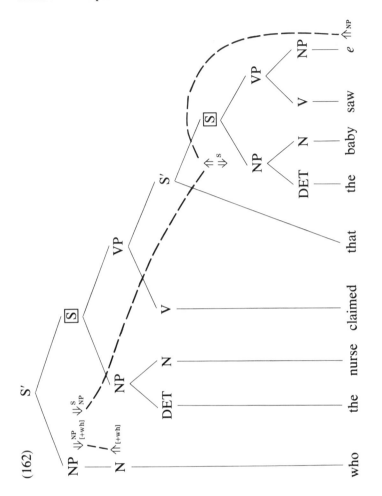

As we will see, the nodes in the VP' in this example lie within two control domains, one rooted in the VP' in the sentential complement of *tough* and the other rooted in the S after *which*. Before exploring the interactions in this sentence, we sketch a grammar for simple *tough-*movement constructions.

A predicate like *tough* is an adjective that can occur as the head of an adjective phrase. Among the alternative expansions for AP is one that allows the adjective to be followed by a sentential complement:

(164)
$$AP \rightarrow A \qquad S'$$
$$(\uparrow \text{SCOMP}) = \downarrow$$

The VP must of course permit APs as complements to copular verbs, but the details of the VP grammar do not concern us here. *Tough* predicates take infinitival sentential complements, so the category S' must also have an alternative expansion. Rule (165) allows S' to expand as a *for*-complementizer followed by a subject NP and a VP':

(165)
$$S' \rightarrow for \qquad NP \qquad\qquad VP'$$
$$(\uparrow \text{SUBJ}) = \downarrow \qquad \uparrow = \downarrow$$
$$(\uparrow \text{TOPIC}) = \Downarrow_{\text{NP}}^{\text{VP}'}$$

The TOPIC schema identifies the TOPIC with an NP controller meta-variable whose corresponding controllee must be inside the VP'. Sentences such as (166), where the subject of *tough* has a clause-internal function in an embedded *that*-complement, justify treating this as a constituent control dependency:

(166)
Mary is tough for me to believe that John would ever marry ____.

In some respects the TOPIC function is like the FOCUS function introduced earlier for indirect questions. It raises an entity with a clause-internal function to a canonical position in the f-structure hierarchy, providing an alternative access path for various anaphoric rules (cf. note 23). There are substantive differences between TOPIC and FOCUS, however. The FOCUS relation marks new information in the sentence or discourse and therefore is not identified with any other elements. The TOPIC function is a place-holder for old information; its value *must* be linked, either functionally or anaphorically, to some other element. For *tough* predicates, the TOPIC is functionally controlled by a schema in the adjective's lexical entry:[30]

(167)

tough: A, (↑ PRED) = 'TOUGH⟨(↑ SCOMP)⟩'
         (↑ SCOMP TOPIC) = (↑ SUBJ)

With these specifications, the c-structure for the simple *tough*-movement sentence (168) is as shown in (170), and its f-structure is displayed in (169):

(168)

The sonata is tough for her to play ____ on the violin.

(169)

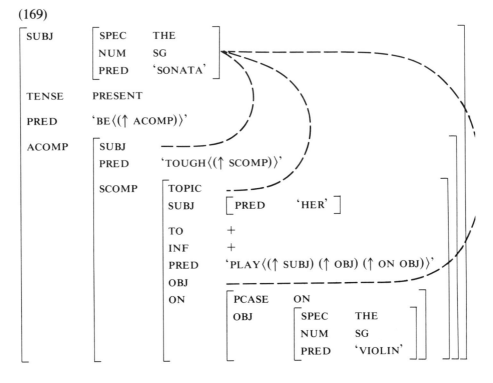

We are now ready to examine the double dependency in (163). In this sentence, *violin* has become the FOCUS of an indirect question. The c-structure for the complement of *wonder* is shown in (171). Since the VP' domain is introduced without a bounding node, there is nothing to block the correspondence between the object NP of *on* and the NP

(170)

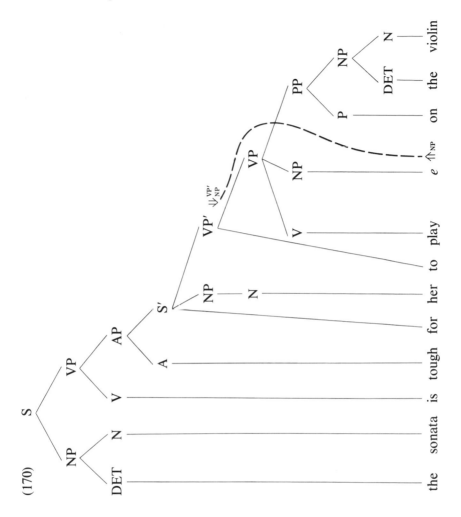

(171)

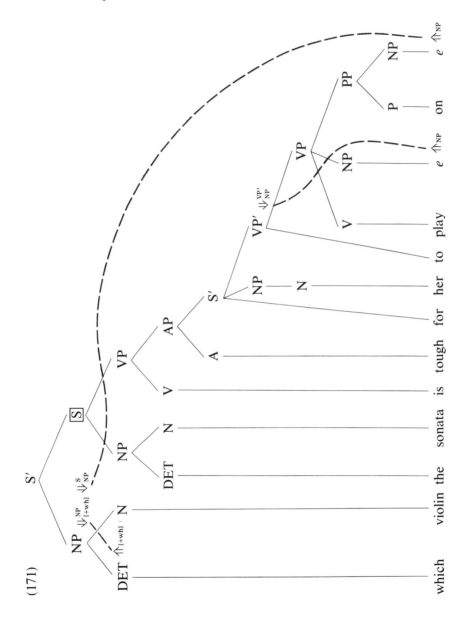

controller for *which violin*. The correspondence for the TOPIC metavariables in *tough*'s complement is established just as in the simpler
example above. Thus, the metavariables can be properly instantiated,
and the intuitively correct f-structure will be assigned to this sentence.

As has frequently been noted, the acceptability of these double dependencies is sensitive to the relative order of controllees and controllers. If *sonata* is questioned and *violin* is the *tough* subject, the result is
the ungrammatical string (172):

(172)
*I wonder which sonata the violin is tough for her to play ____ on ____ .

The reading of this sentence in which *which sonata* is the object of *on*
and *violin* is the object of *play* is semantically unacceptable, but the
semantically well-formed reading of our previous example (163) is not
available. Similarly, Bach 1977 observes that potentially ambiguous
sentences are rendered unambiguous in these constructions. Sentence
(173) can be assigned only the reading in which *doctor* is understood as
the object of *to* and *patient* is the object of *about,* even though the
alternative interpretation is equally plausible:

(173)
Which patient is that doctor easiest to talk to ____ about ____ ?

As Baker 1977, Fodor 1978, and others have pointed out, there is a
simple and intuitive way of characterizing the acceptable dependencies
in these examples. If a line is drawn from each gap to the various lexical
items that are candidates for filling it, then the permissible dependencies are just those in which the lines for the separate gaps do not cross.
Or, to use Fodor's terminology, only nested dependencies seem to be
allowed.

The nested pattern of acceptable dependencies is an empirical consequence of the requirement (147e) that corresponding metavariables
be nearly nested. However, this restriction in our definition of proper
instantiation is strongly motivated by independent theoretical considerations: as we point out in section 4.8, this requirement provides a
sufficient condition for proving that lexical-functional languages are
included within the set of context-sensitive languages. Thus, our restriction offers not only a description of the observed facts, but also a
formal basis for explaining them.

As the first step in formalizing the notion of a nearly nested correspondence, we establish an ordering on the bounded domination meta-

variables attached to a c-structure. We order the c-structure nodes so that each node comes before its daughters and right-sister (if any), and all its daughters precede its right-sister. If the node that one metavariable is attached to precedes another metavariable's node, then we say that the first metavariable precedes the second. The ordering of metavariables can be described more perspicuously in terms of a labeled bracket representation of the c-structure tree. If metavariables are associated with the *open* brackets for the nodes they are attached to, then the left-to-right sequence in the labeled bracketing defines the metavariable ordering. This is illustrated with the (partial) bracketing for sentence (163) shown in part (a) of figure 4.1. We see from this representation that the $\Downarrow_{NP}^{S}$ on the fronted NP is ordered before the $\Downarrow_{NP}^{VP'}$ and that *play*'s direct object $\Uparrow_{NP}$ is ordered before the controllee after *on*.

Drawing lines between corresponding metavariables as ordered in part (a) of figure 4.1 illustrates the intuitive contrast between nested and crossed dependencies. The lines are shown in part (b) of figure 4.1 for the acceptable nested reading of (163) and in part (c) for the unacceptable crossed dependency. A precise formulation of this intuitive distinction can be given in terms of the definition of a crossed correspondence:

(174)

Definition of Crossed Correspondence

The correspondence of two metavariables m_1 and m_2 is *crossed* by a controller or controllee m_3 if and only if all three variables have compatible categorial subscripts and m_3 but not its corresponding controllee or controller is ordered between m_1 and m_2.

Obviously, a correspondence is nested if and only if it is not crossed. All the correspondences in the acceptable readings for the examples above are nested according to this definition, but the correspondences in the unacceptable readings are not.

Metavariable correspondences can be allowed limited departures from strict nesting without undermining the context-sensitivity of lexical-functional languages. We associate with each metavariable correspondence an integer called its *crossing degree*. This is simply the number of controllers and controllees by which that correspondence is crossed. A correspondence is strictly nested if its crossing degree is zero. Further, for each lexical-functional grammar we determine an-

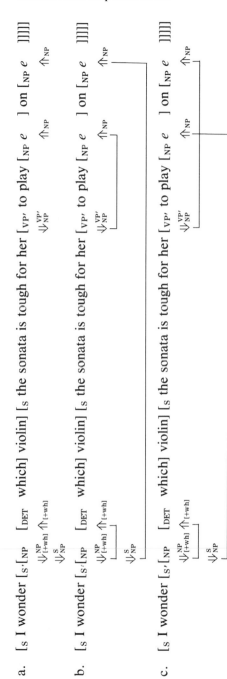

Figure 4.1

other number, the *crossing limit* of the grammar. A nearly nested correspondence is then defined as follows:

(175)
Definition of Nearly Nested Correspondence
A metavariable correspondence is *nearly nested* if its crossing degree does not exceed the grammar's crossing limit.

The significant formal implication of this definition and the nearly nested restriction on proper instantiation is that for any string the degree of departure from strict nesting is bounded by a constant that is independent of the length of that string.

The examples above suggest that the crossing limit for English is zero. This limit can be maintained even in the face of apparent counterexamples to the nesting proposals of other theories. Since our definition of crossed correspondence (174) only involves metavariables with compatible categorial subscripts, we have no difficulty with acceptable sentences containing crossed dependencies of different categories. Other classes of counterexamples involve interactions of functional and constituent control, but our restrictions are imposed only for constituent control dependencies. Thus, there is no real cross-over in sentences such as (176):

(176)
How nice a man would John be ____ to marry ____?

The *man* NP is linked to the first gap, while *John* is linked to the second. In our theory there is a functional identification between *John*, the SUBJ of the complex predicate *how nice a man*, and the TOPIC of its SCOMP. The controller for the second dependency is thus ordered *after* the first gap. Icelandic stands in contrast to English in having constituent control dependencies that can be described correctly only on the hypothesis that the crossing limit for that language is one (Maling and Zaenen to appear).

We have presented in this section the major formal mechanisms for characterizing the long-distance dependencies of natural language. We have motivated and illustrated our formal apparatus with simple and plausible fragments of English grammar. Constituent control is a syntactic phenomenon of considerable complexity, and there are many empirical and theoretical issues that we have not touched on and some that are still to be resolved. No doubt future research in this area will lead to both substantive and formal refinements of our theory. However, we expect the broad outline of our approach to remain unchanged: lexical-functional grammar treats long-distance dependencies as part of the procedure for producing properly instantiated f-descriptions. These dependencies are governed by c-structure configurations and are not directly sensitive to the f-structures that are ultimately constructed.

4.8 Generative Power

We have seen that lexical-functional grammar offers considerable expressive power for describing linguistic phenomena. In this section we examine the position of LFG in the Chomsky hierarchy of generative capacity. The most important result is that our formal system, with two well-motivated restrictions on c-structure derivations that we discuss below, is *not* as powerful as a general rewriting system or Turing machine. In fact, lexical-functional languages are included within the class of context-sensitive languages. On the lower end of the scale, we show that LFG has greater generative power than the class of context-free grammars.

For a string to be a member of the language generated by a lexical-functional grammar, it must satisfy five requirements:

(177)

a. It must be the terminal string of a valid c-structure derivation.

b. There must be a properly instantiated f-description associated with that derivation.

c. The f-description must be consistent and determinate, with a unique minimal solution.

d. The minimal f-structure solution must satisfy all constraints in the f-description.

e. The f-structure must be complete and coherent.

Given a single c-structure derivation for a string of length n (a tree to whose nodes the appropriate functional schemata are attached), there are finite procedures for deciding whether or not (177b)–(177e) hold. Determining proper instantiation for immediate domination metavariables is trivial. Since the given tree has only a finite number of finite control domains, it is also computable whether or not the bounded domination metavariables are properly instantiated. The instantiated f-description has a finite number of statements in it, so the algorithm outlined in section 4.4 and in the appendix produces its unique minimal solution, if it is consistent and determinate. Evaluating a constraining statement requires only a finite traversal of the f-structure,[31] and the Completeness and Coherence Conditions can similarly be checked by a finite computation on the f-structure.

Thus, all that is needed to prove that the grammaticality of any string is decidable is a terminating procedure for enumerating all possible c-structures for the string, so that the functional correctness of each one can then be verified. C-structures are generated by context-free grammars, and there are well-known decision procedures for the membership problem of grammars in this class. That is, there exist algorithms for determining whether there is *at least one* way of deriving the string. Deciding that a string is derivable, however, is not the same as enumerating for inspection all of its derivations. Indeed, there are grammars for which neither the number of derivations that a given string might have nor the number of nodes in a single derivation is bounded. While it may be determined that such a string has one derivation and thus belongs to the language of the c-structure grammar, there is no way of deciding whether or not there exists among all of its derivations one that satisfies the functional requirements of our theory. Suppose that at some point we have examined all derivations with less than m nodes and found them all to be functionally deviant. This does not mean that all derivations with $m + 1$ nodes will also be unsatisfactory. Since this can be true for any m, the grammaticality of that string cannot be decided in a finite number of steps. (This difficulty arises not just with our formalism but with any system in which the definition of grammaticality involves an evaluation or interpretation of the context-free derivations.)

A context-free grammar can produce an unbounded number of derivations of arbitrary size for a string, either because its rules permit a single category to appear twice in a nonbranching chain, or because expansions involving the empty string are not sufficiently restricted. The rules in (178) illustrate the first situation:

(178)
X → Y
Y → Z
Z → X

Any string which has a derivation including the category X will be infinitely ambiguous. There is a larger derivation with the domination chain X–Y–Z–X replacing the single X, and a still larger one with one of those Xs replaced by another chain, and so on. The derivations that result from rules of this sort are in a certain sense peculiar. The non-branching recursive cycles permit a superstructure of arbitrary size to be constructed over a single terminal or group of terminals (or even over the empty string). The c-structure is thus highly repetitive, and the f-description, which is based on a fixed set of lexical schemata and arbitrary repetitions of a finite set of grammatical schemata, is also. While the c-structure and f-structure can be of unbounded size, they encode only a finite amount of nonredundant information that is relevant to the functional or semantic interpretation of the string.

Such vacuously repetitive structures are without intuitive or empirical motivation. Presumably, neither linguists nor language learners would postulate rules of grammar whose purpose is to produce these derivations. However, linguists and language learners both are likely to propose rules whose purpose is to express certain surface structure generalizations but which have derivations of this sort as unintended consequences. For example, suppose that the grammar that includes (178) also has a large number of alternative rules for expanding Y and Z. Suppose further that except for the undesired cyclic X–Y–Z–X chain, X can dominate everything that Y and Z dominate. Only the intended derivations are permitted if X expands to a new category Y′ whose rules are exactly the same as the rules for Y except that another new category Z′ appears in place of Z in (178). The rules for Z′ are those of Z without the X alternative. This much more complicated grammar does not make explicit the almost complete equivalence of the Y–Y′ and Z–Z′ categories. Except for the one spurious derivation, the original grammar (178) is a much more revealing description of the linguistic facts.

The following rules illustrate how derivations of arbitrary size may also result from unrestricted empty string expansions:

(179)
P → P P
P → *e*

If a P dominates (either directly or indirectly) a lexical item in one derivation, there will be another derivation in which that P has a mother and sister which are both P, with the sister expanding to the empty string. Without further stipulations, rules of this sort can apply an indefinite number of times. We introduced empty strings in section 4.7 to represent the lower end of long-distance dependencies. These e's have controllee metavariables and thus are uniquely associated with the lexical signature of a control domain. The possibility of arbitrary repetitions does not arise because derivations for a string of length n can have no more than n controlled e's. An empty string may appear in a c-structure rule for another reason, however. It can alternate with other rule elements in order to mark them as optional. An *optionality e* is a generalization of the standard parenthesis notation for c-structure optionality; it permits functional schemata to be introduced when the optional constituents are omitted. An optionality e does not have the controllee metavariable that inhibits repetitions of controlled e's and, according to the standard interpretation of context-free rules, may appear in derivations indefinitely many times with no intervening lexical items. These derivations are redundant and unmotivated, just like those with nonbranching dominance cycles. The possibility of repeating rule elements with fixed schema sets and no new lexical information is, again, an unintended consequence of a simple notational device for conflating sets of closely related rules.

Having argued that the vacuous derivations involving nonbranching dominance chains and repeated optionality e's are unmotivated and undesired, we now simply exclude them from functional consideration. We do this by restricting what it means to be a "valid" c-structure derivation in the sense of (177a):

(180)
Definition of Valid Derivation
A c-structure derivation is valid if and only if no category appears twice in a nonbranching dominance chain, no nonterminal exhaustively dominates an optionality e, and at least one lexical item or controlled e appears between two optionality e's derived by the same rule element.

This definition, together with the fact that controlled e's are associated with unique lexical signatures, implies that for any string the size and number of c-structure derivations relevant to our notion of grammaticality is bounded as a function of n, even though no such bounds exist according to the standard interpretation for context-free grammars. Note that this restriction on derivations does not affect the language of the c-structure grammar: it is well known that a string has a valid c-structure with no cycles and no e's if and only if it has any c-structure at all (see Hopcroft and Ullman 1969).

With the validity of a derivation defined as in (180), the following theorem can be proved:

(181)
Decidability Theorem

For any lexical-functional grammar G and for any string s, it is decidable whether s belongs to the language of G.

We observe that algorithms exist for enumerating just the finite number of valid derivations, if any, that G assigns to s. A conventional context-free parsing algorithm, for example, can easily be modified to notice and avoid nonbranching cycles, to keep track of the source of optionality e's and avoid repetitions, and to postulate no more controlled e's than there are words in the string. With the valid derivations in hand, there are algorithms, as outlined above, for determining whether any of them satisfies the functional conditions (177b)–(177e). Theorem (181) is thus established.[32]

Theorem (181) sets an upper bound on the generative capacity of lexical-functional grammar: only the recursive as opposed to recursively enumerable languages are generable. It is possible to set a tighter bound on the generative power of our formalism. Because of the nearly nested restriction on proper instantiation, for any lexical-functional grammar G a nondeterministic linear bounded automaton can be constructed that accepts exactly the language of G. Lexical-functional languages are therefore included within the context-sensitive languages. The details of this construction are quite complicated and will be presented in a separate publication. In brief, the c-structure with attached schemata for any string of length n can be discovered and represented by an automaton with a working tape whose size is bounded by a linear function of n. This automaton, however, cannot introduce actual variables and substitute them for metavariables as the instantiation procedure specifies, since that would require a nonlinear amount of space (roughly proportional to $n \log n$). Instead, it uses the arrangement of metavariables in the c-structure to determine the implicit synonymy relations that the actual variables would simply make explicit. The nearly nested restriction guarantees that these relations can be computed using a linear amount of working storage.[33] With synonymous metavariables identified, the functional well-formedness conditions (177c)–(177e) can also be verified in a linear amount of space.

The generative power of lexical-functional grammar is obviously bounded from below by the class of context-free grammars. Any given context-free grammar is a legitimate c-structure grammar with no grammatical schemata. As noted above, the strings with valid c-structure derivations are exactly those that belong to the context-free language. The sets of schemata for those derivations are empty and are vacuously instantiated to produce an empty f-description whose unique minimal solution is the null f-structure. The functional component thus does no filtering, and the c-structure grammar under our interpretation is weakly equivalent to the grammar interpreted in the ordinary context-free way.

In fact, LFG has greater generative power than the class of context-free grammars, for it allows grammars for languages that are known not to be context-free. The language $a^n b^n c^n$ is a classic example of such a language. Its strings consist of a sequence of a's followed by the same number of b's and then c's. A grammar for this language is shown in (182):

(182)

$$S \rightarrow \begin{array}{ccc} A & B & C \\ \uparrow=\downarrow & \uparrow=\downarrow & \uparrow=\downarrow \end{array}$$

$$A \rightarrow \left\{ \begin{array}{cc} & a \\ & (\uparrow \text{COUNT})=0 \\ a & A \\ & (\uparrow \text{COUNT})=\downarrow \end{array} \right\}$$

$$B \rightarrow \left\{ \begin{array}{cc} & b \\ & (\uparrow \text{COUNT})=0 \\ b & B \\ & (\uparrow \text{COUNT})=\downarrow \end{array} \right\}$$

$$C \rightarrow \left\{ \begin{array}{cc} & c \\ & (\uparrow \text{COUNT})=0 \\ c & C \\ & (\uparrow \text{COUNT})=\downarrow \end{array} \right\}$$

The c-structure rules produce a's, b's, and c's in sequences of arbitrary length, as illustrated by the c-structure for *aaabbc* in (183):

(183)

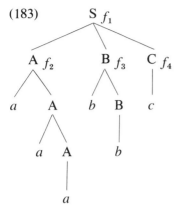

The lengths of those sequences, however, are encoded in the f-structure. For each of the A, B, and C nodes in the tree, the number of COUNT attributes in the ↓ f-structure of that node is a count of the elements in that node's terminal sequence. Thus, the f-structures shown in (184) for the f_2, f_3, and f_4 nodes have three, two, and one COUNTs, respectively.

(184)

$$f_2 \begin{bmatrix} \text{COUNT} & \begin{bmatrix} \text{COUNT} & \begin{bmatrix} \text{COUNT} & 0 \end{bmatrix} \end{bmatrix} \end{bmatrix}$$

$$f_3 \begin{bmatrix} \text{COUNT} & \begin{bmatrix} \text{COUNT} & 0 \end{bmatrix} \end{bmatrix}$$

$$f_4 \begin{bmatrix} \text{COUNT} & 0 \end{bmatrix}$$

The attempt to equate these three f-structures in accordance with the schemata on the S rule leads to a violation of the Uniqueness Condition, and the string is marked ungrammatical. Only if the terminal sequences are all of the same length can the f-structures be combined.

The f-structure in this grammar records the one string property, sequence length, that is crucially needed for this particular context-sensitive test. If instead we let the f-structure be a complete, isomorphic image of the c-structure tree, we can describe a repetition language, another classical example of a non-context-free language. This is a language whose sentences are all of the form $\omega\omega$, where ω stands for an arbitrary string over some vocabulary. We start with a simple context-free grammar for the strings ω, for example, the rule in (185a).

(185)

a. W → L $\begin{pmatrix} W \\ (\uparrow w) = \downarrow \end{pmatrix}$

b. S → W   W
       ↑=↓ ↑=↓

All words in the vocabulary are assumed to belong to the lexical category L, so this rule generates arbitrary strings under right-branching tree structures. If for every word x there is a distinct symbol x, and if x has $(\uparrow L) = x$ as its only lexical schema, the $\downarrow$ f-structure of a W node will be an exact image of its subtree. For example, (186) shows the c-structure that this grammar would assign to the ungrammatical string *abcdbc*, and (187) gives the f-structures for the two topmost W nodes:

(186)

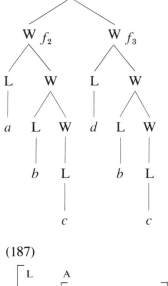

(187)

$$f_2 \begin{bmatrix} L & A \\ W & \begin{bmatrix} L & B \\ W & \begin{bmatrix} L & C \end{bmatrix} \end{bmatrix} \end{bmatrix}$$

$$f_3 \begin{bmatrix} L & D \\ W & \begin{bmatrix} L & B \\ W & \begin{bmatrix} L & C \end{bmatrix} \end{bmatrix} \end{bmatrix}$$

These f-structures contradict the schemata on the S rule, which assert that they are identical. The f-structures for the two Ws in sequence will be the same only if their subtrees and hence their terminal strings are also the same.

We can thus characterize within our formalism at least some of the non-context-free context-sensitive languages. There is nothing devious or obscure about the grammars for these languages: they use ordinary functional mechanisms in perfectly straightforward ways. The additional generative power comes from two features of LFG, functional composition and the equality predicate. Function composition permits f-structures to encode a wide range of tree properties, while the equality predicate can enforce a match between the properties encoded from different nodes. We can be even more specific about the source of our context-sensitive power. If all schemata in a grammar equate attribute values only to constants (e.g., schemata of the form $d_1 = d_2$, where d_2 designates a symbol or semantic form), then a weakly equivalent context-free grammar can be constructed. In this grammar the information contained in the f-structure is encoded in an enlarged set of context-free categories. The additional power of lexical-functional grammar stems from schemata that equate two f-structures, for example, the identification schemata in the examples above.

We have shown that lexical-functional languages properly include the context-free languages and are included within the context-sensitive languages. LFG's generative capacity is both a strong point of our theory and also something of an embarrassment. Huybregts 1976 has argued that dependencies of the sort illustrated by (185) are quite productive in Dutch,[34] and such phenomena have been claimed to exist in other languages as well (e.g., Mohawk (Postal 1964) and the English *respectively* construction). Mechanisms of this power must therefore be a part of any adequate theory of human language.

On the other hand, the problem of recognizing languages with context sensitivities can be computationally much more complex than the recognition problem for context-free languages. If our system turns out to have full context-sensitive power, then there are no known solutions to the recognition problem that require less than exponential computational resources in the worst case. It might therefore seem that, contrary to the Competence Hypothesis, lexical-functional grammars cannot be naturally incorporated into performance models that simulate the apparent ease of human comprehension.

There are several reasons why this conclusion does not necessarily follow. First, an explanatory linguistic theory undoubtedly will impose a variety of substantive constraints on how our formal devices may be employed in grammars of human languages. Some candidate constraints have been mentioned in passing (e.g., the constraints on functional control schemata and the principle of functional locality), and others are under current investigation. It is quite possible that the worst case computational complexity for the subset of lexical-functional grammars that conform to such constraints will be plausibly subexponential. Second, while the Competence Hypothesis asserts that a grammar will be a significant component of a performance model, the grammar is not identified with the processor that interprets it. An adequate theory of performance might impose certain space and time limitations on the processor's capabilities or specify certain nongrammatical heuristic strategies to guide the processor's computations (see for example the scheduling heuristics described in chapter 11). Given these further assumptions, the performance model might actually exhibit the worst case behavior very rarely and then only under special circumstances. Finally, it is quite possible that the exponential explosion is in fact psychologically realistic. For our formal system, this processing complexity is not the result of a lengthy search along erroneous paths of computation. Rather, it comes about only when the c-structure grammar assigns an exponential number of c-structure ambiguities to a string. To the extent that c-structure is a psychologically real level of representation, it seems plausible that ambiguities at that level will be associated with increased cognitive load.

We conjecture, then, that the generative power of our system is not only necessary for adequate linguistic descriptions but is also compatible with realistic models of psycholinguistic performance. In keeping with the Competence Hypothesis, we believe that performance models that incorporate linguistically justified lexical-functional grammars will ultimately provide an explanatory account of the mental operations that underlie human linguistic abilities.

Appendix: F-Description Solution Operators

An intuitive description of our f-description solution algorithm was presented in section 4.4. The algorithm involves three basic operators: Locate, Merge, and Include. If d_1 and d_2 are designators, then an f-description equality of the form $d_1 = d_2$ is processed by performing Merge[Locate[d_1], Locate[d_2]], and a membership statement of the form $d_1 \in d_2$ is processed by performing Include[Locate[d_1], Locate[d_2]]. We now give the formal definitions of these operators.

Locate, Merge, and Include all cause modifications to a collection of entities and variable assignments C, either by modifying an already existing entity or by substituting one entity for every occurrence of another. We specify substitution as a separate suboperator, since it is common to all three operators:

(188)

Definition of Substitute

For two entities *old* and *new*, Substitute[*new, old*] replaces all occurrences of *old* in C with *new*, assigns *new* as the value of variables that previously had *old* as their assignment (in addition to any variables that had *new* as their value previously), and removes *old* from C.

Applying the Substitute operator makes all previous designators of *old* and *new* be designators of *new*.

The Locate operator takes a designator d as input. If successful, it finds a value for d in a possibly modified entity collection.

(189)

Definition of Locate

a. If d is an entity in C, then Locate[d] is simply d.

b. If d is a symbol or semantic form character string, Locate[d] is the symbol or semantic form with that representation.

c. If d is a variable,

If d is already assigned a value in C, Locate[d] is that value.

Otherwise, a new place-holder is added to C and assigned as the value of d. Locate[d] is that new place-holder.

d. Otherwise, d is a function-application expression of the form $(f\ s)$.

Let F and S be the entities Locate[f] and Locate[s], respectively.

If S is not a symbol or place-holder, or if F is not an f-structure or place-holder, the f-description has no solution.

If F is an f-structure:

If S is a symbol or place-holder with a value defined in F, then Locate[d] is that value.

Otherwise, S is a place-holder or a symbol for which F has no value. F is modified to define a new place-holder as the value of S. Locate[d] is that place-holder.

Otherwise, F is a place-holder. A new f-structure F' is constructed with a single pair that assigns a new place-holder value to S, and Substitute[F', F] is performed. Locate[d] is then the new place-holder value.

(189a) provides closure by allowing an entity to serve as a designator of itself. The recursive invocations of Locate that yield F and S in (189d) enable the values of all functional compositions to be obtained. The consistency check is specified in the first clause of (189d). A Locate attempt fails if it requires an entity already known not to be an f-structure to be applied as a function, or an entity known not to be a symbol to be used as an argument.

The Merge operator is also defined recursively. It takes two entities e_1 and e_2 as input. Its result is an entity e, which might be newly constructed. The new entity is substituted for both e_1 and e_2 in C so that all designators of e_1 and e_2 become designators of e instead.

(190)

Definition of Merge

a. If e_1 and e_2 are the same entity, then Merge$[e_1, e_2]$ is that entity and C is not modified.

b. If e_1 and e_2 are both symbols or both semantic forms, the f-description has no solution.

c. If e_1 and e_2 are both f-structures, let A_1 and A_2 be the sets of attributes of e_1 and e_2, respectively. Then a new f-structure e is constructed with

$$e = \{\langle a, v \rangle \mid a \in A_1 \cup A_2 \text{ and } v = \text{Merge}[\text{Locate}[(e_1\ a)],$$
$$\text{Locate}[(e_2\ a)]]\}.$$

Substitute$[e, e_1]$ and Substitute$[e, e_2]$ are both performed, and the result of Merge$[e_1, e_2]$ is then e.

d. If e_1 and e_2 are both sets, then a new set $e = e_1 \cup e_2$ is constructed. Substitute$[e, e_1]$ and Substitute$[e, e_2]$ are both performed, and the result of Merge$[e_1, e_2]$ is then e.

e. If e_1 is a place-holder, then Substitute$[e_2, e_1]$ is performed and the result of Merge$[e_1, e_2]$ is e_2.

f. If e_2 is a place-holder, then Substitute$[e_1, e_2]$ is performed and the result of Merge$[e_1, e_2]$ is e_1.

g. Otherwise, e_1 and e_2 are entities of different types, and the f-description has no solution.

The consistency check in (190b) ensures that nonidentical symbols and semantic forms are not combined, and the checks in (190c,d) guarantee that entities of different known types (i.e., excluding place-holders) cannot be merged. The recursion in (190c) propagates these checks to all the substructures of two f-structures, building compatible values for common function names as it proceeds down level by level until it reaches non-f-structure values.[35]

The Include operator has a particularly simple specification in terms of the Merge operator. It takes two entities e and s as input and is defined as follows:

(191)

Definition of Include

Perform Merge [$\{e\}$, s].

The first entity given to Merge is a new set with e as its only member. The set-relevant clauses of the Merge definition are thus applicable: if s is also a set, for example, (190d) indicates how its other elements will be combined with e.

With these operator definitions, the fundamental theorem that our algorithm produces solutions for all and only consistent f-descriptions can easily be proved by induction on the number of statements in the f-description. Suppose an entity collection C is a solution for an f-description of $n - 1$ statements. Then the collection after successfully performing Merge[Locate[d_1], Locate[d_2]] is a solution for the description formed by adding $d_1 = d_2$ as an nth statement, and the collection after successfully performing Include[Locate[d_1], Locate[d_2]] is a solution for the description formed by adding $d_1 \in d_2$ as an nth statement. If the Locate, Merge, or Include operators fail, the larger f-description is inconsistent and has no solution at all.

Notes

We are indebted to Martin Kay, Beau Sheil, and Tom Wasow for valuable suggestions and fruitful discussions over a period of several years. We also wish to thank Ken Church, Elisabet Engdahl, Kris Halvorsen, and Annie Zaenen for commenting on earlier drafts of this chapter. This work was supported in part by a grant from the Alfred P. Sloan Foundation for research in cognitive science at the Massachusetts Institute of Technology.

1. Kaplan 1975a,b gives an early version of the Competence Hypothesis and discusses some ways in which the grammatical and processing components might interact. Also see chapter 11 of this volume.

2. Semantic forms with a lexical source are often called *lexical forms*. Less commonly, semantic forms are produced by syntactic rules, for example, to represent unexpressed pronouns; this will be illustrated in section 4.6 in the discussion of English imperative subjects.

3. This chapter is not concerned with the details of the semantic translation procedure for NPs, and the specifications for the SPEC and common noun PRED features are simplified accordingly. With more elaborate expressions for these features, NPs can also be translated into a higher-order intensional logic by a general substitution procedure. For instance, suppose that the symbol A is taken as an abbreviation for the semantic form '$\lambda Q \lambda P \exists x \langle Q \langle x \rangle \wedge P \langle x \rangle \rangle$', which represents the meaning of an existential quantifier, and suppose that 'GIRL' is replaced by the expression '($\uparrow$ SPEC)$\langle$GIRL'$\rangle$'. Then the translation for the SUBJ f-structure would be a formula in which the quantifier is applied to the common noun meaning. See Halvorsen forthcoming for an extensive discussion of f-structure translation and interpretation.

4. This correlation of rule properties is a significant difference between lexical-functional grammar and Relational Grammar (see for example the papers in Perlmutter in press). The two approaches are similar, however, in the emphasis they place on grammatical relations. Bell 1980 offers a more extensive comparison of the two theories.

5. There is an equivalent formulation in which the grammatical relation symbols SUBJ, OBJ, etc., are taken to be the names of functions that apply to f-structure arguments. We would then write SUBJ(f_1) instead of f_1(SUBJ), and the left- and righthand elements of all our expressions would be systematically interchanged. Even with this alternative, however, there are still cases where the function is an unknown (see for example the discussion below of oblique objects). The conceptual consideration underlying our decision to treat f-structures as the formal functions is that only total, finite functions are then involved in the characterization of particular sentences. Otherwise, our conceptual framework would be populated with functions on infinite domains, when only their restriction to the sentence at hand would ever be grammatically relevant. Only this intuition would be affected if the alternative formulation were adopted.

6. Another convention for lexical insertion is to attach the schemata directly to the terminal nodes. While the same functional relationships can be stated with either convention, this alternative requires additional identification schemata in the common case where the preterminal category does not correspond to a distinct functional unit. It is thus more cumbersome to work with.

7. If a schema containing $\uparrow$ is attached to a node whose mother has no $\downarrow$-variable, the $\uparrow$ cannot be properly instantiated and the string is marked ungrammatical. This situation is not likely to occur with immediate domination metavariables but provides an important well-formedness condition for bounded domination. This is discussed in section 4.7.

8. In effect, the instantiation procedure adds to the schemata information about the tree configurations in which they appear. As shown in section 4.4, the f-structure for the sentence can then be inferred without further reference to the c-structure. An equivalent inference procedure can be defined that does not require the introduction of variables and instead takes into account the relative position of schemata in the tree. This alternative procedure searches the

c-structure to obtain the information that we are encoding by variables in instantiated schemata. It essentially intermixes our instantiation operations among its other inferences and is thus more difficult to describe.

9. An attribute in an f-structure is thus a special kind of designator, and the notion of a designator's value generalizes our use of the term *value*, which previously referred only to the entity paired with an attribute in an f-structure.

10. This algorithm is designed to demonstrate that the various conditions imposed by our theory are formally decidable. It is unlikely that this particular algorithm will be incorporated intact into a psychologically plausible model of language performance or even into a computationally efficient parser or generator. For these other purposes, functional operations will presumably be interleaved with c-structure computations, and functional data representations will be chosen so as to minimize the combinatoric interactions with the nondeterministic uncertainty of the c-structure rules.

11. Our c-structure rules thus diverge from a strict context-free formalism. We permit the righthand sides of these rules to be regular expressions as in a recursive transition network, not just simply-ordered category sequences. The * is therefore not interpreted as an abbreviation for an infinite number of phrase structure rules. As our theory evolves, we might incorporate other modifications to the c-structure formalism. For example, in a formalism which, although oriented toward systemic grammar descriptions, is closely related to ours, Kay 1979 uses patterns of partially ordered grammatical relations to map between a linear string and his equivalent to an f-structure. Such partial orderings might be particularly well-suited for free word-order languages.

12. The case-marking entry is distinct from the entry for *to* when it serves as a predicate in its own right, as in prepositional complements or adjuncts.

13. Our general Uniqueness Condition is also the most crucial of several differences between lexical-functional grammar and its augmented transition network precursor. ATN SETR operations can arbitrarily modify the f-structure values (or "register contents," in ATN terminology) as they are executed in a left-to-right scan of a rule or network. The register SUBJ can have one value at one point in a rule and a completely different value at a subsequent point. This revision of value assignments is not allowed in LFG. Equations at one point cannot override equations instantiated elsewhere—all equations must be simultaneously satisfied by the values in a single f-structure. As we have seen, the properties of that f-structure thus do not depend on the particular sequence of steps by which schemata are instantiated or the f-description is solved.

14. In a more detailed treatment of morphology, the schemata for *handing* would be derived systematically by combining the schemata for *hand* (namely, the PRED schema in (65)) with *ing*'s schemata (the PARTICIPLE specification) as the word is formed by suffixation.

15. A marking convention account of the defining/constraining distinction would have to provide an alternative lexical entry for each value that the vaguely specified feature could assume. A vague specification would thus be treated as an ambiguity, contrary to intuition.

16. In the more refined theory of lexical representation presented in chapters 1 and 3 of this volume, the relevant functions are those that appear in the function-assignment lists of lexical predicates. The two characterizations are essentially equivalent.

17. Unless, of course, the element is also the nonset value of another attribute. The point is that the element is inaccessible in its role as adjunct. An interesting consequence of this representation is that no cooccurrence restrictions between temporal adverbs and tense can be stated in the syntax, a conclusion justified independently by Smith 1978.

18. There is sometimes a preferred ordering of adjuncts and oblique objects. Grammatical descriptions might not be the proper account of these biases; they might result from independent factors operating in the psychological perception and production processes. See chapter 11 for further discussion.

19. The term *grammatical control* is sometimes used as a synonym for *functional control*. This kind of identification is distinct from *anaphoric control*, which links pronouns to their antecedents, and *constituent control*, which represents long-distance dependencies. Constituent control is discussed in section 4.7; for discussions of functional and anaphoric control, see chapters 5, 6, and 7.

20. In any event, the schemata in these alternatives violate the substantive restriction on functional control mentioned above. They also run counter to a second substantive restriction, the principle of *functional locality*. This principle states that for human languages, designators in lexical and grammatical schemata may specify no more than two function-applications. This limits the context over which functional properties may be explicitly stipulated. The recursive mechanisms of the c-structure grammar are required to propagate information across wider functional scopes. The locality principle is a functional analogue of the context-free nature of our c-structure grammars.

21. Grimshaw 1979a has argued that the sentential complement is restricted to be interrogative by the semantic type of the predicate WONDER. A separate functional specification of this restriction is therefore unnecessary.

22. Our controlled *e* is a base-generated analogue of the traces left by Chomsky's 1977b rule of *Wh* Movement. However, controlled *e*'s are involved only in the description of constituent control, whereas Chomsky's traces are also used to account for functional control phenomena.

Our controller and controllee metavariables also resemble the HOLD action and the virtual/retrieve arcs of the ATN formalism. Plausible processing models for both systems require similar computational resources to locate and identify the two ends of the control relationship. Thus, the experimental results showing that ATN resource demands predict human cognitive load (Wanner and Maratsos 1978, Kaplan 1975a) are also compatible with lexical-functional grammar. However, we discuss below certain aspects of our theory for which standard ATN notation has no equivalents: the appearance of controllees in the lexical entries of fully realized items, the root node specifications, and the bounding node conventions. Moreover, our theory does not have the characteristic left–right asymmetry of the ATN notation and thus applies equally well to languages like Basque, where constituent ordering is reversed.

23. Note as an aside that we have changed the Q-FOCUS identification schema from (135a) to (141) because the questioned element is no longer the ↓ f-structure of the fronted NP. The new schema places the interrogative semantic form in a canonical f-structure location that is independent of its degree of embedding. The complete fronted NP is also recorded in a canonical f-structure location, as the value of the function FOCUS. That NP is accessible as the FOCUS of the question as well as through its clause-internal function OBJ, as indicated by the connecting line in (143). These separate access paths define the scope of different rules for interpreting anaphors. The FOCUS path in the f-structure for sentence (i) permits the ordinary pronoun *she* to be coreferential with *Sally*, even though this is not permitted by its clause-internal object function, as shown by (ii):

(i)   Which of the men that Sally dated did she hate ____?
(ii) *She hated one of the men that Sally dated.
(iii) I wonder how proud of herself Bill thinks Sally is ____.

The clause-internal function governs the interpretation of reflexive pronouns; (iii) would otherwise be unacceptable because the reflexive is not a clause-mate of the antecedent *Sally*. The problem posed by the contrast between examples (i) and (ii) was observed originally by Postal 1971. The solution sketched here is developed in greater detail by Zaenen 1980.

24. The lexical signature requirement and its formal implications are somewhat reminiscent of Peters's 1973 Survivor property and Wasow's 1978b Subsistence property, two restrictions that have been proposed to guarantee the recursiveness of transformational grammars. Those conditions are imposed on the input and output trees of a transformational cycle, whereas (147f) stipulates a property that must hold of a single c-structure.

25. Chomsky 1977b proposes to derive such examples by restructuring rules that move the *of*-PP and *that*-complement outside of the *picture* and *claim* NPs before the *Wh* Movement rule applies. But such a reanalysis in all the relevant cases cannot be justified, as Godard forthcoming shows for French.

26. Constituent control dependencies for relative pronouns also penetrate the genitive NP. This would follow automatically from the hypothesis that relative metavariables share the [+wh] subscript. The well-known distributional differences between relative and interrogative items would be accounted for by additional features in the categorial subscripts for the relative and interrogative dependencies and more selective specifications on the linking schemata associated with other bounding nodes.

27. Our use of linking schemata has some of the flavor of Chomsky's Subjacency Condition and COMP to COMP movement (Chomsky 1977b). We mentioned above that our specifications of bounding nodes differs from Chomsky's, but there are other significant differences in our approaches. For one, we do not *move* constituents from place to place; we merely assert that a functional equivalence obtains. That equivalence enters into the f-description and is

reflected in the ultimate f-structure, but it is never visible in the c-structure. Thus, we have a simple account of cases where *unmoved* constituents are subject to the bounded domination constraints, as in Chinese interrogatives (Huang 1980); in such cases, the theory of Chomsky 1977b fails to provide a uniform explanation.

28. We also leave open the possibility that a given controller has several domain roots. If several daughters of the controller node's mother are labeled with the controller's categorial superscript, then each such daughter becomes the root of a domain that must contain one corresponding controllee. This distributes the instantiation requirement to each of the domains independently. This suggests a plausible account for the across-the-board properties of coordinate structures, but more intensive investigation of coordination within the lexical-functional framework is needed before a definitive analysis can be given.

29. Chomsky 1977b has proposed an analysis of these sentences that does not involve a double dependency. He suggests an alternative phrase structure for examples of this type whereby the *on* PP belongs somewhere outside the *play* VP. Bach 1977 and Bresnan 1976c point out that this proposal has a number of empirical shortcomings.

30. The preposed item in relative clauses is also a TOPIC. Although the relative TOPIC might be functionally controlled when the clause is embedded next to the NP that it modifies, it must be linked anaphorically when the relative is extraposed.

31. The evaluation uses operators similar to Locate, Merge, and Include except that they return False whenever the corresponding solution operators would modify the f-structure.

32. Given the functional apparatus of our theory, we can demonstrate that the restrictions in (180) are necessary as well as sufficient for recursiveness. If nonbranching dominance cycles are allowed, there is a straightforward way of simulating the computation of an arbitrary Turing machine. The Turing machine tape is encoded in the f-structure, each level of which corresponds to one cell and has up to three attributes, CONTENTS (whose value is drawn from the TM's tape vocabulary), LEFTCELL (whose value is an encoding of the cell to the left), and RIGHTCELL. Each state of the TM is represented by a nonterminal category, and a transition from state q_i to q_j is represented by a rule rewriting q_i as q_j. A single rule expands the starting category of the grammar to the initial state of the machine, and that rule has schemata that describe the TM's input tape. Starting at the top of the c-structure, each node in the nonbranching tree represents the next transition of the machine, and the f-structure at each node is the tape at that transition. The tape operations of a transition appear as schemata on the corresponding c-structure rule. They inspect the contents of the mother f-structure and produce an appropriate daughter f-structure. The lexical categories correspond to the final states of the machine, and the f-structure for a prelexical node is an encoding of the TM's output tape.

33. Certain other restrictions on metavariable correspondences will also provide this guarantee. For example, a nearly *crossed* restriction would also suffice, but it would entail more cumbersome models of processing. Formally, what must be excluded is arbitrary degrees of nesting and crossing.

34. Bresnan, Kaplan, and Zaenen forthcoming discuss the formal consequences of the Dutch dependencies and provide a simple lexical-functional description of them.

35. The recursive specification in (190c) must be slightly complicated if f-structures are allowed to be cyclic, that is, to contain themselves as one of their attribute values, either directly or indirectly through some intervening f-structure levels. Structures of this kind would be induced by equations of the form $(f \alpha) = f$. If a Merge of two such structures is attempted, the recursive sequence might never reach a non-f-structure and terminate. However, any infinitely recursive sequence must repeat the merger of the same two f-structures within a finite number of steps. Merges after the first will have no effect, so the sequence can be truncated before attempting step (190c) for the second time. The Merge operator must simply keep a record of which pairs of f-structures it is still in the process of merging. The Locate operator is immune to this problem, since the number of its recursions is determined by the number of function-applications in the designator, which, being derived from the grammar or lexicon, is finite. While presenting no major formal difficulties, cyclic structures seem to be linguistically unmotivated.

Chapter 5

Control and Complementation

Joan Bresnan

This chapter develops a theory of control and complementation based on the lexical–functional theory of grammar, LFG, presented in this volume. A formal theory of grammar, such as the theory of LFG, is not itself a substantive linguistic theory. Rather, it is a language for precisely expressing descriptive rules and universal postulates of grammar. The choice of such a formal theory of grammar is extremely important. If the formal theory contains the appropriate concepts and representations, then linguistic principles and grammatical descriptions expressed within it will immediately generalize along the right dimensions, simplifying both descriptive rules and theoretical postulates. An inappropriate formal theory will require a host of auxiliary concepts and definitions, and may obscure the underlying regularities that optimal grammars must express. Having no formal theory at all will lead to vague and inconsistent formulations at both the theoretical and the descriptive levels. Despite its importance, however, a formal theory of grammar is only one step in the construction of a substantive linguistic theory of universal grammar. The present work adds to the formal theory of LFG a set of substantive postulates for a universal theory of control and complementation. Not all of the relevant phenomena could be treated here, but the central concepts of function, category, syntactic encoding of function in categorial structure, government, and functional and anaphoric control are discussed, and comparisons are made with alternative theories including the government and binding theory of Chomsky 1981.

The basic assumptions of the theory of control are articulated in the initial sections: first, grammatical functions are universal primitives of syntax, not derived from phrase structure representations or from semantic notions; second, grammatical functions are lexically encoded in predicate argument structures in varying ways; third, constituent structure categories are universally decomposed into features and types, the features being definable in terms of the primitives SUBJ, OBJ; and fourth, grammatical functions are syntactically encoded directly in surface representations of phrase structure, according to structural configurations or morphological features. In lexical–functional theory, the grammatical relations of a sentence—that is, the set of associations between its surface syntactic constituents and its semantic predicate argument structure—are represented by a functional structure (*f-structure*), which is separate from the representation of constituency relations (*c-structure*). F-structures represent grammatical relations in a universal format, while constituency relations vary radically across languages and even across constructions within a single language. In this chapter it will be argued that the syntactic conditions on government and control are properly stated in terms of f-structure representations, not c-structure representations. Evidence will be presented to choose between alternative theories of government and control, and a number of major generalizations will be derived from the present theory.

This study presupposes the material in chapters 1, 2, and 4 of this volume.

5.1 Grammatical Functions

In lexical–functional theory, grammatical functions are universal, syntactically primitive elements of grammar. Although grammatical functions are basic concepts in traditional grammars as well as in recent studies of a wide variety of languages (Perlmutter in press), some researchers have objected to taking grammatical functions as primitives at the level of syntactic representation.

The theory of universal grammar, like other theories, can be axiomatized as a set of basic concepts and a set of postulates from which the explanatory results of the theory are deducible as theorems; all grammatical concepts of the theory can be defined in terms of the basic set of concepts, which are taken to be primitive, or undefined. In general, there are many alternative sets of primitives in terms of which theories can be axiomatized. However, Chomsky 1981 asserts that we are not free to choose our primitives in constructing an explanatory theory of universal grammar; in order to explain the fact of language acquisition, we must require that the primitives of our formal grammatical theory correspond directly to categories of prelinguistic experience. This he calls the criterion of *epistemological priority*. He then suggests that the primitive concepts in terms of which constituent structure has been defined may be "epistemologically prior" to the primitives in terms of which grammatical relations have been defined. This is the basis of Chomsky's 1981:10 conclusion that "we should . . . be wary of hypotheses that appear to assign to grammatical relations too much of an independent status in the functioning of rule systems."

However, Chomsky's suggestion that the primitives of categorial or constituent structure are epistemologically prior to the primitives of relational or functional structures is unsupported; no evidence or argumentation is offered for this view. Indeed, this view is implausible, for if it is assumed that the primitives of constituent structure are epistemologically prior, and that grammatical relations are derived from them as defined concepts, then it is difficult to explain the invariance of grammatical relations across the radically varying constituent structures of different languages. If constituency primitives were epistemologically prior, the appearance of universal grammatical relations in languages which lack sufficient constituent structure to support configurational definitions (see Perlmutter in press, Hale 1979, and chapter 8 of this volume) would be completely mysterious.

A more fundamental problem is the criterion of epistemological priority itself. In chapter 10 of this volume and in Pinker and Lebeaux 1981, it is shown that there is a natural inductive basis for the elementary concepts of category and function that are assumed in the lexical–functional theory of syntax; for example, the notion of SUBJ is grounded in the concept of animate agent or actor. However, this inductive basis is supplemented by a distributional learning algorithm that can infer the existence of nonagent subjects. As a result, according to the Pinker–Lebeaux model, the mature grammar eventually acquired by the language learner is *not* represented in terms of formal primitives that correspond directly to prelinguistic notions such as animate agent or actor. Pinker and Lebeaux argue that this model can not only explain the fact of language acquisition, which is the goal of learnability models, but also account for the course of language acquisition; that is, the model provides a consistent and coherent account of the evidence from studies of child language. In short, since well-motivated language acquisition procedures can induce classes of formal grammars whose primitive concepts bear no direct correspondence to prelinguistic categories, the criterion of epistemological priority is simply irrelevant to the goal of constructing an explanatory linguistic theory.

The doctrine that theories of higher cognitive processes should be formulated in terms of primitives that correspond directly to categories of primary experience derives from empiricist theories of knowledge that have long since been rejected in the psychology of language and perception, and which in fact have never been accepted in generative linguistic theory. The evidence suggests, on the contrary, that the human mind is innately endowed with powerful conceptual structures and operations that are only abstractly and indirectly related to "primary experience" (Miller and Johnson-Laird 1976); elsewhere, Chomsky has also championed this view (Chomsky 1969). The fact is that many elementary linguistic concepts play an important theoretical role in rule systems and yet cannot be reduced to primary experience as required by the criterion of epistemological priority. For example, *stress* is a basic concept of Chomsky and Halle's 1968 theory of English phonology, although phonetic research had already shown that stress has no reliable acoustical correlate in amplitude, duration, or fundamental frequency of sound (Lehiste 1970). What *is* required of an explanatory theory of grammar is not that it be axiomatizable in terms of such "epistemologically prior" primitives, but rather that its knowledge representations can be naturally embedded in substantive theories of the processes of language acquisition and use. The theory of syntax adopted here has already begun to meet this requirement; see Pinker and Lebeaux 1981, as well as chapters 10, 11, and 12 of this volume.

A different form of objection to considering grammatical functions as primitives could be based on *constructive elimination*, by constructing from constituency primitives alone a syntactic theory which is capable of explaining the universal properties of grammatical relations. Research in relational grammar (Perlmutter in press), as well as the work presented in this volume and elsewhere (Mohanan 1981a, Marantz 1981, Rappaport 1980, Roberts 1981, Simpson and Bresnan 1982), shows that the invariance of grammatical relations across languages and across constructions with radically varying constituency relations is not explained by purely structure-based theories. In fact, to express certain universals, recent versions of transformational grammar now make explicit or tacit appeal to grammatical relations that cannot be eliminated through definitions in terms of independently motivated constituent structure configurations (see Chomsky 1980a, 1981, Mohanan 1981a).

These objections to considering grammatical functions as primitives at the level of syntactic representation can therefore be rejected. The question remains, however, whether grammatical functions can be reduced to nonsyntactic notions at other levels of linguistic representation. The important work of Dowty (to appear) bears on this question. Dowty proposes a definition of the grammatical functions in terms of their universal roles in the semantic composition of sentences (assuming the framework of Montague 1973). For example, the *object* is the argument that combines with a verb meaning to produce an intransitive verb phrase meaning, and the *subject* is the argument that combines with an intransitive verb phrase meaning to produce a sentence meaning.

A successful definition in these terms would be a welcome advance in grammatical theory. However, while it is possible to identify semantic notions that can be put into correspondence with syntactic concepts, what must be shown in order to claim that the syntactic concepts can be eliminated is that this correspondence is explanatory rather than arbitrary. In other words, the syntactic properties of grammatical functions—such as their roles in reflexivization, causativization, passivization, and control—should not be arbitrarily associated with the proposed semantic definitions, but should be shown to follow from the appropriate semantic characterizations. Unless this is done, syntactically primitive grammatical functions will not have been eliminated by these definitions, but only renamed. For example, in terms of the semantic composition of sentences, the subject plays the same semantic role with both transitive and intransitive verbs. Yet causativization in Malayalam (as in many languages) affects the subjects of transitive and intransitive verbs in syntactically distinct ways: the subject of an intransitive base verb behaves syntactically like the object of the causativized form of the verb, but the subject of a transitive base verb behaves syntactically like an oblique instrumental of the causativized verb (Mohanan 1981a). Since the semantic properties of the causativized subjects are the same regardless of whether they function syntactically as objects or as oblique instrumentals, there is no principled semantic distinction between these two grammatical functions. The proposed semantic definitions of grammatical functions do not explain the syntactic properties of objects and obliques (although one could of course stipulate arbitrary differences in the semantic composition of causativized transitives and intransitives in order to match the syntactic differences.) We therefore conclude that the definitions do not elimi-

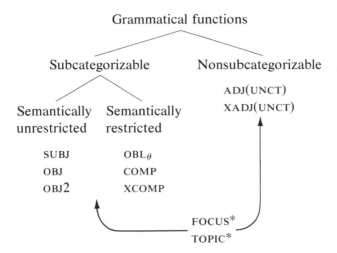

Grammatical functions

*The subcategorizability of these functions is a parameter that distinguishes "subject-oriented" from "topic-oriented" languages.

Figure 5.1
Classification of grammatical functions assumed in this theory

nate grammatical functions, but merely rename them in semantic terms. (See Mohanan 1981a for a similar argument with respect to recent attempts to define grammatical functions in terms of Chomsky's government and binding theory.)

Because grammatical functions in the present theory play an important role both in lexical representations and in semantically interpreted syntactic representations, it is of course possible that lexical or sentential semantics (or both) may ultimately provide true nonsyntactic definitions of these concepts, just as many of the elementary features of phonology are definable in terms of phonetic theory. But the elimination of functions as primitives is no more necessary to an explanatory theory of grammar than is the elimination of phonological features.

The grammatical functions assumed in this study are classified in figure 5.1. The functions XCOMP and XADJ(unct) are distinguished as *open grammatical functions;* all others are *closed.* (Slightly different notations are used elsewhere in this volume; for example, the symbol COMP is used in chapter 8 for XCOMP, and the symbols VCOMP and SCOMP appear in chapters 1 and 4 for XCOMP and COMP, respectively.) The distinction between open and closed functions plays a role in the theory of control (section 5.8). The *subcategorizable* functions in figure

5.1 correspond to the *governable* functions of chapter 4; these are the only functions to which lexical items can make reference.

Not all aspects of this classification are universal; in particular, the subcategorizability of TOPIC and FOCUS appears to be a typological property that distinguishes "subject-oriented" from "topic-oriented" languages. In addition to these functions, there is assumed to be a universal set of functional features, including CASE, TENSE, NUMBER, GENDER, PERSON, FINITE, PRED, and SPEC. In the formal representation of functional structures (chapter 4), function and feature names are formally distinguished by the types of their values.

The role of grammatical functions in the lexical–functional theory of syntax is to provide the mapping between surface categorial structure and semantic predicate argument structure. This is done by assigning the grammatical functions semantic roles in the lexicon and syntactic realizations in the categorial component of the syntax. A fundamental constraint on all references to functions and functional features, whether by lexical or by syntactic rules and representations, is the *principle of functional locality:* designators in lexical and grammatical schemata can specify no more than two function applications (see chapter 4). This principle means that function designators can refer only to functions and features or to immediate subfunctions and features of the f-structure to which they apply.

5.2 Lexical Encoding of Grammatical Functions

In the lexical–functional theory of syntax, lexical items subcategorize for function, not constituent structure categories, and lexical items exert their selectional restrictions on a subset of their subcategorized functions. Lexical subcategorization for function rather than structure explains the fact that when a function is freely realizable in a set of different phrase structure positions, the subcategorization restrictions of any lexical item that subcategorizes that function are satisfied by the entire set of positions (see chapter 2, Grimshaw 1981, Montalbetti 1981). Moreover, it provides an invariant theory of subcategorization for configurational and nonconfigurational grammars alike (section 5.4).

The *predicate argument structure* of a lexical item lists the arguments for which there are selectional restrictions; the *grammatical function assignment* lists the syntactically subcategorized functions (without repetitions) and may include a null symbol ϕ;[1] the *lexical form* pairs arguments with functions. This study employs the notations given in

(1), which differ slightly from those in chapters 1, 3, and 4. (The notation given here provides a simple formal interpretation of the coherence condition; see section 5.5.) (1) gives notation for representing properties of the lexical item *seem* as it is used in sentences like *John seems sick to Mary*.

(1)

a. predicate argument structure: SEEM$\langle 1,2 \rangle$
b. grammatical function assignment: $\{(\text{XCOMP}),(\text{OBL}_{GO}),(\text{SUBJ})\}$
c. lexical form: 'SEEM-TO$\langle(\text{XCOMP})(\text{OBL}_{GO})\rangle$
                                       (SUBJ)'

In this usage *seem* has a dyadic predicate argument structure, whose first argument denotes a state of affairs (e.g., John's being sick) and whose second argument denotes a perceiver of that state of affairs (e.g., Mary). (1b) gives the functions that are subcategorized by *seem*. In (1c) the function XCOMP is assigned to the state-of-affairs argument, and the function (OBL$_{GO}$) is assigned to the perceiver argument. The notation in (1c) indicates that *seem* subcategorizes three functions but exerts its selectional restrictions only on the XCOMP and OBL$_{GO}$ functions. The SUBJ in (1c) is a "nonlogical" or "nonthematic" function, upon which *seem* imposes no selectional restrictions. Its relation to the XCOMP is determined by the theory of control (section 5.8). The material inside the angled brackets in (1a,c) is called the *argument list* of the predicate; this lists the predicate's semantic arguments, which give rise to its "selectional restrictions" (see chapter 1).

Although example (1) shows a verb that does not impose selectional restrictions on its subject, it is well established that lexical items may also impose semantic selectional restrictions on subjects. In (2) and (3), for example, *admire* selects an animate subject while *frighten* selects an animate object.

(2)
a. *Mary* admires John.
b. #*Sincerity* admires John.

(3)
a. Mary frightens *John*.
b. #Mary frightens *sincerity*.

It has been argued that certain semantic asymmetries between subjects and nonsubjects justify the suppression of the "logical" subject argument from lexical predicate argument structure (Marantz 1981).

(The term *logical subject* involves a confusion of distinct levels of representation, as pointed out in chapter 1. In what follows, the term *logical subject argument* will be used to refer to the thematic argument of a predicate that has SUBJ assigned to it in the unmarked active lexical form.) According to this view, the selectional restrictions in (2) would be attributed, not to the verb *admire,* but to the meaning of the verb phrase *admires John.* Nevertheless, many selectional restrictions imposed on the subject ultimately reduce to properties of the lexical item, for subject selection occurs when the only content of the verb phrase is the lexical predicate itself, as in (4).

(4)
a. *Mary* will relax.
b. #*Sincerity* will relax.

The question is not, then, whether subject selection is a property of lexical items, but whether this property is represented by the same predicate argument structure that represents nonsubject selection.

Two rationales have been given for an asymmetrical representation of the logical subject argument and other arguments in predicate argument structure (Marantz 1981:50–51). First, the "choice of object (or other argument of a verb) affects the semantic role of the logical subject while choice of logical subject does not affect the semantic role of the object," and second, there exist object idioms but no subject idioms with free arguments. (Arguments similar to Marantz's have been attributed to Chomsky in lectures.) That is, while many idioms express properties which are noncompositionally derived by combining a verb and an object (these are the so-called "object idioms"), there are claimed to be no idioms that express properties which are noncompositionally derived by combining a verb and a subject (these would be "subject idioms"). Examples like (5a–d) are given by Marantz to illustrate these points.

(5)
a. kill an insect
b. kill a conversation
c. kill a bottle (i.e., empty it)
d. kill an audience (i.e., wow them)

The wide range of predicates expressed by the examples in (5), including literal, figurative, and idiomatic senses of *kill,* depends upon the choice of object of the verb.

As we will see, neither of these considerations is well-founded factually, but it must also be recognized that the logic of the argument that is based upon them is faulty. Note that both of these considerations are based upon the compositional semantics of sentences. The assumption is that if the subject is always the *last* argument to be semantically composed with the predicate, one can explain the generalization that the choice of nonsubject arguments does not depend on the choice of the subject argument. By suppressing the subject argument from the verb's predicate argument structure, one prevents the subject from being combined directly with the verb before the verb and its nonsubject arguments have been assembled into a predicate; the subject can then be semantically composed only with a completely formed predicate. But the issue of whether or not the subject argument has a special role in the semantic composition of the sentence is logically independent of the issue of whether or not a subject argument position should appear in lexical predicate argument structure. For example, in Dowty's theory (Dowty to appear), the subject is always the last argument to be semantically composed with the predicate; yet the lexical function that expresses the meaning of a transitive verb in his theory contains variables for both the subject and the object arguments. In short, one could capture the subject/nonsubject generalizations without affecting the lexical representation of predicate argument structure, simply by giving the subject a distinguished role as final argument in the semantic composition of the sentence.

We will not take this approach, however, because the subject/nonsubject generalization itself is factually ill-founded, as mentioned above. First, there are in fact subject idioms with free nonsubject arguments: for example, *The cat's got x's tongue* ('x can't speak'), *What's eating x?* ('What is making x so irritable?'), *Time's up (for x)* ('The time (for x) has expired'), *x's goose is cooked* ('x is in trouble and there is no way out'). Second, there are clear cases in which the semantic choice of a nonsubject argument does depend upon choice of the subject. Consider, for example, (6a–c).

(6)
a. The ceiling caved in on John.
b. The wall caved in on John.
c. The roof caved in on John.

Example (6c) has a figurative or metaphorical sense ('Everything went wrong for John') as well as the literal sense that part of the structure of a house collapsed on John; but examples (6a,b) are unambiguously literal. Thus, the choice of *the roof* as subject of *caved in* gives rise to a special meaning. Under this special meaning, one can choose as the object of *on* an abstract noun phrase which cannot occur with the literal meaning:

(7)
a. #The ceiling caved in on John's dreams.
b. #The wall caved in on John's dreams.
c. The roof caved in on John's dreams.

How do we know that it is not the object of *on* which gives rise to the special meaning and thereby determines the choice of the subject *the roof?* When we omit the *on*-phrase altogether, we find that *The roof caved in* still has the figurative sense 'Everything went wrong' while *The ceiling caved in* and *The wall caved in* lack it. It is not difficult to find other examples which support the same conclusion (e.g., *A truck hit John* vs. *An idea hit John,* pointed out by K. P. Mohanan).

In conclusion, there is no justification for suppressing the subject argument from predicate argument structure. Moreover, theories of lexical representation which omit the subject argument from predicate argument structure so as to give it the special status of final argument in the semantic composition of the sentence are incompatible with the evidence of subject idioms and the subject-determined selection of non-subject functions.

By separating the predicate argument structure from the grammatical function assignment, as in (1a,b), we open the possibility of finding principles which will enable us to predict the possible function–argument correspondences and so derive, or at least narrowly constrain, the set of lexical forms. Current research in lexical representation suggests that there are universal constraints on the function–argument pairings in lexical forms. One constraint which is discussed elsewhere in this volume is *function–argument biuniqueness:* in each lexical form, the predicate arguments and the functions they are paired with must be in one-to-one correspondence (see chapters 2 and 3).

Recent research suggests that there are also *semantic constraints on function–argument pairings:* there are semantically restricted functions that can only be paired with arguments of specified semantic types (see Rappaport 1980). The specified types of arguments may include the thematic relations AG(ent), TH(eme), EXP(eriencer), SO(urce), GO(al), LOC(ation), DIR(ection), BEN(eficiary), INSTR(umental), as well as MNR (manner), MEANS (a secondary TH), CAUSEE (a secondary AG), PART, PATH, QUANT(ity), and PROP(opositional). (Nothing rests on the details of the classification of argument types; see Jackendoff 1976 and Amritavalli 1980 for some discussion.) To enforce the semantic constraints on function–argument pairings, it is convenient to assume that there is a labeling function from the argument types to the predicate arguments of each predicate argument structure. As illustrated in (8), a single argument may bear more than one label (Jackendoff 1972).

(8)

a.   SEEM-TO⟨PROP,GOAL⟩
                        EXP

b.   BUY⟨AG,TH,SO⟩
            GO

c.   SELL⟨AG,TH,GO⟩
              SO

A semantically restricted function, then, can be paired only with an argument one of whose labels matches its semantic type. In particular, the oblique functions can be paired only with an argument type whose index they carry: for example, OBL_{AG} must be paired with an AG argument; OBL_{GO}, with a GO; and OBL_{LOC}, with a LOC. The open and closed complement functions XCOMP and COMP can be paired only with what may be broadly referred to as "propositional" arguments (those labeled PROP). COMP and XCOMP differ in their syntactic encoding properties (section 5.4) and in their control properties (sections 5.8, 5.9). The null symbol ϕ is not a function; it appears only in argument positions, where it signifies that the argument is lexically interpreted and no function is assigned (footnote 1). For example, in (9) ϕ indicates that the AG is semantically filled in the mediopassive lexical form of *read,* and in (10) it indicates that the TH is filled in the intransitivized lexical form of the same verb:

(9)

a.   The novel reads easily.

b.   READ⟨ϕ (SUBJ)⟩
            AG   TH

(10)

a.   John reads frequently.

b.   READ⟨(SUBJ) ϕ⟩
            AG   TH

We can formulate these restrictions as follows. Let G be a semantically restricted function and R its associated argument type. A *designator of G* is any functional designator in the sense of chapter 4 which mentions the function G: for example, (↑SUBJ) is a designator of SUBJ. Now we will require that in every lexical entry, every lexical designator of G must be assigned to an argument of type R, either by appearing in an argument list at an argument of that type or by being equated with another lexical designator that does so. (The latter condition allows an extraposed COMP function, for example, to be equated with a SUBJ.) Note that these restrictions specify the *only* possibilities for lexical items to refer to semantically restricted functions; this will have consequences for the theory of control (section 5.8), for it restricts the set of lexically induced functional controllers ((20)) and the set of lexically introduced functional anaphors ((35)). Because the open functions have broader syntactic properties, their designators may also appear in certain other contexts (see sections 5.4, 5.8, 5.9).

Unlike the semantically restricted functions, the semantically unrestricted functions SUBJ, OBJ, OBJ2 may be paired with any argument type or remain unpaired with an argument (as in the case of "nonlogical" subjects). There are nevertheless important constraints on their assignment to lexical forms. In particular, there appears to be a hierarchy for the assignment of SUBJ, OBJ, and OBJ2 to predicate argument structures: in the unmarked case, OBJ2 is assigned only if OBJ has been assigned, and OBJ only if SUBJ has been (cf. Rappaport 1980 and chapter 3 of this volume).

Lexical rules can alter the assignment of functions to predicate argument structures, and only lexical rules can do so, given the principle of direct syntactic encoding (chapter 1). Lexical rules are motivated elsewhere in this volume; see also Roberts 1981, Rappaport 1980, Neidle in preparation.

5.3 Categories

Constituent structure categories are decomposed into a *type*, or level of structure, and a *feature matrix* of universal categorial features as in Bresnan 1975, 1976b. The features and types of major categories assumed in this study are shown in figures 5.2 and 5.3, respectively, with their common notations. As we will see (section 5.4), the categorial features "predicative" and "transitive" of figure 5.2 can be defined in terms of the functional primitives SUBJ and OBJ. Hence, we can elimi-

	"predicative"	"transitive"	
V	+	+	verbal
P	±	+	pre- or postpositional
N	±	−	nominal
A	+	−	adjectival
S	−		sentential

Figure 5.2
Feature matrices of major categories

type	0	1	2
category	V	V′	V″ (VP)
	P	P′	P″ (PP)
	N	N′	N″ (NP)
	A	A′	A″ (AP)
		S	$\overline{\text{S}}$

Figure 5.3
Major category types

nate primitive categorial features from our theory altogether. For simplicity in representing c-structure trees in what follows, the convention will be adopted that when a nonsentential category of type 1 is exhaustively dominated by a category of type 2 or exhaustively dominates a category of type 0, the type 1 category will be suppressed.

The categories of type 0 are called *lexical categories;* the categories of types 1 and 2 are called *projections;* projections of the highest type (i.e., type 2 in figure 5.3) are called *maximal projections;* and lexical categories and their projections are all considered *major categories.* S and $\overline{\text{S}}$ are considered to be major categories which are projections of no lexical category (Hornstein 1977, McCloskey 1979). There are also *minor categories* of null or degenerate type, including DET and COMP (Bresnan 1975, 1976b) and certain uses of P(reposition) (see section 5.4). Not all languages have instantiations of all categories. For example, Warlpiri does not instantiate the category A; instead, the category

N functions as both A and N (Nash 1980, Simpson in preparation). Nor do all languages distinguish all types in every category; for example, many VSO languages do not instantiate V' or V''. In short, the instantiation of both types and features of categories is a source of variation among languages.

C-structure rules are context-free rewriting rules (or recursive transition networks) defined over the vocabulary of major and minor categories. The set of possible rules is narrowly constrained, as discussed in the next section. Natural classes of categories and rule schemata can be designated by the X-bar (X-prime) notation as in Bresnan 1975, 1976b. For example, $\underset{[+t]}{X} = \{V,P\}$ and $\underset{[+p]}{X''} = \{VP,PP,NP,AP\}$.

5.4 Syntactic Encoding of Grammatical Functions

Grammatical functions are assigned to the particular c-structure rules and inflectional features of each language. The possible syntactic encodings of functions into structure are highly constrained. In *configurational encoding* a basic form of c-structure rule is, for any categorial feature matrix X, $X^{n+1} \to C_1 \ldots X^n \ldots C_m$, where $n \geq 0$ and C_i is either a minor category or a maximal projection. (Falk 1980 suggests that this basic rule form is further decomposed into separate specifications of dominance and precedence relations.) For this rule form, the basic principle of configurational encoding is to associate a function-assigning equation $(\uparrow G) = \downarrow$ with each C_i if and only if C_i is a maximal projection, and to associate the equation $\uparrow = \downarrow$ elsewhere. A major category bearing the equation $\uparrow = \downarrow$ is called the *head*. Hence, according to the basic principle of configurational encoding, all and only the maximal projections of categories can bear functions, every phrase has a unique head, and the functional features of a phrase are identified with those of its head. It follows immediately that in predominantly configurational languages, only maximal projections of categories will appear to be subcategorized for (section 5.1); this is a widely recognized characteristic of subcategorization.

The X-bar theory must be elaborated to permit other rule forms such as those for coordinate structures and for exocentric constructions (Bloomfield 1933). The syntax and semantics of coordination in the present theory are discussed in Andrews 1981, Peterson 1981a, and Halvorsen forthcoming. Among the exocentric constructions of English are the sentence (e.g., *John walks slowly*) and the gerund phrase (e.g., *John's walking slowly*); in these the head is VP, a maximal projection of V, while the dominating category is not a projection of V. Examples are given in (11) and (12). (Here I am adapting the analysis of the English S proposed by Falk 1980a.) In the gerund construction of rule (12), the case-marking constraints are omitted.

(11)
$$S \rightarrow \quad NP \qquad VP$$
$$\quad\quad (\uparrow SUBJ)=\downarrow \ \uparrow=\downarrow$$

(12)
$$NP \rightarrow \quad NP \qquad 's \ VP$$
$$\quad\quad (\uparrow SUBJ)=\downarrow \qquad \uparrow=\downarrow$$

Because it is the projection of no lexical category, S is an exocentric category in all languages. S can be headed by VP (as in English and other SOV languages), by V (as in VSO languages), by nominals (as in Walpiri (Simpson in preparation)), and by adjectival phrases (as in Russian (Neidle in preparation)).

Exocentric rules fall under the rule form $X^n \rightarrow C_1 \ldots C_m$, where $n > 0$ and C_i is either a minor category (e.g., *'s*) or a maximal projection of a lexical category. The principle of function assignment for rules of this form is to associate the equation $\uparrow = \downarrow$ with a single major category (the head) and to any minor categories, and to associate a function assignment equation $(\uparrow G) = \downarrow$ with all other maximal projections. Consequently, for both exocentric and endocentric categories, the head is a major category annotated with $\uparrow = \downarrow$, while all other major categories (and only these) are annotated with $(\uparrow G) = \downarrow$. Thus, it remains true that in configurational encoding, only the maximal projections of categories can bear functions, every phrase has a unique head, and the functional features of a phrase are identified with those of its head.

In *nonconfigurational encoding*, the basic form of c-structure rule is $C \rightarrow X^*$, where C is a major nonlexical category and X is a lexical or nonlexical category. The basic principle of nonconfigurational encoding is to associate pairs of function-assigning and feature-assigning equations of the form given in (13a) with arbitrary X:

(13)

a. $\begin{cases} (\downarrow F) = v \\ (\uparrow G) = \downarrow \end{cases}$

b. $\uparrow = \downarrow$

In (13a), G is a function selected by the value v of the feature F. For example, taking F to be CASE and v to be NOM or ACC, $(\downarrow\text{CASE}) = \text{NOM}$ could be associated with $(\uparrow\text{SUBJ}) = \downarrow$, and $(\downarrow\text{CASE}) = \text{ACC}$ with $(\uparrow\text{OBJ}) = \downarrow$. These pairs of schemata are arbitrarily associated with categories in c-structure rules; see chapter 8 for a detailed example. The schema $\uparrow = \downarrow$ in (13b) is also associated arbitrarily with categories in c-structure rules. (The association with $\uparrow = \downarrow$ could also depend on some inflectional feature.) The *head* of C is defined to be any major category which is annotated with $\uparrow = \downarrow$ and which has a PRED. It follows from the consistency condition (section 5.5 and chapter 4) that the head is unique.

In nonconfigurational encoding, as in configurational encoding, every phrase has a unique head, and the features of a phrase are identified with those of its head. However, in nonconfigurational encoding, functions need not be assigned to maximal projections; instead, they may be assigned to submaximal projections, or even to single lexical categories, as in the example given in figure 5.4. This example is based on the analysis of Warlpiri given in Simpson and Bresnan 1982. Although alternative assignments of functions to categories are possible in figure 5.4, the conditions on well-formedness of f-structures (section 5.5) eliminate "incorrect" assignments, admitting only those that yield consistent, coherent, and complete f-structures.

In sum, the fundamental difference between configurational and nonconfigurational syntactic encoding lies in the surface realizations of grammatical functions. In configurational encoding, functions are identified by the category and by the order of maximal constituents within the immediately dominating phrase, while in nonconfigurational encoding, functions are identified by the case and other inflectional features of unordered, possibly submaximal, constituents. It follows from this theory that in predominantly nonconfigurational languages, only the case marking of constituents will appear to be subcategorized for, and not their phrase structure configurational properties.

Languages may employ both types of encoding, as observed by Mohanan 1981a. In English, the OBJ and OBJ2 are configurationally encoded. Rule (14) illustrates this.

(14)

$$V' \rightarrow V \begin{pmatrix} NP \\ (\uparrow\text{OBJ})=\downarrow \end{pmatrix} \begin{pmatrix} NP \\ (\uparrow\text{OBJ2})=\downarrow \end{pmatrix} \begin{array}{c} PP^* \\ \left\{ \begin{array}{l} (\uparrow\text{OBL}_\theta)=\downarrow \\ (\downarrow\text{PCASE})=\text{OBL}_\theta \end{array} \right\} \end{array}$$

with $\uparrow = \downarrow$ under V.

c-structure

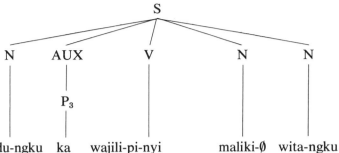

kurdu-ngku   ka   wajili-pi-nyi   maliki-∅   wita-ngku
child-erg   asp   running-do-nonpast   dog-abs   small-erg
'The small child is chasing the dog.'

syntactic encoding of functions

$$\left\{ \begin{matrix} (\uparrow\text{SUBJ})=\downarrow \\ (\downarrow\text{CASE})=\text{ERG} \end{matrix} \right\} , \left\{ \begin{matrix} (\uparrow\text{OBJ})=\downarrow \\ (\downarrow\text{CASE})=\text{ABS} \end{matrix} \right\} , \text{etc.}$$

f-structure

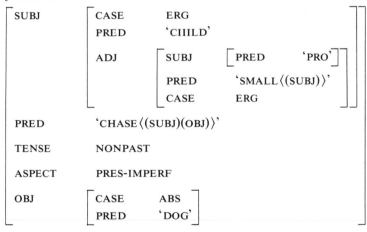

Any order of constituents is possible (so long as AUX is second); the grammatical relations of the sentence remain invariant. The functions are syntactically encoded by case. (Simpson and Bresnan 1982)

Figure 5.4
Nonconfigurational encoding in Warlpiri

In (14), the function names OBJ and OBJ2 are assigned, respectively, to the first and second NPs immediately dominated by VP. However, the OBL_θ function names are assigned on the basis of the features of the unordered PPs. The pair of equation schemata assigned to PP* in (14) actually abbreviates the disjunction of a finite set of pairs, one for each value of θ: $\{(\uparrow OBL_{AG}) = \downarrow, (\downarrow PCASE) = OBL_{AG}\}$ or . . . or $\{(\uparrow OBL_{GO}) = \downarrow,$ $(\downarrow PCASE) = OBL_{GO}\}$. The PCASE features are borne by prepositions, which can serve as case markers in English (Bresnan 1979). For example, the preposition *to* carries the lexical information $(\uparrow PCASE) = OBJ_{GO}$ and the preposition *by* carries the equation $(\uparrow PCASE) = OBL_{AG}$. Since the value of the PCASE feature is always identical with the function name of the PP in rule (14), we can abbreviate the disjunction of these pairs of equations by substituting equals for equals. Thus, we replace the symbol OBL_θ in $(\uparrow OBL_\theta) = \downarrow$ by the designator $(\downarrow PCASE)$, whose value is OBL_θ: the result is the single equation $(\uparrow(\downarrow PCASE)) = \downarrow$ that appears in rule (15).

(15)

$$V' \rightarrow \quad V \quad \begin{pmatrix} NP \\ (\uparrow OBJ)=\downarrow \end{pmatrix} \begin{pmatrix} NP \\ (\uparrow OBJ2)=\downarrow \end{pmatrix} \quad \begin{matrix} PP* \\ (\uparrow(\downarrow PCASE))=\downarrow \end{matrix}$$

$$\uparrow=\downarrow$$

We see, then, that despite its superficial dissimilarity from the schemata in (14), the English PP schema in (15) (which is discussed in chapter 4) is an instance of nonconfigurational encoding. (It should be remembered that the rules just discussed are not the only sources of PP in English; there are PP adjuncts and complements as well (see Bresnan 1979 and chapter 3 of this volume). The introduction of various types of PPs under different nodes, such as S, VP (V''), and V', may give rise to some ordering constraints among prepositional phrases.)

A second example of mixed configurational and nonconfigurational encoding in one grammar is the rule $S \rightarrow X$ AUX X* of Warlpiri, where the minor category AUX has a fixed position in the configuration of S (Hale 1979); in addition, there is evidence that Warlpiri has optional phrasal constituency in nominals as well as infinitival phrase constituents (Nash 1980, Simpson and Bresnan 1982, Simpson in preparation).

Fundamental to X-bar theory are the principles of syntactic encoding which relate possible functions to categorial features. For example, it was pointed out in Bresnan 1975, 1976b that the "verbal" $([+V])$ categories V and P take direct object NPs while the "nominal" $([+N])$ categories A and N do not. Subsequently, Jackendoff 1977 made the important observation that the categories of natural language are better defined in terms of their relations to the subject and object functions than in terms of the categorial features $[\pm N]$, $[\pm V]$ of Chomsky 1970. This insight has a very natural expression in lexical–functional theory. The "intransitive" (i.e., $[-t]$) categories are those which do not permit $(\uparrow OBJ) = \downarrow$ to be annotated to any symbol within the phrase structure rules that expand the intransitive category. This means that adjectival phrases and noun phrases may not contain phrasal direct objects, while verb phrases and pre- or postpositional phrases may.[2] The "predicative" (i.e., $[+p]$) categories are those which do not permit $(\uparrow SUBJ) = \downarrow$ to be annotated to any symbol within the phrase structure rules that expand the predicative category. This means that VP, AP, and predicative NP and PP cannot contain phrasal subjects, while S and nonpredicative NP and PP may. (We have already seen that S and NP may contain phrasal subjects; a possible example in English of a PP which contains a phrasal subject is the absolute PP construction involving *with*: *With John impossible to talk to, Mary left the room, With John away, Mary was happy*.) Thus, we see that we can eliminate primitive categorial features from our theory altogether.

Not only can the basic phrase structure categories of natural language be defined in terms of the primitive functions SUBJ and OBJ, but the function of a category is a fairly good predictor of what are likely to be the categorial and case features of the category. For example, knowing that a category C is a SUBJ, OBJ, or COMP, one can predict that C is likely to be (respectively) a nominative NP, an accusative NP, or an $\bar{S}$, although $\bar{S}$ can also have the SUBJ function, and PP, the OBJ function (Grimshaw 1981), and although nominative NPs can be objects and accusative NPs, subjects (see chapters 7 and 8). Where function and category diverge from their typical correlations, it is the function that correctly predicts the direction in which linguistic rules generalize in such domains as subcategorization, agreement, and control (Grimshaw 1981, Neidle in preparation, Simpson in preparation, Simpson and Bresnan 1982; see also chapters 2 and 8). To express the typical, or unmarked, relations between function and category, however, we postulate substantive constraints on the pairing of functions with categorial and case features. For example, we may say that NOM case is the unmarked feature encoding the SUBJ function. Similarly, we may postulate substantive constraints on the pairing of functions with categories. In particular, the predicative/nonpredicative categorial feature is correlated with the open/closed function distinction.

There are two logically possible ways of pairing the predicative/nonpredicative categories with the open/closed functions: we could say that the predicative categories must have closed functions, and the nonpredicative categories, open functions; or the opposite. It turns out that other properties of our theory dictate which correlation is correct: *a category is predicative if and only if it can be assigned an open function*.[3] This principle of association is motivated by very general conditions on f-structures: only by the function–category associations asserted in this principle can it be ensured in all cases that the f-structures of categories will be consistent and complete (section 5.5) with respect to their subject functions. For predicative categories lack structural subjects; the assignment of an open function to them induces functional control, which obligatorily provides a subject from a category-external source (section 5.8). If these categories were assigned closed functions, a subject could not always be ensured. In contrast, nonpredicative categories may have structural subjects; the assignment of a closed function to them precludes functional control and thereby prevents the assignment of a subject from an external source, which could create inconsistent f-structures. As we will see below in section 9, this principle of function–category association has a number of explanatory consequences.

We digress briefly to point out that the analysis of PPs given here differs in two ways from the analysis presented in chapter 4. First, wherever possible, the PCASE values used here are drawn from a universal set of feature values $\{OBL_{G\acute{O}}, OBL_{AG}, OBL_{INST}, \text{etc.}\}$ rather than from the English-particular set $\{TO, BY, WITH, \text{etc.}\}$. This is motivated by the need for a universal format for representing grammatical relations (see Bresnan 1981, Halvorsen forthcoming, and chapter 10 of this volume). The choice of which prepositions mark which oblique functions appears to depend upon the meaning of the prepositions in their predicative uses. In *This road is to London,* the preposition *to* designates a semantic relation between the SUBJ (*this road*) and the prepositional OBJ (*London*), in which the object is the goal of some motion. Similarly, in *This work is by a famous sculptor,* the preposition *by* designates a semantic relation between the SUBJ (*this work*) and the prepositional OBJ (*a famous sculptor*), in which the object is the agent of some action. We can therefore assume that each case-marking preposition is selected from the set of semantically related predicative prepositions. That is, the preposition that serves as a formal marker of the OBL_{θ} function is chosen from the set of prepositions whose lexical forms associate their prepositional OBJ with the argument type θ. This assumption supports the "semantic bootstrapping" theory regarding acquisition of grammars described in chapter 10 and also accounts for the fact that the case-marking uses of prepositions appear to be related to their predicative uses cross-linguistically. There do, however, appear to be some idiosyncratically marked oblique objects. To account for these, we will extend our notation to OBL$_{\text{FORM}}$, where FORM is a specific preposition name. (For example, in *John relies on Mary,* we could say that *on Mary* is an OBL$_{\text{ON}}$.) Future research may reveal a semantic motivation for these apparently idiosyncratic markings.

The second difference between the analyses of PP given here and in chapter 4 is that the oblique PP is treated here as an exocentric constituent in which the NP actually functions as the head of the PP and the P is a minor category that contributes only the PCASE feature. Thus, it is assumed that in structures of the form [$_\text{PP}$ P NP], either P is the head and NP is an OBJ (yielding the endocentric, predicative PP) or else P is a minor category and NP is the head (yielding the exocentric, oblique PP). The motivation for this is to eliminate compound names (e.g., TO OBJ in chapter 4) for oblique objects. In chapter 7 it is shown that Icelandic verbs which subcategorize for oblique prepositional objects may also govern the case marking of the NP within the PP; if the oblique prepositional object had a compound name, the case-marking restriction on this NP would violate the functional locality principle (for example, no verb could specify "($\uparrow$TO OBJ CASE) = (ACC)").[4]

In conclusion, this theory of syntactic encoding has three main results. First, it provides a characterization of the syntactic notion *head of a phrase* which holds universally for endocentric and exocentric constituents and for configurational and nonconfigurational structure types. Second, it unifies the theories of lexical subcategorization for configurational and nonconfigurational languages. And third, it identifies the basic parameter of syntactic variation for configurational and nonconfigurational languages (see Simpson and Bresnan 1982).

5.5 Representation of Grammatical Relations

The lexical and syntactic encodings of grammatical functions determine a mapping, or a set of associations, between the word and phrase configurations of a language and its semantic predicate argument structures. The grammar of the language assigns to each sentence a set of these associations between surface form and predicate argument structures; these are the *grammatical relations* of the sentence.

Grammatical relations are formally represented by f-structures, which are pairs of *fnames* and *fvalues*. (This differs from the terminology used in chapter 4, where *fnames* and *fvalues* are referred to as *attributes* and *values*.)

(16)
$$\begin{bmatrix} \text{fname}_1 & \text{fvalue}_1 \\ \vdots & \vdots \\ \text{fname}_n & \text{fvalue}_n \end{bmatrix}$$

The *uniqueness* condition on f-structures (also called *consistency*) requires that every fname have a unique value. An *fname* is a symbol denoting one of a universal set of features and functions; an *fvalue* is a symbol (denoting one of a universal set of feature values), a semantic form, an f-structure, or a set of fvalues. Semantic forms differ from symbols in that they are uniquely instantiated when their designators are instantiated (see chapter 4). Consequently, two otherwise identical f-structures with separately instantiated semantic forms are formally distinct. For linguistic motivation for this property, see chapter 2 and Montalbetti 1981. There are two kinds of semantic forms: those with argument lists—called *lexical forms*—and those without.

Certain f-structures are distinguished as *clause nuclei;* these contain an fname PRED whose fvalue is a lexical form (i.e., a predicate argument structure paired with a grammatical function assignment). For example, the f-structure shown in figure 5.5 has two clause nuclei, the f-structure labeled f_1 and its subsidiary f-structure labeled f_2. (The f-structure of figure 5.4 contains three clause nuclei.)

The clause nucleus is the domain of lexical subcategorization in the sense that it makes locally available to each lexical form the grammatical functions that are subcategorized by that form. Lexical subcategorization is enforced by the requirement that every f-structure be both *coherent* and *complete*. An f-structure is locally coherent if and only if all of the subcategorizable functions that it contains are subcategorized by its PRED; an f-structure is then (globally) coherent if and only if it and all of its subsidiary f-structures are locally coherent. Similarly, an f-structure is locally complete if and only if it contains values for all of the functions subcategorized by its PRED; and an f-structure is then (globally) complete if and only if it and all of its subsidiary f-structures are locally complete. This treatment of coherence and completeness permits a very simple formal interpretation: to be locally complete and coherent, an f-structure must contain subcategorizable functions $G_1, ..., G_n$ if and only if it contains a PRED whose value is a lexical form with the grammatical function assignment $\{G_1, ..., G_n\}$.[5]

The level of f-structure differs crucially from representations of constituent structure in that it represents grammatical relations universally, locally with respect to lexical subcategorization, and compositionally with respect to semantic interpretation (Bresnan et al. forthcoming, Simpson and Bresnan 1982). See Halvorsen forthcoming for a compositional procedure for the semantic interpretation of f-structures, which accounts for quantification, adverb scope, control, the distribution of intensional objects, and the interpretation of idiom chunks and grammatical expletives.

5.6 Representation of Constituency

The representation of grammatical relations by f-structures rather than by c-structures permits a massive simplification in the representation of the constituency relations of natural language. These can now be represented by a context-free phrase structure grammar (or a recursive transition network), defining a single level of c-structure representation

a. *c-structure*

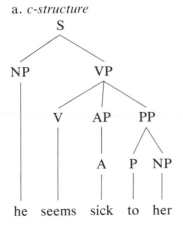

Figure 5.5
Clause nuclei

b. *c-structure annotated with functional schemata*

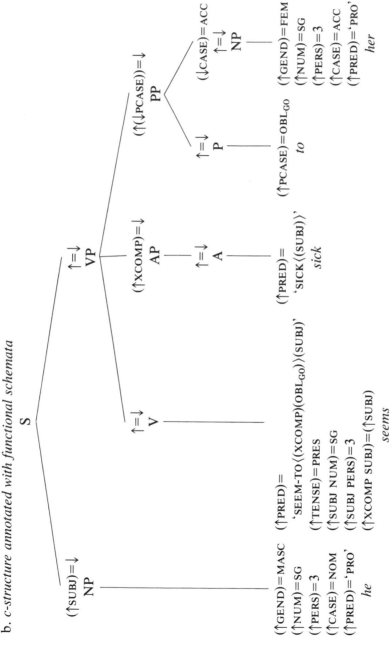

Figure 5.5 (continued)

c. *f-structure*

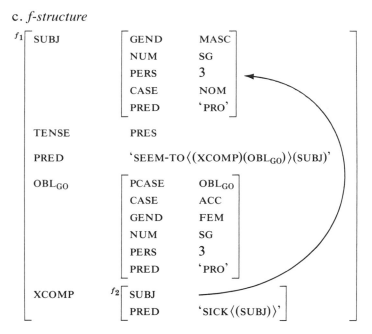

f_1 and f_2 are clause nuclei

Figure 5.5 (continued)

over a small set of universal features and types.[6] The form of c-structure rules is largely predictable from the theory of syntactic encoding, and the categorial features are defined in terms of the primitives SUBJ and OBJ (section 5.4). Since there is only a single level of c-structure to represent the syntactic constituency relations among the words of a sentence, syntactic operations that restructure the dominance or precedence relations among the words and their affixes are eliminated. Consequently, only fully inflected and morphologically complete words are lexically inserted into phrase structures, as Selkirk 1981, Lieber 1980, Lapointe 1980, Nash 1980, and Mohanan 1982 have argued on independent grounds. A further consequence is that any "restructuring" rules that alter word structure (as proposed by Chomsky 1977b, Hornstein and Weinberg to appear) must be presyntactic rules of morphology, as justified by Rothstein 1981, Peterson 1981b, and chapter 1 of this volume. In addition, it follows that there are no structure-dependent operations that map c-structures into c-structures, although there are structure-dependent operations that map c-structures into f-structures, and there may be restricted kinds of operations that map c-structure rules into c-structure rules in a function-preserving fashion (cf. Gazdar to appear b and chapters 1 and 4 of this volume). Thus, syntactic transformations are eliminated.

Finally, the use of null c-structure can be virtually eliminated, restricting both the expressive and the generative power of grammars (see chapter 4). The formal theory of grammatical representation permits a nonterminal node to exhaustively dominate the empty terminal string *e* only in cases of *constituent control,* the long-distance structure-dependent relation that characterizes "*wh*-movement" and similar constructions, as illustrated in figure 5.6.

a. *c-structure*

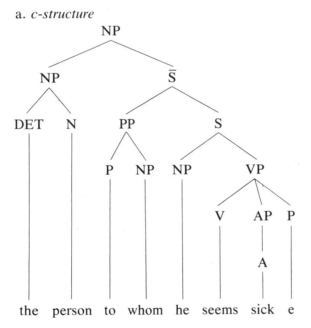

Figure 5.6
Constituent control

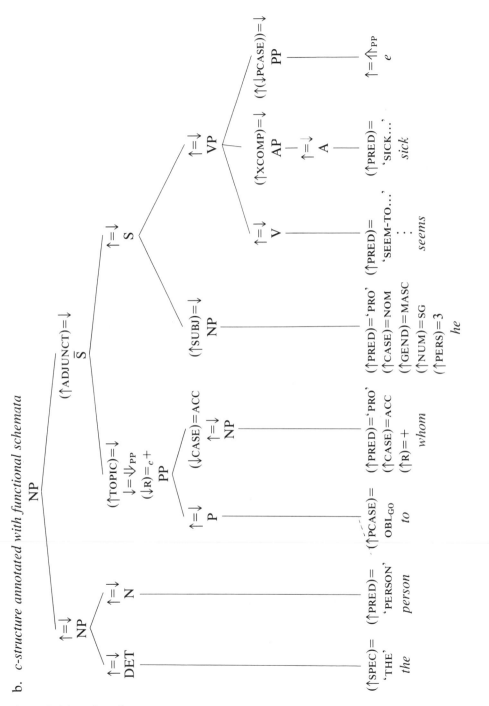

b. *c-structure annotated with functional schemata*

Figure 5.6 (continued)

c. *f-structure*

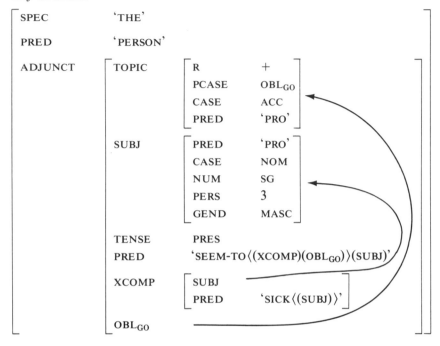

Figure 5.6 (continued)

5.7 Government

Government refers to the ability of lexical items to determine the features of other constituents. The term *agreement* is often used in preference to *government* when an inflectional morpheme of a word and an inflectional morpheme of a governed constituent have mutually constraining features. Prepositions govern the case of their objects (chapter 7); verbs and adjectives govern the case, person, or number marking of their subjects, objects, and oblique objects (chapters 7 and 8 of this volume, Mohanan to appear a, Maling 1980, Craig 1977, Roberts 1981, Robertson 1976); complementizers and verbs may govern the finiteness, mood, and constituent control features of their clauses (Zaenen 1981, McCloskey 1979).

The fundamental problem of government is to explain the observed structural relations between governing morphemes and the constituents they govern. The theory of syntax developed in the preceding sections already provides a solution to this problem. Inflectional affixes are lexical items which must be combined with other lexical items prior to lexical insertion (see chapter 1 of this volume, Selkirk 1981, Lieber 1980, Mohanan 1982). Syntactic information may be encoded in any lexical item in the form of functional features; inflectional affixation sums the feature set of the inflectional morpheme and the feature set of the lexical category that it inflects (chapter 1). After lexical insertion, the features of a word become the features of the phrase of which the word is either the head or a minor category (as defined in section 5.4). Thus, referring to figure 5.6b, we see that the features of the preposition become features of the PP that dominates it, the features of the determiner become features of the NP, and the features of the verb become features of the $\bar{\text{S}}$.

Consider in particular how a verb bearing the present tense inflectional affix -s governs (i.e., agrees with) features of the subject. As in chapters 1 and 4, -s encodes the information that the SUBJ person is 3 and the SUBJ number is singular. When -s is affixed to *seem*, this information becomes part of the feature set of *seems*. When *seems* is lexically inserted into V in figure 5.6b, the feature set is propagated up the tree: by the $\uparrow = \downarrow$ equations, the features of the (f-structure of the) V become features of the (f-structure of the) VP, and the features of (the f-structure of) VP become features of (the f-structure of) S and ultimately of $\bar{\text{S}}$. The uniqueness principle guarantees that any subject that the clause contains will have the features required by the verbal affix and vice versa. Now suppose, hypothetically, that a morpheme similar to -s had been affixed to *whom*, the prepositional object of *to*. At lexical insertion, the features of this hypothetical *whom-s* bearing the information about the number and person of the SUBJ would again be propagated up the tree—but only as far as the PP dominating *whom*. Because this PP is neither a head nor a minor category in $\bar{\text{S}}$ or VP, its features will not propagate to $\bar{\text{S}}$. Hence, the syntactic information borne by the affix will remain within the PP without affecting the SUBJ of the clause.

Our theory of syntax thus provides an explanation for the fact that governing morphemes appear either in the heads (of heads (of heads . . .)) or in minor categories of the phrases whose constituents they govern. There is no need to stipulate what the domains of government are, as much recent work does (Chomsky 1981); the possible governing relations follow from the lexical theory of inflectional affixation (section 5.6) and the theory of syntactic encoding (section 5.4)— both of which are independently motivated subtheories.

This theory has a further consequence of interest. Because government relations follow from the functional relations of categories and not from a set of stipulated structural configurations, the same kinds of government relations can appear in languages with very different c-structure configurations as well as in different c-structures within the same language. Figure 5.7 illustrates several different configurations in which verbal affixes govern (i.e., agree with) the person and number or case features of the SUBJ (and OBJ): number and person agreement in English (figure 5.7a); case and person agreement in the Mayan language Jacaltec (figure 5.7b) (see Craig 1977:108); animacy and person agreement in the Athapaskan language Navajo (figure 5.7c). In this last example, the same affix *-yi-* determines the number and person of the SUBJ and OBJ (Roberts 1981). Figure 5.8 illustrates two configurations in Dutch in which the verb *glimlachen* 'to smile' governs the oblique PP object, determining the choice of the preposition *naar* 'at'; for justification of these structures, see Evers 1975 and Bresnan et al. forthcoming. In both structures 5.8a,b, V_3 governs the preposition, but this similarity is not captured at the level of c-structure representation; rather, it is expressed in the *functional* relation between the verb *glimlachen* and its oblique object, which holds regardless of the very different structural configurations that express it. This result follows from the uniqueness principle: the functions in each functional structure must be unique; hence, the XCOMP within the XCOMP in figure 5.8b, though it is described in discontinuous c-structure positions (namely, at both VP_3 and V_3), forms a single functional unit containing both the OBL_θ and the PRED of *glimlachen*. See Bresnan et al. forthcoming for details.

We see, then, that a word may govern the functions in the f-structure that immediately contains the word's features. No set of c-structure categories provides an invariant universal characterization of this domain of government. However, given the syntactic encoding of functions into the c-structure rules of a particular language or language type, one can predict in which c-structure configurations government relations will hold in that language or type.

These results—the explanation of the distribution of governing morphemes, the uniform cross-configurational characterization of government relations, and the predictability of the actual structural configurations in which government relations can appear—depend on the assumption that verbs govern their subjects. But this assumption is in fact a necessary consequence of the theory of syntax adopted here.

a. *English (number and person agreement)*

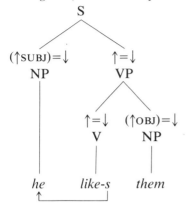

b. *Jacaltec (case and person agreement)*

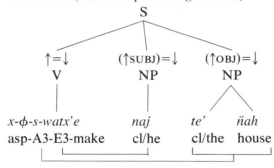

'He made the house.'

c. *Navajo (animacy and person agreement)*

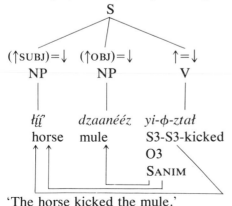

'The horse kicked the mule.'

Figure 5.7
Verbal inflections governing (agreeing with) properties of SUBJ

Recall from the theory of lexical encoding that lexical items exert selectional restrictions on a subset of their subcategorized functions (section 5.2), and that verbs impose selectional restrictions on their subjects. Thus, verbs are subcategorized for their subjects. But then it follows from the completeness and coherence conditions (section 5.5) that f-structures which contain the PREDs of verbs must also contain SUBJS (unless, of course, a particular verb in question is subjectless, as in cases of "spontaneous demotion" (Comrie 1977, Sridhar 1979)). Therefore, verbs govern their subjects.

a. *c-structure 1*

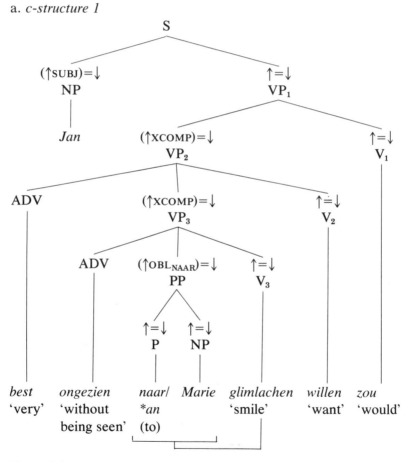

Figure 5.8
Verb governing oblique object in Dutch

b. *c-structure 2*

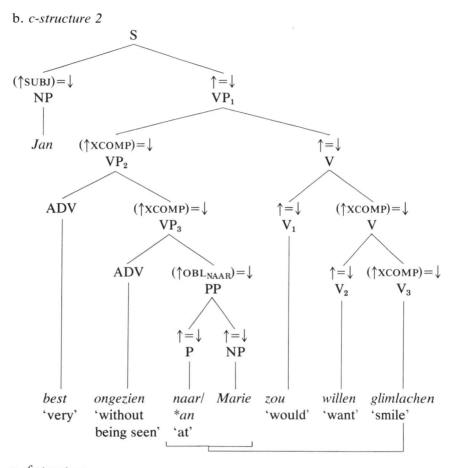

c. *f-structure*

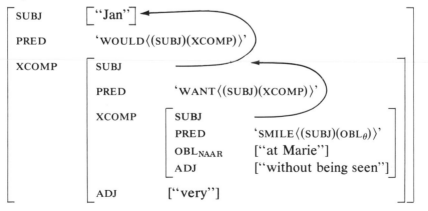

Figure 5.8 (continued)

By the same reasoning, we can establish the more general consequence that *lexical items govern all of their subcategorized functions.*
Since we have assumed that the only functions that can be referred to
in lexical entries are the subcategorizable functions (section 5.1), it
follows that the subcategorizable functions and the governable functions are one and the same. This is an extremely strong substantive
constraint on government which further research must test and may
perhaps modify.

To summarize, we see that several major results follow from the
theory of syntax proposed here: first, that governing morphemes universally appear either in the heads (or heads (of heads . . .)) or in minor categories of the phrases whose constituents they govern; second, that similar government relations are instantiated in configurationally dissimilar structures; and third, that the types of structural
configurations which instantiate government relations in a particular
language (type) are predictable from the syntactic encoding of functions in that language (type).

This theory contrasts with what may be called *configurational* theories of government, which stipulate a set of possible governing relations
in terms of phrase structure configurations. For example, it is assumed
in the theory of government and binding (Chomsky 1981) that government is a structural relation between a major type 0 category and an NP
which is dominated by a projection of that category and that V and
INFL (the category of the tense and subject-agreement morpheme) are
distinct major type 0 categories having separate syntactic projections
(VP and S, respectively). Verbs govern their objects, but not their
subjects, which lie outside of the VP (i.e., outside of the projections of
V). However, subjects are governed by the finite inflectional morpheme
in INFL (or by certain superordinate verbs and prepositions that are
exceptionally permitted to govern the subjects of a subordinate clause).

While it is easy to stipulate sets of possible government relations in
terms of various c-structure configurations, this does not solve the
fundamental problem of government, which is to *explain* the observed
structural relations between governing morphemes and the constituents they govern. Why, for example, are the case, number, and person
of the subject of a sentence recorded in the affix of its verb and not,
say, in the affix of a prepositional object of the verb? Why is it that
verbs and complementizers govern the finiteness of their clauses, while
the determiners of direct objects do not? Why do the same kinds of

government relations appear in unrelated languages with radically different constituent structures? Our theory provides principled answers to these questions.

5.8 Control

Control refers to a relation of referential dependence between an unexpressed subject (the *controlled* element) and an expressed or unexpressed constituent (the *controller*); the referential properties of the controlled element, including possibly the property of having no reference at all, are determined by those of the controller. The term *controlled clause* is also applied to the clause whose subject is controlled. To illustrate, two control relations appear in examples (17a,b).

(17)
a.   At the moment, the goal of the police is to try to prevent a riot.
b.   At the moment, the goal is to try to prevent a riot.

In (17a), the unexpressed subject of *try* is controlled by *the police,* and the unexpressed subject of *prevent* is controlled by the (unexpressed) subject of *try*. In (17b), the unexpressed SUBJ of *try* lacks an antecedent, but this is often viewed as a degenerate control relation, called *arbitrary control.*

Theoretical Considerations
Theories differ according to what are considered the major generalizations to be derived, and what are taken as basic assumptions. For example, Chomsky's 1981 theory of control is designed to obtain the following generalizations as theorems.

(18)
Only subjects are controlled.

(19)
Only nonfinite clauses have controlled subjects.

To derive these results, it is assumed in Chomsky's theory that government is a structural relation, as summarized in section 5.7. It is further stipulated that all NPs must be governed, except for the controlled NP ('PRO'), which must not be governed. Verbs govern their objects, but not their subjects, which lie outside of the VP. However, subjects are governed by the finite inflectional morpheme in INFL (or by certain

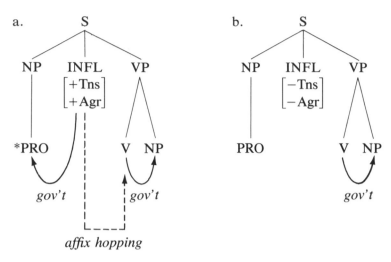

Figure 5.9
A configurational theory of control (Chomsky 1981)

superordinate verbs and prepositions that are exceptionally permitted to govern the subjects of a subordinate clause). Therefore, the controlled NP 'PRO' can occur only in the ungoverned position of subject of a nonfinite clause. The main idea of this theory is illustrated in figure 5.9. Because phrase structure configurations are used to express government and control relations, this can be referred to as a *configurational* theory of control.

It is evident that these assumptions are incompatible with the lexical–functional theory of syntax. In this theory, government is a functional, not a phrase-structural, relation (section 5.7); verbs must govern their subjects (section 5.7); bound inflectional morphemes must be affixed prior to lexical insertion into phrasal structure (section 5.6); and null structure appears only in cases of constituent control (section 5.6), that is, only in cases of unbounded, structure-dependent syntactic binding relations (cf. Bresnan and Grimshaw 1978 and chapter 4 of this volume).

We have already seen that these properties of the theory adopted here lead to several explanatory results in the theories of subcategorization, inflection, and government (section 5.7). The same results do not follow from the assumptions of the configurational theory of control without further stipulations. Since in that theory only the inflectional affix of the verb and not the verb itself governs the subject, and since government is a structural relation that associates each governing category with a distinct phrasal domain, it follows that the phrase structure representation in terms of which government relations are stated will be distinct from the representation of the surface constituency relations of the morphemes in a sentence. Therefore, a separate component of "affix hopping" or "morphological spelling" or "realization" rules must be postulated to map between these two phrase structure representations. As in figure 5.9, one can stipulate that such rules must place the morpheme dominated by INFL on the morpheme dominated by V, but any other stipulation is equally possible. Thus, in the configurational theory of control, it is only an accident that the inflectional affixes that govern the subject in figures 5.7a–c are *verbal* affixes.

Similar considerations show that the invariance of government relations across such configurationally different structures as those in figures 5.7 and 5.8 does not follow from the configurational theory without additional stipulations. Indeed, if government were a structural relation between phrasal nodes, and if such structural relations determined the distribution of 'PRO', one would predict that in languages that lack VPs, subjects could not be controlled (because in such languages verbs would always govern their subjects). However, research on Irish, a VSO language (McCloskey 1980, 1981), and Malayalam, a verb-final language having "flat" clausal structure (chapter 8 and Mohanan to appear a), falsifies this prediction. To maintain the configurational theory, one could draw the procrustean conclusion that there is an underlying phrasal structure in terms of which government is invariantly defined for all languages and that it resembles English surface structure prior to affix hopping as in figure 5.9 (Chomsky 1981). With this move, however, the claim that government is a phrase-structural relation is emptied of its most interesting and falsifiable content. The stipulation of a further level of abstract phrase structure representation complicates the theory with the addition of yet another component of realization rules to map the English-like abstract phrase structure onto the internally motivated phrase structures of each language.

The contrasting properties of the lexical–functional theory of syntax have strong independent justification, in addition to the above explanatory results. First, careful research on the syntax of Irish (McCloskey 1980, 1981) and Malayalam (chapter 8 and Mohanan to appear a), taking into account the various options for configurational theories of control, has yielded clear evidence that verbs govern their subjects; and in Icelandic (chapter 7) and Russian (chapter 6), controlled subjects show evidence of case marking governed by the verb or by the nonfiniteness of the clause. Second, the research of Selkirk 1981, Nash 1980, Lapointe 1980, Lieber 1980, and Mohanan 1982 supports the more constrained lexicalist theory of inflectional morphology over the transformationalist theory. Third, the constraints on null structure are supported by research into null anaphora in Malayalam (Mohanan 1981b), Navajo (Hale 1979), and English (Grimshaw 1979a, chapters 3 and 9 of this volume).

It would therefore be a mistake to suppose that the configurational theory of control, in deriving generalizations (18) and (19) from other assumptions, is more "explanatory" than other theories. In fact, we have just seen that its assumptions lead to the loss of major generalizations which follow instead from the theory described here.

An important further difference between the configurational theory of control and the one presented here is the treatment of the controlled element. As a structuralist theory, the configurational theory of control cannot make direct reference to grammatical functions such as SUBJ. Instead, it takes the property of not being governed to be a universal defining property of the controlled element. Thus, to derive generalization (19), the configurational theory first stipulates that 'PRO' cannot be governed and then that the NP immediately dominated by nonfinite S (i.e., the subject position of a nonfinite clause) is an NP position that is not governed. The latter property is just as much a stipulation as the former, because there is no reason *in principle* why the type 0 category of the nonfinite S—the [−agr] or [−tns] INFL in figure 5.9b—should not be just as much a governor as the [+agr, +tns] INFL in figure 5.9a; but if it were, 'PRO' could never appear in subject position. Similarly, there is no reason *in principle* why verbs are always taken to govern their objects. The category V could bear a syntactic diacritic feature exactly as the category INFL does, which would make it an optional governor of its object; but if it were, 'PRO' could appear in nonsubject positions.

In contrast, the theory of control adopted here can make direct reference to grammatical functions. Instead of stipulating that not being governed is the defining property of the controlled element 'PRO', our theory assumes that the property of being a SUBJ is a defining property of the functionally controlled element. (The qualification "functionally controlled" is explained below.) Similarly, instead of stipulating that the only domain in which the controlled element can appear is nonfinite S, our theory assumes that only the open functions XCOMP and XADJ can denote functionally controlled clauses. We turn now to the precise expression of these assumptions within the formal system of grammatical representation. We will then see that a number of major generalizations follow from the present theory of control relations.

Recall that control has been characterized as a relation of referential dependence between an unexpressed subject and an expressed or unexpressed controller. The characterization of control relations in terms of referential dependence captures their semantic similarity, but masks an important underlying grammatical difference. Where the referential dependence is accompanied by the complete identity of all functional features of the controller and the controlled element, we have *functional control* (also called *grammatical control* elsewhere in this volume). Where the referential dependence implies no identity of grammatical features, we have *anaphoric control*. That is, functional control entails identity of f-structures of the controller and controlled elements, while anaphoric control entails mere "identity of reference" (i.e., only referential dependence). The next two sections articulate the theory of functional and anaphoric control. The reader is referred to figure 5.14 for a schematic summary of the theory.

Functional Control

In *functional control relations*, the controlled element is the SUBJ function and the controlled clauses are designated by the open grammatical functions XCOMP and XADJ. Thus, the term *controlled clause* refers to a clause at the level of f-structure: a *clause nucleus* (section 5.5). The control relation is expressed by a control equation, a functional schema which equates the f-structures of the controller and the controlled element. Functional control relations are either *lexically induced* or *constructionally induced*, depending on whether the control equation is part of a lexical entry or a c-structure rule annotation. The range of possible controllers depends upon whether the functional control relation is lexically or constructionally induced.

In lexically induced functional control, the control equation is part of a lexical entry. The control relation is defined in terms of functions that are subcategorized by the lexical item that induces functional control. Thus, the controlled clause (that is, the function whose subject is controlled) is the XCOMP (the predicative or open complement). The controller is specified by a control equation of the form $(\uparrow G) = (\uparrow \text{XCOMP SUBJ})$, which is added to the lexical entry of the item. From the severe constraints on the lexical encoding of semantically restricted functions (stated in section 5.2), it follows that these functions cannot be lexically induced functional controllers. Hence, only SUBJ, OBJ, and OBJ2 are possible functional controllers, or values of G, in the above control equation. The unmarked choice of controller is predictable from the following universal rule:

(20)
Lexical Rule of Functional Control
Let L be a lexical form and F_L its grammatical function assignment. If XCOMP $\in F_L$, add to the lexical entry of L:
($\uparrow$OBJ2) = ($\uparrow$XCOMP SUBJ) if OBJ2 $\in F_L$;
otherwise:
($\uparrow$OBJ) = ($\uparrow$XCOMP SUBJ) if OBJ $\in F_L$;
otherwise:
($\uparrow$SUBJ) = ($\uparrow$XCOMP SUBJ).

That is, the XCOMP of a lexical form is functionally controlled by the OBJ2 if there is one, otherwise by the OBJ if there is one, otherwise by the SUBJ.

This rule of unmarked lexical control is interpreted as a redundancy rule; that is, the rule obligatorily expands an eligible lexical entry which lacks a control equation, but it blocks if the otherwise eligible lexical entry already has a control equation. For example, rule (20) specifies that the controllers of the predicative complements of *appear* and *regard* in (21) and (22) are the SUBJ and OBJ, respectively, but the rule is blocked by the lexically marked control equation for *strike* in (23).

(21)
a.　John seems sick to Mary.
b.　($\uparrow$PRED) = 'SEEM$\langle$(XCOMP)(OBJ$_\theta$)$\rangle$(SUBJ)'

(22)
a.　John regards Mary as friendly.
b.　($\uparrow$PRED) = 'REGARD$\langle$(SUBJ)(OBJ)(XCOMP)$\rangle$'

(23) ·
a.　John strikes Mary as friendly.
b.　($\uparrow$PRED) = 'STRIKE$\langle$(SUBJ)(OBJ)(XCOMP)$\rangle$'
　　($\uparrow$SUBJ) = ($\uparrow$XCOMP SUBJ)

An example of lexically induced functional control by OBJ2 is given in (24).

(24)
Tom will serve you the fish raw.

The adjective in (24) is a *state predicate,* an optional predicative complement to a verb, which describes a state of one of the verb's arguments at the time of the action denoted by the verb. There are strong lexical restrictions on the introduction of a state predicate as complement to a verb. For example, the predicate must describe an objective state (cf. **Tom will serve you the fish tasty*), the verb's argument must be a THEME (cf. **Tom will give the fish a sauce raw*), and the verb must denote an action rather than a state (cf. **I envy Tom the fish raw*). Within these lexical restrictions, any of SUBJ, OBJ, or OBJ2 are possible functional controllers:

(25)
a.   The package arrived unopened.
b.   John will serve the fish to you raw.
c.   I sent you the letter sealed.

Our theory predicts that only SUBJ, OBJ, and OBJ2 are possible controllers in cases of lexically induced functional control; hence, the ungrammaticality of examples like 26a,b)—noted by Williams 1980a—is explained.

(26)
a.   I presented it to John dead.
b.   *I presented John with it dead.

The verb *present* in (26) allows its THEME argument to be expressed either as OBJ or as OBL$_\theta$; however, as predicted by our theory, only the object can control the state complement. These state complements are a special type of XCOMP; they differ from the XADJs to be described directly.

In constructionally induced functional control, the control equation is part of a c-structure rule annotation. The controlled clause is the XADJ (the predicative or open adjunct), and the controller is specified by a functional schema of the form $(\uparrow G) = (\downarrow SUBJ)$, which is added to the functional annotations of the adjunct. Because the control equation is syntactically, rather than lexically, specified, it is not constrained by the restrictions on lexical encoding of functions; this means that a wider range of controllers is available in principle. The set of possible controller functions Γ appears to be a parameter of variation across languages. In Malayalam, $\Gamma = \{\text{SUBJ}\}$ (Mohanan 1981b), while in Russian (chapter 6 of this volume) and in English, $\Gamma = \{\text{SUBJ}, \text{OBJ}, \text{OBJ2}, \text{OBL}_\theta\}$. The rule of constructional control is given in (27).

(27)
Constructional Rule of Functional Control
If $(\uparrow\text{XADJ}) = \downarrow$ is a syntactically encoded functional annotation, conjoin it to the disjunction of the schemata $\{(\uparrow\text{G}) = (\downarrow\text{SUBJ}) \mid \text{G} \in \Gamma\}$.

Rule (27) is interpreted as a syntactic redundancy rule: if a predicative adjunct lacks a controller, rule (27) obligatorily specifies the set of possible controllers; but if an adjunct construction is marked for a particular controller, the rule's application is blocked.

To illustrate the effect of rule (27), let us consider examples of predicative adjuncts in English. (This discussion disregards other kinds of adjuncts, such as relative or appositional adjuncts.) In (28), either the SUBJ *Mary* or the OBJ *John* can be the controller of *drunk as usual,* although there may be a slight preference to interpret *Mary* as the controller:

(28)
Mary passed John in the hall yesterday drunk as usual.

The following example brings out the interpretation in which the OBJ *John* is the controller, because we assume that Mary would probably not describe herself as "drunk as usual":

(29)
Mary said she passed John in the hall yesterday drunk as usual.

Note that in contrast to the cases of lexically controlled state complements, the controller of these predicative adjuncts is not restricted to one thematic argument of the verb. Moreover, in (30) we see that an OBL_θ can control the adjunct, for it is possible for *drunk as usual* to be predicated of the OBL_{AG} *Mary* as well as the SUBJ *John:*

(30)
John was passed by Mary in the hall yesterday drunk as usual.

Again, a reportive example such as (31) brings out the interpretation in which the subject is not the controller, for once again we assume that John would probably not describe himself as "drunk as usual":

(31)
John said he was passed by Mary in the hall yesterday drunk as usual.

Furthermore, these adjuncts modify a much wider range of lexical predicates than the complements do and can describe nonobjective states. For example, in contrast to *John will serve you the fish tasty, we find *Mary caught a glimpse of the fish lying on the table, tasty and fragrant with herbs* and even *John will serve you the fish, tasty and fragrant with herbs*. The distinction between these XADJs and the state predicate XCOMPs previously discussed corresponds to Halliday's 1967 distinction between "conditional attributes" and "depictive attributes." Halliday observes that multiple conditional attributes can occur in a simple sentence, while only one depictive attribute may. This is exactly what the analysis in terms of XCOMPs and XADJs predicts (see chapters 3 and 4).

While functionally controlled XADJs generally have a range of possible controllers, including OBL$_\theta$ as we have just seen, there is one construction in English in which functional control of the XADJ is restricted. This is the clause-initial position of the adjective phrase adjuncts shown in (32) and (33).

(32)
a.   Sure of winning, Mary entered the competition yesterday.
b.   #Sure of winning, the competition was entered by Mary yesterday.

(33)
a.   #Sure of winning, the competition excited Mary yesterday.
b.   Sure of winning, Mary was excited by the competition yesterday.

In all of (32a,b) and (33a,b), *sure of winning* is controlled by the SUBJ of the sentence; where the SUBJ denotes an inanimate entity, the result is semantically anomalous (signaled by #). Thus, we will assume that SUBJ-control is a marked property of the clause initial XADJ construction shown in (34). ((34) is one instance of a more general rule introducing S-initial adjuncts of various categories.)

(34)
$$S \rightarrow \left(\begin{cases} (\uparrow \text{XADJ})=\downarrow \\ (\uparrow \text{SUBJ})=(\downarrow \text{SUBJ}) \end{cases} \right) \quad \begin{array}{cc} \text{NP} & \text{VP} \\ (\uparrow \text{SUBJ})=\downarrow & \uparrow=\downarrow \end{array}$$

Since the functional controller of the adjunct has been marked in the clause-initial construction given in (34), the rule of constructionally induced functional control (27) is blocked from applying there.

Because functional control relations have been formalized by equations identifying the controlled SUBJ with the controller, the f-structures of controller and controlled will be "merged" into one and the same f-structure; as a result, the controlled SUBJ will have all of the grammatical features (CASE, PERSON, NUMBER, etc.) of the controller. The referential dependence of the controlled SUBJ upon the controller follows from the semantic interpretation of the functional control relation by "quantifying in" (Halvorsen forthcoming).

Anaphoric Control

Anaphoric control relations arise from the presence of a functional anaphor ('PRO') which is not expressed in c-structure. The functional anaphor is created by an optional functional schema of the form ($\uparrow$G PRED) = 'PRO' for any function G. The possible occurrences of these schemata are quite limited by independent principles. 'PRO' is a semantic form, and all semantic forms are introduced in the lexicon (Halvorsen forthcoming). Hence, the optional schema (($\uparrow$G PRED) = 'PRO') must belong to some lexical entry. That cannot be the entry for a null NP, for our theory does not permit the use of null c-structure to represent local grammatical relations (section 5.6). Therefore, since (($\uparrow$G PRED) = 'PRO') lacks its own lexical entry as a null category, it must be introduced as part of the lexical entry of a lexical form that governs G (section 5.1) and G must be a subcategorizable function. Moreover, for any lexical entry L to which an equation (($\uparrow$G PRED) = 'PRO') is added, the completeness and coherence conditions restrict G to the particular functions subcategorized by the lexical form of L. The constraints on lexical encoding of functions (section 5.2) further restrict G to be one of the set of semantically unrestricted functions {SUBJ, OBJ, OBJ2}. Finally, a language-particular parameter may restrict G to a subset Δ of the set of semantically unrestricted functions. We will further assume that only [$\pm$FIN] lexical items permit the functional anaphor, and that the value of the feature [αFIN] is a language-particular parameter. These properties are incorporated in rule (35).

(35)
Rule of Functional Anaphora
For all lexical entries L, for all G $\in$ Δ, assign the optional pair of equations {(($\uparrow$G PRED) = 'PRO'), ($\uparrow$FIN) $=_c$ α} to L.

By fixing the parameters α = $-$ and Δ = {SUBJ}, we derive the rule of functional anaphora for English. Thus, the functional anaphor 'PRO' arises in English only as the subject of a nonfinite verb (infinitive or gerund).

An *anaphor* is a grammatical element which may be assigned an antecedent by the rules of sentence grammar. Semantically, anaphors are either coreferential with or referentially dependent upon their antecedents. 'PRO' is an anaphor similar (but not identical) in its interpretation to the indefinite pronouns *her, he, they*, etc. The so-called control relation between 'PRO' and its controller is actually an anaphoric relation between 'PRO' and its antecedent; we designate this relation *anaphoric control* to distinguish it from functional control. Note that the term *anaphor* as used here applies both to those pronouns that are obligatorily assigned antecedents within the sentence, such as the reflexive pronoun *herself*, and to those pronouns that are only optionally assigned antecedents within the sentence, such as the definite pronoun *her*. The former can be distinguished as *bound anaphors*.

In contrast, in the government and binding theory, *anaphors* are distinguished from *pronominals* in that anaphors "have no capacity for 'inherent reference'" (Chomsky 1981:188). The semantic content of this notion of "inherent reference" is unclear, but what appears to be meant by it is that anaphors lack the independent capacity to refer to specific extrasentential referents. For example, in *We thought Mary should have the operation. *However, herself is the only one that can make that decision,* the anaphor *herself* cannot refer by itself to the extrasentential referent Mary; but in *We thought Mary should have the operation. However, she herself is the only one that can make that decision,* the pronominal *she* can refer to Mary. Anaphors and pronominals are distinguished by the "binding conditions" of the government and binding theory, which assert (A) that an anaphor must be bound within its minimal governing category (NP or S), and (B) that a pronominal must be free within its minimal governing category (Chomsky 1981:188ff). Thus, *herself* in *Mary voted for herself* is an anaphor, while *her* in *Mary voted for her* is a pronominal. As Chomsky (1981:191) writes, 'PRO' is considered to be both a pronominal and an anaphor:

Consider next pronominals without a phonetic matrix, i.e., PRO. Note that PRO is like overt pronouns in that it never has an antecedent within its clause or NP. PRO also resembles anaphors in that it has no intrinsic referential content but is either assigned reference by an antecedent or is indefinite in interpretation, lacking specific reference. It is reasonable, then, to regard PRO as a pronominal anaphor. If so, it is subject to both the binding conditions (A) and (B). Then PRO is bound and free in its governing category, a contradiction if PRO has a governing category. Therefore PRO has no governing category and is therefore ungoverned. We therefore derive the principle (20) [that PRO is ungoverned], which . . . is the essential property of PRO.

Thus, the motivation for the claim that 'PRO' is an anaphor is that when it does not derive its reference from an antecedent within the sentence, it lacks definite reference, as in *It is unclear what to do*. (This is the so-called arbitrary control.) The claim that 'PRO' is an anaphor (as well as a pronominal) in turn motivates the crucial assumption that it is ungoverned, from which follow its most essential properties for the government and binding theory. In particular, it follows that 'PRO' can be the subject of a nonfinite clause (in which INFL does not govern the subject), but not an object or a subject of a finite clause (in which INFL does govern the subject).

However, the assumption that 'PRO' is an anaphor in the sense of the government and binding theory presents a serious problem: unlike anaphors, but like pronominals, 'PRO' does have the capacity to refer independently to specific extrasentential referents. In English, many examples arise in the context of indirect discourse, as (36) illustrates.

(36)
a.   Mary was happy and excited. To have involved herself in the group was a risky action. But it was proving that she could change her life.
b.   Tom felt sheepish. Pinching those elephants was foolish. He shouldn't have done it.
c.   She sighed and looked around the empty room. It was unclear what to do with herself now that Molly was gone.

In these examples, the PRO subjects of the infinitives are respectively understood as referring to Mary, Tom, and the referent of *she*. Examples of definite reference of 'PRO' also occur in other discourse contexts such as (37).

(37)
Frankly, I'm worried about Mary. What has she gotten herself into? Don't get me wrong: I think it was fine to join the group. But getting herself photographed with those starving wolves was dangerous.

Here, too, the PRO subjects of the infinitive and gerund refer specifically to Mary. Like expressed pronouns, 'PRO' can also be understood as referring to a specific referent which is presented in the nonverbal context of an utterance. Consider a situation in which two observers have witnessed a young man commit suicide by leaping from a fortieth-floor window. One observer can say to the other, "I think that killing himself was a terrible mistake," speaking specifically of the young man and meaning by this that his killing himself was a terrible mistake.

In general, the reference of reflexive pronouns is determined by their antecedents. In the above examples, the reflexive pronouns refer to specific individuals, and their antecedents are 'PRO'. Furthermore, in these examples, 'PRO' does not derive its reference from an antecedent within the sentence. Thus, we are led to the conclusion that 'PRO' does have the capacity to refer independently to specific extrasentential referents. (This argument is due to P.-K. Halvorsen.) Thompson 1973 argues convincingly that the interpretation of 'PRO' as definite or generic is predictable from temporal or aspectual and contextual properties of the sentence in which it occurs; in contexts of specific temporal reference such as (36) and (37), 'PRO' may have a definite interpretation, but in contexts of nonspecific temporal reference such as (38), it has the generic interpretation.

(38)
a.   To involve oneself in that kind of group is risky.
b.   Pinching elephants is foolish.

The fact that 'PRO' can have definite reference in the previous examples shows that it cannot be an anaphor in the sense of the government and binding theory. However, if 'PRO' is not an anaphor in this sense, then there is no motivation for the stipulation that it must be ungoverned; 'PRO' should occur in ungoverned positions, such as object position, like other nonanaphors in English. Even if we assumed that 'PRO' is ambiguous, being either [+anaphoric, +pronominal] or [−anaphoric +pronominal], the government and binding theory would be unable to account for the fact that 'PRO' has the same syntactic distribution in English (namely, subject of nonfinite clause) when it is an anaphor as when it is a nonanaphor. Thus, "the essential property" of 'PRO' for the government and binding theory—its being ungoverned—remains unexplained.[7]

Note that the government and binding theory cannot adopt our definition of anaphors as grammatical elements that may be assigned antecedents by the rules of sentence grammar. That definition would admit pronouns as anaphors, because pronouns can, and sometimes must, be assigned sentential antecedents (as in *Louise craned her neck*); by Chomsky's reasoning given above, it would then follow (contrary to fact) that pronouns could occur only in ungoverned positions. The alternative of defining anaphors as grammatical elements that *must* be assigned sentential antecedents would also fail, because 'PRO' need not have such an antecedent; for example, it lacks an antecedent in *It is unclear what to do* and *I think that killing himself was a terrible mistake*.

In the theory proposed here, 'PRO' is not a bound anaphor, but a pronominal element. It must be distinguished from the expressed definite pronouns, however, because it has special restrictions on its anaphoric relations (to be discussed below). Let us therefore assume that there is some feature—call it U (for *unexpressed morphologically*)—which separates 'PRO' from other pronouns. The functional structures for 'PRO' and *she* will therefore resemble (39a,b).

(39)

a.
$$\begin{bmatrix} \text{PRED} & \text{'PRO'} \\ \text{U} & + \end{bmatrix}$$

b.
$$\begin{bmatrix} \text{PRED} & \text{'PRO'} \\ \text{U} & - \\ \text{GEND} & \text{FEM} \\ \text{NUM} & \text{SG} \\ \text{PERS} & 3 \\ \text{CASE} & \text{NOM} \end{bmatrix}$$

Given that 'PRO' is an anaphor which need not be bound, how can we explain the contrast between (40a) and (40b)?

(40)

a.   Mary wished to vote.

b.   Mary wished for her to vote.

The government and binding theory attributes the contrast to the analysis of 'PRO' as a bound anaphor and *her* as a pronominal. Assuming that the complementizer *for* exceptionally governs *her* in (40b), the minimal governing category of the pronominal *her* is extended to include both the matrix clause and the complement clause. The minimal governing category now includes *Mary;* thus, *her* must be free in this domain and disjoint from *Mary*. In contrast, the 'PRO', as a (bound) anaphor, must be bound within the sentence or assigned the *arb* (indefinite) interpretation. Presumably, lexical properties of *wish* force the bound interpretation.

The present theory provides a natural alternative to the above analysis. Note that in these examples, the [+U] anaphor ('PRO') is bound to the SUBJ *Mary,* while the [−U] anaphor (*her*) cannot be bound to the SUBJ. This is reminiscent of the phenomenon known in many languages as *obviation,* by which certain pronouns exclude coreference with specified types of antecedents (Hale 1978). We therefore formulate the *Obviation Principle* given in (41). This formulation should not be regarded as a maximally general statement of obviation across languages, but rather as an alternative hypothesis to the claim of the government and binding theory (Chomsky 1981) that (40b) is an instance of disjoint reference (i.e., of a pronoun being free within its minimal governing category). In fact, (41) can be derived from a general theory of pronominal obviation, but this topic is beyond the scope of our present concerns. See Simpson and Bresnan 1982 and the references cited there.

(41)
Obviation Principle
If P is the pronominal SUBJ of an obviative clause C, and A is a potential antecedent of P and is the SUBJ of the minimal clause nucleus that properly contains C, P is or is not bound to A according to whether P is + or −U, respectively.

In English, an obviative clause is any clause that can be marked by the complementizer *for.*[8] Since the infinitival complement to *wish* can be marked by the complementizer *for,* it is an obviative clause, and given our analysis of pronominals, principle (41) immediately explains the contrast between (40a) and (40b).

Our hypothesis that a type of pronominal obviation is involved in examples like (40a,b) makes a strikingly different prediction from the government and binding theory of pronominals and anaphors. In our theory, obviation is a functional relation which holds between matrix subjects and complement subject pronominals. In the government and binding theory, by contrast, the property of being free within a minimal governing category is a structural relation which prohibits *all* NPs within the matrix clause—subject and nonsubject NPs alike—from binding the pronominal subject of the *for–to* complement. The government and binding theory therefore predicts no difference between matrix subject and nonsubject antecedents of a complement subject pronominal; the complement subject should be disjoint from both. The

Obviation Principle in our theory predicts that disjoint reference applies only with subject and not with nonsubject antecedents in the matrix. The evidence given below crucially chooses between the two theories. (Examples (42d) and (43c) contain nonobviative clauses; they are included as minimal contrasts.)

(42)
a. For her to lose after all that effort would really surprise Louise.
    [*her = Louise*, possibly]
b. It would really surprise Louise for her to lose after all that effort.
    [*her = Louise*, possibly]
c. Louise would really be surprised for her to lose after all that effort.
    [*her ≠ Louise*]
d. Louise would really be surprised if she lost after all that effort.
    [*she = Louise*, possibly]

(43)
a. Louise signaled to Ted for him to follow her.
    [*him = Ted* and *her = Louise*, possibly]
b. Louise signaled to Ted for her to follow him.
    [*her ≠ Louise* and *him = Ted*, possibly]
c. Louise signaled to Ted that she would follow him.
    [*she = Louise* and *him = Ted*, possibly]

Examples (42) and (43) show that, contrary to the predictions of the government and binding theory, the complement subject pronoun is disjoint only from the matrix subject, and not from nonsubject arguments of the matrix. (It might be supposed that the extraposed clause in (42b) lies outside the minimal governing category of *Louise*, as would be the case if the extraposed clause were dominated by $\bar{S}$ rather than by VP. However, there is evidence that the extraposed clause is dominated by VP. Note that the extraposed clause in *It would really surprise her for Louise to lose after all that effort* must be c-commanded[9] by the direct object in order to account for the noncoreference of *her* and *Louise* (assuming Reinhart's 1976 formulation of the noncoreference condition); but this example is exactly parallel in structure to (42b). Hence, the extraposed clause in (42b) does lie within the same minimal governing category as the matrix object.)

The present theory also predicts the contrast in the following examples.

(44)

a. To be able to shave oneself at five years of age would really sur-
    prise one's father.
b. It would really surprise one's father to be able to shave oneself at
    five years of age.
c. One's father would really be surprised to be able to shave *one-
    self/himself at five years of age.

In examples (44a,b), the matrix subject is not a possible antecedent for
the complement 'PRO', so binding is not obligatory by the Obviation
Principle. By contrast, the matrix subject in (44c) *is* a possible antecedent, and the binding of 'PRO' is obligatory, as is shown by the fact that
the reflexive pronoun must agree with *one's father*.[10]

    It must be noted that the Obviation Principle (41) does not provide
the only conditions under which anaphoric control of 'PRO' by a matrix
argument may be obligatory. It has frequently been observed that the
semantic or thematic structure of the matrix predicate can induce control of a complement 'PRO'. This appears to account for the examples in
(45), which indicate that 'PRO' is obligatorily bound to the GOAL argument of *signal*.

(45)

a. Louise signaled to Ted to shave himself.
b. *Louise signaled to Ted to shave oneself.
c. *Louise signaled to Ted to shave herself.

The Obviation Principle is inapplicable to (45) even though *Louise* is a
subject, because *Louise* is thematically excluded as a possible antecedent A of the complement 'PRO'.

    'PRO' is further distinguished from expressed definite pronouns by a
universal condition on anaphoric control which is due to K. P. Mohanan 1981b. We formulate this condition as (46).

(46)

Universal Condition on Anaphoric Control
If A is a grammatically assigned antecedent of P, where the value of P is
[PRED 'PRO', U +], then A must f-command P.

F-command is a relation on f-structures defined as follows:

(47)

F-command

For any occurrences of the functions α, β in an f-structure F, α f-commands β if and only if α does not contain β and every f-structure of F that contains α contains β.

To illustrate the effect of the Universal Condition on Anaphoric Control, figure 5.10 shows the f-structure for the sentence *People who know John often discuss working too hard.* We see in this figure that the SUBJ α_1 f-commands the SUBJ β, while OBJ α_2 does not f-command SUBJ β. Hence, it follows from the Universal Condition on Anaphoric Control that $\langle \alpha_1, \beta \rangle$ but not $\langle \alpha_2, \beta \rangle$ is a possible control relation. This explains why the PRO subject of *working* in (48a) can be interpreted as *people* but not as *John;* (48b) shows that the universal condition applies only to the unexpressed 'PRO' and not to definite personal pronouns.

(48)

a.   People who know John often discuss working too hard.

b.   People who know John often discuss his working too hard.

Similarly, the Universal Condition on Anaphoric Control explains why, in (49a), *Mr. Jones* does not anaphorically control the PRO subject of *contradicting,* even though *Mr. Jones* can be a grammatically assigned antecedent of the pronoun *his* in (49b).

(49)

a.   *Contradicting himself will demonstrate that Mr. Jones is a liar.

b.   His contradicting himself will demonstrate that Mr. Jones is a liar.

Example (49a) is ill-formed when the PRO subject of *contradicting* is taken to be *Mr. Jones.* The reason is that in the f-structure for (49a), shown in figure 5.11, the SUBJ *Mr. Jones* does not f-command 'PRO'. In contrast, *Mr. Jones* can anaphorically control 'PRO' in (50).

(50)

Contradicting himself will discredit Mr. Jones.

In (50), the object of the verb *discredit* does f-command the 'PRO' complement subject; see figure 5.12.

These examples also show very clearly that f-command, and not c-command, is the determining factor in the universal condition (46) on anaphoric control relations, for in neither of the examples *Contradicting himself will discredit Mr. Jones* and **Contradicting himself will*

c-structure

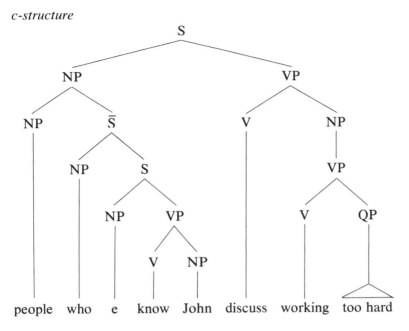

f-structure

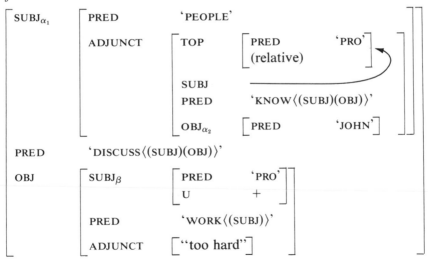

SUBJ_{α_1} f-commands SUBJ_β

OBJ_{α_2} does not f-command SUBJ_β

Figure 5.10
The F-Command Condition on anaphoric control

c-structure

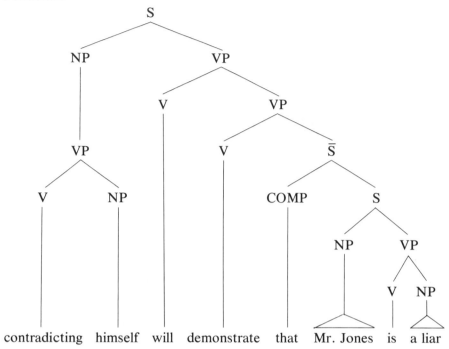

f-structure

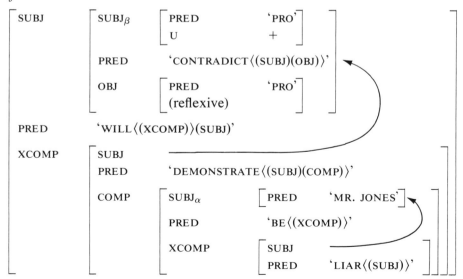

SUBJ$_\alpha$ does not f-command SUBJ$_\beta$

Figure 5.11
F-Command Condition on anaphoric control

c-structure

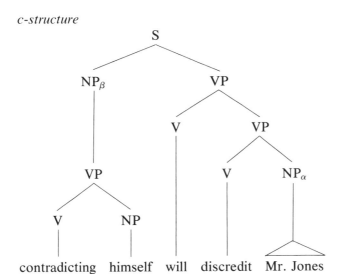

NP$_\alpha$ does not c-command NP$_\beta$

f-structure

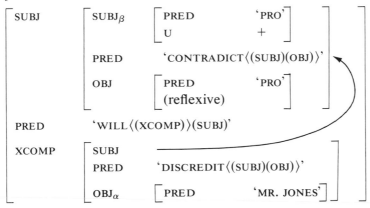

OBJ$_\alpha$ f-commands SUBJ$_\beta$

Figure 5.12
F-command vs. c-command

demonstrate that Mr. Jones is a liar does *Mr. Jones* c-command the complement subject position (see figures 5.11 and 5.12). Similarly, in *Improving himself seems important to John,* the OBJ$_{GO}$ *John* f-commands, but fails to c-command, the SUBJ of *improving himself;* see figure 5.13.

Because 'PRO' can refer to discourse antecedents, as we have seen, the possibility arises that both 'PRO' and another referential phrase in the sentence may refer to the same antecedent in discourse. When this happens, 'PRO' is not anaphorically controlled by the other phrase (because the other phrase has not been grammatically assigned as the antecedent to 'PRO'). In just these cases, apparent counterexamples to the F-Command Condition may appear. As an initial example of this situation, consider (51).

(51)
Contradicting himself will demonstrate that he is a liar.

Example (51) is parallel in structure of (49a), yet *he* and 'PRO' can corefer, where *Mr. Jones* and 'PRO' could not. The reason is that *he,* more easily than *Mr. Jones,* can be taken as referring to an implied discourse antecedent; *he* could even have 'PRO' as its antecedent. However, there are certain conditions under which a nonpronominal noun phrase like *Mr. Jones* could be coreferential with 'PRO'. In general, unstressed definite noun phrases can refer to discourse antecedents much more easily than can stressed noun phrases; unstressed phrases are usually taken as designating old information, and stressed phrases, new information. The contrast between (52a) and (52b) illustrates this phenomenon.

(52)
a. John was unhappy. ??The Nobel Prize had prevented the discovery of a vaccine by John.
b. John was unhappy. The Nobel Prize had prevented John's discovery of a vaccine.

In these examples, we see that the possessive *John's* in (52b) can refer to a discourse antecedent much more easily than can the prepositional object *by John* in (52a). The prepositional object, unlike the genitive prenominal NP, is in a stressed position. On the basis of this difference, we therefore expect the contrast in (53).

c-structure

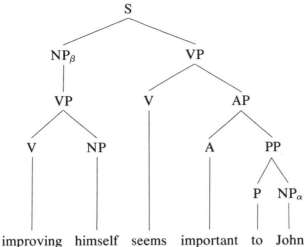

improving himself seems important to John

NP$_\alpha$ does not c-command NP$_\beta$

f-structure

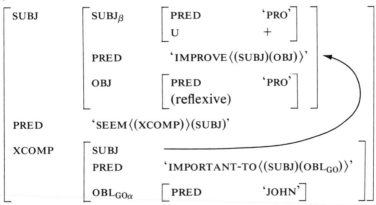

OBL$_{GO\alpha}$ f-commands SUBJ$_\beta$

Figure 5.13
F-command vs. c-command

(53)

a.   Winning the Nobel Prize had prevented John's discovery of a vaccine.

b.   ??Winning the Nobel Prize had prevented the discovery of a vaccine by John.

In (53a), but much less so in (53b), *John* and the PRO subject of *winning* may be coreferential with an implied discourse antecedent. Hence, in (53b) 'PRO' can easily refer to *John* only if 'PRO' is assigned *John* as an antecedent within the sentence; but this is ruled out by the Universal Condition on Anaphoric Control. *John* is properly contained within the object of the main clause, and so clearly fails to f-command the complement subject. Therefore, in (53b) it is very difficult to interpret the PRO subject of *winning* as *John*.

We see, then, that the analysis of 'PRO' as an unexpressed pronoun which is subject to the Obviation Principle (41) and the Universal Condition on Anaphoric Control (46) better expresses the generalizations that govern its behavior than the theory that it is an ungoverned pronominal anaphor. It is of interest that nothing in our theory of anaphoric control predicts that 'PRO' cannot occur in so-called governed positions, such as subject of a finite sentence or object or second object of a verb. In this respect, the theory presented here differs crucially from Chomsky's 1981 government and binding theory, which was designed to derive that generalization as a theorem. Our theory predicts that 'PRO' may have any of the semantically unrestricted functions SUBJ, OBJ, OBJ2. It would therefore be of crucial theoretical interest to know whether there are languages in which this occurs. Let us now suppose that such a language is found. Note that a possible response for the government and binding theory would be that the elements in question are not true instances of 'PRO'. Of course, in bringing evidence to bear on the choice between alternative theories of control of 'PRO', one must have clear criteria for identifying an instance of 'PRO' other than its conformity to one of the theories in question. What, then, are the independent criteria for identifying 'PRO'? Taking into account the above discussion, we can propose the following properties as collectively criterial for 'PRO':

(i) 'PRO' is an unexpressed pronoun.

(ii) 'PRO' may have either definite or indefinite reference, depending upon the context.

(iii) 'PRO' is not assigned an antecedent within its minimal clause.

(iv) 'PRO' may be obligatorily bound to certain thematically or grammatically specified antecedents.

(v) An antecedent grammatically assigned to 'PRO' must be superordinate to 'PRO' in the clause structure representing grammatical relations (in our theory, the antecedent must f-command 'PRO').

(vi) 'PRO' has a restricted set of grammatical functions (either {SUBJ} alone as in the government and binding theory, or a subset of {SUBJ, OBJ, OBJ2} as in the lexical–functional theory).

It might be questioned whether (v) should be admitted as a theory-independent property of 'PRO', since there is no alternative to the F-Command Condition. (Although it has been suggested in passing by Chomsky 1981 that the controller must be an argument of the matrix of the controlled complement, this requirement cannot replace the F-Command Condition (cf. note 16 and the discussion of examples (141a–c) below).) In fact, a condition similar to the F-Command Condition was embodied in the earliest generative analyses of PRO phenomena, which hypothesized a cyclic Equi NP Deletion transformation. The condition of strict cyclicity limited the application of cyclic rules so that no rule could analyze material solely contained within previous cycles, a constraint that had essentially the same effect as (v).

Malayalam provides crucial evidence regarding the existence of governed 'PRO's as defined by the above criteria (Mohanan 1981b). First, Malayalam has unexpressed pronouns. Second, these pronouns may have either generic or definite reference, depending on context. Third, they cannot have antecedents within their minimal clauses. Fourth, they may be obligatorily bound to certain functionally or thematically specified antecedents. An example given by Mohanan (personal communication) is (54).

(54)
ellaawarkkum [r̄aawile kuḷik'k'unnatə] iṣtamaaṇə
all-dat   morning bathe-pres-it   liking-be-pres
'Everyone likes bathing in the morning.'

In example (54), the PRO subject of 'bathing' is obligatorily bound to the matrix subject 'everyone'; in contrast, the expressed pronoun subject in (55) is not obligatorily bound to 'everyone'.

(55)
ellaawarkkum [awar   r̄aawile kuḷik'k'unnatə] iṣtamaaṇə
all-dat   they-nom morning bathe-pres-it   liking-be-pres
'Everyone likes their bathing in the morning.'

Fifth, the Malayalam unexpressed pronouns, unlike the expressed pronouns, must be f-commanded by their grammatically assigned antecedents within the sentence. Example (56), from Mohanan 1981b, illustrates this point.

(56)
[[joon   meeriye   ummawecca] kaaryam] awal/φ   arootum
  John-nom Mary-acc kiss-past   thing   she-nom/PRO anyone
paraññilla
say-past
'She$_i$/*PRO$_i$ did not tell anyone that John had kissed Mary$_i$.'

Sixth, and crucially, these unexpressed pronouns can be SUBJ, OBJ, and OBJ2, but not OBL$_\theta$ or ADJ. Examples of a PRO OBJ having definite and indefinite interpretations are given in (57) and (58) (from K. P. Mohanan, personal communication).

(57)
wakkiilanmaar caticcu
lawyer-nom-pl cheat-past
'The lawyers cheated [definite pronoun: him, her, them, me, etc.].'

(58)
wakkiilanmaar catik'k'um
lawyer-nom-pl cheat-fut
'Lawyers will cheat one.'

An example illustrating the F-Command Condition on an OBJ 'PRO' is given in (59) (from K. P. Mohanan, personal communication).

(59)
[joon   nulliyappool]   meeriyute acchan karaññu
[John-nom pinch-past then] Mary-poss father cry-past
'Mary$_i$'s father$_j$ cried when John pinched him$_j$/*her$_i$.'

For further discusion of the F-Command Condition and evidence that the C-Command Condition does not hold, see Mohanan 1981b. Finally, an example illustrating that 'PRO' cannot be OBL$_\theta$ in Malayalam is given in (60) (from Mohanan 1981b).

(60)
raajaawə waal   etuttu. addeeham mantriye   wadhiccu
king-nom sword-nom take-past he-nom   minister-acc kill-past
'The king took the sword. He killed the minister (*with it).'

As indicated in the gloss of (60), it is not possible to interpret the second sentence as having a dcfinitc 'PRO' as instrumental. (Further examples are given in Mohanan 1981b.) In Malayalam, the criterial properties of 'PRO' are shared by the unexpressed subjects, objects, and second objects of finite clauses (Mohanan 1981b and personal communication).

Thus, the evidence from Malayalam crucially favors the present theory of anaphoric control over the government and binding theory of 'PRO' as an ungoverned pronominal anaphor. For Malayalam, the parameters α and Δ of the universal Rule of Functional Anaphora (35) are fixed as $\alpha = +$ and $\Delta = \{\text{SUBJ, OBJ, OBJ2}\}$.

Our theory of functional and anaphoric control is summarized in figure 5.14.

5.9 Consequences of the Theory of Control

Interpretation, Function, and Agreement
From this theory of functional and anaphoric control, there follow a number of interesting generalizations. First, from the conditions on functional control (section 5.8), it follows immediately that anaphoric and arbitrary control of subject arise only in closed functions (and, depending on the finiteness parameter, in matrix clauses). Thus, the indefinite or antecedentless interpretation of the controlled subject arises only in SUBJ, OBJ, OBL$_\theta$, or COMP clauses (or in main clauses, as in Malayalam); it never occurs in the predicative complement (XCOMP) or open adjunct (XADJ).

An alternative hypothesis concerning the *arb* (arbitrary) interpretation of 'PRO' is Chomsky's proposal that in the structure ... V ... [$_{\bar{S}}$ COMP PRO ...] ..., where V strictly governs $\bar{S}$, (i) if COMP(lementizer) is not null and V has no controller, then PRO is assigned the index *arb;* otherwise (ii) PRO is assigned the index *i* of a controller (Chomsky 1980). In other words, arbitrary control arises only in complement clauses with nonnull complementizers, such as *It is unclear what to do, It is difficult to leave.* (It is assumed in this theory that a nonnull complementizer *for* occurs in the latter example; this complementizer, through its exceptional government of the subject, is what is supposed to sanction the presence of a lexical NP subject of the infinitive in examples like *It is difficult for us to leave* (cf. section 5.7).)

The fact that arbitrary control does arise in complement clauses with nonnull complementizers follows as a special case of our theory, for by the principles of syntactic encoding (section 5.4) $\bar{S}$-complement clauses

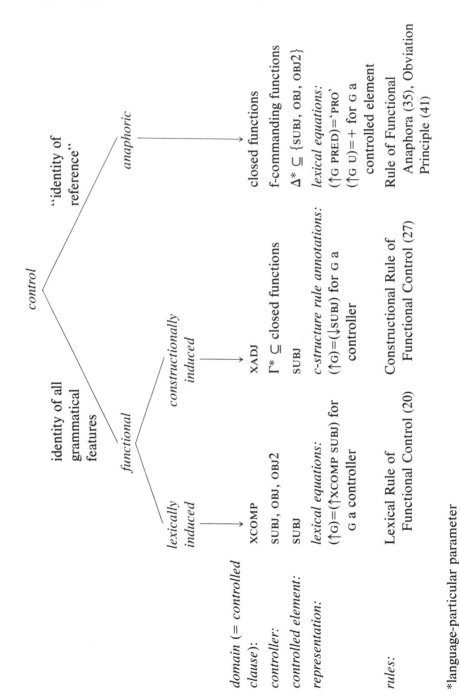

	lexically induced	*constructionally induced*	*anaphoric*
domain (= controlled clause):			
controller:	XCOMP	XADJ	closed functions
controlled element:	SUBJ, OBJ, OBJ2	Γ* ⊆ closed functions	f-commanding functions
representation:	SUBJ	SUBJ	Δ* ⊆ {SUBJ, OBJ, OBJ2}
	lexical equations: (↑G)=(↑XCOMP SUBJ) for G a controller	*c-structure rule annotations:* (↑G)=(↓SUBJ) for G a controller	*lexical equations:* (↑G PRED)='PRO' (↑G U)=+ for G a controlled element
rules:	Lexical Rule of Functional Control (20)	Constructional Rule of Functional Control (27)	Rule of Functional Anaphora (35), Obviation Principle (41)

control

"identity of reference"

anaphoric

identity of all grammatical features

functional

*language-particular parameter

Figure 5.14
The theory of control

can only be assigned closed functions such as SUBJ, OBJ, OBL$_\theta$, or COMP. In contrast to Chomsky's proposal, however, our theory predicts that arbitrary control can arise in clauses that lack nonnull complementizers, so long as these clauses have closed functions. There is evidence from Italian that confirms our theory. Manzini 1980 has observed that arbitrary control occurs in infinitival clauses in Italian, despite the fact that these infinitival clauses lack nonnull complementizers. An example is given in (61).

(61)
E' difficile andarsene.
'It is difficult to leave.'

In (61), the infinitive *andarsene* functions as either the SUBJ of *difficile* or an extraposed COMP, which is bound to the SUBJ. In either case, it has a closed function, and given the absence of an anaphoric controller, arbitrary control arises. The fact that these infinitival clauses never have nonnull complementizers is irrelevant to the determination of control.

Another consequence of our theory of control is that when a lexical item agrees with (or governs) grammatical features of its SUBJ, it must also agree with (or govern) functional controllers of its SUBJ; but it need not agree with *anaphoric* controllers of its SUBJ. English has only vestigial systems of case marking and agreement, and so provides little illustration of this consequence. However, research on Modern Arabic (Fassi Fehri 1981), Icelandic (Andrews to appear; see also chapter 7 of this volume), and Russian (Neidle in preparation; see also chapter 6) bears out the predictions of the theory. For example, Andrews and Neidle show that there are predicative adjuncts in both Russian and Icelandic that agree in case with the subject of the clause in which they occur. In controlled clauses, these adjuncts show two patterns of case marking: in one pattern, the adjunct necessarily agrees in case with the controller of the clause; in the other, the adjunct may appear in a case (nominative in Icelandic, dative in Russian) distinct from that of the controller, the case of the subject of the controlled clause. It turns out that agreement with the controller is necessary just where there is independent syntactic evidence of functional control. No special rules of agreement are required to account for these facts; this is exactly the result that our theory predicts. Similarly, Fassi Fehri's careful syntactic analysis of Modern Arabic shows that predicative adjectives exhibit different patterns of agreement depending upon whether they are anaphorically or functionally controlled. (Note that while agreement with a functional controller is necessary, agreement with an anaphoric controller is not prohibited; however, it must be effected by a further rule.)

These results of the theory of control reveal a surprising interrelation among semantic interpretation, syntactic function, and morphological agreement. Theories which give a uniform syntactic representation to all control relations—for example, theories which treat the controlled element everywhere as a pronominal anaphor 'PRO'—leave this deep relation among interpretation, function, and agreement unexplained.

NP Subjects and Split Antecedents

Our theory implies that lexical NPs cannot appear as the subjects of functionally controllable clauses (sections 5.4, 5.8). Moreover, given the consistency condition, it follows that functionally controllable clauses cannot have split antecedents. (A pronoun that refers to more than one noun phrase is said to have *split antecedents;* for example, in *Tom told Mary that they should leave, Tom* and *Mary* can be split antecedents of *they*.) Functional control by split antecedents is impossible, for the f-structures of each of the functional controllers would be merged with that of the controlled subject, resulting in a clash of features. In contrast, anaphorically controllable clauses may have lexical NP subjects, and (provided that the conditions on anaphoric control permit) they may also have split antecedents, since nonreflexive anaphors in general allow this. Thus, our theory predicts the following correlation: if a controlled clause can have a lexical NP subject, then (subject to conditions on anaphoric control) it can have split antecedents.

In English, both participle phrases and adjective phrases can function as predicative adjuncts, controlled by some element of the clause:

(62)
a.   Angry at John, Mary left.
b.   Being angry at John, Mary left.

Unlike the adjectival adjuncts (which, as we have seen in section 5.8, are functionally controlled XADJs), the participial adjuncts have optional NP subjects, as shown by the contrast between (63a) and (63b).[11]

(63)
a.   *John angry, Mary left.
b.   John being angry, Mary left.

Thus, if the participles in (62b) and (63b) are instances of the same construction, it cannot be the functionally controlled XADJ. Rather, it must be a closed ADJ having an internal structure similar to the one shown in (64):

(64)
$$S \rightarrow \begin{pmatrix} NP \\ (\uparrow SUBJ)=\downarrow \end{pmatrix} \quad \begin{matrix} VP \\ \uparrow=\downarrow \\ (\downarrow PART)=ing \end{matrix}$$

Given this analysis, our theory then predicts that, unlike the open adjectival adjuncts, the closed participial adjuncts will show anaphoric and arbitrary control:

(65)
a.   *Hatless, it is unnecessary to bow.
b.   Having taken off your hat, it is unnecessary to bow.

(Some speakers of English reject examples like (65b); it is unclear whether this is because they class the participial adjuncts (62b) with the phrasal XADJS (62a) rather than with the absolute (sentential) ADJS (63b), or because they wish to avoid the stylistic stigma of "dangling participles.") Our theory further predicts that, since the PRO subject of the participial adjuncts is a nonreflexive anaphor, these adjuncts may have split antecedents (conditions on anaphoric control permitting):

(66)
a.   *Mary lost track of John because, angry at each other, he had gone one way and she the other.
b.   Mary lost track of John because, having been angry at each other, he had gone one way and she the other.

(Again, there are speakers who react to (66) as to (65).)

Note that the converse of this generalization does not hold. It is true that if the subject position of a clause is functionally controlled, then it cannot be replaced by a lexical NP. But it is not true that if the subject position of a clause cannot be replaced by a lexical NP, the subject is functionally controlled. The reason is that other factors than functional control may prevent lexical expression of the subject of a clause. For example, the subject of infinitival $\bar{S}$ in English can be lexically expressed if and only if the complementizer *for* is present, as illustrated in (67).

(67)
a.   Louise gestured/said for me to follow her.
b.   *Louise gestured/said me to follow her.
c.   *Louise gestured/said for to follow her.
d.   Louise gestured/said to follow her.

However, since *wh*-phrases in English exclude the presence of *for,* the subjects of *wh*-infinitival clauses cannot be lexically expressed:

(68)
a.   Whether to grant equal rights to women is under debate.
b.   *Whether men to grant equal rights to women is under debate.

Nevertheless, it is clear that the *wh*-infinitival clause of (68a) cannot be functionally controlled, because it bears the closed function SUBJ and has the indefinite interpretation of arbitrary control. Similarly, there exist lexically governed cases of obligatory anaphoric control in nominals (Kisala in preparation).

Functional Restrictions on Controllers
A further generalization of control follows from this theory. Recall that in lexically induced functional control relations, OBL_θ cannot be a controller. Since the oblique functions are marked by prepositions in English (Bresnan 1979), it follows that prepositional objects cannot be lexically induced functional controllers in English. The following examples were previously given to illustrate this point.

(69)
a.   I presented *it* to John *dead.*
b.   *I presented John with *it dead.*

There are apparent counterexamples to this generalization, such as (70a,b):

(70)
a.   Louise signaled to Ted to follow her.
b.   Mary relies on John to dress himself.

However, these are either cases of anaphoric control or cases of Verb – Preposition Incorporation (V–P Incorporation; see chapter 1). For example, the fact that we find *Louise signaled to Ted for him to follow her,* in which the subject is a lexically expressed NP, indicates that the complement of *signal* must be anaphorically, not functionally, con-

a.
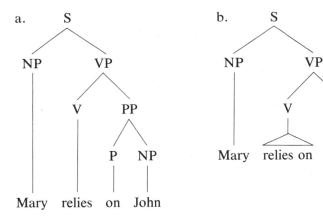

b.

Figure 5.15
Verb–Preposition Incorporation

trolled in (70a). As for *rely on*, it is subject to the rule of V–P Incorporation, which produces the two lexical forms shown in (71).

(71)
a. $[rely]_V$,   ($\uparrow$PRED) = 'RELY-ON$\langle$(SUBJ)(OBL$_{ON}$)$\rangle$'
b. $[rely\ on]_V$,   ($\uparrow$PRED) = 'RELY-ON$\langle$(SUBJ)(OBJ)$\rangle$'

The verb with lexical form (71a) is inserted into the structure shown in figure 5.15a; the verb with lexical form (71b) is inserted into the structure shown in figure 5.15b.

   In the structure shown in figure 5.15a, *on John* is a constituent, while in the structure shown in figure 5.15b, it is not. Moreover, *John* is an OBL$_{ON}$ in figure 5.15a, but an OBJ in figure 5.15b. The former structure accounts for the possibility of *It is on John that Mary relies*, in which the constituent *on John* is clefted; the latter structure accounts for *John is relied on by Mary*, in which *John* as an OBJ has passivized (chapter 1). The theory of control adopted here predicts that functional control of a complement to *rely on* should be possible only when the preposition is incorporated into the verb as in figure 5.15b. Hence, if the functionally controlled complement is present, *on John* must fail to form a constituent. This explains the contrast between (72a) and (72b) and the possibility of (72c).

(72)
a. *It is on John that Mary relies to dress himself.
b. It is John that Mary relies on to dress himself.
c. John is relied on by Mary to dress himself.

It is interesting to compare this explanation with an alternative proposal, due to Williams 1980a. Williams proposes the *C-Command Condition,* which states that in obligatory control relations, the controller
must c-command 'PRO'. Let us first observe that Williams's "obligatory
control" corresponds to our functional control. That is, the central
properties that Williams takes to be characteristic of obligatory control
follow from our theory of functional control. First, Williams stipulates
that in obligatory control there must be an antecedent. In our theory,
this property follows from the completeness condition (section 5.5); if
the functional controller is omitted from a sentence in which functional
control obtains, the f-structure value of both the controller and the
controlled subject will be missing, producing an incomplete f-structure.
Second, Williams stipulates that in obligatory control, lexical NPs cannot appear in the position of the controlled subject. As we have seen,
this property follows from our theory of categories and functional control (sections 5.4, 5.8). Next, in Williams's obligatory control the antecedent must be thematically or grammatically uniquely determined.
In our theory, this property follows directly from the lexical rule of
Functional Control (20). In cases of constructionally induced functional
control, as we have seen in examples (28)–(31), the choice of grammatical controller is not uniquely determined; it remains true, however,
that any function which is chosen as a functional controller must be
unique (i.e., "split antecedents" are impossible). Williams suggests as a
further property that the antecedent must precede the controlled subject position, but indicates that this property may be accidental to
English. This property is *not* implied by our theory. In fact, the property does not hold even for English, as examples (32) and (33) show.
The final property of Williams's obligatory control is that the antecedent must c-command the controlled subject position. This property of
course does not follow from our theory, since the restrictions on the
controller are functional, not structural. Nevertheless, because of the
way functions are encoded in English constituent structure, certain
effects of the C-Command Condition already follow from our theory.

Since NP objects of prepositions will fail to c-command nodes outside of the PP, the C-Command Condition could also account for the
above examples. However, it is easy to distinguish the two explanations empirically: the theory adopted here defines control in terms of
relations between functions; the alternative theory defines it in terms of
relations between constituent structure positions. Now it happens that

in English, the OBL$_\theta$ function is syntactically realized as PP and the OBJ function as NP immediately dominated by VP, but this is not universally the case. There are languages in which oblique objects are syntactically realized as case-marked NPs and languages in which direct objects are syntactically realized as prepositional objects. In such languages, the predictions of the C-Command Condition diverge from those of the present theory of control.

In Icelandic, oblique objects can be realized as case-marked NPs which are not dominated by the node PP (see chapter 7 of this volume; Levin and Simpson 1981). If our theory is correct, the oblique objects in Icelandic cannot be lexically induced functional controllers; but if the c-command hypothesis is correct, these oblique NPs can be obligatory controllers, since they c-command the controlled subject. The evidence given in (73) and (74), cited by Levin and Simpson 1981, confirms our theory. These are examples of *state predication,* discussed in section 5.8, in which a complement is predicated of a theme of the main verb.

(73)
Hann   rændi *matnum*   *hráum* frá   mér.
he-nom stole   the-meat-dat raw-dat from me-dat
'He stole the meat from me raw.'

(74)
*Hann   rændi mig   *matnum*   *hráum*.
he-nom robbed me-acc the-meat-dat raw-dat
('He robbed me of the meat raw.')

Levin and Simpson argue on independent grounds that in (73) *matnum* 'meat' is a direct object of the verb, while in (74) it is an oblique object of the verb. For example, the direct object passivizes, while the oblique object does not. Thus, it is the function of the NP, and not the c-command relation, that correctly predicts its possible control relations.

Spanish provides a case in which an NP does not c-command constituents of the verb phrase but does have the OBJ function. In Spanish, animate direct objects are realized as objects of the preposition *a*. According to the c-command hypothesis, these animate objects should not be possible obligatory controllers; according to our theory, they should be. The evidence below (provided by M. Montalbetti, personal communication) favors the functional theory.

(75)

   Juan la   encontró a *ella borracha.*
   Juan CL-acc met   her   drunk-fem
   'Juan met her drunk.'

(76)

*Juan le   habló a *ella borracha.*
   Juan CL-dat spoke to her drunk-fem
   ('Juan spoke to her drunk.')

In (75) the NP *ella* 'her' does not c-command *borracha* 'drunk', but control is nevertheless possible. The presence of the doubled accusative clitic *la* shows that *ella* is the direct object of the verb 'meet' in (75). Example (76) illustrates that the OBL$_{GO}$ fails to be a possible controller, as both theories would predict.

   This evidence from Icelandic and Spanish shows that it is the function and not the c-structure position that determines the eligibility of an "obligatory" controller in functional control relations. Furthermore, we can see even in English that the C-Command Condition cannot be a necessary property of obligatory controllers. We have already seen examples of constructionally induced functional control, such as (77), which show an obligatory control relation between an NP and a predicate that it fails to c-command. (In this respect, AP adjuncts differ from participial adjuncts.)

(77)

John said he was passed by *Mary* in the hall yesterday *drunk.*

Note that a controller of the predicative AP in (77) is required in the sentence, and that a lexical NP in place of the controlled subject is not possible in the AP construction:

(78)

*It was raining outside drunk.

(79)

*John was passed in the hall, Mary drunk.

Hence, the C-Command Condition is both too weak and too strong. Where objects and oblique objects happen to be syntactically encoded as NPs and PPs, respectively, the C-Command Condition will appear to hold, but the underlying restrictions on "obligatory" controllers are functional, not structural.

Visser's Generalization

Another consequence of our theory is that the controllers of lexically induced functional control relations must change under lexical operations on function assignments. Consider, for example, the verb *keep* as used in *John kept laughing;* its lexical entry includes the lexical form shown in (80a).

(80)

a. 'KEEP⟨(SUBJ)(XCOMP)⟩'

b. (↑SUBJ) = (↑XCOMP SUBJ)

The lexical rule of Functional Control obligatorily adds the unmarked control equation shown in (80b) to the lexical entry for *keep*. Now, like other intransitive verbs in English, *keep* undergoes a lexical rule of Causativization. Causativization adds a new AGENT argument, which is assigned the function SUBJ, and the SUBJ of the intransitive verb becomes the OBJ of the causativized verb by the rule (OBJ) → (SUBJ) (cf. chapter 8 of this volume and Mohanan 1981a). Because Causativization replaces lexical occurrences of (SUBJ), or (↑SUBJ), by (OBJ), the control equation changes as shown in (81).

(81)

a. 'KEEP$_{caus}$⟨(SUBJ)(OBJ)(XCOMP)⟩'

b. (↑OBJ) = (↑XCOMP SUBJ)

The result is to shift control to the object of the causativized verb, as in *Mary kept John laughing*.

The transfer of control in the examples *John kept laughing* and *Mary kept John laughing* could also be obtained if Causativization simply asserted that the THEME argument is the controller of predicative complements (cf. Anderson 1977). However, this alternative formulation fails to account for the fact that *nonthematic* subjects can also become objects under Causativization; compare *Tabs started being kept on celebrities* and *What started tabs being kept on celebrities?*

Predictably, control is also transferred under the lexical operation of Passivization: (OBJ) → (SUBJ). For example, Passivization of the transitive active lexical entry given in (81) produces the intransitive lexical entry shown in (82). (For detailed formulation and discussion of the rule, see chapter 1.)

(82)

a. 'KEEP$_{caus}$⟨(OBL$_{AG}$)(SUBJ)(XCOMP)⟩'

b. (↑SUBJ) = (↑XCOMP SUBJ)

Accordingly, we find that in *John was kept laughing by Mary,* control has transferred to the passive subject.

The theory of control predicts, however, that Passivization of a verb whose SUBJ is a (lexically induced) functional controller should be impossible, for Passivization shifts the semantically unrestricted function (SUBJ) to the semantically restricted function (OBL_θ) or to ϕ, and these cannot be functional controllers. This explains *Visser's generalization* (pointed out in Bresnan 1976a)—the observation that verbs whose complements are predicated of their subjects do not passivize (Visser 1963–1973, part III.2:2118). Consider, for example, the contrast between (83) and (84).

(83)
a.   His friends regard him as pompous.
b.   Aunt Mary made the boys good little housekeepers.
c.   Her friends had failed her in some unclear way.
d.   The vision struck him blind.
e.   Frank persuaded Mary to leave.

(84)
a.   He strikes his friends as pompous.
b.   The boys made Aunt Mary good little housekeepers.
c.   Max failed her as a husband.
d.   The vision struck him as a beautiful revelation.
e.   Mary promised Frank to leave.

The verbs in (83) have objects as functional controllers; those in (84) have subjects as functional controllers. Only the former type has corresponding well-formed passives:

(85)
a.   He is regarded by his friends as pompous.
b.   The boys were made good little housekeepers by Aunt Mary.
c.   She had been failed by her friends in some unclear way.
d.   He was struck blind by the vision.
e.   Mary was persuaded to leave by Frank.

(86)
a.   *His friends are struck (by him) as pompous.
b.   *Aunt Mary was made good little housekeepers (by the boys).
c.   *She was failed (by Max) as a husband.
d.   *He was struck (by the vision) as a beautiful revelation.
e.   *Frank was promised to leave (by Mary).

Note that the examples in (86) are ill-formed whether or not the agentive *by*-phrase is expressed.

Where the complement subject is not functionally controlled, Passivization should be possible. This accounts for the contrast between (87) and (88).

(87)
a.   John promised Mary to bc on time.
b.   *Mary was promised by John to be on time.

(88)
a.   John promised Mary that he would be on time.
b.   Mary was promised by John that he would be on time.

The following observations explain the contrast in more detail. The lexical form for *promise* in (88) is 'PROMISE⟨(SUBJ)(OBJ)(COMP)⟩'; the COMP (closed complement) is not a functionally controllable clause. In contrast, the lexical form for *promise* in (87) has an open XCOMP, which must be grammatically controlled. However, this is a marked control relation, for even though *promise* has an object, it evinces subject control.

(89)
'PROMISE⟨(SUBJ)(OBJ)(XCOMP)⟩'
(↑SUBJ) = (↑XCOMP SUBJ)

In (89), Passivization would substitute (OBJ$_{AG}$) or ϕ for (↑SUBJ), yielding an impossible functional control relation, since only the semantically unrestricted functions can be functional controllers.

Certain apparent exceptions to the conditions on grammatical control relations are actually instances of anaphoric control. Examples are given in (90).

(90)
a.   Mary was ncver promised to be allowed to leave.
b.   It was never promised to Mary to be allowed to leave.
c.   To be allowed to leave was never promised to Mary.

(90a) appears to contradict Visser's generalization, in that a subject control verb (*promise*) passivizes, but (90b,c) show that *to be allowed to leave* behaves like a closed COMP, which cannot be functionally controlled. Unlike XCOMPs, closed COMPs may undergo *It* Extraposition ((90b)) and may appear as the subjects of finite clauses ((90c)). Thus, (90) is analogous to (91).

(91)
a. Mary was never promised that she would be allowed to leave.
b. It was never promised to Mary that she would be allowed to leave.
c. That she would be allowed to leave was never promised to Mary.

In contrast, the infinitival complement in (92) does not behave like a
COMP.

(92)
a. John promised Mary to be on time.
b. *It was promised to Mary to be on time.
c. *To be on time was promised to Mary.

The reason that *to be on time* in (92) is interpretable as an XCOMP but
not as a COMP may be that there is a subtle difference between the
meaning of *promise...to* and *promise...that*. To promise . . . to . . . is
to commit oneself to someone to act in some way. In *X promised Y to Z*,
X is an agent, Y is a goal or beneficiary, and Z is an action. If the action
Z is not in X's power to perform, the result is odd: cf. *#John promised
Mary to be tall, #John promised Mary to be allowed to feed himself*. But
to promise . . . that . . . is to commit oneself to a (possibly abstract)
transfer of some benefit to someone. In *X promised Y that Z*, X is an
agent and perhaps source as well, Y is a goal, and Z is a theme. This
sense of *promise* is comparable to its sense in *John promised Mary an
apple,* which means 'John promised Mary that she could have an
apple'. With *promise...that,* if the theme Z is not transferable to the
goal, the result is odd. This would account for the difference between
(90a), *Mary was never promised to be allowed to leave,* and (87b), *Mary
was promised by John to be on time; to be allowed to leave* can be interpreted as an abstractly transferable benefit ("permission to leave"),
but *to be on time* cannot. In short, the semantic content of the complement biases the choice of predicates *promise-to* or *promise-that*.
Thematic constraints on anaphoric control imply that a theme will be
anaphorically controlled by its goal, experiencer, or possessor (Bresnan 1979); hence, this analysis of *promise-that* subsumes the interpretation of (90) under the same rule that interprets (93).[12]

(93)
a. No one ever promised Mary permission to leave.
b. Mary was never promised permission to leave.
c. Permission to leave was never promised to Mary.

The unexpected deviance of some examples of the type in (87) had occasionally been noticed in the literature of transformational grammar (Chomsky 1965:229, Jenkins 1972:200ff). However, its significance has only recently been appreciated, since it was an assumption in transformational grammar so long and widely maintained as to seem a truism, that however passives may differ from actives in scope relations, discourse function, or stylistic effect, the *grammatical relations* relevant to the semantic interpretation of passive sentences are identical to those of corresponding active sentences.[13] Indeed, this is the fundamental reason for postulating a Passive transformation. Visser's generalization shows that this truism is false. In the lexical analysis of passivization required by our theory, grammatical relations do vary under passivization while the basic predicate argument structure remains invariant (see chapters 1 and 8 of this volume, Roberts 1981, Halvorsen forthcoming). This offers a straightforward explanation of Visser's generalization, as we have just seen.

Since the significance of Visser's generalization was first pointed out (Bresnan 1976a), there have been several attempts to provide an account for it that is consistent with transformational theories of passivization (Wasow 1977, Anderson 1977, Chomsky 1977a, 1980, Williams 1980), but none of them is satisfactory. The first attempt in transformational grammar to explain the deviance of examples like (87) appears to be that of Jenkins 1972:200ff, who proposed a constraint stating that the object of *by* cannot be coreferential with an implicit or expressed subject of a complement. If this were true, it would itself require explanation, but the following examples show that this *by*-phrase constraint does not express the correct generalization:

(94)
a.   John had been promised by Mary that she would meet him at the station.
b.   John expects a promise by Mary to remain faithful to him.
c.   An attempt by the gang of four to advance themselves now would be foolhardy.

In all of these examples, the object of *by* is or can be understood as coreferential with the subject of the complement. In (94a) the complement subject *she* is expressed, while in (94b,c) the subjects of the infinitival complements are implicit. Moreover, the *by*-phrase constraint fails to account for the persisting deviance of examples (86a–e) and (87b) when the *by*-phrases are omitted. In contrast, our theory

correctly distinguishes examples like (94a–c) from the deviant example
(87b). In (94a), the *that*-complement is a (closed) COMP, which cannot
be functionally controlled. In (94b,c), the nominals *promise* and *attempt* cannot have undergone Passivization, since derived nominals
lack both SUBJ and OBJ (Rappaport 1980).[14] The anaphoric relations
between the objects of *by* and the implicit subjects of the infinitives are
similar to those in (95).

(95)
a. John awaits a promise from Mary to remain faithful to him.
b. An attempt on the part of the gang of four to advance themselves
    now would be foolhardy.

Anaphoric control in nominals is analyzed in Kisala in preparation.

Anderson 1977 also attempts to explain Visser's generalization. He
formulates a thematic control rule which states that a complement is
attributed to the theme of its clause (Anderson 1977:375–376) and implies that the passivized subject in (87b) is not thematic. However, this
account provides no insight into the contrast between *Mary was promised to be allowed to leave* and **Mary was promised to be on time,* for in
neither example can *Mary* be considered the theme. Moreover, Anderson's hypothesis, like Jenkins's, fails to explain why the infinitival
clause can be predicated of a nontheme in (94b,c). Finally, as mentioned above in the discussion of *Tabs started being kept on celebrities,*
complements *can* be predicated of nonthematic subjects and objects.
As Borkin 1974 has observed, in many idiolects of English, examples
like (96a) are found alongside the construction (96b).

(96)
a. There struck me as being too few women in positions of power.
b. Too few women struck me as being in positions of power.

Our theory explains why these examples fail to passivize:

(97)
a. *I was struck (by there) as being too few women in positions of
    power.
b. *I was struck (by too few women) as being in positions of power.

However, Anderson's hypothesis offers no explanation for the contrast
between (96a) and (97a) and for the parallel behavior of (96a,b) and
(97a,b), for in neither (96a) nor (97a) is the complement predicated of a
theme.

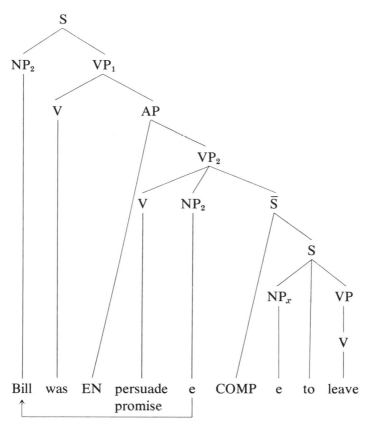

In this structure, *promise* has no subject, so control of its complement's subject is impossible; the object of *persuade* controls its complement's subject.

Figure 5.16
A configurational account of Visser's generalization (Chomsky 1977)

Still another recent attempt to explain Visser's generalization in a way consistent with transformational theory is found in Chomsky 1977a, 1980. Chomsky proposes that passive sentences have the structure shown in figure 5.16 (see Chomsky 1977a:13). As indicated in the figure, an NP Movement transformation has shifted the object *Bill* of the verbs *promise, persuade* into position as subject of *be;* NP Movement leaves a trace NP_2 which is coindexed with the moved NP_2. The NP_x in the $\overline{S}$-complement to *promise* and *persuade* is a 'PRO' which must be coindexed with a subject or object NP of these verbs. Chomsky 1977a:13–14 writes:

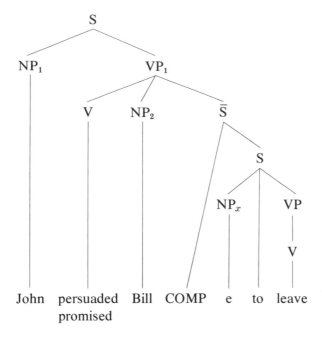

Control of complement's subject is possible for both *promise* and *persuade* in this structure.

Figure 5.17
Examples of control in active structures

The rule of control for *persuade* applies within VP_2, assigning to x of NP_x the value 2, as before, *persuade* being the main verb of VP_2 with NP_2 as its object. But the rule of control for *promise* is inapplicable since *promise* in [figure 5.16] is not the main verb of VP_1 with the surface subject *Bill;* compare in contrast [figure 5.17], where *promise* [is] the main verb of the VP sister to the matrix subject.

Since NP_x cannot be assigned subject control for *promise* in figure 5.16, the passive sentence *Bill was promised to leave* is ungrammatical. Chomsky concludes, "More generally, it follows that a verb with subject control (*promise, strike,* etc.) cannot appear in the passive" (p. 14). This account is technically inadequate in certain ways that are corrected in Chomsky 1980. However, the basis for Chomsky's explanation of Visser's generalization remains that "there is no subject under passive, hence no way for control to be assigned [to passivized verbs of obligatory subject control]" (Chomsky 1980), and this account is carried over in Chomsky's subsequent government and binding theory (Chomsky 1981:75–76).

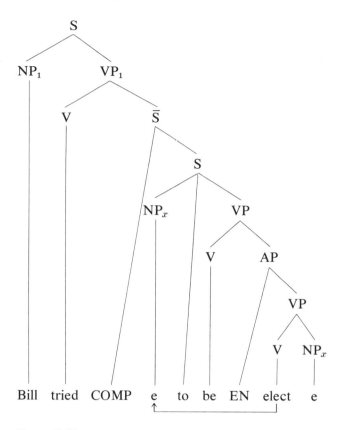

Figure 5.18
Passivization by NP Movement in the complement

Thus, for Chomsky, the apparent subject of a passive verb—e.g., *Bill* in figure 5.16—is actually only the subject of *be;* it is related to the deep object of the passivized main verb only by the trace left by NP Movement. Hence, when a passive verb is embedded in the complement to any verb that assigns control to its complement subject, what is assigned control is the PRO subject NP$_x$ of *be*, as figure 5.18 illustrates. The binding relation between the subject of *be* and the object of *elect* is accomplished by the transformation of NP Movement. The rule of control for *try* will thus assign both occurrences of *x* in figure 5.18 the value 1.

The key assumption in Chomsky's explanation for Visser's generalization is that passivized VPs by themselves have no subject. From this assumption it follows straightforwardly that such VPs could not be

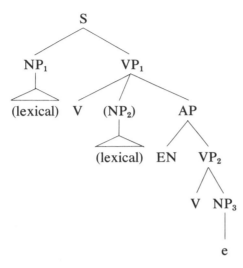

Figure 5.19
An impossible configuration

direct complements to verbs that assign complement subject control; this situation is schematized in figure 5.19. Here, neither NP₁ nor NP₂ can control the subject of VP₂, because VP₂, by hypothesis, *has* no subject. Thus, the ungrammaticality of (98a,b) is consistent with Chomsky's assumption.

(98)
a. *Bill tried elected.
b. *Mary forced Bill examined by a doctor.

The ill-formed example *Bill tried elected* contrasts with the well-formed example *Bill was elected* because *try,* unlike *be,* assigns a thematic role to its subject, precluding NP Movement into the subject position. (Formally, this would be ruled out by the Theta Criterion (Chomsky 1981).)

However, examples like (98a,b) could be ill-formed simply because *try* and *force* require infinitival complements in their intended uses here, while *be* clearly does not. To control for this possibility, we should find verbs that resemble *try* and *force* in having thematic subjects and objects, but differ from these verbs in permitting noninfinitival phrase complements to be predicated of their arguments. Sample verbs that would fit into the main verb position of structures like figure

5.19 with ordinary AP complements would be *stay*, *keep*, *feel*, and *get* in examples like the following:

(99)

a. The room stayed empty.

b. She kept the room empty.

c. John felt glum.

d. That got John glum again.

These verbs have dyadic or triadic predicate argument structures, assigning thematic roles to their subjects and to their objects (in addition to their predicative complements):

(100)

a. *The tables have stayed turned on us.
    (= Our roles have stayed reversed.)

b. The tables have been turned on us.
    (= Our roles have been reversed.)

(101)

a. *The reporters will keep the cat out of the bag.
    (= The reporters will keep the secret exposed.)

b. The reporters will consider the cat out of the bag.
    (= The reporters will consider the secret exposed.)

(102)

a. *Our goose feels cooked.
    (= We feel in trouble with no way out.)

b. Our goose is cooked.
    (= We are in trouble with no way out.)

(103)

a. *Trying to help his friends got excessive advantage taken of John.
    (= Trying to help his friends got John taken advantage of excessively.)

b. I consider excessive advantage to have been taken of John by his friends.
    (= I consider John taken advantage of excessively by his friends.)

(Example (103b) is ill-formed without *to have been* because *consider* takes AP complements, and a thematic condition on adjectival passives rules out semantically empty subjects (see chapter 1 for a detailed account). In contrast, the addition of *to be* in (103a) does not improve the example.)

Of course, the selectional restrictions of the AP-complement verbs
are not *identical* to those of the infinitival-complement verbs; the latter
often require animate arguments where the former require only themes.
Contrast *The situation stayed/felt unbearable* with #*The situation tried
to be unbearable,* and *She kept/got the room warm* with #*She forced the
room to be warm.* Nevertheless, in their imposition of selectional restrictions on their subjects and objects, these verbs behave like *try* and
force rather than *seem* and *expect:*

(104)
a.   Our goose seems to be cooked. (idiomatic)
b.   Our goose tries to be cooked. (unidiomatic)

(105)
a.   I expected excessive advantage to be taken of John by his friends.
b.   *I forced excessive advantage to be taken of John by his friends.

If Chomsky's explanation of Visser's generalization is correct, then
passivized VPs should not appear as direct complements to the verbs
stay, keep, feel, and *get* as used above. NP Movement from the complement object position is impossible; the passivized VP itself lacks a
subject, and the matrix verb assigns a thematic role to its own subject
and object, precluding NP Movement into these positions. Consider
then the crucial examples (106a–d).

(106)
a.   The wall will stay painted black.
b.   She kept the wall painted black.
c.   John felt betrayed and made to look like a fool by Susan.
d.   That got John handed a can of worms.

Indeed, we have already seen passives embedded in some of the examples given above (e.g., *Trying to help his friends got John taken advantage of*). The passivized VPs or APs in each of these well-formed
examples show that Chomsky's explanation for Visser's generalization
cannot be correct.[15] (The lexical–functional theory of passivization
correctly predicts the existence of such examples (see chapter 1).)

One might think that Chomsky's proposal could be rescued by assuming that a rule of *To Be* Deletion has applied in (107a–d), deleting
the verb *be* from the immediate complement of the main verb. However, there is evidence against an underlying *be* in these examples:

(107)

a.   *The wall will stay *to be* painted black.

b.   *She kept the wall *being* painted black.

c.   *John felt *to be* betrayed and *to be* made to look like a fool by Susan.

d.   *That got John *to be* handed a can of worms.

Moreover, when the phrasal complement of one of these verbs does contain *be*, as in *John felt eager to be on the list,* it may not delete: *John felt eager on the list.* Under the *To Be* Deletion hypothesis, the rule of *To Be* Deletion would have to apply obligatorily and locally to verbs like *stay, feel, keep,* and *get* and yet be inapplicable to verbs like *try* and *force.* These properties of lexical specificity and strict locality are of course precisely the characteristics of lexical subcategorization. In fact, Baker 1979 has argued from considerations of language acquisition that replacing the *To Be* Deletion analysis with the direct subcategorization hypothesis yields a more explanatory theory of grammar. His arguments indicate that rules such as *To Be* Deletion should be eliminated in principle from grammars.

Since Chomsky 1970, 1980 recognizes the theoretical deficiencies of the *To Be* Deletion analysis, the only other recourse would seem to be to assume that the verbs *stay, keep, feel,* and *get* in (106) have sentential complements containing *be* in *logical form,* as Chomsky 1980 has proposed for verbs like *strike.* Accordingly, (106a) would have the logical form sketched in figure 5.20. Note that the circled portion of this figure was not present in the syntactic structure shown in figure 5.19; this is structure that has been created in logical form by lexically governed structure-building rules. A rule of control for the verb *stay* could then assign control to the PRO subject of the logical form $\bar{S}$ which was not present in the transformational derivation of the example. Observe, however, that since the PRO subject NP_2 of *be* was not present in the transformational derivation of the example, it remains unbound to the PRO object of *paint.* Whereas the structure-preserving transformation of NP Movement established this crucial connection in figure 5.18, NP Movement cannot have applied in figure 5.20, because, by hypothesis, no subject NP position existed for the object NP to be moved into in the transformational derivation of the sentence. Hence, there is no explanation for the fact that in *The wall will stay painted black,* the phrase *painted black* has the passive interpretation. The same argument applies, mutatis mutandis, to each of the other examples of (106). We

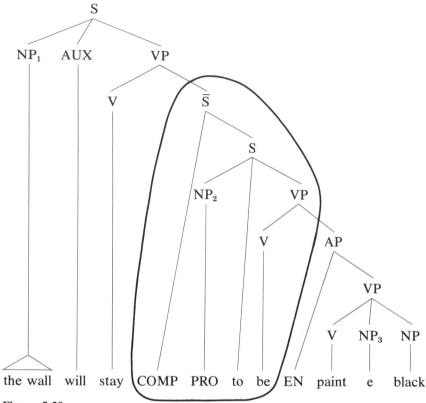

Figure 5.20
Structure-building in "logical form"

might think of adding a new rule of NP Coindexing to logical form to rescue this example by binding the syntactic object of *painted* in figure 5.20 to its logical form subject. However, this would of course make the transformational rule of NP Movement redundant; moreover, it would raise the question of why examples like **John tried examined by a doctor, *Mary forced John examined by a doctor,* and even **Bill was promised to leave* cannot be rescued in the same way, by NP Coindexing in logical form.

Thus, the *To Be* Insertion analysis is just as deficient as the *To Be* Deletion Analysis. In fact, in Chomsky's current government and binding theory, both analyses must be rejected as incompatible with the Projection Principle. However, this leaves the government and binding theory with no explanation at all for Visser's generalization.

Another recent attempt to explain Visser's generalization in a trans-formational theory of passivization is Wasow's 1977:352–353. Wasow suggests that the generalization could be explained if passives were transformationally derived from the "logically subjectless" deep struc-tures proposed in Bresnan 1972:139–143 and in Emonds 1970. Except for the assumption that NP Movement leaves a trace, this analysis of passivization is essentially the one adopted in Chomsky 1977b, 1980, 1981, and it suffers from the same deficiencies.

Williams 1980 offers an account of Visser's generalization based on his C-Command Condition. He observes that in examples like (108a), *Tom* fails to c-command *smart*.

(108)
a.   *Mary was struck by Tom as smart.
b.   *Mary was struck as smart.

Williams also observes that the ill-formedness of (108a) persists when the *by*-phrase is omitted ((108b)), and he therefore adds the stipulation that 'PRO' must have an antecedent in such examples. However, we have already seen in the previous subsection that the C-Command Condition provides neither a necessary nor a sufficient characterization of obligatory control and predication relations; furthermore, the need for an antecedent in (108b) is precisely what must be explained.

We see, then, that despite a concerted effort, no adequate explana-tion for Visser's generalization has yet been found within transforma-tional theories of passivization. The fact that this generalization is among the consequences of our theory counts as very strong support. Before leaving this topic, let us consider a very different approach to the problem.

Bach 1979, 1980 has proposed a novel explanation for Visser's gen-eralization within the framework of Montague grammar as developed by Bach, Dowty, Thomason, and others (Partee 1976). In this frame-work, syntactic structures are represented by a categorial grammar, which projects combinatorial information about sentence structure onto basic lexical categories. For example, the transitive verb *hit* is assigned to the lexical category IVP/NP (something that combines with an NP to form an intransitive verb phrase), while the intransitive verb *die* is assigned to the lexical category IVP (intransitive verb phrase, that is, something with which an NP combines to form a sentence). Similarly, the verb *persuade* is assigned to the lexical category (IVP/ NP)/toVP (something which takes an infinitival VP to form a phrase which takes an NP to form an intransitive VP), while the verb *promise* is assigned to the lexical category (IVP/toVP)/NP (something that takes an NP to form a phrase that takes an infinitival VP to form an intransitive VP). The motivation for this categorial difference between *persuade* and *promise* is in part semantic: unlike *persuade* and like *try*, *promise* is a verb whose complement is predicated of its subject. Bach comments on this classification (1979:518): "Just as *persuade to go* is a complex representative of the category of transitive verb, so *promise Mary* is a complex representative of the same category as *try*." In Bach's terms, *persuade to go* and *hit* are transitive verb phrases and *promise Mary* and *try* are intransitive verb phrases. Bach's explanation for Visser's generalization is then that Passivization applies only to transitive verb phrases and that its effect is to turn them into intransitive verb phrases.

Like the lexical–functional framework, a categorial framework encodes a large amount of surface syntactic information into lexical entries. Because this syntactic information is encoded in the syntactic *categories* of individual lexical items in a categorial framework, however, many cross-categorial lexical generalizations cannot be expressed directly in the lexicon. For example, there is no uniform lexical characterization of the notion *transitive verb,* for *hit* and *persuade* have very different lexical categories (owing to their different combinatorial properties). Hence, a rule such as Passivization that applies to transitive verbs cannot be formulated as a lexical rule. However, the cross-categorial nature of Passivization can be captured by formulating it as a phrasal rule that operates on transitive verb phrases, for at the phrasal level of representation, both *persuade to go* and *hit* are transitive verb phrases.

As evidence in favor of this phrasal analysis of Passivization over a lexical approach, Bach 1979, 1980 cites the existence of infinitivals that may modify transitive verb phrases and passive verb phrases, but not intransitive verb phrases:

(109)
a.   Mary bought it to drive to work in.
b.   It was bought to drive to work in.
c.   *The Dean came in to talk to.

However, the assumption that these infinitivals can modify only *transitive* verb phrases leaves examples like (110a–c) unexplained:

(110)

a. My car is always available (for you) to drive to work in.

b. I am always on hand for students to talk to.

c. It will serve nicely to fix drinks on.

It is clear that these infinitivals are not extraposed infinitival relative clauses, for possessed NPs and definite personal pronouns resist relative clauses for English: *My car (for you) to drive to work in is always available, *I for students to talk to am always on hand, *It to fix drinks on will serve nicely. Nor can the verb phrases containing the adjective available, the idiomatic prepositional phrase on hand, and the intransitive verb serve be naturally analyzed as transitive. Moreover, many transitive verb phrases fail to permit these infinitival modifiers (e.g., *Mary ate it to amuse John with). Thus, it appears that these infinitival modifiers are neither necessary nor sufficient indicators of transitivity. More generally, Halvorsen forthcoming has shown that a variety of arguments for a phrasal passive in the recent literature (Bach 1980, Keenan 1980) dissolve when the lexical analysis of passivization is coupled with a theory of the semantic interpretation of functional structures.

Is there then any evidence at all to choose between Bach's explanation of Visser's generalization and the explanation proposed here? The fundamental difference between the two is that on our account, Passivization fails because the functional control relation between the subject and the complement is destroyed, while on Bach's account, Passivization fails because intransitive verb phrases cannot be passivized. Thus, according to our analysis, the transitivity or intransitivity of the verb undergoing Passivization is irrelevant; the crucial factor is that a (subject or object) AGENT controller of the complement is not syntactically available. Therefore, our analysis would predict that an intransitive verb whose subject functionally controlled a predicative complement could not be passivized, even if intransitive verbs otherwise undergo Passivization. Indeed, in the lexical theory of passivization (see chapter 1), intransitive Passivization can be formulated as a subcase of transitive Passivization, resulting from omission of the optional operation that replaces OBJ by SUBJ:

(111)

(SUBJ) $\rightarrow$ (OBL$_{AG}$)/ϕ

((OBJ) $\rightarrow$ (SUBJ))

In Bach's account, by contrast, transitivity is the crucial factor; the syntactic availability of the AGENT controller is not important. In Bach's theory of passivization, the AGENT is existentially quantified over the passivized verb phrase, as in (112); hence, the AGENT is semantically available as a controller, even if it is not syntactically expressed.

(112)

John is regarded as happy.

$j*(\hat{\ } \lambda x \exists y[[regard' \ (\hat{\ } happy')] \ (\hat{P} \ P(x))](y))$
$= \exists y[[[regard' \ (\hat{\ } happy')] \ (\hat{P} \ P(\hat{\ } j))](y)]$

Thus, Bach's account of Visser's generalization would not generalize to the case of intransitive passives; in particular, if intransitive verbs could undergo Passivization, an *intransitive* verb whose subject controlled a predicative complement could be passivized. (More detailed reasoning in support of this conclusion is given below.)

Intransitive Passivization does exist in a number of languages, Icelandic and Norwegian among them. (The following evidence from Icelandic was provided by Joan Maling.) In Icelandic, intransitive agentive verbs undergo Passivization, as in (113)–(114).

(113)

Allir   keyra   hættulega   í   bænum.
all-nom-masc-pl drive-pl dangerously in town-dat
'Everyone drives dangerously in town.'

(114)

Það er   keyrt   hættulega   í   bænum.
it   be-sg-3 driven-nom-neut-sg dangerously in town-dat
'There is dangerous driving in town.'
[Lit: 'It is driven dangerously in town.']

The morphology of the intransitive passive is the same as that of the transitive passive, except that the passive participle appears in the neuter nominative singular form (the unmarked gender, case, and number). Expression of the agent in intransitive Passivization is marginal. There is evidence that *það* is a syntactic placeholder rather than a subject (Maling and Zaenen 1978).

In Icelandic, a predicative state complement controlled by the subject can appear with intransitive verbs. Unlike an adverb, this complement agrees in gender, case, and number with the subject:

(115)
Allir   keyra fullir   í bænum.
all-nom-masc-pl drive drunk-nom-masc-pl in town
'Everyone drives drunk in town.'

However, no form of this subject-controlled complement can appear in
the passivized form of (115), as (116) shows:

(116)
*Það er   keyrt
 it   be-sg-3 driven-nom-neut-sg
 fullt/fullum/fullir   í bænum.
 drunk-neut-sg/drunk-dat-pl/drunk-nom-pl in town
 ('There is driving drunk in town.')
 [Lit: 'It is driven drunk in town.']

The ungrammaticality of (116) is predicted by our theory, but not by
Bach's. (See below.)
    Similar evidence exists in Norwegian. (The following examples from
Norwegian were provided by Per-Kristian Halvorsen.) In Norwegian,
as in Icelandic, agentive intransitive verbs may undergo Passivization as transitive verbs do, except that the agent is not syntactically
expressed.

(117)
De   kjørte gjennom byen.
they drove through the-town
'They drove through the town.'

(118)
Det ble kjørt   gjennom byen.
it   was driven through the-town
'There was driving through the town.'
[Lit: 'It was driven through the town.']

In Norwegian, a predicative state complement modifying the subject
may appear in the active but not the passive form of the sentence:

(119)
 De   kjørte fulle   gjennom byen.
 they drove drunk-pl through the-town
 'They drove drunk through the town.'

(120)
*Det ble kjørt   fulle/full/fullt   gjennom byen.
 it   was driven drunk-pl/drunk-sg/drunk-neut-sg through the-town
 ('There was driving drunk through the town.')
 [Lit: 'It was driven drunk through the town.']

Thus, the evidence from intransitive passivization in Icelandic and Norwegian confirms our theory that Visser's generalization follows from a syntactic restriction on subject control rather than a condition on transitive verb phrase passivization.

The following reasoning (suggested by P.-K. Halvorsen) supports this conclusion in detail. In general, Bach handles control of infinitival VPs by forming a lambda abstract of the open sentence consisting of the VP and a variable for the subject. Thus, *John persuaded Mary to go* is built up from *persuade to go* and *Mary, John* being added last. Simplifying inessential details, the translation of *persuade to go* is an abstract: $\lambda x[persuade'(\hat{\ }go'(x))(x)]$. When this is combined with the translation of *Mary*, the x is bound and *Mary* will be interpreted to be the subject of the complement *go*. Passivization existentially quantifies the subject and abstracts over the object, producing $\lambda z[\exists y \lambda x[persuade'(\hat{\ }go'(x))(x)](z)(y)]$, which reduces to $\lambda z[\exists y\ persuade'(\hat{\ }go'(z))(z)(y)]$. What would happen in the case of passive intransitives such as *Det ble kjørt* 'There was driving' [Lit: 'It was driven (intrans)'] in Norwegian? The passive intransitive could be translated as $\exists y[drive'(y)]$ (again simplifying inessential details). This is of course the wrong type for an IVP, so let us assume that the translation is $\lambda x \exists y[drive'(y)]$, using vacuous lambda abstraction to perform a type adjustment. When the placeholder subject *det* 'it' is combined with the IVP, the lambda disappears and the translation $\exists y[drive'(y)]$ remains for the sentence *Det ble kjørt*. What if there were a complement? An example such as **Det ble kjørt fulle* [Lit: 'It was driven drunk'] would be built up from *kjørt fulle* and *det*. The active phrase *kjørte fulle* would be translated $\lambda x[drive'(\hat{\ }drunk'(x))(x)]$, in a fashion similar to *try to go*. (Note that, like *try*, *drive* can be used intransitively, transitively, or with a complement. For evidence that state predicates like *drunk* are (controlled) complements rather than adjuncts, see section 5.8 and chapter 6.) The translation rule for passive would then give $\lambda z[\exists y \hat{\ } \lambda x[drive'(\hat{\ }drunk'(x))(x)](y)]$, which reduces to $\lambda z \exists y[drive'(\hat{\ }drunk'(y))(y)]$, which again combines with the placeholder subject *det* to yield the well-formed interpretation $\exists y[drive'(\hat{\ }drunk'(y))(y)]$ 'There was someone driving drunk'.

In conclusion, Visser's generalization follows in its full generality from our theory. Despite proposals by Jenkins 1972, Anderson 1977, Chomsky 1977a, 1980, Wasow 1977, Williams 1980a, and Bach 1979, 1980, other theories leave it unexplained.

Bach's Generalization

In his study of passivization, Bach 1979 has also observed that where the object of a verb is an obligatory controller, intransitivization is impossible. This is illustrated in (121) and (122). In (121), the subject is the controller, and the object may be omitted; in (122), the object is the controller, and may not be omitted.

(121)
a.   Louise promised Tom to be on time.
b.   Louise promised to be on time.

(122)
a.   Louise taught Tom to smoke.
b.   *Louise taught to smoke.

In fact, however, not all cases of obligatory control by an object rule out intransitivization (a fact not explained by Bach's 1979 analysis):

(123)
a.   Louise signaled Tom to follow her.
b.   Louise signaled to follow her.

What is the difference between (122) and (123)? Note that an NP subject can be expressed in the case of (123) but not (122):

(124)
*Louise taught Tom for him to smoke.

(125)
  Louise signaled Tom for him to follow her.

On the basis of this fact, we may tentatively hypothesize that the object in (122a) is a functional controller of its complement, while the object in (123) is an anaphoric controller of its complement. Thus, we can amend Bach's generalization to state that where the object of a verb is a functional controller, intransitivization is impossible. In this form, the generalization appears quite generally to be true:

(126)
a. John called someone.
b. John called.
c. John called someone a fool.
d. *John called a fool.

(127)
a. John painted something.
b. John painted.
c. John painted something black.
d. *John painted black.

This generalization is the counterpart for objects of Visser's generalization for subjects: since only subjects and objects can be functional controllers, it follows that any lexical operations that eliminate subjects or objects will be inapplicable where they would destroy functional control relations. Consider the control relation in example (122). Assuming that *teach* has a basic lexical form 'TEACH$\langle$(SUBJ)(OBJ)(XCOMP)$\rangle$', the lexical rule of Functional Control (section 5.8) obligatorily adds the control relation ($\uparrow$OBJ) = ($\uparrow$XCOMP SUBJ) to the lexical entry. The lexical rule of Intransitivization replaces (OBJ) by ϕ (see chapter 3); it therefore could not apply to *teach* without destroying the functional control relation, since only the semantically unrestricted functions can be functional controllers, and ϕ is not a function (see note 1).

Raising
Raising refers to the type of construction illustrated in (128). The italicized NPs are sometimes referred to as "raised" NPs.

(128)
a. John considered *himself* for a long time to be inferior to his brother.
b. *Mary* seems to like witty women.

Two properties characterize these examples of raising constructions: first, the verb has a predicative complement whose understood subject is referentially dependent upon (in fact, identical to) a pre- or postverbal NP; and second, this pre- or postverbal NP is not a "logical," or thematic, argument of the verb. From the first property we see that raising is a type of control relation (section 5.8). From the second property we see that it must be a *functional* control relation. To see this, suppose that raising involved anaphoric control. The sentences would then be semantically incoherent, containing a subject or object (the "raised" NP) that cannot be bound to any argument position (Halvorsen forthcoming). Thus, raising must be a functional control relation. From our theory of functional control it follows at once that only the SUBJ of a predicative complement can be "raised" and that "raised" NPs can appear only as SUBJ, OBJ, or OBJ2.

Let us now consider the problem of how raising constructions are expressed in c-structure. The government and binding theory of Chomsky 1981 incorporates the *Projection Principle* and *Theta Criterion* as fundamental representational assumptions; together, they imply that all representations of syntactic structure are isomorphic to the representation of thematic structure and reflect the subcategorization properties of lexical items. Given these assumptions, raising constructions must have syntactic structures of the form indicated in (129) and (130). The motivation for this analysis is that in their thematic structures, raising verbs have a propositional argument, and $\bar{S}$ is the syntactic form of such an argument.

(129)
[$_S$ John considered [$_{\bar{S}}$ himself for a long time to be inferior to his brother]]

(130)
[$_S$ Mary seems [$_{\bar{S}}$ [$_{NP}$ e] to like witty women]]

However, this analysis is impossible in our theory, for by the principles of lexical and syntactic encoding (sections 5.2 and 5.4), $\bar{S}$-complement clauses can only be assigned closed functions such as COMP(lement), which cannot be functionally controlled. (Moreover, of course, we are constrained from using null structure to represent local dependencies (section 5.6).) Furthermore, if we assumed that there is no functional control at all in object-raising constructions like (129), we would incorrectly predict that raised objects could not passivize. *John is believed to be smart* would be ill-formed for the same reason that **John is believed is smart* is ill-formed: namely, because *John* is not the object of *believe* in such structures (chapter 1). Hence, the c-structures shown in (129) and (130) are inconsistent with our theory. This analysis also poses a theoretical problem for Chomsky's government and binding theory, because the complement subject NPs must be governed and assigned case, the $\bar{S}$-complements lack finite INFL to assign case, and government from a matrix verb normally cannot cross a maximal projection such as $\bar{S}$. Chomsky therefore postulates a rule which deletes the $\bar{S}$, leaving only S, across which the matrix verbs are supposed to be able to govern the NP subject of a complement (Chomsky 1981:66). However, $\bar{S}$ Deletion has just the properties of strict locality and lexical specificity that characterize lexical subcategorization. It is evident that the use of such lexically governed "pruning transformations" (the term is due to Ross 1969a), like the use of transformational exception features elsewhere (Lakoff 1970), weakens the theory of structure-dependent rules (Bresnan 1975) and circumvents the strong constraint imposed by the Projection Principle. Since such syntactic restructuring processes are prohibited from our much more restrictive theory of constituency relations (section 5.6) in any event, it might seem preferable simply to hypothesize that the raising verbs directly subcategorize for S rather than $\bar{S}$:

(131)
[s John considered [s himself for a long time to be inferior to his brother]]

(132)
[s Mary seems [s[NP e] to like witty women]]

But this option, too, is closed to us, for it follows from our theory of lexically and syntactically encoded functions that in configurational structures, only *maximal* projections can be subcategorized for, and S is submaximal (section 5.3).

Thus, our theory requires that the infinitival complements to raising verbs like *consider* and *seem* be maximal projections other than $\bar{S}$. Since a verb heads these complements in the above examples, the natural choice of category is VP, the maximal projection of V. However, the category VP cannot contain a structural subject (section 5.4). Hence, the only analysis open to us is the one shown in (133), in which the NP *himself* is generated as the object of *considered* outside the predicative VP complement.

(133)
[s John considered [NP himself] for a long time [VP to be inferior to his brother]]

(134)
[s[NP Mary] seems [VP to like witty women]]

Note that our theory requires only that the complement to a raising verb be a maximal projection other than $\bar{S}$. Nothing in our theory requires that it be a VP (as opposed to another phrasal category which is a maximal projection). Hence, in our theory, raising should be possible with phrasal complements other than VP; in fact, both *consider* and *seem* also allow phrasal complements of categories other than VP:

(135)
John considers himself [$_{AP}$ inferior to his brother]

(136)
Mary seems [$_{AP}$ fond of witty women]

Moreover, for many speakers, *consider* and *seem* in these uses may have nonthematic objects and subjects (respectively); compare *Consider your goose cooked,* which can be idiomatic, and *Close tabs seem likely to be kept on celebrities.*

Now according to our analysis, the raising verbs *consider* and *seem* take phrasal complements; they differ in that *consider* is transitive, having a nonthematic object, while *seem* is intransitive, having a nonthematic subject. The phrasal complements in (133)–(136) have the function XCOMP, and the lexical entries for *consider* and *seem* will therefore include the lexical forms given in (137) and (138).

(137)
($\uparrow$PRED) = 'CONSIDER$\langle$(SUBJ)(XCOMP)$\rangle$(OBJ)'

(138)
($\uparrow$PRED) = 'SEEM$\langle$(XCOMP)$\rangle$(SUBJ)'

The lexical rule of Functional Control (section 5.8) will expand these entries with the control equations shown in (139) and (140).

(139)
($\uparrow$PRED) = 'CONSIDER$\langle$(SUBJ)(XCOMP)$\rangle$(OBJ)'
($\uparrow$OBJ) = ($\uparrow$XCOMP SUBJ)

(140)
($\uparrow$PRED) = 'SEEM$\langle$(XCOMP)$\rangle$(SUBJ)'
($\uparrow$SUBJ) = ($\uparrow$XCOMP SUBJ)

Note that it is because the OBJ of *consider* and the SUBJ of *seem* are nonthematic, that they can designate expletives such as *there* and idiom chunks; see chapter 1 for a detailed analysis. In sum, the c-structures and f-structures of our raising constructions must be as shown in figures 5.21 and 5.22.

c-structure

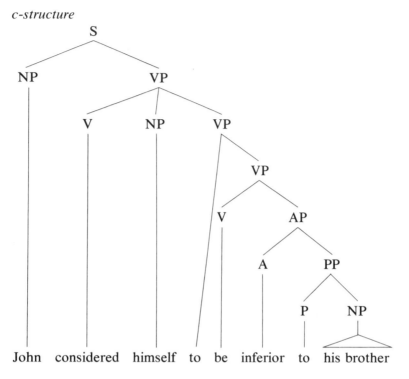

f-structure

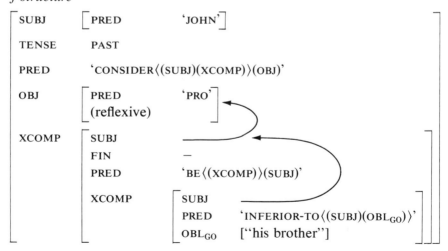

Figure 5.21
A raising-to-object construction

c-structure

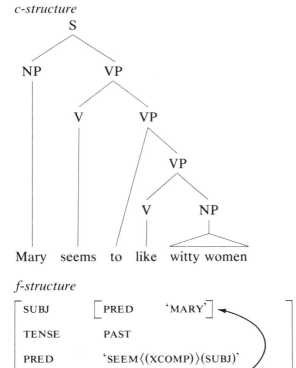

f-structure

$$\begin{bmatrix} \text{SUBJ} & \begin{bmatrix} \text{PRED} & \text{`MARY'} \end{bmatrix} \\ \text{TENSE} & \text{PAST} \\ \text{PRED} & \text{`SEEM}\langle(\text{XCOMP})\rangle(\text{SUBJ})\text{'} \\ \text{XCOMP} & \begin{bmatrix} \text{SUBJ} & \\ \text{FIN} & - \\ \text{PRED} & \text{`LIKE}\langle(\text{SUBJ})(\text{OBJ})\rangle\text{'} \\ \text{OBJ} & [\text{``witty women''}] \end{bmatrix} \end{bmatrix}$$

Figure 5.22
A raising-to-subject construction

However, the analysis of raising required by our theory is incompatible with the basic representational assumptions of Chomsky's 1981 theory (the Projection Principle and the Theta Criterion). The assumptions of each theory require a phrase structure representation of raising constructions which is inconsistent with the assumptions of the other theory. Evidence bearing on the choice of phrasal representations of these constructions would therefore provide grounds for deciding which theory is more explanatory, in the sense of limiting the hypothesis space of grammar construction to the descriptively optimal grammars. In fact, there is strong evidence favoring the analysis of raising constructions given in figures 5.21 and 5.22 over Chomsky's sentential analyses in (129)–(132).

First, because the raised NP in figure 5.21 is an object of the matrix clause, it f-commands the subject in the matrix clause nucleus. If we had adopted the sentential analysis, *himself* would be contained solely within the COMP(lement), in a position where it could not f-command the subject of the matrix clause nucleus. We therefore predict that anaphoric control of a subject clause by the object in a raising construction should be possible (cf. section 5.8). Examples (141a–c) bear out this prediction.

(141)
a.   Contradicting himself will prove Mr. Jones to be a liar.
b.   *Contradicting himself will prove that Mr. Jones is a liar.
c.   Contradicting himself will discredit Mr. Jones.

We see that the object of the raising construction in (141a) behaves like the object of the simple transitive verb in (141c), and not like the subject of the $\overline{S}$-complement in (141b).[16]

Further confirmation for the correctness of our analysis comes from the postposing of a "heavy" postverbal NP to VP-final position (noted in Bresnan 1972). This rule is bounded, in the sense that it can only postpose the postverbal NP over its sister phrases (as observed in Bresnan 1976b):

(142)
a.   I discussed [all those women riding motorcycles nowadays] with my sister.
b.   I discussed with my sister [all those women riding motorcycles nowadays].
c.   *I discussed [riding motorcycles nowadays] with my sister all those women.

(The boundedness property follows at once if the rule operates on the VP phrase structure rule, reordering the categories in a function-preserving manner.) Note in particular that the postverbal NP *all those women* cannot be shifted outside the clause that immediately contains it ((142c)). In our analysis of object raising constructions, the raised NP is the object of the raising verb, and hence may undergo Heavy NP Shift over material in the matrix VP without violating the boundedness of NP Shift. However, if the NP were dominated by an $\overline{S}$- or S-complement of the raising verb, shifting it over material in the matrix verb phrase *would* violate the boundedness of NP Shift. Both *count* and *consider* are object raising verbs in the author's dialect: cf. *I counted there as being more than 20 women on the payroll, I consider there to be too many fools in this committee*. The following examples confirm our analysis.

(143)

a.   I'll count [as being dead] from now on any corpse more than 3 days old.

b.   I will consider [to be fools] in the weeks ahead all those who drop this course.

These examples are naturally paraphrased as "From now on, I'll count any corpse . . . as being dead" and "In the weeks ahead, I will consider all those . . . to be fools," with the adverbial material modifying the matrix clauses as shown. They demonstrate that in c-structure, the raised NP must not form a constituent with the verbal phrase that is predicated of it. (Postal 1974 makes a slightly different argument from NP Shift; his 1977 response to objections by Bresnan 1976d indicates that his argument for a "raised" NP position in the VP is also valid.)

A third source of confirmation for our analysis is the rule of Right Node Raising, which permits a constituent of any category to be omitted from two conjoined clauses and positioned to their right, as shown in (144).

(144)

a.   Mary admired Peter the Great, and Catherine disliked Peter the Great.

b.   Mary admired, and Catherine disliked, Peter the Great.

In the author's dialect, nonconstituent sequences of categories cannot undergo Right Node Raising.[17] Accordingly, examples (145a,b) contrast with (144a,b).

(145)

a.   Mary gave Peter the grape, and Catherine did not give Peter the grape.

b.   *Mary gave, and Catherine did not give, Peter the grape.

Right Node Raising is a very useful test for constituency because it applies to all categories, including S (Bresnan 1974):

(146)

It is possible that, but it isn't obvious that, your theory is right.

In our analysis of object raising constructions, the raised NP and the predicative phrase that it controls do not form a constituent in c-structure; hence, we correctly predict the following contrasts in the restrictive dialect (cf. note 17):

(147)
a.   Mary believes Peter to be fat, but Catherine doesn't believe Peter to be fat.
b.   *Mary believes, but Catherine doesn't believe, Peter to be fat.

A similar argument has been made by Postal 1974.

To account for these facts in the government and binding framework, it has been proposed that a verb can assign case only to an *adjacent* NP; Right Node Raising is held to destroy the connectivity of case assignment by violating the Adjacency Condition (Stowell 1981, Chomsky 1981). Since, in fact, an object NP can be right-node-raised away from its governing verb (as in (144b)), the claim must be that case is transmitted to such an NP from its trace under Right Node Raising, and that there is no trace left of an NP (such as *Peter* in (147b)) which is properly contained within a right-node-raised constituent. Thus, we have two competing hypotheses to account for the ungrammaticality of examples like (147b). Our theory claims that *Peter to be fat* is a nonconstituent NP VP sequence; it therefore fails to undergo Right Node Raising (in the restrictive dialect) for exactly the same reason that other nonconstituent sequences (e.g., (144b)) fail to do so. The alternative theory claims that (147b) and (144b) are ill-formed for unrelated reasons. Example (144b) is said to be ill-formed (in the restrictive dialect) because it is a nonconstituent sequence, but *Peter to be fat* in (147b) is a constituent S, according to this theory. However, *Peter* is not case-marked by *believes* because Right Node Raising destroys the connectivity of case assignment.

Can we find evidence to distinguish between the constituency hypothesis and the connectivity hypothesis? Such evidence could take the form of a construction which required exceptional case marking (in terms of the government and binding theory) and yet behaved as a constituent under Right Node Raising. This evidence exists. Consider the "acc–*ing*" construction, illustrated in (148).

(148)
a.   All his friends worry about Fred losing again.
b.   Doctors disapprove of children smoking.

"Acc-*ing*" constructions are similar in their interpretation to "poss-*ing*" (gerund) clauses, but they lack the genitive marker *'s* to assign case to their subject NPs (*Fred* in (148a), *children* in (148b)). In the government and binding theory, these NPs must be assigned case. Given that the acc-*ing* clauses lack a finite INFL, there are only two possible mechanisms for doing this: either the position of the subject NP is inherently case-marked, or it receives case exceptionally from a governing verb or preposition outside the clause. Now if the NP position were inherently case-marked, the acc-*ing* construction would occur in positions where exceptional government by a verb or preposition does not hold, such as the subject position of a finite clause. However, if the NP position were exceptionally case-marked, the acc-*ing* construction would not occur in subject position. Examples like (149) indicate that the subject of the acc-*ing* construction must be exceptionally governed.

(149)
a.   *Fred losing again is worried about by all his friends.
     (cf. Fred's losing again is worried about by all his friends.)
b.   *Children smoking is disapproved of by doctors.
     (cf. Children's smoking is disapproved of by doctors.)

It is generally true that an acc-*ing* construction cannot function as a subject, even in nonfinite clauses:

(150)
*I'd like for Fred losing again not to bother you.
 (cf. I'd like for Fred's losing again not to bother you.)

In this respect, then, acc-*ing* constructions resemble object raising constructions. They differ crucially, however, in that the acc-*ing* construction gives every evidence of forming a single constituent:

(151)
a.   It's Fred losing that I can't stand the thought of.
b.   What doctors really disapprove of is children smoking.

Indeed, this assumption (together with some version of the A-over-A Condition (Bresnan 1976b)) is needed by the government and binding theory to explain the failure of NP Movement in examples like *Children are disapproved of smoking by doctors*. We see now, though, that both clefting (151a) and pseudoclefting (151b) preserve the connectivity of exceptional case marking. And in fact, so does Right Node Raising:

(152)

a. Mary's not looking forward to, and I can't stand the thought of, Fred losing again.

b. Doctors disapprove of, and parents worry about, children smoking.

Since these examples are perfectly well-formed, we must reject Stowell's and Chomsky's hypothesis, and conclude that Right Node Raising, like other dislocation rules, does preserve the connectivity of exceptional case marking. This conclusion gains plausibility because Right Node Raising preserves connectivity in general; for example, it preserves the lexically governed control relations in (153a,b).

(153)

a. Mary regards Bill, but Sue doesn't regard Bill, as too fond of himself.

b. Mary strikes Bill, but she doesn't strike Peter, as too fond of herself.

Consequently, failure of connectivity cannot be the explanation for the ungrammaticality of (147b) *Mary believes, but Catherine doesn't believe, Peter to be fat. The nonconstituency hypothesis, which is the simpler account, provides a superior explanation.

In summary, our theory requires an analysis of raising constructions in which raising verbs take nonthematic subjects or objects and predicative phrasal complements. There is strong evidence that the analysis of raising constructions required by our theory is optimal for the grammatical description of English. The discussion in chapter 8 shows that the essential features of this analysis are supported by raising constructions in Malayalam, a non-Indoeuropean language which differs strikingly from English in its constituent structure properties. Since the optimal grammatical descriptions of raising constructions are required by the representational assumptions of our theory, but inconsistent with those of the government and binding theory, we conclude that our theory is the more explanatory.

Pro-Drop

Pro-drop is a widespread linguistic phenomenon in which, under certain conditions, a structural NP may be unexpressed, giving rise to a pronominal interpretation. Given our constraints on the use of null c-structure categories (section 5.6) and our postulate that all semantic

forms are introduced lexically (section 5.8), it follows that in the unmarked case, pro-drop should arise for the functions SUBJ, OBJ, and
OBJ2. The reasoning is exactly analogous to that given for the representation of the controlled ($[+u]$) 'PRO' in section 5.8. Moreover, it
follows from our theory of syntactic encoding that when these functions are nonconfigurationally encoded, pro-drop should always be
possible. The reason is that nonconfigurational encoding pairs functional schemata with arbitrary X expanded by rules of the form
$C \rightarrow X^*$ (section 5.4). Hence, the categorial expression of the SUBJ,
OBJ, or OBJ2 is always optional. From functional completeness (section
5.5) it follows that when the categorial expressions of SUBJ, OBJ, or OBJ2
are omitted, the optional functional anaphors carried by the governing
lexical forms will be required. Thus, in the unmarked case, pro-drop of
SUBJ, OBJ, and OBJ2 will always be possible in nonconfigurational
languages.

Investigating this consequence will require careful descriptive studies of nonconfigurational encoding, distinguishing between pro-drop
and the rather different phenomena of morphologically incorporated
oblique pronouns (as in Navajo (Roberts 1981)) and oblique pronominal
clitics (as in Warlpiri auxiliaries (Simpson in preparation)). However,
Hale has already observed that extensive pro-drop is a hallmark of
nonconfigurational languages (Hale to appear), and research on nonconfigurational encoding in Malayalam (chapter 8 and Mohanan 1981b)
and Warlpiri (Simpson and Bresnan 1982, Simpson in preparation)
bears out this consequence of our theory.

5.10 Conclusion

All theories of grammar can be regarded as theories of *grammatical
relations* in the broad sense, that is, theories of the relations between
the surface constituents of sentences and their semantic predicate argument structures. One of the most important issues in current linguistic theory concerns the nature of grammatical relations: are they
completely derivative of representations of constituent structure and
semantic predicate argument structure, or do they have an independent
representation definable in terms of syntactically primitive grammatical
functions (e.g., SUBJ, OBJ)? While this issue will undoubtedly continue
to be debated, one conception of the problem must be rejected as
fundamentally mistaken. That is the view that theories which take only
structuralist concepts as syntactic primitives are inherently simpler

and more explanatory than theories which take functions as syntactic primitives, because the latter theories involve an extra level of representational concepts. This view is mistaken because in constructing a theory of grammar, we are free to take any set of concepts as primitive, defining in terms of these a larger set of derivative concepts; and the linguistic concepts of function, category, government, argument, case, and constituent structure are so closely interrelated as to be interdefinable. In particular, the structuralist concept of category can be reduced to more primitive functional concepts. Thus, in the theory presented in this study, the grammatical functions (SUBJ, OBJ, etc.) are taken as syntactic primitives and the phrase structure categories (NP, VP, etc.) are derivative notions. Contrary to this common but erroneous view, there is simply no a priori basis for preferring a structuralist theory of grammatical relations to a theory which employs grammatical functions as syntactic primitives. On the contrary, there appears to be good reason to prefer the function-based theory, since only in this type of theory has it been shown explicitly that there is a universal representation of grammatical relations for both configurational and nonconfigurational language types, and that the radical differences in the structural expressions of subcategorization, government, and control relations in these languages are predictable from a single parameter of variation: the surface realization of grammatical functions by c-structure configuration or by morphological case.

It is the axioms, or postulates, of a theory which give meaning to its primitive concepts. For example, our theory postulates a narrowly constrained set of relations between functions and lexical predicate argument structures, on the one hand, and between functions and phrasal and morphological structures, on the other hand. From these we have derived several significant generalizations. For example, it follows from these assumptions of our theory that in configurational structures, (a) the head of a phrase governs the maximal projections that are immediately dominated by any of the projections of the head and (b) lexical items will appear to subcategorize for maximal projections of categories. In nonconfigurational structures, it follows (a) that lexical items will appear to subcategorize for morphological case and not for phrase structure order, and (b) that (in the unmarked case) pro-drop of SUBJ, OBJ, and OBJ2 will always be possible.

Similarly, our theory postulates that the set of grammatical functions is partitioned into classes which differ in their lexical encoding properties; in particular, the semantically restricted functions are lexically encoded in much more limited ways than the semantically unrestricted functions. All lexically represented grammatical relations are thereby constrained, including lexically induced control relations and lexically carried functional anaphors. Among the various consequences we have enumerated, it follows in our theory (a) that only SUBJ, OBJ, and OBJ2 are possible as lexically induced functional controllers; (b) that morphosyntactically unexpressed 'PRO's can bear only these functions; and (c) that lexical transformations of control relations—such as Passivization (Visser's generalization) and Intransitivization (Bach's generalization)—are severely restricted.

Finally, our theory postulates that the SUBJ function is universally the controlled element in functional control relations, and that functional control must be distinguished from anaphoric control. Evidence has been given that in anaphoric control relations, objects as well as subjects can be controlled, as our theory predicts. While other theories of control have been based on rather different assumptions, our theory appears to offer a much more constrained and explanatory account of government, anaphoric control, and raising. For example, we have obtained an explanation of the distribution of governing morphemes, a uniform cross-configurational characterization of government relations, and the predictability of the actual structural configurations in which government relations can appear. This is achieved within a narrowly constrained theory of constituency relations, which precludes the use of "Affix Hopping" and other structure-deforming rules. Similarly, we have shown that anaphoric control relations are subject to a condition definable on f-structure, namely, f-command, but not on c-structure. And last, we have seen that our theory predicts the essential properties of raising constructions: that only subjects undergo raising, that the subjects are raised only into subject or object positions in the matrix clause, and that the propositional complement of the raising predicate is expressed in c-structure discontinuously, in the form of a nonthematic subject or object constituent and a separate phrasal complement constituent. This last result is of particular interest, since it is inconsistent with the assumption that phrase structure relations directly reflect semantic predicate argument structure (as in the Projection Principle and Theta Criterion of Chomsky 1981).

Notes

I wish to thank K. P. Mohanan, Per-Kristian Halvorsen, Ronald Kaplan, and Marilyn Ford for detailed comments on earlier drafts of this study. I am also grateful to Jane Grimshaw, Lorraine Levin, Malka Rappaport, and Jane Simpson for suggesting several improvements. This study is based upon work supported by the National Science Foundation under Grant No. BNS 80–14730 to MIT and also by the Cognitive and Instructional Sciences Group of the Xerox Palo Alto Research Center.

1. It is important to note that ϕ is *not* a grammatical function, but a lexical symbol indicating that an argument is semantically filled in the lexicon and is not assigned any function (see chapter 3 of this volume and Halvorsen forthcoming). See examples (8) and (9).

2. It is clear that As and Ns may have oblique NP objects (Maling 1980). In Russian, adjectives appear to have NP objects; whether or not they must be analyzed as direct objects deserves further investigation.

3. Fassi Fehri 1981 has proposed the further restriction that only $\bar{S}$ can be assigned the closed COMP function.

4. Chapter 7 presents an analysis of PPs that differs from the one assumed here. Given our revision, case marking by a preposition can still be distinguished in f-structure from case marking by a nominal inflection, in that the former is expressed by PCASE and the latter by CASE. An example of the need for this distinction is the use of prepositional and nominal instrumentals in Malayalam (see chapter 8); to express OBL_{INSTR}, the instrumental case and the instrumental postposition are used in free variation; to express the OBL_{AG} in passives, only the instrumental case is used; and to express the causativized SUBJ, only the postposition is used.

5. Note that in this formulation of the coherence condition, *local* is interpreted to mean 'in the same f-structure.' There is an alternative formulation of coherence, based on the functional locality principle (section 5.1), which interprets *local* to mean 'in the f-structure that immediately contains or is contained in this f-structure': an f-structure is locally coherent if and only if the values of all of the subcategorizable functions that it contains are subcategorized by a PRED; by the functional locality principle, only a local PRED (in the second sense) can subcategorize these function values (cf. chapter 4). The two formulations have empirically distinguishable consequences; for example, the formulation adopted in the text above is inconsistent with the use of compound function names such as "TO OBJ". Further research is required to determine which interpretation of coherence is optimal. Note also that, to give a uniform definition of *head*, we have adopted the instantiation procedure presented in note 6 of chapter 4.

6. By themselves, context-free grammars are not sufficient to represent the constituency relations of natural language. Bresnan et al. forthcoming show that there is no context-free phrase structure grammar that strongly generates just the set of empirically motivated c-structure representations for Dutch. However, the correct representation of constituency relations can be strongly generated by letting the lexical subcategorization conditions on f-structures filter the associated c-structures.

7. The implications of this analysis of 'PRO' for the government and binding theory were pointed out by K. P. Mohanan (personal communication).

8. We conjecture that the subjunctive complementizer in Romance languages is also an obviative clause marker. In other words, we propose that examples like *Marie veut qu'elle parte,* wherein *elle* must be disjoint from *Marie,* are instances of subject–subject obviation parallel to *Mary would like for her to leave* in English. Since the subjunctive clause of French is finite, the [+U] 'PRO' does not arise in it, but the [−U] pronouns are nevertheless subject to the principle. Simpson and Bresnan 1982 show that complementizers can be obviative markers in Warlpiri.

It is possible that the Obviation Principle (41) should be reformulated to apply only to [−U] pronouns, for the obligatory assignment of an antecedent to the [+U] 'PRO' in examples like (40a) could be attributed to lexical properties of the matrix verb, which could induce "thematic binding" of [+U] 'PRO' (Kisala in preparation). Until further research decides this question, the present formulation of the Obviation Principle will be tentatively maintained.

9. A c-structure node N_1 c-commands a c-structure node N_2 if N_1 does not dominate N_2 and every node that dominates N_1 dominates N_2.

10. If, however, we adopt the alternative formulation of the Obviation Principle suggested in note 8, the contrast between (42a,b) and (42c) would have to be attributed to lexical differences between the verb *surprise* and the deverbal adjective *surprised*.

11. Jane Simpson has pointed out that Stump 1981 discusses absolutives which might seem to be counterexamples. However, his examples fall into several classes that appear to have special properties. One class includes examples which could be analyzed as verbal participles, such as *Her hair braided, Mary began to put on make-up.* A second class includes such examples as *The children asleep, Bill watched TV;* it is well known that *asleep* belongs to a marked class of predicates, including *awake, aglow,* which have mixed adjectival and nonadjectival properties. For example, in contrast to most adjectives, *asleep* cannot occur prenominally and does allow modification by *right* in standard dialects of English: contrast *an angry child,* *an asleep child* and *%The child became right angry, The child fell right asleep.* A third class consists of true adjectives which modify body parts or possessions of the subject: an example is *Her face scarlet, Mary left the room.* These examples appear to be semantically restricted in ways that require further study: contrast the previous examples with *??Her lobster scarlet, Mary left the kitchen* and *?Her dog sick, Mary left the room.* In general, the existence of exceptions to categorial generalizations, including the generalization that adjectives and nouns lack direct objects (Maling 1980), supports a markedness interpretation of the category definitions.

12. Although the passives *Mary was never promised permission to leave* and *Mary was never promised to be allowed to leave* are both judged grammatical by many speakers, the actives *Fred promised Mary permission to leave* and *Fred promised Mary to be allowed to leave* differ, the latter being less acceptable for many. It is unclear exactly why this should be so. Perhaps the infinitival marker

to creates a strong lexical bias toward the *promise-to* reading, which is incompatible with the content of the infinitival phrase (cf. chapter 11).

13. Recall that we use the term *grammatical relations* in a theory-neutral way to refer to the mapping between semantic predicate argument structure and syntactic constituent structure. Thus, *grammatical relations* are to be distinguished from *grammatical functions*.

14. According to Rappaport's analysis, passivization appears to apply in derived nominals because (1) nominalized verbs inherit the predicate argument structures of their base verbs, but not the grammatical function assignments of those verbs; (2) the grammatical function assignments of nominals include only POSS(essor) and the semantically restricted functions. Thus, in *the destruction of the city by the Romans* the *of*-phrase is an OBL$_{TH}$ and the *by*-phrase is an OBL$_{AG}$. Rappaport's analysis explains why both types of phrases appear with nominalizations of intransitive verbs: *the arrival of John, a loud sneeze by Bill*. *John* is the THEME of the nominal *arrival* and the AGENT of the nominal *sneeze*. It also explains why the nominalizations corresponding to *Mary destroyed John* and *Mary surprised John* differ in form: *Mary's destruction of John, *Mary's surprise of John, John's surprise at Mary*. *John* is the TH of *destroy*, but the EXP of *surprise*.

15. It is easy to verify that the VP complements in these examples contain passivized verbs: only Vs and As in English can take direct NP complements (Wasow 1977, Bresnan 1978), and *made* in *made to look like a fool* has the verbal sense 'caused' and not the adjectival sense 'created'. In any event, however, adjectival passives pose exactly the same problem for the NP Movement theory as do verbal passives, for it has been shown in chapter 1 that adjectival passives are formed by conversion from verbal passives and that there is no separate lexical process of adjectival passivization distinct from verbal passivization. This means that the NP Movement approach can express the relation between adjectival and verbal passives only by assuming that both are derived by the same NP Movement rule, as Fiengo 1977 proposes (in violation of the lexicalist hypothesis; see chapter 1 for a discussion of problems inherent in Fiengo's analysis). Thus, whether they contain adjectival or verbal passives, examples like *John felt betrayed by Mary* are inconsistent with Chomsky's explanation of Visser's generalization.

16. These facts also show that it is insufficient to state the constraint on anaphoric control as a condition that the controller must be an *argument* of the matrix of the controlled complement (cf. Chomsky 1981). Clearly, *Mr. Jones* is not a semantic argument of *prove* in *Contradicting himself will prove Mr. Jones to be a liar*.

17. Unlike the author, some speakers do weaken the condition on Right Node Raising to allow nonconstituent sequences (cf. Abbott 1976, Peterson 1981b). Thus, the Right Node Raising judgments of these speakers cannot be used as a test for constituency.

Chapter 6

Case Agreement in Russian

Carol Neidle

The study of case, once primarily of interest to philologists, has only recently begun to receive the attention it deserves from syntacticians. There are still many open questions concerning the nature of case assignment and agreement. Given the degenerate case system of English, the evidence crucial to an eventual understanding of the grammar of case should be sought elsewhere—in languages such as Russian, where overt case marking plays an important role.

Moreover, since case is a reflex of structural and grammatical relations, case marking and agreement can provide good evidence about the nature of such relations. Thus, an understanding of case can contribute to the resolution of seemingly unrelated syntactic questions.

In this chapter, I will propose a strong correlation between case and grammatical control in Russian, on the basis of some interesting facts about the agreement of Russian "second predicates" within postverbal infinitival clauses presented in Comrie 1974. Not unlike the phenomena of "long-distance" agreement in Icelandic and Greek (discussed by Andrews in chapter 7 of this volume), these data pose problems for the transformational framework of the early 1970s. However, when these facts are considered within the theoretical framework that has been developed in earlier chapters, it becomes apparent that many of the seemingly aberrant phenomena can be explained by more general considerations of predicate complements and grammatical control in Russian. If my analysis is correct, the simplicity and naturalness with which case agreement of modifiers follows from the grammatical representation lend support to the theoretical framework of this volume.

I will begin by presenting the curious facts about the agreement of second predicates in Russian. In section 6.2, before proceeding to an analysis of the same facts in the current framework, I will provide background information about the organization and mechanics of this framework and about the treatment of case assignment that it permits. There we will see that functional structure provides a level of representation which integrates the information that is relevant to the determination of case. Finally, in section 6.3, I will argue that the case of modifiers then follows to a large extent from the grammatical representation. Within this framework, case agreement is precisely that: the modifier shares the case of its functional antecedent. Agreement is a natural consequence of the consistency of lexical information within functional structure.

6.1 Data

Second Predicates

Comrie 1974 considers the distribution of the dative second predicate within infinitival clauses. The term *second predicate* refers to modifiers which are detached from the noun phrase to which they refer. As Comrie points out, words occurring in second predicate position of ordinary short sentences may either (a) agree in case with the noun they modify, or (b) occur in the instrumental case. He presents the following illustrations:

(1)
Ivan   vernulsja ugrjumyj/ugrjumym.   (= Comrie's (1))
Ivan(nom) returned gloomy(nom/instr)

(2)
Mne   nužno   bylo streljat' pervomu/pervym.
(for) me(dat) (it) necessary was to shoot first(dat/instr)
   (= Comrie's (4))

Odin and *Sam*

Curiously, though, there are two words which occur in the second predicate position (of very common short sentences) only if they agree in case with their antecedent: *odin* 'alone' and *sam* 'oneself'. For these modifiers, as Comrie states (p. 124), "the noninstrumental Second Predicate is not only possible, not only preferred, but absolutely required."

(3)
Ivan   vernulsja odin/*odnim.   (= Comrie's (5))
Ivan(nom) returned alone(nom/*instr)

(4)
Mne   nužno   bylo idti   odnomu/*odnim.
(for) me(dat) (it) necessary was to go alone(dat/*instr)
  (= Comrie's (8))

According to Comrie (p. 124), "in stating the rules for modern Russian, then, we must indicate that these items are exceptions to the general rule putting Second Predicates optionally, and preferably, into the instrumental."

Second Predicate within Infinitival Clauses
Comrie is primarily interested in studying the second dative, which is often found in embedded infinitival clauses, although the antecedent in the matrix sentence may appear in a different case. Since the instrumental is excluded from the second predicate position with *odin* and *sam*, Comrie focuses, for the sake of simplicity, on sentences containing *odin* and *sam* in the embedded infinitival clause. In this position, however, not only the instrumental case is excluded: the accusative, genitive, and locative are also ruled out (although the antecedent of *odin* or *sam* may appear in any of these cases). Only the second nominative and the second dative are permitted in this context.

Second Nominative with Subjective Infinitives   The second nominative is required within the infinitival clause if the subject of the infinitive is understood to be the same as the subject of the matrix sentence. (Such constructions are referred to as *subjective infinitives* and are distinguished from *objective infinitives,* whose subject is understood to be coreferential with the object of the matrix sentence.) Examples include:

(5)
Vanja   xočet prijti   odin/*odnomu.   (= Comrie's (24))
Vanja(nom) wants to come alone (nom/*dat)

(6)
Ljuda   priexala pokupat' maslo sama/*samoj.   (= Comrie's (28))
Ljuda(nom) came   to buy   butter herself(nom/*dat)

Second Dative with Objective Infinitives   When, however, *odin* or *sam* occurs with an objective infinitive (regardless of the case marking of the matrix object with which the second predicate is understood to be coreferential), *odin* or *sam* is invariably in the dative.

(7)

a. Ja   velel emu   prijti   odnomu.   (= Comrie's (12))
   I(nom) told him(dat) to come alone(dat)

b. Direktor   posovetoval mne   napisat' stat'ju
   the director(nom) advised   me(dat) to write the article(acc)

   odnomu.
   alone(dat)

(8)

a. My   poprosili Ivana   pojti odnomu/*odnogo.
   we(nom) asked   Ivan(acc) to go alone(dat/*acc)
        (= Comrie's (33))

b. U   Koli   net   sil   prijti
   around Kolja(gen) (there is) not (the) strength to come

   samomu/*samogo.   (= Comrie's (34))
   alone(dat/*gen)
   'Kolja doesn't have the strength to come alone.'

Second Dative with Overt Complementizers *Odin* and *sam* must also
be in the dative if there is an overt complementizer preceding the
infinitive, as in (9) and (10):

(9)
Volodja   ne byl tak samonadejan, čtoby   samomu
Volodja(nom) not was so presumptuous as to(Comp) himself(dat)

gnat'sja za   ordenom.   (= Comrie's (37))
chase   after (a) medal
'Volodja wasn't so presumptuous as to chase after a medal himself.'

(10)
Prežde čem samomu   vyprygnut' iz samolëta,   on velel
before Comp himself(dat) jump out   of (the) airplane he told

vyprygnut' mne.   (= Comrie's (40))
jump   me(dat)
'Before jumping out of the airplane himself, he told me to jump out.'

Note that the presence of an overt complementizer, even with a "subjective infinitive," necessitates second dative. Consider the following
minimal pair:

(5)
Ljuda   priexala pokupat' maslo sama/*samoj.   (= Comrie's (28))
Ljuda(nom) came   to buy   butter herself(nom/*dat)

(11)
Ljuda   priexala, čtoby   pokupat' maslo
Ljuda(nom) came   in-order-to(Comp) buy   butter

*sama/samoj.
herself(*nom/dat)

Second Dative with Passive   Furthermore, in passive constructions (which are often rather unnatural in Russian), the second dative is strongly favored within the embedded infinitival clauses. Consider (12):

(12)
On   byl ugovorën prijti   *odin/?odnomu.   (= Comrie's (110))
he(nom) was persuaded to come   alone(*nom/?dat)

Nevertheless, there are examples like (13):

(13)
Ja   byl prinuždën borot'sja odin.   (= Comrie's (111))
I(nom) was forced   to fight   alone(nom)

How can these facts be explained? This is a question to which I will return after describing how case is treated within the framework of this volume.

6.2 Background

Inflection
In the theory presented here, the terminal elements of the constituent structure are fully formed words. Inflection is not accomplished by syntactic derivation; rather, all inflected forms are produced by lexical rules. (See Lieber 1980 for a discussion of the nature of the lexicon under this assumption.) Morphological regularity is captured by lexical redundancy rules.

The Lexicon
As discussed in previous chapters, each lexical entry contains a categorial specification, a predicate (which approximates meaning), a predicate argument structure with indication of corresponding grammatical functions, and a list of features that will be promoted to the

node under which the item will appear in constituent structure. Each lexical item, then, contributes information to the functional structure (f-structure) of the sentence by means of the lexical schemata. The entry for *čelovek* 'person', for example, would contain the following information:

(14)
čelovek: N, (↑PRED) = 'PERSON'
　　　　　(↑NUM) = SG
　　　　　(↑GEND) = M

The metavariable ↑ (read 'mother's') is to be instantiated by the variable of the immediately dominating node (according to the algorithm presented in chapter 4). Thus, the features of *čelovek* will be transmitted to the node (N) which immediately dominates the word. Furthermore, since the N is the head of the NP, by the unmarked assignment ↑ = ↓ these features will percolate to the NP node as well.[1]

　　Following chapter 4, we may call the equations in (14) *defining equations*. The information they provide will be built into the functional structure. There is another type of equation, called a *constraint equation*, which does not add information, but merely checks to see that the information is already present. Constraint equations, written with the symbol "=$_c$", provide a filtering mechanism, since the functional structure will be well-formed only if the constraint equation is satisfied.

　　So far, no mention has been made of the case features which are contained within the lexical entries of nouns and adjectives. First, we should consider the representation of case within the grammar in general.

The Representation of Case

In his article on the case system of Russian, Jakobson 1971 argues for a feature decomposition of case on the basis of semantic considerations and the extensive use of case syncretism within each of the many declension classes of Russian. He proposes a neat, 3-feature binary system for Russian case. The use of such a system results in economy, both within the phrase structure component and, especially, within the lexicon (as "lexicon" is understood here).

　　While the names of the features might be improved upon and while the question of universal case features is worthy of further investigation, Jakobson's case system will be useful for the purposes of this discussion. He chooses the features [±marginal, ±quantifying, ±as-

Table 6.1
Assignment of features to cases

	Marginal	Quantifying	Ascriptive
Nominative	−	−	−
Accusative	−	−	+
Genitive$_1$	−	+	+
Genitive$_2$	−	+	−
Locative$_2$	+	+	−
Locative$_1$	+	+	+
Dative	+	−	+
Instrumental	+	−	−

criptive] (where the negative value is assumed to be unmarked) and assigns them to the cases as shown in table 6.1. If cases are considered to be bundles of features, then feature matrices themselves may be assigned to [+N] constituents (using the notation of X-prime (X-bar) theory).

Assignment of Case
Within this framework, *structurally predictable case* is assigned by grammatical rules (by means of annotations which associate grammatical functions and case). I am assuming that the PS rules for Russian generate the unmarked word order with the appropriate case-marking annotations and that scrambling rules may operate on the PS rules to provide the relatively free surface word order of Russian. (An alternative would be that the PS rules generate unordered sets. Nothing crucial hinges on the assumption of ordering.) *Structurally unpredictable case* (that is, idiosyncratic or inherent case) is assigned through lexical information. (I will not be discussing irregular case assignment in Russian in this chapter. See Andrews's study of Icelandic case in chapter 7 of this volume for an analysis of irregular case within lexical interpretive theory.)

Case is checked by a constraint equation, which every [+N] form in the lexicon must contain. For example, the lexical entry for *ja* 'I' specifies that it may be used only in a position which is marked nominative:

(15)
ja: PRO, ($\uparrow$PRED) = 'I'
        ($\uparrow$CASE) =$_c$ $(-,-,-)$

See table 6.1 for the interpretation of $(-,-,-)$; nominative case is unmarked for all three features.

Notice the great economy within the lexicon that derives from feature decomposition of case. Every declension class contains some degree of case syncretism. To account for the fusion of various cases within each paradigm, constraint equations need not contain arbitrary disjunctions, but merely feature specifications.[2] Consider, for example, the class of plural adjectives. There are four endings: *-ye, -yx, -ym,* and *-ymi.* The first is used for nominative and accusative, the second for genitive$_1$, genitive$_2$, locative$_1$, and locative$_2$, the third for dative, and the last for instrumental. Thus, they would be associated with constraint equations (16a,b,c,d), respectively, where $\alpha,\beta = +$ or $-$.

(16)

a. $(\uparrow\text{CASE}) =_c (-,-,\alpha)$
b. $(\uparrow\text{CASE}) =_c (\alpha,+,\beta)^3$
c. $(\uparrow\text{CASE}) =_c (+,-,+)$
d. $(\uparrow\text{CASE}) =_c (+,-,-)$

Further decomposition of nominal and adjectival endings could produce even greater economy and generalization through use of features; the above example is intended solely to illustrate how constraint equations would control the use of case-marked nouns and adjectives.

Phrase Structure Annotation   Previous chapters have illustrated the use of PS annotation to represent grammatical functions. For example, (17) is a possible PS expansion:

(17)
$$VP \rightarrow V \quad NP \quad NP$$
$$(\uparrow\text{OBJ})=\downarrow \quad (\uparrow\text{OBJ2})=\downarrow$$

Structural case assignment is accomplished within this framework by PS redundancy rules stated in terms of grammatical functions, SUBJECT (SUBJ), OBJECT (OBJ), OBJECT2 (OBJ2), X-COMPLEMENT (XCOMP), etc. *Indirect objects,* for example, appear in the dative case, and there will be a PS redundancy rule which assigns the annotation OBJ2 along with the case marker:

(18)
$$...(\uparrow\text{OBJ2}) = \downarrow \qquad ...$$
$$(\downarrow\text{CASE}) = (+,-,+)$$

Structural case marking assigns the unmarked case for structural positions. However, particular lexical items may impose irregular case requirements on their objects, and these then override the structural assignment. This can be accomplished by making structural case assignment optional (as indicated by parentheses around the case-assigning equations), while irregular lexical case assignment is obligatory. Consider the possibilities:

(A) If structural case is not assigned, and irregular case is assigned by a particular lexical item, for example as in (19),

(19)
XXXXX: V, (↑PRED)   = 'XXXXX((SUBJ),(OBJ))'
        (↑OBJ CASE) = (X,Y,Z)

then the case of the object will be assigned by the lexical item.

(B) If the structural case *is* assigned, and irregular case is also assigned as above (in the verb *xxxxx,* equation 2), then the sentence is ruled out by the principle of *consistency* (which requires that, in an f-structure, a particular function name (such as CASE) must have a unique value).

(C) If structural case is assigned, and no irregular case information is received from any lexical item, then all is well. (This is the unmarked case.)

(D) If, however, structural case marking fails to apply, and no irregular case is assigned, then the constraint equation contained in the lexical entry of a case-marked noun will not be satisfied, and, again, the sentence will be ruled out.

In other words, only cases A and C will result in well-formed f-structures, and case will be assigned either by idiosyncratic lexical information (if and only if such information is provided) or else by the PS redundancy rules.

The *direct object* in Russian occurs most often in the accusative case. However, in negative sentences, it frequently occurs in the genitive. The genitive is used systematically with quantifiers in Russian, with overt quantifiers (such as *monoge* 'many/much' and *skol'ko* 'how many/ much') as well as with the implicit quantification of partitive constructions. Like the partitive, negation can add implicit quantification. The relation between positive and negative sentences with respect to the case of the direct object may be captured by means of a feature Q:

(20)

a. Assign to   ... *ne* Verb ...
    the annotation (($\uparrow$Q) = +)[4]

b. Assign to   ... ($\uparrow$OBJ) = $\downarrow$ ...

    the annotation $\begin{pmatrix} (\downarrow\text{CASE}) = (-,\alpha,+) \\ (\uparrow\text{Q}) =_c \alpha \end{pmatrix}$

    where both occurrences of α must have the same value

Interestingly, this feature of quantification can be introduced either syntactically, through negation, or semantically, through specific lexical items which include a notion of quantification in their meaning. Some verbs take genitive objects (either optionally or obligatorily); for these verbs, the use of the genitive case for the object correlates with the "attenuation," or indefinite, nonabsolute nature, of the object. "Intentional objects" (as discussed by Quine 1960:219–222) occur in the genitive as well. Verbs taking genitive objects include those listed in (21) (from Pul'kina and Zakhava-Nekrasova n.d.:64):

(21)

a. dobivat'sja 'to achieve', dostigat'/dostignut' 'to attain or reach', želat' 'to wish', dožidat'sja 'to wait for', and others, which require a genitive object

b. xotet' 'to want', ždat' 'to wait', iskat' 'to look for', prosit' 'to ask for', trebovat' 'to demand', and others, which appear with the genitive or the accusative (the latter being used to denote a generic or specific object or person)

Complements are, by definition, specified within the predicate argument structure of the lexical items with which they occur. The subject of the complement is grammatically controlled (this relation being expressed by means of a control equation in the lexicon). The symbol XCOMP is used to designate the set of adjective complements (ACOMPs), noun complements (NCOMPs), prepositional complements (PCOMPs), and verbal complements (VCOMPs). Consider, for illustration, the English sentence (22), discussed earlier in chapters 1 and 5:

(22)

John strikes them as a fool.

(23) gives the partial lexical entry of *strike:*

(23)

strike: V, (↑PRED) = 'STRIKE-AS ((SUBJ),(OBJ),(XCOMP))'

(↑SUBJ) = (↑XCOMP SUBJ)   (control equation)

Similar constructions in Russian occur with the NCOMP or ACOMP obligatorily in the instrumental. Consider *sčitat'* 'to consider' and *najti* 'to find', whose OBJ grammatically controls the SUBJ of the complement; or *okazat'sja* 'to turn out to be' and *stat'* 'to start to be', which have subject control over the complement's subject.

(24)

a. On   eë   sčital   *krasivoj.*
    he(nom) her(acc) considered *pretty(instr)*
    'He considered her pretty.'

b. On   eë   našël *umnoj.*
    he(nom) her(acc) found *clever(instr)*
    'He found her clever.'

(25)

a. On   okazalsja   *durakom.*
    he(nom) turned-out-to-be (a) *fool(instr)*

b. On   stal   *lenivym.*
    he(nom) became *lazy(instr)*

The italicized words can occur in no other case.

This generalization about the case of (case-bearing) complements can be stated quite simply within the present framework, since case marking is formulated in terms of grammatical functions. The following PS redundancy rule will account for the case marking of complements:[5]

(26)

Assign to the expansion   ... XP ...

                                 (↑XCOMP)=↓

the annotation   (↓CASE) = (+,−,−)

(*XP* abbreviates the set of categories NP, PP, AP, VP (cf. Jackendoff 1977 and Bresnan 1977).)

Russian Phrase Structure Rules   The simplified PS rules (27) and (28) illustrate PS rules complete with their annotations. (I temporarily omit the case marking of subjects, but I will discuss it in section 6.3.)

(27)

S → NP   VP
    $(\uparrow\text{SUBJ})=\downarrow$ $\uparrow=\downarrow$

(28)

VP →

$$\begin{pmatrix} ne \\ ((\uparrow\text{Q})=+) \end{pmatrix} \text{V} \begin{pmatrix} \text{NP} \\ (\uparrow\text{OBJ})=\downarrow \\ \begin{pmatrix} (\downarrow\text{CASE})=(-,\alpha,+) \\ (\uparrow\text{Q})=_c\alpha \end{pmatrix} \end{pmatrix} \left\{ \begin{pmatrix} \text{NP} \\ (\uparrow\text{OBJ2})=\downarrow \\ (\downarrow\text{CASE})=(+,-,+) \end{pmatrix} \\ \begin{pmatrix} \text{XP} \\ (\uparrow\text{XCOMP})=\downarrow \\ (\downarrow\text{CASE})=(+,-,-) \end{pmatrix} \right\} \text{(PP*) (XP)}$$

Summary

To summarize, then, lexical rules produce fully inflected forms. [+N] constituents contain constraint equations which ensure that case-marked forms are inserted into positions which have been assigned case. Case may be assigned either by grammatical rules of PS annotation, or else by verbs which impose lexical restrictions on the case of the grammatical functions they govern.

With this as background, let us now consider the case marking of the second predicate in Russian.

6.3 Proposed Analysis of Agreement

Second Predicates

As mentioned previously, the so-called second predicates may either (a) agree in case with the noun they modify, or (b) occur in the instrumental case. The term *second predicate* fails to distinguish between at least two fundamentally different types of constructions. When the adjective takes the instrumental, the second predicate is functioning as an adjective complement (ACOMP in the framework of chapter 5, for example). On the other hand, when the adjective functions as an adjunct, it must agree in case with the noun to which it refers.

Complements differ crucially from adjuncts in that the former must be specified in the predicate argument structure of the lexical item, whereas the latter are not lexically specified. Indeed, only certain verbs can take the second predicate in the instrumental case.

(29)
Ivan   vernulsja ugrjumym.
Ivan(nom) returned gloomy(instr)

(30)
*Ivan   čitaet ugrjumym.
 Ivan(nom) reads gloomy(instr)

(31)
*Ivan   igraet ugrjumym.
 Ivan(nom) plays gloomy(instr)

No similar restriction applies to detached attributes agreeing in case with the noun they modify. Being adjuncts, they can occur freely with any verb.

(32)
Ivan   čitaet(,) ugrjumyj.[6]
Ivan(nom) reads(,) gloomy(nom)

(33)
Oni   prišli domoj ustalye.
they(nom) came home tired(nom)

So, adjuncts agree in case with their antecedent, while complements occur only with a limited class of verbs and appear only in the instrumental. Furthermore, it is not surprising that complement second predicates are marked as instrumental, since noun and adjective complements always take the instrumental case in Russian (as discussed earlier).

Restrictions on the Distribution of *Odin* and *Sam*

Comrie observes that *odin* and *sam* cannot occur as second predicates in the instrumental. There is, however, a more general constraint: *odin* and *sam* (on the readings under discussion[7]) cannot occur as ACOMPS.

(34)
*Ona   sčitala   menja   odnoj.
 she(nom) considered me(acc) alone(instr)

(35)
*Ona   okazalas'   odnoj.
 she(nom) turned-out-(to-be) alone(instr)[8]

The distinction between complements and adjuncts is useful, and indeed necessary, to properly account for the distribution of second predicates. It is clearly more adequate than the "general rule putting Second Predicates optionally, and preferably, into the Instrumental," suggested by Comrie 1974:124. Such a rule treats *odin* and *sam* as being anomalous, thus failing to capture the generalization that they are excluded from all complement positions.

Adjuncts within Infinitival Clauses
By focusing his attention on *odin* and *sam*, Comrie in effect limits the class of second predicates under consideration to a subclass: adjuncts. He shows that adjuncts within subjective and objective infinitives act differently. (It should be noted that *odin* and *sam* are the only adjuncts that can occur within infinitival clauses.) Adjuncts within subjective infinitival clauses agree in case with the nominative matrix subject, while those occurring with objective infinitives do not agree in case with the matrix object with which they are coreferential, appearing instead obligatorily in the dative.

Subject of Nontensed Clauses In order to account for the dative adjuncts, Comrie postulates underlying dative subjects of infinitival clauses. In this way, here as elsewhere, the adjuncts agree in case with their antecedents. Comrie justifies his suggestion by introducing evidence from Old Church Slavonic, where datives could appear on the surface as infinitival subjects, and by showing that even in Modern Russian, the dative subject can occasionally be overt, as in the following example he gives from Gorky:

(36)
A nedavno, pered tem kak   vzojti   lune,   po nebu
recently   before   Comp rise(inf) moon(dat) about sky
letala   bol'šuščaja čërnaja ptica.
was flying huge   black   bird
'Recently, before the moon was to rise, a huge black bird was flying about the sky.'

However, dative subjects of infinitives not only occur in archaic literary Russian, but also are common in standard Modern Russian in expressions like (37):

(37)
Kak mne skazat'?
how I(dat) say(inf)
'How could I say?'

In all cases but one,[9] whenever the pronominal subject of an infinitive appears, it is in the dative. Comrie proposes a general rule making the subject of infinitives dative, analogous to the rule making the subject of tensed verbs nominative. Such a case rule is not unusual. The dative case used for infinitive subjects in Russian is not unlike the *for*-phrase used in English;[10] Quicoli 1972b has argued that the subjects of infinitives in Ancient Greek are marked with the accusative case.[11]

Such a rule may be stated within the current framework as follows:

(38)
Assign to $S^{(')} \rightarrow$ ... VP ...
the annotation $(\downarrow \text{SUBJ CASE}) = (\alpha, -, \alpha)$
                      $(\downarrow \text{TENSE}) = -\alpha$

This rule indicates that case is assigned within either S or S' clauses (cf. rule (57) below).

Given this analysis, all adjuncts have antecedents within the same clause, with which they agree in case. Since the adjunct's subject is not always uniquely determined, it is not grammatically controlled by the matrix verb. Following Andrews in chapter 7, we may assign as its subject a variable x, which is permitted to range over grammatical functions (SUBJ, OBJ, OBJ2, etc.). This is not a true variable, but serves to abbreviate a range of possible subject assignments. The annotation $(\downarrow \text{SUBJ}) = (\uparrow x)$ ensures that the assigned subject is contained within the same clause nucleus as the adjunct. (*Clause nucleus* is the functional structure equivalent of a simplex sentence. As defined in chapter 5, it is the minimal f-structure which contains both a SUBJ and a PRED as function names.) The grammar must further specify, as in (39), that the adjunct and its subject agree in case.

(39)
Assign to $S \rightarrow$ ... XP ...
                      $(\uparrow \text{ADJ}) = \downarrow$
the annotation $(\downarrow \text{SUBJ}) = (\uparrow x)$
                      $(\downarrow \text{CASE}) = (\downarrow \text{SUBJ CASE})$

The revised phrase structure rules for Russian appear in table 6.2.

Table 6.2
Revised phrase structure rules for Russian

(i)

$$S \;\rightarrow\; NP \qquad VP$$

$$(\uparrow SUBJ)=\downarrow \quad (\downarrow SUBJ\ CASE)=(\alpha,-,\alpha)$$
$$(\downarrow TENSE)=-\alpha$$
$$\uparrow=\downarrow$$

(ii)

$$VP \rightarrow \left(\begin{array}{c} ne \\ ((\uparrow Q)=+) \end{array}\right) Verb \left(\left(\begin{array}{c} NP \\ (\uparrow OBJ)=\downarrow \\ (\downarrow CASE)=(-,\alpha,+) \\ (\uparrow Q)=_c \alpha \end{array} \right) \left\{ \begin{array}{c} NP \\ (\uparrow OBJ2)=\downarrow \\ (\downarrow CASE)=(+,-,+) \\ XP \\ (\uparrow XCOMP)=\downarrow \\ (\downarrow CASE)=(+,-,-) \end{array} \right\} \right) (PP^*) \left(\begin{array}{c} XP \\ (\uparrow ADJ)=\downarrow \\ (\downarrow CASE)=(\downarrow SUBJ\ CASE) \\ (\downarrow SUBJ)=(\uparrow X) \end{array} \right) \left(\begin{array}{c} S' \\ (\uparrow SCOMP)=\downarrow \end{array} \right)$$

However, if adjuncts agree in case with an antecedent within the same clause and if infinitival subjects are dative, why do dative adjuncts not occur within subjective infinitival clauses? This is a consequence of the representation of grammatical control, as I will now argue.

Grammatical Control   The proposal is that *sam* or *odin* always agrees in case with the functional subject of the infinitive, which is normally dative. However, in the case of subjective infinitives, the subject of the infinitive is grammatically controlled by the subject of the matrix verb. The lexical entry for the verb *xotet'* 'to want', for example, includes the following information:

(40)
xotet': V, ($\uparrow$PRED) = 'WANT((SUBJ),(VCOMP))'
    ($\uparrow$SUBJ) = ($\uparrow$VCOMP SUBJ)   (control equation)

Grammatical control entails identity of all features (and, in particular, of case). This identity is an essential property of the representation of grammatical control, asserted by the control equation (which is required for lexical forms containing a complement (XCOMP)).

 Therefore, in sentence (41)

(41)
On xotel pojti odin.
he(nom) wanted to go alone(nom)

the subject of the infinitive is identical with the subject of *xotel* and is therefore nominative. It is with this nominative functional subject of the infinitive that the adjunct *odin* agrees. Given the PS rules in table 6.2 and the mini-lexicon in table 6.3, we can construct the functional structure for (41) as follows:

(42)

On xotel pojti odin.

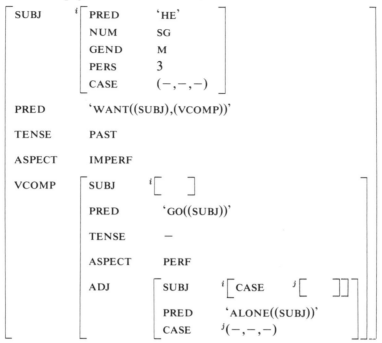

To summarize: the adjunct *odin* must be nominative, since it must agree with its antecedent—the subject of the infinitive, which is grammatically controlled by the nominative matrix subject.

The theory presented in chapter 5, which discusses the principles of control, distinguishes *grammatical control* from *anaphoric control*. The difference is that the former involves identity of f-structures, while the latter involves identity of reference, as I will briefly describe.

Grammatical control is expressed by a control equation in the lexical form of any item whose PRED contains a complement (XCOMP). This will be of the form (43):

(43)

a. Subject Control: $(\uparrow\text{SUBJ}) = (\uparrow\text{XCOMP SUBJ})$

b. Object Control: $(\uparrow\text{OBJ}) = (\uparrow\text{XCOMP SUBJ})$

Any lexical rule applying to a lexical form also applies necessarily to the control equation, if there is one.

Table 6.3
Mini-lexicon 1

on: PRO, ($\uparrow$PRED) = 'HE'[12]
              ($\uparrow$NUM) = SG
              ($\uparrow$GEND) = M
              ($\uparrow$PERS) = 3
              ($\uparrow$CASE) =$_c$ $(-,-,-)$

odin: ADJ, ($\uparrow$PRED)   = 'ALONE((SUBJ))'
              ($\uparrow$SUBJ NUM) = SG
              ($\uparrow$SUBJ GEND) = M
              ($\uparrow$CASE)   =$_c$ $(-,-,-)$

pojti: V,   ($\uparrow$PRED)   = 'GO((SUBJ))'
             ($\uparrow$TENSE) = $-$
             ($\uparrow$ASPECT) = PERF

xotel: V,   ($\uparrow$PRED)   = 'WANT((SUBJ),(VCOMP))'
             ($\uparrow$SUBJ)   = ($\uparrow$VCOMP SUBJ)
             ($\uparrow$SUBJ NUM) = SG
             ($\uparrow$SUBJ GEND) = M
             ($\uparrow$TENSE)   = PAST
             ($\uparrow$ASPECT)   = IMPERF

Anaphoric control is freer than grammatical control. An anaphorically controlled subject is represented as a free anaphor, having the feature [+PRO] within functional structure. No control equation is provided to determine the value of the subject, but there are certain conditions on anaphoric control (some of which follow from independent conditions on anaphora). Certain thematic, semantic, and pragmatic conditions will govern the interpretation of the anaphors, and although these conditions may force a particular reading in a particular context, the antecedent of the anaphor need not be uniquely determined and need not even be present in the f-structure.

Object Control   If the analysis of subject control is correct, why, then, is there no case agreement in objective infinitives between the matrix object and the pronominal subject of the infinitive (with which *sam* or *odin* agrees)? I will argue that this follows from a more general property of control in Russian, namely, that there is no "object control" of

VCOMPS. This is equivalent to claiming that there is no control equation in the lexicon of the form (↑OBJ) = (↑VCOMP SUBJ).

The verbs that take objective infinitives include those listed in (44):

(44)
prosit' 'to ask', ugovarivat' 'to persuade', zastavljat' 'to force', učit' 'to teach', taking accusative objects; prikazyvat' 'to order', velet' 'to order', sovetovat' 'to advise', poručat' 'to entrust', predlagat' 'to offer', zapretit' 'to prohibit', razrešat' 'to permit', taking dative objects

For *prosit'*, which seems fairly representative, there is no grammatical control of the infinitive. Consider (45) and (46):

(45)
Ja   poprosil*a*   ego   ne   byt'
I(nom) asked (*having feminine subject*) him(acc) not to be

žestokim.
cruel(instr masc)

(46)
Ja   poprosil*a*   ego   ne   byt'
I(nom) asked (*having feminine subject*) him(acc) not to be

isključënnoj   iz   školy.
expelled(instr fem) from school

In (45) the subject of *žestokim* is interpreted as the matrix object *ego*, while in (46) the subject of *isključënnoj* is the matrix subject, *ja* (which is also the semantic object of the verb 'expel'). (The gender markings on the verb make these the only readings.) Since the interpretation of the subject of the embedded verb depends on the context, the subject is not grammatically controlled. *Prosit'* can also occur without any overt object, as in (47):

(47)
On   prosil   pomolčat'.
he(nom) asked (pro=them, e.g.) to be quiet

The absence of a possible controller in (47) again shows that there is no grammatical control.

The claim that grammatical control over VCOMP by objects is impossible in Russian is a strong one,[13] and it makes certain testable predictions. It would eliminate the possibility in Russian of constructions which are very common in other languages, involving verbs like the

English *believe,* whose object (although not contained in the predicate argument structure) controls the subject of its VCOMP.

(48)

a. I believed him to have gone.

b. believe: V, (↑PRED) = 'BELIEVE((SUBJ),(VCOMP))'

    (↑OBJ) = (↑VCOMP SUBJ)

Indeed, there is no equivalent structure in Russian. A translation of sentences like (48a) or (49) requires overt complementizers:

(49)

I heard them cry.

(50)

Ja slyšala, kak oni kričali.

I heard how(that) they cried

 Crucially, *believe* differs from *persuade*-type verbs in that it does not contain an OBJ in predicate argument structure.

(51)

persuade: V, (↑PRED) = 'PERSUADE((SUBJ),(OBJ),(VCOMP))'

    (↑OBJ) = (↑VCOMP SUBJ)

(As Bresnan discusses in chapter 1, this is shown by the fact that *believe*'s object is not subject to selectional restrictions, unlike the object of *persuade*.) Thus, while a Russian equivalent of *persuade* could exist hypothetically with anaphoric control, without the option of grammatical control by an OBJ over a VCOMP, no equivalent of *believe* is possible. If the OBJ is mentioned neither in predicate argument structure nor in a control equation, then the functional structure for a sentence like (48a) would be "incoherent";[14] therefore, the theory rules out the possibility of such constructions in Russian.

 If my analysis of case marking is correct, then the following contrast indicates that there is no grammatical control by the subject of a passive over the subject of the infinitival clause:

(52)

*On byl ugovorën prijti odin. (= Comrie's (110))

 he(nom) was persuaded to come alone(nom)

(53)

?On byl ugovorën prijti odnomu.

 he(nom) was persuaded to come alone(dat)[15]

The theory in fact predicts this. Since Passivization is a lexical rule that replaces OBJ by SUBJ throughout the lexical entry, if there can be no control equation ($\uparrow$OBJ) = ($\uparrow$VCOMP SUBJ), then it follows that passivized object control cannot be obtained:

(54)

Passivization

$$\xrightarrow{\times} (\uparrow\text{SUBJ}) = (\uparrow\text{VCOMP SUBJ})$$

In cases where there is apparently a passive construction and an acceptable occurrence of *odin*(nom) in the embedded infinitival clause, I would suggest (as would Comrie) that we are dealing with an adjective which has been formed from a past participle, but which has been lexicalized (with subject control). (That is, it has become an independent lexical item, unlike passivized forms that are related to active forms by a productive lexical redundancy rule.) Many past participles have been lexicalized in a similar fashion and are listed independently as adjectives. Consider (55) (= (13)):

(55)
Ja   byl prinuždën   borot'sja odin.   (= Comrie's (111))
I(nom) was obliged(forced) to fight   alone(nom)

Comrie cites this example from Borras and Christian (1971) and explains (p. 144) that it has the meaning "I had to fight alone, not that anyone actually directly forced me to do something, thus not the same as [(56)]":

(56)
Menja prinudili   borot'sja odnomu.
I(acc) (they (someone)) forced to fight   alone(dat)
'They forced me to fight alone.' [16]

Therefore, although subject control of infinitives is permitted, the subjects of passive sentences cannot exert grammatical control over infinitives, since the precursor from which such a control relation would be derived is not well-formed in Russian.

Let us now return to the verb *prosit'* 'to ask' and consider what its lexical entry would look like. Since the subject of the embedded infinitive is not grammatically controlled, the infinitive itself is not a VCOMP. It must rather be an SCOMP, whose subject is controlled anaphorically. Assuming a PS rule expanding S' as follows,

(57)

S′ →   VP

  (↑SUBJ PRED)=PRO

  (↑TENSE)=−

  (↑SUBJ CASE)=(+,−,+)[17]

  ↑=↓

the lexical entry would then be (58):

(58)

prosit': V, (↑PRED) = 'ASK((SUBJ),(OBJ),(SCOMP))'[18]

Given the mini-lexicon in table 6.4, the derivation of sentence (59) is now straightforward:

Table 6.4
Mini-lexicon 2

ego: PRO, (↑PRED) = 'HE'

          (↑NUM) = SG

          (↑PERS) = 3

          (↑GEND) = M

          (↑CASE) $=_c$ $(-,\alpha,+)$

odnomu: ADJ, (↑PRED)   = 'ALONE((SUBJ))'

          (↑SUBJ NUM) = SG

          (↑SUBJ GEND) = M

          (↑CASE) $=_c$ $(+,-,+)$

ona: PRO, (↑PRED) = 'SHE'

          (↑NUM) = SG

          (↑GEND) = F

          (↑PERS) = 3

          (↑CASE) $=_c$ $(-,-,-)$

pojti: V,   (↑PRED)   = 'GO((SUBJ))'

          (↑TENSE)   = −

          (↑ASPECT) = PERF

poprosila: V,   (↑PRED)   = 'ASK((SUBJ),(VCOMP))'

          (↑TENSE)   = PAST

          (↑SUBJ NUM) = SG[19]

          (↑SUBJ GEND) = F

          (↑ASPECT)   = PERF

(59)

Ona	poprosila	ego	pojti	odnomu.
she(nom)	asked	him(acc)	to go	alone(dat)

(60)

$$
\begin{bmatrix}
\text{SUBJ} & \begin{bmatrix} \text{PRED} & \text{`SHE'} \\ \text{NUM} & \text{SG} \\ \text{GEND} & \text{F} \\ \text{PERS} & 3 \\ \text{CASE} & (-,-,-) \end{bmatrix} \\[2em]
\text{PRED} & \text{`ASK((SUBJ),(OBJ),(SCOMP))'} \\[1em]
\text{TENSE} & \text{PAST} \\[1em]
\text{ASPECT} & \text{PERF} \\[1em]
\text{OBJ} & \begin{bmatrix} \text{PRED} & \text{`HE'} \\ \text{NUM} & \text{SG} \\ \text{GEND} & \text{M} \\ \text{PERS} & 3 \\ \text{CASE} & (-,-,+) \end{bmatrix} \\[2em]
\text{SCOMP} & \begin{bmatrix}
\text{SUBJ} & {}^{j}\begin{bmatrix} \text{PRO} & + \\ \text{CASE} & (+,-,+) \end{bmatrix} \\[1.5em]
\text{PRED} & \text{`GO((SUBJ))'} \\[1em]
\text{TENSE} & - \\[1em]
\text{ASPECT} & \text{PERF} \\[1em]
\text{ADJ} & \begin{bmatrix}
\text{SUBJ} & {}^{j}\begin{bmatrix} \text{GEND} & \text{M} \\ \text{NUM} & \text{SG} \\ \text{CASE} & {}^{k}[\ \ ] \end{bmatrix} \\[1.5em]
\text{PRED} & \text{`ALONE((SUBJ))'} \\[1em]
\text{CASE} & {}^{k}[(+,-,+)]
\end{bmatrix}
\end{bmatrix}
\end{bmatrix}
$$

Overt Complementizers Since sentential complements lack grammatical control, when there is an overt sentential complementizer associated with an infinitive, there is no grammatical control of the subject of the infinitival clause. The subject of the infinitive can be understood to refer to a noun which is not the matrix subject, or the coreferential noun may be omitted entirely.

(61)

U   nego   sliškom malo deneg, čtoby   kupit'

around him(gen) too   little money in-order-to(Comp) buy

sebe   mašinu.

himself(dat) (a) car

'He has too little money to buy himself a car.'

(62)

Sliškom   xolodno, čtoby   ostat'sja zdes'.

(it is) too cold   in-order-to(Comp) stay   here

'It is too cold to stay here.'

Thus, anaphoric rather than grammatical control is operative in these sentences, and any adjuncts should be in the dative. This prediction holds true, as may be seen in (63), where the adjunct agrees with the dative functional subject of *idti*.

(63)

On   ne   takoj durak, čtoby   idti tuda odnomu.

he(nom) (is) not such (a) fool as-to(Comp) go   there alone(dat)

Other Cases of Control   This analysis makes the correct predictions for the case marking of adjuncts occurring in embedded infinitival clauses (A) with adjectives whose subject grammatically controls that of the following vcomp, and (B) with deverbal nominals, whose infinitival subjects are anaphorically controlled.

First, consider adjectives like *dolžen* 'must', *objazan* 'obliged', *vynužden* 'forced', *gotov* 'ready', *nameren* 'intends', *rad* 'glad', and *sčastliv* 'happy'. These adjectives can take vcomps, whose subjects are grammatically controlled by the adjective's own subject. Our theory then predicts that *sam* or *odin* would occur as adjuncts in the nominative case, as in fact they do:

(64)

On   gotov   pojti odin/*odnomu.

he(nom) (is) ready to go alone(nom/*dat)

(65)

Ona   dolžna pomoč' tovarišču   sama/*samoj.

she(nom) must   help   (her) comrade(dat masc) herself(nom/*dat)

Moreover, not all instances of grammatical control involve nouns in the nominative. As mentioned in footnote 13, objects *can* control the subjects of PCOMPs, NCOMPs, and ACOMPs. When, for example, an object grammatically controls an ACOMP which consists of one of the above adjectives followed by a VCOMP (whose subject is controlled by the ACOMP's subject, which itself is controlled by the matrix object), one would expect an adjunct within the embedded clause to appear in the accusative, in agreement with the matrix object. While many speakers do not accept such constructions, those who do accept them show the expected pattern:

(66)

Ona   sčitala   ego

she(nom) considered him$_i$(acc)

$$
\text{gotovym} \quad \text{putešestvovat'} \left\{ \begin{array}{ll} \text{*odnim} & \text{instr} \\ \text{*odin} & \text{nom} \\ \text{*odnomu} & \text{dat} \\ \text{odnogo} & \text{acc} \end{array} \right\}.
$$

[^{i}[ ] ready [^{i}[ ] to travel ^{i}[ ] alone(acc)]]

Now consider deverbal nominals which take infinitival complements. There is no grammatical control of their infinitival complements' subjects, since often the subject is not coreferential with any other noun in the sentence. Since the subject of a nontensed verb is dative and the subject of the infinitive is anaphorically controlled, we would expect adjuncts within the infinitival clause to appear in the dative as well. This prediction also holds true, as (67)–(69) show:

(67)
Samoe   važnoe   —   umenie   rabotat'
(the) most important-(thing)-(nom) (is the) ability(nom) to work
*odin/odnomu.
 alone(*nom/dat)

(68)
Popytka   ispravit' ètu ošibku *odin/odnomu
(the) attempt(nom) to correct that error   himself(*nom/dat)

ne uvenčalas'   uspexom.
was not crowned with success

(69)

U   nego   bylo   želanie   zanimat'sja muzykoj
around him(gen) (there) was (the) desire(nom) to take up   music

*sam/samomu.
 himself(*nom/dat)

'He had the desire to take up music himself.'

Summary

In this chapter I have presented and discussed some data about case agreement in Russian. First, I have shown that the distinction between complement and adjunct is essential to any examination of second predicates in Russian. The case restriction placed on *sam* and *odin* follows from the fact that they cannot occur in complement position. Second, I have considered the agreement of second predicates within the framework of this volume. The seemingly strange distribution of second datives—with objective infinitives, and with subjective infinitives when and only when there is an overt complementizer—turns out to be a simple consequence of the difference between grammatical and anaphoric control.[20] This analysis makes the correct predictions for infinitives dependent on adjectives and deverbal nominals.

Conclusions

As we have seen, functional structure integrates information about syntactic structure and lexical properties. Thus, within the lexical interpretive theory, constituent structure and propositional structure (predicate argument structure) belong to two different components, and grammatical relations mediate between the two. On the contrary, transformationalists have traditionally considered that, at least at the level of deep structure, propositional and constituent structure should be made to coincide. Where they do *not* coincide, however, exceptional mechanisms are required.

Subjective and objective infinitival clauses in Russian provide a case where, although propositional structures are the same, the constituent structures seem to differ (as the agreement facts indicate). Comrie tried to account for this divergence, within the transformational framework of 1974. He (rather tentatively) suggested a rule of restructuring, which he called the *Cohesion Principle*.[21] This rule was to apply only to subjective infinitives and would be blocked from applying by an intervening object or overt complementizer. To quote his proposal (from Comrie 1974:134):

I should like to argue that a main verb lacking any object, but having a subjective infinitive, forms a particularly cohesive unit, i.e. from the underlying structure:

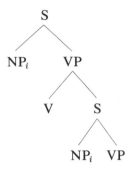

we get ultimately:

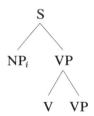

There are problems with this proposal, however. The Cohesion Principle is at best imprecise. If rules for cohesion and case agreement were stated explicitly, it seems that the analysis would have to assume (a) that case agreement must be performed at a stage before the deletion of the underlying dative pronouns, and (b) that case agreement must take place at a stage after the deletion of the subjects of subjective infinitives, in order to permit "the treatment of the whole as a simple unit, i.e., any predicate of the embedded VP is treated as a matrix predicate" (Comrie 1974:135). But this implies that pronoun deletion is not accomplished by a single rule of Equi. The necessity of abandoning a unitary rule of Equi calls the analysis into question.

Even if this problem could be resolved, there would be other difficulties, very similar to those pointed out by Andrews 1971 and by Quicoli 1972b in his discussion of rule interaction in Greek. If Equi is a cyclic rule (as has generally been assumed), then in sentences which contain deeply embedded second predicates, the agreement is dependent on structures contained in higher cycles. However, by the time the appropriate rules apply on the upper cycles, the pronoun which determines agreement would already have been deleted by Equi and would be unavailable for determining the case agreement of the adjunct.

Furthermore, the Cohesion Principle provides no account for the passive agreement facts.

Within our framework, however, constituent structure and functional structure are autonomous levels of representation. Therefore, the correct syntactic distinctions can be formulated within constituent structure, while, at the same time, the correct propositional representation is ensured in functional structure by the principles of control. Notice that if all infinitivals were sentential, there would be no explanation for the fact that infinitival subjects which are subject-controlled fail to be marked dative like other subjects of tenseless Ss. The analysis given here obviates this problem by distinguishing between VP and S' infinitivals (where the former are VCOMPs whose subjects are supplied within functional structure by the control equations).

Agreement of adjuncts within functional structure is then quite straightforward: an adjunct agrees in case with its functional subject, which is identical with some other grammatical function within its clause nucleus.[22]

We have also seen that the system of representation of the lexical interpretive theory permits us to articulate the grammatical distinctions required for a simple account of case agreement. The puzzling distribution of second predicates is explained by more general considerations of case marking, predicate complements, and grammatical control. Given the principles of grammatical control, it becomes apparent that adjuncts merely reflect the case of their functional subject. Just in case this subject is grammatically controlled by a grammatical function of the matrix predicate, the adjunct will agree in case with the matrix antecedent as well. Thus, agreement of adjuncts is explained on the level of functional structure with great simplicity.

Notes

I would like to express my thanks and much appreciation to Joan Bresnan for many helpful discussions, comments, and suggestions, and for her encouragement. I would also like to thank those who read and criticized previous versions of this chapter: Joan Bresnan, Ken Hale, Morris Halle, Alec Marantz, Anne Rochette, Barry Schein, and especially Catherine Chvany, whose suggestions and corrections were of great help. Thanks also to David Pesetsky for suggesting the topic and to Jane Simpson for interesting discussions and assistance with data collection. I am grateful to Catherine Chvany, Volodja Gitin, and Larissa Levin for their Russian insights. Needless to say, all mistakes are my own.

1. The notation is discussed fully in chapter 4. The unmarked assignment in the phrase structure expansion of X' is (i),

(i)
$$X' \rightarrow \ldots X \ldots$$
$$\uparrow = \downarrow$$

where $\uparrow$ is instantiated by the variable assigned to the X'-node and $\downarrow$ by the variable assigned to the X-node. Accordingly, all of the features of the head percolate up.

2. The feature decomposition has some predictive power in determining what cases are likely to be fused. While case syncretism of nominative and accusative or of accusative and genitive is quite common, cases which are compositionally quite different do not share forms. See Jakobson 1971 for discussion.

3. Actually, this is only when the head noun is inanimate. For animate nouns, the -ye ending is used for the nominative, and -yx is used for the accusative (and genitive and locative). The same difference in case fusion is found for nouns. To account for this, an additional equation would be required:

(i)
$(\uparrow \text{CASE}) =_c (-,\alpha,+)$
$(\uparrow \text{ANIMATE}) = \alpha$

This is not relevant to the point under discussion, however.

4. If one were to account for the dialect in which all objects of negative sentences must be genitive, then this annotation would be obligatory rather than optional. In some treatments, this rule is considered to be obligatory, and the output is subject to neutralization under some discourse conditions.

5. In addition to accounting for the types of complements mentioned, the assignment of instrumental to complements is consistent with the facts about sentences containing byt' 'to be'. Byt' can have either of two meanings: (a) an equative, definitional sense, and (b) an attributive, predicative reading. When byt' is overt, these differences correspond to differences in the case marking of the following noun or adjective. Compare:

(i)
On   byl pisatel'.
nom   nom
'He was a writer (by profession).'

(ii)
On   byl pisatelem.
nom   instr
'He was a writer (temporarily).'

The question of the semantics is beyond the scope of this chapter, but both the type of reading and the case marking are consistent with an analysis in which *byt'* occurs with an XCOMP in (ii) but not in (i). When *pisatel'* has the temporary, predicative sense, it is functioning as a complement and is regularly marked with the instrumental. In construction (i), however, the copula is functioning as a grammatical formative, and the main predicate is contributed by the post-copular phrase.

This dual analysis of the copula construction may generalize to other languages. Milsark 1977 and Stowell 1980 argue that the same distinction between *be* sentences expressing temporary states and those expressing essential properties is relevant in English. Stowell proposes that the former should be analyzed as raising-type constructions (e.g., *a man was [t sick]*) and that *be* is a raising verb. (When raising fails to occur, we get *there was [a man sick]*.) Within the lexical interpretive theory, this is equivalent to saying that *be* can take an XCOMP, which is precisely what is suggested for Russian by the instrumental marking of *pisatelem* in (ii) above.

6. Adjuncts are often separated from the rest of the sentence by pauses. Syntactic detachment, indicated by the optional pause, is not relevant here.

7. *Odin* is also the numeral 'one' (as in *odin iz nix* 'one of them') and, as such, it can occur as a complement:

(i)
On   okazalsja   odnim   iz...
he(nom) turned-out-(to-be) one(instr) of...

8. Restrictions on what can occur as an ACOMP may follow from independent principles. It appears that ACOMPs must be interpreted as "qualifying" (as opposed to "quantifying"). *Odin* and *sam* do not really qualify the noun; under the relevant reading, they cannot occur within the NP in the normal adjectival position (which in English and Russian is prenominal). It is interesting that while this is true in English and Russian, in French, where *seul* 'alone' can occur as a normal noun modifier, it can also appear as an ACOMP. The same is true of the related Russian adjective *odinokij* 'lonely'.

(i)
a.   *the alone man
b.   *I consider him alone.

(ii)
a.   *odin   čelovek
     (the) alone person

b.   *Ja sčitaju   ego odnim.
     I   consider him alone

(iii)
a.   la fille seule
     the girl alone

b.   Je la   crois   seule.
     I   her believe alone
     'I believe her (to be) alone.'

(iv)

a. odinokij   čelovek
    (the) lonely person

b. Ja sčitaju   ego odinokim.
    I consider him lonely
    'I consider him (to be) lonely.'

9. Infinitives do appear with nominative subjects in what Jakobson 1963 refers to as elliptical constructions.

(i)
A   oni   kričat'.
and they(nom) cry(inf)

(Such constructions are also extensively discussed in Birnbaum 1965.) One might propose structures for such sentences containing a null verb (with a meaning like 'start').

10. Many Russian datives would have English equivalents with *for*-phrases. The deeper relations between prepositional phrases and case marking are worthy of further study.

11. The generalization that datives occur regularly as the subject of nontensed predicates might be extended to include what have been termed "dative experiencers" that occur with adverbials. These have been much discussed in the literature (see G. C. Rappaport 1978 or Chvany 1975) and have many subject-like properties. The dative experiencer can be the antecedent of a reflexive, as in Chvany's 1975:67 example:

(i)
Ivanu   bylo žal' sebja   i   svoju   sobaku.
Ivan(dat) felt sorry (for) himself and his(refl) dog

It can also be interpreted as coreferential with the subject of an adverbial participle, as in G. C. Rappaport's 1978:3 example:

(ii)
Slušaja   ètot rasskaz, mne   bylo strašno.
listening to this story   I(dat) was terrified

At any rate, *if* one wishes to consider these as subjects, then the generalization might be stated that dative subjects should occur with predicates which do not themselves bear tense markers. (With adverbials, tense *may* be borne by *byt'*, which usually follows the adverbial and is stressless. The predicate *žal'*, for example, itself bears no tense markers.)

"Tensed" is not precisely the right notion, however. Notice that the class of verb forms which assign nominative to their subjects must include the (present and past) adverbial participles, although the markers on these forms are aspectual. Evidence for the nominative subjects of adverbial participles comes from the agreement of adjuncts.

(iii)
Podbežav k stancii   odin,   Ivan...
having run to the station alone(nom) Ivan(nom)

Here *odin* agrees with the subject of the participle, rather than with *Ivan*, since even when *Ivan* is missing from the sentence, *odin* must be nominative. The following sentence is acceptable for many speakers in less formal speech (G. C. Rappaport 1978:6):

(iv)
Podbežav k stancii,   poezd   uže   otošël.
having run to the station the train already left

Odin can still occur only in the nominative case.

(v)
Podbežav k stancii   odin,   poezd   uže   otošël.
having run to the station alone(nom) the train already left

12. The choice of features given here for number, gender, and person is intended to simplify exposition. In fact, these features (like those for case) could be analyzed with respect to markedness and assigned binary values (as suggested by Jakobson) to provide greater economy. In any event, notice that given such lexical representations, agreement is an automatic consequence of the consistency of lexical information within functional structure. Agreement (of number, gender, and person) is obtained by means of information that verbs and adjectives contain in their lexical forms about their subjects. The lexical representation for *govorit* 'says', for example, would include the following information:

(i)
govorit: V, ($\uparrow$PRED)   = 'SAY((SUBJ))'
          ($\uparrow$SUBJ NUM) = SG
          ($\uparrow$SUBJ PERS) = 3

As with information about case, lexical redundancy rules would relate particular suffixes, and the information they convey, to the lexical items which contain them.

The question arises, Should the equations listed above for *govorit* be constraint or defining equations? I have chosen defining equations, because it seems that for Russian, the endings truly carry information. In the absence of an overt subject, the information from the verbal ending is transferred to the pronominal subject. In (ii), for example, *I* is understood to be the subject, because of the ending on the verb:

(ii)
Prijdu.
(I) will-come(1sg)

This interpretive device is particularly common with the third person plural form of the verb. The subject is then understood to be the indefinite *they* or *someone* (something like the French *on*).

(iii)
Govorjat,   čto...
(they, someone) say(s) that...
'It is said that...'

The third person singular form of the verb is used when the subject is presumed to be inanimate. (This distinction plays a crucial role in Turgenev's short story "Stučit!" (meaning 'some*thing* is knocking'), from *Zapiski Oxotnika* (*A Sportsman's Sketches*).)

Languages may well differ in whether the number/gender/person information is represented by means of constraint or defining equations.

A noun or pronoun contains information within its lexical form as to number/gender/person, and this is added to the information received from the verb or adjective of which it is the subject. Agreement, then, is guaranteed by the principle of "consistency." No function is permitted to have more than one value, and therefore conflicting information would not produce a well-formed functional structure. Sentence (iv) contains inconsistent information about the subject's number, and is therefore ruled out by the principle of consistency.

(iv)
*Oni   govorit.
 pronoun(3pl) talk(3sg present)

13. Two remarks are in order here:

(a) The limitation in question permits the control equations for VCOMPs to be filled in by a redundancy rule, since they must be SUBJ-controlled.

(b) It would be nice if this unacceptability of OBJ in Russian control equations applied equally to all complements, but with some verbs the object can control ACOMP, PCOMP, and NCOMP. Example: *sčitat'* 'to consider'.

14. *Coherence* is a well-formedness condition which requires that every semantic form contained within the f-structure be the PRED value of a grammatical function mentioned (either in the predicate argument structure or a constituting equation) in some other semantic form. (See chapter 4.)

15. Notice that the dative adjunct is agreeing with the dative functional subject of *prijti* (which is regularly case-marked, since it is not subject to grammatical control). *Ugovorit'* 'to persuade' is assumed to have the predicate argument structure ((SUBJ),(OBJ),(SCOMP)), and the subject of the SCOMP will be marked dative, like the subject of any other infinitival S or S'.

16. Interestingly, Rochette 1980 has evidence from French that the equivalent past participles *forcé* and *obligé* have been lexicalized as adjectives with subject control over the following VCOMP (as has the English *obliged*).

17. Notice that this is a special case of the generalization that tenseless clauses have dative subjects, which is represented by the PS redundancy rule (38) (here $\alpha = +$).

18. The choice of complementizer (e.g., *čto*, which, like *that* in English, introduces tensed clauses; *čtoby*, which introduces subjunctive or infinitival clauses; and/or the null infinitival complementizer) would be governed by more general semantic and pragmatic considerations, which are beyond the scope of this work.

19. Actually, an additional feature is necessary to distinguish *ty*, the informal singular 'you', from *vy*, the form of 'you' which may be used with the singular

in formal contexts, or with the plural. One might propose an additional feature [±Formal] to capture the opposition of the two singular forms.

This treatment of agreement then permits a natural treatment of the apparent agreement paradox pointed out by Babby 1973a. He shows that *vy* requires the "plural" form of verbs:

(i)

a. Vy prišli. 'You came.'   Oni prišli. 'They came.'
b. *Vy prišël.   On prišël. 'He came.'
c. *Vy prišla.   Ona prišla. 'She came.'

Adjectives, however, behave differently. Long form adjectives agree in number with the sense of *vy*, and may be singular or plural, while short form adjectives are always plural. This gives the following paradigm when *vy* is taken to be masculine singular, for 'you are indifferent':

(ii)

a. Vy ravnodušny.   (short form, pl.)
b. *Vy ravnodušen.   (short form, masc. sg.)
c. *Vy ravnodušnye.   (long form, pl., nom)
d. Vy ravnodušnyj.   (long form, masc. sg., nom)

It is apparent that verbs and short form adjectives exhibit one type of agreement, which Babby calls *formal agreement*, while long form adjectives involve another, *agreement in sense*. The latter operates in the presence of a case feature.

Surely it is not coincidence that short form adjectives behave in some ways like verbs. Many are derived from verbs. However, the similarities between short form adjectives and verbs derive not from the fact that they have the same constituency, but rather from the fact that they share the same morphological endings. It is the endings which encode the information relevant to agreement. The past tense and past participle endings are almost identical with those which occur on short form adjectives.

There is, then, a simple solution to the apparent agreement paradox within the present framework. The ending *-li* or *-ly,* for adjectives which have plural nouns or *vy* as the subject, includes the following specifications,

(iii)

$(\uparrow \text{SUBJ NUM}) \quad = \alpha \text{PL}$
$(\uparrow \text{SUBJ FORMAL}) = -\alpha$

while the long form adjectival ending *-ye* has the marking

(iv)

$(\uparrow \text{SUBJ NUM}) = \text{PL}$

Obviously, these would be distinguished from the endings *-la, -aja:*

(v)

a. *-la:* $(\uparrow \text{CASE}) \quad =_c -$
         $(\uparrow \text{NUM}) \quad = \text{SG}$
         $(\uparrow \text{GEND}) \quad = \text{F}$
         $(\uparrow \text{FORMAL}) = -$

b. *-aja:* ($\uparrow$CASE) $=_c (-,-,-)$
        ($\uparrow$NUM) $=$ SG
        ($\uparrow$GEND) $=$ F

This lexical representation also provides simple solutions to other agreement paradoxes pointed out by Babby within the transformational framework.

If this analysis is adopted, then *poprosila* should also contain the specification ($\uparrow$FORMAL) $= -$.

20. There is a problem, however, in accounting for sentences with *obeščat'* 'to promise'. When there is no object in the matrix sentence, *obeščat'* acts like any other verb with subject control. However, when a direct object intervenes, the data are very fuzzy. To some extent, the sentence-final *odin* is acceptable in either the dative or the nominative. All of these sentences are somewhat unnatural, and speakers prefer to use a complementizer. I would be forced to postulate two separate entries for *obeščat'*, one in which the subject controls the embedded infinitive, and one in which the verb takes an SCOMP. (Even in English, the semantics of these two are somewhat different. Similar problems also arise in French; see Rochette 1980.) More data are necessary, since there seems to be a good deal of dialect variation. Although Comrie generally preferred the dative to the nominative,

(i)
Volodja   obeščal   materi vernut'sja odnomu/??odin.   (= Comrie's (64))
Volodja(nom) promised mother to return alone(dat/??nom)

my informants showed the reverse preference (consistent with grammatical subject control). I leave this as a problem for further research.

21. Similar restructuring rules have been proposed to account for quantifier movement in French. Rochette 1980 argues that the French phenomena as well are nicely explained in the lexical framework in terms of grammatical control and infinitival complement structure.

22. This analysis assumes that *odin* and *sam,* when they occur within infinitival clauses in the dative case, are agreeing with a dative infinitival subject. One might consider an alternative approach, whereby nouns in ungoverned position receive the dative case (and *odin* and *sam,* having no antecedent in the same clause, would be marked dative as well). However, such a proposal fails to account for adjuncts agreeing in case with (ungoverned) nominative subjects of adverbial participles (as discussed in footnote 11). The following contrast indicates that *sam* and *odin* should indeed be viewed as agreeing with their (functional) antecedents:

(i)
Čtoby   pojti odnomu...
in order to go alone(dat)

(ii)
Podbežav k stancii   odin, ...
having-run to the station alone(nom)

Chapter 7

The Representation of Case in Modern Icelandic

Avery D. Andrews

Case marking and agreement are a central component of grammatical structure, which any adequate linguistic theory must come to grips with. In this chapter I will examine the interactions of case marking and agreement with the complement system in Modern Icelandic. We will see that the lexical interpretive theory of this volume provides a simple and highly explanatory analysis of these data, many of which have resisted insightful treatment in other frameworks.

Some of the phenomena we will be considering have been argued by Andrews 1976 and Thráinsson 1980 to require a transformational analysis of the complement system. Others have been put forth by Andrews 1973 as evidence for global rules in syntax. We will find, however, that the theory of functional structure developed and independently motivated in this volume provides exactly what is needed to account for the data, without the excess power of transformations or global rules. The distinction which this theory makes between functional (or grammatical) and anaphoric control will prove to be the crucial factor in the analysis.

In section 7.1 I will introduce certain basic features of Icelandic inflection and sentence structure. In section 7.2 I will present a lexical interpretive analysis of the complement system, including a treatment of "global" or "long-distance" case agreement. This material will for the most part be a reanalysis of data presented in Andrews 1973, 1976 and Thráinsson 1980, and will serve to motivate and delineate the distinction between functional and anaphoric control in Icelandic syntax. In section 7.3 I will turn to the case marking of NP, showing that the theory explains the way in which case marking interacts with the principles of agreement and the complement system.

7.1 Basic Sentence Structure

Basic Icelandic sentence structure is similar to that of English. There is an initial subject NP, followed by a sequence of one or more verbs, the first of which is finite, the others appearing in nonfinite forms determined by the immediately preceding verb. The final verb is generally considered to be the main verb, the others auxiliaries. I shall, however, analyze the auxiliaries as main verbs taking subjectless complements. After the verbs there appear from zero to two NP objects, followed by any number of prepositional objects (with idiomatically selected preposition), followed by any number of prepositional and adverbial adjuncts.

There is no real evidence for a VP node dominating the verb and following complements. In fact, as we will see below, to postulate such a node would complicate the account of the major alternate word order. We may thus take (1) to be the basic rule of sentence structure:

(1)

$$\text{S} \rightarrow \quad \text{NP} \quad \text{V} \quad \text{(NP)} \quad \text{(NP)} \quad \text{(PP)}^*$$
$$(\uparrow\text{SUBJ})=\downarrow \quad \uparrow=\downarrow \quad (\uparrow\text{OBJ})=\downarrow \quad (\uparrow\text{OBJ2})=\downarrow \quad (\uparrow(\downarrow\text{PCASE}))=\downarrow$$

Having nothing of substance to say about adjuncts, I have omitted them from (1).

Icelandic differs from English in having a lively case-marking system. There are four cases—nominative, genitive, accusative, and dative—which are for the most part distinct morphologically. Case marking usually reflects the grammatical relations, with nominative appearing on the subject and accusative on the object. But some verbs select accusative, genitive, and dative subjects, while others take dative, genitive, and even nominative objects. Explaining the behavior of irregularly case-marked NPs will be a major concern of subsequent sections.

Adjectives, participles, and predicate nominals agree in case with the NP they modify, sometimes over arbitrarily long stretches of intervening material. This phenomenon, highly reminiscent of the "global agreement" of Ancient Greek (Andrews 1971), will be explained in the latter part of section 7.2.

Nouns, adjectives, and participles are also inflected for gender (masculine, feminine, and neuter) and number (singular and plural). In section 7.3 I will make proposals about the representations of these and other inflectional categories that draw heavily on the concept of markedness formulated in Jakobson 1932, 1936. Nouns are furthermore inflected for definiteness with a suffixed definite article.

Given the rich case-marking system of Icelandic, one would expect the word order to be significantly more fluid than that of English, and this expectation is borne out. The principal alternate word order is the *inverted word order,* in which the subject follows the verb. Inverted word order is obligatory in matrix questions (though impossible in embedded questions) and in clauses in which a constituent has been preposed under Topicalization. In main clauses (but not subordinate) it may also appear spontaneously, conveying an effect of "narrative style."

Some of these points are illustrated below:

(2)

a. Drengurinn(N) kyssti stúlkuna(A) í bílnum(D).
    the-boy   kissed the-girl   in the-car
    'The boy kissed the girl in the car.'

b. Kyssti drengurinn stúlkuna í bílnum.
    'Did the boy kiss the girl in the car?'
    'The boy kissed the girl in the car.'

(3)

a. Þeir(N) segja að   drengurinn kyssti stúlkuna í bílnum.
    they   say   that the-boy   kissed the-girl in the-car

b. *Þeir segja að kyssti drengurinn stúlkuna í bílnum.

(4)

a. Stúlkuna(A) kyssti drengurinn(N) í bílnum(D).
    'The boy kissed the girl in the car.'

b. *Stúlkuna drengurinn kyssti í bílnum.

(5)

a. Þeir segja að í bílnum kyssti drengurinn stúlkuna.
    'They say that the boy kissed the girl in the car.'

b. *Þeir segja að í bílnum drengurinn kyssti stúlkuna.

(2a) is in normal word order, while (2b) is in inverted order with no constituent preposed (other than the verb). (2b) could be an interrogative, or a declarative in narrative style. These possibilities would be distinguished by intonation in speech. (3a,b) show that such spontaneous inversion is impossible in subordinate clauses. (4a) has inversion with preposing of the object under Topicalization. The prepositional phrase could have been preposed instead. (4b) demonstrates that inversion is obligatory under Topicalization. (5a,b) show that Topicalization is possible in certain subordinate clauses, and that it continues to require inverted word order.

Topicalization and related structures are discussed in detail in Thráinsson 1980:59–70, while the principles governing inverted word order are discussed in Maling and Zaenen 1979.

Inverted word order provides an argument against postulating a VP node in Icelandic. Given (1), we may generate the inverted order with a simple transformation of the phrase structure rules:

(6)
NP V → V NP

If the main verb in Icelandic were buried within a VP constituent, (6) would have to be a transformation of sentence structures rather than of the phrase structure rules. Perhaps the fact that English has evidence for VP is related to the fact that its major inversion rule, Subject–Auxiliary Inversion, does not move main verbs.

7.2 The Complement System

We now take up the analysis of the complement system. This has been treated in great detail by Thráinsson 1980, henceforth T, to which I will be making extensive references.

Complement clauses may be finite or nonfinite. Finite clauses appear in the indicative or subjunctive moods, subjunctive being the normal mood, the indicative being reserved for clauses that are presupposed. In finite clauses, the subject appears obligatorily. Depending on the matrix verb, the clauses may be introduced by the complementizer *að* (equivalent to *that*) or by a *wh*-word (*hv-* in Icelandic morphology). Thráinsson argues at great length that finite clauses are all NPs. They appear in virtually all NP positions, including object of preposition, and there are syntactic tests that single out *að*-clauses and noncontroversial NPs against all other constituent types (T:71–90).

Nonfinite clauses are predominantly in the infinitive mood. Semantically, infinitives correspond to *að*-clauses, *wh*-infinitives being absent. Infinitives never take an overt subject. The infinitives fall observationally into two classes, those with and those without the marker *að* (homophonous with the finite complementizer, but perhaps a different element). Infinitives with *að* share the NP-like syntactic behavior of *að*-clauses and invite a transformational analysis in terms of Equi. In the theory of this volume, they have functional subjects under anaphoric control. Infinitives without *að* lack NP properties, would be transformationally described as involving Raising, and demand to be analyzed as functionally controlled in our lexical interpretive theory. Certain other structures, such as passive verb phrases and complements to the perfective auxiliary, will also be described as structures of functional control.

In the first subsection I will examine *að*-infinitives and show that they demand anaphoric control. In the second I will show that the unmarked infinitives take functional control, while in the third I will analyze the passive construction in Icelandic. In the fourth I will formalize the main points of the analysis. In the following three subsections I will examine the phenomenon of long-distance agreement, whose behavior strongly supports the distinction between anaphoric and functional control. In the last subsection I will summarize the argument.

Anaphoric Control of Að-Infinitives

Að-infinitives are typically optional alternants with *að*-clauses, appearing in all the basic NP positions, such as subject, first object, second object, and object of preposition:

(7)

a. $\begin{Bmatrix} \text{Að við sendum þig heim aftur} \\ \text{Að senda þig heim aftur} \end{Bmatrix}$ væri langbest.

$\begin{Bmatrix} \text{that we send you home back} \\ \text{to send you home back} \end{Bmatrix}$ would be best

b. Þeir ákváðu $\begin{Bmatrix} \text{að þeir skyldu vitja Ólafs} \\ \text{að vitja Ólafs} \end{Bmatrix}$.

they decided $\begin{Bmatrix} \text{that they should visit Olaf} \\ \text{to visit Olaf} \end{Bmatrix}$

c. Hún skipaði honum(D) $\begin{Bmatrix} \text{?að hann færi} \\ \text{að fara} \end{Bmatrix}$.[1]

she ordered him $\begin{Bmatrix} \text{that he go} \\ \text{to go} \end{Bmatrix}$

d. Ég vonast til $\begin{Bmatrix} \text{að ég fái bílinn} \\ \text{að fá bílinn} \end{Bmatrix}$.

I hope to(P) $\begin{Bmatrix} \text{that I get the-car} \\ \text{to get the-car} \end{Bmatrix}$

Furthermore, there are no verbs analogous to English *love, hate,* and *despise,* which take NP but reject S: *I despise his smoking/*I despise that he smokes.* Therefore, neither base nor subcategorization phenomena provide much comfort to an attempt to deny NP-hood to these clauses and infinitives (there are some restrictions in complex sentences, however, which will be discussed below).

"Derived" NP positions, such as cleft, topic, and dislocated positions, tell the same story. Particularly impressive are the right-dislocation and *það*-relative constructions, which take only noncontroversial NPs, *að*-clauses, and *að*-infinitives as focus (T:71–90):

(8)

a. Hún skipaði honum það, $\begin{cases} \text{að hann færi} \\ \text{að fara} \end{cases}$.

    she ordered him it $\begin{cases} \text{that he go} \\ \text{to go} \end{cases}$

b. Það sem hún skipaði honum var $\begin{cases} \text{að hann færi} \\ \text{að fara} \end{cases}$.[2]

    that which she ordered him was $\begin{cases} \text{that he go} \\ \text{to go} \end{cases}$

All of the five NP displacement constructions discussed by Thráinsson also apply to complement clauses and infinitives, but some of them apply to adjectives and other non-NP constituents as well.

There are only three NP positions in which the clauses and infinitives are blocked: complement subject, complement topic, and object controller of a VCOMP. T:99–108 argues that these phenomena should be explained in terms of the NP-over-S constraint of Ross 1967:33, Kuno 1973, and Grosu and Thompson 1977:129. Indeed, only such an account can explain why it is precisely these rather than some random collection of NP positions from which the clauses and infinitives are blocked.

The lexical interpretive theory postulates a basic distinction between closed and open grammatical functions, the latter requiring functional control, the former rejecting it. The basic NP functions (such as subject and object) must be closed, since their values are typically NPs which do not take functional control. Since the *að*-infinitives seem to bear such grammatical functions, they cannot take functional control, so their missing subjects must be supplied by anaphoric control.

Fortunately, there is a great deal of independent evidence for this conclusion. In (7a), for example, we see an infinitive without overt controller, a sign of anaphoric control. Far more evidence to the point is found by Thráinsson, who shows that *að*-infinitives obey pronominalization restrictions.

Controlled *að*-infinitives have a more restricted distribution than uncontrolled. T:59–64 discusses three "leftward movement" rules affecting NP: Topicalization, Contrastive Dislocation, and Left Dislocation. These constructions are illustrated in (9b–d):

(9)

a. Ólafur(N) lofaði   Maríu(D) þessum hring(D).
    Olaf   promised Mary   this   ring

b. *Topicalization*
    Þessum hring(D) lofaði   Ólafur(N) Maríu(D).
    this   ring   promised Olaf   Mary

c. *Contrastive Dislocation*
    Þessum hring(D), honum(D) lofaði   Ólafur(N) Maríu(D).
    this   ring   it   promised Olaf   Mary

d. *Left Dislocation*
    Þessi hringur(N), Ólafur(N) lofaði   Maríu(D) honum(D).
    this   ring   Olaf   promised Mary   it

Topicalization preposes the NP, and its case is preserved. Contrastive Dislocation preposes the NP and adds a preposed pronoun, both in the case appropriate to the NP's function in the clause. In Left Dislocation, the NP is preposed in the nominative, and its position within the clause is occupied by a coreferential pronoun.

Controlled *að*-infinitives appear freely with Topicalization and Contrastive Dislocation, but not Left Dislocation:

(10)

a. Þeir ákváðu að vitja Ólafs.
    they decided to visit Olaf

b. Að vitja Ólafs ákváðu þeir.
    to visit Olaf decided they

c. Að vitja Ólafs, það ákváðu þeir.
    to visit Olaf it decided they

d. ??Að vitja Ólafs, þeir ákváðu það.
    to visit Olaf they decided it

To explain the relative unacceptability of (10d), Thráinsson (T:114–116) observes that backward anaphora is in general not possible in Icelandic, although this constraint is abrogated in Topicalization and Contrastive Dislocation constructions:

(11)

a.   Peysuna sína$_i$ finnur Ólafur$_j$ hvergi.
     sweater self's finds Olaf   nowhere

b.   Peysuna sína$_i$, hana finnur Ólafur$_i$ hvergi.
     sweater self's it   finds Olaf   nowhere

c.   ??Peysuna sína$_i$/hans$_i$, Ólafur$_i$ finnur hana hvergi.
     sweater his/self's Olaf   finds it   nowhere

d.   Peysuna hans Ólafs$_i$, hann$_i$ finnur hana hvergi.[3]
     sweater his Olaf's he   finds it   nowhere

The acceptability of the pronouns (which are obligatorily reflexive, being coreferential with a clause-mate subject) in Topicalization and Contrastive Dislocation structures probably results from their greater syntactic "connectivity," as the case marking shows as well. One would suppose that the foci of topicalization and contrastive dislocation constructions actually bear functions in the clause, while the focus of left dislocation is merely coreferential with a pronoun in the clause.

The following additional examples provide an interesting manifestation of these principles:

(12)

a.   ??Að vitja Ólafs var ákveðið.
     to visit Olaf was decided

b.   Það var ákveðið að vitja Ólafs.
     it   was decided to visit Olaf

The passive in (12a) is somewhat unnatural, while it is saved by extraposition in (12b). The difference between (12a) and (7a) in terms of control is that, semantically, the infinitive of (12a) is controlled by the implicit agent of the passive verb, which has been ellipsed. The infinitive in (7a), on the other hand, is under "discourse control," the extralinguistic context determining who is to perform the action of the complement verb. The passive verb *ákveðið* seems to function as antecedent for the purposes of the principles of anaphora that operate in (12).

This entire discussion is strongly reinforced by Thráinsson's observation that examples like (10d) are much improved by being placed in contexts that would tend to ameliorate backward anaphora:

(13)
A: Hvað ákváðu þeir?
    what decided they

B: Að heimsækja Ólaf, þeir ákváðu það.
    to visit   Olaf they decided it

We thus have considerable evidence that the understood subjects of *að*-infinitives are represented by something like a pronoun at some level of structure. In the present theory, this means that the infinitives are under anaphoric control. I have recounted Thráinsson's evidence at such length because of the support it provides for anaphoric control, and because of the importance of this concept in the sections that follow.

Virtually all verbs whose semantics are appropriate take *að*-clauses. *Að*-infinitives, on the other hand, are far more restricted. For example, they never appear with verbs of cognition or perception such as *telja* 'believe', *vita* 'know', or *sjá* 'see'. Although it seems likely to me that an adequate semantic account of the distribution of *að*-infinitives could be formulated, none has been so far. In most cases, the *að*-infinitive is an alternant, sometimes highly preferred, to a subjunctive *að*-clause. There are a few verbs, however, which require an *að*-infinitive and absolutely reject a finite clause. These include *ætla* 'intend', *reyna* 'try', *byrja (á)* 'begin', and *hætta* 'stop'. T:273 shows that the complements of these verbs are otherwise exactly like *að*-infinitives that do alternate with finite clauses, showing the usual NP-like behavior.

Functional Control of Unmarked Infinitives

The principal variety of infinitive without *að* is what is traditionally called the "accusative plus infinitive" construction, which I shall often refer to as *ACI*. ACI constructions occur with verbs of thinking and saying, verbs of perception, a few semifactives such as *vita* 'know', and the verb *láta* 'let, allow, cause'. Except with *láta*, they alternate freely with *að*-clauses.

Some ACI constructions and their *að*-clause alternatives are illustrated below:

(14)

a. Þeir segja $\begin{Bmatrix} \text{að Haraldur(N) elski Maríu} \\ \text{Harald(A) elska Maríu} \end{Bmatrix}$.

   they say $\begin{Bmatrix} \text{that Harold loves Mary} \\ \text{Harold to-love Mary} \end{Bmatrix}$

b. Þeir telja $\begin{Bmatrix} \text{að María(N) hafi skrifað ritgerðina} \\ \text{Maríu(A) hafa skrifað ritgerðina} \end{Bmatrix}$.

   they believe $\begin{Bmatrix} \text{that Mary has written the(her)-thesis} \\ \text{Mary to-have written the(her)-thesis} \end{Bmatrix}$

c. Þeir sáu $\begin{Bmatrix} \text{að drengurinn(N) hefði kysst stúlkuna} \\ \text{drenginn(A) hafa kysst stúlkuna} \end{Bmatrix}$.

   they saw $\begin{Bmatrix} \text{that the-boy had kissed the-girl} \\ \text{the-boy to-have kissed the-girl} \end{Bmatrix}$

The infinitive and clausal constructions are not precisely equivalent semantically: infinitives are more naturally associated with direct perception, for example. But the semantic principles remain to be worked out. It is also worth observing that the subjunctive clauses obey a sequence-of-tenses principle: when the main verb is present, present subjunctive is used, when it is past, past.

Thráinsson offers substantial evidence that the infinitive structures of (14) involve a transformation of Subject-to-Object Raising. Within the present framework, this translates into evidence that they are object-controlled complements in which the controller does not serve as a predicate argument in the matrix.

One of the more useful arguments that the controllers are matrix rather than complement constituents comes from the placement of the subject-modifying adverbial *í barnaskap X* 'in X's foolishness', where X is a possessive pronoun coreferential with the subject.[4] When modifying the complement subject, this adverbial may appear on either side of the complement auxiliary, but when modifying the matrix subject, it may only precede the complement auxiliary, not follow it (T:389–393):

(15)

a. Jón telur   mig(A) í barnaskap mínum/sínum hafa
   John believes me   in foolishness my/his(self's) to-have

   étið   hákarlinn.
   eaten the-shark

b. Jón telur   mig(A) hafa   í barnaskap mínum/*sínum
    John believes me   to-have in foolishness my/*his

    étið   hákarlinn.
    eaten the-shark

These facts make no sense at all if the accusative *mig* and the following
infinitive phrase are taken to be a constituent. On the other hand, if
mig(A) is the matrix object with a sister infinitival complement, then
the facts follow from the generally valid prohibition against placing
matrix adverbials inside complements.

That the accusative is not a matrix predicate argument is supported
by the characteristic evidence, such as active–passive synonymy, the
lack of matrix-imposed selection restrictions, and idiom-chunk and
weather-*it* phenomena (T:352–360). Finally, data from irregular case
marking will provide strong evidence that the controllers of the infinitives of (14)–(15) are not matrix predicate arguments.

Subject-controlled complements also appear. With verbs of seeming,
such as *virðast, þykir* 'seem, appear', *reynast* 'prove, be proven',
kallast 'be called', etc., the matrix subject is not a matrix predicate
argument. There are others, however, mostly derived by the Middle
Rule (see the discussion surrounding (44) below) from verbs taking
object-controlled complements, in which the matrix subject is a predicate argument of both the matrix and the complement. Examples
would be *þykjast* 'to consider oneself' (basic) and *segjast* 'to say oneself' (derived from *segja*). This construction is illustrated below:

(16)
a. Hann virðist elska   hana.
    he   seems to-love her

b. Skipstjórinn reyndist (vera) fífl.
    the-captain   proved (to-be) a-fool

c. Jón þykist   (vera) vinsæll.
    John thinks-self (to-be) popular
    'John believes himself (to be) popular.'

d. Haraldur segist   hafa   skrifað ritgerðina.
    Harold   says-self to-have written the-thesis
    'Harold says that he has written his thesis.'

(16b,c) illustrate the general fact of the optionality of the copula in
functional control structures, which will shortly be accounted for. It is
interesting to note that subject but not object functional controllers can

be matrix predicate arguments, all instances of control by object predicate arguments being anaphoric.

When the controller of an infinitive is not a predicate argument in the clause in which it appears in constituent structure, it cannot be an anaphoric controller, since the matrix structure would then be incoherent. Hence, the complements must be functionally controlled and bear open rather than closed grammatical functions. They will therefore not be subjects, objects, objects of preposition, etc., and will fail all NP tests, as indeed they do. This failure extends to subject-controlled structures such as (16b–d), in which the controller is a matrix argument as well as a complement argument.

In addition to the bare infinitive functionally controlled complements, there are several aberrant subvarieties, which seem to be restricted to cases of control by the subject. A few aspectual and modal auxiliary-like verbs take what appear to be functionally controlled complements with *að*-infinitives, while the verbs *hafa* (perfect auxiliary) and *geta* 'be able' (also *fá* 'be able' in literary style) take such complements in a verb form called the *supine,* homomorphous with the impersonal passive participle (neuter nominative–accusative singular):

(17)

a. Það er farið   að vetra   snemma.
    it is begun to winter early
    'Winter is beginning early.'

b. Ég get ekki talað   Íslezku.
    I can not spoken Icelandic
    'I can't speak Icelandic.'

The grammar of these auxiliary-like verbs is largely unexplored and contains many puzzles, however.

There are also a few cases of bare infinitives taking anaphoric control. This happens with the subject-control verb *vilja* 'will, want, hope', on whose complement *að* cannot appear. *Að* is also optionally omitted with the object-controlled complements of *biðja* and *beiða* 'request'. That the infinitives in question are anaphorically controlled in spite of their appearance is revealed by the fact that they may be clefted away, in which case *að* reappears (T:346).

The principal special variety of functionally controlled complement, however, is the passive participial phrase, to whose analysis we now turn.

Functional Control of Passive Participles

Passives of transitive verbs in Icelandic are similar to those in English, except for the complications following from the richer inflectional system of Icelandic. The "logical subject" becomes an optional dative object of the preposition *af* 'from', the "logical object" becomes subject (if accusative, changing to nominative); while the verb becomes a passive participle inflected for the gender, number, and case of its new nominative subject, preceded by the auxiliary *vera* 'be' or *verða* 'become'. Thus, corresponding to the active (18a) we get the passives of (18b):

(18)

a. Stúlkan kyssti drengina.
   N-f-sg 3-sg   A-m-pl
   the-girl kissed the-boys

b. Drengirnir voru/urðu   kysstir (af stúlkunni).
   N-m-pl   3-pl   N-m-pl D-f-sg
   the-boys   were/became kissed (by the-girls)

The significance of the *vera/verða* distinction is not clear. Sometimes it seems to be a matter of time-reference; the present tense of Icelandic verbs normally may refer to present or future time, but the present of *vera* is restricted to present time, *verða* providing a future copula: *Ég verð ríkur* 'I will be rich', *Drengirnir verða kysstir* 'The boys will be kissed'. But this principle cannot explain past tense appearances of *verða*.

We shall derive passive participles by a lexical operation analogous to the one for English (cf. chapter 1 of this volume):

(19)

(SUBJ) $\mapsto$ (AF DAT)/ϕ

(OBJ) $\mapsto$ (SUBJ)

AF DAT characterizes the oblique argument as dative object of the preposition *af* in a manner specified in section 7.3 in the discussion of case-marking rules. *Vera* and *verða* will be treated as subject-control verbs taking passive complements. (19) represents the simplest case of Passivization, the rule also being developed more fully in section 7.3.

As in English, Passivization can apply to verbs taking object-controlled complements:

(20)

a. Haraldur(N) er sagður(N) elska   Maríu.
    Harold   is said   to-love Mary

b. María(N) er talin(N) hafa   skrifað ritgerðina.
    Mary   is believed to-have written the-thesis

Such complements can themselves be passives, with *hafa verið* 'to-have been' optional:

(21)
Þeir segja Maríu(A) (hafa verið) kyssta(A).

Formalization of the Analysis
Under the analysis developed in this volume, functionally controlled complements in English are introduced as VPs bearing the function VCOMP, an instance of XCOMP. However, we have seen that a VP constituent is not a welcome addition to Icelandic grammar. It thus seems necessary to introduce these complements as subjectless Ss. This may be achieved by making the subject position of (1) optional, but associating its presence with the equation ($\uparrow$FIN) = +. Introducing XCOMP Ss with ($\downarrow$FIN) = − will force them to lack subjects in constituent structure. The general optionality of the copula *vera* 'to-be' (and *hafa verið* 'to-have been') may be naturally described by introducing AP and NP as bearers of XCOMP. There are also verbs taking only predicate adjectives or nominals, which may be dealt with by specifying ACOMP and NCOMP functions in their lexical forms. The resulting revision of (1) may be written as (22), adopting the abbreviatory conventions of chapter 2 of this volume for equations on PS rules:

(22)

$$
S \rightarrow \underset{\substack{\text{SUBJ} \\ \text{FIN}=+}}{\text{(NP)}} \quad V \quad \underset{\text{OBJ}}{\text{(NP)}} \left(\left\{ \begin{array}{c} \underset{\text{OBJ2}}{\text{NP}} \\ \underset{\substack{\text{XCOMP} \\ (\text{PART}=\text{PASS}) \\ \text{FIN}=-}}{\left[\begin{array}{c} S \\ AP \\ NP \end{array} \right]} \end{array} \right\} \right) \quad \underset{(\uparrow(\downarrow\text{PCASE}))=\downarrow}{\text{(PP)}^*}
$$

(22) itself may be further simplified by using the X-bar theory of categories.

To constrain the use of verb forms to the appropriate contexts, we may proceed as follows. Let finite verbs bear the constraint equation ($\uparrow$FIN) $=_c$ +, nonfinite verb forms ($\uparrow$FIN) $=_c$ − (this latter condition will prove to be eliminable). Thus, the finite forms will appear only where (22) provides an NP (SUBJ), the nonfinite forms where it does not.

The nonfinite forms will then fall into three types: infinitives, supines, and passive participles.

Infinitives are clearly the "unmarked form" for nonfinite verbs. Passive participles may appear freely as VCOMP, but cannot appear as the nonfinite form after *að* in the *að*-infinitive construction. When serving as a copula, *vera* and *verða* are unique in requiring their VCOMP to be passive (they also appear noncopulatively as progressive auxiliaries). The supine form appears only in VCOMP to *hafa* (perfect auxiliary), *geta* 'be able', and *fá* 'be able'.

I shall distinguish the nonfinite verb forms with the grammatical feature PART, taking values PASS (passive), SUP (supine), and − (infinitive). Since the supine and passive participles have restricted distribution, the contexts allowing or requiring them will introduce the specifications PART PASS and PART SUP with defining equations. (22) optionally adds the defining equation ($\downarrow$PART) = PASS to the specifications of a VCOMP. The copulas *vera* and *verða* will bear defining or constraining equations (it does not matter which) ($\uparrow$VCOMP PART) = PASS. *Hafa, geta,* and *fá* will have defining equations ($\uparrow$VCOMP PART) = SUP. Now the supine and passive participle forms of verbs will have the constraining equations ($\uparrow$PART) $=_c$ SUP and ($\uparrow$PART) $=_c$ PASS. Thus, they will be able to appear only where defining equations have already provided the appropriate PART features.

It remains to prevent infinitives from appearing in contexts requiring passive participles and supines, while allowing them to appear freely in other nonfinite contexts. Mechanically, this can be done by equipping them with a defining equation ($\uparrow$PART) = −. Then if an infinitive is introduced in an environment which other defining equations have specified as having PART = PASS or SUP, feature clash will rule the structure out. Infinitives will otherwise appear freely in nonfinite environments.

This solution, although mechanically adequate, is explanatorily unsatisfactory, since it offers no principled reason for the existence of intuitively unmarked options. In section 7.3 we will develop some ideas concerning inflection that will permit us to dispense with the − value for PART and to treat infinitives as unmarked for both PART and FIN.

(22) provides for main clauses and functionally controlled complements, but does not treat *að*-clauses and *að*-infinitives. Under normal principles, these would be introduced as S′ (S-bar) under NP by the trivial rule NP → S′ . More interesting is the rule expanding S′. We

$$(\uparrow = \downarrow)$$

must provide for two possibilities: *að* + finite clause and *að* + infinitive, the latter with anaphoric control of the subject. A simple way of achieving this is the rule (23):

(23)

$$S' \to a\eth \; (\begin{Bmatrix} (\uparrow\text{FIN})=- \\ (\uparrow\text{SUBJ PRED})=\text{PRO} \end{Bmatrix}) \; S$$

The material in braces between *að* and S introduces a nonlexical subject, as described in chapter 5 of this volume. If such a subject is chosen, FIN is also set to −, so we cannot introduce a subject with (22). Thus, the S will automatically have FIN −. If the PRO subject is not generated by (23), then the S expanded by (22) must have a subject in order to be complete; the clause will have FIN + and will be finite.

(23) says that *að* is the same element in both infinitive and finite constructions. While this might be true, there are certain differences. *Að* with finite clauses can be fairly freely deleted in speech under conditions that I do not presently understand, while *að* with infinitives can be deleted only with a few verbs, as noted above. I shall, however, ignore these issues here.

A matter which we will omit for the moment is the treatment of agreement. Finite verbs (considered briefly at the end of section 7.3) agree with the subject in person and number; passive participles agree with their functional subjects in gender, number, and case, as we will see in the next three subsections.

I will close this subsection with an example. Consider first sentence (21). In addition to the phrase structure rules already given, we will need the following lexical entries for *segja, hafa, verið,* and *kyssta,* ignoring person, number, gender, and case marking:

(24)

a.   segja: V, (↑PRED) = 'SEGJA((SUBJ),(VCOMP))'
$$(\uparrow\text{FIN}) =_c +$$
$$(\uparrow\text{VCOMP SUBJ}) = (\uparrow\text{OBJ})$$

b. hafa: V, (↑PRED) = 'HAFA((VCOMP))'
        (↑FIN) =$_c$ −
        (↑VCOMP SUBJ) = (↑SUBJ)
        (↑VCOMP PART) = SUP

c. verið: V, (↑PRED) = 'VERA((VCOMP))'
        (↑FIN) =$_c$ −
        (↑PART) =$_c$ SUP
        (↑VCOMP SUBJ) = (↑SUBJ)
        (↑VCOMP PART) = PASS

d. kyssta: V, (↑PRED) = 'KYSSA((AF DAT)/ϕ,(SUBJ))'
        (↑PART) =$_c$ PASS
        (↑FIN) =$_c$ −

Given these lexical entries, (21) will receive the constituent structure (25) (some functional annotations have been added for clarity):

(25)

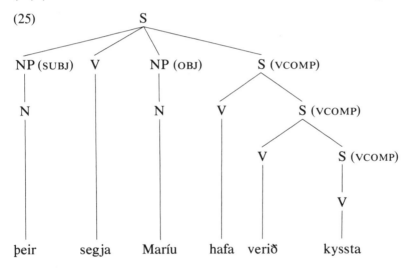

The resulting functional structure will be (26):

(26)

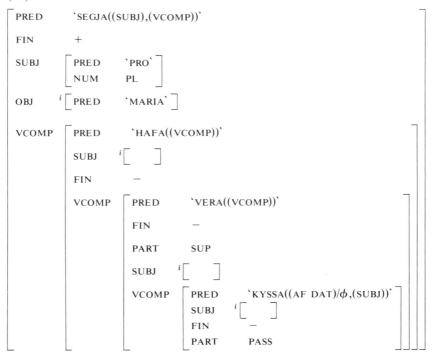

The superscripts in front of the square brackets represent functional control, as discussed in chapters 4 and 5 of this volume. We can obtain (21) without *hafa verið* by generating the passive VCOMP *kyssta* directly as VCOMP of *segja,* as the rules clearly permit. On the other hand, we could not omit just *verið:* **Þeir segja Maríu hafa kyssta.* This is because *hafa* requires a supine, which the passive participle *kyssta* is not (being inflected for gender, number, and case). In a transformational analysis with some form of *to be* deletion, it would be inexplicable that *hafa* should delete along with *verið.* In the following subsection on long-distance agreement, I will work through further examples, including some with anaphoric control.

We have now discerned two types of complement infinitive in Icelandic, bare infinitives and *að*-infinitives. The theory has forced us to analyze the former as having functional control, the latter anaphoric control. In the next three subsections we will see that this treatment explains certain aspects of predicate modifier agreement.

Agreement of Functionally Controlled Predicate Complements

Icelandic adjectives and participles participate in two kinds of agreement phenomena. Within the NP, adjectives agree with their head noun in gender, number, case, and definiteness (via a "strong" vs. "weak" opposition similar to that of German). Our concern will be with another sort of agreement, however, that between NP and predicate modifiers. Predicate adjectives and participles agree with the NP they modify in gender, number, and case. Predicate nominals agree with the NP they modify in case and perhaps number, having their own inherent gender. What is remarkable is that this agreement may obtain over arbitrarily long stretches of intervening material.

This is illustrated in (27a–e):

(27)

a. Hún(N) er vinsæl(N).
    she   is popular

b. Þeir segja hana(A) (vera) vinsæla(A).
    they say   her   to-be popular

c. Hún(N) er sögð(N) (vera) vinsæl(N).
    she   is said   to-be popular

d. Þeir telja   hana(A) (vera) sagða(A) (vera) vinsæla(A).
    they believe her   to-be said   to-be popular

e. Hún(N) er talin(N) (vera) sögð(N) (vera) vinsæl(N).
    she   is believed to-be said   to-be popular

In transformational terms, (27) shows the underlying subject of the adjective *vinsæl* being moved away from it by successive applications of Raising and Passive. The adjective manifests whatever case the NP acquires by virtue of its final position, apparently necessitating a rule of case agreement over a variable. The rule also applies to the passive participles of (27c–e).

In transformational terms, we would clearly have an unbounded rule whereby an adjective agrees in case with the first NP to its left. While such a treatment is descriptively adequate for most of the data from Icelandic, it is quite unsatisfactory from an explanatory point of view. Clearly, the real generalization is that predicate adjectives are agreeing with the NP they modify, which is by chance almost always the first NP to the left. (The sole exception will be discussed below.) To formulate agreement as relating an adjective and the first NP to the left implies that, if the word order were different, adjectives might agree with NPs they do not modify. This is a clearly absurd conclusion, and one that is contradicted by the facts from Ancient Greek, which has similar agreement phenomena but no fixed word order (Andrews 1971).

Consider now the treatment that the lexical interpretive theory provides for (27). It is a basic principle of the theory that all predication relations are represented in functional structure. Thus, if an adjective predicates something of an entity referred to by some NP, then that adjective must have an argument in functional structure referring to the same entity. Hence, in an example such as (27a) *vinsæl* must have as argument either the NP *hún* itself or a functional structure pronoun coreferential with *hún*.

There are three ways in which this could be achieved. First, the adjective could be the functional head, with the copula serving merely as a mood- and tense-bearing element. Second, the copula could be a head taking the adjective as a complement under functional control. Third, the copula could be a head taking the adjective as a complement under anaphoric control.

The first analysis is intrinsically plausible, but to argue for or against it would require a detailed treatment of auxiliary-like verbs in Icelandic. I shall therefore simply assume that it is ruled out on metatheoretical grounds. If it did turn out to be the correct analysis, however, our conclusions about agreement would not be affected in any way.

The present choice is therefore between the second and third analyses. Consider the third. The adjective would bear some sort of closed grammatical function, call it x, to the copula. It would also have a functional PRO subject, coreferential to the overt matrix subject. The resulting structure would be (28):

(28)

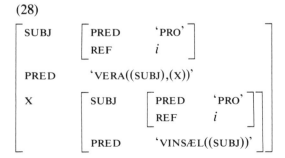

REF has as value a referential index. Inflectional features are omitted.

This structure requires that the copula be a predicate relating an NP and a proposition. Were SUBJ not a predicate argument of the copula, the structure would be incoherent. But there is no reason to suppose that the copula takes the SUBJ as a predicate argument, since it does not itself predicate anything of it. (28) thus meets with disfavor on semantic grounds.

Since the copula predicates nothing of the subject, the subject should not be treated as its argument. But in order for the resulting structure to be coherent, the subject must then be the functional controller of the adjective complement. The complement cannot be a VCOMP, since bare infinitives do not follow the copula. Since some verbs will turn out to take only adjectival complements and others predicate nominals (see below), we may set up one open grammatical function ACOMP to be borne only by AP, and another, NCOMP, for NP. Letting the pre-adjectival copula have the sole argument ACOMP and the control equation ($\uparrow$ACOMP SUBJ) = ($\uparrow$SUBJ), we derive the following functional structure for (27a):

(29)

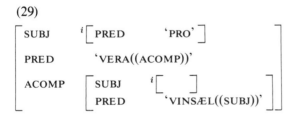

Consider now the question of agreement. Varying the gender and number of the subject of (27a) would induce corresponding variations in the form of the adjective. Given the basic structure (29), this is most naturally accommodated by setting up inflectional features GEND and NUM with the appropriate values. A pronoun like *hún* would introduce GEND F and NUM SG. The adjectival form *vinsæl* would then have the equations ($\uparrow$SUBJ GEND) = F and ($\uparrow$SUBJ NUM) = SG. By contrast, *vinsælir,* which requires a masculine plural subject, would bear the restrictions ($\uparrow$SUBJ GEND) = M, ($\uparrow$SUBJ NUM) = PL. For the present these could be either defining or constraining equations, though in section 7.3 we will resolve the choice in favor of the latter.

Turning now to case, examples of the form (27a) prove nothing about the existence of case agreement for predicate adjectives, since even though the adjectives are nominative in form, this could simply be a property of the predicate adjective construction, having nothing to do with agreement. But (27b) shows that this idea is false for Icelandic. Given our previously motivated treatment of sentence structure, (27b) would have the functional structure (30) (only certain relevant inflectional features are included):

(30)

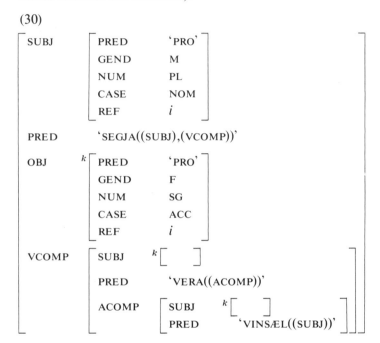

Given this structure, motivated by our previous discussion of bare infinitive complements and the copula, the overt accusative pronoun *hana* is the SUBJ of the adjective *vinsæla*. The case agreement may then be most naturally accommodated by establishing a function CASE for NP, and giving adjectives SUBJ CASE specifications along with their gender and number restrictions. In addition to the feminine and singular restrictions, *vinsæl* will thus have (↑SUBJ CASE) = NOM and *vinsæla* will have (↑SUBJ CASE) = ACC. (I might point out that in addition to being the feminine singular nominative form, *vinsæl* is also neuter plural nominative/accusative and *vinsæla* is also masculine plural accusative.)

The same account will clearly hold for (27b) with the copula omitted: the functional structure will be (31), even simpler than (30) (inflection omitted):

(31)

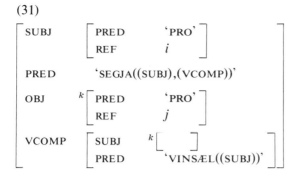

The accusative NP is again the SUBJ of the adjective, so the agreement restrictions apply as desired.

The treatment motivated by the instances of "local" case agreement, (27a,b), clearly extends to the nonlocal instances of (27c–e). In each case, the adjective simply agrees with its SUBJ. This is clearly true of the passive participles as well. Nonlocal, "long-distance" agreement is thus simply an elementary consequence of the sentence structure and the morphology. It is an effect, not a rule.

Such agreement phenomena can be seen with verbs taking complements other than VCOMP. Consider the verb *vilja* 'want', which takes an NP object in the accusative followed by an accusative adjective, but not an NP or a V:

(32)

a.   Ég vil   hann(A) dauðan(A).[5]
     I   want him   dead

b.   *Ég vil   hann vera dauðan.
     I   want him   to-be dead

c.   *Ég vil   hann (vera) skipstjóra.
     I   want him   (to-be) captain

If we treat *vilja* as taking an object-controlled ACOMP, the appearance of the accusative on the adjective is explained. It is unclear to me whether the accusative is a predicate argument of *vilja* or not, that is, whether *vilja*'s lexical form is 'VILJA((SUBJ),(OBJ),(ACOMP))' or 'VILJA((SUBJ),(ACOMP))' with object control of the ACOMP in these examples.

The verb *kjósa* 'choose, elect', on the other hand, takes an object-controlled NCOMP:

(33)

a. Við kusum Höskuld(A) skipstjóra(A).
    we chose Höskuldur captain

b. Höskuldur(N) var kosinn(N) skipstjóri(N).
    Höskuldur   was chosen   captain

c. *Við kusum hann vera skipstjóra.

d. *Við kusum hann (vera) dauðan.

The passive (33b) shows that the accusative form of *skipstjóra* in (33a) is due to agreement rather than some sort of accusative case marking of an object NP. (33c,d) show that verbal and adjectival complements are excluded. *Kjósa* is thereby indicated as taking an object-controlled NCOMP.

Predicate modifier agreement is thus implemented by restrictions on grammatical features of the SUBJ placed by the morphology of the modifier. So far our treatment of the nature of the morphological mechanisms has been sketchy, but it will be further discussed in the section on the theory of agreement. It is worth pointing out that our mechanism for predicate adjective agreement is presumably different from whatever is involved in agreement within the noun phrase. This seems reasonable, inasmuch as predicate modifier and NP-internal agreement frequently behave differently. In Icelandic, for example, there is NP-internal adjective agreement for definiteness, but no predicate modifier definiteness agreement. In German, NP-internal adjectives agree in gender, number, case, and definiteness, but predicate adjectives do not agree at all.

We now have a full explanation of long-distance agreement in ACI structures.

Agreement in Anaphorically Controlled Constructions
In functional control structures, predicate modifiers always agree in case with their overt controllers. Informants are never in doubt, in structures of manageable complexity, and extensive observation of literature, radio broadcasts, and natural speech by Friðjónsson 1977 yielded no counterexamples to this claim. When we turn to agreement under anaphoric control, we find a different picture.

Anaphoric controllers may be nominative, accusative, or dative in case. A predicate adjective modifying the subject of an anaphorically controlled complement may appear either in the nominative or in the case of the controller. Various instances of this are presented in (34):

(34)

a. Hún(N) lofaði   honum(D) að vera góð(N).
   she   promised him   to be   good

b. Hún(N) bað   hann(A) að vera góðan(A)/góður(N).
   she   requested him   to be   good

c. Hún(N) skipaði honum(D) að vera góður(N)/góðum(D).
   she   ordered him   to be   good

The cases indicated for the adjective are the only ones possible, with the preferred alternative listed first.

Given our theory of anaphoric control, the expected phenomenon is that the adjective will appear in some invariant case. (34b), for example, would have the functional structure (35):

(35)

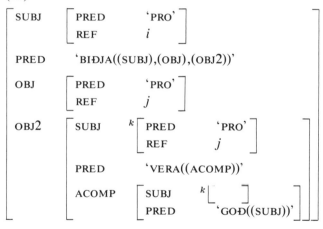

The functional subject of the adjective is the SUBJ of the OBJ2, which is a functional structure pronoun. This is what the adjective should agree with in case. In terms of the basic theory, there is no reason why the adjective should agree with the anaphoric controller of the functional pronoun, which is the OBJ. And in fact it need not.

There are two things we need to explain about (34). First, why is the nominative always possible, rather than some other case, such as the accusative? Second, why do the adjectives sometimes agree with the anaphoric controllers of their SUBJ? An answer to the first question emerges from the thesis discussed in the section on case marking that nominative is the unmarked case. A nominative NP will be represented as one with no value for the CASE function.

Since *að*-infinitives never have overt subjects, there is no evidence for any special rule depositing a case feature on their functional structure subjects, so these automatically appear in the unmarked case, which is the nominative.

Given this account of the nominative, it is the expected case in (34), and it is the appearance of the accusative and dative that is unexpected. Following Quicoli 1972a in his account of similar circumstances in Ancient Greek, I shall call this phenomenon *case attraction*. The major question, I believe, is whether the explanation for case attraction belongs in the theory of grammar or is part of the theory of performance.

Linguistic performances are presumably the result of the interaction of a number of cognitive systems, only one of which is the grammar. The acceptability and occasional production of a class of sentences may therefore be due to something other than the grammatical system per se. What evidence might there be that attraction is extragrammatical? Three considerations, examined at more length below, suggest this: (a) the overt evidence bearing on attraction is very sparse in normal performance; (b) the conditioning of the process is complex, "squishy," and variable from speaker to speaker; and (c) essentially the same phenomenon seems to exist with similar conditioning in Ancient Greek.

In an extensive study of agreement in infinitive constructions in Icelandic, Friðjónsson 1977 found that examples of predicate adjectives in *að*-infinitive constructions were extremely rare. He was forced, apparently much against his inclinations, to make considerable use of informants' judgments of acceptability, rather than relying solely on collected examples. I might add that I have not come across a single example of the relevant structure in my own reading of Icelandic. Hence, if attraction were a rule, it would be learned on the basis of extremely sparse evidence. If the rule were simple, this might not be an obstacle, but the rule is not simple.

The factors conditioning attraction have been extensively discussed by Friðjónsson 1977 and Thráinsson, especially T:361–363. I will mention some of the major points, adding a few of my own.

First, attraction is much more likely with an accusative object controller than with a dative object controller. In fact, I have in the past (Andrews 1973, 1976) erroneously claimed that attraction is obligatory with an accusative object controller, finding that my informants up to that time seemed to require it.

Dative controllers, on the other hand, are far weaker attractors. Many informants reject a dative adjective in (34c), and Friðjónsson reports that instances of such attraction are especially rare.

Attraction remains highly likely when a subject-controlled *að*-infinitive is embedded as an accusative-plus-infinitive construction:

(36)

a. Ég(N) vonast til   að vera vinsæll(N).
   I   hope   toward to be   popular

b. Þeir telja   mig(A) vonast til   að vera vinsælan(A)/vinsæll(N).
   they believe me   to-hope toward to be   popular

Attraction is blocked, however, over an intervening noun phrase. Hence, if we embed (34a) as an accusative-plus-infinitive, the nominative remains the only possible case for the adjective:

(37)

Þeir telja   hana(A) hafa   lofað   honum að vera
they believe her   to-have promised him   to be

góð(N)/*góða(A).
good

Of course, as long as the subject is the controller of the infinitive, it is impossible for the adjective to agree with the object. Hence, though (38) is permissible for those speakers who accept attraction into the dative, it has a different meaning, *lofa* in this case meaning 'to allow' and taking an object-controlled complement. (The nominative *góður* is perfectly acceptable here, and is for many speakers preferable.)

(38)

Hún(N) lofaði   honum(D) að vera góðum(D).
she   allowed him   to be good

It is this phenomenon that shows that we cannot merely stipulate that predicate modifiers agree with the first NP to their left; they do so only if they in some sense modify that NP.

A further point is that predicate nominals and passive participles are more resistant to attraction than predicate adjectives. When, for example, *að* is optionally omitted with *biðja,* attraction of the adjective into the accusative becomes stronger. Friðjónsson in fact reports it to be obligatory. Thráinsson (T:363–363) gives the following data:

(39)

a. Ég bað Maríu(A) vera ?góð(N)/góða(A).
   I asked Mary   to-be good

b. Ég bað Maríu(A) vera góða stúlku(A)/góð stúlka(N).
   I asked Mary   to-be good girl

c. Ég bað Maríu(A) vera tekin(N)/??tekna(A) af lögreglunni.
   I asked Mary   to-be taken   by the-police

A nominative predicate adjective is somewhat unacceptable in (39a), but the nominative predicate nominal in (39b) is all right. In (39c) the accusative passive participle approaches unacceptability, though the accusative is permitted with predicate adjectives and nominals. Thráinsson gives further evidence that when *að* is present, a nominative adjective in (39a) becomes fully acceptable, and the accusative participle in (39c) becomes impossible. An accusative predicate nominal remains possible when *að* is present, however.

We can see from this that there is a hierarchy of attractability: predicate adjective > predicate nominal > passive participle. The omission of *að* renders attraction more likely. Furthermore, since dative is a weaker attractor than accusative, we should not be surprised to learn that Thráinsson finds attraction of participles and predicate nominals into the dative to be unacceptable.

A final factor is whether or not the attractor is a surface subject. Icelandic has verbs taking *að*-infinitive complements controlled by accusative and dative subjects. That these oblique controllers are in fact subjects will be shown in section 7.3. Friðjónsson finds attraction questionable with such controllers. (I have changed the gender of the subject pronoun from that of Friðjónsson's original example so that the morphology will reflect the case marking.)

(40)
?Hana(A) langar að vera rík(N)/?ríka(A).
 her   longs to be   rich
'She longs to be rich.'

I have found some informants who approve sentences like (40), however, so they perhaps have some measure of acceptability.

Putting all this together, in addition to our hierarchy of attractability, we can propose a hierarchy of attractiveness: accusative object > dative object > oblique subject. We may also characterize intervening *að* as a somewhat inhibiting factor, and an intervening NP as an absolutely inhibiting factor.

The "squishiness," complex conditioning, and judgmental uncertainty of agreement under anaphoric control is in marked contrast with the absolute character of agreement under functional control. It is furthermore implausible to suggest that people could actually learn the conditioning factors on the basis of the very sparse evidence that normal performance provides.

Further difficulty for the hypothesis that the conditioning for attraction is learned comes from the nature of predicate modifier agreement in Ancient Greek, as described by Andrews 1971 and Quicoli 1972a. Although these authors opt for an account in terms of global rules and indexing devices, respectively, it is quite apparent that the facts they present call for a treatment in terms of functional structure very much like the one we have presented for Icelandic. Within such an analysis, Greek would have attraction under anaphoric control just as Icelandic does. Quicoli discusses the relevant data with especial thoroughness. Attraction appears to be obligatory into the nominative and accusative, and optional into the genitive and dative. Furthermore, predicate adjectives seem to be more likely to attract than predicate nominals. Some of the same sorts of conditioning factors thus seem to have similar effects in Greek and Icelandic, although attraction is generally more prevalent in Greek. Perhaps this is because Greek is a free word order language, so that agreement bears a greater burden in the expression of grammatical relations.

Exiling attraction from the realm of grammar does not absolve me of the responsibility for making some suggestion about what it is. I would suggest that attraction happens when a structure of anaphoric control is treated like a structure of functional control by the agreement restrictions on the predicate modifier. Thus, (35) behaves as if the OBJ and OBJ2 SUBJ were functionally identical rather than functionally distinct. The predicate adjective will then agree with the overt OBJ in (34b) rather than the covert OBJ2 SUBJ.

This account is essentially the one suggested by Friðjónsson, translated into our theoretical framework. Friðjónsson suggests that attraction occurs because the *að*-infinitive construction analogizes to the accusative-plus-infinitive construction, where agreement with the controller is obligatory. This explains why attraction is often better in structures which more closely resemble accusative-plus-infinitives. Hence, absence of *að* strengthens attraction, and accusative is a stronger attractor than dative, since datives do not functionally control agreeing modifiers, as we shall see below. Likewise, oblique subjects do not functionally control agreeing modifiers, so attraction is weak here as well. I suggest that this misanalysis of the sentence structure by the agreement restriction is a more or less automatic consequence of the grammatical pattern of the language and the properties of the performance mechanism.

Further support for this idea comes from Neidle's discussion of case agreement in Russian (chapter 6 of this volume). Given Neidle's analysis, there is no attraction, at least by objects, in Russian. This can be explained by the fact that there is no evidence for functional control of VCOMPs by objects in Russian.

From a linguistic point of view, the plausibility of this account depends on the discovery of more phenomena that can be explained by this kind of "misanalysis." From a psychological point of view, it depends on the formulation of a performance model that predicts the effect. Both of these tasks I leave to the future.

Regardless of the fate of attraction, our theory has a clear success in accounting for the agreement differences between structures with functional control and those with anaphoric control, and it thus achieves a substantial measure of explanatory power.[6]

Agreement of Complements to Middle Verbs
Nonagreement with the controller in (34) is predicted by the distinction between functional and anaphoric control. However, there is another difference between the structures of (34) and the functional control structures we have considered so far. In the functional control structures discussed earlier, the controller is not an argument in the matrix, while in the anaphoric control structures, it is. In transformational terms, our functional control structures involve subject movement, our anaphoric control structures subject deletion. Could this be the distinction crucial for agreement? Evidence to the contrary is provided by the "middle voice" construction of Icelandic.

Icelandic has a conjugation of verbs consisting of the normal verb endings plus -st, which fuses phonologically with the preceding ending. This -st was originally the reflexive pronoun sik, and forms the middle voice. Middle forms have a variety of uses in Modern Icelandic, discussed in Valfells 1970; they are for the most part like those of the Romance reflexive, discussed in chapter 2 of this volume. Some middle forms are completely arbitrary from a synchronic point of view, such as *nálgast* 'approach' and *óttast* 'fear', which are both transitive verbs taking accusative objects. Other middle forms represent intransitive counterparts of transitive forms, usually with a passive, reflexive, or reciprocal sense. There seems to be a reasonably productive rule deriving reflexive middles from transitive counterparts: most transitive verbs seem to have middles that can be interpreted reflexively in at least some contexts, although passive and reciprocal senses are generally dominant if present.

The middle construction seems to be especially productive with verbs taking the ACI. We thus have pairs such as these:

(41)

a. Þeir sáu sig hlaupa.
    they saw self to-run

b. Þeir sáust   hlaupa.
    they saw-selves to-run
    'They saw themselves run.'

(42)

a. Hann(N) telur   sig(A) (vera) sterkan(A).
    he   believes himself to-be strong

b. Hann(N) telst   (vera) sterkur(N).
    he   believes-self to-be strong
    'He believes himself to be strong.'

(43)

a. Þú(N) kallar þig(A)   prest(A).
    you   call   yourself priest

b. Þú(N) kallast prestur(N).
    you   call-self priest
    'You call yourself a priest.'

In the (a) sentences, the complement SUBJ is functionally controlled by the accusative form of appropriate pronoun. In the (b) sentences, the pronoun vanishes and the verb acquires the *-st* ending. When a third person object pronoun is coreferential with the subject, it is reflexive, so (41a), (42a) have *sig*, the accusative third person reflexive (invariant for number and gender). Other persons lack a reflexive, using the normal personal pronoun. Hence, *þig* in (43a) is merely the accusative of *þú*. But middle verb forms are possible for all persons and numbers.

Note the agreement of the predicate modifiers in (42), (43), which we shall explain in a moment.

Within the lexical interpretive theory, the optimal analysis for these middle voice constructions is to derive the matrix verbs by a lexical rule, the Middle Rule, which operates on the grammatical function assignment as follows:

(44)

Middle Rule

(OBJ) $\mapsto$ (SUBJ)

The relevant aspects of the entry for *telja* in (45a) will thus be changed to those for *teljast* in (45b):

(45)

a. telja: V, PRED = 'TELJA((SUBJ),(VCOMP))'
             ($\uparrow$VCOMP SUBJ) = ($\uparrow$OBJ),...

b. teljast: V, PRED = 'TELJA((SUBJ),(VCOMP))'
             ($\uparrow$VCOMP SUBJ) = ($\uparrow$SUBJ),...

The effect of the Middle Rule on lexical entries like that of *telja* will be to change the control equation ($\uparrow$VCOMP SUBJ) = ($\uparrow$OBJ) to ($\uparrow$VCOMP SUBJ) = ($\uparrow$SUBJ). I leave it to the reader to construct the resulting functional structures for the (b) examples of (41)–(43).

Observe now that the agreement phenomena of (42)–(43) are automatically accounted for. Given the entry (45b) for *teljast,* for example, the nominative *hann* will end up as the SUBJ of *sterkur* 'strong' in (42b). Thus, the adjective must be nominative. Given the preceding discussion of *að*-infinitives, one might suggest that these nominatives are instances of some sort of nonagreement. This idea may be dispelled by embedding the (b) examples in the accusative-plus-infinitive construction:

(46)

a. Ég held hann(A) teljast   (vera) sterkan(A)/*sterkur(N).
    I   hold him   to-believe-self to-be strong

b. Hann(N) segir þig(A) kallast   prest(A)/*prestur(N).
    he   says you   to-call-self priest

When the SUBJ of the adjective becomes accusative, the adjective becomes accusative obligatorily, in contrast to what happens with *að*-infinitives in such examples as (34b) or (36b). Passive participles also

obligatorily switch to the accusative, in contrast to their behavior in the
að-infinitive:

(47)

a. Hann(N) segist   (hafa   verið) skoðaður(N).
   he   says-self to-have been   examined

b. Ég heyrði hann(A) segjast (hafa   verið)
   I   heard him   say-self to-have been

   skoðaðan(A)/*skoðaður(N).
   examined

The lexical interpretive theory explains this contrast in agreement. In
a transformational theory, on the other hand, the *að*-infinitives and
middle voice constructions would both be derived by deletion rules,
and there would be no reason to expect them to behave differently in
the way they do. Hence, the lexical interpretive theory has a decided
explanatory edge.

Ordinary transitive verbs also possess middle voice forms. Hence,
from *raka* 'to shave', we find *rakast* 'to shave oneself'. The PRED of
raka would be 'RAKA((SUBJ),(OBJ))'. (44) applying to this will produce
'RAKA((SUBJ),(SUBJ))'. But given the results of Grimshaw's work on
Romance reflexives in chapter 2 of this volume, this is an illegal PRED,
calling for two instances of the SUBJ function (that is, two SUBJS), which
violates single valuedness of grammatical function.

Hence, reflexives from ordinary transitives must arise by some different set of operation on lexical items, presumably the binding operation formulated by Grimshaw as Reflexivization:

(48)
Reflexivization (example (37) of chapter 2)
Predicate $(x, ..., y, ...) \rightarrow$
    Predicate$_{\text{refl}}$ $(x, ..., x, ...)$

(48) operates on the predicate argument structure of the lexical item (cf.
chapter 3 of this volume) rather than on the grammatical function assignment, and has the effect of binding the variable associated with an
object argument to the one associated with the SUBJ. The object argument expression is thereby automatically changed to ϕ, so that the
predicate becomes intransitive, exactly as Grimshaw describes for
Romance languages. Hence 'RAKA((SUBJ),(OBJ))' with predicate argu-
                         x y

ment structure 'SHAVE(x,y)' becomes 'RAKAST((SUBJ),ϕ)' with predi-
$$x \quad x$$
cate argument structure 'SHAVE(x,x)'.

But just as the Middle Rule (44) produces wrong results when applied to simple transitive verbs, so Grimshaw's Reflexivization will not apply correctly to ACI verbs: the accusative that is suppressed is not an argument of the predicate, so no operation on the predicate argument structure of the predicate can have any effect on it. The lexical form of *telja* is 'TELJA((SUBJ),(VCOMP))', with control equation
$$x \qquad y$$
($\uparrow$VCOMP SUBJ) = ($\uparrow$OBJ). If Reflexivization were to apply at all here, it would create an intransitive lexical form 'TELJAST((SUBJ),ϕ)', with no
$$x$$
VCOMP, and the control equation ($\uparrow$VCOMP SUBJ) = ($\uparrow$OBJ) would necessitate the appearance of an OBJ which did not serve as an argument to anything, rendering the structure incoherent.

Although all productively derived middle verbs are grammatically intransitive, with the subject of the derived verb interpreted in some sense as the object of the base verb, this is achieved by different lexical rules, including (44) and (48). Our theory thus leads to the surprising conclusion that the Icelandic reflexive middle is not a unified construction, different rules being involved with ACI and ordinary transitive verbs. If further work on the middle supports this claim, it will be a striking confirmation for the theory that predicted it.

Summary

In this section we have seen that the lexical interpretive theory of this volume predicts the main features of "long-distance" agreement. First we discovered that the theory requires us to analyze bare infinitives as structures of functional control, *að*-infinitives as structures of anaphoric control. In the latter part of the section we saw how this leads to correct predictions about the behavior of agreement in these complement constructions.

Other syntactic frameworks known to me do not draw a natural distinction between structures of functional and anaphoric control. Rather, they draw a natural distinction between "movement" constructions, in which the controller is not a matrix argument, and "deletion" constructions, in which it is. But it is anaphoric versus functional control, rather than "movement" versus "deletion," that is important for agreement. The theory of functional structure is thus superior in explanatory power.

7.3 Case Marking of NPs

We will now take up the analysis of case marking of NPs. Our basic concern will be to explain the differences between the behavior of regularly case-marked NPs (nominative subjects and accusative objects, and, it turns out, nominative objects) and irregularly case-marked NPs. We shall examine in succession irregularly case-marked subjects, irregularly case-marked objects, the peculiarities of irregularly case-marked NPs, the essentials of our analysis of case marking, the case-marking rules, and the mechanisms of inflection. I summarize the argument in the last subsection.

Oblique Subjects

Andrews 1976 first argued that Icelandic had nonnominative subjects, and this conclusion was accepted and the arguments improved and extended by Thráinsson (T:462–476). Below is a selection of examples of putative oblique subjects, chosen to give an idea of the semantic range of the constructions:

(49)

a. Mig(A) langar að fara til Íslands.
   me　　longs to go　to Iceland

b. Hana(A) dreymdi um　hafið.
   her　　dreamed about the-sea

c. Mig(A) velgir　　við setningafræði.
   me　　is-nauseated at　syntax
   'Syntax turns my stomach.'

d. Mig(A) klæjar lófann(A).
   me　　itches the-palm

e. Mig(A) kelur.
   me　　is freezing
   'I am freezing/getting frostbitten.'

f. Snjóa(A) leysir á　fjallinu.
   snow　　melts on the-mountain

g. Bátinn(A) rak　á　land.
   the-boat　drifted to land

h. Hrútana(A) flæddi.
   the-rams　　flooded
   'The rams were caught by the flood-tide.'

i.   Drengina(A) vantar mat(A).
     the-boys   lacks   food

(50)

a.   Honum(D) mæltist vel í kirkjunni.
     him   spoke well in the-church
     'He spoke well in the church.'

b.   Henni(D) áskotnaðist bíll(N).
     her   lucked-onto car
     'She got possession of a car by luck.'

c.   Stúlkunni(D) svelgdist   á   súpunni(D).
     the-girl   mis-swallowed on the-soup
     'The girl swallowed the soup wrong.'

d.   Bátnum(D) hvolfdi.
     the-boat   capsized

e.   Eldingu(D) sló   niður í   húsið.
     lightning struck down into the-house
     'Lightning struck the house.'

f.   Óveðrinu(D) linir.
     the-storm   abates

g.   Landinu(D) hallar niður að sjó.
     the-land   slopes down to sea

h.   Mér(D) sýndist   álfur(N).
     me   thought-saw elf
     'I thought I saw an elf.'

i.   Mér(D) sýnist hann(N) (vera) góður drengur.
     me   seems he   (to-be) good fellow
     'He seems to me (to be) a good fellow.'

j.   Mér(D) býður   við setningafræði.
     me   is-nauseated at syntax
     'I abhor syntax.'

k.   Mér(D) kólnar.
     me   is-getting-cold
     'I am getting cold.'

l.   Barninu(D) batnaði   veikin(N).
     the-child recovered-from the-disease

m. Honum(D) svipar   til frænda(G) síns.
   him   resembles to cousin   self's(his)
   'He resembles his cousin.'

n. Mér(D) er kalt.
   me   is cold
   'I am cold.'

(51)

a. Verkjanna(G) gætir   ekki.
   the-pains   is-noticeable not
   'The pains are not noticeable.'

b. Konungs(G) var þangað von(N).
   of-the-king was thither expectation
   'The king was expected there.'

A not-too-compulsively executed search of Zoega's Icelandic–
English dictionary revealed about 70 verbs taking accusative subjects,
120 taking dative subjects, and 1 taking the genitive (though there were
some additional fixed expressions taking the genitive). There are also
predicate adjectivals and nominals taking genitive and dative subjects,
but none with accusatives. I will not investigate the nonverbal constructions here.

The semantics of these constructions are not entirely arbitrary. First,
they are all nonagentive, the nearest thing to an exception being the
"dative of success" in (50a) (there are other similar verbs). But success
in a venture is not entirely up to the person who succeeds, so the dative
here is not fully agentive. Accusatives seem to appear with essentially
physiological states (including intense desires and dreams), while the
dative tends to be associated with psychological states. Hence, *velgja
við* in (49c) is more suggestive of physical, *bjóða við* in (50j) of mental
nausea. Likewise, *kala* in (49e) suggests physical damage or difficulty,
such as frostbite, whereas *kólna* in (50k) speaks merely of feeling cold.
Accusatives are also associated with aimless, gradual motions, as in
(49g) and perhaps (49f), while datives are associated with sharp, sudden motion, as in (50c–e). We find the accusative with various verbs of
lacking, as in (49i), the dative with verbs of waning, as in (50f,g). Dative
as opposed to nominative tends to appear with verbs of false or unsure
perception, as in (50h,i). I have nothing to say about the semantics of
genitive subjects.

These examples show that while there is a good deal of systematicity to case selection, there is no invariant meaning that one can assign each case which will then provide an explanation of its distribution. Rather, case selection is basically lexical and idiosyncratic, but subject to regularities keyed to the semantics of the matrix verb.

Why should we believe that the initial oblique NPs above are actually subjects? One problem with this view is that their agreement is aberrant: while finite verbs agree with nominative subjects in person and number, the verb forms with oblique subjects are third person singular (except in certain cases involving agreement with the object, as we shall see). The most straightforward way to explain this failure of case agreement would be to claim that the initial oblique NPs are not subjects.

Since Thráinsson presents the arguments for the subjecthood of initial obliques in great detail, we need not outline them all here. Immediately below I present two arguments deriving from the syntax of the complement system of Icelandic which are quite sufficient to establish the point within the present theory.

First, the oblique subjects may appear as functional controllers of the infinitives selecting them:

(52)

a. Hann telur mig(A) (í barnaskap sínum) vanta peninga(A).
   he believes me (in his foolishness) to-lack money

b. Hann telur barninu(D) (í barnaskap sínum) hafa
   he believes the-child (in his foolishness) to-have

   batnað veikin(N).
   recovered-from the-disease

c. Hann telur verkjanna(G) (í barnaskap sínum) ekki
   he believes the-pains (in his foolishness) not

   gæta.
   to-be-noticeable

(53)

a. Hana(A) virðist vanta peninga(A).
   her seems to-lack money

b. Barninu(D) virðist hafa batnað veikin(N).
   the-child seems to-have recovered-from the-disease

c. Verkjanna(G) virðist ekki gæta.

   the-pains   seems not to-be-noticeable

Placement of *í barnaskap sínum* 'in his foolishness' shows that the obliques are indeed matrix constituents in (52). The word order establishes the same point in the subject-controlled structures of (53) (cf. (16) and accompanying discussion).

Needless to say, such constructions are totally impossible with, say, topicalized or other clearly nonsubject NPs (see also Maling and Zaenen 1978). Within the present theory, these examples alone are enough to force us to treat the initial obliques as SUBJS. Note that it is obligatory that the controller NP show whatever case the complement verb calls for.

Particularly striking are the dative subject–nominative object structures like (50b,h,l). When these are embedded in the ACI construction, the nominative stays nominative and remains after the verb, as in (52b). It is quite impossible to change the case of the nominative, even if we switch the order:

(54)

a. *Hann telur   barninu(D) hafa   batnað   veikina(A).

   he   believes the-child   to-have recovered-from the-disease

b. *Hann telur veikina(A) hafa batnað barninu(D).

Given the relatively fluid word order of Icelandic, various rearrangements of the superficial order of (52)–(53) are possible, but they all "feel derived" to native speakers.

The other argument from complement structure for the subjecthood of initial obliques is that they may be replaced by functional subject anaphors under anaphoric control:

(55)

a. Ég vonast til $\begin{cases} \text{að mig vanti ekki efni í ritgerðina} \\ \text{að vanta ekki efni í ritgerðina} \end{cases}$.

   I hope to(P) $\begin{cases} \text{that I lack not material for the-thesis} \\ \text{to lack not material for the-thesis} \end{cases}$

b. Ég vonast til $\begin{cases} \text{að mér mælist vel í kirkjunni} \\ \text{að mælast vel í kirkjunni} \end{cases}$.

   I hope to(P) $\begin{cases} \text{that I speak well in the-church} \\ \text{to speak well in church} \end{cases}$

Not all speakers like infinitives in examples like (55a,b), but a reasonable number find them passable (see T:300–305). But that they have any measure of acceptability at all is very strong evidence for calling their initial obliques subjects in some sense. Below we shall suggest an explanation for their relative unacceptability. Again, needless to say, topics and other noncontroversial nonsubjects cannot be replaced by functional subject anaphors in infinitives.

We see in (55) a substantial difference between functional and anaphoric control: under functional control the controller takes the case selected by the complement verb, while under anaphoric control the controller is in the case selected by the matrix verb. Dative or accusative matrix subjects would be quite impossible with the infinitives of (55). This difference will prove to follow from our theory of sentence structure.

Oblique Objects

Objects also have nonstandard case marking. Many verbs take genitive or dative objects:

(56)

a. Þeir björguðu stúlkunni(D).
   they rescued   the-girl

b. Þeir luku   kirkjunni(D).
   they finished the-church

(57)

a. Stúlkan beið   mín(G).
   the-girl awaited me

b. Við vitjuðum Ólafs(G).
   we visited   Olaf

Sometimes the oblique objects alternate with prepositional objects, as with *bíða* (taking also *eftir* + D) and *ljúka* (taking also *við* + A). Other times they do not, as with *bjarga* and *vitja*. I have not done any dictionary counts of oblique object verbs, although they are clearly greatly outnumbered in the basic vocabulary by verbs taking accusative objects.

Evidence that the oblique objects are indeed OBJs is provided by the Passivization rule. (58a–d) are the passives of (56)–(57):

(58)

a. Stúlkunni(D) var bjargað.
   the-girl   was rescued

b. Kirkjunni(D) var lokið.
   the-church   was finished

c. Mín(G) var beðið.
   me   was awaited

d. Ólafs(G) var vitjað.
   Olaf   was visited

The usual arguments show that these initial obliques are in fact subjects. They may be functional controllers:

(59)

a. Hann segir stúlkunni(D) (í   barnaskap sínum) hafa   verið
   he   says the-girl   in foolishness self's to-have been

   bjargað.
   rescued

b. Hann segir mín(G) (í   barnaskap sínum) hafa   verið beðið.
   he   says me   in foolishness self's to-have been awaited

Also, they may be replaced by functional subject anaphors under anaphoric control:

(60)

a. Ég vonast til   að verða bjargað.
   I   hope   to(P) to be   rescued

b. Ég vonast til   að verða vitjað.
   I   hope   to(P) to be   visited

These latter examples are as usual questionable for many speakers.

Passives thus provide us with an argument that there are nonaccusative OBJs as well as nonnominative SUBJs, in addition to giving us more examples of the behavior of irregularly case-marked NPs.

Properties of Irregularly Case-Marked NPs

Let us now concentrate on the peculiarities of irregularly case-marked NPs. With anaphoric control, the case of the controller, regular or not, has no relationship to the case of the controlled. Hence, in (34c) we have a dative object controller (these are in fact the commonest kind, although some verbs take accusatives) and in (49a) an accusative subject controller. Dative subject controllers also appear: *þér(D) leyfist ekki að sofa í tímanum* 'you are-permitted not to sleep in the-class'. In all these cases the anaphorically controlled NP would be nominative (as supported by the agreement facts reported in the previous section). On the other hand, (55) and (60) show regular nominatives controlling dative and accusatives. Since the controller and the controlled are different entities in functional structure, there is no reason to expect them to share the same case, any more than there is such a reason for ordinary pronoun–antecedent pairs.

In the passive and functional control structures, an irregularly case-marked NP shows the case called for by the verb of which it is an argument, violating the regular principles of case marking. Thus, a genitive or dative object becomes a genitive or dative subject under passivization, though the accusative object becomes nominative. Again, the accusative, dative, or genitive subject stays in its oblique case in the "subject raising" constructions, rather than becoming nominative when subject, accusative when object.

This "case preservation" effect also obtains when an object controller is passivized:

(61)

a. Mig(A) er talið   vanta   peninga.
    me   is believed to-lack money
    'I am believed to lack money.'

b. Barninu(D) er talið   hafa   batnað   veikin(N).
    the-child   is believed to-have recovered-from the-disease

c. Verkjanna(G) er talið   ekki gæta.
    the-pains   is believed not to-be-noticeable

Note that the accusative is retained in (61a) even though the accusative in the corresponding active (52a) is observationally regular.

The other major effect is of course the general failure of agreement. Not only do finite verbs fail to agree with oblique subjects, but passive participles do as well; hence, the participles in (58) and (61) are all neuter nominative–accusative singular. With finite verbs, we could say that agreement is restricted to the nominative: this would have no explanatory value, but it would work. No such trick will be success-ful with the participles though, since they must agree with *regular* accusatives:

(62)
Þeir telja(A) drengina(A) hafa   verið kyssta(A).
they believe the-boys   to-have been kissed

The participle in (62) is accusative because the accusative on *drengina* is due to its being an object, rather than due to irregular case marking as in (61).

We can even find an agreement contrast between regular and irregular accusatives in object position:

(63)
a. Þeir segja drengina (vera) talda   elska   stúlkurnar.
                  A-m-pl   A-m-pl
    they say   the-boys (to-be) believed to-love the-girls
b. Þeir segja drengina (vera) talið/talda vanta   peninga.
                  A-m-pl   N/A-n-sg
    they say   the-boys (to-be) believed   to-lack money

The nonagreeing *talið* is impossible in (63a), while informants are not so clear about the impossibility of agreeing *talda* in (63b). This may be explained by the implications of the linear order for processing: on encountering *talda* in (63b), one does not yet know that the accusative on *drengina* is irregular, and since it is more likely to be regular, it seems legitimate to simply assume that it is, and agree. The irregularity of an initial accusative such as the one in (61a) is immediately evident, however, so agreement with it is out of the question.

The basic peculiarities of irregularly case-marked NPs are thus: (a) predicate modifiers of which they are the functional SUBJs do not agree with them; (b) a functional controller of a verb taking an irregularly case-marked SUBJ appears in that case; and (c) the SUBJ of a passive derived from a verb taking an irregularly case-marked OBJ appears in that case. The "case preservation" and "nonagreement" effects seem to be suspended under anaphoric control. In particular, the attraction phenomenon for some speakers permits a predicate modifier to agree in case with an irregularly case-marked anaphoric controller.

The Theory of Case Marking
In looking for an analysis to explain these facts, the first idea that might spring to mind is that verbs governing irregular case carry equations like ($\uparrow$SUBJ CASE) = DAT, ($\uparrow$OBJ CASE) = GEN. But this theory fails to explain agreement phenomena. The most natural treatment of agreement

would be that it works by constraint equations such as ($\uparrow$SUBJ PERS) $=_c$ 1, ($\uparrow$SUBJ NUM) $=_c$ PL. The value of SUBJ CASE is irrelevant to the satisfaction of such a restriction (this result is preserved if the agreement equation is defining rather than constraining). Hence, the agreeing forms will have to carry ad hoc restrictions like ($\uparrow$SUBJ CASE) $=_c$ NOM.

But this ad hoc move cannot even account for, let alone explain, the difference in agreement between regular and irregular accusatives exhibited in (63). Yet the exotic nature of the contrast in (63) is a virtual guarantee that it must be explained by the theory rather than engineered into the formulation of some rule, for it is highly improbable that Icelanders learn this contrast on the basis of direct experience with examples of this structure.

Furthermore, we will run into problems when we try to write the regular case-marking rules. I will shortly advocate that nominative be considered an unmarked case, so that in effect there is no nominative case-marking rule. But objects will call for a restriction to the effect that their CASE be ACC: subtending the equation ($\uparrow$CASE) $=$ ACC to the OBJ term of (22) will do to begin with. But this regular case-marking rule will now lead to the rejection of irregularly case-marked OBJs.

If we did not have functional control constructions to deal with, this could be evaded by taking care of all case marking in the lexicon, ($\uparrow$OBJ CASE) $=$ ACC being added as an "elsewhere case" to lexical entries that had an OBJ but failed to specify a case for it. But examples like (52b,c), (59) spoil this suggestion: verbs like *telja* with object-controlled VCOMP would need to pick up the ($\uparrow$OBJ CASE) $=$ ACC equation, but here one sees them with genitive and dative OBJs.

A third possibility would be to treat regular case marking as optional: one optional rule would assign CASE NOM to SUBJ, another would assign CASE ACC to objects. By feature clash, these rules would be blocked when the verb had an irregular case specification. If a verb said nothing about case, on the other hand, they would have to apply, because all lexical entries for nouns would have a constraint equation for some case. While having a certain appeal, this analysis would still fail to solve our problems with agreement. Furthermore, Jakobson 1936 has made a classic argument that the nominative in Indo-European languages is an "unmarked" case, representing not some value of case, but an absence of case.

The idea that nominative is unmarked is supported in Icelandic by a number of facts. First, in such constructions as Left Dislocation (cf.

(9d), above, and T:59–63), in which the dislocated constituent does not show the case appropriate to the position it binds in the body of the clause, the constituent appears in the nominative. Second, predicate modifiers that fail to agree with anything show up in a nominative form (actually, neuter nominative–accusative singular). Furthermore, as explained above, we can explain the appearance of the nominative on predicate modifiers in anaphoric control structures by treating nominative as absence of CASE. Subtler indications of the correctness of Jakobson's view will emerge in following arguments. The explanatory consequences of Jakobson's treatment cannot be captured in an analysis where NOM is a value of CASE, which seems inevitable if regular case marking is to be optional.

Irregular cases are somewhat like verbally governed prepositions in the semisystematic way in which they are selected. Furthermore, in many languages, cases overtly resemble prepositions, being manifested as particles before or after the NP as a whole. Indeed, it is sometimes difficult to motivate a distinction between case markers and pre- or postpositions.

This suggests that we imitate the treatment of verbally governed prepositions set forth in chapter 4 of this volume. There these PPs are introduced with the equation $(\uparrow(\downarrow\text{PCASE})) = \downarrow$. The PP as a whole thus bears the grammatical function whose name appears as the value of PCASE, this value being supplied by the lexical entry of the preposition itself. A PCASE value such as WITH thus serves both as value of a grammatical feature and as the name of a grammatical function.

Applying this sort of treatment to case, we propose that the values of CASE, which are ACC, DAT, GEN, appear both as oblique grammatical functions borne by NPs and as values of CASE. Irregularly case-marked NPs will thus appear in functional structure as values of ACC, GEN, and DAT, as called for by the lexical form of the governing verb. But we have seen that these NPs also function as SUBJ and OBJ (and OBJ2).

The conflict may be resolved by treating irregularly case-marked NPs as bearing composite grammatical functions such as OBJ DAT for a dative object, SUBJ ACC for an accusative subject. This is again similar to a representation such as TO OBJ for an idiomatic object of *to*. On the other hand, regularly case-marked NPs will bear the simple grammatical functions SUBJ, OBJ, and OBJ2. As a consequence of this representation, the "extra layer" of functional structure associated with irregularly case-marked NPs will serve to "protect" them from agreement restrictions and regular case-marking rules.

An important special consideration is nominative objects. Nominative objects appear only with dative subjects, and no other case on the object is possible with such a subject. For this and other reasons to follow, we will regard nominative as the regular case on the OBJ when there is SUBJ DAT. Hence, nominative objects will bear the simple function OBJ. Our theory will prove to have considerable explanatory power for these objects.

A lexical item such as *bjarga* 'to rescue', with a nominative subject and dative object, will thus have the lexical form 'BJARGA((SUBJ), (OBJ DAT))'. *Batna* 'to recover from', with dative subject and nominative object, will have 'BATNA((SUBJ DAT),(OBJ))'. *Vanta* 'to lack', with accusative subject and accusative object, will have 'VANTA((SUBJ ACC), (OBJ ACC))', while *gæta* 'to matter' with a genitive subject will have 'GÆTA((SUBJ GEN))'. A regular transitive verb such as *kyssa* 'kiss', on the other hand, will have 'KYSSA((SUBJ),(OBJ))'. A case-marking rule to be formulated later will ensure that the OBJ appears in the accusative. The lexical form for a verb will thus specify, for each argument, whether the NP bearing that argument has regular or irregular case; and, if and only if the case is irregular, the form will also specify what case appears.

A sentence such as (50 l), *Barninu batnaði veikin,* will now receive the functional structure (64) (some details omitted):

(64)

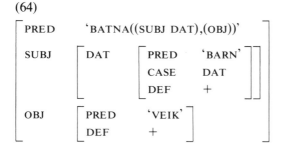

In conformity with our previous discussion, we treat the nominative *veikin* as unmarked for CASE. The manner in which the constituent structure rules produce the functional structures will be described below. For the moment, let us concern ourselves with the way in which the lexical entry of the verb selects the appropriate grammatical functions.

Given the argument expression SUBJ DAT in the lexical form of the verb, this composite function must have a value in the structure. Hence, if it contained simply [SUBJ [PRED 'BARN']], it would be incomplete; the same would be true for a composite function such as [SUBJ [GEN...]] with the wrong case. Suppose, on the other hand, that we had a composite grammatical function for the OBJ; say [OBJ [GEN [PRED 'VEIK']]]. The lexical form 'BATNA((SUBJ DAT),(OBJ))' would call for an OBJ as argument, but the value of OBJ would be [GEN [PRED 'VEIK']]. This structure returning no value for PRED, it would be unsatisfactory as an argument, so the structure would be incomplete. Further, since the [PRED 'VEIK'] substructure would not be serving as an argument, it would be incoherent. Hence, the completeness and coherence conditions force the subject to be a SUBJ DAT and the object to be a simple OBJ, as required.

Let us see what this analysis has to say about the peculiarities of irregularly case-marked NPs. First, consider anaphoric control. Inasmuch as an irregularly case-marked NP can be antecedent to an overt pronoun, there is no reason why one should not antecede a covert functional pronoun and thus be an anaphoric controller. And indeed this happens. On the other hand, we should expect anaphoric control of a covert oblique subject to be dubious. For the rule (23) that produces anaphorically controlled covert SUBJs will not manufacture composite grammatical functions without being appropriately extended. A reformulation along the lines of (65) is necessary:

(65)

$$S' \rightarrow a\delta \,(\left\{ \begin{array}{l} (\uparrow\text{SUBJ}\langle\alpha\rangle) = \begin{bmatrix} \text{PRED PRO} \\ \langle\text{CASE }\alpha\rangle \end{bmatrix} \\ (\uparrow\text{FIN}) = - \end{array} \right\}) \; S$$

The angle-bracket notation is interpreted so that the option α is taken if and only if the option CASE α is taken. Given this additional complexity, it is not surprising that speakers would be uncertain about sentences such as (55) or (60) which require this formulation rather than the simpler one of (23).

An indication that the anaphorically controlled subjects are in fact oblique for the speakers who accept them is provided by the fact that one can actually have an element in the $a\delta$-infinitive showing case agreement with the irregularly case-marked subject. Such examples were first discussed by Andrews 1976 and have been further investigated by Thráinsson (T:301–303). Typical instances are (66) and (67):

(66)

Ég(N) vonast til   að vanta ekki einan(A) í tímanum.
I   hope   toward to lack   not alone   in class
'I hope not to be the only one missing from class.'

(67)

Ég vonast til   að verða vitjað eins(G).
I   hope   toward to be   visited alone

In (66), *einan* 'alone' is accusative, since that is the case that *vanta* 'lack' selects for its subject, which *einan* modifies. In (67), *eins* is genitive, since that is the case of the subject of the passive participle *vitja* 'visited'. These examples are directly generated by (65), together with the rule introducing adjuncts.

Note also that *ein* 'alone' is able to agree with an indirect NP. This is presumably because it is an adjunct, not a complement (see chapter 6 of this volume).

Consider now a simple functional control structure, such as (53a), *Hana virðist vanta peninga* 'She seems to lack money'. *Virðast* 'seems' has the lexical entry PRED = 'VIRÐAST((VCOMP))' with control equation (↑VCOMP SUBJ) = (↑SUBJ). *Vanta* 'lack', on the other hand, will have the entry 'VANTA((SUBJ ACC),(OBJ ACC))'. Putting these requirements together, the only solution is the functional structure (68):

(68)

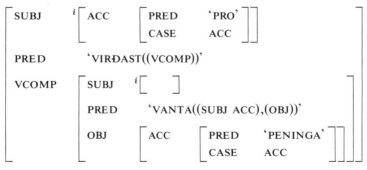

Since the matrix SUBJ is the complement SUBJ, and the complement's lexical form calls for a SUBJ ACC, we must have SUBJ ACC in the matrix. The same account obviously extends to the object-controlled complements of (52).

Note that because the functional controllers in (52), (53) are not matrix predicate arguments, the matrix verb has nothing to say about their case. Therefore, we expect that if the functional controller were a matrix predicate argument, its case would be fixed by the matrix verb, rather than varying according to the demands of the complement verb. We can test this prediction with the middle voice construction. A lexical item such as *segjast* 'to say oneself to be' will (by the theory of the preceding section) have the lexical form 'SEGJA((SUBJ),(VCOMP))' and the control equation ($\uparrow$VCOMP SUBJ) = ($\uparrow$SUBJ). We therefore predict the examples of (69) to be starred under the reflexive interpretation, as indeed they are:[7]

(69)
a. *Hana(A) segist   vanta   peninga(A).
    her   says-self to-lack money

b. *Barninu(D) telst   hafa   batnað   veikin(N).
    the-child   believes-self to-have recovered-from the-disease

We should also get unacceptable results if we put the controller in the nominative, since the complement verb's demand for a SUBJ ACC or SUBJ DAT will go unsatisfied:

(70)
a. *Hún(N) segist vanta peninga(A).
b. *Barnið(N) telst hafa batnað veikin(N).

While not as bad as (69), these are clearly worse than the anaphoric control structures of (60). The theory thus successfully predicts the interaction of the Middle Rule with oblique subjects.

Another difference between functional and anaphoric control is that anaphoric control verbs frequently govern irregular case on the controllers of their complements, while functional control verbs never do. Imagine a verb which takes an accusative subject as functional controller of its VCOMP. If the controller is not a matrix argument, the only way in which the matrix verb can impose the restriction is with a control equation ($\uparrow$VCOMP SUBJ) = ($\uparrow$SUBJ ACC). But in chapter 5 of this volume, Bresnan argues that functional controllers can be only SUBJ or OBJ. Thus, this situation is ruled out. The same holds if the controller is a matrix predicate argument permitting complement verbs taking regularly case-marked subjects. We could, however, imagine a matrix verb with arguments ((SUBJ ACC),(VCOMP)) and control equation ($\uparrow$VCOMP SUBJ) = ($\uparrow$SUBJ). Such a verb would allow only complement verbs selecting accusative subjects. Although permitted by our formalism, this seems highly unlikely on functional grounds, so there is no point in excluding it formally.

What now of the passive? A verb such as *bjarga* 'rescue', with a nominative subject and dative object, will have the arguments ((SUBJ),(OBJ DAT)). Passivization (19) will apply to this to produce ((AF DAT)/ϕ,(SUBJ DAT)), which is what we need for *bjargað* in (58a). Hence, the irregular case of objects will be "preserved" under passivization, as required.

Consider oblique subject verbs. The lexical form of *batna* 'recover from' is 'BATNA((SUBJ DAT),(OBJ))'. Applying Passivization to this would yield 'BATNA(((AF DAT)/ϕ DAT),(SUBJ))', which is both ill-formed and unsatisfiable. Taking the non-ϕ material as present, we have 'BATNA((AF DAT DAT),(SUBJ))', which cannot be satisfied because the c-structure rules will not produce the required functional structure. Taking ϕ, the null grammatical function, the form is unsatisfiable because the value of ϕ is nothing, which cannot return a value for DAT.

The resulting prediction—that passivizing an oblique-subject verb will yield an ungrammatical structure—is borne out.

(71)

a. *Veikin(N) var bötnuð   (af öllum börnunum).
   the-disease was recovered-from (by all   the-children)

b. *Peninga(A) er vantað⎫
   *Peningir(N) eru vantaðir⎭ (af öllum stúdentum).
   money   is lacked   (by all   students)

Of course, the English counterparts to these sentences are also questionable, but the Icelandic examples seem to be impossible. The theory thus correctly predicts the behavior of irregularly case-marked SUBJ and OBJ under passivization.

Finally, consider agreement. In a sentence such as (61b), we have a SUBJ [DAT [...]]. Given the previously developed theory of agreement, a passive participial form agreeing with the dative *barninu* would carry a restriction such as ($\uparrow$SUBJ CASE) $=_c$ DAT. But the SUBJ of (61a) would not satisfy this restriction, since it is the SUBJ DAT CASE that is DAT, rather than the SUBJ CASE, which is simply undefined. The extra layer of functional structure we have associated with irregularly case-marked NPs will thus protect them from the normal agreement rules. It remains to explain why we find third person singular, neuter nominative–accusative forms with these NPs. This we shall undertake in a later section on the theory of agreement.

This theory of irregular case relates in an interesting way to the idea that the nominative is unmarked: if there is no value NOM of CASE, then no such value can be used as a grammatical function in our irregular case structure. Appearances of the nominative will thus all have to be instances of regular case marking, bearing simple grammatical functions such as SUBJ, OBJ, and OBJ2. In particular, nominative objects will have to be products of regular case-marking principles, bearing simple grammatical functions. This prediction will turn out to be confirmed.

Case marking thus results from an interaction of the lexical forms of verbs with a case-marking rule which marks objects accusative. The part of the lexical form that is relevant is the grammatical function assignment (cf. chapter 3 of this volume), the expression that associates the arguments of the lexical item with the grammatical functions carried by the NPs that bear them. For convenience, I shall henceforth refer to grammatical function assignments as *argument frames*.

Case-Marking Rules
Let us now work out the actual rules of case marking. Siegel 1974 has argued that NPs in general have a structure of the form NP′ → NP (C), where C is a case marker. C appears overtly in some NPs, such as genitives in English or all NPs in Japanese, but does not appear in others. However, given the hypothesis that constituents always have the same number of levels (the Uniform Level Hypothesis of Jackendoff 1977), NP′ and NP will be present in the constituent structure of all NPs.

Siegel's structural hypothesis provides us with what we need to produce the composite grammatical functions of irregularly case-marked NPs. Consider the following NP′ rule:

(72)
$$\text{NP}' \rightarrow \qquad \text{NP}$$
$$\left(\left\{\begin{array}{c} (\uparrow(\downarrow\text{CASE}))=\downarrow \\[1ex] (\downarrow\text{CASE})=\left\{\begin{array}{c}\text{ACC}\\\text{DAT}\\\text{GEN}\end{array}\right\}\end{array}\right\}\right)$$

If the material in the curly brackets is omitted, we have a structure which may be represented as (73a). If on the other hand it is included, we have the structure (73b):

(73)

a.   NP'   (F)
       |
       NP

b.   NP'   (F)
       | ⎧ ACC ⎫
       NP   (α), α = ⎨ DAT ⎬
     CASE α   ⎩ GEN ⎭

It should be obvious how (72) produces (73a). The material in the
brackets being absent, the equation ↑=↓ is understood, in accordance
with the conventions for annotating equations on PS rules developed in
chapter 2 of this volume. The generation of structures like (73b) is more
complex, but works in the same general way as the introduction of
PCASE functions, discussed in chapter 4. The (↓CASE)—that is, the CASE
of the functional structure correspondent of the NP—is chosen as ACC,
DAT, or GEN; then the ↓—that is, the NP—bears whatever grammatical function the (↓CASE) is to the ↑, that is, the NP'. It is sometimes
convenient to call the NP structure of (73a) a "direct" NP, that of (73b)
an "indirect" NP.

Replacing NP with NP' in the S-rule (22), we may derive functionally
annotated constituent structure diagrams (74a) and (74b) for *Stúlkan(N)
bjargaði drengnum(D)* 'The girl rescued the boy' and *Barninu(D) batnaði veikin(N)* 'The child recovered from the disease':

(74)

a.

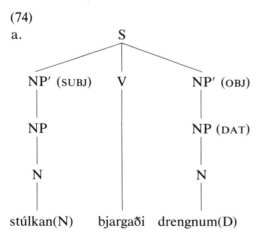

b.

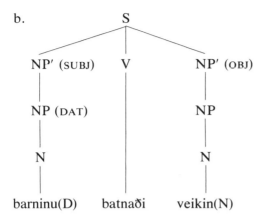

(72) will thus produce the two kinds of NP functional structure that we postulated in the previous subsection. The distribution of the types is of course controlled by the argument frames of the verbs, as described above. (72) thus completes our theory of irregular case marking. Note that (72) does not introduce NOM (nominative), since NOM is not a value of CASE, but the absence of CASE.

We now turn to the regular case-marking rule. As mentioned above, the most obvious idea would be to subtend the equation $(\downarrow\text{CASE}) = \text{ACC}$ to the OBJ term in (22). But this suggestion turns out to be wrong. The evidence against it comes from nominative object constructions, and the most telling difficulty arises with the passive construction for ditransitive verbs.

The commonest sort of ditransitive has a dative first object and an accusative second object. These are generally verbs of giving, showing, etc., in which the recipient is in the dative and the thing given is in the accusative. But with a dative first object one can also have a genitive or dative second object, again with the "personal" object first and the nonpersonal second:

(75)

a. Ég(N) sýndi   henni(D) bílinn(A).
    I   showed her   the-car

b. Ég(N) lofaði   henni(D) bílnum(D).
    I   promised her   the-car

c. Ég(N) neitaði henni(D) peninganna(G).
    I   denied her   the-money

We can also have accusative first object with genitive or dative second object:

(76)

a. Ég(N) svipti   hana(A) peningunum(D).
   I   deprived her   of-the-money

b. Ég(N) leyndi   hana(A) staðireyndanna(G).
   I   concealed her   the-facts
   'I concealed the facts from her.'

There are also double-accusative verbs, but these seem to involve either predicate nominals or idiomatic nominal–verb combinations such as *höggva einhvern(A) högg(A)* 'to strike someone a blow'. Thus, double-accusative verbs do not seem to involve two true arguments. Finally, genitives never appear as first objects together with a second object.

Our theory encounters no difficulty in providing argument frames (grammatical function assignments) for (75b,c) and (76a,b). For example, *lofa* 'promise' in (75b) would have the frame ((SUBJ),(OBJ DAT), (OBJ2 DAT)), while *leyna* in (76b) would have ((SUBJ),(OBJ),(OBJ2 GEN)). Furthermore, Passivization will apply as desired: we can passivize OBJ but not OBJ2, and the accusative OBJ changes to nominative (78a) but the dative OBJ does not (77a):

(77)

a.   Henni(D) var lofað bílnum(D).
b. *Bílnum(D) var lofað henni(D).

(78)

a.   Hún(N) var leynd staðireyndanna(G).
b. *Staðireyndanna(G) var leynt hana(A)/hún(N).

(75a), however, creates problems. We could account for its accusative OBJ2 either by assigning it the argument frame ((SUBJ),(OBJ DAT), (OBJ2 ACC)), or by subtending OBJ2 with ($\downarrow$CASE) = ACC and using the argument frame ((SUBJ),(OBJ DAT),(OBJ2)). Either way, we would expect the OBJ2 to remain accusative while the OBJ became SUBJ.

In fact, sentences like (75a) have two passives, one in which the OBJ becomes SUBJ, another in which the OBJ2 becomes SUBJ. In either case, however, the accusative becomes nominative:

(79)

a. Henni(D) var sýndur(N) bíllinn(N).
   her   was showed   the-car

b. Bíllinn(N) var sýndur henni(D).
   the-car   was showed her

Not only does the accusative become nominative whether or not it moves into subject position, but also the participle agrees with it.

That our diagnosis of (79) as showing different choices for converting an object to subject is correct is made clear by what happens when we embed such structures as ACI:

(80)

a. Þeir telja henni(D) hafa verið sýndur(N) bíllinn(N).
b. Þeir telja bílinn(A) hafa verið sýndan(A) henni(D).

When *henni* is preverbal, *bíllinn*(N) 'the car' remains in the nominative. When 'the car' is preverbal, however, it becomes accusative. Furthermore, the participle agrees accordingly.

Exotic as these phenomena may seem at first, we have already done the groundwork for a natural and elegant analysis of them. Recall first that since, by the markedness theory, nominative does not represent a value of CASE, the nominative objects with dative subjects in sentences like (50b,l) cannot be directly induced by argument frames such as ((SUBJ DAT),(OBJ NOM)). Rather, the argument frame must be ((SUBJ DAT),(OBJ)), the nominativity of the OBJ being then an automatic consequence of the case-marking rules. The most obvious way to achieve this is to mark the OBJ with CASE ACC *only when the* SUBJ *is direct* (bearing a simple grammatical function like SUBJ rather than a complex one like SUBJ DAT). Turning to a verb like *gefa*, with dative OBJ and accusative OBJ2, all we need to do is extend the case-marking rule for OBJ to OBJ2: *gefa* will have the lexical form 'GEFA((SUBJ), (OBJ DAT),(OBJ2))'. When Passivization applies, it gives either 'GEFA ((AF DAT)/ϕ,(SUBJ DAT),(OBJ2))' for (79a), or 'GEFA((AF DAT)/ϕ, (OBJ DAT),(SUBJ))' for (79b). In either case, the OBJ former accusative argument will be nominative.

In fact, the markedness theory and our theory of the representation of irregular cases actually predict the nominative OBJ2 phenomenon. Of the various object case combinations for ditransitive verbs, dative OBJ–accusative OBJ2 is the commonest. Given that OBJ remains dative when it becomes SUBJ, it must bear the lexically governed composite grammatical function OBJ DAT, rather than resulting from a regular case-marking rule marking OBJ dative. To achieve maximal economy in the specification of argument frames in the lexicon, we must now treat the accusative on OBJ2 as regular, so that the OBJ2 of verbs like *gefa* will bear a simple grammatical function OBJ2 rather than OBJ2 ACC. But now the simplest way to explain the accusative case is to extend the case-marking rule for OBJ to OBJ2. It is therefore predicted that an accusative OBJ2 will become nominative if a dative OBJ is passivized. The nominative OBJ2 in (79a) is thus a consequence of two of our theoretical ideas about the representation of case.[8]

This analysis of case with ditransitive verbs also gives a straight-forward account of which objects may be passivized. We may stipulate that OBJ in an argument expression rewrites as SUBJ regardless of whether it is direct or indirect, while OBJ2 will rewrite as SUBJ only if it is indirect. Assuming that the idiomatic *höggva einhvern (A) högg(A)* 'strike someone a blow' constructions do not involve an OBJ OBJ2 sequence, we may let the presence or absence of material after OBJ2 in the lexical argument expression be the deciding factor in whether OBJ2 can be rewritten as SUBJ: the dative–accusative verbs are the only ditransitives with simple OBJ2, and the only ones that permit passivization of OBJ2.

A similar restriction on passivization appears in other languages as well. For example, when the German verb *helfen,* with a dative object, is passivized, the result is either (81a) or (81b):

(81)
a.   Es wurde mir(D) geholfen.
     it   was   to-me helped

b.   Mir(D) wurde geholfen.
     to-me was   helped

The dative OBJ clearly fails to become a SUBJ in (81a), while the correct analysis of (81b) is obscure: perhaps *mir* is SUBJ, or perhaps it is merely a topicalized OBJ. Unfortunately, the syntax of German makes it virtually impossible to tell which is the case. It is clear, however, that change of the dative OBJ to SUBJ is at best optional. This is what we would expect if an object undergoing passivization is normally required to be a direct NP and if the irregular dative object here is indirect.

I thus tentatively reformulate Passivization in Icelandic as (82):

(82)

(SUBJ) $\mapsto$ (AF DAT)/ϕ

$\begin{cases} (\text{OBJ}) \mapsto (\text{SUBJ}) \\ (\text{OBJ2}) \mapsto (\text{SUBJ}) \text{ only if OBJ2 is direct} \end{cases}$

Of course, considerably more work will be necessary on the interactions of Passivization and case marking to confirm this or any other formulation. From ((SUBJ),(OBJ DAT),(OBJ2)), (82) will produce either ((AF DAT)/ϕ,(SUBJ DAT),(OBJ2)) or ((AF DAT)/ϕ,(OBJ DAT),(SUBJ)), but from a frame like ((SUBJ),(OBJ DAT),(OBJ2 DAT)) it will produce only ((AF DAT)/ϕ,(SUBJ DAT),(OBJ2 DAT)).

Our treatment of the passive is still incomplete. Passivization also applies to intransitive verbs, both those having no non-SUBJ argument and those having only prepositional object arguments. These structures are described in Andrews 1976 and T:477–484. Another matter we have not dealt with is the agreement of the passive participle with the OBJ2 in (79a). Both of these subjects will be discussed briefly in the next subsection.

Passives thus show explanatory consequences of the markedness and irregular case representation theories in the treatment of nominative objects. A further demonstration of explanatory power is provided by the existence of VCOMPs controlled by nominative objects, discussed in T:426–427. This construction appears with verbs of seeming, such as *virðast*, and of false or unsure perception, such as *missýnast* 'to mistakenly see' and *heyrast* 'think one hears'. The following set of examples illustrates the major properties of the construction:

(83)

a. Mér(D) virðist Haraldur(N) (í barnaskap mínum) hafa
   me   seemed Harald   (in my foolishness)   to-have

   gert þetta vel.
   done that well
   'Harald seems to me (in my foolishness) to have done that well.'

b. Jón telur   mér(D) virðast Haraldur(N) hafa   gert þett vel.
   John believes to-me to-seem Harald   to-have done that well

c. Mér(D) virðist hana(A) vanta   peninga.
   me   seems her   to-lack money
   'She seems to me to lack money.'

As before, the fact that *í barnaskap mínum* can be interposed in (83a) shows that the nominative does not form a constituent with the infinitive. Were we to treat such nominative objects as bearing composite grammatical functions, we would have a counterexample to the claim that only SUBJ and OBJ can be functional controllers of complements. (83b) confirms the fact that the nominative controller is not the matrix subject, while (83c) shows that the controller can have complement-governed irregular case. Note that the contrast between (83a) and (83c) is precisely what is predicted by our theory: the indirect subject of *virðast* prevents its direct object from receiving accusative case; the object therefore assumes the unmarked form, which is nominative (as in (83a)), unless the complement governs a marked case on its subject, which will then be functionally identical to the object of *virðast* (as in (83c)).

Let us now consider the nature of the Accusative Rule. An issue that we have not yet dealt with explicitly is whether or not CASE features on lexical items involve defining or constraining equations. The formulation of rule (72) is in fact suggestive of the latter, for it introduces a CASE feature with values ACC, GEN, DAT. Lexical items would then most naturally be thought of as bearing constraining equations ($\uparrow$CASE) $=_c$ ACC, DAT, GEN, and UNDEFINED. The Accusative Rule would then add the CASE ACC restriction to functional structures under the appropriate circumstances.

The principal difficulty with this proposal is that we must explicitly list the CASE values introduced by rule (72). This claims that it is an accident that *all* the marked values of CASE can be grammatical functions. Suppose, on the other hand, that CASE were introduced on nouns by defining equations. Then (72) could be simplified to (84):

(84)
NP$'$ $\rightarrow$ NP
                        $((\uparrow(\downarrow\text{CASE}))=\downarrow)$

The CASE values would then be supplied by the lexical entry of the head N, rather than by the NP$'$ Rule.

I believe it to be a linguistic universal that all marked CASE values can serve as oblique grammatical functions. I shall thus propose (84) as the correct NP$'$ Rule, and assume CASE features to be introduced by defining equations on lexical items.

We are now led to think of the accusative case-marking rule as a constraint on functional structures. The most natural formulation would be (85):

(85)

($\uparrow\alpha$CASE) $=_c$ ACC if ($\uparrow$SUBJ PRED) & ($\uparrow\alpha$PRED), where α = OBJ/OBJ2

We shall consider (85) to be a general constraint on functional structures that applies along with the constraining equations from lexical
items and phrase structure rules. It says that CASE must be ACC on a
direct OBJ or OBJ2 when SUBJ is direct. Note that a function is direct if it
has a PRED value, as required by the existential constraints on the
righthand side of the biconditional (85); cf. chapter 4. For example, in
the functional structure derived from (74b), the value of SUBJ would not
have a PRED, being [DAT [PRED 'BARN' ...]]. Similarly, the constraint
would not apply to the structure from (74a), since the OBJ would not
have a PRED. But (85) will require CASE ACC on direct OBJ and OBJ2
when SUBJ is direct.

We now face the problem of ensuring that only nominative appears
where neither (84) nor (85) calls for a CASE. The following presumably
universal convention seems appropriate:

(86)

CASE *Convention*[9]

CASE appears in a functional structure only if there is a rule or constraint which requires it.

In effect, (86) says that CASE is a marked feature, which must be
specified by some rule or constraint; otherwise, there will be no CASE at
all. To see how (86) applies, suppose that we attempted to derive a
functional structure from the string (87) (cf. 74b)).

(87)

*Barnið(N) batnaði veikin(N).

Taking the initial N as nominative, with no CASE, we cannot derive a
well-formed functional structure given the lexical form ((SUBJ DAT),
(OBJ)). If we apply the complex version of (84), we get the equation
$(x(y \text{ CASE})) = y$ in the functional description, but since nothing specifies
a value for $(y \text{ CASE})$, there is no solution. Thus, CASE does not appear in
the SUBJ of (87), but the completeness of the f-structure requires it;
CASE DAT, in contrast, will be acceptable on the SUBJ in this example.
Suppose we had the string (88), on the other hand:

(88)

*Barninu(D) batnaði veikina(A).

There is no rule or constraint requiring the presence of CASE ACC on the OBJ of this example, or of any other value of CASE, so by (86) the only possibility is the nominative.

Consider further (89):

(89)
Ég tel   drengina(A) elska   stúlkuna(A).
I   believe the-boy   to-love the-girl

(89) will have annotated constituent structure (90) and functional structure (91):

(90)

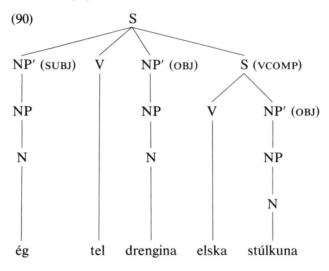

(91)

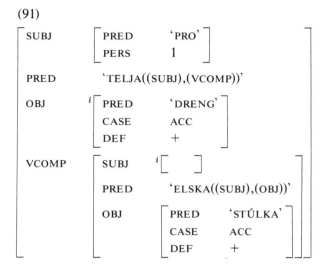

The appearance of accusative case in (89) is permitted by (86), because the Accusative Rule (85) requires it. Observe that because the Accusative Rule is a restriction on functional structure, the absence of a SUBJ in the constituent structure of the VCOMP S does not block the accusative.

Universal grammar must specify which grammatical features are subject to conditions like (86). Number on N, for example, is obviously not subject to such a convention.

CASE features are thus introduced by defining equations on N, and controlled by the argument frames of verbs, via the rules (84) and (85) and the convention (86).

We have now completed our theory of case marking of verbal arguments in Icelandic. There are, however, some additional varieties of case marking in the language which deserve mention: case marking in prepositional phrases, and what is sometimes called "adverbial case."

Aside from case marking, Icelandic PPs seem to be exactly like their counterparts in English. A few examples are given below:

(92)

a.   Drengurinn(N) kyssti stúlkuna(A) í   bílnum(D).
     the-boy   kissed the-girl   in the-car

b.   Stúlkan(N) beið   eftir   mér(D).
     the-girl   waited after (= for) me

The PP *í bílnum* in (92a) is an adjunct, giving the location of the event reported by the sentence. This locative sense of *í* takes the dative case. In (92b) the PP *eftir mér* is an idiomatic PP, *eftir* not functioning semantically as a predicate, but simply formally like a case marker. With *bíða* 'wait for', *eftir* + D is in free variation with a genitive object.

Prepositions select the case of their objects: *til* 'toward' takes only the genitive, *um* 'around, about' only the accusative, *af* 'from, by' only the dative. Some prepositions take the accusative or the dative, depending on their sense. Thus, directional *í* 'in, into' takes the accusative, locative *í* the dative. Nominative never appears on the object of a preposition.

There seems to be no motivation for settling on any particular case as the unmarked one for objects of prepositions. Furthermore, since prepositions take only one NP object, there is no need to set up a grammatical function "object of preposition." Rather, we can suppose that the objects of prepositions bear the case functions to the prepositions. This may be achieved by writing the PP Rule as follows:

(93)
PP → P NP′

Since no functional equations are subtended to the constituents of PP, the conventions of chapter 2 treat them as having the equation ↑ = ↓.

The lexical form of *í* 'in' in its adjunct usage might then be í(*, DAT). Semantically, í says that the first argument is located within the second argument, while the * means that the first argument is not a value of any grammatical function. Semantically, it is the event reported by the clause containing the PP. (In general, the adjunct lexical form can be derived from the complement lexical form by replacing (SUBJ) with *.) To satisfy this lexical form, the PP in (92a) would be given the annotated constituent structure (94) and the functional structure (95):

(94)

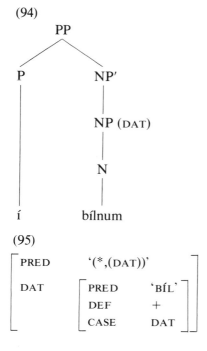

(95)

$$\begin{bmatrix} \text{PRED} & \text{'(*,(DAT))'} \\ \text{DAT} & \begin{bmatrix} \text{PRED} & \text{'BÍL'} \\ \text{DEF} & + \\ \text{CASE} & \text{DAT} \end{bmatrix} \end{bmatrix}$$

Idiomatic PPs are taken to be introduced as in English (cf. (1)). The PP is subtended with the equation $(\uparrow(\downarrow\text{CASE})) = \downarrow$, and the lexical entry of the P specifies a value for the function PCASE, each preposition having a distinct PCASE value. (92b) could thus receive the annotated constituent structure (96):

(96)

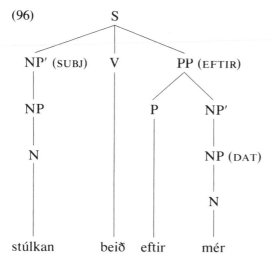

We can thus give *bíða* 'wait for' the argument frame ((SUBJ),
(EFTIR DAT)), in addition to the ((SUBJ),(OBJ GEN)) frame that allows the
verb to take genitive objects. Given such a lexical form for *bíða*, (92b)
will have the functional structure (97):

(97)

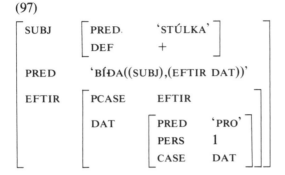

The argument expression AF DAT introduced in Passivization will in the
same way call for a dative object of the preposition *af*.

It is an interesting fact about idiomatic PPs that the matrix verb can
specify the case that appears with the preposition. At the same time,
that case must be one that is governed by one of the nonidiomatic uses
of the preposition. *Eftir,* for example, appears only with the dative and
accusative: we could not have a verb taking idiomatic *eftir* with the
genitive. It thus seems that even though the PRED of the P does not
appear in the idiomatic PP functional structure, still the selection of
case imposed by its argument frame is preserved in the lexical form of
the verb that governs it.

Note further that if we had introduced an OBJ function for objects of
prepositions, our treatment of idiomatic PPs would be complicated: we
would have to do something to avoid treating a dative *eftir*-object as an
EFTIR OBJ DAT, for example.

An important aspect of cases which we will mention only fleetingly in
this study is "adverbial case." Sometimes case-marked NPs seem to
function adverbially as adjuncts. For example, an accusative NP in
Icelandic can function as an adverb of duration:

(98)
Ég var þar   tvo(A) daga(A).
I   was there two   days

Although a serious study of adverbial case is beyond the scope of this chapter, our treatment of PPs suggests a simple formal theory. Suppose that adverbial case NPs were PPs with a lexically empty head. An annotated constituent structure for *tvo daga* in (98) would then be (99):

(99)

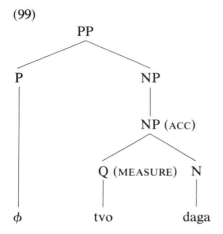

To provide the correct semantic interpretation, we can set up a lexical entry for the null preposition such as (100):

(100)
ϕ: P, ($\uparrow$PRED) = 'ϕ(*,(ACC)),...'

The semantic form associated with the lexical form 'ϕ(*,(ACC))' would say that the second argument gives the duration of the first (the adverbial accusative would have other semantic forms as well). It is perhaps not necessary that the null preposition actually be represented by [$_P$ ϕ] in the constituent structure, if the appropriate functional structures were produced by general convention when the head of the PP is omitted.

The functional structure of *tvo daga* in (98) would then be (101):

(101)

$$
\begin{bmatrix}
\text{PRED} & \text{'}\phi(*,(\text{ACC}))\text{'} \\
\text{ACC} & \begin{bmatrix} \text{PRED} & \text{'DAG'} \\ \text{NUM} & \text{PL} \\ \text{CASE} & \text{ACC} \end{bmatrix}
\end{bmatrix}
$$

Prepositional and adverbial case marking thus fit fairly smoothly into the theory. Furthermore, our approach explains why only marked cases appear with prepositions.

The Theory of Agreement

We now take up the analysis of agreement. The present problem is to explain why oblique SUBJs elicit third person singular, neuter nominative forms on elements that would normally agree with the SUBJ. We find our answer in Jakobson's 1932, 1936 concept of markedness for grammatical features.

I begin with person and number agreement on finite verbs. In addition to proposing that nominative is the unmarked case, Jakobson argues that singular is the unmarked number and third the unmarked person in universal grammar. There is a variety of morphological and syntactic evidence for these claims.

A typical piece of morphological evidence is the fact that in many languages third person is represented by the absence of an overt person mark, singular number by the absence of a number mark. This is nicely illustrated by the following paradigm of the verb 'to run' in Crow (a Siouan language of southern Montana):

(102)

	Singular	Plural
1	ba:-xalúšši-k	ba:-xalúss-u:-k
2	da-xálušši-k	da-xáluss-u:-k
3	xalúšši-k	xalúss-u:-k

The first person marker is *ba:-*, the second person marker *da-,* and the plural marker *-u:-.* *-k* is the declarative sentence marker. Third person and singular numbers lack marks.

On the syntactic side, there is a general propensity for verbs to appear in the third person singular when what one would normally expect them to agree with does not exist. This propensity is illustrated in Icelandic not only by verbs taking oblique SUBJs, but also by verbs that lack a SUBJ argument. Some of these are meteorological and seasonal predicates that have no arguments at all. There are also some semantically one-place verbs whose argument appears as a prepositional object.

Such verbs take *það* 'it' in initial position, the verb appearing in a third person singular form:

(103)

a. Það dimmir nú.
    it   dims   now
    'It is getting dark.'

b. Það vetrar   snemma.
    it   winters early
    'Winter is coming early.'

(104)

a. Það kveður að honum(D).
    it   imports at him
    'He is important.'

b. Það glampaði á   sverðið.
    it   gleamed on the-sword
    'The sword gleamed.'

The grammar of *það* in these constructions has various peculiarities, discussed in T:477–484 and Maling and Zaenen 1978, 1979.

This sort of impersonal construction is also produced when Passivization applies to an intransitive verb. The intransitive verbs may lack any sort of object argument, or have only a prepositional object argument:

(105)

a. Það var dansað.
    it   was danced
    'There was dancing.'

b. Það var beðið   eftir mér.
    it   was waited for   me
    'I was waited for.'   (cf. (96))

The version of Passivization producing these structures eliminates the SUBJ (overt agent phrases being quite impossible):

(106)

Passivization-with-Intransitives

(SUBJ) ↦ φ

Það is introduced whenever a predicate lacks a SUBJ argument in its lexical form, and in such cases the verb forms are always third person singular (and neuter nominative).

A natural account of the person and number agreement phenomena is to let first person pronouns introduce PERS1 by defining equation, and second person pronouns PERS2. Third person pronouns and ordinary Ns will on the other hand introduce no PERS. Plural nouns and pronouns will introduce NUM PL; singulars will introduce nothing. Verb forms will then have constraint equations governing the value of SUBJ PERS and SUBJ NUM. Plural forms will have the constraint ($\uparrow$SUBJ NUM) $=_c$ PL, first person forms ($\uparrow$SUBJ PERS) $=_c$ 1, and second person forms ($\uparrow$SUBJ PERS) $=_c$ 2.

What of the third person and singular forms? One possibility is to equip them with the equations ($\uparrow$SUBJ PERS) $=_c$ U, ($\uparrow$SUBJ NUM) $=_c$ U, where U means 'undefined'. A sentence such as (49i), *Drengina vantar mat* 'The boys lack food', would receive the functional structure (106):

(106)

$$
\begin{bmatrix}
\text{SUBJ} & \begin{bmatrix} \text{ACC} & \begin{bmatrix} \text{PRED} & \text{'DRENG'} \\ \text{NUM} & \text{PL} \\ \text{DEF} & + \\ \text{CASE} & \text{ACC} \end{bmatrix} \end{bmatrix} \\
\text{PRED} & \text{'VANTA((SUBJ ACC),(OBJ ACC))'} \\
\text{OBJ} & \begin{bmatrix} \text{ACC} & \begin{bmatrix} \text{PRED} & \text{'MAT'} \\ \text{CASE} & \text{ACC} \end{bmatrix} \end{bmatrix}
\end{bmatrix}
$$

Clearly, the SUBJ NUM in this structure is undefined, although the SUBJ ACC NUM is PL. Hence, the singular verb form would be used. Likewise, even if the SUBJ ACC PERS were 1, the SUBJ PERS would remain undefined, so the third person verb form would continue to be appropriate.

Although such constraint equations would suffice for our present purposes, there is another solution more in keeping with the universal tendencies illustrated in (102). Suppose that the singular verb forms had no number specification, the third person forms no person specification. These forms would continue to be the only ones that could be used when SUBJ NUM and SUBJ PERS were undefined. But how could we prevent singular forms from appearing in plural contexts, and third person forms from appearing in first or second person contexts? A possible answer is an "elsewhere" condition due essentially to Pāṇini via Kiparsky 1973, which we may formulate as follows:

(107)

Morphological Blocking Condition

If the constraint equations of a form A are a subset of those of a form B from the same paradigm, and the equations of B are satisfied at a position X, then A may not be inserted at X.

(107) forces us to insert into a given position the most heavily restricted form that will go into that position.

Given (107), the forms of the present indicative of *elska* 'to love' would have the following agreement restrictions:

(108)

elska	(↑SUBJ PERS) $=_c$ 1	elskum	(↑SUBJ PERS) $=_c$ 1
			(↑SUBJ NUM) $=_c$ PL
elskar	(↑SUBJ PERS) $=_c$ 2	elsku	(↑SUBJ PERS) $=_c$ 2
			(↑SUBJ NUM) $=_c$ PL
elskar		elska	(↑SUBJ NUM) $=_c$ PL

If a sentence had, say, *ég* 'I' as subject, we could not use the third singular form *elskar* because its constraint equations are a subset of those of the first singular form *elska,* and these would be satisfied with *ég* as subject. On the other hand, we could not use the first plural form *elskum* under these circumstances, since the equation (↑SUBJ NUM) $=_c$ PL would not be satisfied, so *elska* is appropriate in this position even though its constraints are a subset of those of *elskum.* (107) thus simplifies the structure of inflectional forms, and perhaps eliminates the need for equations specifying features as undefined.

(107) makes crucial reference to the notion "paradigm." When are forms from the same paradigm? Or, essentially the same question: What is the difference between inflectional and derivational morphological processes? Although it is an important question, I shall leave it unanswered here.

Turning now to participle and adjective agreement, we have the additional features of case and gender to deal with. We have already decided to introduce CASE with defining equations on N, nominatives failing to introduce a CASE value just as singulars fail to introduce a NUM value. Likewise, for gender, the obvious decision is to set up a GEND function with marked values M and F and unmarked value neuter. Basic lexical entries for nouns will have inherent GEND specifications and will acquire NUM and CASE specifications by inflection. As with CASE, the specifications for NUM and GEND will take the form of defining equations.

The agreement restrictions on adjectives and participles will now be expressed by constraint equations. A masculine singular form such as *sagður* (passive participle of *segja* 'to say') will have ($\uparrow$SUBJ GEND) $=_c$ M. The corresponding accusative will have in addition ($\uparrow$SUBJ CASE) $=_c$ ACC. The blocking condition (107) will correctly control the distribution of agreeing forms, keeping the nominative from appearing when the accusative is possible.

Given our markedness assignments, the neuter singular nominative–accusative form will be the one bearing no agreement restrictions. Hence, it will be the one used when SUBJ{GEND, NUM, CASE} are undefined, either because the N in question is neuter singular nominative, or because the SUBJ is irregularly case-marked. The agreement differences between direct and indirect NP are thus explained.

In this chapter we have introduced CASE by defining equations on N. This necessitated a special convention (86) to ensure that only nominative appears in environments where no rule requires CASE. There is an alternative approach in which (107) does the work of (86). Taking this choice, we would keep (72) rather than (84) as the formulation of the NP' Rule, and we would interpret the accusative rule (85) as a rule adding CASE ACC to functional structures, rather than as a well-formedness constraint. Then case inflection on N would be considered as the addition of constraining equations ($\uparrow$CASE) $=_c$ ACC, etc., with nominative forms lacking any case constraints. Nominatives would thus be the only forms that could appear when neither (72) nor (85) put a CASE in the structure. (107) would then prevent nominative from appearing in positions where one of these rules had placed a CASE feature.

Although this alternative deserves serious consideration, I have rejected it for three reasons. First, the cases that are introduced in (72) must be explicitly listed, destroying the generalization that they are exactly the marked cases. Second, it is more congenial to the spirit of the present theory to treat (85) as a constraint on functional structure rather than as an addition rule which applies after the defining equations have produced a structure and before the constraining equations check it. Treating (85) as a function addition rule is in fact tantamount to introducing transformations into the theory of functional interpretation, violating the principle of direct syntactic encoding (chapter 1). Finally, the approach I have adopted permits us to treat all N features as being added by defining equations, a pleasant uniformity.

In addition to having defining equations for gender, number, and case, N may be inflected for definiteness. Ns with the suffixed article have DEF +; Ns without the article are unmarked for DEF. Definiteness is not involved in predicate modifier agreement, though it is involved in agreement within the NP.

One final problem we can solve with (107) is the selection of verb forms in complement constructions. We had two functions, FIN with values + and −, and PART with values PASS, SUP, and −. We can now dispense with the − values. Suppose that finite verb forms bear the constraint $(\uparrow \text{FIN}) =_c +$, and that FIN + is introduced into the sentence structure together with the subject by defining equation, as in rule (22). Suppose that in addition there are conventions blocking the expansion of a subject under S in the functional and anaphoric control structures. If the nonfinite forms bear no FIN restrictions, they will be appropriate in these constructions, while the finite forms will not be. We have already proposed that PART PASS and PART SUP features are introduced by defining equations on governing verbs or the S-Structure Rule (22). Hence, infinitives have already been characterized as the forms used when no PART feature has been placed. In section 7.2 this was accomplished by giving them a defining equation $(\uparrow \text{PART}) = -$, but if we accept (107) we can achieve it simply by giving infinitives no constraints for FIN or for PART. Hence, they will be appropriate where and only where no rule has put these features into the functional structure. The elimination of FIN − depends on the existence of conventions for the suppression of subjects under S in control structures. Since such conventions must certainly exist, we may regard FIN − as eliminated in principle, although not perhaps in technique. The elimination of PART − is on the other hand unconditional. Verbs will also have MOOD and TENSE, which I will not discuss here.

The markedness theory, together with the Blocking Condition (107), permits us to simplify the structure of inflectional forms substantially, and at the same time to account for the agreement facts with irregularly case-marked SUBJs.

The reader will observe that we have not adopted a completely Jakobsonian approach to markedness: in the works cited, Jakobson did not think of inflected forms as involving values of possibly multivalued features. Rather, he regarded the features themselves as accumulations of marks. First and second person forms, for example, shared the mark "personal," while first person forms had the additional mark "ego." Although Jakobson's original approach is followed in chapter 6, I have

not done so in the present context because the arguments for the decomposition of feature values into marks seem on the whole more
difficult to motivate than those for considering one value of a grammatical feature as unmarked.

Finally, we have the agreement-with-OBJ2 in (79a) to deal with. First
of all, such agreement is not limited to passives. T:466 observes that
number agreement with a nominative object is sporadic for dative
subject–nominative object verbs in general. But full gender, number,
and case agreement with a nominative OBJ2 seems to be obligatory for
passive participles (which are, of course, the only forms that have
nominative OBJ2). Thus, whatever our account is, it will involve something that is optional for an OBJ with a SUBJ DAT, but obligatory for such
an OBJ2.

Two possibilities come to mind. First, the inflectional specifications
of passive participles with a SUBJ DAT might determine the properties of
OBJ2 rather than SUBJ: *sýndur* would then have ($\uparrow$OBJ2 GEND) $=_c$ M
when its argument frame is ((AF DAT)/ϕ,(SUBJ DAT),(OBJ2)), and
($\uparrow$SUBJ GEND) $=_c$ M when its frame is ((AF DAT)/ϕ,(OBJ DAT),(SUBJ)).
Another, more daring possibility is to say that the inflectional specifications are ($\uparrow$SUBJ GEND) $=_c$ M in both cases, but that equations are
added which copy the OBJ2 GEND and OBJ2 NUM onto SUBJ when there
is a SUBJ DAT. Adding the equations ($\uparrow$SUBJ NUM) = ($\uparrow$OBJ2 NUM) and
($\uparrow$SUBJ GEND) = (OBJ2 GEND) to the lexical entries of passive participles
with a SUBJ DAT would suffice. (79a) would then have the following
functional structure (certain details omitted):

(109)

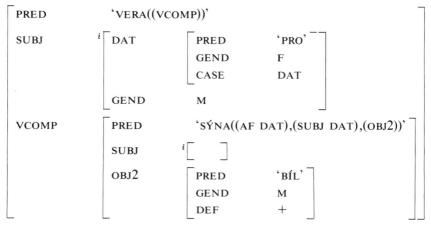

Even though the SUBJ GEND is M, the fact that *henni* is feminine is not problematic, since its F is the value of SUBJ DAT GEND, not SUBJ GEND.

One indication that this latter solution might be correct is that the copula with a passive also partakes in this agreement:

(110)
Henni(D) voru(pl) sýndir(m-pl) bílarnir(pl).
her   were   shown   the-cars

If the passive participle *sýndir* is causing the number feature of the OBJ2 to be copied onto the SUBJ, the plurality of the copula requires no further explanation. Yet more evidence comes from the fact that sentences like (111) seem to be at least somewhat acceptable:

(111)
Henni eru(pl) taldir(pl) hafa   verið sýndir(pl) bílarnir(pl).
her   are   believed to-have been shown   the-cars

Here the matrix copula and passive participle appear in agreement with the complement OBJ2. Such structures are not at all embarrassing to the analysis illustrated in (109), but they would seem to confound the first analysis above in which the inflectional restrictions refer directly to the properties of OBJ2.

Whatever analysis is chosen, the prospects for a synchronic explanation of the agreement in (79a), (110), and (111) would seem dim within the present theory. For better or worse, the theory characterizes these constructions as synchronically complex and unexpected, though their historical source is transparent (cf. footnote 8).

Summary

In this section, facts about case marking, agreement, and the complement system have been shown either to follow from or to fit naturally into an analysis dominated by two major ideas: first, that irregularly case-marked NPs bear composite grammatical functions, the first member of which is an ordinary grammatical relation, the second member being the irregular case; second, that grammatical functions generally have unmarked values, nominative being the unmarked case, singular the unmarked number, and neuter the unmarked gender.

The markedness and case-representation theories jointly predict that verbs, adjectives, and participles will not agree with irregularly case-marked NPs. They also entail that nominative objects must be regular, thereby predicting certain properties of these objects.

Other facts follow from the interaction of the case-representation theory with the principles of the complement system developed in section 7.2. It is predicted that functional control of a verb governing irregular case on the subject will be impossible unless the controller shows the case governed by the controlled verb. On the other hand, it is predicted that there will be no such "case preservation" effect with anaphoric control. The interactions of the ACI, middle-governed, and *að*-infinitive complements with irregular case marking are thus predicted by our representations of case.

An important explanatory task still remains. Our case representations predict many phenomena, but on what basis would language learners adopt these representations? If they need all the evidence we have looked at, our treatment is insufficiently explanatory. To explain the data, we need principles that will induce language learners to adopt the representations we have proposed on the basis of minimal evidence. These principles must determine nominative as the unmarked case, singular the unmarked number, and third the unmarked person, without reference to the nonagreement facts. Likewise, they must lead us to treat a given irregularly case-marked NP as bearing its case as a grammatical function to its clause.

To settle on a particular collection of explanatory principles would require deep study of a substantial number of languages. I shall nonetheless proffer some hypotheses, based on our analysis of Icelandic and some incidental observations about language typology.

Consider first questions of markedness. Fairly generally, singular seems to be the unmarked number and third the unmarked person. Since these categories are so firmly attached to semantics, we may suppose that the unmarkedness of third person and singular number is due to axioms of the theory of semantic interpretation. At present, I see little point in trying to derive them from deeper principles.

As for the nominative, a plausible principle would be that the normal case of an argument of a one-argument sentence is the unmarked case. Since nominative is indeed the normal case of the argument of a one-argument sentence in Icelandic, it is selected as the unmarked case. This principle will also correctly select absolutive as the unmarked case in ergative languages. (See Dixon 1979 for an important discussion of markedness and grammatical relations.) The prospects for deriving this principle as a theorem seem reasonably good. The basic principle might be a tendency to minimize the markedness of structures in performance.

The representation of irregular case makes a knottier problem. What we need to rule out is the possibility of a lexical item like *vanta* 'lack' simply having an equation ($\uparrow$SUBJ CASE) = ACC in its lexical entry. The problem is that precisely this equation is attached to lexical items by agreement rules, and equations of similar form appear on verbs to control the FIN and PART features of their clausal complements. The relevant principle would thus appear to have to be somewhat complex.

The grammatical features we have considered in this study seem in fact to fall into at least two classes. First, there are the "nominal features," such as GEND, DEF, PERS, NUM, and CASE. These are introduced by defining equations on N and are frequently subject to constraint equations imposed by agreement rules in inflectional morphology. They do not, however, seem to be mentioned in constraint equations associated with basic lexical entries. Hence, there are no stems that call for grammatically plural subjects, for example (although selection for semantic plurality is common).

Second, there are the "verbal features," notably PART and FIN. Verb stems do seem to carry restrictions on the PART and FIN values of their complements. But restrictions involving complement values of these features seem never to be placed by inflectional rules. For example, there is no inflectional ending that, when placed on a verb, requires its subject to be an infinitive.

We may incorporate these observations into the theory by hypothesizing a universal division of features into nominal and verbal (and perhaps other sorts as well). The nominal features will be universally characterized as being introduced on N by defining equation, and it will be universally permitted to impose restrictions on their complement values in the inflectional morphology, but not in the basic lexical entries that are the input to the inflectional morphology.

Given these restrictions, the most economical way for the language learner to implement irregular case marking would seem to be to adopt rule (84) interacting with verbal argument frames in the manner we have proposed. The agreement and complement system phenomena are then to a substantial degree predicted.

Notes

My major acknowledgments are to Joan Bresnan, for persuading me that the theory was right and helping work through many aspects of the analysis, and to Höskuldur Thráinsson for answering innumerable questions about Icelandic. I have also received assistance with Icelandic from Inga Black, Inga Cott, Jón

Bjarnason, Guðmundur Ágústsson, Sveinn Ólafsson, Vígfúss Jakobson, Sigur-
ður Helgason, Jóhann Jóhannsson, Baldur Jónsson, Valgi Gould, and Magnús
Fjalldal. All errors are of course my own.

This work was made possible by the Outside Studies Program of the Australian National University, and pleasant by the hospitality of the MIT Linguistics
Department.

1. *Að*-clauses here are somewhat unnatural, but not really ungrammatical, as
was erroneously claimed in Andrews 1976. Verbs that are unnatural with *að*-
clauses take them more easily if they are clefted or dislocated.

2. *Sem* is here not a relative pronoun, but rather an invariable complementizer.

3. Pronouns sometimes appear as determiners before proper names, particularly in the possessive construction.

4. Possessive pronouns acquire gender, number, and case inflections agreeing
with the possessed, except for the third person nonreflexive, which is an invariable genitive. Hence *sínum* consists of the genitive of the reflexive (*sín*) plus the
dative masculine singular or plural adjectival ending. Allen 1975 describes the
same phenomenon in Old English.

5. *Vera* may in fact be acceptable in (32b,c), but only with a slightly different
meaning for *vilja*. If (32b) is acceptable, it expresses a mere wish that some-
body die, while (32a) orders an execution.

6. Ostler 1976 and Lieber 1978 have presented treatments of agreement in
Ancient Greek within the framework of Bresnan 1978, the predecessor to the
present theory of functional structure. Since this framework did not have such
a clear-cut conception of functional structure, they could not attain the explanatory power of the present treatment.

7. These sentences may have passive interpretations, 'She is said to lack
money' and 'The child is believed to have recovered from the disease'. These
would arise from an *st*-Passivization rule which binds the variable associated in
the semantic form with SUBJ to an existential quantifier, and rewrites OBJ as
SUBJ as in chapters 2 and 3. Such a rule could apply freely to simple transitives
and ACI verbs alike without violating any conditions of functional structure.
Though I am unsure of the status of the passive interpretation, a reflexive
interpretation is definitely blocked.

8. Our pleasure in this explanation must be tempered by the knowledge that the
real reason this construction exists is almost certainly the historical development of the language. Once upon a time the case marking was presumably a
faithful reflection of the grammatical relations of the language, nominatives
being subjects, and verbs and participles agreeing with subjects (Cole et al.
1978). As word-order restrictions emerged or changed, the grammatical relations fell out of alignment with the case marking, rendering the case-marking
and agreement rules more complex. What our synchronic explanation does do
is predict that the language will not come to allow accusatives in the OBJ2
position of (79a) unless its case-marking system changes in other respects as
well.

9. (86) describes the intended effect of a convention, but is of unclear formal status. I now prefer (i):

(i)

($\uparrow\alpha$CASE) is undefined unless a case constraint requires it to be defined, for $\alpha =$ SUBJ/OBJ/OBJ2.

(i) will require direct NP to be caseless unless the conditions of (85) apply. (i) will not rule out an indirect NP structure such as [ACC [CASE ACC,...]] since, although ($\uparrow\alpha$CASE) = ACC, $\alpha \neq$ SUBJ/OBJ/OBJ2, but rather $\alpha =$ ACC.

Chapter 8

Grammatical Relations and Clause Structure in Malayalam

K. P. Mohanan

8.1 Introduction

One of the basic insights of lexicalist grammar as presented in this volume and relational grammar (Perlmutter in press) is that there exist various phenomena in natural languages which are best accounted for in terms of grammatical relations such as "subject-of" and "object-of", and not in terms of syntactic configurations or cases. In this chapter I will provide further evidence for this hypothesis by examining, in some detail, the clause structure of Malayalam, a Dravidian language spoken in southern India.

In the recent literature, there has been an interest in the typological distinction between *configurational* and *nonconfigurational* languages (see Hale 1979, Farmer 1980, Nash 1980, Simpson 1980). Configurational languages, which may be loosely referred to as "fixed word order" languages (such as English), are those in which grammatical relations can be identified from word order; nonconfigurational languages, or so-called "free word order" languages, are those in which word order does not provide the relevant information regarding grammatical relations. Extreme cases of nonconfigurational languages are languages such as Walpiri, in which the words in a sentence can occur in almost any order. These have been referred to as *W* languages* in Hale 1979, as their grammars make use of the rule S → W* (that is, "Expand S into any number of words in any order"). I shall show that in order to bring out the fundamental similarities between configurational and nonconfigurational languages, linguistic theory must necessarily incorporate the level of grammatical relations.

I shall examine in some detail a mass of phenomena that are not typically amenable to a categorial treatment, and show that in addition to universal considerations of explanatory adequacy, even the language-specific considerations of descriptive adequacy force us to incorporate grammatical relations into syntactic theory. In some sense, therefore, this chapter can be considered an exemplification of such an approach to Malayalam syntax within the lexicalist framework.

Two Approaches to Grammatical Relations

Broadly speaking, we isolate two opposing viewpoints with respect to the role of grammatical relations in linguistic theory. The first view, proposed as early as Chomsky 1965 and held as late as Chomsky 1979a,b, 1980, claims that grammatical relations such as subject-of and object-of can be equated with configurational relations in the deep structure.[1] Thus, "subject" can be universally defined as the NP that is directly dominated by S, and "object" as the NP directly dominated by VP. This theory makes the following implicit claims:

(1)
a. Nonconfigurational languages do not exhibit processes which are typically dependent on grammatical relations.
b. All the relevant generalizations associated with grammatical relations in those languages which have them can be stated in terms of configurations.
c. Grammatical relations are a property of the deep structure alone, and not that of the surface structure.

The alternative theory, as embodied in relational and lexicalist grammars, makes the following assumptions:

(2)
a. All natural languages, configurational and nonconfigurational, exhibit processes which are crucially dependent on grammatical relations.
b. It is not always possible, or insightful, to state the processes associated with grammatical relations in terms of configurations or cases.

As stated earlier, I intend in this chapter to provide further confirmation of (2a). I will show that the grammar of Malayalam lacks configurational structures for subject, object, etc., but exhibits fundamental processes that are dependent on grammatical relations.

Basic Assumptions

One of the basic assumptions that I shall make in this chapter is that linguistic theory provides for the following levels of description:

(3)

a. A *categorial level,* which must include at least (i) phrase markers with primes such as NP, VP, PP, and a set of precedence and dominance relations, (ii) case features, with primes such as nominative, accusative, and (iii) agreement features, with primes such as gender, number, and person. The phrasal categories (NP, VP, PP, etc.) can themselves be derived from the sets of category features and types given by X' (X-bar) theory (cf. Chomsky 1972, Jackendoff 1977, Bresnan 1977).

b. A *relational level* with primes such as subject, object, complement.

c. A *thematic level* with primes such as experiencer, goal, theme.

The theory must also provide for the following functions:

(4)

a. A *category–relation* function that relates levels (3a) and (3b).

b. A *relation–role* function that relates levels (3b) and (3c).

I shall also assume that grammatical relations are relations with universal properties, both syntactic and semantic, encoded in natural languages in terms of either (i) phrase markers or (ii) morphological features (case, agreement; cf. Keenan 1976). Therefore, it is important that there should be a universal alphabet of grammatical relations, though languages differ with respect to the way the relations are formally encoded, that is, in the details of the category–relation function. This will allow us to state universal generalizations at the level of grammatical relations, the formal properties associated with them, such as movement or case change, being mechanical consequences of the encoding function.

If this assumption is correct, we would expect configurational languages like English and nonconfigurational languages like Malayalam to show similar behavior with respect to processes involving grammatical relations such as passivization, causativization, anaphora, and control. This would in turn provide a powerful argument for incorporating the level of grammatical relations into linguistic theory as distinct from categorial and thematic levels.

A Preview

In the sections that follow, I shall present a fragment of Malayalam grammar that is worked out within the lexicalist theory of this volume. The general objective of section 8.2 will be to demonstrate that Malayalam is a nonconfigurational language; that is, that grammatical relations in Malayalam are not expressed in terms of phrase marker configurations. In this section I will formulate a set of PS rules that will characterize the clause structure of the language, showing that it has no VP node that dominates the verb and the object, but not the subject.[2] I shall argue that its clause structure is to be characterized by a rule that looks essentially like (5), generating structures such as (6):

(5) S → NP* V

(6)

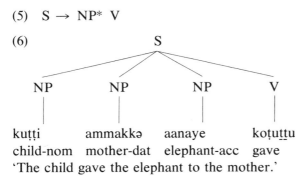

kuṭṭi   ammakkə   aanaye   koṭuttu
child-nom   mother-dat elephant-acc gave
'The child gave the elephant to the mother.'

The symbol NP*, which is an adaptation of Hale's 1979 W* notation, is to be interpreted as 'any number of NPs, including none'. By way of motivating this structure, I shall examine phenomena related to scrambling, clefts, certain kinds of verbal constructions, pronominal non-coreference, and quantifier scope.

   In section 8.3 I will be concerned with mapping these categorial structures generated by phrase structure rules onto functional structures. In configurational languages like English, the principles for picking out grammatical relations can be encoded into the PS rules themselves, which give the configurational structure. I shall argue that grammatical relations in Malayalam, on the other hand, have a morphological encoding. I shall propose a set of interpretive principles that pick out grammatical relations on the basis of case features. With this minimal difference, the rest of the machinery set up for English can be used for Malayalam as well.

   Section 8.4 demonstrates the advantages of this model, using data from passivization, causativization, anaphora, and control.

8.2 Constituent Structure

The Flat Structure Hypothesis
The Scrambling Phenomena   Word order in Malayalam has generally been looked upon as being "free." The positional freedom of subject, object, and verb is illustrated by the sentences in (7), all of which mean 'The child saw the elephant'.

(7)
a. kuṭṭi   aanaye   kaṇṭu.   (SOV)
    child-nom elephant-acc saw
b. aanaye kuṭṭi kaṇṭu.   (OSV)
c. aanaye kaṇṭu kuṭṭi.   (OVS)
d. kaṇṭu aanaye kuṭṭi.   (VOS)
e. kaṇṭu kuṭṭi aanaye.   (VSO)
f. kuṭṭi kaṇṭu aanaye.   (SVO)

I shall represent the structure of, say, (7a) as follows:

(8)

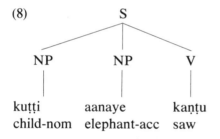

The reasons for not representing it as (9) will be discussed at a later point.

(9)

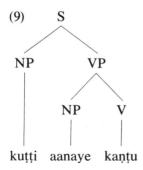

I shall also assume that the rule responsible for the structure is something like (5), repeated here.

(5)

S → NP* V

The NPs expanded by rule (5) can be interpreted as subjects, direct objects, indirect objects, etc., on the basis of their case features.

Rule (5) accounts for the freedom of word order of all constituents of S except V. I shall assume that the freedom of the verb to appear in nonfinal positions can be accounted for in terms of a scrambling rule. This rule, as well as the reason for making a distinction between subject–object freedom and verb freedom, will be discussed later.

The freedom of word order extends to indirect objects and various kinds of adjuncts, as illustrated by (10) and (11):

(10)

a. kuṭṭi   aanaye   ammakkə koṭuṭṭu.
   child-nom elephant-acc mother-dat gave
   'The child gave the elephant to the mother.'

b. ammakkə kuṭṭi aanaye koṭuṭṭu.

(11)

a. kuṭṭi innale   skuuḷileekkə ṭaniye pooyi.
   child yesterday school-to   alone went
   'The child went alone to school yesterday.'

b. skuuḷileekkə kuṭṭi ṭaniye pooyi innale.

We shall therefore revise rule (5) as follows:

(12)

S → X′* V

Rule (12) expands S into any number of constituents at the X′ level (N′, P′, ADV′, etc.), followed by a verb. This rule needs to be constrained somewhat. First, we observe that if X′ is interpreted as V′, it will result in ungrammatical sentences such as (13):

(13)

*kuṭṭi   amma   uraṇṇi ciriccu.
 child-nom mother-nom slept   laughed

Second, adjectives in Malayalam are not directly dominated by S; that is, they do not occur in the "predicative position." Thus, Malayalam does not have structures of the form [NP AP V]$_S$, where *AP* denotes an adjective phrase. In order to block these structures, we shall first assume the following feature classification:

(14)

[+V] = verbs and adjectives

[−V] = nouns, postpositions, adverbs, and S

We can now revise rule (12) as follows:

(15)

$$S \rightarrow \underset{[-V]}{X'*} \; V$$

Rule (15) says, "Expand S into any number of X' constituents, and a verb at the end, as long as the X' constituents do not have the feature [+V]."

Why Verb-Final?   Rule (15) claims that Malayalam is a verb-final language, the freedom of the verb to appear nonfinally being described in terms of scrambling. An alternative hypothesis would be that even the position of the verb is not fixed in phrase structure, thereby building verb scrambling as well into the PS rules. For example, we could formulate an alternative PS rule such as (16):

(16)

$$S \rightarrow \underset{[-V]}{X'*} \; V \; \underset{[-V]}{X'*}$$

The choice between (15) and (16) does not affect the central thesis of this chapter. However, I shall present data that lend support to the view that (15) is the better solution. First, we note the following facts about Malayalam:

(17)

a.   Noun modifiers always precede the noun.

b.   Complementizers occur at the end of the clause.

c.   Auxiliaries always follow the main verb.

d.   P follows N'; in other words, Malayalam is a postpositional language.

If we assume that (i) Malayalam is a verb-final language, (ii) V is the head of a clause, and (iii) COMP is the head of S, we can state the facts in (17) as a single generalization:

(18)

In all structures, the head occurs at the end.

In order to account for the facts in (17), we shall formulate the following set of PS rules for Malayalam:

(19)

a. S′ → S COMP

b. S   → X′* V
        [−V]

c. N′ → $\begin{Bmatrix} \text{(POSS) (DEM) (QUANT) A′* N} \\ \text{S′ N′} \end{Bmatrix}$

d. P′ → N′ P

In addition to capturing the generalization in (18), rule (19b) also ties in neatly with the following facts. First, verbs behave differently from the other constituents of S when not final. Thus, while the semantic and phonological consequences of switching the subject and object or direct and indirect objects are often hardly noticeable, putting the verb in a nonfinal position tends to (i) place a heavy nuclear pitch accent on the verb, wiping out all the word melodies that occur after the nuclear accent, and (ii) lengthen the final vowel of the verb. Second, nonfinal verbs have heavy contrastive meanings not necessarily associated with the shifting of other constituents. In short, nonfinal verbs are clearly in marked positions.

The rule of *Verb Scrambling* can be formulated as an operation on the PS rule that expands S. Since X′* = X′* X′*, the operation X′* X′* V ⇒ X′* V X′* derives rule (20) from (19b).

(20)

S → X′* V X′*
      [−V]   [−V]

By formulating Verb Scrambling as an operation on PS rule (19b), we explain why the verb can be scrambled only with respect to its sisters in S: all symbols to the right of → are dominated by the symbol to the left, and hence are sisters.

Yet another phenomenon that supports our decision to treat Malayalam as a verb-final language is the existence of certain kinds of embedded clauses in which the verb cannot be scrambled away from the final position. These typically involve complementizer affixes which are morphologically suffixed to the verb. Compare, for example, the behavior of the complementizer suffix *-aal* 'if' with the complementizer word *eŋgil* 'if':

(21)

a.   ₛ′[kuṭṭi   aanaye   nuḷḷiyaal] amma kaṟayum.
        child-nom elephant-acc pinched-if mother cry-will
        'If the child pinches the elephant, mother will cry.'

b.   *ₛ′[kuṭṭi nuḷḷi aanaye -aal] amma kaṟayum.

c.   *ₛ′[kuṭṭi nuḷḷiyaal aanaye] amma kaṟayum.

(22)

a.   ₛ′[kuṭṭi   aanaye   nuḷḷi   eŋgil] amma kaṟayum.
        child-nom elephant-acc pinch-past if   mother cry-will
        'If the child pinches the elephant, mother will cry.'

b.   ₛ′[kuṭṭi nuḷḷi aanaye eŋgil] amma kaṟayum.

c.   *ₛ′[kuṭṭi nuḷḷi eŋgil aanaye] amma kaṟayum.

   I can think of two ways of accounting for this phenomenon. The first
is to say that (21a) and (22a) have the following structures:

(23)

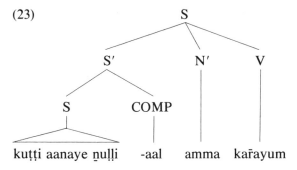

(24)

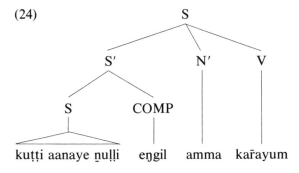

Since -aal is a suffix, it would necessarily be attached to the verb. If the
verb is scrambled away from the final position, the suffix will remain
unattached, which would account for the ungrammaticality of (21b).

However, the complementizer in (22b) is not a suffix, so that Verb Scrambling is possible there. Both (21c) and (22c) are ungrammatical for the same reason, namely, that none of our rules allows clause-internal *-aal* or *eŋgil*.

This solution requires the adjunction of an affix to follow the generation of scrambled structures. It is therefore incompatible with the lexicalist theory, which does not allow processes of word formation (inflectional or derivational) to apply in syntax (cf. chapter 1 of this volume and Lieber 1980). An alternative solution would be to derive V + *-aal* prior to lexical insertion, and formulate the scrambling rule to apply to V and not to V + *-aal*. Lexical insertion could then place V + *-aal* only in the S-final position, while simple Vs would be allowed S-internally as well. Unlike the previous one, this solution is compatible with the lexicalist hypothesis that affixation is the product of lexical word-formation rules.

Theoretical consistency constrains us to select the former rule, (19b), which allows the lexicalist solution to verb-final clauses.

The [X′ V]$_{V'}$ Construction   There exists a small class of verbs in Malayalam such as *aa* 'be', *uḷ* 'have', *waṟ* 'come', *cey* 'do', which combine with NPs, PPs, etc., to form verbal structures. One of their characteristic properties is that they cannot be moved away from the constituent to which they are attached. I shall illustrate the behavior of these verbs using the verb 'be':

(25)

a.   kaẓuṭa   oṟə mrəgam   aaṇə.
      donkey-nom one animal-nom is
      'The donkey is an animal.'

b.   oṟə mrəgam aaṇə kaẓuṭa.   (= (25a))

c.   *aaṇə kaẓuṭa oṟə mrəgam.

d.   *aaṇə oṟə mrəgam kaẓuṭa.

e.   *kaẓuṭa aaṇə oṟə mrəgam.

f.   *oṟə mrəgam kaẓuṭa aaṇə.

Notice that in copula constructions, we have only two options, rather than six, which suggests that they involve only two constituents under the S node. One way of accounting for this behavior of 'be' is to say that, unlike regular verbs, 'be' is not a constituent of S, but rather a form that creates a verb by attaching itself to some other constituent such as N′, P′, S′, etc. Under this analysis, the structure of (25a) would be as follows:

(26)

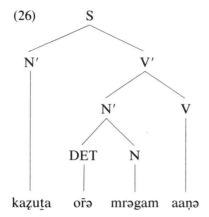

kaẓuṭa   oͬə   mrəgam   aaṇə

Two more examples of this construction are given in (27) and (28):

(27)

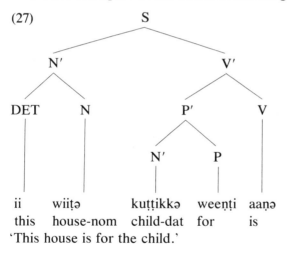

ii   wiiṭə   kuṭṭikkə   weeṇṭi   aaṇə
this   house-nom   child-dat   for   is
'This house is for the child.'

(28)

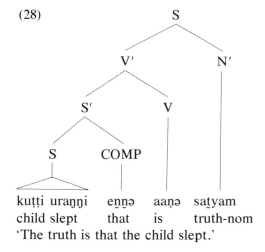

kuṭṭi uraṇṇi enṇǝ aaṇǝ saṭyam
child slept   that   is   truth-nom
'The truth is that the child slept.'

In all these cases, scrambling within the matrix is restricted to permutation between the sister constituents X' and V'.

We shall supplement (19a–d) with the following rules, in order to account for constructions like (26)–(28).

(29)

a.   S   → X'* V'   (= (19b))
         [–V]

b.   V' → (X') V

We must also be able to account for the optionality of the copula in the present tense. Thus, (30a–c) are alternate versions of (26)–(28).

(30)

a.   kaẓuṭa oṝǝ mrǝgam.
     donkey one animal
     'The donkey is an animal.'

b.   ii wiiṭǝ kuṭṭikkǝ weeṇṭi.
     this house child-dat for
     'This house is for the child.'

c.   saṭyam kuṭṭi uraṇṇi enṇǝ.
     truth child slept that
     'The truth is that the child slept.'

Following the notation of chapter 4 of this volume, we shall incorporate the optionality of the copula into the PS rule as follows:

(31)
V′ → (X′)   (V)
        (↑COPULA)=+
        (↑TENSE)=PRES

The notation (α) is to be interpreted as 'α, otherwise γ'. Thus, rule (31)
        γ
says, "Choose a verb; if not, include the features [+copula] and present tense." This notation encodes the fact that sentences without
verbs are interpreted as having the meaning of present tense copula
constructions.

As stated earlier, there are other verbs that can occur in the structure
[X′ V]$_{V′}$. A few examples are given below:

(32)
cey 'do'
a. kuṭṭi nrəṭṭam   ceyṭu.
    child dance-nom did
    'The child danced.'

b. kuṭṭi ammaye   šalyam   ceyṭu.
    child mother-acc annoyance-nom did
    'The child annoyed the mother.'

(33)
war̃ 'come'
a. kuṭṭikkə ṭalaweeḍana wannu.
    child-dat headache   came
    'The child got a headache.'

(34)
uḷ 'have'
a. kuṭṭikkə muunnə ṭala unṭə.
    child   three   head have
    'The child has three heads.'

The principles responsible for blocking undesirable verbs from entering
into the [X′ V]$_{V′}$ structure will be dealt with in section 8.3. At this
point, I shall simply give, by way of illustration, the structure of (32b).

(35)

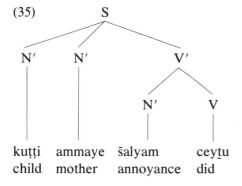

kuṭṭi	ammaye	šalyam	ceytu
child	mother	annoyance	did

The [V′ V]$_{V''}$ Construction   The strategy implicit in our treatment of the [X′ V] construction was to treat those elements which cannot be scrambled away from each other as belonging to the same constituent, thus keeping the generalization that only the immediate constituents of S are order-free. We shall now go on to examine the kind of scrambling restrictions exhibited by verbs like *kaṇakkaakk* 'consider', *teraññeṭukk* 'select', etc. Consider (36):

(36)

1	2	3

raajaawə	kuṭṭiye	kaḷḷan	aayi	kaṇakkaakkunnu
king-nom	child-acc	thief-nom	was	consider-pres

'The king considers the child to be a thief.'

What is interesting about this construction is that the elements marked 1, 2, and 3 can be scrambled with respect to each other, but the order of the words within 3 is absolutely rigid.

(37)

a. kuṭṭiye raajaawə *kaḷḷan aayi kaṇakkaakkunnu.*
b. *kaḷḷan aayi kaṇakkaakkunnu* raajaawə kuṭṭiye.
c. kuṭṭiye *kaḷḷan aayi kaṇakkaakkunnu* raajaawə.

(38)

a. *kaṇakkaakkunnu* raajaawə kuṭṭiye *kaḷḷan aayi.*
b. *raajaawə kaṇakkaakkunnu* kuṭṭiye *kaḷḷan aayi.*
c. *kuṭṭiye kaṇakkaakkunnu kaḷḷan aayi* raajaawə.
d. *kaṇakkaakkunnu* kuṭṭiye *kaḷḷan aayi* raajaawə.

(39)
a. *kaḷḷan aayi ṛaajaawə kuṭṭiye kaṇakkaakkunnu.
b. *ṛaajaawə kaḷḷan aayi kuṭṭiye kaṇakkaakkunnu.

The construction illustrated in (36) and (37) has a number of peculiar properties. First, the past tense form of 'be', aayi, must appear before the main verb. Further, the copula cannot be omitted as in (30). Finally, the construction cannot be nested, unlike the comparable construction in English. (I am grateful to Mark Liberman for pointing this out to me.)

(40)
The king considered the child to be elected to be the next leader.

As the first step toward a solution, notice that the $[X' \ V]_{V'}$ construction that we set up in the previous section is already present in the sentences above. In order to block (38) and (39), what we must do is to add one more level to V', and analyze (36), for example, as follows:

(41)

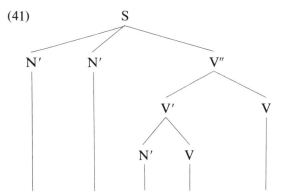

ṛaajaawə kuṭṭiye kaḷḷan aayi kaṇakkaakkunnu
king   child   thief   was   considers
'The king considers the child to be a thief.'

We shall therefore expand (29) further as follows:

(42)
a. $S \rightarrow X'^* \ V''$
         $_{[-V]}$

b. $V'' \rightarrow \left\{ \begin{array}{l} \begin{array}{ll} V' & V \\ (\downarrow TENSE) = PAST \\ (\downarrow COPULA) = + \end{array} \\ \\ V' \end{array} \right\}$ ....(i)[3]

....(ii)

c. $V' \rightarrow (X') \quad (V)$
$(\uparrow COPULA) = +$
$(\uparrow TENSE) = PRES$

One may make the following parenthetical remark about the V'' construction in Malayalam. Notice that the object of the matrix sentence in (36), *kuṭṭiye* 'child-acc', has no thematic role associated with the matrix verb *kaṇakkaakk* 'consider'; the interpretation of the sentence should be (43):

(43)
The king considers [the child is a thief].

The *consider* construction in English is faced with a similar problem:

(44)
The king considers $\begin{Bmatrix} \text{the child} \\ \text{him} \end{Bmatrix}$ to be a thief.

The difficulty is that *him* is in the accusative case and is disjoint in reference with *king*, which suggests that it is the object of the matrix sentence; yet in terms of thematic role assignment, it belongs to the lower clause. Two alternative solutions would be (a) to assume that *him* is the subject of the lower clause (which accounts for the thematic role assignment), and that it is exceptionally case-marked by the higher clause verb (which accounts for its accusative case and disjoint reference (cf. Chomsky 1979a,b)), or (b) to assume that *him* is the object of the higher clause (which would account for its case and disjoint reference), and that it is in a position for a grammatical relation that receives its thematic role from the lower verb (cf. chapter 5 of this volume). The same discrepancy between grammatical relations and thematic role appears in the Malayalam example, but unlike the English case, there is only one solution open to us, namely, to assume that *kuṭṭiye* 'child-acc' belongs to the matrix. If we assumed that it is the subject of the verb 'be', we would have no way of accounting for the scrambling freedom of *kuṭṭiye*. This conclusion is, in fact, reinforced by the restrictions on clefting, which will be discussed shortly.

What the Malayalam example shows, then, is the legitimacy of postulating grammatical relations that do not have thematic role assignments in the same clause nucleus, which shows, indirectly, the legitimacy of treating *him* as the object of *consider* in (44).

Predicative Adjectives   Since the treatment of "predicative adjectives" is important for the analysis of clefts in the next section, it is necessary to make an addition to our PS rules to explain the behavior of adjectives. With the exception of a few adjectives like *ciitta* 'bad' and *pacca* 'green', as opposed to *nalla* 'good', adjectives in Malayalam cannot occur as "predicate" adjectives, that is, in X' V structures. Thus, even though *nalla* 'good' occurs in the prenominal position, as in (45), (46) is ungrammatical:

(45)
nalla kuṭṭi
good child

(46)
*kuṭṭi nalla aaṇə.
 child good is

The strategy that Malayalam uses to express the kinds of meanings involved in (46) is to attach a pronoun to the adjective and convert it into a nominal:

(47)
kuṭṭi nallawan aaṇə.
child good-he is
'The child is a good one.'

(48) illustrates the same phenomenon:

(48)
a.   paẓaya pusṭakam
      old   book

b.   *pusṭakam paẓaya aaṇə.
      book   old   is

c.   pusṭakam paẓayatə aaṇə.
      book   old-it   is
      'The book is old.'

We shall assume that (48c) has the following structure:

(49)

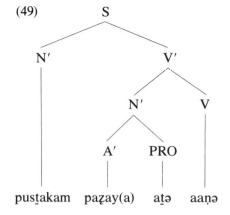

pustakam   paẓay(a)   atə   aaṇə

Additional examples of this structure are given below:

(50)

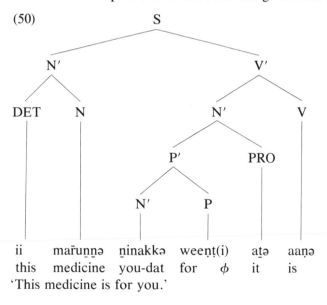

ii	maṟunnə	ninakkə	weeṇṭ(i)	φ	atə	aaṇə
this	medicine	you-dat	for		it	is

'This medicine is for you.'

(51)

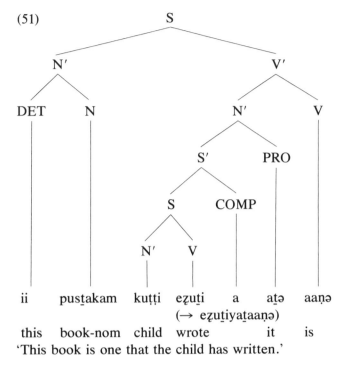

ii	pustakam	kuṭṭi	eẓuti	a	atə	aaṇə
			(→ eẓuṭiyataaṇə)			
this	book-nom	child	wrote		it	is

'This book is one that the child has written.'

The atə constructions extend to verbs as well:

(52)
pustakam cumaṇṇatə aaṇə.
book   reddened-it is
'The book is red.'

(53)

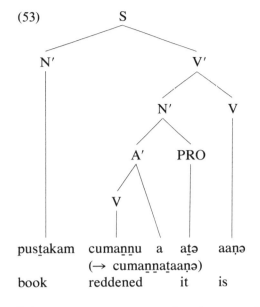

pustakam   cumaṇṇu   a   atə   aaṇə
              (→ cumaṇṇataaṇə)
book   reddened   it   is

It is necessary to assume that these are [X′ PRO] constructions rather than [X′ N′], since [A′ N′] is impossible. In order to account for them, we would need the following rules:[4]

(54)
a.   N′ → X′ PRO
b.   A′ → V -*a*

We can now list all the PS rules we have set up in this section:

(55)
a.   S′ → S COMP

b.   S → X′* V″
      [−V]

c.   V″ → $\begin{cases} \text{V′} \qquad\qquad \text{V} & ....(i) \\ (\downarrow\text{TENSE})=\text{PAST} \\ (\downarrow\text{COPULA})=+ \\ \text{V′} & ....(ii) \end{cases}$

d.   V′ → (X′)   (V)
                (↑COPULA)=+
                (↑TENSE)=PRES

e. $N' \rightarrow \begin{cases} \text{(POSS) (DEM) (QUANT) A'* N} & ....\text{(i)} \\ S' \ N' \\ X' \ \text{PRO} & ....\text{(ii)} \end{cases}$

f. $P' \rightarrow N' P$

Arguments against VP

Preliminary Arguments   Instead of using flat clause structures, we could conceivably set up a VP node in Malayalam and account for the freedom of word order with a stylistic scrambling rule of the kind proposed in Chomsky and Lasnik 1977. Thus, instead of having structures like (56), we could as well imagine structures like (57):

(56)

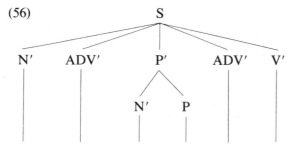

kuṭṭi iṇṇale   skuuḷileekkə ṭaniye pooyi
child yesterday school-to   alone   went
'The child went to school alone yesterday.'

(57)

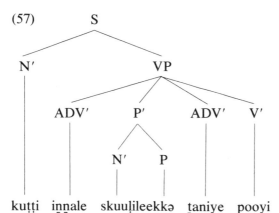

kuṭṭi iṇṇale skuuḷileekkə ṭaniye pooyi

Why is it better to assume the flat structure hypothesis rather than a VP node? First, as far as I know, there are no rules or distributional regularities in Malayalam that require a VP node. In the absence of positive evidence for a VP node, (57) would be an unmotivated artifact. Second, the existence of a VP node would unnecessarily complicate the word order phenomena, obscuring the generalization that it is only the sister constituents directly dominated by S that are order-free. I shall leave this statement for the reader to verify. Third, a VP node in Malayalam grammar would require us to postulate stylistic scrambling rules in order to arrive at surface word order. The organization of grammar assumed in Chomsky and Lasnik 1977 and Chomsky 1980 requires that stylistic rules and rules of logical form be mutually independent. However, in Malayalam, surface word order—the output of scrambling—would be the input to rules of logical form such as those involving pronominal noncoreference and quantifier scope. Therefore, if stylistic scrambling rules are of the kind proposed by Chomsky and Lasnik, they cannot determine surface word order in Malayalam, which argues for the base generation of these structures without a VP node.

The noncoreference rule for Malayalam can be stated as follows:

(58)
If NP_1 precedes NP_2, and NP_1 is a pronoun while NP_2 is not, then NP_1 and NP_2 are noncoreferential.

Consider the effects of scrambling on noncoreference:

(59)
a. $joon_i$ $awante_i$ bhaaīyaye ṇuḷḷi.
    John-nom his   wife-acc   pinched
    'John pinched his wife.'

b. *$awante_i$ bhaaīyaye $joon_i$ ṇuḷḷi.

As shown by (59), the rule of noncoreference operates upon the surface word order. That quantifier scope also is dependent on surface word order is illustrated by the following examples:

(60)
a. ellaawaīum   cilaīe   ṇuḷḷi.
    everyone-nom some-acc pinched
    'For all x, there is some y such that x pinched y.'

b. cilaīe ellaawaīum ṇuḷḷi.
    some everyone   pinched
    'There is some y such that for all x, x pinched y.'

(61)

a. amma   ellaa kuṭṭikaḷkkum cila   puṣṭakam koṭuṭṭu.
    mother all   children-dat some book   gave
    'For all children x, there is some y such that mother gave y to x.'

b. amma   cila   puṣṭakam ellaa kuṭṭikaḷkkum koṭuṭṭu.
    mother some book   all   children-dat gave
    'There is some y such that for all children x, mother gave y to x.'

(62)

a. ellaawaṙum cilaṙe patti   aaloociccu.
    everyone   some about thought
    'For all x, there is some y such that x thought about y.'

b. cilaṙe patti   ellaawaṙum aaloociccu.
    some about everyone   thought
    'There is some y such that for all x, x thought about y.'

The principle governing the interpretation of *ellaa* 'all' and *cila* 'some' is: the preceding quantifier has the wider scope. It is clear that the orders subject/direct object and direct object/subject (as in (60)), subject/direct object/indirect object and subject/indirect object/direct object (as in (61)), etc., are relevant for quantifier interpretation, as they are for pronominal noncoreference.

Thus, if stylistic scrambling rules do not affect the rules of logical form, then the phenomenon of free word order in Malayalam cannot be handled in terms of scrambling. The only other alternative is to assume that free word order is the result of a movement rule (Chomsky 1980). However, one of the restrictive properties of movement rules is that they are structure-preserving. Notice that the free word order phenomenon in Malayalam involves the permutation of NPs, PPs, S, and ADVPs. Furthermore, there is no particular position such as "topic" outside of S to which these various elements can move. Therefore, even within the framework of the revised extended standard theory (REST), free word order in Malayalam must be built into the PS rules.[5]

Clefts   Clefts offer the strongest support to the flat structure hypothesis. To begin with, we observe that only order-free constituents can be clefted. Within our framework, this simply means that only the immediate constituents of S can be clefted. As we shall see, however, even such a statement is unnecessary in this theory, since clefting will be shown to require no additional rule or restriction, being already described by PS rule (55b). If we use the VP hypothesis, on the other hand, we will not only have to set up ad hoc restrictions on clefting, but also have to face the fact that these restrictions are identical to those on scrambling.

Clefted sentences in Malayalam are formed by attaching *aṭə* 'it' to the verb and a form of *aa* 'be' to the clefted constituent, which has to be a direct constituent of the S node. Thus, the subject cleft of (63a) is (63b).

(63)

a.   kuṭṭi uraŋŋi.
      child slept

b.   kuṭṭiyaaṇə uraŋŋiyatə.
      child-is   slept-it
      'It was the child who slept.'

Some of the clefted sentences corresponding to (64) are given in (65):

(64)

kuṭṭi   innale   ammakkə aanaye   koṭuttu.
child-nom yesterday mother-dat elephant-acc gave
'The child gave an elephant to the mother yesterday.'

(65)

a.   kuṭṭiyaaṇə innale ammakkə aanaye koṭuttatə.
      child-is   gave-it
      'It was the child who gave an elephant to the mother yesterday.'

b.   kuṭṭi innaleyaaṇə ammakkə aanaye koṭuttatə.
           yesterday-is
      'It was yesterday that the child gave an elephant to the mother.'

c.   kuṭṭi innale ammakkaaṇə aanaye koṭuttatə.
                 mother-is
      'It was to the mother that the child gave an elephant yesterday.'

d.   kuṭṭi innale ammakkə aanayeyaaṇə koṭuttatə.
                              elephant-is
      'It was an elephant that the child gave to the mother yesterday.'

The clefting of the verb requires the use of *cey* 'do'. *aṭə* is attached to the verb after changing it into the infinitival form. The verb cleft for (64) is given below:

(66)

kuṭṭi iṇṇale ammakkə aanaye koṭukkukayaaṇə ceyṭaṭə.
                                      give(inf)-is   did-it

I shall assume the following structure for, say, (65b).

(67)

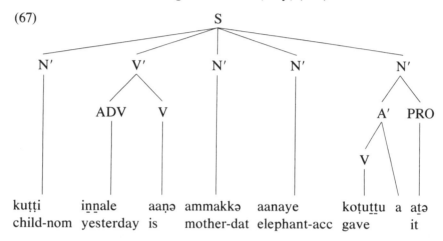

kuṭṭi   iṇṇale   aaṇə ammakkə   aanaye   koṭuttu a aṭə
child-nom yesterday is   mother-dat elephant-acc gave   it

As our analysis predicts, the relative order of the sister constituents
kuṭṭi, ammakkə, aanaye, and *koṭuttaṭə* in (67) is free, and the verb
iṇṇale aaṇə can be scrambled freely amongst them.

It must be pointed out that, unlike the English clefts, Malayalam
clefts do not involve a gap or a binding relation. Clefts and nonclefts are
identical except for the additional presence of *aaṇə* and *aṭə*. Now,
the PS rules we set up in (55) in order to account for independent
constructions are already capable of describing clefts as well. For example, (55d) (V′ → X′ V) will generate the structure of *iṇṇaleyaaṇə*
'yesterday-is', and (55e–ii) (N′ → X′ PRO) gives us *koṭuttaṭə* 'gave it'.

That independently motivated rules account for the entire clefting
phenomenon points to the correctness of this approach. As mentioned
earlier, it is only the immediate constituents of S that can be clefted,
which is precisely what our analysis predicts. As illustration, compare
the following grammatical and ungrammatical clefts:

(68)

a.   kuḷattil weccə jooninte kuṭṭi aanaye   ṇuḷḷi.
       pond   at   John's   child elephant pinched
       'John's child pinched the elephant at the pond.'

b. kuḷattil weccaaṇǝ jooṇinte kuṭṭi aanaye ṉuḷḷiyatǝ.
          at-is   pinched-it
    'It was at the pond that John's child pinched the elephant.'

c. *kuḷattil aaṇǝ weccǝ jooṇinte kuṭṭi aanaye ṉuḷḷiyatǝ.
    pond   is

Although the PP in (68b) can be clefted, the NP in (68c) cannot. As a comparison of the two structures will show, this contrast follows directly from our analysis:

(69)

a. (= (68b))

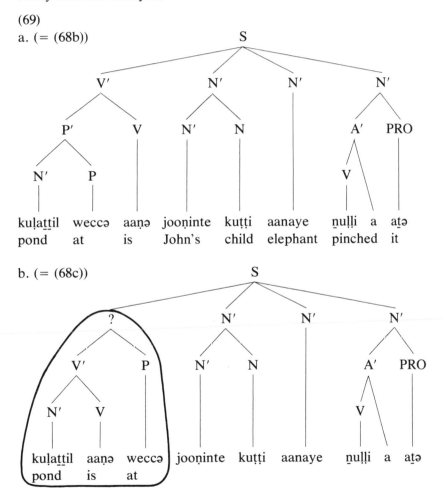

b. (= (68c))

There are two things wrong with (69b). First, it does not have a verb under S (which violates (55b)). Second, it has a postposition that is illegally attached to a verb (see the circled construction).

Consider now the following contrast:

(70)

a.   kuḷattil weccə jooṇinte kuṭṭiyaaṇə aanaye ṇuḷḷiyatə.
             John's   child-is
      'It was John's child that pinched the elephant at the pond.'

b.   *kuḷattil weccə jooṇinteyaaṇə kuṭṭi aanaye ṇuḷḷiyatə.
             John's-is   child

In (70a), the NP *John's child* is clefted; in (70b), it is impossible to cleft the possessive *John's*.

(70b) would have the following structure:

(71)

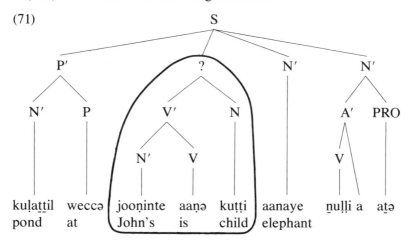

Once again, this structure is not allowed by our PS rules. Even though [POSS V] is a legitimate construction, there is no verb under the S node, which rules out (71).

Consider now the behavior of V″ constructions under clefting:

(72)

a.   ṛaajaawə kuṭṭiye kaḷḷan aayi kaṇakkaakki.
      king   child   thief   was considered
      'The king considered the child a thief.'

b.   ṛaajaawaaṇə kuṭṭiye kaḷḷan aayi kaṇakkaakkiyatə.
      king-is   considered-it
      'It was the king who considered the child a thief.'

c.   r̄aajaawə kuṭṭiyeyaaṇə kaḷḷan aayi kaṇakkaakkiyatə.
       child-is
   'It was the child that the king considered a thief.'

d.   r̄aajaawə kuṭṭiye kaḷḷan aayi kaṇakkaakkukayaaṇə ccytatə.
               thief   was   consider(inf)-is   did-it
   'What the king did was to consider the child a thief.'

No other clefts are possible for this sentence. Recall that on the basis of scrambling, we had set up the following structure for (72a):

(73)

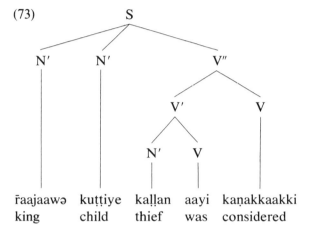

r̄aajaawə   kuṭṭiye   kaḷḷan   aayi   kaṇakkaakki
king   child   thief   was   considered

The fact that we can cleft only the three constituents directly dominated by S provides additional support for our analysis.

One of the characteristics that distinguish Malayalam clefts from English clefts is that they do not exhibit any of the long-distance movement properties. Unlike English clefting, Malayalam clefting is clause-bound. Thus, in English we can have (74a,b):

(74)
a.   The child said that the mother pinched the elephant.
b.   It was the elephant the child said the mother pinched.

A corresponding sentence is impossible in Malayalam.

(75)
a.   amma   aanaye   ṇuḷḷi   ennə kuṭṭi paraññu.
   mother elephant pinched that   child said

b.   *amma   aanayeyaaṇə ṇuḷḷi   ennə kuṭṭi paraññatə.
   mother elephant-is   pinched that   child said-it

To use the movement metaphor, what (75b) means is that clefting cannot extract items from embedded clauses. But in our analysis, clefts involve nothing that corresponds to extraction. The grammar correctly predicts the ungrammaticality of (75b).

(76)

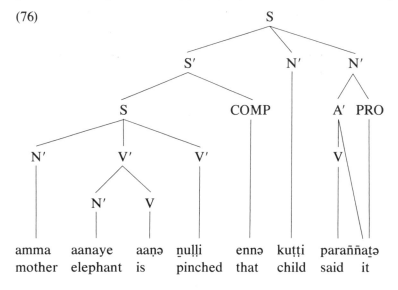

amma	aanaye	aanə	nuḷḷi	ennə	kuṭṭi	paraññatə
mother	elephant	is	pinched	that	child	said	it

The sentence is ungrammatical because the lower clause has two verbs and the higher has none.

Note that an entire clause can be clefted:

(77)
àmma   aanaye   nuḷḷi   ennə aanə kuṭṭi   paraññatə.
mother-nom elephant-acc pinched that is   child-nom said-it
'What the child said was that the mother pinched the elephant.'

It is also possible to have separate clefts in the matrix and the embedded clauses:

(78)
amma   aanayeyaanə nuḷḷiyatə ennə aanə kuṭṭi   paraññatə.
mother-nom elephant-acc-is pinched-it that is   child-nom said-it
'What the child said was that it was the mother who pinched the elephant.'

Note that the grammaticality of (77) is predicted by our X' V rule, which allows the S' in (77) to be attached to *aan* (V).

(79)

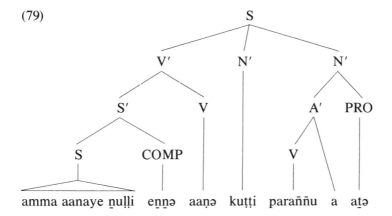

amma aanaye ṇuḷḷi enṇə aaṇə kuṭṭi paraññu a aṭə

If we accept the flat structure hypothesis, we can account for all these peculiarities of clefts by base-generating them in terms of rules that are necessary elsewhere in the language.

The facts that clefting in Malayalam does not leave a gap and that unbounded clefting is impossible show clearly that it does not involve a movement rule. Since questions, passives, relative clauses, etc., do not involve any overt movement, this is precisely what we would expect.

It must be mentioned that sentences like (80),

(80)
amma   mooṣṭiccu enṇə kuṭṭi paraññaṭə ii   puṣṭakam aaṇə.
mother stole   that child said-it   this book   is
'This is the book the child said the mother stole.'

which do involve long-distance binding, are not clefts but relative clauses. Thus, the structure of (80) is as follows:

(81)

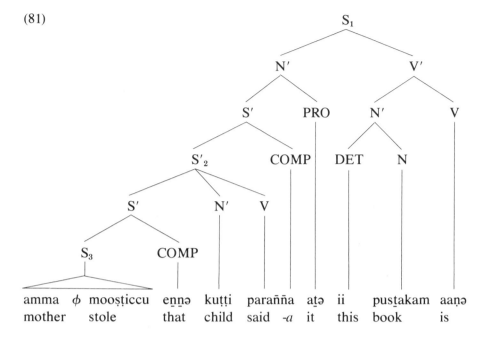

amma φ mooṣṭiccu enṇə kuṭṭi parañña aṭə ii pusṭakam aaṇə
mother   stole   that child said -a it this book   is

The V' *ii pusṭakam aaṇə*, for example, cannot be placed within S_3, where the gap is, contrary to what happens in clefts:

(82)

*[[amma ii   pusṭakam aaṇə mooṣṭiccu] enṇə] kuṭṭi parañ̃aṭə
  mother this book   is   stole   that child said- it

There are several other reasons why the structure in (81) should be distinguished from clefts, but I shall not go into the details, as they are not directly relevant to our concerns in this chapter.

8.3 Functional Structure

Having made a sketch of the PS rules that would generate the c-structures of Malayalam, we shall now turn our attention to how the c-structures can be mapped onto functional structures (f-structures). Note that rule (55) overgenerates. How do we block ungrammatical sentences like (83a–c), which our PS rules allow?

(83)

a. *kuṭṭi   aana   aṭiccu.
     child-nom elephant-nom beat

b. *kuṭṭi   aanaye   uraŋŋi.
   child-nom elephant-acc slept

c. *kuṭṭi   aanaye   acchane   ammaye   ṇuḷḷi.
   child-nom elephant-acc father-acc mother-acc pinched

Within the framework we are using, the answer is that these sentences are ungrammatical because they cannot receive any grammatical interpretation. That is, the word-formation component assigns cases to nouns and provides the syntactic component with nouns which already have case features. Interpretive rules assign nominal expressions to the argument positions of the verb by interpreting the case features. Thus, (83a–c) are ungrammatical because (83a) has an "uninterpreted" nominative, (83b) has an uninterpreted accusative, and (83c) has two uninterpreted accusatives.

In this section, I shall outline a mechanism that will take care of overgenerations such as (83a–c). Essentially, the strategy will involve mapping case features onto grammatical relations. We shall see in section 8.4 that this case–relation mapping, in addition to blocking ungrammatical strings, allows us to formulate generalizations for a number of syntactic processes in an insightful manner.

In order to show how the interpretive mechanism works, it is necessary to first give a brief account of the case system in Malayalam.

Case in Malayalam

The case inflections in Malayalam are illustrated in (84):

(84)

Case	Inflection	'he'	'tree'	'elephant'
Nominative	φ	awan	maṟam	aana
Accusative	-e	awan-e	maṟa-tt-in-e	aana-e
Dative 1	-ə	awan-ə	maṟa-tt-in-ə	aana-kk-ə
Dative 2	-ooṭə	awan-ooṭə	maṟa-tt-in-ooṭə	aana-ooṭə
Genitive	-ṭe/-uṭe	awan-te	maṟa-tt-in-te	aana-uṭe
Instrumental	-aal	awan-aal	maṟa-tt-in-aal	aana-aal
Locative	-il	awan-il	maṟa-tt-il	aana-il

Following Lieber 1980, I shall assume that case inflections (CI) are attached freely to nouns in the word-formation component. The relevant word-formation rule can be stated thus:

(85)

N → N (CI)

Now, case inflections will be listed in the lexicon, bearing equations, as follows:

(86)
a. -e: CI, (↑CASE) = ACC
b. -ə: CI, (↑CASE) = DAT1
c. -ootə: CI, (↑CASE) = DAT2
d. -uṭe: CI, (↑CASE) = GEN
e. -aal: CI, (↑CASE) = INSTR
f. -il: CI, (↑CASE) = LOC

Thus, the attachment of *case inflections* such as *-e, -uṭe,* etc., in word formation causes *case features* such as ACC, GEN, etc., to be assigned to the nouns. These features are automatically promoted upward to the category dominating the root, as a consequence of the notation implicit in (85):

(87)
N →   N   (CI)
      ↑=↓ ↑=↓

Recall that ↑=↓ says, in the formulation of chapter 2, that features of the mother are features of the ego. As a result of the same feature promotion process, the functional structure of the N′ illustrated in (88) will have the features PL and GEN.

(88)

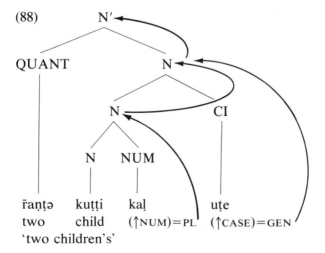

ranṭə   kuṭṭi   kaḷ   uṭe
two   child   (↑NUM)=PL   (↑CASE)=GEN
'two children's'

I shall assume that the equation ($\uparrow$CASE) = NOM is used whenever rule (85) is expanded without CI; that is, the feature NOM is assigned to nouns without case inflections. Rule (85) will therefore be revised as follows:

(89)

N → N   (CI)
$\qquad$ ($\uparrow$CASE)=NOM

(89) is to be interpreted using the notation (α) explained for rule (31).

γ

In this account of case inflections and case features, I have assumed that (a) case inflections are attached to nouns in word formation; (b) it is the attachment of inflections that assigns case to nouns; (c) case features of the noun percolate upward to NP (=N'); and (d) the feature "nominative" is assigned whenever no case inflection is attached to a noun. (For similar approaches to case within the lexicalist theory, see chapters 7 and 9 of this volume.)

As mentioned above, case features in Malayalam serve to indicate grammatical relations. Cases are also triggered by postpositions. A few examples of this use of case are given below:

(90)

a. kuṭṭi   aanaye   waṭi   koṇṭə aṭiccu.
   child-nom elephant-acc stick-nom with   beat
   'The child beat the elephant with the stick.'

b. kuṭṭi   aanayuṭe   kuuṭe skuuḷil   pooyi.
   child-nom elephant-gen with   school-loc went
   'The child went to school with the elephant.'

c. kuṭṭi   aanaye   patti aaloociccu.
   child-nom elephant-acc about thought
   'The child thought about the elephant.'

d. awan ṇaalaṇakkə weeṇṭi manuṣyane kollum.
   he   a coin-dat1 for   man-acc   will kill
   'He will kill a man for a quarter.'

e. kuṭṭi   kaṭayil   weccə aanaye   ṇuḷḷi.
   child-nom shop-loc at   elephant-acc pinched
   'The child pinched the elephant while at the shop.'

The postposition *patti* 'about' takes a noun inflected for accusative case (90c); *weeṇṭi* 'for' takes dative 1 (90d); *kuuṭe* 'with' takes genitive (90b) or dative 2; *konto* 'with' takes nominative (90a) or accusative. These case inflections are dictated by the idiosyncratic features of the post-position and have nothing to do with the general system for interpreting grammatical relations. To account for the case inducement of postpositions, we shall use equations such as the following:

(91)
a. patti: P, ($\uparrow$OBJ CASE) = ACC
b. weenṭi: P, ($\uparrow$OBJ CASE) = DAT
c. konṭə: P, ($\uparrow$OBJ CASE) = NOM
d. kuuṭe: P, ($\uparrow$OBJ CASE) = GEN

Mapping Case Features onto Grammatical Relations
First Approximation   Having outlined an approach to lexical case assignment, I shall now relate case features to grammatical relations.

As a first approximation, one may say that subjects are in the nominative case, direct objects are in the accusative case, and indirect objects are in the dative case (dative 1 or dative 2, depending upon the verb). The following sentences illustrate these statements:

(92)
a. kuṭṭi   aanaye   nuḷḷi.
    child-nom elephant-acc pinched
    'The child pinched the elephant.'

b. aana   ammakkə   kaaśə   koṭuttu.
    elephant-nom mother-dat1 money-nom gave
    'The elephant gave mother some money.'

c. amma   kuṭṭiyooṭə kaaśə   cooḍiccu.
    mother-nom child-dat2 money-nom asked
    'Mother asked the child for money.'

Verbs like *koṭukk* 'give', *praarṭhikk* 'pray', *wilkk* 'sell', etc., take dative 1 as indirect objects, and verbs like *paray* 'say', *cooḍikk* 'ask', etc., take dative 2 instead.

It is not always the case that nominative NPs are subjects, or that subjects are always nominative. The problem cases are nominative objects and dative subjects, discussed in the next two sections.

Nominative Objects   Notice that the direct object *kaaśə* 'money' in (92b) and (92c) is in the nominative case. This is because inanimate nouns in Malayalam take the nominative case when they are direct objects. Consider the following sentences:

(93)

a. puucca eliye   tinnu.
    cat-nom rat-acc ate
    'The cat ate the rat.'

b. *puucca eli   tinnu.
              rat-nom

(94)

a. *puucca rottiye   tinnu.
    cat   bread-acc ate

b. puucca rotti   tinnu.
    cat   bread-nom ate
    'The cat ate the bread.'

(95)

a. awal   awane kantu.
    she-nom he-acc saw
    'She saw him.'

b. *awal awan   kantu.
              he-nom

(96)

a. *awal   pustakattine kantu.
    she-nom book-acc   saw

b. awal pustakam kantu.
            book-nom
    'She saw the book.'

Similar "double" (or triple) nominatives are found in temporal adjuncts:

(97)

a. kutti   oru maasam   pustakam waayiccu.
    child-nom one month-nom book-nom read
    'The child read the book for a month.'

b. kutti   awasaanam kuppi   potticcu.
    child-nom end-nom   bottle-nom broke
    'The child broke the bottle in the end.'

The absence of the accusative inflection in these cases cannot be treated as an instance of the accusative case being realized as zero inflection (e.g., plural in the English *sheep*). Thus, inanimate nouns do take the accusative case with the accusative inflection when they appear with postpositions:

(98)

a.   puṭakaṭṭine patti
       book-acc   about
       'about the book'

b.   *puṭakam patti

Dative Subjects   There is a class of verbs in Malayalam that require the subject to be in the dative case. Consider the following examples:

(99)

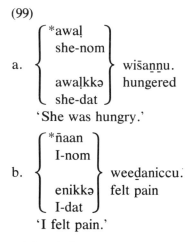

a.   { *awaḷ / she-nom / awaḷkkə / she-dat }   wiśannu. / hungered
       'She was hungry.'

b.   { *ñaan / I-nom / enikkə / I-dat }   weeḍaniccu. / felt pain
       'I felt pain.'

The dative subject is an idiosyncratic property of the verb. It cannot, for example, be correlated with thematic roles. Thus, the verbs *taḷaṟ* 'be tired' and *santooṣikk* 'be happy', which presumably have the same thematic roles as *wiśakk* 'be hungry' and *weeḍanikk* 'feel pain', take nominative and not dative subjects:

(100)

a.   { awaḷ / she-nom / *awaḷkkə / she-dat }   taḷarnnu. / was tired
       'She became tired.'

b. $\begin{Bmatrix} \tilde{\text{n}}\text{aan} \\ \text{I-nom} \\ \text{*cnikkə} \\ \text{I-dat} \end{Bmatrix}$ santoosiccu.
was happy

'I was happy.'

In contrast to the verb *santoosikk* 'be happy', the phrase *santoosam war* 'be happy' (an [X' V] construction, from *santoosam* 'happiness' and *war* 'come'), takes a dative subject:

(101)

$\begin{Bmatrix} \text{*}\tilde{\text{n}}\text{aan} \\ \text{I-nom} \\ \text{enikkə} \\ \text{I-dat} \end{Bmatrix}$ santoosam wannu.
happiness came

'I was happy.'

There are also modal suffixes like *-anam* and *-aam* which impose the same restriction on the subject, depending on the meaning of the modal. Thus, *-aam* in the sense of 'permission' demands that the subject be in the dative, as opposed to *-aam* in the sense of 'promise', which takes a nominative subject:

(102)

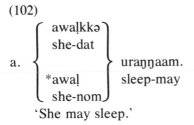

a. $\begin{Bmatrix} \text{awalkkə} \\ \text{she-dat} \\ \text{*awal} \\ \text{she-nom} \end{Bmatrix}$ uraŋŋaam.
sleep-may

'She may sleep.'

b. enikkə uraŋŋaam.
I-dat sleep
'I have permission to sleep.'

c. ñaan uraŋŋaam.
I-nom sleep
'I promise to sleep.'

-anam takes the nominative case if it is speaker-oriented (= logocentric) or epistemic, and the dative case if it is subject-oriented.[6]

(103)

a. kuṭṭi aanaye   ṇuḷḷaṇam.
    child elephant-acc pinch
    'The child must pinch the elephant.'
    (= 'I insist that the child . . .' or 'It is necessary . . .')

b. kuṭṭikkə aanaye   ṇuḷḷaṇam.
    child-dat elephant-acc pinch
    'The child wants to pinch the elephant.'

To account for the exceptional behavior of these verbs and modals, I shall use the following kind of lexical entry:

(104)

a. wišakk: ($\uparrow$SUBJ CASE) = DAT
b. -aam (permission): ($\uparrow$SUBJ CASE) = DAT

Principles of Case Interpretation   The principles of interpreting NPs as subjects, objects, etc., can be given as follows:

(105)

Principles of Case Interpretation

a. Interpret accusative case as the direct object (OBJ).
b. Interpret dative 2 case as the indirect object (OBJ2).
c. Interpret dative 1 case as either the indirect object (OBJ2) or the subject (SUBJ).
d. Interpret nominative case as either the subject (SUBJ) or the direct object (OBJ) if the NP is [−animate]; otherwise, interpret nominative case as the subject (SUBJ).

The principles in (105) can be formally encoded in this framework in terms of sets of functional equations, as follows:

(106)

a. ($\uparrow$OBJ)   = $\downarrow$
    ($\downarrow$CASE) = ACC
    ($\downarrow$ANIM) = +
b. ($\uparrow$OBJ2) = $\downarrow$
    ($\downarrow$CASE) = DAT2
c. ($\uparrow$OBJ2) = $\downarrow$
    ($\downarrow$CASE) = DAT1
d. ($\uparrow$SUBJ) = $\downarrow$
    ($\downarrow$CASE) = DAT1

e. $(\uparrow \text{OBJ}) \quad = \downarrow$
   $(\downarrow \text{CASE}) = \text{NOM}$
   $(\downarrow \text{ANIM}) = -$
f. $(\uparrow \text{SUBJ}) \quad = \downarrow$
   $(\downarrow \text{CASE}) = \text{NOM}$

If we adopt the featural analysis of case proposed by Jakobson 1971 (see chapter 6), these equations can be further abbreviated. Assuming that DAT1 and DAT2 in Malayalam are featurally equivalent to DAT and LOC1 in Russian, we would have NOM $= [- - -]$, ACC $= [- - +]$, DAT1 $= [+ - +]$, and DAT2 $= [+ + +]$. As a result of this analysis, certain sets of cases can be represented by the same feature matrix, for $\alpha = +$ or $-$. Thus $\{\text{DAT1}, \text{DAT2}\} = [+ \alpha +]$, $\{\text{DAT1}, \text{NOM}\} = [\alpha - \alpha]$, and $\{\text{ACC}, \text{NOM}\} = [- - \alpha]$. The six sets of equations in (106) then reduce to the three sets in (107), where α has the same values $+$ or $-$ in each set.

(107)
a. $(\uparrow \text{SUBJ}) \quad = \downarrow$
   $(\downarrow \text{CASE}) = [\alpha - \alpha]$
b. $(\uparrow \text{OBJ}) \quad = \downarrow$
   $(\downarrow \text{CASE}) = [- - \alpha]$
   $(\downarrow \text{ANIM}) = \alpha$
c. $(\uparrow \text{OBJ2}) \quad = \downarrow$
   $(\downarrow \text{CASE}) = [+ \alpha +]$

Any of these sets can be assigned to any of the X′ constituents dominated by S. The appropriateness of case features will be ensured by the principles governing functional structure (to be discussed below). Oblique functions such as the instrumental can be identified by a further equation discussed later in the section on causativization in transitives.

Some explanation is in order at this point. The crucial assumption behind my approach to the problem of case in Malayalam is that case is assigned to a noun as part of inflectional morphology in the word-formation component, and that this inflectional case must match the grammatical case assigned by functional rules such as those in (104) and (107). A functional equation such as $(\uparrow \text{SUBJ CASE}) = \text{DAT1}$ guarantees that the subject's case cannot be anything other than DAT, for if the subject's head noun bears any other inflectional case than DAT, the promotion of this feature will result in a clash of case values and an ill-formed functional structure.

One of the advantages of this approach is that it allows grammatical relations to be associated with no inflectional case at all. Thus, in Malayalam, constituents bearing nuclear grammatical relations (i.e., subjects, objects, and indirect objects) can freely be absent, as in the following sentences:

(108)

a. wišakkuṇṇu.
   hungers
   '*I* am hungry.'

b. kuṭṭi ewiṭe? wiiṭṭil   pooyi.
   child where home-loc went
   'Where is the child? *He* (*the child*) went home.'

c. roṭṭi ewiṭe? kuṭṭi ṭiṇṇu.
   bread where child ate
   'Where is the bread? The child ate *it* (*the bread*).'

When an optional constituent bearing a nuclear grammatical relation G is omitted from the c-structure but required by a lexical form, the grammatical relation G is interpreted as an anaphor. (This interpretation can be provided by the equation ($\uparrow$G PRED) = PRO. In this case, the functional structure contains a grammatical relation which corresponds to no structural constituent. Although this functional grammatical relation lacks inflectional case, it is compatible with the equation ($\uparrow$SUBJ CASE) = DAT. It would not be compatible with the constraint equation ($\uparrow$SUBJ CASE) $=_c$ DAT; see chapter 4.

Another advantage of this approach is that it allows nonnominals to have no case at all. Consider, for example, the sentential objects in (109):

(109)

amma   [kuṭṭi   uraṇṇi ennə] paraññu.
mother-nom child-nom slept   that   said
'Mother said that the child slept.'

The embedded sentence *kuṭṭi uraṇṇi ennə* has no inflectional case, which is allowed by the equations in (107), because they block only constituents that are wrongly case-marked, not constituents that have no case marking. Had the equations in (107) been constraint equations, on the other hand, they would have incorrectly required case on sentential objects.

The grouped equations in (106) derive functional structures from categorial structures. In order to explain how the equations work, it is necessary to refer to the well-formedness conditions governing functional structures, namely, completeness, coherence, consistency, and functional uniqueness. (For a statement of these principles, see chapter 4 of this volume.)

I shall assume, following chapters 1 and 3, that the lexical entries of verbs specify (i) the thematic roles they express, and (ii) the grammatical relations that express them. A few sample entries are given below:

(110)

a. uraŋŋ: V,   PRED = 'SLEEP ((SUBJ))'
                                experiencer

b. ṭinn: V,   PRED = 'EAT((SUBJ), (OBJ))'
                                agent patient

c. wilkk: V,   PRED = 'SELL((SUBJ), (OBJ),(OBJ2))'
                                agent theme goal

d. wiśakk: V,   PRED = 'BE HUNGRY ((SUBJ))'
                                experiencer
                                ($\uparrow$SUBJ CASE) = DAT

e. kiṭṭ: V,   PRED = 'RECEIVE ((SUBJ), (OBJ))'
                                recipient theme
                                ($\uparrow$SUBJ CASE) = DAT

f. -aam: MODAL, 'PROMISE'

g. -aam: MODAL, 'PERMISSION'
                    ($\uparrow$SUBJ CASE) = DAT

Consider the following sentences:

(111)

a. kuṭṭi   ammaye   ṉuḷḷi.
   child-nom mother-acc pinched
   'The child pinched the mother.'

b. *kuṭṭi ammaye ooṭi.
   child mother   ran
   *'The child ran the mother.'

As stated earlier, the grouped equations in (106) can be attached freely to any of the X' constituents dominated by S. If we chose to attach

(106f) to the first N' and (106a) to the second N' in (111a), we would have the following result:

(112)

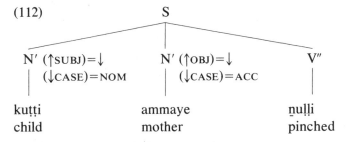

The lexical entry for *nuḷḷi* specifies that it has a subject argument and a direct object argument. Similarly, *kuṭṭi* and *ammaye* have the following equations attached to them:

(113)
a. kuṭṭi: (↑CASE) = NOM
b. ammaye: (↑CASE) = ACC

All this information is relevant for the derivation of the functional structure. For the purposes of exposition, I shall represent the information as follows:

(114)

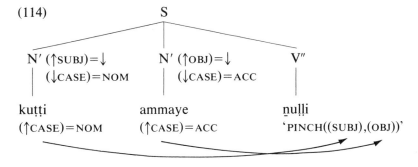

Thus, we have the following well-formed functional structure for (111a).

(115)

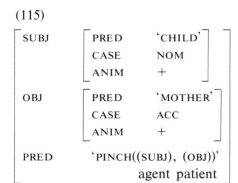

If, on the other hand, we choose to attach equation (106a) to the first and the second N's of (111a), the functional structure (116) results:

(116)

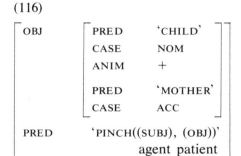

(116) is incomplete because the subject slot of 'pinch' does not have a corresponding argument. In addition, the case equation in (106a), ($\downarrow$CASE) = ACC, is also violated by the nominative case of the lexical entry for 'child'. The reader can verify that choosing other alternatives to (115) would result in similar ill-formed functional structures.

For a sentence to be grammatical, there should be at least one well-formed functional structure associated with it. (111b) is ungrammatical because it cannot be associated with any well-formed f-structures. *Ammaye* 'mother-acc' satisfies the equations in (106) only if it is interpreted as a direct object, but the verb has no object slot. F-structure (117) thus violates the principle of coherence, and is ruled out as ill-formed.

(117)

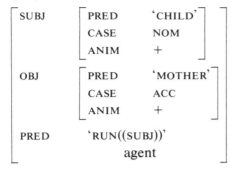

Consider now the following sentences:

(118)

a. kuṭṭikkə wiśannu.
    child-dat hungered
    'The child was hungry.'

b. *kuṭṭi   wiśannu.
    child-nom hungered

(118a) can be interpreted by attaching the paired equations in (106d) to the N', namely, (↑SUBJ) = ↓, (↓CASE) = DAT1, thereby deriving a well-formed f-structure. Intuitively, (118b) is ungrammatical because *wiśannu* demands that its subject be in the dative case, while *kuṭṭi* is nominative. More formally, if we chose (106f), we would get (119):

(119)

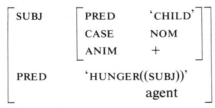

(119) violates the case equation attached to the verb *wiśakk,* namely, (↑SUBJ CASE) = DAT; thus, since no well-formed f-structure can be found for (118b), the grammar rejects it.

The opposite result is found in (120):

(120)

a.   kuṭṭi   uraṇṇi.
      child-nom slept
      'The child slept.'

b.   *kuṭṭikkə uraṇṇi.
      child-dat

I shall leave it for the reader to verify that (120a) has a well-formed f-structure.

How can we block sentences like (120b)? What is intuitively obvious is that *uraṇṇi* takes a nominative subject and *kuṭṭikkə* is in the dative case. Note that the equations in (106d) allow a dative N' to be interpreted as a subject, and there is nothing in the lexical specifications of *uraṇṇi* that tells us that it cannot have a dative subject. But verbs in Malayalam are strictly divided into two mutually exclusive classes: the marked class with dative subjects, and the unmarked class with nominative subjects. Thus, for the unmarked class, the case value of the subject is lexically predictable. Given that the unmarked class does not take dative subjects, N' in (120b) cannot be interpreted as the subject, thereby denying the sentence a well-formed f-structure.

Consider now the following sentences:

(121)

a.   kuṭṭi   coorə   ṭinnu.
      child-nom rice-nom ate
      'The child ate the rice.'

b.   kallə   kuppi   poṭṭiccu.
      stone-nom bottle-nom broke
      'The stone broke the bottle.' *or* 'The bottle broke the stone.'

Ignoring the technical details of f-structures for smoother exposition, we may note that we are allowed to interpret *coorə* 'rice' in (121a) as either the subject or the direct object of the sentence (by (106f) and (106e), respectively). However, since *kuṭṭi* 'child' can be interpreted only as the subject (by (106f), not (106e)), choosing *coorə* as subject would result in an ill-formed f-structure that is both incomplete and incoherent. Therefore, the only possible interpretation for (121a) has *kuṭṭi* as the subject and *coorə* as the object. On the other hand, both *kallə* 'stone-nom' and *kuppi* 'bottle-nom' in (121b) can be interpreted as either the subject or the object of the sentence (by (106e,f)). We can therefore assign (121b) to two distinct f-structures. The sentence, as a result, is ambiguous.

The following sentences illustrate another instance of ambiguity:

(122)

a. kuṭṭikkə aanaye   ṭinnaṇam.
child-dat elephant-acc eat-*aṇam*
'The child wants to eat the elephant.'

b. kuṭṭi   kaarə   ammakkə   wittu.
child-nom car-nom mother-dat sold
'The child sold the car to the mother.'

c. kuṭṭikkə kaarə   ammakkə   wilkkaṇam.
child-dat car-nom mother-dat sell-*aṇam*
'The child wants to sell the car to the mother.' *or* 'The mother wants to sell the car to the child.'

The equations in (106a) interpret the accusative 'elephant' in (122a) as the direct object, and (106f) interprets the nominative 'child' as the subject. (106a) and (106e) allow the nominative 'car' in (122b) to be either the subject or the direct object, but the former reading would be blocked, as the nominative 'child' would then receive no interpretation. Thus, (122b) is unambiguous. On the other hand, (122c) is ambiguous, because (106c) and (106d) allow us to interpret either of the two datives as the subject and the other as the indirect object.

The Functional Structure of [X′ V]ᵥ′ Constructions
In section 8.2, we proposed the analysis in (123b) for the sentence in (123a).

(123)

a. kuṭṭi   kaḷḷan   aaṇə.
child-nom thief-nom is
'The child is a thief.'

b.   S

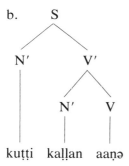

kuṭṭi   kaḷḷan   aaṇə

The first problem regarding the [X' V]$_{v'}$ construction concerns the number of arguments that can appear under V', and their grammatical relations. Consider, for example, the behavior of *cey* 'do':

(124)

a.   kuṭṭi   nrəṭṭam   ceyṭu.
      child-nom dance-nom did
      'The child danced.'

b.   *kuṭṭi ammaye   nrəṭṭam ceyṭu.
            mother-acc
      *'The child danced the mother.'

(125)

a.   *kuṭṭi šalyam   ceyṭu.
      child annoyance-nom did
      *'The child annoyed.'

b.   kuṭṭi ammaye šalyam   ceyṭu.
      child mother   annoyance did
      'The child annoyed the mother.'

In order to account for (124) and (125) and to derive the appropriate f-structures for them, it is necessary to clarify some of my assumptions regarding lexical representations. To begin with, I assume that verbs, adjectives, and nouns share properties of predicate argument structure, as illustrated by the following examples:

(126)

a.   John sleeps.

b.   John is asleep.

(127)
a. John is human.
b. John is a human.

(128)
a. John fears Mary.
b. John is afraid of Mary.

One may assume, without causing any serious controversy, that the sentences in (126) and (127) have the logical form given in (129a), and that those in (128) have the logical form in (129b).

(129)
a. F(j) where j = John, F = sleep, asleep, human
b. F(j,k) where j = John, k = Mary, F = fear

If this is so, the lexical entries for these words would roughly be (130a–f):

(130)
a. sleep: V, 'SLEEP   ((SUBJ))'
                        experiencer
b. asleep: A, 'SLEEP   ((SUBJ))'
                        experiencer
c. human: A, 'HUMAN((SUBJ))'
                        theme
d. human: N, 'HUMAN((SUBJ))'
                        theme
e. fear: V, 'FEAR   ((SUBJ),   (OBJ))'
                        experiencer theme
f. afraid: A, 'FEAR   ((SUBJ),   (OBJ))'
                        experiencer theme

This proposal would essentially require that elements such as auxiliary, *be*, etc., be represented without any predicate argument structure. We shall regard them as grammatical formatives which convert nonverbal predicates into verbs for categorial purposes, sometimes modifying the meaning of the predicate they are attached to.

The following sentences illustrate the need for yet another assumption.

(131)
a. The child is asleep.
b. John is a child.

If these sentences are interpreted as shown in (132),

(132)
a. SLEEP (child)
b. CHILD (John)

we will have to assume that nouns can be either predicates, as in (132b), or terms, as in (132a).

Given these assumptions, we can tackle the transitivity problem of *cey* 'do' constructions as follows. First, we note that *nrəṭṭam* 'dance' has a monadic predicate, while *śalyam* 'annoyance' has a dyadic predicate:

(133)
a. nrəṭṭam: N, 'DANCE((SUBJ))'
                     agent
b. śalyam: N, 'ANNOY((SUBJ),(OBJ))'
                     source goal

Next, we assume that verbs like *cey* 'do' and *aa* 'be' have no predicate argument structure associated with them in the lexicon. If so, the notation ↑ = ↓ implicit in the PS rules will automatically promote the properties of X′ upward to V′. From this, it follows that 'dance-do' is intransitive, while 'annoy-do' is transitive.

(134)

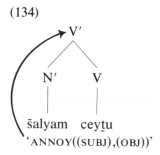

It must be noted that some of these nominal predicates are specified for indirect object rather than direct object:

(135)

a. kutti   {awaḷkkə / she-dat | *awaḷe / she-acc}   upakaaṟam ceytu.
   child   help   did

'The child helped her.'

b. kutti   {awaḷootə / she-dat | *awaḷe / she-acc}   kṣamaayaacanam ceytu.
   child   pardon request   did

'The child apologized to her.'

We can account for these nouns in terms of the following type of lexical entry:

(136)
a. upakaaṟam: N, 'HELP((SUBJ),(OBJ2))'
b. kṣamaayaacanam: N, 'REQUEST PARDON((SUBJ),(OBJ2))'

There is evidence that some information from V should also be promoted upward. Thus, *aa* 'be' and *uḷ* 'there is', unlike *cey* 'do', induce the dative case on their subjects:

(137)

a. {kuttikkə / child-dat | *kutti / child-nom}   saŋkatam / sorrow-nom   {aaṇə / is | uṇtə / is}.

'The child is unhappy.'

b. {kuttikkə / child-dat | *kutti / child-nom}   aanaye weruppə / elephant-nom hatred-nom   {aaṇə / is | uṇtə / is}.

'The child has hatred toward the elephant.'

In order to account for the behavior of these verbs, we will postulate the following lexical entries:

(138)

a. aa: V, (↑SUBJ CASE) = DAT
b. uḷ: V, (↑SUBJ CASE) = DAT
c. waṛ: V, (↑SUBJ CASE) = DAT

It must be pointed out that the verb *waṛ* 'come', when used as a full verb with its own predicate argument structure as in (139a), does not induce dative subjects, as the empty *waṛ* does as in (139b):

(139)

a. kuṭṭi   waṇṇu.
    child-nom came
    'The child came.'

b. kuṭṭikkə ṭalaweeḍana waṇṇu.
    child-dat headache   came
    'The child got a headache.'

Similarly, *aa* used as an equative verb does not induce the dative. I shall ignore these details here.

The situation can now be summarized as follows. In the [X′ V]_V′ structure, (i) the V has no predicate argument structure associated with it; (ii) the lexical form of X′, which contains the specification of the grammatical relations it can take, is promoted upward to V′; and (iii) the information about the case feature of the subject is promoted from V to V′. All of this is automatically taken care of by the notation ↑ = ↓ implicit in the PS rule V′ → X′ V:

(140)

V′ → X′   V
      ↑=↓ ↑=↓

Predicative Adjectives

How do we arrive at the functional structures of constructions like the following?

(141)   S

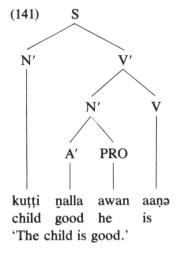

kuṭṭi ṉalla awan   aaṇə
child good   he   is
'The child is good.'

Let us assume that the sentence is understood as (142):

(142)
GOOD (child)

If so, what we need is a device to promote the lexical form of *ṉalla* 'good' upward to V':

(143)
ṉalla: V, PRED = 'GOOD((SUBJ))'

Observe that any theory of grammar needs to distinguish between referential pronouns, as in (144), and nonreferential or empty pronouns, as in (145):

(144)
a. *It* is moving.
b. *It* told him that Mary was alive.

(145)
a. *It* is raining.
b. *It* occurred to him that Mary was alive.

Granted that this is so, all we have to do to account for (141) is to assume that the pronoun in [X' PRO]$_{N'}$ is an empty one. Given our assumptions regarding the unmarked notation ↑ = ↓, the properties of the adjective, along with its lexical form, will be promoted upward to N', which in turn will be promoted to V':

(146)

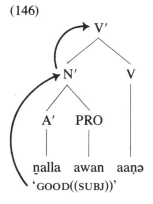

nalla awan aaṇə
'GOOD((SUBJ))'

Thus, we arrive at the following functional structure for (141):

(147)

$$\begin{bmatrix} \text{SUBJ} & \begin{bmatrix} \text{PRED} & \text{'CHILD'} \\ \text{CASE} & \text{NOM} \\ \text{ANIM} & + \end{bmatrix} \\ \text{PRED} & \begin{array}{c} \text{'GOOD((SUBJ))'} \\ \text{theme} \end{array} \end{bmatrix}$$

Interpretation of Clefts

Consider the following pair of sentences:

(148)

a. kuṭṭi aanaye ṇuḷḷi.
    child elephant pinched
    'The child pinched the elephant.'

b. kuṭṭiyaaṇə aanaye ṇuḷḷiyatə.
    child-is   elephant pinched-it
    'It was the child who pinched the elephant.'

Ignoring details, (148a) has the following functional structure:

(149)

$$\begin{bmatrix} \text{SUBJ} & \text{'CHILD'} \\ \text{OBJ} & \text{'ELEPHANT'} \\ \text{PRED} & \text{'PINCH((SUBJ),(OBJ))'} \end{bmatrix}$$

What we want is the same functional structure for (148b). In other
words, we would like to have the derivation of functional structure
ignore the addition of *aanə* to *kuṭṭi* and treat it as a noun, and ignore the
addition of *aṭə* to *ṉuḷḷi* and treat it as a verb, thus making *aanə* and *aṭə*
transparent for functional interpretation.

Notice that this is precisely what happens in the grammar, given our
assumptions regarding $[X'\ V]_V$, and $[X'\ PRO]_N$, structures, which we
found to be necessary independently of clefts:

(150)

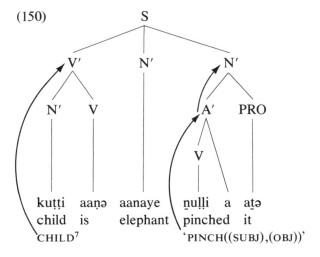

Thus, we find that neither the categorial structure nor the functional
structure of clefts in Malayalam requires us to set up any special rules.[8]
All the peculiarities of clefts are fully accounted for by base-generating
clefts using the PS rules and interpretive mechanisms that are needed
elsewhere in the grammar.

Interpretation of [V′ V]ᵥ′ Constructions
How do we arrive at the functional structure of (151)?

(151)

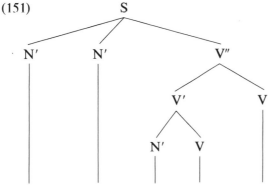

ṛaajaawə	kuṭṭiye	kaḷḷan	aayi	kaṇakkaakki
king-nom	child-acc	thief	was	considered

I shall assume that the sentence is understood as (152)

(152)
CONSIDER (king (THIEF (child)))

and that *kaṇakkaakk* 'consider' has the following lexical form:

(153)
kaṇakkaakk: V, PRED = 'CONSIDER((SUBJ),(COMP))'
                                    agent theme
                                    (↑OBJ) = (↑COMP SUBJ)

The lexical entry in (153) says that *kaṇakkaakk* takes a subject, a direct object, and a complement, and that it is only the subject and the complement that are associated with thematic roles. The details of this notation are found in chapters 1 and 4 of this volume.

The functional equation (↑OBJ) = (↑COMP SUBJ) says that the direct object *kuṭṭi* 'child' is interpreted as the subject of the complement *kaḷḷan aayi* 'thief was'.

To complete the picture, we must add the following equation to rule (55c–i).

(154)
V″ →   V′   V
       (↑COMP)=↓

The lexical entry (153), along with the equation in (154), gives the following functional structure for (151):

(155)

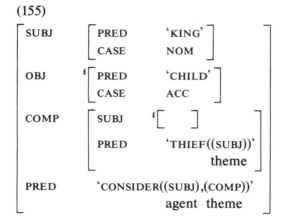

The Problem of 'Become'

The verb *aa* 'become', though homophonous with *aa* 'be', behaves quite differently from 'be'. Consider, for example, the morphological differences:

(156)

	Present	*Past*	*Future*
aa 'be'	aanə, aakunnu	aayiṙunnu	aakum
aa 'become'	—	aakunnu	aayi	aakum

Another difference between the two *aa*s is that the negative particle *illa* can be attached to 'become', and not to 'be':

(157)

a. kuṭṭi kaḷḷan aakunnu.
    child thief   becomes/is
    'The child becomes/is a thief.'

b. kuṭṭi kaḷḷan aakunnilla.
    child thief   becomes/*is
    'The child does not become a thief.'[9]

The third difference between the two verbs is that 'become' allows clefting, while 'be' does not:

(158)

a. kuṭṭiyaaṇə kaḷḷan aakuṇṇatə.
    child-is   thief becomes/*is-it
    'It is the child who becomes a thief.'

b. kuṭṭi kaḷḷanaaṇə aakuṇṇatə.
        thief-is   becomes/*is-it
    'It is a thief that the child becomes.'

The fact that both *kuṭṭi* and *kaḷḷan* can be clefted suggests the following analysis for (157a) under the 'become' reading:

(159)   S

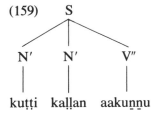

kuṭṭi kaḷḷan aakuṇṇu

I shall give the form of 'become' as follows:

(160)
aa: V, PRED = 'BECOME((SUBJ),(COMP))'

This would require an interpretive principle that allows nominative NPs to be interpreted as complements:

(161)
($\uparrow$COMP) = $\downarrow$
($\downarrow$CASE) = NOM

Note that the nominative case on complements is not an instance of case agreement. (Malayalam has no agreement phenomena of any sort.) Thus, even when the subject is dative, the complement remains nominative:

(162)
kuṭṭikkə kaḷḷan   aakaṇam.
child-dat thief-nom become-*aṇam*
'The child wants to become a thief.'

Following chapter 2 of this volume, I shall assume that relations such as subject, object, etc., correspond to simple logical terms, while COMP corresponds to a logical predicate. Thus, the 'become' reading of (157a) will be (163):

(163)
BECOME (child, THIEF (child))

I shall therefore represent the functional structure of (159) as follows:

(164)

$$
\begin{bmatrix}
\text{SUBJ} & ^i\begin{bmatrix} \text{PRED} & \text{`CHILD'} \\ \text{CASE} & \text{NOM} \end{bmatrix} \\
\text{COMP} & \begin{bmatrix} \text{SUBJ} & ^i[\quad] \\ \text{PRED} & \text{`THIEF((SUBJ))'} \end{bmatrix} \\
\text{PRED} & \text{`BECOME((SUBJ),(COMP))'}
\end{bmatrix}
$$

What we need to derive this functional structure is the following equation:

(165)
aa: V, PRED = 'BECOME((SUBJ),(COMP))'

$$(\uparrow\text{COMP SUBJ})=(\uparrow\text{SUBJ})$$

At this point, I will not give any serious argumentation for this analysis of complements, but I do want to point out that this approach would explain why there are rules that raise and lower subjects and objects, but hardly any rules that raise or lower complements. The advantage of treating complements in this fashion will become clear when we come to causatives.

I must point out that there is a strong tendency for the first NP in the 'become' construction in Malayalam to be interpreted as subject. However, there are, in fact, ambiguous cases which show that either of the two NPs can be freely chosen as the subject.

(166)
ṛaajaawə kaḷḷan   muunnu kollam munpə aayi.
king-nom thief-nom three   year   before became
'The king became a thief three years ago.' *or* 'The thief became a king three years ago.'

8.4 The Need for Grammatical Relations

Direct and Relationally Mediated Evaluation
The assumption implicit in our approach to the interpretation of thematic roles can be stated as follows:

(167)
Thematic roles are a property of grammatical relations, and are linked to categorial structure through the intermediacy of these relations.

I shall refer to this as the hypothesis of *relationally mediated evaluation* (RME).

An alternative would be to deny that the level of grammatical relations plays any independent role at all in natural languages, making the following assumption:

(168)
Thematic roles are a property of phrase markers, case, or agreement, and are linked to these categorial units directly.

I shall refer to this as the hypothesis of *direct evaluation* (DE) (cf. Ostler 1979).

As far as Malayalam is concerned, the difference between RME and DE can be represented schematically as follows:

(169)

RME   case features ⟷ grammatical relations ⟷ thematic roles

DE   case features ⟷ thematic roles

A device that made use of DE for Malayalam would be, though not impossible, as uninsightful as a phonological theory which, using brute force, applies all the rules simultaneously to underlying representations and maps them directly onto phonetic representations.

How does the DE approach work? To begin with, it has to account for the fact that case features such as nominative or accusative can take up roles such as agent, experiencer, theme, etc.:

(170)
a.   waaṭil   aṭaññu.
     door-nom closed

                                        (nom. subj. = theme)

     'The door closed.'
b.   kuṭṭi waaṭil aṭaccu.
     child door   closed

                                        (nom. subj. = agent)
                                        (nom. dir.obj. = theme)

     'The child closed the door.'

c.   amma   kuṭṭiyekkoṇṭə waaṭil aṭappiccu.
     mother child-instr   door   make-close-past

$$\text{(nom. subj. = causer)}$$
$$\text{(nom. dir.obj. = theme)}$$
$$\text{(instr. = agent)}$$

     'The mother made the child close the door.'

d.   kuṭṭi kayarə   kaṇṭu.
     child rope-nom saw

$$\text{(nom. subj. = experiencer)}$$
$$\text{(nom. dir.obj. = theme)}$$

     'The child saw the rope.'

e.   kuṭṭi aanaye   kaṇṭu.
     child elephant saw

$$\text{(nom. subj. = experiencer)}$$
$$\text{(acc. dir.obj. = theme)}$$

     'The child saw the elephant.'

According to the DE hypothesis, the lexical entries of these verbs would presumably be as follows:

(171)
a.   aṭay: V, PRED = 'CLOSE' (NOM)
                              theme
b.   aṭakk: V, PRED = 'CLOSE' (NOM, NOM)
                              agent theme
c.   aṭappikk: V, PRED = 'MAKE X CLOSE Y' (NOM, NOM, INSTR)
                                      causer agent instr.
d.   kaaṇ: V, PRED = 'SEE' (NOM, NOM)
                              ACC
               exper. theme

These examples indicate that the relation between case features and thematic roles is far from being direct. I shall illustrate this with a single problem, from which the reader can extrapolate the impossibility of trying to relate case features directly to roles.

   A corollary of principle (105d) can be stated as follows:

(172)
[+nominative] NPs cannot be objects if they are [+animate].

This corollary blocks sentences like (173), while allowing (170d,e):

(173)
*kuṭṭi   aana   kaṇṭu.
child-nom elephant-nom saw

The corresponding version of principle (172) in DE would be something like (174):

(174)
[+nominative] NPs cannot be role *j* if they are [+animate].

Role *j* cannot be causer, agent, or experiencer, as (170a–e) indicate. The only way to block (173), then, would be to list under each verb a condition on animacy for one of its nominative arguments. Thus, (172) cannot be stated in DE.

Consider another objection. In DE, in order to avoid referring to direct objects, we would have to use circumlocutions such as

(175)
Those NPs which, if animate, are accusative, and if inanimate, nominative.

Note that this statement is not simply a disjunction. Thus, rules that apply to direct objects cannot be stated as applying to "either nominatives or accusatives," for such a statement would incorrectly include nominative subjects and nominative complements. Similarly, a rule applying to subjects will have to be stated as applying to

(176)
Those NPs which, for marked verbs, are dative, and for unmarked ones, nominative.

Such an approach is, indeed, uninsightful, if there are a number of rules that must refer to subjects and objects for their application. As the following sections show, this is clearly the case: there exist a number of rules in Malayalam that refer crucially to grammatical relations like subject and object. If we do not incorporate the level of grammatical relations in the theory, we will be forced to continue to refer to them in a roundabout manner, using illegitimate descriptions such as (175) and (176).

One of the alternatives to a nonrelational syntactic theory is to set up an unmotivated fixed word order for Malayalam (ignoring the objections I raised in section 8.2), with or without a VP. "Subject" can then be defined as the first NP in a clause, and "object" as the one next to the verb. The sole justification for such a move would be to avoid using the terms "subject" and "object." This solution is at best a notational variant, and I shall not discuss it further here.

Another possibility is to set up abstract case features which are invisible on the surface. Thus, all direct objects, animate or inanimate, can be assigned the accusative case, with a rule that changes it into nominative on the surface in the case of inanimate NPs. Similarly, dative subjects can start out as nominatives and then be changed to datives by a later rule. Given the freedom to use cases as diacritical features in this manner, one can think of various ingenious ways of avoiding reference to grammatical relations. Like the previous alternative, I shall not pursue this one any further.

Reflexives

One of the crucial properties of reflexives in Malayalam (which it seems to share with most modern Indian languages) is that their antecedents can only be subjects. In fact, this can be used as a test for subjecthood in Malayalam. Consider the behavior of *swaṇṭam* 'self's' in the following sentences, for example:

(177)

a.   ṛaajaawə swaṇṭam bhaaṛyaye ṇuḷḷi.
      king-nom self's   wife-acc   pinched
      'The king pinched his (the king's) wife.'

b.   *ṛaajaawine swaṇṭam bhaaṛya ṇuḷḷi.
      king-acc   self's   wife   pinched
      'The king's wife pinched him (the king).'

(177b) is ungrammatical because the antecedent of *swaṇṭam* is not a subject. Now, if we use (177b) as an embedded clause, we get grammatical results:

(178)

ₛ′[ṛaajaawine swaṇṭam bhaaṛya ṇuḷḷi   enṇə] bhaṭane   maṇṭri
    king-acc   self's   wife   pinched that   soldier-acc minister
wiśwasippiccu.
made believe
'The minister convinced the soldier that the minister's/*soldier's/
*king's wife pinched the king.'

The condition on the antecedent of reflexives cannot be stated in terms of case features, for the following reasons. First, it would be incorrect to say that nominative NPs are the antecedents of reflexives, since nonsubject nominatives cannot be their antecedents. Thus, though one can say (179), (180) is ungrammatical.

(179)
tiiyə   wirakə   caampalaakki.
fire-nom logs-nom burnt
'The fire burnt the logs.'

(180)
*swantam tiiyə wirakə caampalaakki.
 self's   fire logs   burnt
'The logs' fire burnt them (the logs).'

Semantic reasons force the reading of 'fire' as subject, and 'logs' as object. Therefore, *swantam* cannot refer to 'logs' in (180).

Second, it would be incorrect to say that reflexives can be bound only by nominative NPs, because dative subjects (but not dative indirect objects) can serve as antecedents for reflexives:

(181)
a.   ɾaajaawinə swantam bhaaɾyaye iṣtamaaṇə.
      king-dat   self's   wife-acc   liking-is
      'The king likes the king's wife.'

b.   *ɾaajaawə makaḷkkə   swantam bhartaawine koṭuttu.
      king-nom daughter-dat self's   husband-acc gave
      'The king gave his daughter self's husband.'

In (181a), the reflexive has a dative subject as its antecedent. (181b) is ungrammatical because semantics forbids the subject to be the antecedent of the reflexive (*king's husband*), which cannot be bound to the indirect object.

Control

Another test for subjecthood in Malayalam is control. Here I shall restrict the discussion to the control phenomena of *koṇṭə* 'while' adverbial clauses, the control equation for which can be informally stated as, "The subject of the matrix controls the subject of the embedded clause":

(182)

[φ kuṭṭiye ṇuḷḷikkoṇṭə]   amma puṭakam waayiccu.
    child   pinched-while mother book   read
'The mother read the book while pinching the child.'

Examples (183a–c) show that the controller cannot be an object, whether in the nominative, accusative, or dative case.

(183)

a.   [φ kaṭṭilil kiṭannukoṇṭə] acchanə   amma   kaaśə koṭuttu.
        bed-loc lay-while   father-dat mother-nom money gave

     'Mother gave money to father, while $\begin{Bmatrix} \text{she} \\ \text{*he} \end{Bmatrix}$ lay on the bed.'

b.   [φ kaṭṭilil kiṭannukoṇṭə] acchane   amma   ṇuḷḷi.
        bed-loc lay-while   father-acc mother-nom pinched

     'Mother pinched father, while $\begin{Bmatrix} \text{she} \\ \text{*he} \end{Bmatrix}$ lay on the bed.'

c.   [φ cuuṭə piṭiccukoṇṭə] kuṭṭi uppeeṙi iḷakki.
        heat caught-while child veg.dish stirred

     'The child stirred the vegetable, while $\begin{Bmatrix} \text{he} \\ \text{*dish} \end{Bmatrix}$ got hot.'

(184) shows that the controller can be a dative subject, though (as (183a) makes clear) not a dative indirect object.

(184)

[φ puṭakam waayiccukoṇṭə] kuṭṭikkə uraṇṇaṇam.
    book-nom read-while   child-dat sleep-modal
'The child wants to sleep while he reads a book.'

Thus, we find that the controller for *koṇṭə* adverbial clauses is the dative or nominative subject, but not a dative, nominative, or accusative object. It is also the case that the victim of control is the subject, nominative or dative, and not the object. The examples given above show that a nominative subject can control the embedded subject; given below are examples that show that dative subjects can be controllers as well:

(185)

a.   kuṭṭikkə wiśaṇṇu.
        child-dat hungered
        'The child was hungry.'

b. [ϕ wišaṇṇukoṇṭə] kuṭṭi pusṭakam waayiccu.
    hungered-while child book   read
    'The child read the book while he was hungry.'

(186) and (187) show that the victim cannot be a nonsubject, whatever its case:

(186)

a. acchanə amma   kaašə   koṭuṭṭu.
    father-dat mother-nom money-nom gave
    'Mother gave money to father.'

b. *[ϕ amma kaašə koṭuṭṭukoṇṭə] acchan sukhamaayi iṛuṇṇu.
     mother money gave-while   father happily   sat
    'Father lived happily, while mother gave him money.'

(187)

a. kuṭṭi   uppeēṛi   iḷakki.
    child-nom vegetable-nom stirred
    'The child stirred the vegetable dish.'

b. *[kuṭṭi ϕ iḷakkikkoṇṭə] uppeēṛi   kaṛiññu.
    child   stirred-while vegetable got burnt
    'The vegetable dish got burnt, while the child stirred it.'

It is observed that in all natural languages, it is only the subject position that can be controlled. A theory that incorporates the level of grammatical relations has a natural way of stating this universal restriction. On the other hand, if we try to state it in terms of phrase markers and case features, we will obscure the underlying generalization by making unrelated statements for configurational and nonconfigurational languages.

Causatives

A phenomenon that offers strong support to the framework developed here is *morphological causativization*, a feature that has been generally recognized as a common property of Southeast Asia as a linguistic area (see Masica 1976). Many of the theoretical points I make in this section have already been made, though in a different fashion, by Comrie 1976, but it seems worthwhile to offer the Malayalam data as additional support for this analysis.

    Malayalam uses three morphological processes to indicate causation: (i) morpholexical processes (cf. Lieber 1980) such as gemination and denasalization, (ii) infixation of *-ippi-*, and (iii) suffixation of *-ikk*. The relevant morphological structure of a verb would be:

(188)

```
V →    stem      (cause) (cause)  tense
        |           |       |
     primary      -ippi-   -ikk
        or
     derived
```

Since the stem itself may contain a "cause" if it is derived through gemination or denasalization, a verb can take three causes, as the following example illustrates:

(189)

a. ṭinnum   'will eat' (*-um:* Future)
b. ṭiittum   'will feed'
c. ṭiittikkum   'will make *x* feed *y*'
d. ṭiittippikkum   'will make *x* feed *y*'

It is clear that causativization is a part of word formation in Malayalam. I shall assume that it is a lexical process involving three independent aspects: (i) the morphology of causation (restrictions involved in (188)); (ii) the semantics of causation (prediction of the semantic structure of the resultant words),[10] and (iii) the syntax of causation (prediction of grammatical relations, cases). I shall leave aside problems (i) and (ii) and proceed directly to the issue of the syntax of causation.

Causativization in Intransitives The simplest kind of causativization is the one that changes intransitive verbs (verbs without any object in the lexical form) to transitive verbs (those that have objects). The process is illustrated in (190) and (191):

(190)

a. kuṭṭi kaḷikkuṇṇu.
    child plays
    'The child is playing.'

b. acchan   kuṭṭiye   kaḷippikkuṇṇu.
    father-nom child-acc makes play
    'The father makes the child play.'

(191)

a. kuppi   poṭṭi.
   bottle-nom broke
   'The bottle broke.'

b. kuṭṭi   kuppi   poṭṭiccu.
   child-nom bottle-nom broke
   'The child broke the bottle.'

The relation between the primary and derived verbs in these cases can be described as follows:

(192)

primary   *derived*
PRED((SUBJ)) $\mapsto$ PRED((SUBJ), (OBJ))
     | | |
   term$_i$ causer term$_i$

As the first step, the lexical rule of Causativization can be formulated as follows:

(193)
Causativization (First Formulation)
((SUBJ)) $\mapsto$ ((SUBJ), (OBJ))
    | | |
  term$_i$ causer term$_i$

It must be pointed out that rule (193) is independent of case features and thematic roles. Thus, it applies to both nominative and dative subjects:

(194)

a. kuṭṭi   dukkhiccu.
   child-nom sorrowed
   'The child was sad.'

b. amma   kuṭṭiye   dukkhippiccu.
   mother-nom child-acc sad-caused
   'The mother made the child sad.'

(195)

a. kuṭṭikkə wiśannu.
    child-dat hungered
    'The child was hungry.'

b. amma   kuṭṭiye wiśappiccu.
    mother-nom child-acc hunger-caused
    'The mother caused the child to be hungry.'

Similarly, the object of the causative may be either nominative or accusative:

(196)

a. kaaṭə   kaṭṭi.
    forest-nom burned
    'The forest caught fire.'

b. iṭiminnal   kaaṭə   kaṭṭiccu.
    lightning-nom forest-nom burnt
    'The lightning burnt the forest.'

Any analysis of causativization that seeks to account for causatives in terms of case features will have to repeat the disjunction involved in dative subjects and nominative objects while making reference to the other case features in the system. The examples above should make it clear that the subjects that are demoted to objects by Causativization may be experiencers ((194), (195)) or themes ((191), (196)). The following examples show that they can be agents as well:

(197)

a. pakṣi   parannu.
    bird-nom flew
    'The bird flew.'

b. kuṭṭi   pakṣiye parappiccu.
    child-nom bird-acc fly-caused
    'The child made the bird fly.'

As can be expected, the subject of the noncausative, once demoted to the object position through Causativization, does not exhibit any of the subject properties with respect to rules sensitive to subjecthood. Thus, the noncausative–causative pair exhibits precisely the predicted behavior with respect to control in *koṇṭə* adverbial clauses. (The subject of the matrix controls the subject of the embedded clause.)

(198)

a.   kuṭṭi   [φ wiśannukoṇṭə]   skuuḷil   pooyi.
     child-nom hungered-while school-loc went
     'The child went to school feeling hungry.'

b.   amma   [φ kuṭṭiye   wiśappiccukoṇṭə]   skuuḷil   pooyi.
     mother-nom child-acc made hungry-while school-loc went
     'The mother went to school, causing the child to be hungry.'

c.   *kuṭṭi   [amma φ   wiśappiccukoṇṭə]   skuuḷil   pooyi.
     child-nom mother-nom made hungry-while school-loc went
     'The child went to school, while the mother caused the child
     to be hungry.'

Note that the demoted subject ('child') can no longer act as the control
site in the causative structure (198b,c). Nor can the demoted subject
act as the controller, as shown by the following examples:

(199)

a.   kuṭṭikkə [φ kḷassil   iṛunnukoṇṭə] wiśannu.
     child-dat   class-loc sat-while   hungered
     'The child was hungry while the child sat in class.'

b.   amma   kuṭṭiye [φ kḷassil   iṛunnukoṇṭə] wiśappiccu.
     mother-nom child-acc   class-loc sat-while   made hungry
     'The mother made the child hungry, while she sat in the class.'

The behavior of reflexives points to the same conclusion:

(200)

a.   kuṭṭi   swantam kaṭṭilil iṛunnu.
     child-nom self's   bed-loc sat
     'The child sat on the child's bed.'

b.   amma   kuṭṭiye   swantam kaṭṭilil iṛutti.
     mother-nom child-acc self's   bed-loc sat-caused
     'The mother made the child sit on $\left\{ {\text{mother's} \atop \text{*child's}} \right\}$ bed.'

'Child' is eligible to be the antecedent of *swantam* in (200a), but not in
(200b).

Causativization in Transitives   Causativization of transitive verbs typically involves the demoting of the primary subject to the instrumental
adjunct position. Consider the following examples:

(201)

a. kuṭṭi   waaṭil   aṭaccu.
   child-nom door-nom closed
   'The child closed the door.'

b. amma   kuṭṭiyekkoṇṭə waaṭil   aṭappiccu.
   mother-nom child-by   door-nom close-made

(202)

a. raaṇi   maṇtriye   nuḷḷi.
   queen-nom minister-acc pinched
   'The queen pinched the minister.'

b. r̃aajaawə raaṇiyekkoṇṭə maṇtriye   nuḷḷiccu.
   king-nom queen-by   minister-acc pinch-made
   'The king made the queen pinch the minister.'

The relation between the primary and derived stems in these cases may be described as follows:

(203)

primary   *derived*
PRED((SUBJ), (OBJ)) $\mapsto$ PRED((SUBJ), (INSTR), (OBJ))
          | | | | |
       term$_i$ term$_j$ causer   term$_i$ term$_j$

The Causativization rule can now be expanded as follows:

(204)

Causativization (Second Formulation)
((SUBJ),X) $\rightarrow$ ((SUBJ),(OBJ)/(INSTR),X)
       | | |
    term$_i$ causer   term$_i$

The rule says, "When a verb is causativized, attach a causer subject and demote the noncausative subject to either the direct object or the instrumental adjunct function."

Two points must be noted: (i) If the primary predicate has a direct object, the demoted subject does not become the direct object. This is predicted by the principle of function-argument biuniqueness, which rules out any lexical form that contains two occurrences of the same grammatical relation (see chapter 3). (ii) If the primary predicate does not have an object, the demoted subject becomes an object. This result should also be derivable from general principles. I do not, however, have any definite proposals about this.

The demoted subject that becomes an instrumental is optional:

(205)

a. amma   kuṭṭikkə puṣṭakam koṭuṭṭu.
    mother-nom child-dat book-nom gave
    'The mother gave a book to the child.'

b. acchan   (ammayekkoṇṭə) kuṭṭikkə puṣṭakam koṭuppiccu.
    father-nom mother-by   child-dat book-nom give-made
    'Father caused the child to be given a book (by mother).'

In order to account for the optionality of INSTR, we shall revise (204) as follows:

(206)

Causativization (Final Formulation)

$$((\text{SUBJ}),\text{X}) \rightarrow ((\text{SUBJ}),(\text{OBJ})/\begin{Bmatrix}(\text{INSTR})\\ \phi\end{Bmatrix},\text{X})$$

$$\underset{\text{term}_i}{|} \qquad \underset{\text{causer}}{|} \quad \underset{\text{term}_i}{|}$$

Malayalam has a free variation between the instrumental case *-aal* and the instrumental postposition *koṇṭə*, as in (207a,b):

(207)

a. amma   kuṭṭiye waṭiyaal aṭiccu.
    mother-nom child-acc stick-instr beat
    'The mother beat the child with a stick.'

b. amma   kuṭṭiye waṭikoṇṭə aṭiccu.
    mother-nom child-acc stick-with beat
    'The mother beat the child with a stick.'

However, when the demoted subject becomes an INSTR in causatives, it is always instantiated as an instrumental postpositional phrase, not as instrumental case:

(208)

a. amma   kuṭṭiye ṇulḷi.
    mother-nom child-acc pinched
    'The mother pinched the child.'

b. acchan $\begin{Bmatrix}\text{ammayekkoṇṭə}\\ \text{mother-by}\\ \text{*ammayaal}\\ \text{mother-instr}\end{Bmatrix}$ kuṭṭiye ṇulḷiccu.
    father-nom   child-acc pinch-made
    'The father made the mother pinch the child.'

This information can be encoded in the causative rule by specifying that SUBJ is replaced by an instrumental object (INSTR OBJ).

(209)

$$((\text{SUBJ}),\text{X}) \quad \rightarrow \quad ((\text{SUBJ}),(\text{OBJ})/\left\{\begin{matrix}(\text{INSTR OBJ})\\ \phi\end{matrix}\right\},\text{X})$$

$$\begin{matrix}| & & | & & | \\ \text{term}_i & & \text{causer} & & \text{term}_i\end{matrix}$$

The reason is that P' but not N' takes objects (cf. (91)). As shown in (210a), the instrumental postposition *koṇṭə* governs the nominative case of its object, but carries the instrumental case itself. Through rule (210b) the instrumental case is promoted to the f-structure of P'. The case interpretation equation (210c) assigns the function INSTR to any X' bearing the case feature INSTR.

(210)
a.   *koṇṭə:* P, ($\uparrow$OBJ CASE) = NOM
                 ($\uparrow$CASE) = INSTR
b.   P' $\rightarrow$ N'   P
             ($\uparrow$OBJ)=$\downarrow$ $\uparrow$=$\downarrow$
c.   ($\uparrow$($\downarrow$CASE)) = $\downarrow$

Accordingly, rule (210c) will apply both to any P' whose P is *koṇṭə* and to any N' whose head noun is inflected with *-aal*. Thus, the functional structures of instrumental P's will fit the composite functional name (INSTR OBJ), while the functional structures of instrumental N's will fit the simple functional name (INSTR). Consequently, rule (209) changes subjects to instrumental P' and not to instrumental N'. By collapsing these functional names to (INSTR (OBJ)), we can refer to both *-aal* phrases and *koṇṭə* phrases in functional structure.

Causatives and Complements   In chapter 2 of this volume, Grimshaw points out that French causativization shows an interesting contrast between *devenir* 'become', which does not take an object, and transitive verbs, which take objects, in spite of the fact that they are dyadic and have the structure [V NP] in the VP. The general mechanism is: *faire* 'make' demotes subjects to objects in intransitive sentences, and to dative adjuncts in transitive sentences. The process is very similar to the one outlined here for Malayalam: subjects are demoted to objects if no object is already present, and if it is, to dative adjuncts. Interestingly enough, *devenir* 'become', which takes a complement and not an object, has its subject demoted to an object under causativization, exactly as the theory predicts. Now, the same phenomenon is found in Malayalam, in spite of the syntactic dissimilarities between French and Malayalam.

Consider the following examples:

(211)

a. kuṭṭi   kaḷḷan   aayi.
    child-nom thief-nom became
    'The child became a thief.'

b. kuṭṭi   kaḷḷane   konnu.
    child-nom thief-acc killed
    'The child killed the thief.'

We might ask why we should correlate this formal distinction in case features (nominative vs. accusative) with a distinction in grammatical relations (complement vs. object), as we did in the earlier section on *aa* 'become'. The answer is that it makes the correct predictions for the causative and, as we shall see, for the passive. The Malayalam passive morpheme, -*appeṭ*, can be attached to any transitive verb, without lexical exceptions. It cannot, however, be attached to 'become':

(212)

a. *kaḷḷan   (kuṭṭiyaal) aakappeṭṭu.
     thief-nom child-instr become-pass-past
    *'The thief was become by the child.'

b. kaḷḷan   (kuṭṭiyaal) kollappeṭṭu.
    thief-nom child-instr kill-pass-past
    'The thief was killed by the child.'

If we assume that the distinction in case corresponds to the distinction in grammatical relations (which is a perfectly natural assumption to make), we need not say anything about the fact that 'become' cannot be passivized: it cannot take the passive suffix because its lexical entry does not contain an object. This independently necessary assumption explains the apparently strange behavior of 'become' in causatives as well. Since 'become' does not have an object, its subject becomes an object under causativization.

Compare the causativization of 'cut' in (213) and (214) with that of 'become' in (215) and (216):

(213)

a. kuṭṭi   { maṛam / tree-nom ; *maṛattine / tree-acc } weṭṭi.
    child-nom   cut

'The child cut the tree.'

b. amma   kuṭṭiyekkoṇṭə { maṛam / tree-nom ; *maṛattine / tree-acc } weṭṭicu.
    mother-nom   child-by   cut-made

'The mother made the child cut the tree.'

(214)

a. kuṭṭi   { *puucca / cat-nom ; puuccaye / cat-acc } weṭṭi.
    child-nom   cut

'The child cut the cat.'

b. amma   kuṭṭiyekkoṇṭə { *puucca / cat-nom ; puuccaye / cat-acc } weṭṭiccu.
    mother-nom   child-by   cut-made

'The mother made the child cut the cat.'

(215)

a. { kuṭṭi / child-nom ; kallə / stone-nom } { maṛam / tree-nom ; *maṛattine / tree-acc } aayi.
                                                                                             became

'The { child / stone } became the tree.'

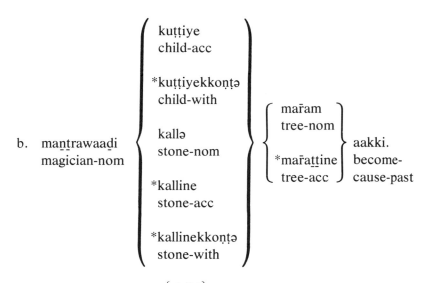

b. mantrawaaḍi
   magician-nom

| kuṭṭiye
child-acc |
| *kuṭṭiyekkoṇṭə
child-with |
| kallə
stone-nom |
| *kalline
stone-acc |
| *kallinekkoṇṭə
stone-with |

| maṟam
tree-nom |
| *maṟattine
tree-acc |

aakki.
become-
cause-past

'The magician turned the { child / stone } into a tree.'

(216)

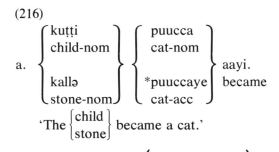

a.

| kuṭṭi
child-nom |
| kallə
stone-nom |

| puucca
cat-nom |
| *puuccaye
cat-acc |

aayi.
became

'The { child / stone } became a cat.'

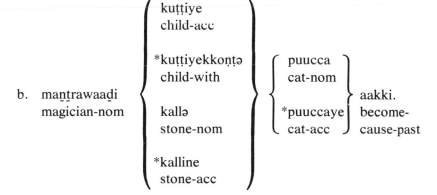

b. mantrawaaḍi
   magician-nom

| kuṭṭiye
child-acc |
| *kuṭṭiyekkoṇṭə
child-with |
| kallə
stone-nom |
| *kalline
stone-acc |

| puucca
cat-nom |
| *puuccaye
cat-acc |

aakki.
become-
cause-past

'The magician turned the { child / stone } into a cat.'

The complex facts about case change in these examples follow directly from our analysis. A theory that tries to account for them in terms of case features, however, has to explain the following phenomena: both 'become' and 'cut' can take nominative NPs as the second (= nonsubject) argument. However, in 'cut', the NP becomes accusative if animate. This difference correlates with the following facts: (a) 'Become' cannot be passivized, while 'cut' can be. (b) One of the nominative arguments of 'become' is picked out for case change. Assuming that there is a principled way of making this selection, we still have to state that after causativization, the argument selected imitates the behavior of the second argument of noncausative 'cut': it is nominative if inanimate, and accusative if animate. On the other hand, the argument selected for case change in the causativized 'cut' is the nominative one, whether animate or inanimate. This argument changes into an instrumental after causativization. I do not think that there is any non-ad hoc way of handling these facts in terms of cases alone.

Yet another phenomenon demands special attention. Notice that *maṟam* 'tree' is interpreted as referring to 'child'/'stone' in (215a); in (215b), the coreference continues, even though 'child'/'stone' is the object. Recall that in our framework, 'become' has the following lexical entry:

(217)
aa: V, PRED = 'BECOME((SUBJ),(COMP))'
$$(\uparrow\text{COMP SUBJ}) = (\uparrow\text{SUBJ})$$

Causativization, which demotes subjects to objects, is to be interpreted as saying, "Replace all symbols of the form $(\uparrow\text{SUBJ})$ with symbols of the form $(\uparrow\text{OBJ})$." (See chapter 4 for details.) This rule will derive (218) from (217):

(218)
aakk: V, PRED = 'CAUSE TO BECOME((SUBJ),(OBJ),(COMP))'
$$(\uparrow\text{COMP SUBJ}) = (\uparrow\text{OBJ})$$

Note that, within our framework, the control equation for COMP SUBJ is changed automatically as a consequence of the application of causativization, thus taking care of the interpretation of *maṟam* 'tree' in (215a,b).

Notice also that these are exactly the same control relations that we find in the *faire* causatives in French (see chapter 2 of this volume). Our theory predicts that French and Malayalam should behave in the same manner with respect to causativization, in spite of the fact that causativization results in reordering in French and not in Malayalam. This syntactic difference is to be expected, since grammatical relations are encoded configurationally in French and morphologically in Malayalam, and any rule that affects grammatical relations should change the configuration in French and the case features in Malayalam. A theory that deals with French causativization in terms of movement transformations and Malayalam causativization in terms of case change will not explain why Malayalam 'become' and French 'become' behave exactly alike under causativization.

Passivization

The Rule of Passivization   Another rule that has to make crucial reference to subjects and objects is Passivization, which is triggered by the attachment of the passive suffix *-appeṭ*. The position of the passive suffix with respect to causative and tense suffixes is as follows:

(219)

stem (cause) (cause) (passive) tense
     | | |
   -ippi- *-ikk* *-appeṭ*

The rule of Passivization can be universally characterized as shown in (220):

(220)
Passivization
(OBJ) ↦ (SUBJ)

Following chapter 1, we shall interpret the rule as saying, "Wherever the name OBJ occurs, replace it with the name SUBJ."

As I just mentioned, Passivization in Malayalam is triggered by the attachment of the passive morpheme *-appeṭ* to the verb. The demoted subject becomes an instrumental:

(221)
a. kuṭṭi   aanaye   aaṛaadhiccu.
    child-nom elephant-acc worshipped
    'The child worshipped the elephant.'

b. kuṭṭiyaal aana   aaṛaadhikkappeṭṭu.
    child-instr elephant-nom worship-pass-past
    'The elephant was worshipped by the child.'

The change in the lexical entry of *aařaaḍhikk* effected by Passivization can be represented as follows:

(222)

aařaaḍhikk: PRED((SUBJ), (OBJ)) ↦
                agent theme

    aařaaḍhikkappeṭ: PRED((SUBJ),(INSTR))
                     theme agent

Note that the only changes that Passivization in Malayalam effects are those of (i) the attachment of the passive morpheme, and (ii) the realignment between grammatical relations and thematic roles. The fact that verbs that cannot take an accusative argument (i.e., direct objects) cannot be passivized, as well as the fact that passivized verbs do not take accusative arguments, is a consequence of the rule (OBJ) ↦ (SUBJ). There is no apparent NP movement, nor the attachment of a copula, as there is in English; and yet, as we shall see later, the consequences of Passivization for processes like control and anaphora are identical in Malayalam and English. This suggests that Passivization is, indeed, a rule involving grammatical relations: what looks like NP movement is a consequence of grammatical relations' being encoded in terms of configurations in English.

As (220) implies, Passivization in Malayalam can advance only direct objects (OBJ) and not indirect objects (OBJ2) to the subject position:

(223)

a.   amma   kuṭṭikkə puṣṭakam koṭuttu.
       mother-nom child-dat book-nom gave
       'The mother gave the book to the child.'

b.   ammayaal   kuṭṭikkə puṣṭakam koṭukkappeṭṭu.
       mother-instr child-dat book-nom give-pass-past
       'The book was given to the child by the mother.'

c.   *ammayaal   kuṭṭi   puṣṭakam koṭukkappeṭṭu.
       mother-instr child-nom book-nom give-pass-past
       'The child was given a book by the mother.'

A fact that must be stated in the grammar is that the demoted subject (= subject of the active) becomes an instrumental N', unlike the demoted subject of the causative, which becomes an instrumental P':

(224)

a. kuṭṭi   ammayaal   aṭikkappeṭṭu.
    child-nom mother-instr beat-pass-past
    'The child was beaten by the mother.'

b. *kuṭṭi ammayekkoṇṭə aṭikkappeṭṭu.
    child mother-with   beat-pass-past

This restriction can be expressed as shown in (225):

(225)
Passivization
(SUBJ) ⟼ (INSTR)/ϕ
(OBJ) ⟼ (SUBJ)

When the intransitive 'become' is causativized and passivized, the original subject retains its subjecthood (first (SUBJ) ⟼ (OBJ) by Causativization; then (OBJ) ⟼ (SUBJ) by Passivization); however, when a transitive verb is causativized and passivized, the new subject is the original direct object ((SUBJ) ⟼ (INSTR); then (OBJ) ⟼ (SUBJ)). Consider the following examples that show this contrast:

(226)

a. ammayaal   kuṭṭi   kaḷḷan   aakkappeṭṭu.
    mother-instr child-nom thief-nom become-cause-pass-past
    'The child was made a thief by the mother.'

b. *ammayaal   kuṭṭi   kaḷḷane kollikkappeṭṭu.
    mother-instr child-nom thief-acc kill-cause-pass-past
    *'The child was killed the thief by the mother.'

Passives, Dative Subjects, Reflexives, and Control The interaction of passives with other rules that involve grammatical relations supports our decision to formulate Passivization in terms of subjects and objects. Thus, the modals that induce datives on subjects behave exactly as predicted:

(227)

a. kuṭṭiye   pooliissukaar ikkiḷiyaakki.
    child-acc policemen-nom tickled
    'The policemen tickled the child.'

b. kuṭṭiye   pooliissukaarkkə ikkiḷiyaakkaṇam.
    child-acc policemen-dat   tickle-*aṇam*
    'The policemen want to tickle the child.'

(228)

a. kuṭṭi   pooliissukaaṟaal ikkiḷiyaakkappeṭṭu.
   child-nom policemen-instr tickle-pass-past
   'The child was tickled by the policemen.'

b. kuṭṭikkə pooliissukaaṟaal ikkiḷiyaakkappeṭaṇam.
   child-dat policemen-instr tickle-pass-*aṇam*
   'The child wants to be tickled by the policemen.'

The modal in (227) induces the dative case on *pooliissukaar*. Once the verb undergoes Passivization, however, the dative is induced on *kuṭṭi* ((228)).

There is a similar shift in the antecedent of reflexives. Consider the following sentences:

(229)

a. ṟaajaawə swaṇtam bhaaṟyaye ṇuḷḷi.
   king-nom self's   wife-acc   pinched
   'The king pinched self's wife.'

b. *ṟaajaawinaal swaṇtam bhaaṟya   ṇuḷḷappeṭṭu.
   king-instr   self's   wife-nom pinch-pass-past
   *'The self's wife was pinched by the king.'

(230)

a. *ṟaajaawine swaṇtam bhaaṟya   ṇuḷḷi.
   king-acc   self's   wife-nom pinched
   *'The self's wife pinched the king.'

b. ṟaajaawə swaṇtam bhaaṟyayaal ṇuḷḷappeṭṭu.
   king-nom self's   wife-instr   pinch-pass-past
   'The king was pinched by the self's wife.'

(229b) is ungrammatical because *ṟaajaawinaal,* which is no longer the subject after Passivization, cannot serve as the antecedent of *swaṇtam.* On the other hand, *ṟaajaawə* in (230b), which has acquired subjecthood after Passivization, is now eligible to be an antecedent.

Consider now the interaction between Passivization and control:

(231)

a. [ɸ kuṭṭiye   ikkiḷiyaakkikkoṇṭə] pooliissukaar biiḍi waliccu.
      child-nom tickle-while   policemen-nom beedi smoked
   'The policemen smoked beedi, while they tickled the child.'

b. *[pooliissukaar   φ ikkiḷiyaakkikkoṇṭǝ] kuṭṭi   biiḍi waliccu.
    policemen-nom   tickle-while   child-nom beedi smoked
    'The child smoked beedi while the policemen tickled the child.'

(232)

a. *[φ kuṭṭi   ikkiḷiyaakkappeṭṭukoṇṭǝ] pooliissukaar   biiḍi
    child-nom tickle-pass-past   policemen-nom beedi

    waliccu.
    smoked
    'The policemen smoked beedi while the child was being tickled
    by them.'

b. [pooliissukaaṙaal φ ikkiḷiyaakkappeṭṭukoṇṭǝ] kuṭṭi   biiḍi
    policemen-instr   tickle-pass-past-while   child-nom beedi

    waliccu.
    smoked
    'The child smoked beedi, while the child was being tickled
    by the policemen.'

(231b) is ungrammatical because the victim of control, *kuṭṭi,* is the object, but (232b) is grammatical because Passivization has changed *kuṭṭi*
to a subject. (231a) is grammatical; (232a) is not, because *pooliissukaar*
is not a subject.

This subject–object contrast is seen in (233a,b), in terms of the
controller:

(233)

a. [φ meeṡameel iṙunṇukoṇṭǝ] kuṭṭiye   pooliissukaar   ikkiḷiyaakki.
    table-loc   sat-while   child-acc policemen-nom tickled
    'The policemen tickled the child, while the policemen sat
    on the table.'

b. [φ meeṡameel iṙunṇukoṇṭǝ] kuṭṭi pooliissukaaṙaal
    table-loc   sat-while   child policemen-instr

    ikkiḷiyaakkappeṭṭu.
    tickle-pass-past
    'The child was tickled by the policemen, while the child sat
    on the table.'

In (233a), the controller is *pooliissukaar;* Passivization makes *kuṭṭi* the
controller in (233b).

Passives and Causatives   Since Causativization demotes the subject of intransitive verbs to direct objects, we would expect that the derived verbs, unlike the noncausative ones, would be passivizable. The following data confirm the prediction:

(234)

a.   kuṭṭi   uraṇṇi.
     child-nom slept
     'The child slept.'

b.   *kuṭṭi uraṇṇappeṭṭu.
     child sleep-pass-past
     *'The child was slept.'

c.   amma   kuṭṭiye   urakki.
     mother-nom child-acc sleep-cause-past
     'The mother made the child sleep.'

d.   kuṭṭi   urakkappeṭṭu.
     child-nom sleep-cause-pass-past
     'The child was made to sleep.'

(235)

a.   kuṭṭi   kaḷiccu.
     child-nom played
     'The child played.'

b.   *kuṭṭi   kaḷikkappeṭṭu.
     child-nom play-pass-past
     *'The child was played.'

c.   acchan   kuṭṭiye   kaḷippiccu.
     father-nom child-acc play-cause-past
     'The father made the child play.'

d.   kuṭṭi   kaḷippikkappeṭṭu.
     child-nom play-cause-pass-past
     'The child was made to play.'

While the passive suffix cannot be attached to *uraṇṇ* (in (234b)) and *kaḷikk* (in (235b)), their causativized versions *urakk* and *kaḷippikk* are free from this restriction.

Conclusion

We have seen that linguistic theory must incorporate three independent levels of description, schematized as follows:

(236)
Categorial level: Phrase markers, Case features, etc.
                            $\updownarrow$
Relational level: Grammatical relations
                            $\updownarrow$
Thematic level: Thematic roles

This allows us to make the following distinction between configurational and nonconfigurational languages:

(237)
Configurational languages are those in which grammatical relations are encoded in terms of configurations; nonconfigurational languages are those in which grammatical relations are encoded in terms of morphological features (case, agreement).

Grammatical relations can be encoded in terms of configurations only if the language has fixed word order. It follows, therefore, that languages with free word order cannot encode grammatical relations in terms of configurations. In other words, free word order will be possible in a language only if grammatical relations are encoded morphologically. Seen in this light, free word order is a derived property rather than a defining property of W* languages (cf. Hale 1979).

If a language is configurational, it follows that rules which effect a change in grammatical relations will change the configuration as well, thereby producing results which seem like movement. On the other hand, in nonconfigurational languages, the corresponding change will be one of morphology.

It is clear, then, that incorporating the level of grammatical relations into syntactic theory provides a powerful tool for describing the kind of phenomena typically associated with nonconfigurational languages. This level also enables us to capture insightfully the shared properties of human languages, in spite of superficial differences in phrase structure, agreement, or case.

Notes

This chapter owes its greatest debt to Joan Bresnan, but for whom I would not have had the courage to attempt something of this kind. She patiently read through several of its preliminary versions, offering invaluable guidance at every step. I have also benefited a great deal from the comments of Noam

Chomsky, Morris Halle, Ken Hale, Haj Ross, Mark Liberman, Mitch Marcus, and K. A. Jayasheelan. The errors are my own.

1. As far as I know, Chomsky no longer entertains this view (class lectures, MIT, Spring 1980).

2. See Farmer 1980 for evidence that Japanese also lacks a VP node.

3. The entry ($\downarrow$TENSE) = PAST is to block sentences like (i):

(i)

*r̄aajaawə kuṭṭiye kaḷḷan aaṇə kaṇakkaakkuṇṇu.

  king   child   thief   is   considers

(Compare this with (36).) The specification ($\downarrow$COPULA) = + prevents verbs like, say, *kaaṇ* 'see' from entering into this construction, thus blocking (ii):

(ii)

*r̄aajaawə kuṭṭiye kaḷḷan kaṇṭu kaṇakkaakkuṇṇu.

                  saw

I am grateful to K. A. Jayasheelan for bringing this to my notice and rectifying the weakness of the earlier formulation.

I must confess that I do not feel quite happy with rule (42b). Several people who read the draft of this chapter have, understandably enough, objected to its formulation. Unfortunately, however, given the peculiar properties of the construction, I cannot think of a better solution at the moment.

4. (54b) is not a syntactic rule, but a word-formation rule, since -*a,* an affix, is adjoined to the verb before lexical insertion. Hence, this is not a violation of any of the claims of X′ theory, which asserts that the expansion X^n should contain an X^{n-1} with the same categorial feature (cf. Jackendoff 1977).

5. My argument becomes void if the claim made by the binary branching of logical form (LF) and phonetic form (PF) in REST (cf. Chomsky 1980) is found to be false. Mark Liberman has pointed out to me that it may very well be the case that this claim is false, as it is unlikely that there is any language in which pronominal noncoreference and quantifier scope take place independently of stylistic scrambling. What my argument would then prove is that stylistic scrambling rules cannot exist. If, for example, the kind of argumentation I have used for Malayalam scrambling and rules of LF is applicable to English as well, it nullifies the claim made by REST rather than saying anything about Malayalam grammar.

6. In British English, the *shall* in *He shall do it* ('*I* insist that he does it') is "speaker-oriented"; on the other hand, *will* in *He will do it* ('*He* insists that he does it') is "subject-oriented." Similarly, *may* in *He may do it* is "epistemic" or "existential" ('*There exists* a possibility that he does it').

7. It may be noted that in *joon kuṭṭiyaaṇə* 'John is a child', we are assuming that *kuṭṭi* is 'CHILD((SUBJ))' while in (150), we are assuming that it is a term without a lexical form. The choice can be said to be free, *kuṭṭi* giving both alternatives, one of them being rejected in each case by conditions of well-formedness.

8. We do need interpretive rules to assign the feature of "focus" to the clefted constituent. I do not at present know how to outline an appropriate mechanism for this purpose.

9. The negation of 'The child is a thief' is *kuṭṭi kaḷḷan alla*.

10. This would involve problems such as direct and indirect causation, e.g., *eat ~ feed* vs. *eat ~ make x eat*.

Chapter 9

Sluicing:
A Lexical
Interpretation
Procedure

Lori S. Levin

Sluicing is an elliptical construction in which a sentence contains an embedded question consisting only of a *wh*-phrase. In this chapter, the word *fragment* refers to these isolated *wh*-phrases, such as *what, which one,* and *why* in the following examples.

(1)
a. I don't know what.
b. She wouldn't tell us which one.
c. I wonder why.

Fragments take on interpretations with respect to *context sentences.* Context sentences are often conjoined to sluiced sentences, but they need not be; in fact, they can be uttered by a different speaker. *Interpretations* (enclosed here in single quotation marks) are sentences that contain complete embedded questions which express the meaning of a fragment in a particular context.

(2)
a. Someone likes Janet, but I don't know who.   sluicing
   'I don't know who likes Janet.'   interpretation
b. Jenny was eating, but she won't tell us what.   sluicing
   'She won't tell us what she was eating.'   interpretation
c. Speaker A: Jill went home.
   Speaker B: I wonder why.   sluicing
   'I wonder why Jill went home.'   interpretation

   In this chapter I will present a procedure for interpreting sluiced sentences, proposing that fragments be generated as incomplete sentences in constituent structure and that interpretations be built in functional structure by copying pieces from the functional structure of the context sentence.

The analysis of sluicing developed here is based on the formal grammar described in chapter 4 of this volume. In this theory, *constituent structure* (c-structure) is the only level of phrase structure representation. The surface grammatical relations expressed at that level are encoded in *functional structures* (f-structures). Functional structures also take information from the lexicon. In particular, they contain *semantic forms* which essentially encode meanings of sentences by expressing mappings between grammatical functions and logically significant thematic functions. In short, functional structures are conglomerates of syntactic, lexical, and semantic information.

It will be shown later that notions of syntactic, semantic, and lexical compatibility of fragments and contexts are essential in the interpretation of sluicing. The sluicing construction therefore illustrates the usefulness of a level like f-structure which encodes all three types of information.

In section 9.1 I will describe the basic properties of the sluicing construction and consider how they are to be explained. In section 9.2 I will elaborate on lexical issues, focusing on the interaction of sluicing with lexical rules. Finally, in section 9.3 I will present an interpretation procedure for sluicing, along with solutions to the problems raised in the first section.

9.1 Basic Properties of Sluicing

Discourse Ellipsis

Sluicing belongs to a class of discourse ellipsis constructions and shares certain properties with the other members of that class. Discourse ellipsis constructions are incomplete sentences whose interpretation and grammaticality are determined by some other sentence.[1] As applied to sluicing, this means that a given fragment has no inherent interpretation; rather, it takes on a different interpretation in each different context. Notice also that fragments have no inherent grammatical function. *Who* is an object in (3a), a subject in (3b), and a prepositional object in (3c).

(3)

a. Janet likes someone, but I don't remember who.
    'I don't remember who Janet likes.'

b. Someone likes Janet, but I don't remember who.
    'I don't remember who likes Janet.'

c. Janet was talking to someone, but I don't remember who.
    'I don't remember who Janet was talking to.'

The grammaticality of a fragment also depends on the context. A fragment that is acceptable in one context may be completely ungrammatical in another.

(4)

a. Jenny mailed the postcards, but I don't know where to.[2]
b. *Jenny drank six milkshakes, but I don't know where to.

A theory of slucing should provide an explanation for these phenomena that can be applied to other types of discourse ellipsis as well.

Three Types of Sluicing

Fragment *wh*-phrases are assigned grammatical functions with respect to their context predicates in essentially three different ways. A fragment can be coreferential with some element of the context; it can act as a new argument of the context; or it can become an adjunct to the context.

Consider the sentences in (5). In each case, the *wh*-phrase has an *antecedent* in the context (fragments and their antecedents are italicized). The interpretations show that the *wh*-phrases have the same grammatical and thematic functions as their antecedents: *who* and *someone* are both subjects of *love*, *which one* and *one of the boys* are both objects of *kiss*, and *which day* and *one day last week* are both adjunct temporal phrases that are not arguments of the predicate *left*. The fragments actually replace their antecedents and take over their functional roles.

(5)

a. *Someone* loves Janet, but I don't know *who*.
    'I don't know *who* loves Janet.'

b. Jenny kissed *one of the boys*, but she won't say *which one*.
    'She won't say *which one* she kissed.'

c. Jill left *one day last week*, but I don't remember *which day*.
    'I don't remember *which day* Jill left.'

It often happens that the fragment *wh*-phrase does not have an antecedent but nevertheless becomes an argument of the predicate in the interpretation. In (6a), for example, *eat* is intransitive in the context, its only argument being its subject, *Jenny*. In the interpretation, however, it is transitive, taking the fragment *what* as its new object. In the interpretation of (6b), the predicate *slice* takes on a third argument in the form of an instrumental phrase, *with what*.

(6)

a. Jenny was eating, but nobody knows what.
   'Nobody knows what Jenny was eating.'

b. Seymour sliced the salami, but it's not clear with what.
   'It's not clear what Seymour sliced the salami with.'[3]

The *wh*-fragments in (6) correspond to *possible* arguments of the context predicates.

The fragments in (7) also have no antecedents. However, these examples are different from the previous ones in that the fragments are not arguments of their predicates. *When* and *where* are temporal and locative adjuncts. They are not selected by *leave* and *eat* in the way that an object is selected by *eat*, nor are they introduced as arguments by lexical rules as instrumentals are. Adjuncts are not incorporated into semantic forms of verbs (see chapter 4 of this volume).

(7)

a. Jenny left, but it's not clear when.
   'It's not clear when Jenny left.'

b. Janet ate dinner, but she won't tell us where.
   'She won't tell us where she ate dinner.'

Clearly, an adequate theory of sluicing should say something about how to detect the three different context–fragment relationships and how to handle each one. That they do in fact have to be treated differently will become clear below in the section on levels of representation.

Constituent Structure of Sluiced Questions
Sluiced embedded questions could be represented in c-structure as isolated *wh*-phrases, as they are perceived, or they could be represented as full embedded questions, reflecting their interpretation. Transformationalists choose to incorporate both representations in

their analysis; they propose to start with an underlying phrase marker for a full embedded question and apply a deletion rule that produces a truncated phrase marker for the fragment. (Ross 1969, Rosen 1976, and Bechhofer 1976a describe sluicing as a deletion rule.) However, such a derivation is not possible in a nontransformational grammar which has only one level of syntactic representation. Clearly, if one phrase marker has to be chosen, it should be an incomplete one that reflects the phonological shape of fragments. The plausibility of a nontransformational theory of sluicing therefore depends on the hypothesis that there is no need for an underlying syntactic representation of the interpretation.

There is apparently conflicting evidence bearing on this issue. I will argue in this section that sluiced embedded questions behave like S' ($\overline{\text{S}}$) with respect to syntactic rules that apply to S'. However, I will also present evidence showing that *wh*-fragments, unlike the *wh*-phrases in surface embedded questions, are not involved in long-distance syntactic relationships.

The puzzle then is this. Fragments cannot simply be represented as isolated *wh*-phrases, because they behave in some ways as if they were inside an S'. Still, they cannot be inside an S', because they behave in some ways as if they were truly isolated.

S' Behavior   The fact that *wh*-fragments are interpreted as sentences does not necessarily imply that they have to be represented as such syntactically. Furthermore, if fragments are in fact S's, special rules will have to be added to the grammar in order to derive or generate S's whose only surface structure constituent is a *wh*-phrase. Representing fragments as ordinary phrases, on the other hand, would be very easy. For example, the structures in (8) are generated by the usual phrase structure rules that produce such sentences as *I like apples, They spoke to Janet, Eating made Janet fat,* and *Jenny reads quickly.*

(8)

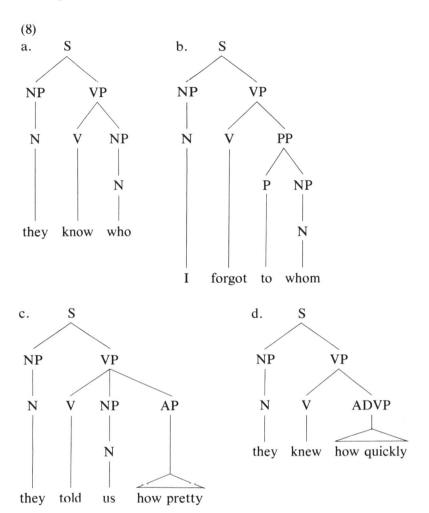

Unfortunately, *wh*-fragments do not behave like other NPs, PPs, APs, and ADVPs (henceforth XPs) with respect to subcategorization, number agreement, extraposition, and, in German, word order. Moreover, in those same situations, *wh*-fragments behave as if they were dominated by S'.

Perhaps the distribution of fragments provides the most convincing evidence that they are dominated by S'. Fragments are distributed like S' in two ways. First, they are subcategorized as if they were S's. That is, predicates that do not subcategorize for S' complements cannot take sluiced complements, and predicates that do take interrogative S' complements can also occur with sluiced complements. A second distributional property that fragments share with S's is that there is no categorial selection of the *wh*-phrase. Predicates that take sluiced complements take the whole range: NP, PP, AP, and ADVP. The evidence strongly suggests, therefore, that what is being selected is an S', not an XP.

Consider first some predicates that subcategorize for XPs, but not for S' complements. These never occur with sluicing. For example, *eat, look,* and *seem* in the (a) sentences of (9)–(11) are shown taking NP, PP, and AP arguments, and *run* in (12a) is shown with an adverbial adjunct. The (b) sentences of (9)–(12) show the same predicates with NP, PP, AP, and ADVP fragments. However, these are ungrammatical. (They are acceptable as echo questions, but that reading is not relevant to this discussion.)

(9)
a.   Janet ate apples.
b.   *Janet ate what.
c.   *Janet ate what on earth John cooked for dinner.[4]

(10)
a.   Jenny looked in the cookie jar.
b.   *Jenny looked in what.
c.   *Jenny looked where on earth she put the cookies.

(11)
a.   Jenny seemed pretty.
b.   *Jenny seemed how pretty.
c.   *Jenny seemed how pretty Janet is.

(12)
a.   Jenny ran home quickly.
b.   *Jenny ran home how quickly.
c.   *Jenny ran home how quickly Janet can run.

If fragments were represented syntactically as XPs, the contrast between the (a) and (b) sentences above would be unexplained: as an XP, a fragment should be able to replace any other XP of the same category. Notice though that in addition to not allowing sluiced complements, the predicates in (9)–(12) do not allow full embedded question complements, as the (c) examples illustrate. If fragments were represented as S's, the ungrammaticality of the (b) sentences would follow from the ungrammaticality of the (c) sentences. The predicates *eat, look, seem,* and *run* simply do not select embedded questions as arguments.

The converse situation is that some predicates do not subcategorize for XPs, but only for interrogative S′ complements. These always take sluiced complements as well. *Wonder* and *have no idea* are predicates of this type. They do not permit XP arguments, (13a) and (14a), but they do take sluiced complements, (13b) and (14b).

(13)

a.   *I wonder $\left\{ \begin{array}{l} \text{apples} \\ \text{in the cookie jar} \\ \text{pretty} \\ \text{quickly} \end{array} \right\}$.

b.   I wonder what.

c.   I wonder what Jenny saw.

(14)

a.   *I have no idea $\left\{ \begin{array}{l} \text{apples} \\ \text{in the cookie jar} \\ \text{pretty} \\ \text{quickly} \end{array} \right\}$.

b.   I have no idea what.

c.   I have no idea what Jenny saw.

If fragments were simply XPs, an exception would have to be made in the subcategorization requirements for *wonder* and *have no idea* in order to permit fragments to appear where no other XP is allowed. On the other hand, the distribution of argument types would be easily explained assuming that sluiced fragments are S′s. (13b) and (14b) are grammatical because *wonder* and *have no idea* take sentential complements, as shown in (13c) and (14c).

Selection of sluiced complements is similar to selection of S′s in another way. Predicates that take embedded question complements do not subcategorize for the category of the *wh*-phrases inside the complement (a fact also discussed in Bresnan and Grimshaw 1978).

(15)

a.   I have no idea *what* Jenny ate.   NP

b.   I have no idea *under what circumstances* they'd arrest him.   PP

c.   I have no idea *how pretty* Janet is.   AP

d.   I have no idea *how quickly* Jenny can run.   ADVP

(16)
a.   I wonder *what* Jenny ate.   NP
b.   I wonder *under what circumstances* they'd arrest him.   PP
c.   I wonder *how pretty* Janet is.   AP
d.   I wonder *how quickly* Jenny can run.   ADVP

Nor do they select the syntactic category of their sluiced complements. Any fragment XP can be interpreted as a sluiced question.

(17)
a.   I have no idea what.   NP
b.   I have no idea under what circumstances.   PP
c.   I have no idea how pretty.   AP
d.   I have no idea how quickly.   ADVP

(18)
a.   I wonder what.   NP
b.   I wonder under what circumstances.   PP
c.   I wonder how pretty.   AP
d.   I wonder how quickly.   ADVP

However, predicates that subcategorize for XP arguments specify the syntactic category of those arguments. For example, objects of transitive verbs must be NPs. Any other XP could not be interpreted as an object.

In summary, there are two ways in which fragments behave like S's with respect to subcategorization: they appear only where embedded questions appear, and the syntactic category of the *wh*-phrase is not subcategorized for by the matrix predicate.

Treating *wh*-fragments as simple XPs would give bad results in two respects. First, nothing could prevent them from appearing after predicates that take XP arguments, thus producing ungrammatical sentences like the (b) examples of (9)–(12). Also, in order to generate sluiced complements for *wonder* and *have no idea,* the syntactic subcategorization restrictions of these verbs would have to be relaxed so as to permit XP complements. But then nothing could prevent using just any XP as an argument, as the ungrammatical (13a) and (14a) demonstrate. Treating *wh*-fragments as S's, on the other hand, correctly predicts their distribution.

Fragments are also subject to semantic selection in addition to being subcategorized syntactically as S's. Sluiced embedded questions are not selected by every predicate that takes S'-complements. Rather, they occur only with those that semantically select interrogative complements.

(19)
a.   It seems that John left.
b.   *It seems why John left.
c.   *It seems why.

(20)
a.   I think that John likes Janet.
b.   *I think who likes Janet.
c.   *I think who.

(21)
a.   It's clear that John left.
b.   It's clear why John left.
c.   It's clear why.

(22)
a.   I know that John likes Janet.
b.   I know who likes Janet.
c.   I know who.

These semantic selection facts suggest a counterproposal to the conclusion that fragments are dominated by S′.

One could argue that fragments are XPs by showing that the data in (9)–(14) are a result of semantic selection alone—not syntactic subcategorization. If this were the case, then fragments could be represented as XPs in c-structure, provided that they are represented semantically as questions. They would then be selected only by predicates that take interrogative S′-complements. (I am assuming here the theory of complement selection described in Grimshaw 1979a. Predicates have syntactic subcategorization and semantic selection frames that operate autonomously. That is, the set of possible complement types for a given predicate is the cross product of the sets of subcategorization and selection frames.)

Notice that this particular representation of fragments implies that *wonder* and *have no idea* subcategorize for XPs as well as for S's. Their semantic selectional restrictions, however, would guarantee that they choose only complements that could be interpreted as questions. That is, they could select embedded question and sluiced complements because both are questions semantically, but choosing ordinary XP complements would violate a selectional restriction and result in an ungrammatical sentence. Conversely, the selectional restrictions on *eat, look, seem,* and *run* do not allow them to take interrogative arguments. Therefore, they could not select sluiced complements.

Unfortunately, allowing *wonder* and *have no idea* to subcategorize for XPs has an undesirable consequence. Grimshaw 1979a points out that there is a construction called a *concealed question,* which consists of a non-*wh* noun phrase which is interpreted as an indirect question. For example, *his name* and *the answer* in the following sentences are roughly synonymous to the corresponding embedded questions *what his name is* and *what the answer is.*

(23)
a. I found out his name.
b. I found out what his name is.

(24)
a. I found out the answer.
b. I found out what the answer is.

Now, if *wonder* and *have no idea* could select *what* as an NP that is semantically a question, they should select concealed questions as well. But, in fact, they do not.

(25)
a. I wonder what.
b. *I wonder his name.
c. *I wonder the answer.

(26)
a. I have no idea what.
b. *I have no idea his name.
c. *I have no idea the answer.

This contrast in grammaticality can be explained only by returning to the original observation that *wonder* and *have no idea* subcategorize only for S'. This, in turn, requires returning to the conclusion that sluiced fragments are dominated by S' and that they are chosen both syntactically and semantically by predicates that select interrogative S' complements.[5]

The second process with respect to which *wh*-fragments do not behave like other XPs is *number agreement.*

Consider the following sentences:

(27)

a.   Which problem isn't clear?

b.   *Which problem aren't clear?

(28)

a.   Which problems aren't clear?

b.   *Which problems isn't clear?

In each of these questions, the subject of *be clear* is a *wh*-phrase which, like any other subject, agrees with its predicate in number.

The subjects of the next examples are embedded questions which also agree in number with their predicates. However, because they are S's, they are all singular with respect to number agreement.

(29)

a.   Which problem we were supposed to do isn't clear.

b.   *Which problem we were supposed to do aren't clear.

(30)

a.   Which problems we were supposed to do isn't clear.

b.   *Which problems we were supposed to do aren't clear.

Sluiced fragments also occur only with singular verbs, regardless of whether the *wh*-phrases are singular or plural. (This is discussed in Ross 1969.)

(31)

a.   We were supposed to do one of the problems for tomorrow, but which problem isn't clear.

b.   *We were supposed to do one of the problems for tomorrow, but which problem aren't clear.

(32)

a.   We are supposed to do some problems for tomorrow, but which problems isn't clear.

b.   *We are supposed to do some problems for tomorrow, but which problems aren't clear.

These data are naturally explained under the assumptions that the fragment *wh*-phrases are contained inside an S' and that it is the S', not the fragment itself, that is the subject of the sluiced sentence.

The third argument concerning the constituency of *wh*-fragments involves *it-extraposition* and *sentential subjects*. Sentential subjects in English appear in two different constructions: either sentence-initial or extraposed.

(33)

a. That Janet will be home early is not likely.

b. It is not likely that Janet will be home early.

(34)

a. What she wants us to do isn't clear.

b. It's not clear what she wants us to do.

NP subjects, however, cannot be extraposed.

(35)

a. Her story is not likely.

b. *It's not likely her story.

(36)

a. The answer isn't clear.

b. *It's not clear the answer.

NP fragments, like S's, can be extraposed (Ross 1969).

(37)

a. She wants us to do something, but what isn't clear.

b. She wants us to do something, but it isn't clear what.

If *what* in (37) were an NP, it would be an exception to the generalization that only sentences extrapose. The *it*-extraposition construction would have to be modified in an ad hoc way to allow extraposed *wh*-NPs, but not extraposed non-*wh*-NPs. However, the following examples would remain unexplained.

(38)

a. It isn't clear how.

b. It isn't clear to who.

c. It's not clear how pretty.

Assuming still that fragments are XPs, these examples require more than just a modification of the *it*-extraposition construction. They would require a modification of c-structure to allow PP, AP, and ADVP subjects. If fragments are dominated by S', however, they can be selected as subjects and extrapose freely without making changes in phrase structure or *it*-extraposition.

The final bit of evidence concerning the sentential nature of fragments comes from *German word order*. The following examples show that in the past tense construction in German, NP objects can only precede the main verb while sentential complements must follow it.

(39)

a.   Ich habe ihm die Wahrheit gesagt.
      I   have him the truth   said
      'I told him the truth.'

b.   *Ich habe ihm gesagt die Wahrheit.

(40)

a.   Ich habe ihm gesagt, wer die Äpfel gestohlen hat.
      I   have him said   who the apples stolen   has
      'I told him who stole the apples.'

b.   *Ich habe ihm, wer die Äpfel gestohlen hat, gesagt.

Sluiced fragments behave like sentential complements in that they can
only follow the main verb. (This was pointed out to me by Ross, personal communication.)

(41)

a.   Jemand   hat die Äpfel gestohlen, und ich habe ihm gesagt wer.
      somebody has the apples stolen   and I   have him said   who
      'Somebody stole the apples and I told him who.'

b.   *Jemand hat die Äpfel gestohlen, und ich habe ihm wer gesagt.

The evidence so far indicates that sluiced fragments are not simply
wh-phrases that float around in isolation. Their syntactic behavior is, in
fact, quite systematic and can be predicted by assuming that they are
contained inside an S'. The data in the next subsection show that
fragments are not involved in long-distance syntactic relationships inside those S's.

Independence from Superbinding   I will use the word *superbinding* as a
convenient name for the long-distance syntactic relationship that holds
between a *wh*-phrase and its trace. In this discussion, I will assume
familiarity with Kaplan and Bresnan's treatment of long-distance dependencies in chapter 4, especially their use of the metavariables $\Uparrow$
and $\Downarrow$.

The superbinding relationship is subject to a variety of syntactic
constraints, which have been widely discussed in the transformational
literature as constraints on the analogous process, *wh*-movement.[6]
Violating the constraints in surface embedded questions, of course,
results in ungrammatical sentences. However, it often happens that
grammatical sluiced sentences have interpretations in which con-

straints are violated. In fact, the only syntactic constraints that apply to interpretations are that the *wh*-phrase itself be well-formed and that it meet the subcategorization restrictions of the context predicate.

(42a–e) are examples of grammatical sluiced sentences with interpretations that are considered ungrammatical by many speakers.

(42)

a. I heard about Rome's destruction of some city, but I don't remember which city.
   *'I don't remember which city I heard about Rome's destruction of.'

b. Janet and one of the boys were holding hands, but I don't remember which one.
   *'I don't remember which one Janet and were holding hands.'

c. I heard the claim that he bit someone, but I don't remember who.
   *'I don't remember who I heard the claim that he bit.'

d. That he'll fire someone is possible, but he won't say who.
   *'He won't say who that he'll fire is possible.'[7]

e. They asked where we bought one of our cars, but I don't remember which one.
   *'I don't remember which one they asked where we bought.'

The interpretations violate the Specified Subject, Coordinate Structure, Complex Noun Phrase, Sentential Subject, and *Wh*-Island Constraints, respectively.[8] Notice that these are all constraints on what can intervene between a *wh*-phrase and its trace: there cannot be a subject of an embedded clause, another *wh*-phrase, more than one bounding node, and so on. Notice also that these are constraints on constituent structure. They deal with phrase structure entities such as NP and S nodes, complex noun phrases, and coordinate structures. The constraints could not operate if those structures were not available.

The data in (42) provide evidence that fragments are not transformationally derived from their interpretations. The phrase structure trees for the interpretations would be ill-formed because they violate constraints on *Wh* Movement. Ill-formed trees would have to be allowed as intermediate stages in derivations that result in grammatical sentences.[9]

However, the data in (42) follow naturally from the assumption that sluiced fragments are directly generated by the phrase structure rules. The fact that interpretations violate constraints on superbinding is a consequence of the fact that they have no phrase structure representations. I am proposing that interpretations be constructed in f-structure, where phrase structure constraints are not applicable. This means that in c-structure, fragments stand alone as *wh*-phrases that are not super-bound to any sentence. It will be shown later that this is not incompatible with the fact that they are dominated by S'.

Further evidence that fragments are isolated in phrase structure is provided by another class of constraints, the left branch and pied piping conditions. These determine what counts as a complete *wh*-phrase in any given sentence. It is assumed here that they operate in basically the following way: the morphological feature [+WH] is assigned to *wh*-words in the lexicon. Then, based on the syntactic properties of the phrase containing the *wh*-word, [+WH] can percolate up from the *wh*-word to higher nodes. Only higher nodes that have the feature [+WH] can sit at the front of an S', and, conversely, if a node is assigned the feature [+WH], it and all of its daughters must come to the front of the S'. The Left Branch Condition specifies how far up [+WH] *must* percolate, preventing *wh*-phrases that are too small. In addition to ruling out phrases that are too small, pied piping conditions rule out phrases that are too big by preventing [+WH] from percolating up too far.

The class of left branch and pied piping conditions can be further divided into two smaller classes. One type of constraint, which sluicing obeys, distinguishes possible from impossible *wh*-phrases. Constraints of the other type, which sluicing violates, determine whether a given well-formed *wh*-phrase is appropriate in a given sentence. The contrast is significant because the first type of constraint, since it deals with *wh*-phrases themselves, can apply to fragments in isolation. The second type, however, must look at structural properties of a sentence in order to operate and, therefore, cannot operate when there is no structure. This indicates again that interpretations have no phrase structure representation.

Consider first some examples in which sluicing obeys left branch and pied piping conditions.

(43)
a. *I know he must be proud of it, but I don't know how.
b.   I know he must be proud of it, but I don't know how proud (of it).

(44)

a.   *John saw pictures of someone, but I don't know pictures of whom.

b.   John saw pictures of someone, but I don't know of whom.

c.   John saw pictures of someone, but I don't know who.

(43a) is ruled out as a violation of the Left Branch Condition. *How,* as a degree modifier, does not constitute a *wh*-phrase by itself.[10] The [+WH] feature percolates up from *how* to the entire adjective phrase, thus producing the *wh*-phrase *how proud (of it),* as in (43b). (44a), on the other hand, violates a pied piping restriction because the *wh*-phrase *pictures of whom* is too large. The [+WH] feature in this case starts on *who,* which is an acceptable *wh*-phrase in itself, and can percolate up to *of whom,* as in (44b), but not to *pictures of whom.*[11]

Sluicing does not obey all pied piping constraints that operate in embedded questions. In particular, it violates those that control preposition stranding. Violations of these constraints are manifested in two ways: prepositions which must be fronted under normal conditions may be omitted in sluiced fragments, and prepositions which cannot be fronted in surface embedded questions can appear with the *wh*-word in sluiced fragments.

The fronting of prepositions in embedded questions is highly restricted. Often, prepositions that can be fronted in matrix questions cannot be fronted in their corresponding embedded questions. For example, in (45)–(47) all of the matrix questions are completely grammatical, but in the embedded questions, stranding is highly preferred over pied piping.

(45)

a.   Who was he invited by?

b.   By whom was he invited?

c.   I forgot who he was invited by.

d.   ?I forgot by whom he was invited.

(46)

a.   What did he hang up the picture with?

b.   With what did he hang up the picture?

c.   I forgot what he hung up the picture with.

d.   ?I forgot with what he hung up the picture.

(47)
a. Who did he talk to?
b. To whom did he talk?
c. I forgot who he talked to.
d. ?I forgot to whom he talked.

Of course, *by whom, with what,* and *to whom* are legitimate *wh*-phrases, as opposed to *how* (as a degree modifier) and *pictures of whom,* which are ill-formed in some sense. Therefore, the awkwardness of the (d) examples of (45)–(47) is not caused by the *wh*-phrases themselves; rather, it is a property of the embedded question construction.

Now notice that the sluiced sentences corresponding to the (d) examples of (45)–(47) are completely grammatical.

(48)
a. I forgot by whom.
b. I forgot with what.
c. I forgot to whom.

The evidence concerning pied piping restrictions so far indicates that, in sluiced embedded questions, it is the form of the *wh*-phrase itself that is important, not the grammaticality of its interpretation.

Certain cases of obligatory pied piping also support the observation that the acceptability of fronted prepositions in fragments is governed by the well-formedness of the *wh*-phrase. Along with the paradigm in (45)–(47) there exists another, shown in (49). In this case, since it is obligatory in the matrix questions to front the prepositions, it is also obligatory in the embedded questions. (There is some dialectal variation on this point. Some speakers accept (49b) and (49d) as grammatical.) (49a) and (49c) are in contrast to the previous examples, where fronting prepositions in embedded questions is not even permitted for many speakers.

(49)
a. Under which circumstances will they report me?
b. *Which circumstances will they report me under?
c. I forget under which circumstances they'd report me.
d. *I forget which circumstances they'd report me under.

Notice that although *which circumstances* is not a big enough *wh*-phrase for these particular examples, it is a good *wh*-phrase in *I don't know which circumstances would be more hazardous.* Accordingly, *which circumstances,* as well as its pied piped version, *under which circumstances,* is an acceptable fragment, even though it is associated with an ungrammatical interpretation.

(50)

a.   They will report me under some circumstances, but I forget under which circumstances.

b.   They will report me under some circumstances, but I forget exactly which circumstances.

It is not always the case, however, that well-formed *wh*-phrases make well-formed fragments. (51) illustrates one situation in which prepositional phrase fragments are prohibited even though they are well-formed. (Similar examples are discussed in Rosen 1976.) The data in (51) do not constitute a counterexample to the pied piping facts described above. Rather, they show that sluicing is sensitive to lexical processes that affect the context predicate and thus support the claim that interpretations are constructed, not in c-structure, but in f-structure where they have access to lexical information.

(51)

a.   *They did away with someone, but I forgot with whom.
     *'I forgot with whom they did away.'

b.   *They were counting on someone, but I don't know on whom.
     *'I don't know on whom they were counting.'

c.   *They heard from someone, but they won't tell us from whom.
     *'They won't tell us from whom they heard.'

d.   *They dealt with some of the issues, but we don't know with which.
     *'We don't know with which issues they dealt.'

The predicates in (51) have undergone lexical reanalysis, a process that produces complex predicates which structurally and lexically incorporate a preposition (see chapter 1 of this volume). The input to reanalysis is a verb that subcategorizes for a prepositional phrase, and the output is a verb–preposition complex that subcategorizes for NP objects. The reanalyzed predicates above are *do-away-with, count-on, hear-from,* and *deal-with.* Notice that the prepositions have actually become part of the verbs and, therefore, can no longer be associated with the following NP. This means that the NP no longer has the grammmatical function POBJ. It is now an OBJ, as shown by the fact that it passivizes.

(52)
a. Some requirements have been done away with.
b. She can be counted on.
c. He hasn't been heard from in ages.
d. These are problems that have to be dealt with.

Recall now that in the interpretation of sluiced sentences, fragments take on the grammatical function of their antecedents. This is not possible in (51) because the antecedents are OBJs while the fragments are prepositional phrases. (51a–d) are ungrammatical for the same reason that (53) is ungrammatical: the fragment does not meet the subcategorization restrictions of the context predicate. Nor can the fragment, a *to*-object, share the same grammatical function with its antecedent, an object.

(53)
*Janet kissed someone, but I don't know to who.

We see, then, that the evidence concerning constraint violations suggests that sluiced fragments are syntactically isolated from any superbinding relationship. The data show that interpretations of fragments are exempt from constraints on the structural properties of sentences that contain *wh*-phrases. That is, interpretations that violate those constraints are often associated with grammatical fragment sentences. The insensitivity of fragments to the structural well-formedness of their interpretations indicates that the two are not related in c-structure but at some other level in the grammar where syntactic constraints on superbinding are not applicable.

Level of Representation
The basic goal of a theory of sluicing is to create a mapping between fragments and interpretations. Toward that end, the first step is to determine what component of the grammar should handle the mapping. This amounts to deciding what properties of the context and the fragment are reflected in the interpretation. For example, many transformational theories of sluicing proposed that only syntactic properties were important. In these analyses, underlying syntactic representations of contexts and interpretations were manipulated in order to produce

fragments in surface structure. The opposite position would be a semantic theory of sluicing which generates fragments directly by phrase structure rules and then constructs interpretations based on the thematic relationships in the context.

It turns out that interpretation cannot be either purely semantic or purely syntactic. The evidence in this section shows that the interpretation procedure must have access to the syntactic, semantic, and lexical properties of the context sentence.

Syntax   The need for syntactic information about the context sentence is best illustrated by case agreement between antecedents and fragments. When there is an antecedent in the context sentence, its surface structure position determines the case of the fragment.

Consider the simple sentences in (54)–(57), assuming a dialect of English in which *who* is ambiguously nominative or objective, *whom* is only objective, and *whose* is genitive.

(54)
a.   Someone kissed Janet, but I don't remember who.
b.   *Someone kissed Janet, but I don't remember whom.
c.   *Someone kissed Janet, but I don't remember whose.

(55)
a.   Janet kissed someone, but I don't remember who.
b.   ?Janet kissed someone, but I don't remember whom.[12]
c.   *Janet kissed someone, but I don't remember whose.

(56)
a.   It was hard to talk to one of the boys, but I don't remember who.
b.   ?It was hard to talk to one of the boys, but I don't remember whom.
c.   *It was hard to talk to one of the boys, but I don't remember whose.

(57)
a.   Someone's mother called, but I don't remember whose.
b.   *Someone's mother called, but I don't remember who.
c.   *Someone's mother called, but I don't remember whom.

The antecedents in (54)–(57) are not morphologically marked for case, but the case of each one can be determined by putting a pronoun which is marked for case in its place. The pronouns in (58) indicate that their corresponding NPs in (54)–(57) are nominative, objective, objective, and genitive, respectively.

(58)
a. He kissed Janet.
b. Janet kissed him.
c. It was hard to talk to him.
d. His mother called.

In (54), where the antecedent is nominative, the only acceptable *wh*-fragment is *who,* which can also be nominative. *Whom* is not permissible, because it can only be objective, nor is the genitive *whose* allowed. Where the antecedents are objective, in (55) and (56), *who* and *whom,* which can both be objective, are acceptable fragments, but *whose* is ungrammatical. And, of course, in (57), where the antecedent is genitive, only *whose* is allowed. In short, fragment *wh*-phrases agree with their antecedents in case, a property that is determined by surface structure position. (The case agreement facts in sluicing were first noticed by Ross 1969.)

It might be objected that there is another possible conclusion to be drawn on the basis of the data in (54)–(57). The case of a fragment could be determined, not by the position of its antecedent, but by its thematic role. That is, nominative fragments could be associated with thematic agents as in (54), objective fragments could be associated with themes and goals as in (55) and (56), and genitive fragments could be possessors of NPs. Further examples show, however, that there is no fixed mapping from the thematic role of the antecedent to the case of the fragment.

(59)

a. Someone was kissed, but I don't remember $\begin{Bmatrix} who \\ *whom \\ *whose \end{Bmatrix}$.

b. One of the boys was hard to talk to, but I don't remember $\begin{Bmatrix} who \\ *whom \\ *whose \end{Bmatrix}$.

c. Someone's singing too loudly annoyed the conductor, but he couldn't determine $\begin{Bmatrix} whose \\ *who \\ *whom \end{Bmatrix}$.

Someone in (59a) has the same thematic role that it had in (55), namely, the theme or "the one who was kissed." The corresponding *wh*-phrase has to be objective in (55), while in (59a) it must be nominative. Similarly, *one of the boys* shares the same thematic role in (56) and (59b). In the former the fragment is objective, while in the latter it must be nominative. Finally, in (59c), although *someone* has a thematic role as agent with respect to *sing,* the fragment is sensitive only to its surface position as a possessor. The examples in (59) show that the fragment is reflecting the surface position of the antecedent, not its thematic role.

The significance of this observation is that some surface syntactic information is used in sluicing. It cannot, therefore, be a purely semantic phenomenon. A semantic theory of sluicing that looked only at thematic relations could not predict the contrasts between (54)–(57) and (59). However, sluicing is not blind to thematic relations, nor is it blind to lexical information about the mapping from thematic to surface grammatical relations. In fact, it makes crucial use of thematic and lexical information and is, therefore, not a purely syntactic phenomenon.

Thematic Arguments and Mappings   (60) shows the inadequacy of syntactic information to completely account for sluicing. The contexts *John ate, John fell,* and *John moved* are syntactically identical, yet the fragment *I don't know what* is acceptable following only the first one. The source for the contrast in grammaticality lies in the lexical entries for the three context predicates. *Eat* differs from *fall* in the number of thematic arguments it has, and it differs from *move* in the way it maps surface grammatical functions onto thematic roles.

(60)
a.   John ate, but I don't know what.
b.   *John fell, but I don't know what.
c.   *John moved, but I don't know what.

Compare first *eat* and *fall.*

(61)
a.   John ate.
b.   John ate apples.
c.   John fell
d.   *John fell apples.

Eat is transitive in (61b). It has two arguments, *John* and *apples*. Each argument has a grammatical function and a thematic function. *John's* grammatical function is SUBJ, and its thematic function can be given the heuristic name *eater*. The grammatical function of *apples* is OBJ, and its thematic function can be called *eatee*.

This information is encoded in one of the semantic forms for *eat* that is found in the lexicon. (The matrix notation used here for semantic forms in the lexicon differs insignificantly from that used in functional structures, in that parentheses around grammatical functions are omitted in the former.)

(62)

$$\text{EAT}\begin{pmatrix} \text{SUBJ} & \text{OBJ} \\ \text{eater} & \text{eatee} \\ a & b \end{pmatrix}$$

Each column in the semantic form characterizes one argument. In this case, a is a referential index for *John* which is associated with the functions SUBJ and *eater*. b here is a referential index for *apples* which is associated with the functions OBJ and *eatee*. In general, the format for a semantic form is

(63)

$$\text{P}\begin{pmatrix} \text{G}_1\ldots\ldots\text{G}_n \\ \text{T}_1\ldots\ldots\text{T}_n \\ x_1\ldots\ldots x_n \end{pmatrix}$$

where P is the name of some predicate, G_i is a grammatical function, T_i is a heuristic name for a thematic function, and x_i is a referential index.

Now look at (61a). There is only one argument, *John*, but there is an entailment. *John ate* entails *John ate something*. This is encoded as follows in another semantic form for *eat*.

(64)

$$\exists x \text{ EAT}\begin{pmatrix} \text{SUBJ} & \\ \text{eater} & \text{eatee} \\ a & x \end{pmatrix}$$

Again, a is a referential index for *John,* the SUBJ and *eater*. The second column, however, says that there exists some x that is the *eatee,* but it has no grammatical function. In other words, even when *eat* is grammatically intransitive, there is a second thematic argument that does not show up on the surface.

Fall in (61c) also has just one grammatical argument. In this case, there is no unrealized second argument. In fact, as (61d) shows, it is impossible for *fall* to take a direct object as a second argument.[13] The semantic form for *fall,* therefore, shows only one thematic role, the *faller.*

(65)

$$\text{FALL} \begin{pmatrix} \text{SUBJ} \\ \text{faller} \\ a \end{pmatrix}$$

Now, in the context sentence of (60a) (repeated below with its interpretation), the intransitive form of *eat* is used, but the interpretation requires *eat* to be transitive. The two arguments of *eat* in the interpretation are *John* and *what.* Of course, no such interpretation is possible for (60b), because *fall* cannot be transitive. Sluicing is sensitive to the fact that *eat* could have two arguments, even though it has only one in the context sentence.

(60)

a'.   John ate, but I don't know what.
      'I don't know what John ate.'

b'.   *John fell, but I don't know what.
      *'I don't know what John fell.'

Sensitivity to possible arguments is not yet the whole story. *Move,* like *eat,* can be either transitive or intransitive.

(66)

a.   John moved.
b.   John moved the chair.

However, the transitive form of *move* cannot appear beside the transitive form in sluicing.

(60)

c'.   *John moved, but I don't know what.
      'I don't know what John moved.'

To see why this is so, compare the two semantic forms for *move.* Intransitive *move* takes one argument whose grammatical function is SUBJ and whose thematic function is *movee.* Transitive *move,* however, associates its SUBJ with the *mover* role and its OBJ becomes the *movee.* In other words, *John* is the thing that changed position or location in

(66a), but in (66b), *John* is only an agent for causing *the chair* to change position or location. Similarly, in (60c'), *John* is the *movee* in the context and the *mover* in the interpretation.

(67)

$$
\text{a.} \quad \text{MOVE} \begin{pmatrix} \text{SUBJ} \\ \text{movee} \\ a \end{pmatrix} \qquad \text{b.} \quad \text{MOVE} \begin{pmatrix} \text{SUBJ} & \text{OBJ} \\ \text{mover} & \text{movee} \\ b & a \end{pmatrix}
$$

Changing thematic roles is not a problem with *eat* because even though the OBJ comes and goes, the SUBJ retains its role as *eater*.

In order to explain the data in (60), the sluicing interpretation procedure must have access to the lexical entries for the predicates involved. In particular, it must be able to determine the number of possible thematic arguments that each predicate can take and how those arguments are mapped onto grammatical functions. The interaction of sluicing with the lexicon is examined in detail in section 9.2.

Semantics Semantics in sluicing is used most in the description of adjuncts. Adjuncts are sentence-modifying phrases expressing notions like time, place, and manner. It was mentioned earlier that they are not arguments of any predicate. Accordingly, they are not associated with any grammatical function and are not governed by the uniqueness condition on grammatical function assignments, which stipulates that a given grammatical function name can have at most one value (see chapter 4 of this volume). That is, there can be any number of adjuncts of any type modifying a given sentence. (68), for example, has five temporal adjuncts.

(68)
Your mother called in the afternoon, at four o'clock, on Tuesday, last week, after you had already left.

The distribution of adjuncts is constrained in some sense, however. When there are multiple adjuncts, they must all describe the same event.

(69)
a.   Your mother called at four o'clock, on Tuesday.
b.   #Your mother called at four o'clock, at three o'clock.
c.   #Your mother called on Tuesday, on Wednesday.

(70)

a.   Janet lives in the Bronx, in New York.

b.   #Janet lives in Philadelphia, in New York.

Notice that compatibility of adjuncts is a purely semantic issue (taking *semantics* in a loose sense to include notions like reference and knowledge about the world, not just logical properties of sentences). (70a) and (70b), for example, are syntactically identical. The distinction in acceptability depends on the knowledge that the Bronx is in New York but Philadelphia is not. All of the sentences in (69) and (70) are syntactically and functionally well-formed. It is not until their functional structures are handed over to the semantic component that they are detected as deviant (# signifies semantic ill-formedness).

Adjunct fragments behave like any other adjunct. They must be compatible with the adjuncts in the context sentence to which they are added.

(71)

a.   Janet lives in Philadelphia, but I don't know exactly where.
      'I don't know exactly where Janet lives in Philadelphia.'

b.   #Janet lives in Philadelphia, but I don't know in what city.
      #'I don't know in what city Janet lives in Philadelphia.'

(72)

a.   Your mother called on Tuesday, but I don't remember at what time.
      'I don't remember at what time your mother called on Tuesday.'

b.   #Your mother called on Tuesday, but I don't remember on what day.
      #'I don't remember on what day your mother called on Tuesday.'

(71a) and (72a) show that sluiced sentences can be interpreted as having multiple temporal and locative adjuncts. The problem with (71b) and (72b) is not that they are functionally ill-formed, but that their interpretations have conflicting adjuncts. In order to detect such conflicts, interpretations, like any other functional structure, must be subject to semantic processing.

Another use of semantics in sluicing is illustrated at the end of section 9.2, where it is shown that fragments must meet the selectional restrictions imposed by their context predicates.

9.2 Sluicing and Lexical Rules

In the previous section some examples were presented in which the predicate in the context of a sluiced sentence had fewer arguments than the predicate in the interpretation. In those examples (repeated here), *eat* becomes transitive in the interpretation and *slice* acquires an instrumental phrase. These changes in polyadicity (the number and type of a predicate's grammatically interpretable arguments) are effected by the lexical rules of Existential Quantification and Instrumentalization, respectively.

(6)
a. Jenny was eating, but nobody knows what.
    'Nobody knows what Jenny was eating.'
b. Seymour sliced the salami, but it's not clear with what.
    'It's not clear what Seymour sliced the salami with.'

It is a general property of sluicing that the predicates in the context and interpretation need not be identical, but may instead be related by a lexical rule.

However, predicates that are related by lexical rules are not always interchangeable. Consider *move* again, for example.

(60)
c'. *John moved, but I don't know what.
     'I don't know what John moved.'

The lexical rule of Causativization relates the intransitive and transitive forms of *move*. Yet when the former is used in the context of a sluiced sentence, the latter cannot be used in the interpretation. In this section I will examine a number of lexical rules affecting polyadicity in relation to compatibility conditions that determine which of them relate predicates that are interchangeable with respect to sluicing.

Mappings between Grammatical and Thematic Functions
Two Types of Lexical Rules   Recall that semantic forms for predicates specify assignments of grammatical functions to thematic argument positions, thus creating pairs of grammatical and thematic functions. Lexical rules change the assignments, thereby producing alternate semantic forms. For the purposes of this discussion, lexical rules are divided into two classes: those that relate *conflicting* semantic forms and those that relate *compatible* semantic forms.

Compatible semantic forms for a given predicate differ only in the presence or absence of one or more grammatical–thematic pairs. (73) is a hypothetical lexical rule that relates compatible semantic forms. The left side of (73) has two pairs, G_1–T_1 and G_2–T_2. The right side has those same two pairs plus a third, G_3–T_3.

(73)

$$P\begin{pmatrix} G_1 & G_2 \\ T_1 & T_2 \\ x_1 & x_2 \end{pmatrix} \Leftrightarrow P\begin{pmatrix} G_1 & G_2 & G_3 \\ T_1 & T_2 & T_3 \\ x_1 & x_2 & x_3 \end{pmatrix}$$

The semantic forms in (74) are also compatible. There is only one pair, G_1–T_1, on the left. T_2 does not participate in a pair because its grammatical function is not specified. Rule (74) assigns a grammatical function to T_2, thereby producing a second pair, G_2–T_2.

(74)

$$P\begin{pmatrix} G_1 & \\ T_1 & T_2 \\ x_1 & x_2 \end{pmatrix} \Leftrightarrow P\begin{pmatrix} G_1 & G_2 \\ T_1 & T_2 \\ x_1 & x_2 \end{pmatrix}$$

Conflicting semantic forms are produced by lexical rules that destroy some already existing pairs and create new ones by combining the grammatical and thematic functions in different ways, perhaps at the same time adding new functions or discarding old ones.

(75)

a.
$$P\begin{pmatrix} G_1 & G_2 \\ T_1 & T_2 \\ x_1 & x_2 \end{pmatrix} \Leftrightarrow P\begin{pmatrix} G_1 & G_2 \\ T_2 & T_1 \\ x_2 & x_1 \end{pmatrix}$$

b.
$$P\begin{pmatrix} G_1 \\ T_1 \\ x_1 \end{pmatrix} \Leftrightarrow P\begin{pmatrix} G_1 & G_2 \\ T_2 & T_1 \\ x_2 & x_1 \end{pmatrix}$$

The distinction between compatible and conflicting semantic forms is the basis of the following principle.

(76)
Principle of Lexical Compatibility I (PLC I)
Only compatible semantic forms are interchangeable with respect to sluicing.

PLC I explains why structurally identical sentences sometimes behave differently in sluicing. Lexical properties of context predicates must be taken into account. In particular, it is important to know what lexical rules apply to the context predicate and what kinds of changes those rules bring about. In the next few pages I will discuss rules that relate compatible semantic forms (Existential Quantification, Passive Existential Quantification, various preposition-incorporating rules), proceeding then to examine rules that relate conflicting lexical forms.[14]

Compatible Forms *Existential Quantification* (EQ) was mentioned earlier as the rule that relates the transitive and intransitive forms of *eat*. In general, it changes transitive predicates into intransitive predicates with implied objects. It is responsible for the following alternations.

(77)
a. Jenny ate apples.
b. Jenny ate.

(78)
a. Jenny sang "As Time Goes By."
b. Jenny sang.

(79)
a. Jenny was reading comic books.
b. Jenny was reading.

(80) is the rule schema for EQ.

(80)

$$\exists y \; P \begin{pmatrix} \text{SUBJ} & \\ T_1 & T_2 \\ x_1 & y \end{pmatrix} \Leftrightarrow P \begin{pmatrix} \text{SUBJ} & \text{OBJ} \\ T_1 & T_2 \\ x_1 & x_2 \end{pmatrix}$$

The presence of T_2 on the left with no grammatical function signifies an entailment that is associated with each of the intransitive sentences. (77b) entails *Jenny ate something*, (78b) entails *Jenny sang something*, and (79b) entails *Jenny was reading something*. This is in contrast to sentences like *John moved* and *John fell*, which do not entail *John moved something* and **John fell something*. Furthermore, the entailed objects in (77)–(79) are unspecified or indefinite, unlike the missing object in *John shaved*, which has a definite, reflexive interpretation along the lines of *himself* or *his face*. The entailed argument in EQ and its indefiniteness are represented by existentially quantifying its referential index.

Notice that EQ relates compatible semantic forms. By assigning the grammatical function OBJ to the second argument position, it simply defines a new pair, OBJ–T_2, without changing the first pair, SUBJ–T_1. Forms that are related by EQ are interchangeable in sluicing, as shown by the following examples where an intransitive predicate in the context is replaced by its corresponding transitive predicate in the interpretation.

(81)

a. Jenny ate, but she won't tell us what.
   'She won't tell us what she ate.'

b. $\exists y \; \text{EAT} \begin{pmatrix} \text{SUBJ} & \\ \text{eater} & \text{eatee} \\ a & y \end{pmatrix} \Rightarrow \text{EAT} \begin{pmatrix} \text{SUBJ} & \text{OBJ} \\ \text{eater} & \text{eatee} \\ a & b \end{pmatrix}$

c. Jenny was singing, but I couldn't tell what song.
   'I couldn't tell what song Jenny was singing.'

d. Jenny was reading, but she won't tell us what.
   'She won't tell us what she was reading.'

Passive Existential Quantification (PEQ) is very similar to EQ, the only difference being that the quantified argument in PEQ is the BY OBJ of a passive predicate. It produces agentless passives.

(82)

a. Janet was kissed by Jimmy.
b. Janet was kissed.

Like EQ, PEQ relates compatible forms which can occur side by side in sluicing.

(83)

a. *Passive Existential Quantification (PEQ)*

$\exists y \; \text{P} \begin{pmatrix} & \text{SUBJ} \\ T_1 & T_2 \\ y & x_1 \end{pmatrix} \Leftrightarrow \text{P} \begin{pmatrix} \text{BY OBJ} & \text{SUBJ} \\ T_1 & T_2 \\ x_2 & x_1 \end{pmatrix}$

b. Janet was kissed, but I don't know by whom.
   'I don't know who Janet was kissed by.'

$\exists y \; \text{KISS} \begin{pmatrix} & \text{SUBJ} \\ \text{kisser} & \text{kissee} \\ y & a \end{pmatrix} \Rightarrow \text{KISS} \begin{pmatrix} \text{BY OBJ} & \text{SUBJ} \\ \text{kisser} & \text{kissee} \\ b & a \end{pmatrix}$

Preposition-Incorporating rules, which add prepositional objects to semantic forms, are described by schema (84).

(84)

$$P\begin{pmatrix} G_1 \ldots \ldots G_n \\ T_1 \ldots \ldots T_n \\ x_1 \ldots \ldots x_n \end{pmatrix} \Leftrightarrow P\begin{pmatrix} G_1 \ldots \ldots G_n & \text{PREP OBJ} \\ T_1 \ldots \ldots T_n & T_{n+1} \\ x_1 \ldots \ldots x_n & x_{n+1} \end{pmatrix}$$

Rules that fit this schema are of basically two types: those that productively introduce a particular prepositional phrase that always has the same thematic function, and those that add prepositional phrases to small classes of predicates that subcategorize for them and select their thematic functions.

Instrumental, benefactive, and comitative phrases are introduced by rules of the first type (see chapter 3 of this volume for evidence that these phrases are, in fact, thematic arguments of their predicates). Each rule brings in a new thematic function that is inherently associated with a particular preposition. The thematic roles *instrument* and *accomplice* are always realized by the grammatical function WITH OBJ, while the *benefactor* role is always realized as a FOR OBJ. The rules that introduce these arguments are illustrated below as they apply to the predicates *slice, bake,* and *eat.*

(85)
a.   Seymour sliced the salami.
b.   Seymour sliced the salami with a knife.
c.   *Instrumental*

$$\text{SLICE}\begin{pmatrix} \text{SUBJ} & \text{OBJ} \\ \text{slicer} & \text{slicee} \\ a & b \end{pmatrix} \rightarrow \text{SLICE}\begin{pmatrix} \text{SUBJ} & \text{OBJ} & \text{WITH OBJ} \\ \text{slicer} & \text{slicee} & \text{instrument} \\ a & b & c \end{pmatrix}$$

(86)
a.   John baked a cake.
b.   John baked a cake for Jimmy.
c.   *Benefactive*

$$\text{BAKE}\begin{pmatrix} \text{SUBJ} & \text{OBJ} \\ \text{baker} & \text{baked} \\ a & b \end{pmatrix} \Rightarrow \text{BAKE}\begin{pmatrix} \text{SUBJ} & \text{OBJ} & \text{FOR OBJ} \\ \text{baker} & \text{baked} & \text{benefactor} \\ a & b & c \end{pmatrix}$$

(87)

a. Jenny ate dinner.
b. Jenny ate dinner with Janet.
c. *Comitative*

$$\text{EAT} \begin{pmatrix} \text{SUBJ} & \text{OBJ} \\ \text{eater} & \text{eatee} \\ a & b \end{pmatrix} \Rightarrow \text{EAT} \begin{pmatrix} \text{SUBJ} & \text{OBJ} & \text{WITH OBJ} \\ \text{eater} & \text{eatee} & \text{accomplice} \\ a & b & c \end{pmatrix}$$

The forms in (85)–(87) are compatible and interchangeable in sluicing.

(88)

a. Seymour sliced the salami, but I don't know with what.
b. John baked a cake, but I don't know for whom.
c. Jenny ate dinner, but I don't know with whom.

The rules illustrated in (85)–(87) are fairly productive. That is, they apply to many different predicates that do not form a natural semantic class. The second type of rule that introduces oblique objects, however, applies to small semantic classes of predicates. Such rules add *to*-phrases to *talk*- and *speak*-type predicates and *at*-phrases to the *laugh, grin, smile* group.

(89)

a. Jenny was talking.
b. Jenny was talking to Janet.

(90)

a. Janet laughed.
b. Janet laughed at Jenny.

In spite of their different nature, idiosyncratic preposition-incorporating rules follow the same schema as the productive ones. It follows, then, that they too relate forms that are compatible and interchangeable.

(91)

a. Jenny was talking, but I don't know to who.
b. Jenny was smiling, but we don't know at what.

Adjuncts have a special status in lexical interpretive theory. They are not assigned grammatical functions, nor are they encoded in semantic forms. The following examples, therefore, trivially illustrate PLC I in that the semantic forms in the contexts and interpretations are identical.

(92)
a. Jenny went home, but nobody knows why.
b. Janet jimmied the lock, but she won't tell us how.
c. Jill is coming to visit, but I don't know when.

Conflicting Forms The lexical rules Causativization, Activo-Passivization, Passivization, and Dative relate conflicting semantic forms, as we will see in the following paragraphs.

Causativization was discussed briefly as the rule that relates the two forms of *move*. ((66) is repeated here as (93).)

(93)
a. John moved.
b. John moved the chair.

It is also responsible for these alternations:

(94)
a. The door opened.
b. Janet opened the door.

(95)
a. The vase broke.
b. Jill broke the vase.

(96a) is the rule schema for Causativization. Clearly, the forms it associates are conflicting. Causativization introduces a new grammatical function, OBJ, and a new thematic function, T_2, but it assigns the new grammatical function to the old thematic function and the new thematic function to the old grammatical function. (96b) shows Causativization as it applies to *move*.

(96)

a. $\quad P \begin{pmatrix} \text{SUBJ} \\ T_1 \\ x_1 \end{pmatrix} \quad \Leftrightarrow \quad P \begin{pmatrix} \text{SUBJ} & \text{OBJ} \\ T_2 & T_1 \\ x_2 & x_1 \end{pmatrix}$

b. $\quad \text{MOVE} \begin{pmatrix} \text{SUBJ} \\ \text{movee} \\ x_1 \end{pmatrix} \quad \Leftrightarrow \quad \text{MOVE} \begin{pmatrix} \text{SUBJ} & \text{OBJ} \\ \text{mover} & \text{movee} \\ x_2 & x_1 \end{pmatrix}$

Now consider more carefully what would happen if the two forms of *move* were interchanged in the sluicing construction. Suppose, as in (60c) (repeated here as (97)), that *John moved* is the context sentence and that *what* is to become the object of *move* in the interpretation.

(97)
*John moved, but I don't know what.

As can be seen on the right side of (96b), the object of *move,* when it is present, is assigned the thematic function *movee,* and the subject is forced to take the *mover* role. The problem with (97), then, is that in the context, *John* is the *movee,* but the interpretation forces *John* to be the *mover.*

   Conversely, suppose that *The chair moved* is a context sentence, as in (98), and that *who* is to become the *mover* in the interpretation.

(98)
*The chair moved, but I don't know who.
 'I don't know who moved the chair.'

The right side of (96b) shows that, when there is a *mover,* its grammatical function is SUBJ; the *movee,* which was the subject of the intransitive form of *move,* must now take the grammatical function of OBJ instead. The ungrammaticality of (98) is due to the fact that *the chair* is the subject of the context sentence and the object of the interpretation.

   Activo-Passivization is the rule that relates the (a) and (b) sentences in (99) and (100). It imposes a passive reading on a predicate while maintaining active morphology.

(99)
a.   This book reads easily.
b.   Janet read the book.

(100)
a.   Novels sell well.
b.   Barnes and Noble sell novels.

(101)
Activo-Passivization

$$Qy \ P \begin{pmatrix} & \text{SUBJ} \\ T_1 & T_2 \\ y & x_1 \end{pmatrix} \Leftrightarrow P \begin{pmatrix} \text{SUBJ} & \text{OBJ} \\ T_1 & T_2 \\ x_2 & x_1 \end{pmatrix}$$

Activo-Passivization is like EQ in that it involves quantification over an implied argument. In this case, however, there is a generic quantifier, Q, which is intended to be read 'people in general' or 'one'. This reflects the fact that activo-passive sentences seem to be generalizations. For example, (99a) means roughly 'People, in general, read this book easily'.

In addition to quantifying one of its arguments, Activo-Passivization, like Causativization, changes the mapping between grammatical and thematic functions, thereby producing incompatible semantic forms. Consider the ungrammatical sluiced sentence (102), which uses the quantified form of (101) in its context and the related transitive form in its interpretation. Notice that *novels* is the subject of the context and the object of the interpretation, while *who* is the subject of the interpretation. Such changes in grammatical function assignment in sluicing are, of course, ruled out by PLC I.

(102)
*Novels sell well, but I don't know who.
'I don't know who sells novels well.'

Another lexical rule that relates conflicting semantic forms is *Passivization*.

(103)

$$
P \begin{pmatrix} \text{SUBJ} & \text{OBJ} \\ T_1 & T_2 \\ x_1 & x_2 \end{pmatrix} \Leftrightarrow P \begin{pmatrix} \text{BY OBJ} & \text{SUBJ} \\ T_1 & T_2 \\ x_1 & x_2 \end{pmatrix}
$$

Unfortunately, Passivization cannot be tested directly for compliance with PLC I. I will discuss examples (104a–e), which are the data that potentially determine whether Passivization confirms or disproves PLC I, and show that they are inconclusive on that point. Then I will show that the function-changing effects of Passivization do show up when it is applied in sequence with Passive Existential Quantification (PEQ), so that, in an indirect way, Passivization does provide supporting evidence for PLC I.

(104a–e) are potential examples of sluicing where the context and the interpretation differ in voice. Some of the examples appear to support PLC I, and some appear to disconfirm it. However, they all have alternative explanations in terms of the relation between the fragments and their antecedents and thus do not decide the issue of whether or not Passivization complies with PLC I.

(104)
a. *Someone kissed Janet, but I don't know by who.
b. Janet was kissed by someone, but I don't know who.
c. Someone was kissed by Janet, but I don't know who.
d. *Someone was kissed by Janet, but I don't know whom.
e. Janet kissed someone, but I don't know who.

Given the interpretation 'I don't know by whom Janet was kissed', (104a) appears to support PLC I. That is, it could be ungrammatical because the active semantic form used in the context conflicts with the passive semantic form in the interpretation. However, there is another explanation. *Someone* and *by who* are in an antecedent–anaphor relationship by virtue of the fact that they bear the same thematic role with respect to *kiss*. But, as shown in section 9.1, fragments must take on the grammatical function of their antecedents, which is impossible here. The ungrammaticality of (104a) need not result from lexical conflict. It could result instead from the fact that the prepositional phrase, *by who,* cannot take over the grammatical function of its antecedent, *someone,* which is a subject.

In contrast to (104a), (104b) might seem to be a counterexample to PLC I if it is given an active interpretation, 'I don't know who kissed Janet', where the fragment, *who,* becomes the subject of the interpretation. If this were the case, the active form of *kiss* in the interpretation would conflict with the passive form of *kiss* in the context, *Janet was kissed by someone,* and PLC I would predict that (104b) is ungrammatical. However, (104b) is grammatical, in apparent violation of the principle.

It turns out that the apparent acceptability of an active interpretation of (104b) is only due to the fact that *who* is ambiguously nominative or objective and could be mistaken for a subject. (104b) could also be assigned a passive interpretation, 'I don't know who Janet was kissed by', where *who* is the object of the stranded preposition, *by.* Under this interpretation, (104b) is consistent with PLC I in that the context and the interpretation are both passive and are therefore compatible. Unfortunately, this tells us nothing about the alternation of active and passive predicates in sluicing.

Also because of the ambiguity of *who,* (104c) could be assigned an active interpretation, 'I don't know who Janet kissed', which would constitute a counterexample to PLC I. However, the alternative interpretation, 'I don't know who was kissed by Janet', is consistent with PLC I because both the context and interpretation are passive. Still, this says nothing about the compatibility of actives and passives in sluicing.

Notice though that for those speakers who accept *whom* as a direct object, (104d) does illustrate the incompatibility of active and passive predicates. Since *whom* is case-marked as objective, only the active interpretation, 'I don't know whom Janet kissed', is possible because in the passive interpretation, '*I don't know whom was kissed by Janet', *whom* would be used incorrectly as a subject. PLC I correctly predicts that (104d) is ungrammatical, because the lexical forms used in the context and interpretation are conflicting.

Unfortunately, this is not a valid example for a great many speakers of English who allow *whom* only as a prepositional object. For those speakers, (104d) is ungrammatical because *whom* is used "incorrectly" as a direct object. The example is, therefore, irrelevant to the question of compatibility of actives and passives.

(104e), like (104b) and (104c), also has two potential interpretations: one that would disconfirm PLC I because the context and interpretation would contain conflicting forms, *I don't know who Janet was kissed by;* and one that is not relevant to the question of compatibility because the context and interpretation have the same semantic form, *I don't know who Janet kissed.*

In short, the data in (104) do not show conclusively whether or not active and passive predicates can be interchanged in sluicing. (104a) could illustrate the incompatibility of active and passive forms, or it could merely illustrate the fact that a prepositional phrase fragment cannot have a noun phrase antecedent. (104b)–(104e) each have one possible interpretation that would disconfirm PLC I and another possible interpretation that is irrelevant to the question of compatibility of actives and passives. (104d) is the only example that might show that actives and passives are not interchangeable, but it is a valid example only for speakers who allow *whom* as a direct object.

Example (105a) shows much more clearly that active and passive predicates are not interchangeable. In the proposed interpretation, the agentless passive of the context is replaced by an active predicate in the interpretation. The quantified agent phrase of the context has been instantiated as a subject rather than a *by*-object (compare (83b)), and the subject of the context has become the object of the interpretation. This effect is achieved by applying Passivization and PEQ in sequence as shown in (105b).

(105)

a.   *Janet was kissed, but I don't know who.
     'I don't know who kissed Janet.'

b. $P \begin{pmatrix} \text{SUBJ} & \text{OBJ} \\ T_1 & T_2 \\ x_1 & x_2 \end{pmatrix} \overset{\text{Pass.}}{\Leftrightarrow} P \begin{pmatrix} \text{BY OBJ} & \text{SUBJ} \\ T_1 & T_2 \\ x_1 & x_2 \end{pmatrix} \overset{\text{PEQ}}{\Leftrightarrow} \exists y\, P \begin{pmatrix} & \text{SUBJ} \\ T_1 & T_2 \\ y & x_2 \end{pmatrix}$

As shown earlier (example (83b)), passives and agentless passives related by PEQ are compatible. The conflict in the derivation (105b) lies in the relation between the active and passive semantic forms. A result of using Passivization in (105b) is that the input and output of the derivation are not interchangeable. (105b) thus provides another piece of supporting evidence for PLC I.

The lexical *Dative* rule also produces conflicting grammatical function assignments and, like Passivization, its effects are not directly observable. Examples (106a) and (106b) are analogous to (104a) and (104b). The first appears to support the prediction that *to*-datives are not interchangeable with double object datives, but its ungrammaticality could alternatively be explained by the fact that the prepositional phrase, *to who,* cannot take over the grammatical function of its antecedent, *someone,* which is an object. (106b), on the other hand, would disconfirm PLC I if it were given the double object interpretation, because it would constitute a grammatical sluiced sentence with conflicting semantic forms. (The ungrammaticality of this interpretation results from the fact that the first object of a double object construction cannot, in general, be questioned.) The second suggested interpretation of (106b) is consistent with PLC I, but says nothing about the *to*-dative–double object alternation because both the context and the interpretation have the same semantic form. Thus, (106a,b) do not decide the issue of whether *to*-datives and double object datives are interchangeable.

(106)

a.   *Janet threw someone the ball, but I don't know to who.
     ?'I don't know to who Janet threw the ball.'

b.   Janet threw the ball to someone, but I don't know who.
     *'I don't know who Janet threw the ball.'
     'I don't know who Janet threw the ball to.'

c.   *Dative*

$$P\begin{pmatrix} \text{SUBJ} & \text{OBJ} & \text{TO OBJ} \\ T_1 & T_2 & T_3 \\ x_1 & x_2 & x_3 \end{pmatrix} \Leftrightarrow P\begin{pmatrix} \text{SUBJ} & \text{OBJ2} & \text{OBJ} \\ T_1 & T_2 & T_3 \\ x_1 & x_2 & x_3 \end{pmatrix}$$

The function-changing effect of the Dative rule becomes apparent when it is used in a derivation. In example (107), the context predicate, a dyadic transitive verb, is replaced by a double object dative in the interpretation. The two conflicting forms are related by the sequence of rules shown in (108).

(107)

*Janet threw the ball, but I don't know who.

*'I don't know who Janet threw the ball.'

(108)

$$P\begin{pmatrix} \text{SUBJ} & \text{OBJ} \\ T_1 & T_2 \\ x_1 & x_2 \end{pmatrix} \overset{\substack{\text{Oblique} \\ \text{Object} \\ \text{Introduction}}}{\Leftrightarrow} P\begin{pmatrix} \text{SUBJ} & \text{OBJ} & \text{TO OBJ} \\ T_1 & T_2 & T_3 \\ x_1 & x_2 & x_3 \end{pmatrix} \overset{\text{Dative}}{\Leftrightarrow} P\begin{pmatrix} \text{SUBJ} & \text{OBJ2} & \text{OBJ} \\ T_1 & T_2 & T_3 \\ x_1 & x_2 & x_3 \end{pmatrix}$$

The first step in the derivation, Oblique Object Introduction, produces compatible forms (see example (91)), but then the Dative rule changes the grammatical function assignments so that the input and output of (108) are conflicting and not interchangeable. This result is consistent with PLC I, which correctly predicts that *to*-datives and double object datives are not interchangeable.

PLC I reflects the fact that the interpretation of a fragment is dependent on the context sentence. By requiring that the interpretation and context specify the same mapping between grammatical and thematic functions, this principle ensures that it is the functional interpretation of the context, not just its structural form, that is used in the interpretation.

Semantic Constraints on Indices

In addition to changing polyadicity, lexical rules can impose semantic constraints on argument positions either by specifying selectional restrictions or by simply assigning a particular fixed value to a referential index. Since fragments, when they are interpreted, actually become arguments of their context predicates, it is reasonable to assume the following principle:

(109)

Principle of Lexical Compatibility II (PLC II)

Fragments must obey semantic constraints imposed by their context predicates.

Reflexive Intransitivization relates transitive predicates to intransitive predicates with reflexive readings. It is schematized as follows:

(110)

$$P\begin{pmatrix} \text{SUBJ} & \text{OBJ} \\ T_1 & T_2 \\ x_1 & x_2 \end{pmatrix} \Leftrightarrow P\begin{pmatrix} \text{SUBJ} \\ T_1 & T_2 \\ x_1 & x_1 \end{pmatrix}$$

As in EQ and Activo-Passivization, the presence of a thematic function without an assigned grammatical function signifies an implied argument. In this case, however, the implied argument is coindexed with the grammatically realized argument, thus indicating that the two are coreferential. As applied to the following examples, this means that the intransitive predicates in the (b) sentences are understood as having reflexive objects.[15] That is, they mean roughly 'John shaved himself', 'Janet washed herself', and 'Janet hid herself'. The transitive predicates in the (a) sentences, however, impose no such restriction on the identity of the object.

(111)
a.   John shaved every man in the barber shop.
b.   John shaved before going to work.

(112)
a.   Janet washed the dishes.
b.   Janet washed.

(113)
a.   Janet hid the cookies.
b.   Janet hid.

Now consider what happens in sluicing when the transitive form of *shave* replaces the intransitive form.

(114)
a.   *John shaved, but he won't tell us who.
     'He won't tell us who he shaved.'

$$ \text{b.}\quad \text{SHAVE} \begin{pmatrix} \text{SUBJ} & \text{OBJ} \\ \text{shaver} & \text{shavee} \\ a & b \end{pmatrix} \Leftrightarrow \text{SHAVE} \begin{pmatrix} \text{SUBJ} & \\ \text{shaver} & \text{shavee} \\ a & a \end{pmatrix} $$

Intransitive *shave,* used in the context sentence of (114a), requires that the *shavee* be identical to *John*, the *shaver*. Transitive *shave*, used in the interpretation, does not stipulate that its arguments be coreferential. *Who* and *John* are, therefore, assigned distinct indices, in violation of the restriction imposed by the context predicate that the *shaver* and *shavee* be coreferential. Principle (109) predicts on the basis of this that (114a) should be ungrammatical, as, in fact, it is.

Reciprocal Intransitivization follows the same schema as Reflexive Intransitivization, except that it imposes a reciprocal reading on its missing object. That is, the (b) sentences in (115) and (116) mean 'Janet and Jenny met each other' and 'They kissed each other'.

(115)
a. Janet and Jenny met Jimmy.
b. Janet and Jenny met.

(116)
a. They kissed all of the boys.
b. They kissed.

Of course, predicates related by Reciprocal Intransitivization, like those related by Reflexive Intransitivization, are semantically incompatible. One form requires its arguments to be identical, while the other asserts that they are different.

(117)
a. *Janet and Jenny met, but they won't say who.
    'They won't say who they met.'
b. *They kissed, but it's not clear who.
    'It's not clear who they kissed.'

Some predicates impose very strong *selectional restrictions* on their optional arguments. *Paint,* for example, has an optional NCOMP or ACOMP that expresses a color.

(118)
a. We painted the wall.
b. We painted the wall red.
c. We painted the wall the color of fire engines.

Selectional restrictions on these XCOMPs are reflected in the way they are questioned. When the NCOMP of *paint* is questioned, the *wh*-phrase clearly specifies the notion of color, as in (119a). (119b) is unacceptable because, out of context, it is hard to interpret *what* as referring to a color. Notice that in the appropriate discourse setting (119b) becomes acceptable: "They painted the living room red, and the bedroom green, but what did they paint the kitchen?"

(119)
a. What color did you paint the kitchen?
b. ?What did you paint the kitchen?

The restrictions on questioning the NCOMP of *paint* also apply in sluicing. The alternate forms of *paint* are compatible in the sense of PLC I,
but they are interchangeable only when the fragment clearly reflects
the selectional restrictions on the NCOMP.

(120)

a.　　We painted the wall, but I don't remember what color.

b.　　?We painted the wall, but I don't remember what.

$$
\text{c.   PAINT} \begin{pmatrix} \text{SUBJ} & \text{OBJ} & \text{NCOMP} \\ \text{painter} & \text{painted} & \text{color} \\ x_1 & x_2 & x_3 \end{pmatrix} \Leftrightarrow \text{PAINT} \begin{pmatrix} \text{SUBJ} & \text{OBJ} \\ \text{painter} & \text{painted} \\ x_1 & x_2 \end{pmatrix}
$$

Cognate object constructions provide another example of strong selectional restrictions. *Live* and *die,* for example, when they take objects, require them to explicitly mention life and death.

(121)

a.　She lived a happy life.

b.　She lived.

(122)

a.　She died a noble death.

b.　She died.

Selection for cognate objects is also reflected in the way they are questioned. The *wh*-phrases *what kind of life* and *what kind of death* clearly
satisfy the selectional restrictions of *live* and *die,* but a simple *wh*-
phrase like *what* is not easily interpretable as a semantically appropriate argument.

(123)

a.　　What kind of life did he live?

b.　　*What did he live?

c.　　What kind of death did he die?

d.　　*What did he die?

This restriction on *wh*-phrases is applicable in sluicing also. Cognate
objects that are introduced by sluicing must explicitly express the appropriate semantic selection.

(124)

a.　　She lived, but nobody knows what kind of life.

b.　　*She lived, but nobody knows what.

c.   He died, but nobody knows what kind of death.
d.   *He died, but nobody knows what.

The fact that fragments comply with semantic selectional properties of the context predicate shows that interpretations must be constructed at a level of representation that is subject to semantic evaluation. F-structure is such a level. The semantic restrictions discussed in this section can be explained by constructing functional representations of interpretations in which fragments are incorporated as arguments of the context predicate. The functional structures that result from sluicing interpretation are then subject to semantic processing just like any functional structure produced by the rules of sentence grammar, and thus reflect the semantic well-formedness conditions of sentence grammar.

9.3 The Interpretation Procedure

In the first section of this chapter we examined the properties of sluiced fragments and the issues that are involved in interpreting them. Briefly: sluicing deals with *wh*-phrases that are dominated by S′ in c-structure but are not involved in superbinding relationships. These *wh*-phrases are meaningless in isolation, but with respect to some context sentence, they are interpreted as embedded questions. However, interpretation is possible only if the fragment and the context are compatible syntactically, semantically, and lexically. Interpretations must, therefore, be constructed at some level in the grammar where all three types of information are available. Fragments that are not compatible with their contexts must be ruled out as ill-formed at that level of representation. These issues are resolved in this section.

One new phrase structure rule is needed to generate sluiced fragments which consist of S′s exhaustively dominating *wh*-phrases. The functional structures produced from these fragments are functionally incomplete in that they have no PRED values and incoherent in that they contain *wh*-phrases that are not arguments of any predicate; therefore, fragment functional structures are meaningless in isolation. Complete and coherent interpretations of fragments can be constructed by copying pieces of the functional structure for the context sentence. Functional structures encode surface syntactic structures, lexical information about mappings between grammatical and thematic functions, and semantic forms that are input to semantic interpretation processes—all of the information necessary for determining compatibility of fragments and contexts. When the compatibility conditions are not met, an interpretation results that is either functionally or semantically ill-formed, reflecting the fact that it is perceived as unacceptable.

Generating Fragments

In the nontransformational grammar developed in this volume, there is one level of syntactic representation that is generated by a set of context-free phrase structure rules. Associated with each rule are functional equations which describe the functional structure corresponding to a given constituent structure. The following is a skeletal set of rules for generating some very simple sentences and their functional structures.

(125)

a. S $\rightarrow$ NP   VP
             $(\uparrow\text{SUBJ})=\downarrow$ $\uparrow=\downarrow$

b. NP $\rightarrow$ DET   N
             $\uparrow=\downarrow$ $\uparrow=\downarrow$

c. PP $\rightarrow$ P   NP
           $\uparrow=\downarrow$ $(\uparrow\text{OBJ})=\downarrow$

d. VP $\rightarrow$ V   (NP)   (PP)   (S$'$)
          $\uparrow=\downarrow$ $(\uparrow\text{OBJ})=\downarrow$ $(\uparrow(\downarrow\text{PCASE}))=\downarrow$ $(\uparrow\text{SCOMP})=\downarrow$

e. S$'$ $\rightarrow$ XP   S
          $(\uparrow\text{Q})=\downarrow$ $\uparrow=\downarrow$
          $(\downarrow\text{WH})=+$
          $\downarrow=\Downarrow$

Rule (125d) generates sentential complements in the verb phrase. Notice that the rule mentions only the node S$'$. Whatever happens to be inside that S$'$ is invisible to the VP. Therefore, generating sluiced fragments under S$'$ ensures that they will appear wherever full S$'$s appear.

Rule (125e) expands S$'$s into full embedded questions. Embedded questions consist of an XP, where X = N, P, A, ADV, followed by a sentence. One functional equation associated with the XP gives it the function name Q in functional structure. The second ensures that the functional substructure for the XP will have a positive value for the morphological feature [WH]. Finally, via the long-distance metavariable $\Downarrow$ in the third functional equation, the XP will be coindexed with a trace (an empty XP) inside its sister S from which it receives a grammatical function. If the $\Downarrow$ variable is not instantiated by some other phrase in the c-structure tree, the embedded question will not have a properly instantiated functional description and is thus ruled out as discussed in chapter 4.

A truncated version of (125e) suffices to generate sluiced fragments.

(126)
$$S \rightarrow \quad XP$$
$$(\uparrow Q) = \downarrow$$
$$(\downarrow WH) = +$$

(126) differs most obviously from (125e) in that the XP has no sister S-node. It follows that the XP could not possibly be involved in long-distance syntactic relationships because there is no syntactic structure that could instantiate the $\Downarrow$ variable. (126) fits the specifications that were laid out in the first section, generating *wh*-fragments that are dominated by S' but are not involved in superbinding relationships.

Since *wh*-fragments generated by (126) are not involved in long-distance dependencies, some other way must be devised for assigning grammatical functions to them. This will occur when interpretations for the fragments are constructed in functional structure.

Constructing Interpretations
Recall from the first section of this chapter that there are basically three different relationships that hold between contexts and fragments: the fragment can have an antecedent in the context, it can be an optional argument of the context predicate, or it can become an adjunct to the context sentence. I will illustrate the interpretation procedure separately for each type so as to bring out the different issues associated with each one.

Fragments with Antecedents The important facts to capture about fragments and their antecedents are that they agree in case and in various other features such as number and animateness, and, furthermore, that the fragment, when it is interpreted, takes over the grammatical and thematic functions of its antecedent. An example will illustrate how these issues are handled.

(127)
A: Janet saw something.
B: I wonder what.

The phrase structure rules, along with the semantic forms for the particular lexical items involved, generate the following c-structure and f-structure for the sluiced sentence *I wonder what*.

(128)

a.

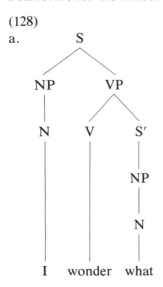

b.

$$
\begin{bmatrix}
\text{SUBJ} & \begin{bmatrix} \text{PRED} & \text{`I'} \end{bmatrix} \\
\\
\text{PRED} & \text{`WONDER} \begin{pmatrix} (\text{SUBJ}), & (\text{SCOMP}) \\ \text{wonderer} & \text{question} \\ a & b \end{pmatrix} \text{'} \\
\\
\text{SCOMP} & \begin{bmatrix} \text{Q} & \begin{bmatrix} \text{PRED} & \text{`WHAT'} \\ \text{WH} & + \end{bmatrix} \end{bmatrix}
\end{bmatrix}
$$

The SCOMP in (128b) is incomplete in that it has no PRED value and incoherent in that the *wh*-phrase, *what*, is not an argument of any predicate. This simply reflects the fact that the fragment is actually perceived as being incomplete. Consider now how this fragment could receive a complete and coherent interpretation from the context sentence, *Janet saw something*.

The first step in interpreting (127) is to establish that *what* refers to *something*. This is indicated by coindexing them in their respective functional structures. (The functional structures in this section are greatly oversimplified for ease of discussion. Most obviously, they do not include tense or morphological features which are not relevant to the discussion.)

(129)

a.
$$\begin{bmatrix} \text{SUBJ} & \begin{bmatrix} \text{PRED} & \text{`JANET'} \end{bmatrix} \\ \text{PRED} & \text{`SEE}\begin{pmatrix} (\text{SUBJ}), & (\text{OBJ}) \\ \text{seer} & \text{seen} \\ a & b \end{pmatrix}\text{'} \\ \text{OBJ} & {}^{i}\begin{bmatrix} \text{PRED} & \text{`SOMETHING'} \end{bmatrix} \end{bmatrix}$$

Janet saw something.

b.
$$\begin{bmatrix} \text{SUBJ} & \begin{bmatrix} \text{PRED} & \text{`I'} \end{bmatrix} \\ \text{PRED} & \text{`WONDER}\begin{pmatrix} (\text{SUBJ}), & (\text{SCOMP}) \\ \text{wonderer} & \text{question} \\ c & d \end{pmatrix}\text{'} \\ \text{SCOMP} & \begin{bmatrix} \text{Q} & {}^{i}\begin{bmatrix} \text{PRED} & \text{`WHAT'} \\ \text{WH} & + \end{bmatrix} \end{bmatrix} \end{bmatrix}$$

I wonder what.

Now, agreement in semantically relevant features such as number and animateness follows trivially from the fact that the fragment and antecedent are coreferential. The predicate of the antecedent can now be deleted because it is no longer needed in the interpretation, and the remainder of the antecedent's functional structure can be merged with that of the fragment.

(130)

$$\begin{bmatrix} \text{SUBJ} & \begin{bmatrix} \text{PRED} & \text{`JANET'} \end{bmatrix} \\ \text{PRED} & \text{`SEE}\begin{pmatrix} (\text{SUBJ}), & (\text{OBJ}) \\ \text{seer} & \text{seen} \\ a & b \end{pmatrix}\text{'} \\ \text{OBJ} & {}^{i}\begin{bmatrix} \quad \end{bmatrix} \end{bmatrix}$$

Next, the context f-structure is copied into the incomplete SCOMP of the fragment f-structure.

(131)

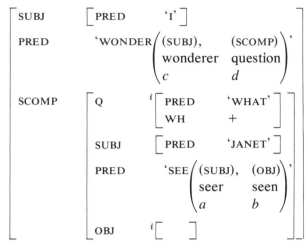

Notice now that this is exactly the functional structure that the grammar would generate for *I wonder what Janet saw,* which is, in fact, the desired interpretation for (127).

So far, case agreement has not been mentioned in this example. Unlike the other agreements, it does not follow from the fact that the fragment and antecedent are coreferential. In general, since the case of a noun phrase depends on the particular syntactic configuration in which it is found, pronouns need not agree in case with their antecedents. In (132), for example, each of the three coreferential pronouns has a different case which is determined by its syntactic location, not by its referential properties.

(132)
He$_i$ went to visit his$_i$ mother. She gave him$_i$ a hug.

Case agreement between fragments and antecedents in sluicing does not follow from the fact that they corefer, but rather from the fact that they have the same grammatical function.

Generating case-marked fragments is not a problem under the assumption that NPs are marked for case in the lexicon. Lexical entries like the following can be inserted freely into c-structure representations of fragments.

(133)

who: N, ($\uparrow$PRED) = 'WHO'
       ($\uparrow$CASE) = NOM
       ($\uparrow$WH)   = +

whom: N, ($\uparrow$PRED) = 'WHOM'
         ($\uparrow$CASE) = OBJECTIVE
         ($\uparrow$WH)   = +

whose: N, ($\uparrow$PRED) = 'WHOSE'
          ($\uparrow$CASE) = GEN
          ($\uparrow$WH)   = +

The problem, of course, is to be sure that the case chosen for the fragment is appropriate to the context.

When surface embedded questions are constructed via phrase structure rules and functional equations, the case of each argument is defined, in English, by an equation that applies to its functional structure.

(125')

a. S $\rightarrow$ NP   VP
               ($\uparrow$SUBJ)=$\downarrow$ $\uparrow$=$\downarrow$
               ($\downarrow$CASE)=NOM

c. PP$\rightarrow$ P   NP
          $\uparrow$=$\downarrow$ ($\uparrow$OBJ)=$\downarrow$
                ($\downarrow$CASE)=OBJECTIVE

d. VP$\rightarrow$ V   (NP)   (PP)   S'
          $\uparrow$=$\downarrow$ ($\uparrow$OBJ)=$\downarrow$ ($\uparrow$($\downarrow$PCASE))=$\downarrow$ ($\uparrow$SCOMP)=$\downarrow$
                ($\downarrow$CASE)=OBJECTIVE

These case equations simply guarantee that objective NPs will appear as OBJS and POBJS and that nominative NPs will appear as SUBJS.

Sluicing interpretations, however, are not built from phrase structure rules with functional equations. Instead, they are copied from previously constructed functional structures. Even though case equations are not involved in their derivation, interpretations do have access to the information they carry, because these equations have marked the antecedent which must be compatible with the fragment.

Case agreement brings out the usefulness of functional structure representations in sluicing. By encoding surface grammatical relations, they enable interpretations, which have no syntactic realization, to have access to syntactic information.

Optional Arguments   Consider again the fragment *I wonder what,* but this time with a different context.

(134)
A: Jenny was eating.
B: I wonder what.

Interpretation starts as before with functional structures for the fragment and the context.

(135)

a.
$$
\begin{bmatrix}
\text{SUBJ} & \begin{bmatrix} \text{PRED} & \text{`JENNY'} \end{bmatrix} \\
\text{PRED} & \text{`}\exists y\ \text{EAT} \begin{pmatrix} \text{(SUBJ)} \\ \text{eater} \quad \text{eatee} \\ a \qquad\ y \end{pmatrix} \text{'}
\end{bmatrix}
$$

Jenny was eating.

b.
$$
\begin{bmatrix}
\text{SUBJ} & \begin{bmatrix} \text{PRED} & \text{`I'} \end{bmatrix} \\
\text{PRED} & \text{`WONDER} \begin{pmatrix} \text{(SUBJ),} & \text{(SCOMP)} \\ \text{wonderer} & \text{question} \\ c & d \end{pmatrix} \text{'} \\
\text{SCOMP} & \begin{bmatrix} \text{Q} & \begin{bmatrix} \text{PRED} & \text{`WHAT'} \\ \text{WH} & + \end{bmatrix} \end{bmatrix}
\end{bmatrix}
$$

I wonder what.

This time, however, *what* does not have an antecedent, so the context is copied as is into the fragment functional structure.

(136)
$$
\begin{bmatrix}
\text{SUBJ} & \begin{bmatrix} \text{PRED} & \text{`I'} \end{bmatrix} \\
\text{PRED} & \text{`WONDER} \begin{pmatrix} \text{(SUBJ),} & \text{(SCOMP)} \\ \text{wonderer} & \text{question} \\ c & d \end{pmatrix} \text{'} \\
\text{SCOMP} & \begin{bmatrix} \text{Q} & \begin{bmatrix} \text{PRED} & \text{`WHAT'} \\ \text{WH} & + \end{bmatrix} \\ \text{SUBJ} & \begin{bmatrix} \text{PRED} & \text{`JENNY'} \end{bmatrix} \\ \text{PRED} & \text{`}\exists y\ \text{EAT} \begin{pmatrix} \text{(SUBJ)} \\ \text{eater} \quad \text{eatee} \\ a \qquad\ y \end{pmatrix} \text{'} \end{bmatrix}
\end{bmatrix}
$$

This functional structure is still incoherent. The semantic form for *eat* can accommodate only one grammatical argument, the subject. *What* is still not an argument of any predicate. However, EQ can apply to the semantic form for *eat,* thus allowing it to take another grammatical argument, OBJ. In order to be incorporated as an argument, though, the functional structure for *what* must be assigned a grammatical function name (Q simply labels the functional structure of the fragment—it is not a grammatical function. That is, it does not define the role played by the fragment in the semantic form of the predicate). Since grammatical function names are assigned by functional equations, one way of naming the fragment is to find the equations that describe its functional structure and then use those equations to build an identical structure with the appropriate name that can be coindexed with the fragment. In this particular example, the functional structure for the fragment is described very simply by the equation $(\uparrow \text{OBJ}) = \downarrow$, which is normally used in the grammar to name functional structures for noun phrases. This equation is then used to generate a functional substructure with the function name OBJ which is coindexed with the fragment. As a result of coindexing, *what* inherits the grammatical function OBJ. Now it can be interpreted as the object of *eat,* because it satisfies the functional and selectional requirements of the second argument position. The result is a well-formed functional structure for *I wonder what Jenny was eating.*

(137)

$$
\begin{bmatrix}
\text{SUBJ} & \begin{bmatrix} \text{PRED} & \text{`I'} \end{bmatrix} \\
\text{PRED} & \text{`WONDER}\begin{pmatrix} (\text{SUBJ}), & (\text{SCOMP}) \\ \text{wonderer} & \text{question} \\ c & d \end{pmatrix}\text{'} \\
\text{SCOMP} & \begin{bmatrix}
\text{Q} & {}^{i}\begin{bmatrix} \text{PRED} & \text{`WHAT'} \\ \text{WH} & + \end{bmatrix} \\
\text{SUBJ} & \begin{bmatrix} \text{PRED} & \text{`JENNY'} \end{bmatrix} \\
\text{PRED} & \text{`EAT}\begin{pmatrix} (\text{SUBJ}), & (\text{OBJ}) \\ \text{eater} & \text{eatee} \\ a & b \end{pmatrix}\text{'} \\
\text{OBJ} & {}^{i}\begin{bmatrix} \quad \end{bmatrix}
\end{bmatrix}
\end{bmatrix}
$$

The usual well-formedness conditions of the grammar guarantee that the correct functional name will be assigned to the fragment. For example, in interpreting (134), the functional equation ($\uparrow$SUBJ) = $\downarrow$ could have been chosen instead of the correct equation, ($\uparrow$OBJ) = $\downarrow$, to describe the fragment *what,* since it too is used in the grammar to name the functional structures associated with noun phrases. However, if the fragment were given the name SUBJ, the resulting functional structure would violate the uniqueness condition on grammatical function assignments because *eat* would have two subjects, *what* and *Jenny.*

The well-formedness conditions of the grammar also guarantee that the appropriate semantic form of the context predicate will be chosen. Suppose, for example, that Instrumentalization rather than EQ had applied to the semantic form of *eat* on (135), thus adding a WITH OBJ instead of an OBJ as the second grammatical argument. The interpretation of (134) would then be incomplete because there would be no substructure named WITH OBJ to satisfy the functional requirements of the predicate, and it would be incoherent because *what* would still not be bound to an argument position of any predicate.

The sluicing interpretation procedure is clearly a process of discourse grammar, since it applies to two sentences at once. The question now arises whether or not discourse grammar imposes its own well-formedness conditions on functional structure. However, if discourse and sentence grammars are to interact smoothly, they must be able to exchange representations of sentences or groups of sentences. It follows that the interpretation procedure, although it is not a part of sentence grammar, uses inputs and outputs that are well-formed by sentence grammar standards.

Consider what would happen if the context sentence that is the input to the interpretation procedure were functionally incomplete. An alternative procedure, for example, might start with the transitive form of *eat* in the context functional structure in order to interpret (134).

(138)

a.

$$\begin{bmatrix} \text{SUBJ} & \begin{bmatrix} \text{PRED} & \text{'JENNY'} \end{bmatrix} \\ \text{PRED} & \text{'EAT} \begin{pmatrix} (\text{SUBJ}), & (\text{OBJ}) \\ \text{eater} & \text{eatee} \\ a & b \end{pmatrix}\text{'} \\ \text{OBJ} & \begin{bmatrix} \quad \end{bmatrix} \end{bmatrix}$$

Jenny was eating.

b.
$$
\begin{bmatrix}
\text{SUBJ} & \begin{bmatrix} \text{PRED} & \text{`I'} \end{bmatrix} \\[2ex]
\text{PRED} & \text{`WONDER} \begin{pmatrix} \text{(SUBJ),} & \text{(OBJ)} \\ \text{wonderer} & \text{question} \\ c & d \end{pmatrix} \text{'} \\[4ex]
\text{SCOMP} & \begin{bmatrix} \text{Q} & \begin{bmatrix} \text{PRED} & \text{`WHAT'} \\ \text{WH} & + \end{bmatrix} \end{bmatrix}
\end{bmatrix}
$$

I wonder what.

Now, no lexical rules need to apply. The context can simply be copied into the fragment f-structure and *what* can be coindexed with the object of *eat*. As before, the result is (137), a well-formed functional structure for *I wonder what Jenny ate*.

Although it works for *eat*, this procedure has undesirable consequences. It will produce a well-formed functional structure for (139), thereby wrongly predicting that it is grammatical. (140) is the derivation of (139).

(139)
*John took, but I know what.

(140)

a.
$$
\begin{bmatrix}
\text{SUBJ} & \begin{bmatrix} \text{PRED} & \text{`JOHN'} \end{bmatrix} \\[2ex]
\text{PRED} & \text{`TAKE} \begin{pmatrix} \text{(SUBJ),} & \text{(OBJ)} \\ \text{taker} & \text{takee} \\ a & b \end{pmatrix} \text{'} \\[4ex]
\text{OBJ} & \begin{bmatrix} \ \ \end{bmatrix}
\end{bmatrix}
$$

John took.

b.
$$
\begin{bmatrix}
\text{SUBJ} & \begin{bmatrix} \text{PRED} & \text{`I'} \end{bmatrix} \\[2ex]
\text{PRED} & \text{`KNOW} \begin{pmatrix} \text{(SUBJ),} & \text{(OBJ)} \\ \text{sage} & \text{fact} \\ c & d \end{pmatrix} \text{'} \\[4ex]
\text{SCOMP} & \begin{bmatrix} \text{Q} & \begin{bmatrix} \text{PRED} & \text{`WHAT'} \\ \text{WH} & + \end{bmatrix} \end{bmatrix}
\end{bmatrix}
$$

I know what.

c.

$$
\begin{bmatrix}
\text{SUBJ} & \begin{bmatrix} \text{PRED} & \text{‘I’} \end{bmatrix} \\[2ex]
\text{PRED} & \text{‘KNOW} \begin{pmatrix} \text{(SUBJ),} & \text{(SCOMP)} \\ \text{sage} & \text{fact} \\ c & d \end{pmatrix}\text{’} \\[4ex]
\text{SCOMP} & \begin{bmatrix}
\text{Q} & {}^{i}\begin{bmatrix} \text{PRED} & \text{‘WHAT’} \\ \text{WH} & + \end{bmatrix} \\[3ex]
\text{SUBJ} & \begin{bmatrix} \text{PRED} & \text{‘JOHN’} \end{bmatrix} \\[2ex]
\text{PRED} & \text{‘TAKE} \begin{pmatrix} \text{(SUBJ),} & \text{(OBJ)} \\ \text{taker} & \text{takee} \\ a & b \end{pmatrix}\text{’} \\[4ex]
\text{OBJ} & {}^{i}\begin{bmatrix} \quad \end{bmatrix}
\end{bmatrix}
\end{bmatrix}
$$

I know what John took. (interpretation)

(139) can be ruled out simply by insisting that the context used by the sluicing interpretation procedure be a complete functional structure. The ungrammaticality of (139) then follows naturally from the ungrammaticality of its context sentence, **John took,* which is functionally incomplete in that there is no PRED value for the object of *take*.

The functional notion of coherence also rules out a large class of ungrammatical sluiced sentences. For example, the sentence **Jenny fell, but I don't know what* has a monadic predicate in its context f-structure. There are, however, no lexical rules that add a noun phrase argument to the semantic form of *fall*. When the context is copied into the fragment f-structure, there will be no argument slot for *what* to fit into, nor can one be created. The resulting functional structure will, therefore, be incoherent.

The uniqueness condition on functional structures filters out sluiced sentences with conflicting semantic forms. It was pointed out earlier that it is the functional interpretation of the context sentence, not just its structural form, that is used in the interpretation of a fragment. Furthermore, it was shown that the surface grammatical relations of the context sentence must be available in order to mark the fragment properly for case. Basically, this means that in sentences like (98) (repeated below), the grammatical function assignments for the context must be included in the functional structure for the interpretation. Each sentence alone has a well-formed functional structure, but consider what happens when their representations are combined. *Move* has two different subjects, *the chair* and *who;* conversely, *the chair* has two grammatical functions, SUBJ and OBJ. Therefore, the two meanings of *move* cannot be conveyed simultaneously without violating the uniqueness condition on functional well-formedness.

(98)
*The chair moved, but I don't know who.
'I don't know who moved the chair.'

In contrast, when the representations for *Jenny ate* and *I don't know what Jenny ate* are combined, the uniqueness condition is not violated. *Eat* has only one subject, *Jenny,* and each argument has only one function—*Jenny* is only a subject and *what* is only an object.

Another segment of sentence grammar that is important in sluicing is the inventory of semantic forms. If the interpretation procedure could make up arbitrary semantic forms, it would be able to generate ungrammatical sentences like (141) below in the following way. The context, as usual, would be copied into the fragment. The resulting structure would be incoherent, because the intransitive semantic form for *open* used in the context cannot accommodate the fragment, *by whom,* as an argument. One way out of this predicament is simply to assign a unique grammatical function name and thematic role to the fragment. The result might look something like (142), which is a well-formed functional structure for **I don't know by whom the door opened.*

(141)

*The door opened, but I don't know by whom.

(142)

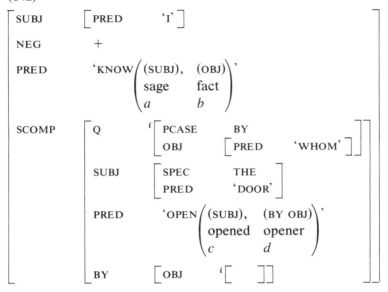

The semantic form for *open* in (142) specifies a subject which is the *opened* and a *by*-object which is the *opener*. This form, however, is not found in the lexicon; that is, there is no such sentence as *The door opened by the girls*. The generation of (141) can be prevented simply by requiring that the interpretation procedure use only naturally occurring semantic forms.

Notice that although interpretations must obey conditions on functional and lexical well-formedness, they have no phrase structure representation. A consequence of this is that interpretations may lack a well-formed c-structure as long as they are functionally well-formed. There were some examples of this in section 9.1 (42a–e), where it was shown that interpretations could violate constraints on *Wh* Movement. (143) and (144) also illustrate this point. Their interpretations lack a well-formed c-structure but are functionally well-formed.

(143)

Bill mentioned his plans to go on vacation, but he didn't say where.
*'He didn't say where his plans to go on vacation.'

(144)
There's a Coke on the table, but I don't know whose.
*'I don't know whose there is on the table.'

The noun phrase *his plans to go on vacation* serves as the context sentence in (143). Although it has nominal morphology, it is a legitimate clause nucleus (substructure with a predicate and arguments) and can be used as such in sluicing. When it is copied into the fragment f-structure, the result is complete and coherent: the predicate *plan* has two arguments that it subcategorizes for, a subject and an infinitive complement, and each argument has a grammatical function. In particular, *where* is an optional argument of *go* inside the complement of *plan*. The only deviant item in the interpretation is the morphological form of the subject, *his,* and the predicate, *plans,* but this has no effect on the functional well-formedness of the sentence.

The interpretation of (144) is also complete and coherent. Its predicate is *be,* which takes the semantically empty subject *there.* (I am assuming familiarity with the analysis of *There* Insertion in chapter 1.) *Whose* is the grammatical object of *be,* and *on the table* is a locative phrase selected by the *there-be*-construction. The ungrammaticality of the interpretation is caused by something other than functional ill-formedness.

Since the interpretations of (143) and (144) are functionally well-formed, the corresponding sluiced sentences are grammatical.

Adjuncts In the lexical interpretive grammar developed in this volume, adjuncts do not receive a unique grammatical function name. Rather, they are accompanied by the functional equation $\downarrow \in (\uparrow \text{ADJ})$, which is to be read, "Down is an element of up's adjunct pool." This makes interpretation of adjunct fragments very easy. Once the context is copied into the SCOMP of the fragment, the *wh*-phrase need only be coindexed with an empty element of the adjunct pool which can be created as described earlier by invoking the appropriate functional equations. The derivation of (145) is shown in (146). The internal f-structure of adjuncts is not treated here; compare chapters 6 and 7.

(145)

Janet called on Tuesday, but I don't know when.

'I don't know when Janet called on Tuesday.'

(146)

a.
$$
\begin{bmatrix}
\text{SUBJ} & \begin{bmatrix} \text{PRED} & \text{'JANET'} \end{bmatrix} \\
\text{PRED} & \text{'CALL} \begin{pmatrix} (\text{SUBJ}) \\ \text{caller} \\ a \end{pmatrix} \text{'} \\
\text{ADJ} & \{\text{"on Tuesday"}\}
\end{bmatrix}
$$

Janet called on Tuesday.

b.
$$
\begin{bmatrix}
\text{SUBJ} & \begin{bmatrix} \text{PRED} & \text{'I'} \end{bmatrix} \\
\text{NEG} & + \\
\text{PRED} & \text{'KNOW} \begin{pmatrix} (\text{SUBJ}), & (\text{OBJ}) \\ \text{sage} & \text{fact} \\ b & c \end{pmatrix} \text{'} \\
\text{SCOMP} & \begin{bmatrix} \text{Q} & \begin{bmatrix} \text{PRED} & \text{'WHEN'} \\ \text{WH} & + \end{bmatrix} \end{bmatrix}
\end{bmatrix}
$$

I don't know when.

c.
$$
\begin{bmatrix}
\text{SUBJ} & \begin{bmatrix} \text{PRED} & \text{'I'} \end{bmatrix} \\
\text{NEG} & + \\
\text{PRED} & \text{'KNOW} \begin{pmatrix} (\text{SUBJ}), & (\text{OBJ}) \\ \text{sage} & \text{fact} \\ b & c \end{pmatrix} \text{'} \\
\text{SCOMP} & \begin{bmatrix} \text{Q} & {}^i\begin{bmatrix} \text{PRED} & \text{'WHEN'} \\ \text{WH} & + \end{bmatrix} \\ \text{SUBJ} & \begin{bmatrix} \text{PRED} & \text{'JANET'} \end{bmatrix} \\ \text{PRED} & \text{'CALL} \begin{pmatrix} (\text{SUBJ}) \\ \text{caller} \\ a \end{pmatrix} \text{'} \\ \text{ADJ} & \left\{ \begin{bmatrix} \text{"on Tuesday"} \end{bmatrix} \\ {}^i\begin{bmatrix} \quad \end{bmatrix} \right\} \end{bmatrix}
\end{bmatrix}
$$

I don't know when Janet called on Tuesday.   *(interpretation)*

Once the interpretation is constructed, it is subject to semantic processing, at which point adjuncts are judged for compatibility.

Discourse and Sentence Grammar   It has been emphasized in this section that sluicing interpretation, although it is a discourse phenomenon, operates within the guidelines of sentence grammar. To begin with, it must have access to the output of sentence grammar processes. That is, the context sentences that it manipulates must be complete, coherent, semantically processed functional structures with encodings of surface grammatical relations and mappings from grammatical to thematic functions. Furthermore, much of the sentence grammar apparatus is used in constructing sluicing interpretations. Like regular sentences, interpretations are represented as well-formed functional structures. In constructing them, the interpretation procedure has access to the inventory of semantic forms and lexical rules and the notions of completeness, coherence, and uniqueness, the functional well-formedness conditions of sentence grammar. Finally, like any other functional structure, interpretations are relinquished to the semantic processor for validation of argument assignments and compatibility of adjuncts.

The benefits of studying discourse constructions like sluicing are two-fold. First, it is presumably desirable that a sentence grammar fit naturally into a larger model of speaker interactions. Toward that end, sluicing brings out the role of the sentence grammar machinery in discourse grammar. It shows how functional structures, functional well-formedness conditions, the lexicon, and lexical rules could be extended beyond their usual realm of operation. Conversely, by making extensive use of the components of sentence grammar, sluicing, even though it is a discourse construction, can provide insights into how they work and thus create a better understanding of sentence grammar.

Notes

Thanks go to Joan Bresnan, Ken Church, Paula Pranka, Alec Marantz, Jay Keyser, Haj Ross, Beth Levin, and many fellow linguistics students for helpful hints and moral support. Thanks also to Dieter Niemitz and Brownell Chalstrom. This work is supported by a fellowship from the National Science Foundation.

1. Other discourse ellipsis constructions are gapping, stripping, and verb phrase deletion. Null complement anaphora and comparative deletion might be included in this group, but they differ from the others in important respects. Null complement anaphora occurs only after predicates that subcategorize for

it (see Grimshaw 1979a), and comparative deletion does not apply across sentence boundaries (Williams 1977).

2. Notice that the preposition and *wh*-phrase in the fragment are in reverse order (*where to* instead of *to where*). This variant of the sluicing construction has been discussed by Van Riemsdijk 1978, Rosen 1976, Bechhofer 1976a,b, and Ross 1969. For the purposes of this discussion, it is simply used as an alternative way to express PP fragments.

3. Notice that the preposition in the fragment of (6b) is apparently pied piped, while in the interpretation it is stranded. The pied piped version of the interpretation sounds quite awkward.

(i)

?It's not clear with what Seymour sliced the salami.

This discrepancy between the fragment and the interpretation is explained in the discussion of examples (45)–(47).

4. The predicates in (9)–(12) can have relative clauses as arguments. For example, in the sentence *Janet ate what Jenny cooked,* the phrase *what Jenny cooked* is an NP analogous to *the food that Jenny cooked.* Headless relatives should not be confused with embedded questions. Bresnan and Grimshaw 1978 discuss criteria for distinguishing between the two constructions.

5. Van Riemsdijk 1978 proposes that fragment *wh*-phrases are X'''s (X-triple bar) and that they are selected for the morphological feature [+WH]. This raises some theoretical questions. First, it seems odd that, at least in English, [+WH] is the only morphological feature that is selected in sluicing. If morphological selection were possible, one would expect fragments to be selected for properties like number and gender as well. Furthermore, it is not clear that morphological selection is needed in the grammar at all if syntactic and semantic selection together are necessary and sufficient.

Clearly, syntactic selection is necessary because predicates do, in general, subcategorize for the syntactic category of their arguments. To take a simple example, *eat* selects NP objects but does not subcategorize for Ss, PPs, APs, or ADVPs as logical arguments. Semantic selection is needed also to distinguish questions from exclamations. Grimshaw 1979a shows that some predicates semantically select one or the other. The complements in (i) are embedded questions, and those in (ii) are exclamations.

(i)
a.   Fred will ask whether he is a fool.   (= Grimshaw's (6a))
b.   *It's amazing whether he is a fool.   (= Grimshaw's (7a))

(ii)
a.   *John will ask what a fool he is.   (= Grimshaw's (5a))
b.   It's amazing what a fool he is.   (= Grimshaw's (4a))

Neither syntactic nor morphological selection could account for the contrasts in (i) and (ii) because questions and exclamations are both S's syntactically and are both morphologically marked by *wh*-phrases.

Given that syntactic and semantic selection are both necessary in general, and that together they account for all of the sluicing data, it seems that calling upon morphological selection would be an unnecessary complication of the grammar.

6. Numerous versions of these constraints have been proposed; however, the fine distinctions among the various theories of constraints are not relevant here. In the following discussion, therefore, I will use whatever name seems most convenient or intuitive for the constraints, and I invite readers to imagine their own favorite versions.

7. There are alternative, grammatical interpretations of (42c,d) in which a lower clause is used as the context sentence.

(i)
I heard the claim *that he bit someone,* but I don't remember who.
'I don't remember who he bit.'

(ii)
That *he'll fire someone* is possible, but he won't say who.
'He won't say who he'll fire.'

It might be argued that these are, in fact, the correct interpretations for (42c,d) and that there is no problem with constraint violation. However, no such alternative interpretations are available for (42a,b,e). Something would still have to be said about constraint violations in those sentences.

In general, multi-clause sentences have ambiguous interpretations. In (iii), for example, either clause of the context can be used in the interpretation.

(iii)
I heard that he bit someone, but I don't remember when.
'I don't remember when I heard that he bit someone.'
'I don't remember when he bit someone.'

In order to keep the generalization that multiple clauses are associated with multiple interpretations, it is desirable to keep (42c,d) as possible interpretations along with (i) and (ii).

8. Ross 1969 gives different examples illustrating the same phenomena. His examples are not completely grammatical, however.

(i)
??Irv and someone were dancing together, but I don't
remember who.   (= Ross's (71b))
  *'I don't know who Irv and were dancing together.'

(ii)
??I believe the claim that he bit someone, but they don't
know who.   (= Ross's (72d))
  *'They don't know who I believe the claim that he bit.'

(iii)
??That he'll hire someone is possible, but I won't divulge
who.   (= Ross's (73b))
  *'I won't divulge who that he'll hire is possible.'

Ross observes that the sluiced sentences are slightly better than their interpretations, but they are still not completely grammatical and should, therefore, not be generated by the grammar. Since he proposes a deletion theory of sluicing, in which fragments are derived from their interpretations, he attributes the ungrammaticality of (i)–(iii) to the fact that they violate constraints in deep structure. He concludes that fragments must be involved in *Wh* Movement in order to make use of island constraints.

I agree with Ross's grammaticality judgments, but I think that the awkwardness of his examples is a pragmatic problem and is not due to constraint violations. Notice that (i)–(iii) differ minimally from (42b,c,d), which are grammatical. It seems, for example, that sentences sound better when the subject of the context and the sluiced sentence are the same person, as in (42c,d). In (ii) and (iii), where the context and sluiced sentence have different subjects, the latter simply sounds irrelevant. Since this is clearly a pragmatic issue, island constraints need not be invoked and it need not be assumed that fragments are involved in movement.

There are other pragmatic constraints in sluicing. (iv), in which the antecedent is embedded under a factive predicate, sounds worse than (v), in which the antecedent is embedded under a nonfactive predicate.

(iv)
?I regret that I bit someone, but I can't remember who.

(v)
I think that I bit someone, but I can't remember who.

Given that there are pragmatic constraints on sluicing, the preferred policy is to generate sentences like (i)–(iv) in addition to (42b–d) and (v) and then rule some of them out on pragmatic grounds. If, on the other hand, (i)–(iv) were ruled out as syntactically ill-formed and were not generated by the grammar, there would be no way to generate the grammatical sentences in (42), which are syntactically indistinguishable from their ungrammatical counterparts.

9. This is in fact what Ross proposes. He suggests that island constraints be thought of as filters on the outputs of derivations. Under this analysis, sentences can pass through ungrammatical stages as long as they are well-formed at the end of the derivation. As applied to sluicing, this means that island constraints could be violated provided that the island was deleted.

There is, however, a problem with this analysis in the current version of the revised extended standard theory. Deletion rules, such as sluicing, map s-structures (trees that have not yet undergone deletion and stylistic rules) onto phonetic representations (PR). Island constraints, on the other hand, apply between surface structure and logical form (LF). Since PR and LF are separate components, island constraints should not be sensitive to whether or not the island was deleted.

10. It might be objected that *which* and *whose* violate the Left Branch Condition in (i) and (ii).

(i)
John likes one of the girls, but he won't tell us which.
*'He won't tell us which he likes one of the girls.'

(ii)
John stole someone's baseball, but he won't tell us whose.
*'He won't tell us whose he stole baseball.'

However, *which* and *whose* need not be determiners. They often stand alone as full *wh*-phrases.

(iii)
a.   Which does he like?
b.   Whose did he steal?

With respect to sluicing, this means that *which* can simply be a pronominal *wh*-phrase like *who* and *what*, taking *one of the girls* as its antecedent. Similarly, *whose*, by itself, could take *someone's baseball* as its antecedent. If this were the case in (i) and (ii), their interpretations would be grammatical.

(iv)
He won't tell us which he likes.

(v)
He won't tell us whose he stole.

There is, in fact, no violation of the Left Branch Condition.

Notice also that *how* can be an acceptable *wh*-phrase when it is a manner adverb as in *I don't know how he did it*.

11. *Pictures of whom* is an acceptable *wh*-phrase in a relative clause.

(i)
They shot Jesse James, pictures of whom were in every post office.

This simply indicates that pied piping restrictions vary from construction to construction.

Bechhofer 1976a, however, points out that *pictures of whom* shows up in constructions that look like sluicing.

(ii)
John bought a picture, but a picture of whom, I don't know.

(= Bechhofer's (79c))

She attributes examples such as these to stripping, a similar discourse construction.

12. Many speakers allow *whom* only as a prepositional object. I will assume, for the sake of discussion, that any objective use of *whom* is acceptable.

13. *Fall* can be followed by a noun phrase, as in *John fell fifty feet*. The noun phrases in such examples are not direct objects but distance phrases. They differ from direct objects in two respects: they do not passivize (**Fifty feet were fallen by John*) and they cannot be questioned by *what* (**What did John fall?*, but *How far did John fall?*).

The second argument of *fall* can be used in sluicing. Compare (60b) to *John fell, but I don't know how far*.

14. The lexical rules in this section are based on Joan Bresnan's 1979 class lectures; see chapters 1 and 3 of this volume and Bresnan in preparation a. No important claims rest on my notation or formulation of particular rules. All formalisms in this chapter were chosen for ease of discussion.

15. In certain contexts the intransitive predicates take on other readings. For example, the object can be understood from the surrounding discourse as in (i) where *Janet washed* means 'Janet washed the dishes'.

(i)
After dinner, Janet and Jenny did the dishes.
Janet washed and Jenny dried.

Part III

COGNITIVE PROCESSING OF GRAMMATICAL REPRESENTATIONS

Chapter 10

A Theory of the Acquisition of Lexical Interpretive Grammars

Steven Pinker

Language learning has always been a central concern of cognitive science, and an explanation of children's and adults' linguistic abilities within a single acquisition theory has always been one of its fondest hopes. But it has also been one of its most notorious disappointments. Theories of adult linguistic competence become strained when applied to child language, and descriptive accounts of child language seem to allow no possibility for development into the full adult grammar. Even the landmark "Degree-2 theory" of the acquisition of transformational grammars (Hamburger and Wexler 1975; Wexler and Culicover 1980), the most ambitious attempt so far at bridging linguistics and language development, has inspired only a moderate amount of interdisciplinary convergence in the five years since it first appeared.

The gulf between linguistic theory and child language has an obvious counterpart in the gulf between linguistic theory and language comprehension and production processes. Bresnan 1978 has diagnosed that problem as resulting in part from an incorrect specification of syntactic competence. In particular, Bresnan suggests that a lexical interpretive grammar (Bresnan 1978; chapter 4 of this volume) may be more congenial to the facts of adult comprehension abilities than the standard theory of transformational grammar (Chomsky 1965) that has guided psycholinguistic research in the past. Recall that in a standard transformational grammar, meaningful grammatical relations are defined by the configuration of phrases in a "deep" phrase structure tree, which is transformed into the "surface structure" tree determining the phonological form of the utterance. The problem is that it has proven to be extremely difficult to formulate a comprehension model that makes use of multiple levels of phrase structure and transformational rules and that is reasonably plausible, efficient, and true to empirical observations in the study of comprehension (Fodor, Bever, and Garrett 1974). In contrast, a lexical interpretive (hereafter "lexical") grammar generates a single phrase structure tree for each sentence and specifies meaningful grammatical relations by the configuration of phrases in the tree and by the lexical entry of the predicate. A lexical grammar can easily be embedded within an efficient left-to-right parser such as Kaplan's General Syntactic Processor (see chapter 11 in this volume), yielding a comprehension model that is consistent with many observed comprehension phenomena (see also Kaplan 1972, Wanner and Maratsos 1978, Wanner in press).

Recently, a diagnosis analogous to Bresnan's has been made for the failure of generative grammars to mesh easily with the facts of language development. Maratsos 1978, Baker 1979, Roeper, Bing, Lapointe, and Tavakolian 1979, and de Villiers in press have all suggested that certain facts about the course of language acquisition resist parsimonious explanation in terms of the acquisition of a standard transformational grammar, but become more tractable when treated within a lexicalist framework. In this chapter, I explore in greater depth the possibility that lexical grammars may succeed where standard transformational grammars have failed in serving as a foundation for a psychologically plausible theory of language acquisition—a theory both adequate in principle to explain the fact of language learning and capable of interpreting the developmental sequence that children pass through on their way to language mastery. I review the prima facie advantages of lexical accounts of acquisition, prove that lexical grammars are learnable in principle, present principles underlying a new theory of language acquisition based on lexical grammar, describe the mechanisms of the theory, and show examples of these mechanisms at work.

10.1 Lexical Interpretive Grammars

The theory of lexical interpretive grammar was introduced in Bresnan 1978 and is outlined systematically in the first four chapters of this volume. However, to facilitate the discussions to follow, I will outline the theory briefly here as well.

A lexical grammar assigns two structures to every sentence. The first is called a *constituent structure* (c-structure) and is basically a familiar surface phrase structure tree. The c-structure determines the phonological form of the sentence. The second structure is called a *functional structure* (f-structure) and specifies explicitly the semantically interpretable information expressed by the sentence. This includes the linking of predicates to their arguments, as well as information about the tense, aspect, number, gender, definiteness, and so on, of the elements of the sentence. The linking of predicates to arguments is accomplished by the mediation of *grammatical functions* such as "subject" (SUBJ), "object" (OBJ), "sentential complement" (SCOMP), and so on. Below are a simplified c-structure and f-structure corresponding to the sentence *The operator told Judy that Elvis died.*

(1)

a.

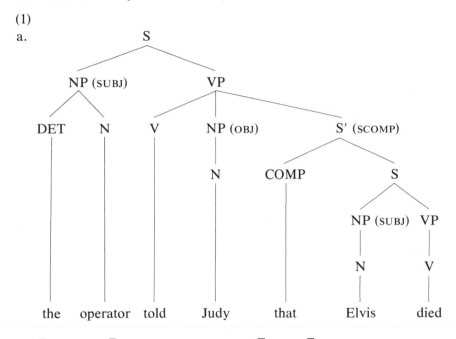

b.

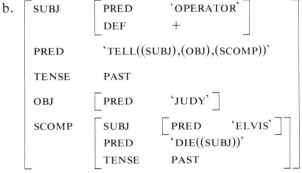

The c-structure and f-structure are generated by *annotated phrase structure rules* in conjunction with *lexical entries*. Annotated phrase structure rules are similar to the base rules of a transformational grammar, but with two important differences. First, since a lexical grammar has no transformational rules, there must be phrase structure rules to generate all surface structures directly. For example, a *"to*-dative" sentence such as *They showed the apteryx to me* is generated in part by the rule VP → V NP PP, whereas a "double-object" dative sentence such as *They showed me the apteryx* is generated in part by the rule VP → V NP NP. In other words, the double-object dative is generated directly; it is not derived by a transformation applying to a *to*-dative form.

The second difference between the base rules of a transformational grammar and annotated phrase structure rules is that in the latter, category symbols on the righthand side of rules can be annotated with grammatical functions. Thus, (1a) was generated by the rules in (2), where the functional annotation is written below the category and parentheses (following the standard notational convention) indicate optionality. The notation follows that of Grimshaw in chapter 2 of this volume.

(2)

a.   S —→ NP   VP
            SUBJ

b.   NP → (DET) N

c.   VP → (NP)   (S′)
            OBJ   SCOMP

d.   S′ → COMP S

A word's lexical entry specifies its syntactic categorization (e.g., noun, verb, adjective), its syntactic features (e.g., GEND(ER) = M(ASCULINE), DEF(INITE) = +, TENSE = PAST, etc.), and the form of its *predicate argument structure*. For a simple predicate like *operator,* the part of the lexical entry indicating its predicate argument structure simply contains a symbol referring to its semantic representation. In the current notation, this semantic symbol consists of the word printed in small capital letters and surrounded by single quotation marks ('OPERATOR', 'JUDY', etc.). For predicates that take one or more arguments, such as verbs and some adjectives and nouns, the lexical entry specifies the number of distinct arguments required (signified by the number of places within a pair of parentheses, each place designating a particular argument) and the grammatical functions that correspond to each of those arguments (signified by placing the name of the function in the appropriate place within the parentheses). Thus, the lexical entries for the words in sentence (1) will look something like this:

(3)

the:	DET,	DEF	= +
operator:	N,	PRED	= 'OPERATOR'
		COMMON	= +
		HUMAN	= +
tell:	V,	PRED	= 'TELL((SUBJ),(OBJ),(SCOMP))'
-ed:	V AFFIX,	TENSE	= PAST
Judy:	N,	PRED	= 'JUDY'
		COMMON	= −
		GEND	= F
		HUMAN	= +
that:	COMP		
Elvis:	N,	PRED	= 'ELVIS'
		COMMON	= −
		GEND	= M
		HUMAN	= +
die:	V,	PRED	= 'DIE((SUBJ))'

The lexical representation for *told* indicates that the first argument (the teller) will be found as the subject in the f- and c-structures, that the second argument (the hearer) will be found as the object, and that the third argument (the tale) will be found as the sentential complement. Thus, the raison d'être of a grammatical function is to mediate between lexical entries and constituent structures, since each function simultaneously labels an argument in a lexical entry and a category in an annotated phrase structure rule. Incidentally, for mnemonic purposes, one can write names for the different arguments below each function, as in (4),

(4)
tell: V, PRED = 'TELL((SUBJ), (OBJ), (SCOMP))'
                              teller hearer   tale

but these names play no direct role in the grammar (aside from a possible role in acquisition, which I discuss later); all that is needed is that the order of functions within the parentheses of a lexical form be fixed.

Earlier I noted that lexical grammars directly generate distinct surface structures for supposedly transformationally related sentence pairs, such as *to*-dative/double-object dative and active/passive. Correspondingly, every verb that can enter into both members of one of these paired constructions has two lexical entries. For example, in addition to the lexical entry for *told* listed here, there will be a second entry corresponding to the verb as it would appear in the passive version of the sentence, *Judy was told by the operator that Elvis died.* The second entry would look like (5),

(5)
tell: V, PRED = 'TELL((BY OBJ),(SUBJ),(SCOMP))'
                                  teller   hearer   tale
      PART(ICIPLE) = PAST

where BY OBJ is a grammatical function annotated to the phrase structure rules that expand the prepositional phrase.

It should be apparent that the lexical entries, together with the c-structure annotated with grammatical functions, uniquely determine the f-structure for any sentence. It is also apparent that the phrase structure rules will generate c-structures for many ungrammatical sentences. In fact, a sentence will be grammatical only if it has both a c-structure *and* an f-structure meeting certain well-formedness conditions, such as having an argument for each grammatical function and vice versa. A more formal presentation would outline the interpretive procedures that build an f-structure and assess its well-formedness, given a c-structure and a lexicon. Such a presentation would require more explicit annotations than simple function names on each phrase structure rule. These annotations, called *functional equations,* specify precisely how the information in the lexical entries is amalgamated with the information in the phrase structure rules to yield an f-structure. See chapter 4 of this volume for details, and see chapter 2 for an account of the relation between Kaplan and Bresnan's functional equations and the simpler annotations used here.

With transformations eliminated, how does a lexical interpretive grammar handle the syntactic phenomena that motivated transformations, such as cross-construction generalizations, indirect mappings from surface structure to meaning, and nonlocal dependencies? There are three sorts of mechanisms that go beyond the rules listed so far. First, the grammar should be capable of expressing the generalization that a large class of predicates can appear in either of two versions of a pair of constructions (e.g., active and passive, *to*-dative and double-object dative, sentential subject and extraposed sentential complement). In the theory as presented so far, there would be two distinct lexical entries for each predicate that can appear in the alternative constructions (e.g., an active entry and a passive entry). This parallelism can be encoded explicitly as a *lexical redundancy rule* (lexical rule), which would relate the alternative lexical entries. Thus, the lexical rule of *Passivization* (performing the same function as a Passive transformational rule in a standard transformational grammar) would state that an OBJ in a predicate argument structure can be converted to a SUBJ and that a SUBJ can simultaneously be converted to a BY OBJ:

(6)
Passivization
(OBJ) $\mapsto$ (SUBJ)
(SUBJ) $\mapsto$ (BY OBJ)
$\mapsto$ PART = PAST

The rule can apply productively, generating new lexical entries from old ones (unless a particular lexical entry prohibits the rule application explicitly).

The second mechanism accounts for the fact that a sentence constituent can serve simultaneously as a certain argument for one predicate in the sentence and as a different argument for a second predicate. This mechanism is a type of functional equation called a *control equation,* which is listed in the lexical entries of the predicates that can appear in such constructions. A control equation asserts an equivalence between one of the functions associated with its own predicate and one of the functions associated with the predicate embedded in a complement constituent. Thus, in (7)

(7)
Irwin tried to leave.

the lexical entry for *try* would indicate that its subject is also the subject of its verb phrase complement (VCOMP; in this case, *to leave*). The entry would look like (8),

(8)
try: V, PRED = 'TRY((SUBJ),(VCOMP))'
        (SUBJ) = (VCOMP SUBJ)

where VCOMP SUBJ is interpreted as 'V-complement's subject'. The
function VCOMP would be introduced by the annotated phrase structure
rule VP → V VP' ; the VP' would be expanded as VP' → to VP;
              VCOMP
and the f-structure would indicate the identity of two substructures by
associating them with the same superscript, as in (9).

(9)

$$
\begin{bmatrix}
\text{SUBJ} & {}^i\begin{bmatrix} \text{PRED} & \text{'IRWIN'} \end{bmatrix} \\
\text{PRED} & \text{'TRY((SUBJ),(VCOMP))'} \\
\text{VCOMP} & \begin{bmatrix} \text{SUBJ} & {}^i\begin{bmatrix} \text{PRED} & \text{'IRWIN'} \end{bmatrix} \\ \text{PRED} & \text{'LEAVE((SUBJ))'} \end{bmatrix}
\end{bmatrix}
$$

This eliminates the grammatical transformation called "Equi NP Deletion." Similarly, one can annotate control equations to other predicates
to do the work of the "Raising" transformation thought to relate (10a)
and (10b).

(10)
a.   I believe Les Canadiens to be the champions.
b.   I believe that Les Canadiens are the champions.

In this case, the lexical entry for the (10a) form of *believe* is (11).

(11)
believe: V, PRED = 'BELIEVE((SUBJ),(VCOMP))'
            (OBJ) = (VCOMP SUBJ)

   Finally, the grammar must be able to account for the syntactically
determined equivalence between "fillers" and "gaps" (also known as
"traces") in sentences such as (12a–c) with relative clauses, *wh*-
questions or complements, and *tough*-movement constructions. (The
gap is indicated by *e;* the filler is italicized.)

(12)
a.   *The singer* I like *e* is blind.
b.   I discovered *what* they meant *e*.
c.   *Zimmer* is easy to hate *e*.

Because these dependencies can span arbitrary distances in the c-structure and are independent of grammatical functions, they cannot be handled by control equations. Instead, a lexical grammar annotates "subjacency metavariables" to certain rewrite rules, in order to accomplish this "long-distance binding" usually attributed to movement transformations. The metavariable ⇓ labels a node in the c-structure as a "binder" and is annotated to the filler in rules like (13a) which generate relative clauses. The metavariable ⇑ labels a node in the c-structure as a "bindee" and is annotated to the rule (13b) generating gaps.

(13)
a. NP →   NP   S′
          ⇓,HEAD MOD(IFIER)
b. NP → e
        ⇑

Whenever there are two constituents within a bounded domain of the c-structure (technically, a "binding" domain), such that one constituent is annotated with ⇓ and the second, lower one is annotated with ⇑, the interpretive procedures link their respective f-substructures. Thus, corresponding to (12a) we have the c-structure (14a) and the f-structure (14b).

(14)
a.

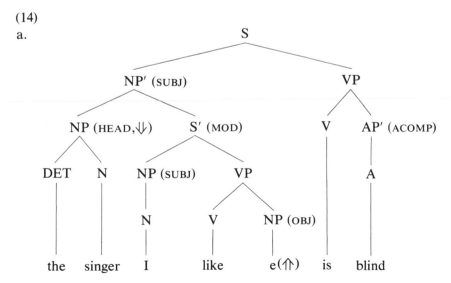

b.

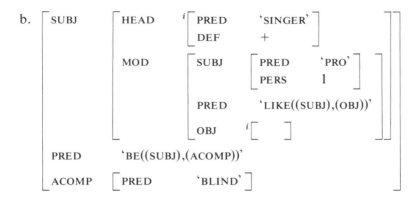

This example has been drastically simplified, but it should illustrate the nature of the mechanisms involved.

10.2 Why a Lexical Theory of Acquisition?

Elsewhere I have claimed that most arguments about language acquisition are unsound unless they refer to mechanisms of well-defined learning models capable in principle of acquiring a correct grammar given exposure to linguistic data (Pinker 1979). Since we do not yet have an explicit model of the acquisition of lexical grammars, the following points in favor of a lexical approach to acquisition will at best serve as plausibility arguments, encouraging the effort to develop a lexical model, but not demonstrating its truth in advance. Later in the chapter I will present an explicit model of the acquisition of lexical grammars. Though I think that this model has certain advantages over acquisition models based on the standard theory of transformational grammar (including the Degree-2 model), here again the model will not license a decisive choice between lexical grammars and contemporary transformational grammars as part of a theory of language acquisition. It may be possible to develop an equally plausible model based on recent versions of transformational grammar (e.g., Chomsky 1980). However, to the degree that the lexical model presented here is consistent with the linguistic and developmental facts, the burden of proof is shifted to those who would claim that a transformational theory is correct. Linguistics long ago issued a promissory note stating that a restrictive theory of grammar would provide psychology with the foundations of an adequate and plausible theory of language acquisition. The fact that the lexical interpretive theory allows the note to be redeemed so easily I think speaks very strongly for the explanatory adequacy and feasibility of the theory.

There are several prima facie reasons to believe that a lexical grammar is a promising foundation for a theory of language acquisition:

The correctness of the theory. A theory that accounts for the acquisition of an incorrect grammar is, of course, an incorrect acquisition theory. Therefore, much of the promise of a lexical acquisition theory will be proportional to the empirical success of lexical grammars in accounting for adults' linguistic judgments. The other chapters in this volume present arguments attesting to that success. But regardless of whether or not *all* the features of lexical grammar will turn out to be correct, it appears that *many* of them will characterize a correct theory, if the current consensus among linguists is justified. For example, in virtually all current theories of generative grammar, much of the descriptive burden shouldered by transformational rules in Chomsky 1965 and subsequent work has been transferred to other components of the grammar, such as phrase structure rules, lexical rules, and interpretive rules (e.g., Chomsky 1970, 1980). Thus, a theory of the acquisition of lexical grammars will probably be applicable in large measure to the acquisition of other sorts of grammar which share its essential features, such as the base generation of surface structures, the use of lexical rules to capture syntactic generalizations, and the use of lexical information in interpreting meaningful grammatical relations.

It is noteworthy that the Degree-2 theory has turned out to be somewhat brittle in this regard. It is not clear how to adapt the model to the acquisition of contemporary grammars in which the role of transformations has been usurped by other components. A particularly thorny problem with the model is that the learner's perceptual and cognitive faculties are assumed to provide access to the deep structure of an utterance, which then is used to help infer the transformations in the target language. But in modern transformational theories, the structures that undergo semantic interpretation (and hence which conceivably could be derived via perception of the speaker's intentions and the nonlinguistic context) are distinct from the structures that trigger grammatical transformations.

Direct incorporation into a perception–production model. The second advantage of a lexical grammar is that it can be embedded as a distinct component of a computational model embodying a theory of on-line sentence comprehension and production (see chapter 11 of this volume). This is in line with Chomsky's prediction (1965:9) that "no doubt a reasonable model of language will incorporate, as a basic component, the generative grammar that expresses the speaker–hearer's knowledge of the language." An explicit performance theory in which distinct grammatical rules are consulted during comprehension and production offers three benefits to language acquisition theory. First, unlike theories that intentionally conflate grammatical rules with comprehension heuristics (e.g., Bever 1970), modular-grammar theories sharply delineate what must be learned from what might be innate. Presumably, properties of the parser, such as whether the scheduler proceeds depth-first or breadth-first or whether a pushdown stack or a well-formed substring table is used, do not differ among speakers of different languages. A theory that separates the grammatical representations defining the difference between English and French from the comprehension algorithms common to all languages allows one to try to account for the induction of the former without worrying about the specification of the latter. Similarly, once the acquisition of grammatical rules for a particular language is explained, the ability to speak, understand, and judge the grammaticality of the sentences of the language immediately follows.[1] If, on the other hand, we tried to account for the acquisition of comprehension heuristics, we would then be faced with the separate problems of accounting for the acquisition of the ability to speak and to judge. In sum, a perception–production model with a distinct grammatical component factors the human language faculty optimally for explaining the acquisition of languages.

The fact that the parsing theory is explicit offers two other advantages to language acquisition research. In interpreting naturalistic and experimental data on the constructions children are most likely to use and understand properly, researchers have been hampered by the fact that any instance of linguistic behavior simultaneously reflects properties of the grammar and of the parsing/producing mechanisms. Thus it is never clear whether a given developmental trend is caused by a change in the grammar, a change in the parsing mechanisms (e.g., an increase in working memory), or both. With an explicit parsing theory, the chances of teasing them apart improve. For example, it appears that certain trends detailed in the child language literature, such as the comprehension of relative clauses (Sheldon 1974, de Villiers, Flusberg, Hakuta, and Cohen 1979), may be at least partially explicable in terms of parsing principles independently motivated by studies of adult comprehension (see Solan and Roeper 1978), rather than in terms of changes in grammatical rules. Discoveries of this sort, incidentally, can only be welcomed: explaining the acquisition and modification of grammatical rules is a tremendously difficult problem, so the less there is to explain, the better.

Finally, having an explicit parsing theory offers the hope of modeling the actual computations that occur at the moment when a child adds a new rule to his or her grammar. It is unlikely that children literally select randomly from among a large set of hypotheses and then test them against the utterances they hear (as is the case in the Degree-2 theory, and countenanced by Erreich, Valian, and Winzemer 1980); rather, they probably enrich their grammar as they try to understand incoming sentences in left-to-right order (much the same way that adults can learn new vocabulary items as they try to understand a sentence in which the item is embedded). If acquisition is driven by the comprehension process, then limitations on comprehension, such as the size of working memory, may constrain the types of rules that may be added to a child's grammar at a given stage of development. Therefore, a theory of the growth of processing mechanisms, which itself depends on there being a distinct theory of processing, may contribute to predictions about the order of acquisition of grammatical rules, something that the field has lacked since the demise of the derivational theory of complexity (discussed below).

Compatibility with child language data. There are three facts about language development that are difficult to interpret if language acquisition consists of the child accumulating transformations. All three can be given straightforward interpretations if language acquisition consists largely of the acquisition of lexical entries, each one specific to a grammatical construction that the word enters into.

Baker 1979 has pointed out that transformational acquisition theories predict a class of overgeneralization errors that no child has been observed to make. Many English transformations, such as Dative Movement, may be applied to sentences containing some verbs, but not others, as sentences (15) and (16) show:

(15)
a. Carter sent a warning to Brezhnev.
b. Carter sent Brezhnev a warning.

(16)
a. Carter announced his policy to Congress.
b. *Carter announced Congress his policy.

If children mastered forms such as (15b) by constructing a transformational rule interchanging the two postverbal noun phrases and deleting the preposition *to*, we would expect them to overgeneralize by uttering ungrammatical strings such as (16b). Such utterances are not to be found in child speech. Furthermore, even if they were, it is unclear how children could ever learn to suppress the overgeneralization, since they have no access to information about ungrammatical sentences in their language (see Brown and Hanlon 1970). In a lexical theory, the dative alternation consists of a predicate's having two lexical entries, one identifying its respective arguments with the subject, object, and *to*-object and one identifying its respective arguments with the subject, second object, and first object. If children enter a lexical form into their grammars *only* upon hearing it in a particular utterance, the fact that they never hear sentences such as (16b) ensures that they will never produce such anomalous constructions. (The issues are in fact considerably more complex than I have portrayed them here. In a later section entitled "Productivity Revisited," I consider in greater detail the facts and theories concerning cross-construction productivity.)

Maratsos 1978 has shown that children not only successfully avoid overgeneralizing to cases such as (16b), they also fail to generalize transformational relations that *legitimately* apply across large classes of predicates. For example, at an age at which children correctly interpret both the active and passive versions of sentences with action verbs such as (17), they understand only the active version of sentences with nonaction predicates such as (18):

(17)
a.   The boy hit the girl.
b.   The girl was hit by the boy.

(18)
a.   The boy liked the girl.
b.   The girl was liked by the boy.

Jill de Villiers and Robin Barr (personal communication) have found that passive sentences with nonaction predicates are rare in parental speech to children, supporting the notion that children acquire "transformational" relations by conservatively adding lexical entries for a predicate to their grammar only when the predicate is encountered in a particular construction (though I again refer the reader to the section entitled "Productivity Revisited").

The lexical specificity of syntactic constructions even seems to be true of children's earliest word combinations. Bowerman 1976 and Braine 1976 have found that young children do not use all the verbs and adjectives in their vocabularies productively at one time. Rather, each item in a form class begins to be used productively at different points in the child's development. Again, it seems that the rules that allow predicates to be combined with other words are stored with the individual predicates.

Finally, a transformation-by-transformation acquisition theory makes two predictions about the order of acquisition of grammatical constructions that child language data have not dealt kindly with. First, constructions derived by the application of a particular transformation should be mastered later than their untransformed counterparts. Second, constructions derived by the application of two transformations should be mastered only after each of the transformations is mastered in isolation. Maratsos 1978 documents the many counterexamples to this "derivational theory of complexity" (see also de Villiers, Flusberg, and Hakuta 1977), such as the pairs in (19)–(23), whose first members, though derivationally more complex according to standard transformational theories, appear earlier than their second members:

(19)
a.   the brown dog
b.   The dog is brown.

(20)
a.   Daddy's chair
b.   Daddy has a chair.

(21)
a.   I want to go.
b.   I want Sam to go.

(22)
a.   The boy was licked.
b.   The boy was licked by the dog.

(23)
a.   Rosie flies a kite and a plane.
b.   Rosie flies a kite and Rosie flies a plane.

In a lexical theory, the (a) and (b) members of each pair are generated by different phrase structure rules, and their orders of acquisition should be predictable from the relative complexity of their underlying f-structures and by the relative availability of appropriate exemplars in parental speech. And in fact, the f-structures underlying the (a) members of (19)–(22) are simpler than those underlying their (b) counterparts; furthermore, (23a) forms seem to be more frequent in maternal speech than (23b) forms (de Villiers, Flusberg, and Hakuta 1977).[2,3]

10.3 The Learnability of Lexical Interpretive Grammars

E. M. Gold's seminal paper on the learnability of classes of languages (Gold 1967) has inspired a number of linguists to evaluate theories of grammar according to whether the classes of languages they define are learnable in principle (Wexler and Culicover 1980, Baker 1979; see Baker and McCarthy in press). Though Chomsky has pointed out that it is not logically necessary for an explanatorily adequate theory of grammar to define a learnable class of languages, there are several reasons why learnability is a desirable property for a grammar to have. First, when a feature of a grammar contributes to a demonstration of learnability, that feature is in some sense explained (Wexler and Culicover 1980, Chomsky 1965). Second, if a feature of the grammar seems to preclude learnability, the theory of grammar may need a revision (Baker 1979). Finally, demonstrations showing which mechanisms are necessary and sufficient for learnability bear strongly on the plausibility of psychological theories of language acquisition (Pinker 1979). In this section, I briefly review the foundations of learnability theory, sketch out a demonstration that lexical theories of grammar define a learnable class of languages (a full proof is included as an appendix), and discuss the implications of the result for a realistic theory of the acquisition of lexical grammars.

Learnability Models
The following discussion is necessarily cursory. For a more detailed presentation of learnability models and their relevance to human language acquisition, see Pinker 1979.

Gold defines a language learnability model as consisting of four parts: a class of target languages defined over a common vocabulary, a method of presentation of information to the learner, a learning strategy, and a success criterion. Given that an infinite number of grammars are consistent with any finite sample of sentences, obviously we cannot require that a learner acquire an arbitrary language based on a finite sample drawn from it. Gold thus defines a more tractable learnability model called "identification in the limit." In a version of this model called "text presentation," the target language is drawn from one of the classes of languages in the "Chomsky hierarchy," such as finite state, context-free, primitive recursive, and so on. Sentences are presented to the learner one at a time, starting at a fixed point and continuing forever, every sentence in the language appearing in the sample at least once. On every trial, the learner must guess a grammar for the target language. Usually the learner arrives at this guess by enumerating grammars in the target class (say, in order of increasing complexity) until coming upon one that can generate every sentence encountered up to that point. If after some trial the learner always guesses the same grammar, and the grammar correctly generates the target language, the learner is said to have succeeded in identifying the language in the limit.

Gold's most notable result was that no infinite class of languages in the Chomsky hierarchy is learnable in the limit in a text presentation situation. A seemingly more positive result was that if the learner has access to all possible strings of vocabulary symbols, with each string labeled as either grammatical or ungrammatical with respect to the target language, then any recursively enumerable class of decidable languages is learnable in the limit. Unfortunately, since children appear to have no access to information about ungrammatical sentences (Brown and Hanlon 1970), that result is of little interest. A genuine positive result stems from the observation that children probably *do* have simultaneous access to a sentence and to the speaker's intended meaning, inferred from the nonlinguistic context of the utterance (Macnamara 1972). Let us use the term *semantic text* to refer to a sample consisting of sentences paired with denumerable symbols (e.g., positive integers) representing their meanings. Let us use the term *semantic-mapping grammar* to refer to a recursive function that maps the grammatical sentences of a language onto their meanings in one-to-one fashion. Using one of Gold's 1967 results, Anderson 1976 has shown that any recursively enumerable class of semantic-mapping grammars is learnable in the limit from semantic text.

It is reassuring to know that semantic-mapping grammars are learnable from semantic text, since the underlying assumptions—that children have access to speakers' meanings, that grammars recursively map sentences onto meanings, and that the class of grammars is recursively enumerable—are accepted by most language acquisition researchers. Of course, one would want to develop learnability models with the more stringent criterion of acquiring grammars in a manner more reminiscent of human children, a criterion sometimes called *feasibility*. For example, unlike Gold's identification in the limit model, Wexler, Culicover, and Hamburger's "Degree-2" learner inspects a single meaning–sentence pair at a time, modifies the hypothesis grammar one rule at a time, and can converge on a correct grammar with fairly simple sentences. Here a criterion is adopted that is intermediate between Gold's and that of Wexler, Culicover, and Hamburger: I attempt to demonstrate that the class of possible lexical grammars is finite in cardinality. This, I show, allows learnability in time far less than the astronomical amounts required by Gold's enumerative learner. In a later section, I argue that by changing some of the usual assumptions about language learnability, one can *informally* account for the acquisition of lexical grammars in a pyschologically realistic manner.

The proof (presented in full in the appendix) consists of two parts. First, since any finite set is recursively enumerable, it is easy to show that a finite set of semantic-mapping grammars is identifiable in the limit from a semantic text, given Anderson's result. This is because any incorrect hypothesis grammar will eventually encounter a semantic structure which it maps onto a different string than the one paired with it in the sample. Thus, all mistaken guesses will sooner or later be rejected. Since there are only a finite number of possible grammars, the learner will eventually hit upon the correct one and will never have to change the guess after that.

The other (lengthier) part of the proof is that the class of possible lexical interpretive grammars is finite. This proof is accomplished by showing that a lexical grammar, formally speaking, has seven parts and that each of these parts can assume a finite number of realizations. The parts are listed in (24).

(24)
a. The terminal vocabulary (root lexical items)
b. The nonterminal vocabulary (lexical and phrasal category symbols)
c. The start symbol ("S")
d. The functional vocabulary (grammatical functions and syntactic features)
e. The functional equation relations (equivalence relations such as "=" used in functional equations)
f. The annotated phrase structure rules
g. The lexical redundancy rules

Part (a) is assumed to be finite for convenience, a standard and innocuous assumption in learnability proofs. Parts (b)–(e) are, according to the theory of universal lexical grammar, subsets of universal finite sets. Since a finite number of subsets can be drawn from any set, there are finitely many possible realizations of parts (b)–(e). Part (f) is shown to be finite with the help of two universal constraints on annotated phrase structure rules: (i) the "no-repetition" condition, which forbids any category symbol together with its annotations to appear more than once in the righthand side of an annotated phrase structure rule; and (ii) the "functional locality" condition, which allows a functional equation to refer to functions separated by no more than one level of embedding in an f-structure (for example, an equation can refer to a VCOMP or a VCOMP('s) SUBJ, but not a VCOMP('s) SUBJ('s) MOD). Each of these constraints is independently motivated by Bresnan and Kaplan in chapter 4 of this volume; (i) complements their "Uniqueness Condition," and (ii) is proposed explicitly in that chapter. Part (g) is finite by virtue of the fact that lexical redundancy rules may replace single grammatical functions with single grammatical functions, the functions being drawn from a universal finite set, as mentioned. Since each of the seven parts of a lexical grammar can come in one of only finitely many forms, the grammar as a whole can come in only finitely many forms.

Although the finiteness of the class of lexical grammars automatically makes the class recursively enumerable and hence learnable, that alone would hardly justify the effort of proving the class finite. After all, one could equip the learner with an enumeration procedure for the entire class of primitive recursive semantic-mapping grammars, which no doubt includes grammars for all languages generated by lexical grammars. That would be sufficient for the learner to identify in the limit a grammar for any lexical language. But showing that the class of possible grammars is finite makes the learnability model more realistic in two ways. First, allowing the learner to enumerate an entire class of grammars in the Chomsky hierarchy would be tantamount to claiming that a human child was capable of learning any of these grammars given exposure to a sample of their strings, for example, COBOL $a^n b^n$ languages, or the Red Sox batting averages 1901–1979. By restricting the learner to the much narrower class of lexical grammars, we are espousing the more reasonable assumption that human language learners can acquire only grammars for natural languages.

Second, restricting the learner's hypothesis class to a finite set allows a reduction of the astronomical amount of time that the learning of grammars would take under a standard enumeration procedure (see Pinker 1979). The amount of time necessary to arrive at a correct grammar is a function of the number of meaning–string pairs that must be inspected before the correct grammar is hypothesized for the first time, the number of computational steps necessary to hypothesize each grammar up to and including the correct grammar, and the number of computational steps necessary to verify whether each grammar is consistent with the input received up to a given point. One reason that the learning time for an enumeration procedure is so unmanageably large is that the learner must enumerate vast numbers of grammars and test each one against the sample before arriving at the correct one. In fact, since any of the grammars in an infinite class could have been chosen as a target language, it is impossible to put a finite bound on the amount of time the learner must spend enumerating grammars before finding the correct one. And not surprisingly, when enumeration procedures are implemented as efficiently as possible in computer programs (e.g., Horning 1969, Wharton 1977, Biermann and Feldman, 1972), they spend vast amounts of time enumerating and testing even the simplest sorts of grammars. If the class of target grammars is finite, as it is in our case, one can put a finite bound on the amount of time the learner will spend enumerating grammars. This bound will be determined by the cardinality of the class and will be approached as the target grammar increases in complexity and so occurs "farther down the list."

In fact, there is a way that enumeration time can be reduced to zero. Imagine a complex learning device consisting of n computational modules operating in parallel, each one "hardwired" with a grammar from the set of possible lexical interpretive grammars, every possible grammar being represented by one module. The modules, in unison, inspect the input pairs and test their grammars against them, and any module whose grammar is inconsistent with the latest input pair "turns itself off" permanently. The modules are wired together so that the lowest-numbered (i.e., simplest) module that is not turned off at a given trial announces its grammar as the learner's hypothesis for that trial. With a device like this, it is easy to see that hypothesization time for each trial will depend only on the longest amount of time required by any of the modules to complete its test. Furthermore, since modules turn themselves off at the earliest evidence that their grammars are inconsistent with the sample, the learner does not have to remember the entire sample, and the modules have to test only a single meaning–string pair on each trial, saving even more time. Neither of these results would be possible with an infinite class of target grammars, since there would have to be an infinite number of modules, violating the key assumption that the learner is a finite creature.

As with many learnability presentations, the account just given has an air of science fiction about it. I am certainly not proposing this contraption as a model of the human learner, not even as an idealization or a first approximation. Rather, the scenario is an illustration of the general point that when the class of target grammars is relatively small, a learner with a rich innate structure can save vast amounts of time and working memory in acquiring a grammar. In the last section of this chapter, I use a more realistic learning procedure to show how the linguistic constraints that guarantee finiteness (e.g., the no-repetition constraint) allow a learner to acquire rules quickly and with a minimum of evidence (see also Pinker in press).

A final note: There is a trivial way of proving that almost *any* class of grammars is finite. For example, one could arbitrarily restrict the length of each rule in a grammar to, say, a hundred symbols or less. This would guarantee the finiteness of the class and would have no detrimental effect on the descriptive adequacy of the grammar. But despite the advantages that finiteness brings, no one imposes restrictions like these, because doing so would advance no substantive claim about the human mind—the restriction could just as easily have been to a thousand symbols, or a million. But when a restriction that entails finiteness of the class of grammars is independently motivated, as in the case of the no-repetition and functional locality conditions, there is a strong suspicion that it reflects some fundamental property of the human language faculty. It is for this reason that the finiteness of the class of lexical grammars is a significant observation.

10.4 Some Properties of a Reasonable Theory of Language Acquisition

Formulating a feasible model of language acquisition requires constraining a mathematical model by a variety of additional factors ranging from the amount of matter in the universe to the amount of short-term memory in the child. In this section I discuss some of the general considerations that will govern the choice of mechanisms for a reasonable learning model; in the section following I sketch a particular theory of what such mechanisms are and show how they operate when confronted with particular linguistic data.

Innate Constraints on Acquisition: Hypothesis-Testing versus Parameter-Setting

Perhaps the most fundamental tenet of modern linguistics is that language acquisition is made possible by strong innate constraints on the form and contents of adult grammar (Chomsky 1965). However, it has never been clear *how* the innate constraints literally operate in the process of rule learning. In *Aspects of the Theory of Syntax,* Chomsky wrote of a *hypothesis-testing* mechanism whose hypothesis grammars were ordered by an innate evaluation metric. As an abstract characterization of language learning, talk of a hypothesis-tester may be useful (just as one could say that the human visual cortex has the "hypothesis" that the visible world is composed mostly of vertical and horizontal edges), but obviously it cannot be taken as a literal description of what happens during language learning. Children do not test a full-blown grammar for Swahili against their input, then a grammar for Rumanian, and so on; rather, they build their grammars rule by rule. The more reasonable Degree-2 hypothesis-tester generates hypotheses at the level of individual transformations instead of whole grammars, but here again one must question whether children literally draw up a large set of hypotheses and select randomly from among them. (This is a particularly severe problem given that the Degree-2 model is intended to be a "reasonable" acquisition model, and in the authors' own presentation is made to conform to various plausibility conditions such as no memory for past data and rule-by-rule acquisition.) But implausibility aside, hypothesis-testing of any sort is an inefficient way for a learner to use primary data. When a hypothesis is disconfirmed by a datum, a hypothesis-testing learner gains only one bit's worth of information and is only minutely more likely to hit upon the correct hypothesis on the next guess. It would be more useful to exploit the *type* and *degree* of discrepancy between hypothesis and datum and to modify the grammar specifically to remedy the discrepancy (as the Degree-2 learner does after deciding to add a transformation). See Braine 1971 for a general discussion of the problems with a literal hypothesis-testing model, such as its need for negative information (which children do not have) and its susceptibility to irreversible error when exposed to noisy data.

In more recent discussions of learnability, Chomsky 1980 has alluded to *parameter-setting,* as opposed to hypothesis-testing, as a mechanism instantiating innate constraints. Here the innate givens would consist of schemata for various types of rules, containing slots or free parameters which would be fixed for a particular language upon exposure to the relevant data. This sort of account is clearly more appealing than literal hypothesis-testing, since the inefficiency of the hypothesis-testing process is eliminated. Because the learner's rule changes must be made in the course of processing a given datum, it is easier to integrate rule learning into the left-to-right comprehension process, instead of forcing the learner to spin hypotheses in vacuo and then juxtapose them against incoming speech.

Unfortunately, getting a parameter-setting model to work in concrete instances is far from easy. The problem is that unless learners have some way of knowing *which* schemata are relevant to a given datum and *which* aspects of the datum justify setting a given parameter in a schema, they must resort to the same trial-and-error method that made the hypothesis-tester so implausible. For example, consider the too-strong theory that universal grammar specifies that languages have identical phrase structure rules except for the left-to-right order of symbols on their righthand sides, it being the learner's task to set the order parameter for each rule. Even if universal grammar contained only two rule schemata, S → {NP, VP} and NP → {N, (DET)} (where {X,Y} means "X Y or Y X"), plus the rule VP → V (NP), the learner would run into trouble even with the simplest cases, as the hypothesized tree and the phrase structure rules in (25) show (the example is adapted from Grimshaw in press):

(25)

a.

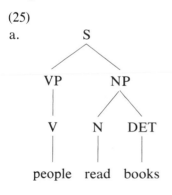

people   read   books

b. S → VP NP   V → people   DET → books
    NP → N DET   N → read

In this artificially constrained case, the learner somehow must know the lexical categories of each word in the input sentence before being able to use that sentence to set the order parameter in each rule to the value defined in the adult grammar. Since individual words vary from language to language, obviously their categorization cannot be specified innately. Similar problems arise in more complicated cases. It seems that innate rule schemata with free parameters are not *sufficient* for a feasible acquisition theory.

The Semantic Bootstrapping Hypothesis

Grimshaw in press and Macnamara in preparation have suggested one way to give learners access to information about which aspects of their innate schemata should be brought to bear on the current inputs. The proposal is to "flag" the elements of each syntactic schema with some feature in the semantic representation of a sentence (since most people agree that the child can construct some version of a semantic representation of an utterance by perceiving its nonlinguistic context). These universal "semantic flags"[4] would not have to represent invariant meanings of syntactic elements in the adult grammar; they would simply serve as parts of the learning mechanism that could become dormant as soon as they had fulfilled their function in setting the relevant parameters. Once a set of parameters was "bootstrapped" into the grammar by these semantic means, the rules thereby fixed could be used in conjunction with further data to set the rest of the parameters in the grammar. For example, imagine that in (25) the learner provisionally assumes that words for perceptible concrete objects are nouns, words for actions are verbs, and words correlated with the specificity of objects in discourse are determiners. Assume further that the learner hears each noun and verb together with its perceptual referent in isolation, then hears determiners plus nouns in situations where the specificity of the noun was already known. Then the categorization of each word could be deduced, and the sentence would suffice to fix the order of each rule in the grammar. Once the rule orders were fixed, they in turn could allow the learner to infer the categorization of more abstract words whose meanings either cannot be deduced from the situation or whose meanings do not flag their categories. For example, upon hearing the sentence *The president stagnates,* the learner could assign *stagnates* the category "verb," because that is the only categorization that would permit a complete analysis of the sentence according to the grammar constructed so far. Let us call rule acquisition relying on semantic flags *semantic bootstrapping* and further acquisition relying on existing rules *distributional learning.*

The "semantic bootstrapping hypothesis" is strongly supported by studies of child language. Children's nouns and verbs display different privileges of occurrence in early sentences and correspond to physical objects and actions, respectively (Brown 1973). This distinction can even be seen in the invented signs of deaf children isolated from other signers: pointing signs correspond to objects, iconic or pantomime signs correspond to actions (Feldman, Goldin-Meadow, and Gleitman 1977). Similarly, in children's early sentences, what seem to be subjects and objects correspond almost entirely to agents and patients of actions (Brown 1973, Bowerman 1973, Maratsos and Chalkley in press). Syntactic constructions that express relatively sophisticated notions like counterfactuals are acquired later than constructions of similar syntactic complexity that express more childlike concepts (Slobin 1973), and constructions in one language that conflate semantic features are acquired later than similar constructions in other languages that map onto the same semantic features in one-to-one fashion (Slobin in press). In fact, the close correspondence between syntax and semantics in early child language is probably the most robust empirical finding in developmental psycholinguistics in the past decade.

Note that the use of semantic flags in syntactic acquisition is different from the frequent claim among developmental psycholinguists that children's early constituents and relations *are* semantic, not syntactic, in nature. The problem with this semantic reductionism is that one still has to explain the acquisition of autonomous syntactic structures in adult language. In such accounts, either the evolution from semantic to syntactic units is attributed to some unspecified process of "abstraction" or "induction," or the syntactic units are said to emerge at a certain maturational stage in a (presumably innately specified) reorganization of the child's language faculty. The former hypothesis is as vague as the latter is ad hoc; clearly both are to be avoided if possible. The present hypothesis—that semantic correlates to syntactic constructions are there to help the learner fix parameters in innate rule schemata—can explain the early correlation between syntax and semantics within an explicit and motivated acquisition theory.

To make the distinction clear, consider the following analogy. Imagine that two dialects of Fortran are in use, one in which a function name must be outside parentheses and its argument within (e.g., "cosine(theta)"), the other having the opposite arrangement ("theta(cosine)"). Computer manufacturers cannot be sure which dialect will be used in a given customer's installation, and so equip their compilers with an acquisition mechanism that interprets the first user program to decide which dialect is used. Since Fortran users may define their own function names and variable names, simply inspecting a function expression within a program statement will not suffice: $X(Y)$ could mean the function X taken at value Y, or vice versa. However, if this learning compiler ignored all function expressions except those containing one of a small set of "library" function names such as SINE, SQUAREROOT, and so on, and if the learner was prohibited from redefining those names, the inference would be simple: the format of the first statement mentioning such a function would identify the dialect. Subsequently, even expressions with arbitrary user-defined functions would be interpretable. And so it might be with language acquisition: children might filter out all meaning–sentence pairs other than those whose semantics give clues to their syntactic analyses; then they might use their syntactic knowledge to interpet utterances whose semantic interpretation is either unavailable at the time or indeterminate with respect to the syntactic rules yet to be learned.

Instantaneous and Noninstantaneous Learners

It has been a working assumption among acquisition-minded linguists that the role of linguistic universals in acquisition can be highlighted in a model of *instantaneous* acquisition (Chomsky 1965), one in which the time dimension can be eliminated or scrambled without altering the operation or the success of the learner. Though children's highly regular acquisition sequence (Brown 1973) suggests that this idealization is false on the face of it, it is unclear exactly what to make of that sequence. To clarify what it means for a language learner to be noninstantaneous, elsewhere (Pinker in press) I have unpacked the instantaneity condition into three subconditions: (a) *Stationarity*—do the acquisition mechanisms themselves change over time (presumably because of maturation)? (b) *Order-sensitivity*—do different orderings of the input sentences affect the success of the learner, the rate of learning, or the form of the grammar at the completion of learning? and (c) *Developmental sequencing*—does the model acquire portions of the grammar in a fixed (though perhaps only partially ordered) sequence, regardless of the order of the input sentences and with its mechanisms stationary? According to this treatment, a model that is either nonstationary, order-sensitive, or developmentally sequenced would be considered a noninstantaneous model.

A learner like the one described, which uses a subset of the data to fix the free parameters in rule schemata with the help of semantic flags and then processes the rest of the data using the partial grammar thus attained, is not instantaneous according to the present definition. It might be thought that such a model is nonstationary, because it initially filters out all sentences except those whose meaning structures uniquely flag a syntactic analysis and then accepts a larger class of sentences. (For instance, in the example presented above, the learner would at first process only sentences containing concrete actions and objects.) However, this fact does *not* necessarily entail nonstationarity (for example, using some sort of semantic filter and then discarding it). It could be that the learner tries to analyze each sentence as completely as possible, using any means available, and will add new rules whenever the analysis exceeds some threshold in completeness. Initially, semantic flags are the only means of analysis available, so only sentences whose meanings can flag their analyses will trigger rule formation. As rules are added, more abstract sentences can be processed, but the actual rule-forming mechanisms remain unchanged throughout. (In the last section of the chapter, I discuss these mechanisms in more detail.) The model could be nonstationary only if a subset of the semantic flags were available to the learner from the outset, the rest emerging later.

The model's order-sensitivity, on the other hand, will depend on whether the data sample repeats sentences an infinite number of times (as in the Degree-2 model) or whether each sentence appears only once (as in identification in the limit). If sentences appear only once (or if the learner cannot remember the entire sample), there may be sample orderings that will prevent our learner from acquiring the entire grammar. For example, if abstract words (e.g., *justification*) always appear in a given construction before concrete words appear in that construction, it may be impossible to identify the syntactic categorization of the abstract words. But even if the learner can recover from such orderings, the learning rate will be slower than in the case where the sample first presents each syntactic construction in a sentence whose semantic representation flags the appropriate rule schemata.

In any case, the surest violation of instantaneity lies in the developmental sequencing inherent in the model. For example, regardless of all else, a semantic-bootstrapping learner cannot acquire the syntactic features of an abstract word before acquiring phrase structure rules that can generate a sentence in which the word can appear. In general, semantically flagged syntactic rules will be learned before other rule types, since the acquisition of nonflagged rules depends on other rules having been mastered in advance.

It may be thought that an instantaneous model is a more tractable idealization of a language learner than a noninstantaneous one. However, this intuition is probably true only of the stationarity criterion. Clearly, it would be impossible to explain language development if the acquisition mechanisms changed in arbitrary ways during the course of acquisition (cf. Pinker 1978). But if the noninstantaneity sprang from intrinsic constraints on the order of the inputs or outputs of the learning mechanisms, the model as a whole would not necessarily be any more complex or opaque than an instantaneous model. In fact, one could argue that by generating predictions about order of acquisition, a noninstantaneous model is more falsifiable than an instantaneous one, which would have to be supplemented with various ordering parameters before it could even be brought to bear on the child's acquisition sequence. This is one of the reasons that the Degree-2 model, important as it is, has been less of a bridge between psychology and linguistics than one might have hoped.

To sum up: the acquisition model that I will outline will not generate hypotheses and then test them against the input. Rather, the rule-learning mechanisms will act directly upon the input meaning–sentence pairs, modifying rules as it tries to parse the sentence. Rule acquisition will consist of filling the slots or setting the parameters of innate rule schemata, and it will depend at first on predictable correlations between elements of syntactic rule schemata and semantic features derivable by perceptual and cognitive faculties. Once a certain number of rules have been "bootstrapped" in this way, other rules can be deduced from a combination of existing rules and subsequent data. As such, the model is noninstantaneous (although it is for all intents stationary) and potentially can generate predictions about the order of acquisition of syntactic rules. I will elaborate all of these points with concrete examples in the next section.

10.5 A Reasonable Theory of the Acquisition of Lexical Grammars

In this section I sketch three aspects of the proposed theory: the innate rule schemata, the "semantic flags" that allow the child to apply rule schemata in the appropriate way to input data, and the procedures that formulate new grammatical rules while processing the input.[5] Even taken together, these specifications do not add up to anything like a complete or formal theory. There is no guarantee that these mechanisms will be sufficient to acquire an entire grammar for any human language. However, at this point it may be more important to show that the model has the potential to be extended to a formally adequate and psychologically plausible acquisition theory than to strive to prove learnability under the current formulation at any price. Perhaps a lesson to be drawn from the Degree-2 effort is that a model's ability to accommodate to evolving characterizations of the grammar and the child may be as much of a virtue as its ability to support a learnability proof under a relatively fixed set of assumptions.

Innate Constraints on Rules

It is assumed that the child is equipped to acquire a lexical interpretive grammar of the sort described in this volume. In particular, it is assumed that the following constraints define the principal degrees of freedom along which languages can vary and which the child will attempt to pin down during acquisition.

Phrase Structure Rules   Here I assume something like Jackendoff's 1977 version of Chomsky's 1970 "X-bar" (here, X-prime) theory of phrase structure rules. Rules are of the general scheme (26),

(26)
$$X^i \rightarrow (Y_1^3)...(Y_k^3) \ X^{i-1} \ (Y_{k+1}^3)...(Y_m^3)$$

where X stands for a major lexical category, X^i stands for one of a set of "projections" of the category (corresponding to the phrasal categories in standard treatments), i is less than or equal to 3, and $Y_1...Y_k$ stands for a series of maximal projections of any category. I assume with Jackendoff that V''' (that is, V triple-bar or V^3) is equivalent to S and that categories flanking the "head" of the phrase (X^{i-1}) correspond either to "specifiers" and "complements," respectively, or to "complements" and "specifiers," respectively, across all rules. (I will discuss the meanings of these terms and the semantic correlates of the different aspects of the rules in the next section.) Finally, I assume that maximal projections of categories in the righthand side of a rule can be annotated with functional equations according to the constraints described in chapter 2 of this volume.

Lexical Entries and Lexical Rules   Lexical entries contain *lexical forms,* which consist of predicate argument structures (n-place functions, $n \leq 4$) and a biunique assignment of arguments to grammatical functions (see chapters 1 and 3 of this volume). Lexical forms are annotated with functional equations specifying the grammatical features of the entry (e.g., its number, gender, person) and the "control equations" associated with it. These control equations can state an identity between the subject of an embedded complement and the object, oblique object, or subject of the clause in which the predicate is found.

Lexical rules may alter every occurrence of one or more grammatical functions in a lexical entry and may add lexical equations to the existing set, so long as biuniqueness is preserved.

Long-Distance Binding   The metavariables $\Uparrow$ and $\Downarrow$, which govern the "long-distance" relations linking "binders" and "bindees" in subjacent clauses, may be appended to a restricted set of nodes in the phrase structure rules. Specifically: (a) the $\Uparrow$ symbol specifying a link to a superior binder must be appended to the rule NP $\rightarrow$ e if it exists (a complete account would specify how it would also be appended to lexical entries for certain words such as *wh*-pronouns); (b) the symbol $\Downarrow$ specifying a link to a lower gap may be appended to any NP which is a sister to an S and a daughter to S'; (c) the equation $\Uparrow = \Downarrow$ transferring a binding relation from clause to clause may be appended to the COMP node, that is, to a non-NP node which is a sister to an S and a daughter to S'.

Semantic Flags for Elements of Syntactic Schemata
I have referred to semantic clues that the child may use to recognize the elements of innate syntactic schemata. Of course, unless these clues or "flags" are spelled out explicitly, a learning theory appealing to them can quickly become circular, since it is always possible to call on some unspecified semantic entity to assist the learner in acquiring some syntactic rule (Pinker 1979). Here I state hypotheses concerning the cognitive or semantic clues that the child innately treats as signaling elements of specific syntactic structures. The reader will note that these hypotheses imply that the child's "language of thought" contains a rich and highly differentiated set of units and relations and not just a small assortment of directed associations (cf. J. R. Anderson 1977).

Syntactic Categories   With Grimshaw in press, I suggest that the child tacitly uses something like the old-fashioned definitions of syntactic categories: a noun is a person, place, or thing; a verb is an action; an adjective is a physical property of a person, place, or thing; a preposition is a direction, path, or spatial relation; a determiner specifies the number and definiteness of objects; an "S" expresses a complete proposition; an auxiliary specifies the temporal, aspectual, and modal aspects of an action; a *wh*-pronoun is an unknown variable in a semantic description; and so on.

Phrase Structure Configurations   The X-bar (X-prime) specifications of possible phrase structure rules outlined above allow a complement phrase to be introduced by three different rules, corresponding to the three possible levels of projection of the lexical head. Jackendoff 1977 has proposed that the level of projection of the rule generating a complement (and hence the point of attachment of the complement phrase to the branch of the phrase structure tree dominating the head) is predictable from the semantic relation between the logical referents of the head and of the complement. If the complement is an argument of the predicate specified by the head (e.g., *the picture of John*), it is generated as a daughter of the first projection of the head (that is, X'); if the complement functions as a restrictive modifier of the head (e.g., *the picture that won the contest*), it is generated as a daughter of the second projection (X''); and if it functions as a nonrestrictive modifier of the head (e.g., *the picture, which was the third one I took*), it is generated as a daughter of the third level of projection (X'''). I propose that the semantic representation that the child constructs by perceiving the nonlinguistic situation captures these semantic distinctions, and that the child uses the correspondences between semantics and phrase structure to fit a tree onto the adult sentence. As we shall see, the tree is used to coin the phrase structure rules of the grammar (as in J. R. Anderson 1977). In the present theory, the semantic input to the child is represented as a language-independent f-structure (see below), and the argument/restrictive modifier/nonrestrictive modifier distinction is explicitly represented there using different function names within that structure: a grammatical function (such as SUBJ(ECT) or OBJ(ECT)) corresponds to a logical argument, and the RESTRICTIVE MODIFIER and UNRESTRICTIVE MODIFIER labels correspond to the other two relevant relations. I refer the reader to Jackendoff 1977 for analogous restrictions on the attachments of specifiers, which I also assume to be part of the learner's innate endowment.

Two other semantic distinctions are relevant to the formulation of syntactic rules. Again it is assumed that the child's representation of a situation captures these distinctions. One is the distinction between specifiers and complements, which allows the child to make cross-category generalizations of the order of terms in the righthand sides of phrase structure rules. In the functional structure, a specifier corresponds to a primitive function value (such as the value for the definiteness of a noun phrase or the tense of a verb phrase), and a complement corresponds to an embedded functional substructure (like the arguments of a verb phrase predicate or the modifiers of a noun phrase). Finally, I assume that one of the arguments of the main verb of the sentence is perceived to be the "topic" or "given" of the sentence within the context of discourse and is distinguished from the other arguments within the f-structure. That argument will be immediately dominated by the S-node in the phrase structure tree and will correspond to the "subject" in languages like English.

Lexical Entries I assume that there is an isomorphism between the predicate argument structure of the children's early lexical entries and the predicate argument structures of the predicates in their abstract "language of thought." For example, the child might conceptualize a situation in terms of a 2-place predicate corresponding to *hit,* with arguments corresponding to the thematic relations "agent" and "patient," and use this predicate as the basis for the lexical entry for the word *hit* upon hearing it.[6] This isomorphism disappears in the adult grammar, where the predicate argument structure of a lexical item cannot always be predicted from semantic or logical considerations (see chapter 3 of this volume). In addition, it is assumed that the arguments of a budding lexical entry are assigned default grammatical functions as follows: if there is a single argument, it must be assigned as SUBJ. If there are more than one, the default functions will be determined by the thematic relations labeling the argument: SUBJ for agent, OBJ for patient, P-CASE OBJ for recipient, SCOMP for a propositional argument, and possibly several others.

Syntactic Features The child is assumed to encode a small number of semantically identifiable and linguistically relevant features of each utterance, such as its tense and aspect, and the number, person, gender, animacy, humanness, and the like, of each of its arguments. The child is assumed to know innately that this small set of features is the linguistically relevant subset of the many features that can be perceived to be true of the referents of an utterance, for instance, temperature, color, size, etc. See Slobin 1979, in press for arguments supporting this sort of assumption.

The Input to the Learner

I assume that the input to the child is a semantic text consisting of strings paired with "uncommitted" f-structures. These f-structures differ from the ones that the adult would assign to sentences in that, clearly, they cannot contain information that is determined by rules that have not yet been learned. However, I assume that they contain information about the propositional structure of the sentence's meaning (such as the correct links between predicates and arguments), the topic–comment distinction defined by the pragmatics of the utterance, and whatever default grammatical information may be associated with the predicates and arguments (for instance, the assignment of SUBJ to agent arguments). Thus, the child may plausibly construct the uncommitted f-structure (27) on the basis of perceiving the nonlinguistic context of the utterance *John convinced the milkman to swat the dog:*

(27)

$$
\begin{bmatrix}
\text{SUBJ} & \begin{bmatrix} \text{PRED} & \text{`JOHN'} \\ \text{NUM} & \text{SG} \\ \text{PERS} & 3 \\ \text{ANIM} & + \\ \text{HUMAN} & + \\ \text{DEF} & + \\ \text{GEND} & \text{M} \\ & \vdots \end{bmatrix} \\
\\
\text{TENSE} & \text{PAST} \\
\\
\text{PRED} & \text{`CONVINCE((SUBJ), (OBJ), (SCOMP))'} \\
& \quad\quad\quad\quad \text{agent } \text{ patient } \text{ proposition} \\
\\
\text{OBJ} & {}^{i}\begin{bmatrix} \text{PRED} & \text{`MILKMAN'} \\ \text{DEF} & + \\ \text{NUM} & \text{SG} \\ \text{PERS} & 3 \\ \text{ANIM} & + \\ \text{HUMAN} & + \\ \text{GEND} & \text{M} \\ & \vdots \end{bmatrix} \\
\\
\text{SCOMP} & \begin{bmatrix} \text{SUBJ} & {}^{i}\begin{bmatrix} \vdots \end{bmatrix} \\ \\ \text{TENSE} & \text{none} \\ \\ \text{PRED} & \text{`SWAT((SUBJ), (OBJ))'} \\ & \quad\quad \text{agent } \text{ patient} \\ \\ \text{OBJ} & \begin{bmatrix} \text{PRED} & \text{`DOG'} \\ \text{HUMAN} & - \\ \text{DEF} & + \\ \text{NUM} & \text{SG} \\ \text{PERS} & 3 \\ \text{ANIM} & + \\ & \vdots \end{bmatrix} \end{bmatrix}
\end{bmatrix}
$$

In this example, the child is assumed to know that *John* is the topic of the utterance (represented by the notational convention of listing its f-substructure first in the overall f-structure), that the principal predicate, *convince,* takes three arguments, corresponding here to *John, the milkman,* and *the milkman swats the dog,* that the predicate *swat* takes two arguments corresponding to *the milkman* and *the dog,* that the same milkman is simultaneously the convinced and the swatter, and that the SUBJ, OBJ, and SCOMP, respectively, correspond to the agent, patient, and proposition arguments of the predicates. In addition, the child encodes the perceptible features of the situation (tense, gender, etc.) which are known innately to be potentially grammatically relevant.

The f-structure that the adult grammar would pair with the sentence differs from this uncommitted structure in three ways. First, features irrelevant to English syntactic rules (e.g., animacy) would not be listed in the adult f-structure. Second, syntactic elements without perceptible referents (e.g., the *to* introducing the complement) *would* be listed in the adult structure. Third, structures could violate the default assignments of grammatical functions to arguments. For example, in the child's f-structure the predicate *try* would take an SCOMP, whereas in the adult's it would take a VCOMP. Similarly, the child's f-structures constructed in the presence of active and passive sentences would be identical (except for the topic–comment distinction), whereas the adult's f-structures for the two constructions would employ different sets of grammatical functions.

The Learning Procedure

In the present theory, the child uses three sets of learning procedures: procedures for the initial acquisition of lexical items, procedures for the acquisition of phrase structure rules, and procedures for the acquisition of the devices that account for grammatical relations not expressible by phrase structure rules, such as lexical redundancy rules, control equations, and long-distance binding. In the standard theory, of course, these rules consist of structure-dependent transformations.

Word Learning   Virtually every explicit model of language acquisition has assumed that the child knows the meaning of words before starting to acquire syntactic rules (e.g., Wexler and Culicover 1980; J. R. Anderson 1977; see Pinker 1979, for a review). This idealization vastly simplifies the task of explaining the acquisition of syntax since, at the very least, the child can link the simple elements of the spoken sen-

tence with the simple elements of the semantic representation underlying the sentence. However, it begs the question of whether the child
can learn lexical items at a time when he or she is ignorant of the
syntactic rules governing the assembly of those words into sentences.
In the case of the parent pointing to a dog and saying *dog,* the idealization seems reasonable (though clearly even here one must assume that
the child brings a rich perceptual and cognitive representational system
to the task of word learning). But in the case of the so-called "grammatical morphemes" such as determiners, inflections, auxiliaries, and
the like, matters become muddier. The parent cannot simply point to
something definite and say *the!* Instead, the child may use the following
four strategies to acquire words and morphemes in advance of knowing
syntactic rules. This proposal, I hope, will allow us to keep the words-
first-then-syntax idealization that makes syntactic acquisition tractable.
Incidentally, in discussing each of these strategies, the idealization is
carried even further by assuming that the child has segmented the
speech wave into words, and words into morphemes (e.g., that /dɔgz/ is
represented as "dog + s"). Perhaps this can be accomplished in part by
purely distributional methods (see Olivier 1968, Wolff 1977).

(a) *The Ostension Strategy.* The child perceives a single entity; the
parent utters a single word; the child links the word to the mental
predicate or concept underlying the perceived entity. This will work for
the doggy example above.

(b) *The Pragmatic Emphasis Strategy.* The child perceives that the
adult is trying to convey information about a single linguistically relevant attribute (e.g., the pastness of an action, the definiteness of an
object, the necessariness of a proposition). The adult gives emphatic
stress to the morpheme signaling that attribute (e.g., *I* was *sleeping,*
Hand me the *toy, You* must *go to bed*). The child links the emphasized
attribute to the stressed word.

(c) *The Odd Feature, Odd Name Strategy* (cf. Carey 1978). Again the
child perceives that the adult is trying to convey information about a
single linguistically relevant attribute, but the corresponding morpheme is not distinguished phonologically in the spoken utterance.
However, if the morpheme is the only one in the sentence that cannot
be understood, the child can safely link it to the emphasized attribute.

(d) *The Abstraction Strategy.* If all else fails, the child can record the
unknown morpheme in memory, together with a list of all the linguistically relevant semantic features of the utterance that were not expressed in the sentence by other, known words. When the word is used

in subsequent sentences, listed features that are untrue of the situation are erased from the list, and eventually only the features actually signified by the morpheme will remain. Later we shall see that the abstraction strategy for word learning is a special case of a more general procedure for the acquisition of syntactic features of words.

The abstraction strategy differs from the other strategies in that the correct rule cannot be acquired with a single exposure to an exemplar. However, unlike the other strategies, it will allow the child to acquire simple morphemes that signify conjunctions of features. The lengthier learning period predicted by this strategy (owing to the greater number of exemplars required) can in fact be observed in language development: Slobin in press has found that when features are conflated into single morphemes in a language, children acquire those morphemes far more slowly than children whose target languages map the same semantic features onto morphemes in one-to-one fashion.

Phrase Structure Rules   The child acquires annotated phrase structure rules by fitting a tree onto the incoming sentence, using the partial grammar acquired so far and the uncommitted f-structure, and by reading the corresponding rewrite rules off the tree. The procedure is as follows:

(P1) Build as complete a tree for the string as possible by parsing it with existing annotated phrase structure rules and existing lexical entries. Alter the uncommitted f-structure as mandated by these existing rules.

(P2) For the parts of the sentence that do not yet subtend branches of the tree, label the words with the lexical categories that are flagged by the semantic properties of the word meaning (e.g., noun for thing, verb for action, etc.). Build a branch extending each lexical category upward to its maximal projection (i.e., X''' according to Jackendoff's formulation of X-bar theory).

(P3) Connect the "topic" noun phrase as the daughter of the root S-node (the maximal projection of the main verb of the sentence).

(P4) Connect the remaining branches according to the information in the f-structure, and the X-bar principles (e.g., functional argument = sister of X, restrictive modifier = sister of X', nonrestrictive modifier = sister of X''; and the analogous conditions for specifiers). If the desired connection is impossible without crossing branches, connect the complement one node higher than the specified node.

(P5) Annotate the maximally projected node of each noun phrase with the grammatical function specified for that argument by the default lexical form. Fill in the metavariables according to the conventions proposed in chapter 2 of this volume.[7]

(P6) Create annotated phrase structure rules corresponding to the tree fit onto the sentence, according to the usual conventions relating trees to rewrite rules.

(P7) Collapse new and old expansions of a category as follows (*symbol* refers here to a category together with a particular set of functional equations): (a) Asterisk any symbol that appears twice in succession in an expansion in one rule. (Note that the no-repetition condition makes this procedure possible.) (b) If a sequence of symbols in one expansion is properly contained within another expansion, combine the two expansions, putting parentheses around the symbols not contained in the smaller expansion. (c) If two expansions are identical except for one symbol that differs between them, collapse the expressions by placing within braces the symbols that are not held in common. (d) If two symbols appear in braces in one rule but successively in the other (the rest of the expansions being identical), discard the braces and retain the symbols in the correct sequence, each within a pair of parentheses.

The following procedures allow the child to acquire the devices (control equations, lexical redundancy rules, long-distance binding metavariables) that perform the computations accomplished by transformations in the standard theory. As such, this part of the theory embodies the claim that a lexical interpretive grammar is the correct theory of human linguistic competence.

Lexical Entries, Control Equations, and Lexical Redundancy Rules
Although the child's f-structure contains a default lexical form for the predicate of a sentence, that form is not yet suitable for entry into the lexicon. Thus, the procedure that enters lexical forms in the lexicon (L2) is deferred until several others have been executed. Additional information such as control equations might have to be appended to the lexical entry, and the functional assignments in the correct adult lexical entry may differ from those in the default form. In fact, certain default forms do not appear at all in the adult lexicon. For example, the predicate *try* takes a propositional argument, which is assigned SCOMP as its default function. Nevertheless, *I tried for me to go* and *I tried that he leave,* in which *try* does appear with an S-complement, are ungram-

matical. Interestingly, errors of this sort have never been observed to occur in child speech (Maratsos 1978).

(L1) If the grammatical functions assigned to arguments in the lexical form in the f-structure differ from those assigned to the corresponding noun phrases in the tree, create a second lexical form for the predicate. In the new lexical form, the arguments should be assigned the functions annotated to the phrase structure tree. Effect the same substitution of new functions for old functions in whatever equations are associated with the old lexical form. Add equations to the new lexical form specifying the morphological features distinguishing this realization of the predicate from the one associated with the old lexical form.

The following three procedures, which add control equations to a lexical form, are applied whenever a predicate takes an argument which is itself a complete proposition, and when that proposition is represented in the tree without its subject by a phrasal category X':

(C1) Connect X''' as a sister of the predicate that contains the propositional argument.

(C2) Create a second lexical entry for the predicate, in which the function SCOMP is replaced by the function XCOMP, where X is the category label of the subjectless proposition.

(C3) Add to the second lexical entry the equation XCOMP SUBJ = FUNCTION, where FUNCTION is the grammatical function annotated to the matrix noun phrase coindexed with the missing subject in the f-structure.

(L2) Add the current lexical form (the form as altered by the procedures above) as an entry to the lexicon.

(L3) Coin a lexical redundancy rule generalizing the function replacements and equation addition performed by L1 and C2–3. For example, for passive constructions, L1 would have replaced an OBJ in a lexical form by a SUBJ and a SUBJ by a BY OBJ, and would have added the equation PART = PAST.[8] Thus, L3 would coin the rule listed as (28).

(28)
(OBJ) $\mapsto$ (SUBJ)
(SUBJ) $\mapsto$ (BY OBJ)
$\mapsto$ (PART) = (PAST)

This procedure is in fact somewhat too general and would lead to the overgeneralizations and rapid correct generalizations that children do not seem to make. In a later section, I discuss how the creation of lexical rules can be tamed in the appropriate way.

Long-Distance Binding   Because of the intricacy of constructions such as relativization and question formation in natural languages, the acquisition of the mechanisms necessary to accomplish long-distance binding cannot be presented here in depth. However, it is possible to sketch out a procedure that will acquire the most important aspects of these rules. Binding relationships must be stated separately for two sorts of paired entities: between empty noun phrases (also known as traces or gaps) and full noun phrases higher up in the tree; and between *wh*-elements (which themselves may be embedded within full noun phrases) and a certain function called Q representing either the "questioned element," or the "focused element" for a relative clause. (The Q function is listed within the modifier f-substructure of a relative clause, where it serves as the anaphoric element associated with the head of the relative clause.) Thus, in *I wonder whose sister Jimmy married e*, the empty noun phrase *e* serving as the object of *marry* must be linked with the full noun phrase *whose sister* (treated here as *who's sister*), and the *wh*-element *who* within *who's sister* must be specified as the unknown element in the complement of *wonder*. Thus, two sets of subjacency metavariables must be acquired: one pair for noun phrases, $\Uparrow_{\mathrm{NP}}$ and $\Downarrow_{\mathrm{NP}}$, and one pair for *wh*-elements, $\Uparrow_{wh}$ and $\Downarrow_{wh}$. The following procedures, executed after P5 and before P6, will acquire the basic annotations needed.

(W1) If a noun phrase in a tree is "missing" (that is, if the phrase structure rules and lexical entry call for a noun phrase in a certain place, but none appears) and if the value of the grammatical function corresponding to the missing element is linked to a Q element in the f-structure, insert a "trace" in that location annotated with $\Uparrow_{\mathrm{NP}}$.

(W2) Add the symbol $\Uparrow_{wh}$ to the lexical entry for any word corresponding to the "questioned variable" (the Q) in an f-structure (this will pick out the *wh*-words).

(W3) Find the category in the tree which is (a) the sister of an S and (b) coindexed with the empty noun phrase, and add the symbol $\Downarrow_{\mathrm{NP}}$ and the equation $Q = \Downarrow_{wh}$ to it. (This is the functional equation that creates the Q-substructure within the f-structure.)

(W4) Add the equation $\Uparrow = \Downarrow$ to any node in the tree between binder and bindee that is a sister to S and dominated by S'.

Examples of the Learning Procedures in Action

This section presents some examples of input pairs consisting of strings and uncommitted f-structures, and shows how they are processed according to the procedures outlined above to yield new grammatical rules. In the examples, the particular procedure used to build a given structure or to coin a given rule will be indicated by its abbreviation (e.g., P3, L2).

The first example shows how phrase structure rules are acquired. It is assumed that no grammatical rules exist yet, except for the various default assignments of grammatical symbols to semantic entities, plus the meanings of individual words.

(29)

a. *F-Structure*

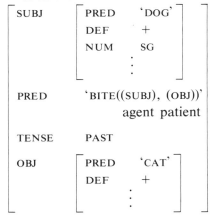

b. *Sentence*

The dog bit the cat.

c.

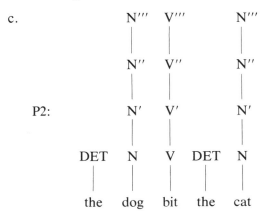

d.

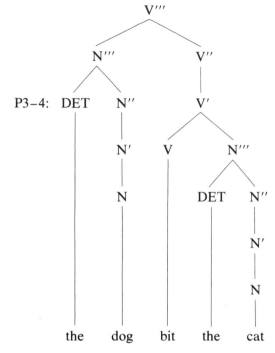

P3–4:

e.

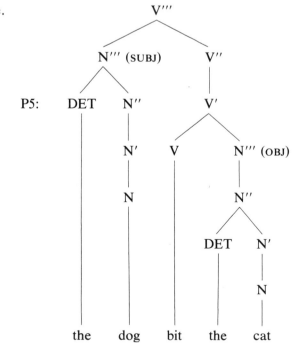

P5:

f.   P6:   V''' → N''' V''   (analogous to the rule: S → NP VP)
                      SUBJ   SUBJ
             N''' → DET N''
             N'' → N'
             N' → N   (analogous to NP → DET N)
             V'' → V'
             V' → V N'''   (analogous to VP → V NP)
                      OBJ   OBJ

g.   L2: bite: V, PRED = 'BITE((SUBJ),(OBJ))'

The second example (30) shows how the procedure would work for a VSO language like Irish. The uncommitted f-structure, of course, is assumed to be the same as for the English example.

(30)
a.

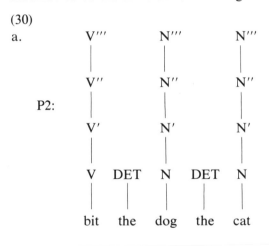

b.

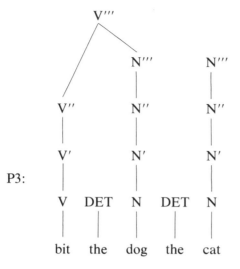

P3:

c.

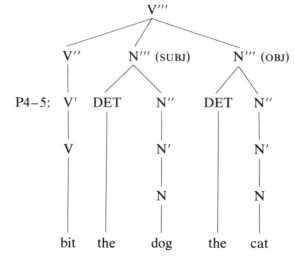

P4–5:

d.   V''' → V'' N''' N'''
                     SUBJ OBJ
        V'' → V' (analogous to S → V NP NP)
                                    SUBJ OBJ
        V' → V

Note that the instruction to attach the "topic" noun phrase to the "S" (V''') ensures that the learner will formulate a branching VP node in SOV and SVO languages, but not in VSO or OSV languages.

A passive sentence like the one in (31) illustrates what happens when the default assignment of grammatical functions to predicate arguments conflicts with the assignment dictated by the phrase structure rules. The functional structure is the same as before, except that the sub-structure corresponding to *the cat* is listed first because it is inferred to be the topic of the sentence.

(31)

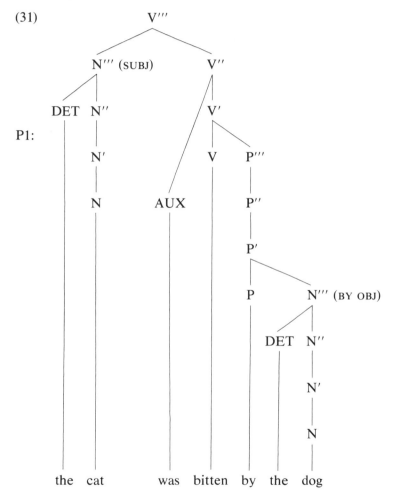

I assume that the child knows that *by* is a preposition and that *was* is an auxiliary. (The details of the latter's attachment to the tree are not important for the present example and would be specified by the relevant aspect of X-bar theory). I also assume that the phrase structure rules label the noun phrase dominated by PP with the default function P OBJ (where P refers to the particular prepositional head and is contributed by the lexical entry for that preposition; see chapter 4 of this volume for details).

In the example, the learner builds up the tree by parsing the sentence with existing phrase structure rules, and hence assigns SUBJ to the *cat* NP and BY OBJ to the *dog* NP. However, the default lexical entry for *bite* assigns the functions OBJ and SUBJ to the arguments corresponding to those noun phrases. The conflict is resolved by rule L1, which creates the new lexical entry 'BITE((BY OBJ),(SUBJ))', which L2 adds to the lexicon. L3 then creates lexical rule (28).

The next example (32) illustrates the annotation of control equations to a lexical form in so-called "raising-to-subject" constructions (many features of the f-structure and lexical forms have been simplified).

(32)

a. *F-Structure*

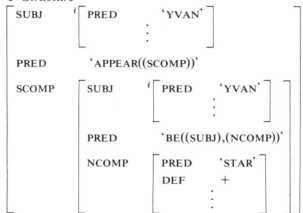

b. *Sentence*
   Yvan appears to be a star.

c.

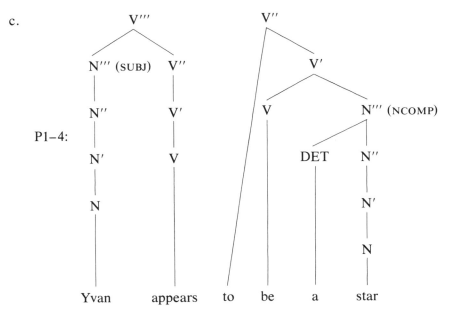

P1-4:

Having analyzed the sentence up to this point, the learner will not know how to complete the tree, because neither *Yvan* nor *to be a star* is an argument or modifier of *appears*. But since *appears* takes a propositional argument in the f-structure that is found without its subject as a constituent in the c-structure, procedures C1–C3 allow the learner to complete the tree and to annotate the entry for *appears,* as is shown in (33).

(33)

a.

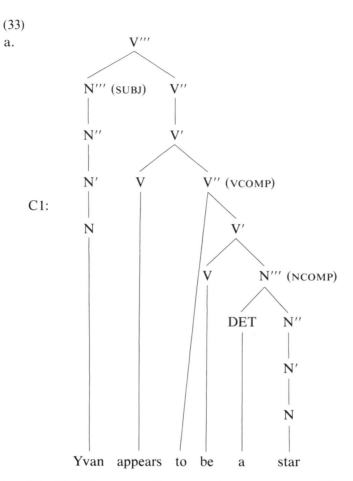

b.   C2, C3, L2: appear: V, PRED = 'APPEAR((VCOMP))'
(SUBJ) = (VCOMP SUBJ)

A second example (34) shows how so-called "object-Equi" constructions are mastered.

(34)

a. *F-Structure*

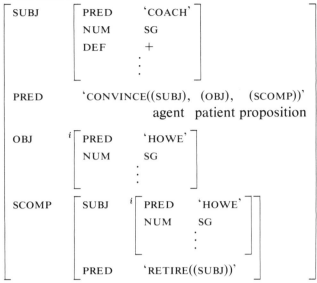

b. *Sentence*

The coach convinced Howe to retire.

c.

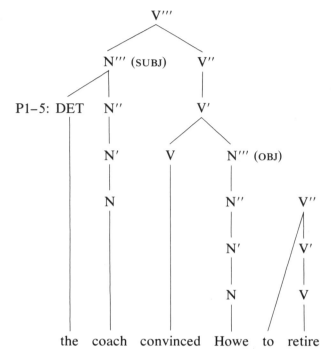

the   coach   convinced   Howe   to   retire

d.

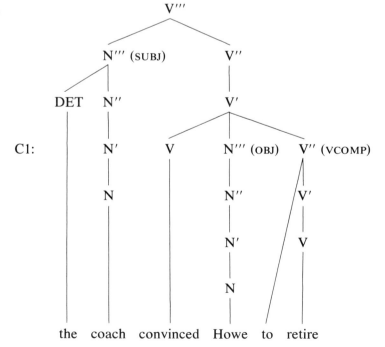

the   coach   convinced   Howe   to   retire

e.   C2, C3, L2: convince: V, PRED = 'CONVINCE((SUBJ),(OBJ),(VCOMP))'
                                           (OBJ) = (VCOMP SUBJ)

The final example (35) shows how the annotations subserving long-distance binding are acquired. (In this example, I assume a version of X-bar theory that would always introduce nonroot Ss with the rule S' → X S, where S = V'''.)

(35)

a.   *F-Structure*

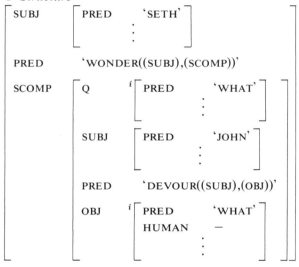

b.   *Sentence*
Seth wondered what John devoured.

c.

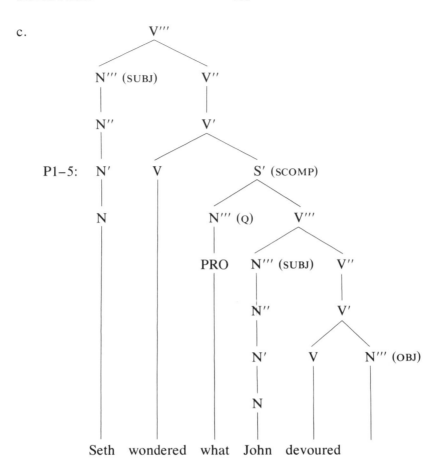

Seth   wondered   what   John   devoured

The fact that *devoured* is a transitive verb forces the learner to expand
the V′ node to include an N‴ OBJ (see the section later in this chapter
on "distributional learning and the parsing process," which sketches
the motivation for this assumption). At this point, W1 forces the learner
to expand that object N‴ as a trace, annotated with ⇑$_{NP}$. W2 is cause
to annotate ⇑$_{wh}$ to the lexical entry for *what*, and W3 and W4 are cause
to annotate the N‴ dominating *what* with ⇓$_{NP}$ and Q = ⇓$_{wh}$. This
yields the rules in (36) and the lexical entry (37).

(36)
a. N →   e
         ⇑$_{NP}$
b. S′ →   N‴   V‴   (recall that V‴ = S)
       Q = ⇓$_{wh}$
       ⇓$_{NP}$

(37)
what: PRO, PRED   = 'WHAT'
        HUMAN = −

     .

     .

     .

$\Uparrow_{wh}$

This account would have to be generalized somewhat to acquire rules generating "*tough* movement" and "pied piping" constructions, but that generalized account would preserve the essentials of the present analysis.

10.6 Some Concluding Comments

In this last section I touch on some of the issues left open in the presentation of the learning procedures.

Miscellaneous Grammatical Rules

Many grammatical phenomena have not been treated in the previous account. Given the richness of language, along with boundedness constraints on book length, this should not be surprising. There is a danger in accounting for the acquisition of selected aspects of grammar, however: the class of mechanisms proposed to account for the subset may be inadequate in some fundamental way to account for the remainder. (See Pinker 1979 for criticisms of several computer models of language acquisition on these grounds.)

It would seem that the present approach can be extended gracefully to account for aspects of grammar that have not been discussed here. Though the study of universal lexical grammar has just begun, it is meeting with success at providing concise statements of the degrees of freedom allowed in various types of rules across the world's languages (see elsewhere in this volume). Furthermore, since lexical explanations of grammatical phenomena tend to invoke mechanisms that are "close to the surface," it has been relatively straightforward to devise plausible data-driven procedures that pin down these degrees of freedom with the help of semantics and of rules already acquired.

Take the example of agreement rules, which have not been discussed so far. In a lexical theory, agreement is accomplished by annotating the lexical entries for affixes or inflections with equations asserting the

gender, number, and so forth, of one of the functional arguments of
the inflected predicate (e.g., its subject, object, etc.). It is already assumed that the learner innately attends to the grammatically relevant
semantic features of an event (the number, gender, tense, animacy,
etc.) and is able to segment words into stems and affixes. A plausible
learning strategy, related to the "abstraction strategy" for word learning mentioned earlier, might be first to annotate a verb affix with every
agreement equation, tense equation, and aspect equation that is logically consistent with the information in its f-structure. Then, if any of
the equations is violated in future sentences, it is discarded from the
entry. Thus, after hearing the sentence *The boy showed flatworms to the
girl,* the child might annotate the affix *-ed* with the equations in (38).

(38)

TENSE	= PAST
ASPECT	= PERF
SUBJ NUM	= SG
SUBJ GEND	= M
SUBJ ANIMACY	= +
SUBJ PERS	= 3
OBJ NUM	= PL
OBJ ANIMACY	= +
OBJ GEND	= ?
OBJ PERS	= 3
TO OBJ NUM	= SG
TO OBJ GEND	= F

.
.
.

Every incorrect equation will eventually be expunged when it is contradicted by information in an f-structure, so in time only the correct
equations will remain.[9] This account is made possible by the lexical
theory's provision that agreement phenomena are stated as annotations
to lexical entries for affixes, by its provision that only a relatively small
set of semantically identifiable features is ever encoded linguistically
(e.g., "gender" and "humanness," but not "color" or "time of day"),
and by its provision that only grammatical functions (e.g., SUBJ and
OBJ, but not arbitrary tree configurations) can enter into the equations.
Provisions of this sort on grammatical rules make the formulation of
acquisition procedures relatively straightforward; thus, the success of

the lexical acquisition theory will depend to a large extent on the success of the theory of universal lexical grammar.

Incidentally, it is noteworthy that the procedure for the acquisition of agreement rules requires the processing of many successive sentences, unlike the acquisition of phrase structure rules and control equations, which in principle can be deduced from single exemplars. It is noteworthy because one of the most striking features about language acquisition is that the learning of agreement and inflections is a drawnout, error-prone process (Brown 1973), whereas, at least in English, the learning of phrase structure rules, complement structures, long-distance linking, and so on, is relatively rapid and accurate once it begins at all (see Maratsos 1978, Maratsos and Chalkley in press).[10] This is consistent with the present account.

The syntactic properties of determiners, auxiliaries, and case markers can be acquired using the same procedure. For example, to acquire case markers, the learner would annotate a noun affix with equations noting all the syntactic features of the noun, plus case equations assigning a default case to the affix according to the noun's thematic relation to the predicate (e.g., "nominative" for agents). For example, a hypothetical affix might tentatively be annotated with the equations in (39):

(39)

CASE   = ACC
NUM   = SG
GEND   = M
DEF   = +
HUMAN   = +

.
.
.

At the same time, the case equation will be annotated to the part of the phrase structure rule that generated the noun phrase (see chapters 2, 6, and 7 of this volume for details). Note that, as before, the acquisition of case markers will require many exemplars relative to the acquisition of phrase structure rules, especially if the sampling-without-replacement variant of the procedure outlined in footnote 9 is used. This correctly predicts that for case-inflected languages, children will utter sentences in the dominant word order (if there is one) and will use the dominant word order as a cue in comprehending sentences, before they have mastered their language's case system (Slobin in press, Hakuta 1979).

Productivity Revisited

Perhaps the chief original motivation for bringing lexical theories to bear on language acquisition was the fact that children generalize syntactic rules to new predicates to a lesser degree than a transformational theory would lead one to expect (Baker 1979, de Villiers in press, Maratsos 1978, Roeper et al. 1979). If transformations are triggered by structural configurations, the argument runs, they should apply freely to all predicates. But children's (and, for that matter, adults') grammars allow only certain predicates to witness transformations (see section 10.2), so some information about a predicate's ability to appear in a transformed construction must be stored with the particular predicate. This information cannot consist of a negative rule feature (e.g., [−Passive]) barring a transformation from applying, since children are not corrected for speaking ungrammatically and so would have no basis for adding the feature to some predicates but not others (Baker 1979). Thus, it is held that children learn conservatively, entering predicate–construction pairs into their lexicon only upon hearing a particular predicate used in a particular construction.[11]

Unfortunately, this solution will not work. It predicts that children will never generalize a known predicate to a new construction; and this prediction is false. Bowerman 1974 documents her young daughter's productive misuse of verbs in causative constructions, along the lines of *I jumped the doll,* meaning 'I caused the doll to jump'. Similarly, Wasow in press observes that his four-year-old daughter once protested *I don't like being falled down on,* overgeneralizing the passive. Nor are children the only ones who generalize beyond what they hear. Wasow points out that possible neologisms such as *I will satellite a letter to you* (meaning that I will transmit a letter to you via satellite) are patently passivizable, as shown by the naturalness of *That letter was satellited to me last week.* And I have caught myself saying *I will xerox you a copy of the paper* and *These circuit boards are daisychained together.* Of course, the use of lexical redundancy rules will create the necessary productivity (and in fact learning procedure L3 creates lexical rules whenever possible), but this simply leads us back to the original question, Why do children undergeneralize the use of certain constructions, and how do they learn which predicates are exceptional in the adult grammar?

It seems then that children are neither purely conservative (item-by-item) nor purely liberal (lexical redundancy rule) learners. The particular undergeneralizations cited in the literature suggest that children generalize along semantic/thematic lines, using a predicate in a new construction only if it is an action predicate. Recall as well that Maratsos 1978 found that children will understand only the active version of nonaction predicates (e.g., *like*) at the same stage at which they understand both the active and the passive versions of action predicates (e.g., *hit*). In addition, de Villiers in press, in an experiment with children who did not yet understand passive sentences, described pictures for the children using passive sentences and either action or nonaction predicates (depending on the picture). Regardless of which sort of passive sentence the children witnessed, when they were induced to describe pictures on their own, they used passive sentences fairly frequently when the picture called for an action verb, but rarely when the picture called for a nonaction verb.

One possible explanation for these data is that children's lexical rules first apply only to narrowly defined semantic or thematic categories such as agent-of-action and patient-of-action. The difficulty with this account is in developing a plausible learning mechanism that will take the child from rules that operate on semantic or thematic symbols to the correct adult rules, which operate on grammatical functions. It could be that this change simply results from maturation, but I think one would want to implicate nonstationary mechanisms only as a last resort.

There is a better solution. One can invoke a certain property of lexical rules that is independently motivated by studies of adult grammar. In some languages, lexical rules may apply only if certain thematic conditions are first met. For example, a Passive lexical rule changing an object to a subject might apply only if the original subject and object were the agent and patient arguments of the predicate (Bresnan personal communication). It could be that when children coin a lexical rule, it operates on grammatical functions, as it does in the adult grammar, but a set of "only if" provisos referring to the thematic relations of the arguments to the predicate is included with the rule, as in (40).

(40)
(OBJ) $\mapsto$ (SUBJ)
(SUBJ) $\mapsto$ (BY OBJ)
$\mapsto$ (PART) = (PAST)
only if:
   (SUBJ) is an agent
   (OBJ) is a patient

If subsequently a sentence is encountered which inspires the learner to form a rule with the same function replacements, but which simultaneously violates one of the "only if" conditions (e.g., *Leon was considered by Cindy to be a fine yodeler*), that "only if" condition is deleted. Thus, the form of the rule remains constant, though its conditions for application might change depending on the particular target language.

Still, one problem remains. There seem to be pairs of semantically similar predicates in English such that only one member of the pair can be operated upon by a lexical rule; for example, Dativization applied to *give* versus *donate, tell* versus *say, show* versus *demonstrate,* and so on. Assuming that there is no subtle semantic/thematic difference between all predicates that can undergo Dativization, for instance, and all those that cannot, one solution to this acquisition problem is to hypothesize some kind of information indirectly available to the learner indicating that a predicate cannot appear as a given lexical form. Elsewhere (Pinker in press), I suggest that in a given context of discourse, the child might have reason to expect the words of a sentence to be spoken in a certain gross order, owing to various pragmatic, semantic, and processing determinants of word order choice. A sentence that violated the expected order in a given situation might be evidence that the sentence's predicate cannot appear in the construction that would have displayed the expected word order. This would allow the learner to append to the predicate, correctly, a feature that blocks the application of the relevant lexical rule.[12] The inelegance of this procedure might simply be one of the concessions we have to make to the recalcitrance of natural language to submit to our acquisition theories.

Distributional Learning and the Parsing Process
Earlier in the chapter it was proposed that language acquisition depends at first on correlations between syntax and semantics, but that later the learner can identify the syntactic properties of more inscrutable elements by observing their distribution within known structures.

However, it is far from a trivial matter to design a procedure that will accomplish this reliably. The problem is that occurrences of an unknown element in a familiar context usually support several analyses and thus allow the grammar to be modified in several ways, only one of them correct. (Recall that children have no access to information telling them that they have made an error, so an acquisition theory must minimize incorrect inductions.) For example, the unknown word in the sentence *She called me blunks* could be a proper singular noun (cf. *Toots*), a common plural noun (cf. *names*), an adverb (cf. *quickly*), or an adjective (cf. *foolish*). In *I glomped the cat on the mat, glomp* could take three arguments like *put* or two like *groomed.* In *I consider Sam to be a fruitcake,* the learner could analyze *Sam* as a direct object and *to be a fruitcake* as a verb phrase complement; alternatively, the learner could analyze *Sam to be a fruitcake* as a sentential complement (an incorrect analysis, according to the lexical theory, but the one the learner would probably choose, given that the phrase corresponds to a propositional argument of *consider* in the f-structure). Even for seemingly nonambiguous phrases like *the ort,* the learner could correctly posit that *ort* is a noun or (just as easily) that *ort* is a verb and that DET V is a possible phrase. (See Pinker 1979 for a general discussion of the problems of distributional learning.)

One solution would be to restrict the learner to making one change to the acquired grammar at a time. Thus, only if the learner knew the categorization of a word could he or she modify a phrase structure rule, and vice versa. For instance, the word *ort* in *the ort* would have to be categorized as a noun, because any other categorization would necessitate coining a new phrase structure rule at the same time. Similarly, because there presumably would already exist a rule expanding the verb phrase as an object plus a VP-complement (to handle sentences like *I convinced Manny to be an accountant*), the child would have to analyze *consider* as taking a VP-complement (the subject being specified by a control equation). That is because the alternative, S-complement analysis would necessitate coining a new rule expanding an S-complement as NP-*to*-VP in addition.

However, this begs the question of how to design a procedure that will discriminate between those contexts that uniquely determine the analysis of an unknown element and those contexts that allow multiple analyses and hence error-prone inferences. Happily, this problem is nicely solved by certain properties of the parsing component of the lexical interpretive theory (the "General Syntactic Processor"; see

Kaplan 1973a, and chapter 11 of this volume). As the parser reaches a given point in a sentence, it "proposes" possible analyses for the rest of the sentence by entering "tasks" onto its "agenda." For example, after it has analyzed a verb, it creates tasks directing it to look for a noun phrase, a VP-complement, an S-complement, and so on; each of these possibilities inspires further predictions down to the level of lexical categories (for example, in the case of the noun phrase, a determiner).

How does this help distributional language acquisition? It seems plausible that for many sentences the parser would make unique predictions about the possible analyses of the unparsed portion of a sentence or phrase. The learner would be safe in positing new grammatical rules, such as the categorization of an unknown word, whenever the parser made a *single* prediction about what that analysis must be. This would allow the child to be fairly sure that the new word in a sentence like *This is an aardvark* was a noun, whereas in *Watch me flambé these raspberries* it is a verb.

Unfortunately, as the child develops, the richness of the grammar acquired will make a great many analyses possible at most points in many sentences. But even this is not an insurmountable problem. At least two sorts of "scheduling principles" will sharply restrict the tasks that the parser will consider. First, the alternative "arcs" of the grammar (that is, alternative symbols in the expansion of a phrase structure rule) may be assigned different "strengths" (Kaplan 1972, Wanner in press), so that certain predictions would be made more salient than others.[13] For example, the noun phrase expansions might include DET N and DET ADJ (as in *the good, the bad, and the ugly*), but the latter would be assigned an extremely low value and would be ignored on most occasions (contributing to the garden path in sentences like *The prime number few*). The second set of scheduling principles might reside in the lexicon. The multiple lexical entries corresponding to a given predicate might be assigned different strengths, and the strongest one might determine which predictions are made at a given point in the parsing of a sentence (see chapter 11 of this volume, for a detailed discussion of this principle). Thus, the intransitive entry for the verb *float* might have a higher value than the transitive entry, biasing the parser against predicting an object noun phrase in sentences containing the verb (and contributing to the garden path in sentences like *The boat floated down the river sank*). With a rich enough set of scheduling principles, the parser might posit only a single analysis of a sentence whose cumulative strength is above a certain minimum, even if it allowed a larger set of possible analyses in principle. The learner could then add a rule to the developing grammar *only* if positing that rule completed a single sufficiently strong prediction of the parser.

A final note: Since the parser is also capable of operating in "bottom-up" fashion (that is, grouping substrings of words into a constituent in advance of knowing how that constituent will fit into the remainder of the sentence), it will be possible to posit phrase structure rules based on the known categorizations of words in a sentence, in addition to positing the categorization of unfamiliar words based on known phrase structure rules. The reader might note that this is exactly what was happening in section 10.5, where it was shown how phrase structure rules were inferred from words whose categorizations were given by their semantic properties. As a result, it would be fairly straightforward to design a parsing algorithm that would perform the inductions licensed by the learning procedures during the left-to-right parsing of a sentence (J. R. Anderson 1977 and Berwick 1980 have implemented learners with this feature). Though this will have to remain a task for the future, the fact that it is feasible at all vindicates the optimistic conjectures reviewed in the first section of this chapter. It seems that a restrictive theory of lexical interpretive grammar, together with an explicit theory of the parsing mechanisms that interact with the grammar, brings within reach the goal of language acquisition research: a theory of how children process the sentences they hear to infer the grammatical structure of the rest of the language.

Appendix

This section contains the proof that the class of lexical interpretive grammars is finite in cardinality and hence learnable (technically, it is the class of languages generated by the grammars that is learnable, though I will refer interchangeably to learning classes of grammars and to learning classes of languages). For clarity's sake, the proof primarily consists of a set of observations, though it will be apparent that each observation states a very elementary point. Note that the notation used here is the full notation of Kaplan and Bresnan (chapter 4 of this volume) and not the simplified version used in the body of this chapter.

Definition 1. A *lexical interpretive grammar* is a 7-tuple consisting of a finite *terminal vocabulary,* a finite *nonterminal vocabulary,* a *start symbol* chosen from the nonterminal vocabulary, a finite *functional vocabu-*

lary, a finite set of *functional equation relations,* a finite set of *annotated phrase structure rules,* and a finite set of *lexical redundancy rules.*

Comment: I have followed the standard convention in formal definitions of grammars of abstracting away from the grammar the computational machinery that actually expands the rewrite rules, solves the functional equations, and so on. See chapter 4 of this volume for a formal presentation of these computations and for a demonstration that, for every lexical grammar, there is an effective procedure that computes the functional structure corresponding to each string generated by the grammar, and vice versa. Thus, the definition of a grammar presented above is all that is needed to identify uniquely any given lexical grammar.

Definition 2. The *terminal vocabulary* for a given grammar is a set of symbols for lexical items and is drawn from a finite universal set.

Comment: Note that this definition treats lexical items as atomic symbols. The representation of the detailed information accompanying each lexical entry will be discussed later. Note also that the definition incorporates the standard assumption of learnability proofs that the number of root lexical items in the class of possible languages is finite. The assumption is probably false in the case of human languages, since there is no grammatically motivated limitation on the number of possible roots in a language. But the violation is innocuous. Because the model of grammar presented here abstracts away from the terminal vocabulary all the grammatical properties of words, the class of grammars defined will include every grammatically distinguishable type of lexical item, even if it (perhaps falsely) restricts the number of possible tokens of each such type that can appear in a grammar. If humans can learn an arbitrary number of words sharing a given set of syntactic properties, that ability will remain outside the scope of the language acquisition device to be described here. But then the device would still seem to be a legitimate idealization of most people's intuitions of what syntactic acquisition is.

Observation 1. There are a finite number of possible terminal vocabularies.

Proof: By definition 2, a terminal vocabulary is a subset of the universal finite set of lexical roots. If the universal set has n members, finitely many (specifically, $2^n - 1$) nonempty subsets can be drawn from it.

Definition 3. The *nonterminal vocabulary* for a given grammar is a set of symbols for lexical and phrasal categories, drawn from a finite universal set.

Comment: The claim embodied in this definition is supported by recent treatments of phrase structure such as X′ (X-bar) theory (Chomsky 1970, Jackendoff 1977), which propose that there are a finite number of possible lexical categories and a small number of phrasal categories (usually set at 3 or 4) corresponding to each lexical category. (Equivalently, we could say that there are a finite number of syntactic features and that each lexical category corresponds to a subset of these features; see Chomsky 1970, Jackendoff 1977).

Observation 2. There are a finite number of possible nonterminal vocabularies.

Proof: Same as for observation 1.

Definition 4. The *start symbol* is the symbol S for all lexical interpretive grammars.

Definition 5. The *functional vocabulary* is a finite set of symbols which can serve either as *function names* (e.g., SUBJECT, OBJECT, TO OBJECT, NUMBER, TENSE, PARTICIPLE, etc.), *function values* (e.g., SINGULAR, MASCULINE, +, PAST, etc.), or as *metavariables* ($\uparrow$, $\downarrow$, $\Uparrow$, $\Downarrow$, $\Uparrow_{NP}$, $\Downarrow_{wh}$, etc.), and *predicates* symbolizing the meanings of lexical items. All are drawn from finite universal sets.

Comment: Each of these restrictions seems justified by descriptive evidence (see Bresnan 1978 and the other chapters in this volume), with the exception of the number of possible predicates or meanings. As in the case of the terminal vocabulary, I adopt this restriction without attempting to justify it. Note also that predicates are being treated as atomic symbols, and the specification of the number of arguments linked to a complex predicate will be accomplished by other means, to be described below. This ensures that every possible type of grammatically distinguishable predicate will be available to the learner, though again the acquisition of arbitrary numbers of tokens of each type will be outside the learner's abilities.

Observation 3. There are a finite number of possible functional vocabularies.

Proof: Same as for observation 1.

Definition 6. The *functional equation relations* are drawn from the universal set $(=, =_c, \neq_c, \epsilon)$, corresponding to declarative equations, constraining equations, negative constraining equations, and set membership equations, respectively.

Comment: In chapter 4 of this volume, Kaplan and Bresnan argue that these four equation relations are adequate to handle all syntactic dependencies.

Observation 4. There are a finite number of possible sets of functional equation relations.

Proof: Same as for observation 1.

Definition 7. An *annotated phrase structure rule* is of the form $A \rightarrow B_1 \ldots B_n$, where A is a single nonterminal vocabulary symbol and B_i is an ordered pair consisting of a single terminal or nonterminal vocabulary symbol plus a *functional equation set,* with the constraint that for all B_i, B_j, $B_i \neq B_j$.[14]

Definition 8. A *functional equation set* is a set of statements of the form $M_1 F_1 F_2$ *eq* $M_2 F_3 F_4$, where $M_{1,2}$ are metavariables, *eq* is a functional equation relation, and $F_{1,2,3,4}$ are function names or function values. Any symbol except the functional equation relation may be null, but there must be at least one symbol on each side of the equation.

Comment: The ordered pairs B_i correspond to symbols such as

$$\begin{array}{c} \text{NP} \\ (\uparrow\text{SUBJ})=\downarrow \end{array}$$

which occur in annotated phrase structure rules such as

$$\text{S} \rightarrow \begin{array}{cc} \text{NP} & \text{VP} \\ (\uparrow\text{SUBJ})=\downarrow & \uparrow=\downarrow \end{array} .$$

That is, the first member of the pair is the category symbol, and the second member is the functional equation set written beneath it.

These definitions embody two substantive claims. Assuming some additional constraints on the distribution of metavariables (for example, as in chapter 2 of this volume), the no-repetition constraint in definition 7 is motivated by Bresnan and Kaplan's Uniqueness Condition, whereby no functional structure may contain a function name that has more than one function value corresponding to it. Thus, rules like (41), which assigns two subjects to a sentence, are prohibited.

(41)

$$\text{S} \rightarrow \begin{array}{ccc} \text{NP} & \text{V} & \text{NP} \\ (\uparrow\text{SUBJ})=\downarrow & & (\uparrow\text{SUBJ})=\downarrow \end{array}$$

Similarly, iterated categories such as locative PPs must be allowed either once or an infinite number of times, the latter by means of the "asterisk" notational convention.[15]

The second constraint is that no more than two function names may appear on either side of a functional equation. This is identical to Kaplan and Bresnan's "functional locality" constraint, which states that no rule in the grammar may refer to symbols separated by more than a single level of embedding in an f-structure.[16]

Note that in this formal definition there is no separate lexicon. Each lexical entry corresponds here to a "lexical insertion" annotated phrase structure rule whose lefthand side is a lexical category symbol and whose righthand side is a terminal vocabulary symbol plus the set of syntactic feature equations and control equations that would be associated with it in the lexicon. Entries for predicates taking a number of arguments can be broken down into a set of equations, each one specifying the grammatical function assigned to one argument of the predicate. Thus, one of the lexical entries for the word *give*, which Bresnan and Kaplan would specify as in (42), would be translated into the annotated phrase structure rule (43):

(42)

give: V, ($\uparrow$PRED) = 'GIVE((SUBJ),(OBJ),(TO OBJ))'

   ($\uparrow$INF)   = +

(43)

V $\rightarrow$ give

   ($\uparrow$PRED) = 'GIVE'

   ($\uparrow$ARG1) = (SUBJ)

   ($\uparrow$ARG2) = (OBJ)

   ($\uparrow$ARG3) = (TO OBJ)

   ($\uparrow$INF)   = +

Multiple lexical entries for a given predicate would be represented as distinct phrase structure rules with identical terminal symbols on the righthand side, but with different equation sets. The lexical theory's restriction of lexical forms to functions of four or fewer places corresponds here to the inclusion of only four primitive symbols for arguments (ARG1, ARG2, ARG3, ARG4) in the universal set of functional vocabulary terms.

Finally, it should be noted that the constraints on annotated phrase structure rules specified here are far weaker than those that *could* be specified in a theory of universal lexical interpretive grammar. For example, X-bar theory would constrain the type and order of categories in the righthand side of a rule, and many conditions on the well-formedness of functional equations could be imposed. Each such constraint reduces the cardinality of the class. Here I state only the constraints necessary to prove the finiteness of the set of possible lexical grammars.

Observation 5. There are a finite number of possible functional equations.

Proof: By definition 7, a functional equation is of the form $M_1F_1F_2$ *eq* $M_2F_3F_4$. By definition 5, $M_{1,2}$ and $F_{1,2,3,4}$ are drawn from finite sets whose cardinalities I will refer to as m and f, respectively. By definition 6, *eq* is drawn from a finite set of cardinality, say, e. Therefore, the number of possible functional equations is no larger than m^2f^4e.

Observation 6. There are a finite number of possible functional equation sets.

Proof: Same as for observation 1.

Observation 7. There are a finite number of possible B_i ordered pairs.

Proof: By definition 7, a B_i consists of a nonterminal or terminal vocabulary symbol plus an equation set. By definition 2, the number of possible terminal symbols is finite; by definition 3, the number of possible nonterminal symbols is finite; by observation 6, the number of possible functional equation sets is finite. The number of possible B_i ordered pairs is no larger than the product of these three finite numbers.

Observation 8. The number of possible annotated phrase structure rules is finite.

Proof: By definition 7, each rewrite rule consists of a lefthand nonterminal symbol and a righthand n-tuple $(B_1...B_n)$. By definition 3, the number of possible nonterminal symbols is finite. I will use B to refer to the set of possible ordered pairs B_i and b to refer to the cardinality of that set. Since by definition 7, no B_i may appear more than once in the ordered n-tuple $(B_1...B_n)$ constituting the righthand side of a rule, the number of n-tuples will be no larger than the number of possible subsets of B times the number of possible orders of the members of each subset. This number is (44),

(44)

$$\sum_{i=1}^{b} \frac{b!}{(b - i)!}$$

which is finite. The number of possible annotated phrase structure rules is no larger than the number of possible lefthand sides times the number of possible righthand sides, a product of finite numbers.

Observation 9. The number of possible sets of annotated phrase structure rules is finite.

Proof: Same as for observation 1.

Definition 9. A *lexical redundancy rule* is a finite set of *function replacement rules* of the form $F_1 \mapsto F_2$, where F_1 and F_2 are function names, plus a finite set of functional equations.

Comment: Lexical redundancy rules operate on lexical insertion rules to produce new lexical insertion rules. The function replacement rules replace each occurrence of a function name in the old insertion rule with a new function. Then the equations listed in the redundancy rule are added to the set.

Observation 10. There are a finite number of sets of function replacement rules.

Proof: By definition 5, there are a finite number f of functions. The number of function replacement rules is thus f^2. The number of nonempty sets of function replacement rules is no larger than $2^{(f^2)} - 1$.

Observation 11. There are a finite number of sets of lexical redundancy rules.

Proof: By definition 9, a lexical redundancy rule is a set of function replacement rules plus a set of functional equations. By observation 10, there are a finite number of the former; by observation 6, there are a finite number of the latter. Therefore, the number of members of the set of possible lexical redundancy rules is the product of these two numbers, and finitely many nonempty subsets can be drawn from that set.

Theorem 1. There are a finite number of lexical interpretive grammars.

Proof: By definition 1, a lexical interpretive grammar is a 7-tuple consisting of a terminal vocabulary, a nonterminal vocabulary, a start symbol, a functional vocabulary, a set of functional equation relations, a set of annotated phrase structure rules, and a set of lexical redundancy rules. By observations 1 and 2, definition 4, and observations 3, 4, 9, and 11, respectively, the number of possible instances of each component is finite. The number of possible lexical interpretive grammars is the product of these 7 finite numbers and hence is itself a finite number.[17]

Comment: The number of possible lexical interpretive grammars according to this definition is very large.

Corollary: The class of languages generated by lexical interpretive grammars is not weakly identical to any class of languages in the Chomsky hierarchy, all of which are infinite in cardinality.

Comment: A common criticism of Augmented Transition Networks, precursors of the current formal system of representation, is that their generative capacity is equivalent to that of Turing machines (e.g., Anderson 1976). In chapter 4 it is shown that the system has sub-Turing power.

Theorem 2. The class of lexical interpretive grammars is identifiable in the limit from a semantic text.

Proof: In chapter 4 of this volume, Kaplan and Bresnan have shown that a lexical interpretive grammar is a semantic-mapping grammar, since there is an effective procedure for each grammar that maps the sentences in the language onto functional structures, which contain the information necessary for semantic interpretation. By theorem 1, the number of lexical interpretive grammars is finite; therefore, the members of the class are recursively enumerable. Anderson 1976 has shown that any recursively enumerable set of semantic-mapping grammars is identifiable in the limit from a semantic text. Therefore, the class of lexical interpretive grammars is identifiable in the limit from a semantic text.

Comment: The learner is assumed to be able to enumerate the class of lexical grammars, say, by consulting a list of them in order of increasing complexity. On each trial, the learner takes an f-structure–string pair (the former deduced from the perceptible nonlinguistic context of the utterance) and uses the highest grammar on the list to generate a string from the f-structure. If the generated string is identical to the string in the input, the learner offers that grammar as the current guess. If the strings differ, or if no string can be generated, the grammar is "crossed off the list" and the next one is tried. Any incorrect grammar will be rejected when it generates the wrong string for an f-structure. Upon reaching a correct grammar on the list, the learner will stick with it forever.[18]

Notes

I am deeply indebted to Joan Bresnan and to Jane Grimshaw for their extensive comments on an earlier draft, for invaluable discussions of the issues raised herein, and for generously sharing their time and knowledge. They deserve credit for whatever is of value in this chapter, but none of the blame for what is not. I am also grateful to Ron Kaplan, Alan Prince, and Joan Ryder for their insightful comments on an earlier draft and to Bob Berwick, Jill de Villiers, Roger Wales, Kenji Hakuta, and Phillip Dale for helpful discussions.

1. Incidentally, the observation that comprehension abilities are usually superior to production abilities is not inconsistent with the claim that a single knowledge representation underlies both. The difference may reflect the relative resource demands of comprehension and production processes, whether or not the two processes access a common pool of syntactic knowledge. To take an analogy from verbal learning, it has long been known that it is harder to recall a word from a memorized list than to recognize it. This does not mean that there are separate word traces underlying recognition and recall performance, only that the processes that search the traces run into different "bottlenecks" in each case (see Anderson and Bower 1973:442).

2. Note that another accurate predictor of acquisition order is length: constructions involving fewer words are learned earlier. This is consistent with an acquisition model in which the processing capacity available to the producing mechanisms increases with development. This also illustrates the bewildering degree of overdetermination of acquisition order in child speech.

3. It seems that more recent formulations of transformational grammar (e.g., Chomsky 1980) would not make the same derivational complexity predictions in sentences 19, 20, 22, and 23 as did the standard theory.

4. The terminology is my own. Grimshaw speaks of various syntactic structures as being the "canonical structural realizations" of certain semantic structures. That is simply the inverse of certain semantic structures serving as the "semantic flag" or, in Macnamara's terms, the "inductive basis," of the elements of various syntactic schemata.

5. Bob Berwick has developed a computer-based acquisition model sharing many assumptions with the theory proposed here. The reader is referred to Berwick 1980 for a detailed presentation.

6. Feldman, Goldin-Meadow, and Gleitman 1977 argue that one can empirically distinguish 1-place, 2-place, and 3-place predicates in the gestural signs invented by the deaf children they studied. Though this conclusion is controversial (see Brown 1978), if supported it would bolster the claim that the predicate argument structures underlying early words are innate.

7. It is likely that there are also structural constraints on grammatical functions that will determine whether the function annotated to a node by the default lexical form will "take." For example, in configurational languages, the subject should be higher in the tree and farther to the left than the other arguments; in case-marked languages, the subject will be the argument lacking a case marker if any arguments are. Functional annotations that violate these constraints will require many exemplars to make them permanent. This prevents possible misanalyses, such as annotating the S-dominated NP as an OBJ and the PP-dominated NP as a SUBJ after processing a passive sentence. It will also give the learner of a "true" ergative language (one in which the function assignments, and not just the morphological case markers, distinguish transitive from intransitive subjects) some of the evidence needed to reassign the agent of a transitive predicate as the OBJ and the patient as the SUBJ.

8. Note that there is a conservative variant of L3: Check the lexicon for predicates with parallel pairs of lexical entries, such that the first member of each pair contains one assignment of grammatical functions to arguments and the second member of each pair contains a second assignment. If the number of such pairs exceeds a critical value, create a lexical redundancy rule generalizing the parallelism. This strategy will lead to a sudden blossoming of the productive use of rules, which is sometimes attributed to a "radical reorganization" of the child's grammar from a semantics-based phrase structure grammar to a formal transformational grammar. The present proposal accounts for the qualitative change by a simple addition to the grammar, not an ad hoc reformulation of it, and hence is more parsimonious.

9. Since the number of possible equations that could be added to an affix at one time may exceed the child's processing capacity, it may be more plausible to posit a sampling-without-replacement version of this procedure. The child could add a random subset of these equations to an affix (perhaps sampling according to some weighting function) every time he or she processed a sentence. When an equation was falsified by a sentence, it would be rejected permanently. Eventually the child would converge on the correct equations for the affix. Indeed, given Slobin's 1979 data that morphemes with one-to-one mappings onto features are acquired earlier than morphemes with one-to-many mappings, it seems that a single equation may be all that a young child can entertain at one time. (See also Brown 1973 for evidence that acquisition order is predictable from the relative syntactic and semantic complexity of the various grammatical morphemes.)

10. Of course, children make many errors in *comprehending* constructions like relative clauses (de Villiers et al. 1979) and Equi and *tough* movement constructions (C. Chomsky 1969). But it seems likely that many of these errors are parsing phenomena, and not grammatical phenomena. For example, in a set of detailed experiments on the comprehension of relative clauses by Japanese children, Hakuta 1979 found no interaction between age and any syntactic variable, only general improvements in comprehension. This suggests that computations that are relatively hard for young children are also relatively hard

for older children, and that the age-related changes may reflect increases in memory and processing capacity rather than changes in grammatical rules.

11. It is possible to make a transformational learner conservative in a similar way. Instead of adding negative features to an exceptional predicate, forbidding the application of a certain transformation to it, a learner could add *positive* features to *non*exceptional predicates, *allowing* the transformation to apply to it (e.g., [+Passive]). Here again, a conservative child could add a positive rule feature to a predicate only upon hearing the predicate used in the appropriate construction. However, Bresnan 1977 has argued that this move would have undesirable consequences for the theory of transformational grammar in general, since it undermines the key assumption of the structure dependence of transformations.

12. This procedure is more consistent with lexical theories than with transformational theories to the extent that negative transformation features on lexical entries are an undesirable addition to transformational theories, as argued by Bresnan 1977 (see also footnote 11).

13. In fact, the scheduling is usually stated in terms of ordering the arcs rather than assigning an interval value to them, but the present description subsumes the usual one and is more adaptable to our purposes here.

14. In some annotated phrase structure rules, a category symbol is accompanied not by one but by a group of functional equation sets, any one of which can be applied in generating a sentence (see chapter 8 of this volume). This does not alter any of the results to follow, since if there are a finite number of possible functional equation sets (which I will show), there can only be a finite number of groups of functional equation sets, namely, the subsets of the set of all functional equation sets.

15. The present definition would have to be modified somewhat to allow asterisks to accompany category symbols in phrase structure rules. One way would be to define each B_i as a triple consisting of a category symbol, an equation set, and an asterisk/no asterisk feature. Since I will show that there are a finite number of possible B_i's, it follows that there are a finite number of B_i*'s as well.

16. The schema outlined here excludes equations in which the expression on the left- or righthand side contains an embedded expression, such as $(\uparrow(\downarrow\text{PCASE})) = \downarrow$, used in chapter 4 and in other chapters in this volume. However, any equation of this sort can be replaced by a finite group of equation sets whose member equations do fit the schema, without altering the strong generative capacity of the grammar. For example, $(\uparrow(\downarrow\text{PCASE})) = \downarrow$ is replaced by $\begin{Bmatrix} (\uparrow\text{TO})=\downarrow \\ (\downarrow\text{PCASE})=\text{TO} \end{Bmatrix}, \begin{Bmatrix} (\uparrow\text{AT})=\downarrow \\ (\downarrow\text{PCASE})=\text{AT} \end{Bmatrix}, \begin{Bmatrix} (\uparrow\text{FOR})=\downarrow \\ (\downarrow\text{PCASE})=\text{FOR} \end{Bmatrix}$, and so on, one equation set for each possible value of the embedded expression. This will yield a finite number of equation sets because (a) cross-linguistic evidence suggests the constraint that only a single level of embedding be permitted within an expression, (b) embedded expressions, like expressions themselves, are of bounded length, and (c) every function can have only finitely many values, each drawn from the universal functional vocabulary.

17. One class of rules has been omitted in this discussion: the structure-changing, function-preserving rules that derive new annotated phrase structure rules from old ones by rearranging the order of their constituents (e.g., scrambling rules, Heavy NP Shift; see chapter 8 of this volume). Note that each such rule can create a finite number of new annotated phrase structure rules (at most, the number of permutations of the constituents of each existing annotated phrase structure rule) and that each of these new annotated phrase structure rules is permitted by the current definition of annotated phrase structure rules, in any event. Thus, for every grammar containing structure-changing rules, there is a strongly equivalent grammar without them satisfying the current definition of lexical interpretive grammars. Therefore, allowing structure-changing rules in lexical grammars does not change the finiteness result.

18. It is assumed here that every f-structure can be used to generate at most one sentence. An alternative (and more plausible) assumption is that several sentences may be generated from an f-structure but that pragmatic, semantic, and processing factors pick out one sentence from the set as the most appropriate, and this one is matched against the input string. See Pinker in press for details.

Chapter 11

A Competence-Based	Marilyn Ford,
Theory of	Joan Bresnan, and
Syntactic Closure	Ronald M. Kaplan

Although a sentence may be structurally ambiguous, it is often the case that perceivers prefer one possible structural analysis over another (see Kimball 1973, Wanner, Kaplan, and Shiner 1975, Frazier and Fodor 1978, Kirby 1979, Wanner 1980, Fodor and Frazier 1980, Holmes 1981). A particularly interesting and important research problem in the development of a theory of sentence perception is to explain the structural biases shown in these ambiguous sentences, since the effects observed reflect the operating principles of the human parsing mechanism very directly. In this study, we examine syntactic bias effects and show that they are a joint function of (i) the linguistic rules which define the structures of sentences, (ii) the predicate argument structures and grammatical functions of lexical items, and (iii) a well-defined interaction between rule-driven and data-driven analysis procedures. The theory that is developed in this study directly incorporates the linguistically motivated rules of the lexical-functional grammar presented in this volume and so supports the competence hypothesis (see the introduction to this volume) in the domain of sentence comprehension.

11.1 Some Phenomena

In this section we will present a few examples of structurally ambiguous sentences and show which of the possible structures for each is preferred. For each of the fully ambiguous sentences discussed in this study, evidence of the preferred reading was obtained from 20 subjects. The data are presented in appendix A, together with a description of how they were gathered. For each of the partially ambiguous sentences, our own intuitions, together with those of colleagues and those presented in the literature, were used. The examples in the present section will give an idea of the kinds of phenomena we are dealing with and will demonstrate just how complicated syntactic bias effects appear to be. While the phenomena seem to be very complicated, this very complexity provides a richness of data for developing a theory of sentence perception.

Sentence (1) is structurally ambiguous, as shown in (2a) and (2b) (the preferred (P) and nonpreferred (N) structures, respectively).

(1)
Joe bought the book for Susan.

(2)
a.   Joe [$_{VP}$ bought [$_{NP}$ *the book*] [$_{PP}$ for Susan]]   (P)
b.   Joe [$_{VP}$ bought [$_{NP}$[$_{NP}$ *the book*] [$_{PP}$ *for Susan*]]]   (N)

In (2a) the Object NP of the verb *bought* closes immediately after *the book,* yielding the interpretation *Joe bought it (the book) for Susan,* whereas in (2b) it closes after *for Susan,* yielding the reading *Joe bought it (the book for Susan).* Although the competence grammar must represent both possible structures of sentence (1), it is usually first perceived as meaning (2a) (see Kimball 1973, Frazier and Fodor 1978, Wanner 1980, appendix A). The consistent preference for structure (2a) across informants suggests that in the perception of this type of example, the Object NP is closed early.[1]

Sentence (3) also suggests that NPs are closed early.

(3)
The girl pushed through the door laughed.

The initial portions of example (3) are locally ambiguous between the simple sentence structure [$_S$ *the girl pushed through the door*] and the reduced relative structure [$_{NP}$ *the girl (who was) pushed through the door*]. Although the ambiguity is resolved by the final word in the sentence, there is a strong preference for the simple sentence structure (Bever 1970), which makes the final word difficult to integrate into the analysis. Note that in the preferred structure, shown in (4a), the Subject NP closes immediately after *the girl,* whereas in the nonpreferred structure, shown in (4b), it closes after *pushed through the door.*

(4)
a.   [$_{NP}$ *the girl*] pushed through the door . . .   (P)
b.   [$_{NP}$[$_{NP}$ *the girl*] [$_{VP}$ *pushed through the door*]] laughed   (N)

Despite sentences (1) and (3), it can be shown that the early closing of phrases is not general. For sentence (5), the lower VP can be closed early (as in (6a), where the PP *at work* attaches to the higher verb), or it can be closed late (as in (6b), where the PP attaches to the lower verb). It is the late closure analysis that is preferred for sentence (5).

(5)
Tom disputed Bill's dying at work.

(6)
a.   Tom disputed Bill's [$_{VP}$ *dying*] at work   (N)
b.   Tom disputed Bill's [$_{VP}$ *dying at work*]   (P)

It is also easy to find sentences where there is a preference to close an NP late. In sentence (7), for example, the Object NP can be closed early (as in (8a), where the PP *on the beach* is associated with the verb), or it can be closed late (as in (8b), where the PP is associated with the NP *the dogs*). The late closure analysis is preferred for sentence (7).

(7)
The women discussed the dogs on the beach.

(8)
a.   the women [$_{VP}$ discussed [$_{NP}$ *the dogs*] [$_{PP}$ on the beach]]   (N)
b.   the women [$_{VP}$ discussed [$_{NP}$[$_{NP}$ *the dogs*] [$_{PP}$ *on the beach*]]]   (P)

We see that even though two sentences may be very similar, as sentences (1) and (7) are, informants' preferences for them may differ. In fact, we can find sentences that differ by only one lexical item and yet still show different preference patterns. In contrast to sentence (7), for example, sentence (9) elicits a preference for early closure of the Object NP.

(9)
The women kept the dogs on the beach.

The same preference holds for sentence (10).

(10)
The women discussed the dogs with the policeman.

The sentences presented in this section give some idea of the syntactic closure phenomena exhibited in structurally ambiguous sentences. A theory of competence must account for all possible structures of an ambiguous sentence. A theory of performance must explain why there is a bias in the actual perception of sentences toward a particular structural analysis. It is obvious that syntactic preferences depend upon very subtle factors, and may indeed vary from person to person and from situation to situation, though we have found a substantial agreement among our subjects with the preferences reported here (see appendix A). This variation itself must be explained by any adequate performance theory. In the next section, we will consider previous explanations of syntactic closure effects. In sections 11.3–11.5, we will present our theory. Appendix A contains the data on which this study is based, and appendix B a computational interpretation of the theory.

11.2 Previous Explanations

Among the various discussions of syntactic bias and closure phenomena in the literature, three influential psycholinguistic proposals have done the most to clarify the issues and the evidence.

Heuristic Strategies

One approach to the problem of syntactic closure effects in structurally ambiguous sentences is to assume that the rules of grammar that characterize linguistic competence are not utilized in the perception of sentences, but that agrammatic heuristic strategies which derive only the preferred analysis are employed instead (Bever 1970, Fodor, Bever, and Garrett 1974). For example, the *Canonical Sentoid Strategy* (see Fodor, Bever, and Garrett) assumes that sentences are first analyzed in terms of lexical classes and that when the sequence N V (N) is encountered it is directly assigned the analysis of a simple sentence, containing Subject Verb (Object). This could account for the bias in interpreting the initial portions of (3) as a simple sentence. However, the strategy does not extend in any obvious way to the other phenomena presented above.

Apart from the fact that proposed heuristic strategies such as the Canonical Sentoid Strategy do not explain the phenomena we have presented, the assumption that heuristic strategies are independent of the rules of linguistic competence fails to explain why it is that *any* of the possible structures of an ambiguous sentence can be perceived given appropriate context. In order to describe this fact, heuristic strategies would either have to duplicate all of the possible structural analyses that the competence grammar already defines or else provide some explicit way of accessing the information in the competence grammar. In the former case, it is not explained why there must be two different representations of the same linguistic information. In the latter case, the probable flow of information between the heuristic processes and the competence-based analysis procedures is unspecified, and the possibility remains that the competence-based analysis procedures themselves would suffice to explain the phenomena. Indeed, this possibility would be theoretically preferable to the heuristic strategies approach—on grounds of its simplicity, generality, and strength.

Despite its theoretical weakness, the heuristic strategies approach does call attention to the fact that factors other than those represented in the rules of grammar do play an important role in sentence comprehension. It is the exact nature of the interaction between these factors and the competence grammar that must be determined.

The Sausage Machine

Frazier and Fodor 1978 maintain that syntactic bias phenomena can be explained by the *architecture* of the sentence processing device—that is, by the structuring of its memory and operations. In particular, they propose a two-stage parsing model, designated the *Sausage Machine*, which makes use of a phrase structure grammar. In the first stage of the parsing process of this model, a Preliminary Phrase Packager (PPP) assigns lexical and phrasal nodes to groups of words within the sentence. In the second stage, the Sentence Structure Supervisor (SSS) combines the resulting "phrasal packages" into a complete phrase structure tree for the sentence. Frazier and Fodor do not specify exactly how the PPP determines the lexical and phrasal nodes or how the SSS combines the resulting phrasal packages. But they hypothesize that the PPP is "shortsighted," being limited to looking at approximately six words at a time, while the SSS can "survey" all of the phrase structure tree that has been compiled so far. An important property of the PPP is thus that it is not only ignorant of what is to come later in a sentence, but also ignorant of what came before, since once a phrasal package is analyzed, the package is "shunted" to the SSS. The PPP therefore fails to recognize certain legitimate ways of attaching constituents.

Frazier and Fodor 1978 illustrate the effect of the two-stage parsing process with ambiguous sentences like (11) and (1).

(11)
Tom said that Bill had taken the cleaning out yesterday.

(1)
Joe bought the book for Susan.

The preference for (11) is to attach *yesterday* to the lower clause, yielding the interpretation *Tom said it (that Bill had taken the cleaning out yesterday).* Frazier and Fodor claim that the higher attachment of the adverb, yielding *Tom said it . . . yesterday,* is difficult to compute because by the time the constituent *yesterday* is reached, the PPP has lost access to *Tom said.* Since sentence (1) is short enough that it would fit within the narrow viewing window of the PPP, both possible ways of attaching the constituent *for Susan* could be seen by the PPP. Thus, it might be expected that both possible structures would be equally acceptable. To explain why the VP attachment of *for Susan* is preferred over the complex NP attachment, Frazier and Fodor 1978:320 propose what they call the *Minimal Attachment* strategy, which stipulates that "each lexical item (or other node) is to be attached into the phrase marker with the fewest possible number of nonterminal nodes linking it with the nodes which are already present." While the preferred structure for sentence (1) conforms to Minimal Attachment, the nonpreferred structure violates it because of the presence of the extra NP node dominating the NP *the book* and the PP *for Susan* (see (2a) and (2b)). In short, Frazier and Fodor 1978:299 claim that the low right adjoining of a constituent, as found with the adverb *yesterday* in (11), sets in only in cases where the constituent is "at some distance from the other daughter constituents of the higher node to which it might have been attached."

Wanner 1980 points out that the two-stage architecture of the Sausage Machine is not necessary to account for the evidence given by Frazier and Fodor, because the normal depth-first recursive analysis of embedded phrasal structure in a top-down parser could produce very similar effects. For example, in a top-down parse, the adverb *yesterday* in (11) would be encountered during the analysis of the embedded clause while the matrix clause is temporarily not being considered. Wanner also argues that the Sausage Machine model is empirically less adequate than his account in certain crucial cases. He has noted that if the tendency for the low right adjoining of a constituent resulted from the narrow viewing window of the PPP, the preference for right attachment should disappear in all cases where a sentence is shortened to approximately six words. However, as Wanner observes, the preference for right attachment does not disappear in sentence (12), for example.

(12)
Tom said Bill died yesterday.

Presumably, since the sentence is so short, the PPP can "see" both possible ways of attaching the adverb *yesterday,* but there is still a marked preference for the low, local, right attachment. The same is true of many other sentences, such as (5).

(5)
Tom disputed Bill's dying at work.

In their reply to Wanner 1980, Fodor and Frazier 1980 accept the idea that the preference for low right attachment of a constituent could not be due to the narrow viewing window of the PPP, but argue that a distinct phenomenon called *Local Association* does result from the narrow window. They claim that it is Local Association that motivates the Sausage Machine model, and they distinguish it from the phenomenon of *Right Association,* that is, the low right attachment of a constituent. For Fodor and Frazier, Local Association refers to the preference to attach a constituent with nearby phrases, while Right Association refers to the preference to attach a constituent low and to the right in the phrase structure. So, while Right Association (which was actually formulated as a principle of parsing by Kimball 1973) makes reference to height of attachment, Local Association does not. Notice that Right Association of a constituent yields a structure that is closed late, but Local Association does not necessarily do so. This is because a constituent may be left-attached with its righthand neighbors, resulting in the early closure of a preceding structure.

As evidence for a distinct phenomenon of Local Association, Fodor and Frazier present sentence (13).

(13)
Though Martha claimed that she will be the first woman president yesterday she announced that she'd rather be an astronaut.

In sentence (13), the subordinate phrase (*Though Martha claimed that . . .*) could be closed late, the adverb *yesterday* being adjoined with *Martha claimed,* or it could be closed early, the adverb being adjoined with its immediate right neighbor *she announced*. Although the latter adjunction would be the higher attachment, it is nevertheless the preferred one. A second type of sentence Fodor and Frazier present as evidence for Local Association is (14).

(14)
Joe took the book that I had wanted to include in my birthday gift for Susan.

According to Fodor and Frazier, in the preferred analysis of (14), the PP *for Susan* attaches low and to the right as a modifier to the head NP *my birthday gift,* yielding the structure [NP[NP *my birthday gift*] [PP *for Susan*]]. That is, the constituent *for Susan* is Right Associated. This preference is dominant despite the fact that it requires one more node than the alternative analyses where *for Susan* is attached with a verb, as in [VP *to include . . . for Susan*]. Thus, even though the PP *for Susan* could be "minimally attached" into the phrase structure, the preference is to "locally" attach it to nearby phrases. The preference is taken as evidence for a phenomenon of Local Association because in contrast to short sentences such as (1), where Minimal Attachment wins out over Right Association, in (14), where there is some distance between the constituent and the node to which it could minimally attach, Right Association wins out over Minimal Attachment.

Fodor and Frazier claim that the preferences in both (13) and (14) follow from the limited capacity of the PPP. They assert that because the PPP cannot "see" much of the phrase marker of a sentence, it cannot "see" that the adverb *yesterday* could be attached to *Martha claimed* in (13) or that the PP *for Susan* could be attached to a distant verb in (14). But what happens if sentences (13) and (14) are shortened so that they would fit within the narrow viewing window of the PPP? The shorter sentences in (15) and (16) have the same structural possibilities as (13) and (14), respectively; contrary to the predictions of the Sausage Machine model, however, the shorter sentences exhibit the *same* syntactic biases as their longer counterparts, as shown in appendix A.

(15)
Forgetting she shouldn't sometimes she ran.

(16)
Joe included my gift for Susan.

For (15), although the adverb *sometimes* could be adjoined either with *forgetting* or with *she ran,* attachment to *she ran* is preferred. For (16), the structure in which the PP *for Susan* is attached as a modifier to the NP *my gift* is still preferred, even though on the alternative analysis the PP would be minimally attached in the VP. Examples (15) and (16) demonstrate clearly that the crucial sentences which are meant to justify the architecture of the Sausage Machine in fact provide *no* motivation for a two-stage parsing process whose first stage is limited to a narrow viewing window. (Note, too, that (16) and (7) are counterexamples to Frazier and Fodor's Minimal Attachment strategy.)

The evidence cited by Frazier and Fodor in favor of the Sausage Machine architecture is contaminated by two factors that they fail to recognize. First, it is a grammatical property of English that S' (S̄ or S-bar) Complements are normally positioned finally in their matrix clauses. It is this fact which explains the contrast between examples (17a) and (17b).

(17)
a. It surprised all of my young science students yesterday *that there are flightless birds*.
b. It surprised all of my young science students *that there are flightless birds* yesterday.

In contrast to example (17a), sentence (17b) seems very awkward. It is initially interpreted as though *yesterday* modified *that there are flightless birds*. The reason why the adverb is attached within the Complement S' even though it leads to a disagreement in tense features is that the required upper attachment of the adverb results in a Complement S' that is nonfinal within its matrix clause. (Note that the same effect occurs even when the phrase *all of my young science students* is shortened to *everyone*.) Categories other than S' are not subject to the clause-final restriction, as illustrated by the contrast between (18a,b), which contain an S' Complement, and (19a,b), which contain a PP Complement.

(18)
a. Martha notified us that Joe died by express mail.
b. Martha notified us by express mail that Joe died.

(19)
a. Martha notified us of Joe's death by express mail.
b. Martha notified us by express mail of Joe's death.

Without special intonation, (18a) is not immediately perceived as synonymous with (18b); rather, it is taken to have the anomalous interpretation according to which *by express mail* modifies *Joe died*. However, (19a) is easily understood as synonymous with (19b).

The clause-final S' restriction by itself could account for the "local association" effect in example (13). If so, we would predict that that effect would disappear in examples like (20) and (21), which have non-S' complements.

(20)
Although an astronaut lectured on many renowned Russian space expeditions at our school the students weren't interested.

(21)
Although the women talked about John's killing his very old father on many occasions they repressed how much they disliked the old man.

The complement to *lectured* in (20) is the PP *on many renowned Russian space expeditions;* the complement to *talked about* in (21) is the gerundive NP *John's killing his very old father*. (On the criteria for distinguishing S' Complements from gerundive NPs, see Emonds 1976.) As in example (13), both complements semantically preclude modification by the adjunct (*at our school* and *on many occasions*). As before, the principle of Local Association predicts that the adjunct should attach with the local phrases on the right. However, the preference is to associate the adjunct with the more distant phrases on the left.[2]

The second unrecognized factor in the evidence for Local Association is that it is conditioned by the choice of lexical items. We have already seen that structurally identical sentences that differ lexically exhibit different syntactic biases; thus, sentence (16) contrasts with sentence (1), and sentence (7) differs from sentences (9) and (10). Further, sentence (22) contrasts with sentence (23).

(22)
Joe arrived on the day that I had wanted to discuss my youngest daughter's difficulties with the teachers.

(23)
Joe arrived on the day that I had wanted to discuss my youngest daughter's difficulties at the school.

In the relevant respects, sentences (22) and (23) are similar in length and structure to (14), but only sentence (23) exhibits the same bias as

(14). In the preferred interpretation of sentence (23), the PP *at the school* modifies *my youngest daughter's difficulties,* and the analysis in which the PP attaches with the preceding verb, yielding the interpretation *discuss them (my youngest daughter's difficulties) at the school,* is less preferred. However, for sentence (22), the preference is to attach the PP *with the teachers* with the verb *discuss* and not with its immediate neighbor, *my youngest daughter's difficulties.* It is clear, then, that the choice of lexical items conditions whether or not a phrase is associated with its neighbors. As we will see, the preferences are accounted for by a theory of lexically induced bias.

In sum, an analysis of the data that Fodor and Frazier give shows that there is no real evidence for a distinct phenomenon of Local Association and hence no motivation for the specific architecture of the Sausage Machine model.[3] Nevertheless, Frazier and Fodor's emphasis on the relation between the phenomena of sentence perception and the architecture of the human sentence processor is important. What our analysis of the data suggests is that an architecture which simply allows the rules of syntactic structure to interact with lexical information provides a better explanation of the data than a two-stage parser whose first stage is limited to a narrow viewing window. (Actually, in an attempt to explain the lexically induced biases discussed in this study, the Sausage Machine could be modified to allow the rules of syntactic structure to interact with lexical information. However, the point is that once this is done, there is no need for the particular architecture of the Sausage Machine. Moreover, we will show later that strict subcategorization features, which are the form of lexical representation assumed in the Sausage Machine model, are inadequate to explain the performance data.)

ATNs

Wanner 1980 argues that Augmented Transition Networks (ATNs) can provide a general description of both "Right Association" and "Minimal Attachment" strategies and their interactions. Although we have seen that there are counterexamples to the "Minimal Attachment" strategy and that closure properties are conditioned by the choice of lexical predicates, it is still worthwhile considering Wanner's account of these closure phenomena because it does contain an important insight.

Frazier and Fodor 1978 assume that it is impossible for ATN parsers to model the "Right Association" and "Minimal Attachment" strategies and their interactions in a *general* way. They claim, for example, that since an ATN's decisions "are determined by the ranking of arcs for specific word and phrase types, rather than in terms of concepts like 'lowest rightmost node in the phrase marker', the parser's structural preferences would have to be built in separately for each type of phrase and each sentence context in which it can appear" (1978:294). But in his reply, Wanner argues that this claim is erroneous (1980:216):

. . . a scheduling rule in an ATN, as described by Kaplan (1975, 1972) and by Wanner and Maratsos (1978), is essentially a specification of the order in which the ATN processor considers the arcs leaving a state in an ATN grammar network. . . . [T]he ATN network includes at least 5 types of arcs:

—WORD arcs that analyze specific grammatical morphemes such as *that* or *to;*

—CAT arcs that analyze grammatical categories such as Noun (N) or Verb (V);

—SEEK arcs that analyze whole phrases or clauses such as NP, VP, or S;

—SEND arcs which terminate a network;

—JUMP arcs which provide a free transition between states, thus expressing the optionality of certain sub-paths through the network.

Given this enumeration of arc types, we can formulate two general constraints on ATN scheduling rules which provide a general description of Right Association and Minimal Attachment:

. . . Right Association: Schedule all SEND arcs and all JUMP arcs after every other arc type . . .

. . . Minimal Attachment: Schedule all CAT arcs and WORD arcs before all SEEK arcs.

In their reply to Wanner 1980, Fodor and Frazier 1980 concede that, contrary to their original argument, Right Association does not follow from the structure or operational characteristics of the Sausage Machine. However, they argue that the scheduling of CAT and WORD arcs before SEEK arcs is less general than Minimal Attachment because it does not account for biases toward Minimal Attachment in cases where there is a choice between which of two SEEK arcs to schedule first. They describe four possible cases where such biases exist. In Wanner's terms, the four crucial examples given by Fodor and Frazier indicate that the SEEK NP arc is scheduled before the SEEK S (or S') arc. It is actually very simple to provide a generalization of Wanner's basic idea that will account for all of the cases. There are at least two general principles which would entail both the CAT-before-SEEK ordering and the ordering of SEEK NP before SEEK S or S'.

First, arcs could be scheduled according to their transition frequencies. It is generally true of natural languages that every nonlexical phrasal node (such as NP) dominates at least one lexical node, and usually more than one. Thus, in analyzing natural language sentences, the lexical (CAT) arcs will be traversed more often than the nonlexical (SEEK) arcs. Moreover, every S or S' dominates at least one NP, and most dominate more than one, while fewer NPs dominate Ss. Thus, SEEK NP will be traversed more often than SEEK S or SEEK S'. Finally, the principle will order frequently occurring constructions before less frequent constructions, such as the nominative absolute construction cited by Fodor and Frazier as one of their crucial cases (*The leader of the gang of thieves having been captured by the police, the others quickly divided up the loot and left the country*).

An alternative principle that would generalize Wanner's ordering strategy can be based on X' (X-bar) theory (see Bresnan 1977, Jackendoff 1977); namely, the ordering of an arc is equal to $1 + n$, where n is the number of primes (bars) in the category labeling the arc. In general, the lower the number of primes on a category C, the closer C will be to the terminal string (that is, the fewer will be the number of nodes that intervene between C and a terminal string). CAT arcs, which have low-level category labels such as N and V, will be ordered before SEEK arcs, which have higher order category labels such as NP ($= N''$) and VP ($= V''$), and SEEK NP ($= N''$) arcs would be ordered before SEEK S ($= V'''$) arcs and S' ($= V''''$) arcs. This principle establishes only a partial ordering of arcs because two arcs may be labeled with different categories that have the same number of bars.

The choice between these two general principles, or other possible principles of arc ordering, is an empirical matter. The important point here is simply that the effects of Minimal Attachment can be derived from a general principle governing the order in which grammatical rules are applied in the analysis of sentences.

Although Wanner does not discuss scheduling in detail, we note here that his Minimal Attachment principle must actually be supplemented by another principle. In sentence (1), *Joe bought the book for Susan,* a decision must be made *after* the determiner (*the*) and the noun (*book*) have been found and analyzed as a simple NP (*the book*): it must be decided whether to attach the simple NP into a VP or a complex NP. The top-down control structure of the ATN will guarantee that the simple NP is attached into the VP. However, a problem will arise in any situation where the structure must be reanalyzed to yield a left-recursive structure, such as [$_{NP}$[$_{NP}$][$_{PP}$]]. ATNs go into a "loop" when analyzing left-recursive structures (see Winograd forthcoming). To avoid this problem, left-recursive structures are usually written in some other form in ATN grammars. However, in the grammar Wanner presents in his discussion of Minimal Attachment, left-recursive structures are permitted, and hence a special principle is required to avoid the usual ATN problem with these structures.

The ATN solution to the problem of the relation between performance and competence differs from both the heuristic strategies and Sausage Machine approaches: the grammars used by the ATN parser give a full specification of linguistic competence, but the order in which rules are applied in the analysis of sentences gives rise to biases shown in performance. Thus, the ATN model presupposes the competence hypothesis, as does the theory we will propose. We have already said that the competence hypothesis is desirable on grounds of its simplicity, generality, and strength. Our proposal is very different, though, from the ATN model: it differs in the theory of competence (see chapters 3 and 4 of this volume), in the computational specification of the performance model, and in the theory of how rule-driven and data-driven analysis procedures interact (see below). Nevertheless, we will make use of the important insight that the biases shown in Minimal Attachment phenomena are explained in part by the order in which rules are applied in the analysis of sentences (Wanner 1980, Wanner and Kaplan 1975). We have already shown that the structural analysis of a sentence is conditioned by the choice of lexical predicates. What is required is a coherent theory of sentence perception which explains how structural analyses are biased by the interaction of syntactic and lexical factors.

11.3 A Theory of Syntactic Closure

Basic Assumptions

Any theory of sentence perception must specify a process that extracts representations of meaningful grammatical relations from strings of words. In keeping with the lexical-functional theory of grammar, we assume that the input to this process consists of strings of lexical items and that the output of the process is a functional structure which represents the meaningful grammatical relations of the sentence. We also assume that the perception process can recover *all* possible functional structures for any sentence. The theory of syntactic closure explains the recovery of the preferred analysis. This theory of syntactic closure is not intended to account for all of the phenomena, such as memory limitations and center embedding difficulties, which a comprehensive theory of sentence perception must explain. However, we expect it to be integrated into a more comprehensive theory. Recent work by Church 1980 and Church and Kaplan forthcoming suggests interesting possibilities for this.

Our theory of syntactic closure assumes (i) that rules of the competence grammar are used to construct the internal representations in sentence perception; (ii) that the order in which these grammatical rules are applied gives rise to closure effects; (iii) that this order is jointly determined by the strengths of alternative lexical forms, the strengths of alternative categories in the expansion of syntactic rules, and the sequence of hypotheses in the parsing process.

(i) The competence grammar assumed here is given by the lexical-functional theory of grammatical representation presented in this volume. The lexicon and the rules of grammar define both a constituent structure and a functional structure for any given sentence. For English, the grammar includes rules like the following:

$$S \rightarrow \quad \underset{(\uparrow\text{SUBJ})=\downarrow}{\text{NP}} \quad \text{VP}$$

$$\text{VP} \rightarrow \text{(AUX)} \quad \text{V} \quad \underset{(\uparrow\text{OBJ})=\downarrow}{\left(\text{NP}\right)} \quad \left(\left\{ \begin{array}{c} \text{NP} \\ (\uparrow\text{OBJ2})=\downarrow \\ \text{XP} \\ (\uparrow\text{XCOMP})=\downarrow \end{array} \right\} \right) \quad \underset{(\uparrow(\downarrow\text{PCASE}))=\downarrow}{\text{PP*}}$$

$$\underset{\downarrow\in(\uparrow\text{ADJ})}{\text{PP*}} \quad \left(\underset{(\uparrow\text{SCOMP})=\downarrow}{\text{S}'} \right)$$

$$\text{NP} \rightarrow \text{(DET)} \quad \underset{\downarrow\in(\uparrow\text{MOD})}{\text{ADJ*}} \quad \text{N}$$

$$\text{NP} \rightarrow \underset{(\uparrow\text{HEAD})=\downarrow}{\text{NP}} \quad \left\{ \begin{array}{c} \text{PP} \\ (\uparrow\text{HEAD})=(\downarrow\text{SUBJ}) \\ \uparrow=\downarrow \\ \text{S}' \\ (\uparrow\text{HEAD})=\Downarrow_{\text{NP}} \\ \uparrow=\downarrow \end{array} \right\}$$

$$\text{NP} \rightarrow \quad \text{NP's} \quad \text{VP}$$
$$(\uparrow\text{SUBJ})=\downarrow$$

$$\text{NP} \rightarrow \quad e$$
$$\uparrow = \Uparrow_{\text{NP}}$$

For ease of exposition, these rules have been simplified in certain ways that do not affect any of our arguments. Rules that are too long for one line have been divided and continued on a second line. For a fuller discussion of the constructions in question, see chapters 4 and 5 and the references cited there. Note that a superscript asterisk on a category indicates that that category may be repeated any number of times, including none.

(ii) The model of grammatical perception implied by the theory includes three basic features concerning the order in which grammatical rules are applied. First, in the course of the syntactic analysis, grammatical rules are applied serially such that only one structure is *initially* obtained, but at each application of a grammatical rule the constituent structure is analyzed and the functional structure is built up at the same time. (This will permit the simultaneous construction of the semantic interpretation as well (see Halvorsen 1980, forthcoming).) Second, functional and lexical information systematically affect syntactic decisions as the sentence is being analyzed. Third, data-driven analysis procedures interact with rule-driven (top-down, left-to-right) analysis procedures.

In the kind of model we have envisioned, there are two types of memory: a memory for what has been discovered so far about the string and a memory for options that could be taken at different points in the string. A processor takes one option at a time and executes the operations appropriate for that option. There are also principles that set the priority of different grammatical rules and thus determine the order in which alternative options are taken. Two types of options can arise during a parse: options for *hypothesizing* possible constituents and options for *attaching* a complete constituent, once it is found, into some structure. In appendix B, we give one explicit computational interpretation of the theory based on the General Syntactic Processor of Kaplan 1981.

(iii) The perceptual theory assumes that the order of application of grammatical rules is determined by two principles and their defaults. Both principles—the principles of Lexical Preference and Final Arguments—are concerned with the strengths of lexical forms and conditions on the well-formedness of functional structures. The default for the Lexical Preference principle makes reference to the strengths of alternative categories in the expansion of syntactic rules, while the default for the Final Arguments principle makes reference to the sequence of hypotheses in the parsing process. The two principles and their defaults govern the choice among alternatives that arise in different circumstances during the parsing process.

The Principles of Syntactic Closure
In this section we give an informal description of the principles of syntactic closure, illustrating them with a few simple examples. (Those interested in a more explicit computational interpretation of the theory should also see appendix B.) In the following section we demonstrate the explanatory power of our theory by applying the principles to more complex closure phenomena and by deriving predictions from the theory. In the final section, we consider the implications of the theory for the nature of linguistic representation.

As we have seen, one of the most crucial aspects of syntactic closure is one which is not explained in the previous literature, namely, that lexical items govern the closure properties of phrases. We have already given examples of sentences that differ by only one lexical item but that show different closure effects. The sentences in (24)–(26) further demonstrate the effect of lexical choice, particularly the choice of verb.

Sentences (24a) and (24b) are both ambiguous between a relative structure [$_{NP}$[$_{NP}$ *the dress*] [$_{PP}$ *on that rack*]] and a complement structure [$_{VP}$ *wanted/positioned* [$_{NP}$ *the dress*] [$_{PP}$ *on that rack*]]. Although (24a) and (24b) differ only in the verb, the relative structure is preferred for (24a), while for (24b) the preferred structure is the complement.

(24)
a. The woman wanted the dress on that rack.
b. The woman positioned the dress on that rack.

(25a) differs from (25b) in just the same way.

(25)
a. The tourists objected to the guide that they couldn't hear.
b. The tourists signaled to the guide that they couldn't hear.

Examples (25a) and (25b) are ambiguous between a relative clause analysis [$_{PP}$ *to* [$_{NP}$[$_{NP}$ *the guide*] [$_{S'}$ *that they couldn't hear*]]] and a complement analysis [$_{VP}$ *objected/signaled* [$_{PP}$ *to* [$_{NP}$ *the guide*]] [$_{S'}$ *that they couldn't hear*]]. While for (25a) the relative clause analysis is preferred, for (25b) the complement analysis is preferred.

Similarly, (26a) and (26b) differ only in the verb, but are ambiguous between a reduced relative analysis [$_{NP}$[$_{NP}$ *the package*] [$_{PP}$ *for Susan*]] and a prepositional object analysis [$_{VP}$ *included/carried* [$_{NP}$ *the package*] [$_{PP}$ *for Susan*]].

(26)
a.   Joe included the package for Susan.
b.   Joe carried the package for Susan.

While for (26a) the relative analysis is preferred, for (26b) the prepositional object analysis is preferred.

Thus, it appears that late closure of a phrase is preferred for (24a), (25a), and (26a), while early closure is preferred for (24b), (25b), and (26b). It is quite evident, then, that the closure effects in these sentences are induced in some way by the choice of the lexical items. Notice that the verb-governed preferences shown in (24)–(26) persist even when potential contextual sources of bias are eliminated. In (27)–(29), the lexical content of the subjects and objects in (24)–(26) has been replaced by pronouns, but the specific syntactic preferences are nevertheless preserved.

(27)
a.   They wanted everything there.
b.   They positioned everything there.

(28)
a.   They objected to everyone that they couldn't hear.
b.   They signaled to everyone that they couldn't hear.

(29)
a.   They included everything for them.
b.   They carried everything for them.

These sentences show that one can observe syntactic biases operating in isolation from context. Further evidence that syntactic biases cannot be explained solely in terms of contextual factors is found in studies by Kirby 1979 (also see Holmes 1979) and Holmes 1981. Kirby found that preferred interpretations of structurally ambiguous sentences were significantly related to certain structures but were *independent* of the judged plausibility of the two unambiguous readings of a sentence. Holmes 1981 showed in a reaction time study that syntactic preferences exist for structurally ambiguous sentences even when both readings of the sentences were judged to be equally plausible. Moreover, in another study, she showed that regardless of whether prior context was consistent with the syntactically preferred or nonpreferred interpretation of a structurally ambiguous sentence, the initial structure assigned to the sentence was the syntactically preferred one. More evidence that syntactic biases exist independently of contextual factors is given in section 11.5.

A plausible hypothesis to account for the closure effects shown in sentences such as (24)–(29) is that within the human memory structure which stores the lexical component of the grammar, the various lexical forms of a given verb have different "strengths" or "saliences," and that the strongest form somehow determines the preferred syntactic analysis. So, for example, the form *want* $\langle$(SUBJ),(OBJ)$\rangle$ may be stronger than the form *want* $\langle$(SUBJ),(OBJ),(PCOMP)$\rangle$, while the form *position* $\langle$(SUBJ),(OBJ)$\rangle$ may be weaker than the form *position* $\langle$(SUBJ),(OBJ), (PCOMP)$\rangle$. The difference in bias between (24a) and (24b), and (27a) and (27b), may be induced in some way by the difference in the strength of the alternative lexical forms of *want* and *position*. It seems perfectly reasonable to assume that lexical forms differ in their strength. It is well known that words themselves vary in their salience. There are many studies which show, for example, that words differ in their ease of recognition depending on their frequency of usage. It is thus plausible that lexical forms also vary in their strength. Moreover, given the assumption that they do vary, our theory of perception will account for certain closure effects that are not explained in the previous literature and will also correctly predict a number of complex interactions. Obviously, we want to find out precisely what determines "strength," but that is a question for future research. It may be that strength is determined by the general frequency of usage in texts and speech in a society and that there is an underlying stability in the human memory structure, thus accounting for the uniformity of judgments for sentences in null context. But it could also be that the immediate context of a sentence might dynamically change the strength of lexical forms as a sentence is being processed. This is an empirical issue which cannot be decided a priori. Present evidence suggests, though, that syntactic biases exist independently of context.

However, this does not mean that context does not have any influence on the interpretation of a sentence. We note here that at least the eventual interpretation of a sentence may be affected by contextual factors, such as semantic plausibility. When we vary the context, we do seem able to alter syntactic biases, as (30a) and (30b) show.

(30)
a.   When he arrived at our doorstep, I could see that Joe carried a package for Susan.
b.   Whenever she got tired, Joe carried a package for Susan.

The preferred structures for (30a,b) are (31a,b), respectively.

(31)
a.   . . . Joe [$_{VP}$ carried [$_{NP}$[$_{NP}$ a package] [$_{PP}$ for Susan]]]
b.   . . . Joe [$_{VP}$ carried [$_{NP}$ a package] [$_{PP}$ for Susan]]

(31a) has the 2-place predicate "NP$_1$ carry NP$_2$," and (31b) the 3-place benefactive predicate "NP$_1$ carry NP$_2$ for NP$_3$." The benefactive predicate would naturally be preferred in a context where someone was helping someone else, as in (30b). But in the context of (30a), which focuses on the direct perception of a concrete situation, the more abstract benefactive predicate is disfavored. The lexical content of the grammatical arguments of a predicate can also influence the bias, as (32a,b) illustrate.

(32)
a.   The Boy Scout carried the package for his pet.
b.   The Boy Scout carried the package for his aunt.

The 2-place predicate is favored in (32a) and the 3-place benefactive predicate in (32b).

We are not concerned with context in the present study. Instead, we are concerned with how the contextually neutral strength of alternative lexical forms governs closure. We thus limit our consideration to the study of ambiguous sentences for which the different readings are equally reasonable in meaning and for which any variation in preference presumably arises from the strength of the alternative lexical forms of a lexical item.

We assume that alternative lexical forms of a verb differ in their strength or salience, perhaps because of variations in frequency of usage. We also assume that the alternative lexical forms are represented together with the verb in the emerging functional structure and that the forms are ranked. The initial ranking is set according to the contextually neutral strength of the forms of the verb. However, if the form that is the strongest is rejected in favor of another form during the analysis of the sentence, this latter form is then taken as the strongest form of the verb for that sentence.

No doubt there is some variation in the strength of lexical forms from person to person, just as there is some individual variation in the strength of words, though the data on intuitions presented in appendix A suggest that there is a substantial degree of consistency among people. What is important to our theory is that the various lexical forms of a verb differ in strength and that these strengths, once established, predictably affect the syntactic closure properties of phrases. Regardless of which particular lexical form is in fact stronger for a given speaker, our theory provides a general explanation of *how* the strength of alternative lexical forms governs syntactic closure.

One basic condition on the well-formedness of functional structures in lexical-functional grammar is *Coherence,* that is, that every governable grammatical function in the functional structure must be in the function-assignment list of the lexical form of its local predicate (see chapter 4 of this volume). A governable grammatical function is one that can appear as an argument to some lexical predicate. We hypothesize that an item's strongest lexical form influences the analysis of a sentence by suggesting which to choose among a set of alternatives in a phrase structure rule so that a coherent functional structure would be obtained if the lexical form were used.

The principle of *Lexical Preference* is informally stated in (33); see appendix B for a precise formulation.

(33)
Lexical Preference
If a set of alternatives has been reached in the expansion of a phrase structure rule, give priority to the alternatives that are coherent with the strongest lexical form of the predicate.

We will use sentence (24b) as an example to illustrate how the Lexical Preference principle influences syntactic choices.

(24)
b. $_1$The$_2$woman$_3$positioned$_4$the$_5$dress$_6$on$_7$that$_8$rack$_9$.

The numbered positions between the words will help us keep track of the parsing process. Let us assume that at some point in the analysis of this string we have found a partial VP constituent of which only the verb *positioned* has been analyzed. At position 4, there is the possibility of an Object NP or no NP. We can represent the partial VP constituent by (34), using notation adapted from Winograd forthcoming. For expository purposes, the rule is simplified. However, the simplification does not affect any of our arguments.

(34)

$$
{}_3\text{VP} \rightarrow \text{V} \quad {}_4\Bigg|\begin{pmatrix} \text{NP} \\ (\uparrow\text{OBJ})=\downarrow \end{pmatrix} \left(\begin{Bmatrix} \text{NP} \\ (\uparrow\text{OBJ2})=\downarrow \\ \text{PP} \\ (\uparrow\text{PCOMP})=\downarrow \end{Bmatrix} \right) \quad \begin{matrix} \text{PP*} \\ (\uparrow(\downarrow\text{PCASE}))=\downarrow \end{matrix} \quad \begin{matrix} \text{PP*} \\ \downarrow\in(\uparrow\text{ADJ}) \end{matrix}
$$

$$
\begin{pmatrix} \text{S}' \\ (\uparrow\text{SCOMP})=\downarrow \end{pmatrix}
$$

The subscript by the VP shows that the VP begins at position 3. Also notice that the material already analyzed by this rule is represented on the lefthand side of the vertical bar and that the other possible constituents of a VP are represented on the righthand side of the bar. An optional symbol is always analyzed as a choice between that symbol and the empty string *e:* thus, (35) is equivalent to (36). (Similarly, X^* can be represented as an alternative between *e* and X^+, which represents one or more Xs.)

(35)

$$
\begin{pmatrix} \text{NP} \\ (\uparrow\text{OBJ})=\downarrow \end{pmatrix}
$$

(36)

$$
\begin{Bmatrix} \text{NP} \\ (\uparrow\text{OBJ})=\downarrow \\ e \end{Bmatrix}
$$

We will assume that the strongest form of the verb *position* is *position* $\langle(\text{SUBJ}),(\text{OBJ}),(\text{PCOMP})\rangle$ and that the form *position* $\langle(\text{SUBJ}),(\text{OBJ})\rangle$ is weaker. Since the strongest form takes a direct object (OBJ), the Lexical Preference principle requires that in the VP rule, priority be given to the expansion of $\begin{smallmatrix} \text{NP} \\ (\uparrow\text{OBJ})=\downarrow \end{smallmatrix}$, over the alternative, *e*. Thus, an NP is hypothesized at position 4. Once the NP ${}_4$*the dress*${}_6$ has been analyzed and attached into the VP with $_3positioned_4$, as in $_1The_2woman_3positioned_4the_5dress_6$ . . . , there would be the possibility of a second NP, a PP Complement, or the alternative, e, at position 6. That is, we have the partial constituent represented in (37).

(37)

$$_3VP \rightarrow V \quad \begin{matrix} NP \\ (\uparrow OBJ)=\downarrow \end{matrix} \quad _6 \left| \left(\left\{ \begin{matrix} NP \\ (\uparrow OBJ2)=\downarrow \\ PP \\ (\uparrow PCOMP)=\downarrow \end{matrix} \right\} \right) \quad \begin{matrix} PP* \\ (\uparrow(\downarrow PCASE))=\downarrow \end{matrix} \quad \begin{matrix} PP* \\ \downarrow \in (\uparrow ADJ) \end{matrix} \right.$$

$$\left(\begin{matrix} S' \\ (\uparrow SCOMP)=\downarrow \end{matrix} \right)$$

Since the strongest lexical form of *position* takes a PCOMP, the Lexical Preference principle requires that priority be given to the expansion of $\begin{matrix} PP \\ (\uparrow PCOMP)=\downarrow \end{matrix}$, over the alternatives, $\begin{matrix} NP \\ (\uparrow OBJ2)=\downarrow \end{matrix}$ and e. Thus, a PP Complement would be hypothesized at 6. Now, for the sake of illustration, let us suppose that the verb in our example was *want*, as in (24a), with the strongest lexical form *want* $\langle$(SUBJ),(OBJ)$\rangle$.

(24)
a. $_1The_2woman_3wanted_4the_5dress_6on_7that_8rack_9.$

In this case, the Prepositional Complement would not be given priority at position 6 and, as we shall see, in the preferred reading the PP *on that rack* would be taken to modify *the dress*.

When the Lexical Preference principle does not choose between alternative categories in the expansion of a rule, its default, which makes use of the strengths of the alternative categories, is employed. This default principle of *Syntactic Preference* is informally stated in (38).

(38)
Syntactic Preference
The (default) order of priority for alternative categories in the expansion of a phrase structure rule is the order of the strengths of the alternative categories.

We assume that the strength of alternative categories is given by a general principle of frequency or category level as described in our discussion of Wanner's ATN. The effect of this principle can be seen in the way the sentence fragment (39), given by Fodor and Frazier 1980, is initially analyzed.

(39)
That silly old-fashioned . . .

Example (39) is ambiguous between a simple subject NP analysis, as in *That silly old-fashioned joke is told too often,* and a sentential subject S' analysis, as in *That silly old-fashioned jokes are told too often is well known.* According to Fodor and Frazier, the former analysis is preferred. Two syntactic analyses of subjects might be proposed. The first is given by the possible rule represented in (40).

(40)

$$
S \rightarrow \left\{ \begin{array}{c} NP \\ (\uparrow SUBJ)=\downarrow \\ S' \\ (\uparrow SUBJ)=\downarrow \end{array} \right\} VP
$$

Since the category NP is ranked higher than the category S' by either frequency or category level, the principle of Syntactic Preference gives priority to the NP analysis for the sentence fragment (39). The second analysis of subjects is given by the rules represented in (41).

(41)

$$
S \rightarrow \quad NP \quad VP \\ \quad (\uparrow SUBJ)=\downarrow
$$

$$
NP \rightarrow \left\{ \begin{array}{ccc} (DET) & ADJ^* & N \\ & \downarrow \in (\uparrow MOD) & \\ S' & & \end{array} \right\}
$$

In this case, the alternative categories for the expansion of the NP are ranked by the principle of Syntactic Preference in the order DET . . . before S', again yielding the preferred analysis.

A second illustration of the effect of the principle of Syntactic Preference is given by (42).

(42)
We discussed running.

This sentence is ambiguous between the structures (43a) and (43b).

(43)

a. we [$_{VP}$[$_V$ discussed] [$_{NP}$[$_N$ running]]]

b. we [$_{VP}$[$_V$ discussed] [$_{NP}$[$_{VP}$[$_V$ running]]]]

In (43a), *running* has the properties of a noun: it can be modified by a prenominal adjective (*excessive running*); it can take a determiner (*the running*); it prohibits the negative adverb *not* (**not excessive running*); and it takes PP but not NP Complements (*the excessive running of races*, **the excessive running races*). In contrast, *running* in (43b) has all the properties of a verb. It can be modified by an adverb (*running excessively*); it can take the negative particle *not* (*not running excessively*); and it permits direct NP Objects (*running races excessively*). (For a discussion of the two kinds of gerunds, see Wasow and Roeper 1972.) There is a bias to analyze sentence (42) as having the structure given in (43a). This bias follows immediately from the Syntactic Preference principle, since in the alternative expansions of NP, the category N would be ranked higher than the alternative category VP, either by frequency or by category level. Although it might be thought at first glance that the bias also follows immediately from Fodor and Frazier's Minimal Attachment strategy, it does not. In both (43a) and (43b), the lexical item *running* is minimally attached given its classification as N or V.

Now that the Lexical Preference principle and its default have been formulated, we can turn to the Final Arguments principle and its default. In our discussion of the Lexical Preference principle, we assumed that the verbs *position* and *want* differ in that while the strongest lexical form of *position* is *position*⟨(SUBJ),(OBJ),(PCOMP)⟩, the strongest form of *want* is *want*⟨(SUBJ),(OBJ)⟩. We will now see how, given these assumptions, the Lexical Preference and Final Arguments principles interact to account correctly for the preferences for sentences (24a) and (24b).

(24)

a. $_1$The$_2$woman$_3$wanted$_4$the$_5$dress$_6$on$_7$that$_8$rack$_9$.

b. $_1$The$_2$woman$_3$positioned$_4$the$_5$dress$_6$on$_7$that$_8$rack$_9$.

We have already suggested that in a sentence such as (24b), the Lexical Preference principle will cause priority to be given to the proposal of an Object NP at 4 and a Prepositional Complement at 6. In sentence (24a), priority would not be given to the proposal of a Prepositional Complement at 6 because the strongest lexical form of *want* takes only two arguments—a Subject and an Object. The Object will be the final argument of *want*. The final argument of a lexical form of a given phrase is a constituent of that phrase which is coherent with the lexical form and which can be followed by no other constituent that is coherent with the form. Thus, the final argument of a lexical form will be the one that is rightmost in the string. Although an Object NP in (24a) is the final argument of the strongest form of *want*, this obviously does not mean that there can be no more words in the string after the simple NP $_4the\ dress_6$. On finding the NP $_4the\ dress_6$, a number of options arise at position 6 that would allow more material to be included in the string. If the simple NP were attached to the VP and the functional structure closed, a mistake would have been made—although the functional structure would be complete, in that it would contain all the governable grammatical functions of *want* ⟨(SUBJ),(OBJ)⟩, some material would have been omitted from the analysis. We hypothesize that in order to avoid such a mistake, there is a delay in attaching to a phrase its final argument; for the same reason, we hypothesize that there is a delay in attaching to a phrase any element subsequent to the final argument. The effect of this delay will be to induce late closure at or after the final argument.[4] The principle of *Final Arguments* is informally stated in (44).

(44)
Final Arguments
Give low priority to attaching to a phrase the final argument of the strongest lexical form of that phrase and to attaching any elements subsequent to the final argument. Low priority is defined here with respect to other options that arise at the end position of the element whose attachment is to be delayed.

The effect of the principle of Final Arguments can be illustrated by sentence (24a). The preference to associate the PP $_6on\ that\ rack_9$ with the NP $_4the\ dress_6$ follows from the principle. Once the simple NP constituent $_4the\ dress_6$ has been analyzed, it could be attached into the partial VP constituent represented in (45).

(45)

$$_3\text{VP} \rightarrow \text{V} \quad _4\Bigg|\left(\begin{array}{c}\text{NP}\\(\uparrow\text{OBJ})=\downarrow\end{array}\right)\left(\left\{\begin{array}{c}\text{NP}\\(\uparrow\text{OBJ2})=\downarrow\\\text{PP}\\(\uparrow\text{PCOMP})=\downarrow\end{array}\right\}\right)\quad\begin{array}{c}\text{PP*}\\(\uparrow(\downarrow\text{PCASE}))=\downarrow\end{array}\quad\begin{array}{c}\text{PP*}\\\downarrow\in(\uparrow\text{ADJ})\end{array}$$
$$\left(\begin{array}{c}\text{S}'\\(\uparrow\text{SCOMP})=\downarrow\end{array}\right)$$

However, the NP, if attached into the VP, would be the final argument of the strongest lexical form of the verb *want*. The Final Arguments principle would thus come into effect, giving low priority to the option for attaching the NP into the VP in favor of other options that arise at the end position of $_4$*the dress*$_6$, that is, at position 6. In the case of sentence (24a), the option of attaching the simple NP $_4$*the dress*$_6$ into a partial complex NP constituent would be given priority and then taken. The partial complex NP constituent into which the simple NP can be attached is illustrated in (46). The NP rule is simplified for expository purposes, but this does not materially affect our discussion.

(46)

$$_4\text{NP} \rightarrow \quad _4\Big|\begin{array}{ccc}\text{NP} & & \text{PP}\\(\uparrow\text{HEAD})=\downarrow & & (\uparrow\text{HEAD})=(\downarrow\text{SUBJ})\\ & & \uparrow=\downarrow\end{array}$$

The simple NP $_4$*the dress*$_6$ is thus now attached directly under an NP node; yielding the partial constituent represented in (47).

(47)

$$_4\text{NP} \rightarrow \quad \begin{array}{ccc}\text{NP} & _6\Big| & \text{PP}\\(\uparrow\text{HEAD})=\downarrow & & (\uparrow\text{HEAD})=(\downarrow\text{SUBJ})\\ & & \uparrow=\downarrow\end{array}$$

A PP will then be hypothesized as a possible completion of the complex NP and the phrase $_6$*on that rack*$_9$ will be analyzed. This PP must now be attached into a phrase structure. Only one option exists for doing this: the PP must be attached into the partial complex NP constituent represented in (47), which requires a PP at position 6. Notice that the PP $_6$*on that rack*$_9$ cannot be attached into the VP because we have only the partial VP constituent represented in (45), which has so far been analyzed only to position 4 in the string and requires an NP or *e* at position

4. The PP is therefore attached as a sister to the simple NP $_4$*the dress*$_6$, to form the complex NP structure (48).

(48)
$_4$[$_{NP}$[$_{NP}$ the dress] [$_{PP}$ on that rack]]$_9$

The complex NP must now be attached to something. There are various options for doing this: for example, it could be attached into the partial VP constituent represented in (45) or into the partial complex NP constituent represented in (46). The former option would attach the final argument of *want* to the VP. Hence, the Final Arguments principle would take effect again, delaying the attachment of the complex NP into the VP and giving higher priority to other options that arise at the end position of $_4$*the dress on that rack*$_9$, that is, position 9. However, none of these other options can lead to a successful analysis. For example, attaching the complex NP (48) into the partial NP constituent represented by (46) would lead to the proposal of a PP at position 9, but the sentence ends at that position. Attaching the simple NP $_7$*that rack*$_9$ as head of a complex NP would also not lead to a successful analysis because the sentence ends at position 9. The option that was delayed by the Final Arguments principle would therefore have to be taken. The complex NP would be attached into the partial VP constituent represented in (45). Eventually, the VP would be attached under the S node.[5]

In contrast to sentence (24a), the Final Arguments principle would not come into effect to delay the VP attachment of the NP $_4$*the dress*$_6$ in sentence (24b), since the Object NP would not be the final argument of the strongest lexical form of *position*.

(24)
b. $_1$The$_2$woman$_3$positioned$_4$the$_5$dress$_6$on$_7$that$_8$rack$_9$.

Instead, the default principle would apply. The default, which we call *Invoked Attachment,* simply gives priority to the attachment of a phrase into the partial constituent that caused the phrase to be hypothesized. The default principle of Invoked Attachment is informally stated in (49).

(49)
Invoked Attachment
When there are alternative options for attaching a phrase into a structure, give (default) priority to the option for attaching the phrase to the partial constituent that caused the phrase to be hypothesized.

When the simple NP $_4$*the dress*$_6$ in (24b) has been analyzed, it must be attached to something. Just as for sentence (24a), there are two options for doing this. The NP could be attached into the partial VP constituent represented in (50) or into a partial complex NP constituent such as (51).

(50)

$$_3\text{VP} \rightarrow \text{V} \quad _4\left|\left(\begin{array}{c}\text{NP} \\ (\uparrow\text{OBJ})=\downarrow\end{array}\right)\right. \left\{\begin{array}{c}\text{NP} \\ (\uparrow\text{OBJ2})=\downarrow \\ \text{PP} \\ (\uparrow\text{PCOMP})=\downarrow\end{array}\right\} \quad \begin{array}{c}\text{PP*} \\ (\uparrow(\downarrow\text{PCASE}))=\downarrow\end{array} \quad \begin{array}{c}\text{PP*} \\ \downarrow\in(\uparrow\text{ADJ})\end{array}$$

$$\left(\begin{array}{c}\text{S}' \\ (\uparrow\text{SCOMP})=\downarrow\end{array}\right)$$

(51)

$$_4\text{NP} \rightarrow \quad _4\left|\begin{array}{cc}\text{NP} & \text{PP} \\ (\uparrow\text{HEAD})=\downarrow & (\uparrow\text{HEAD})=(\downarrow\text{SUBJ}) \\ & \uparrow=\downarrow\end{array}\right.$$

A VP would have been hypothesized at position 3 in the string, and once the verb had been analyzed the partial VP constituent in (50) would have been obtained. This partial constituent would have caused an NP to be hypothesized at position 4: for example, (51) as well as (52) would have been hypothesized.

(52)

$$_4\text{NP} \rightarrow \quad _4\left|\begin{array}{ccc}(\text{DET}) & \text{ADJ*} & \text{N} \\ & \downarrow\in(\uparrow\text{MOD}) & \end{array}\right.$$

The simple NP $_4$*the dress*$_6$ would then have been analyzed. Since the NP, if attached into the partial VP constituent, would *not* be the final argument of the strongest lexical form of *position*, the Final Arguments principle would *not* apply. Instead, the default principle of Invoked Attachment would come into effect, giving the option for attaching the NP into the VP priority over the option for attaching it into the complex NP structure. The partial VP constituent represented in (53) would then be obtained.

(53)

$$_3\text{VP} \rightarrow \text{V} \quad \underset{(\uparrow\text{OBJ})=\downarrow}{\text{NP}} \quad {}_6\Bigg|\Bigg(\left\{\begin{array}{c} \text{NP} \\ (\uparrow\text{OBJ2})=\downarrow \\ \text{PP} \\ (\uparrow\text{PCOMP})=\downarrow \end{array}\right\}\Bigg) \quad \underset{(\uparrow(\downarrow\text{PCASE}))=\downarrow}{\text{PP*}} \quad \underset{\downarrow\in(\uparrow\text{ADJ})}{\text{PP*}}$$

$$\left(\begin{array}{c} \text{S}' \\ (\uparrow\text{SCOMP})=\downarrow \end{array}\right)$$

At position 6 in the string, then, a set of alternatives is reached in the expansion of the VP rule. Since the strongest lexical form of *position* takes a PCOMP, the Lexical Preference principle requires that the expansion of $\underset{(\uparrow\text{PCOMP})=\downarrow}{\text{PP}}$ be given priority over the alternatives. Thus, a PP Complement is hypothesized and the PP $_6$*on that rack*$_9$ is analyzed. If this PP were attached into the partial VP constituent represented in (53), it would be the final argument of the verb *position*. Thus, the Final Arguments principle comes into effect, delaying the PP's attachment into the VP in favor of other options that arise at position 9 in the string. However, none of these leads to a successful analysis since there are no more words in the string past position 9. The PP Complement would thus be attached under the VP node, yielding the structure (54).

(54)
[$_{\text{VP}}$ positioned [$_{\text{NP}}$ the dress] [$_{\text{PP}}$ on that rack]]

Eventually, the VP would be attached under the S node.

Accounting for the Closure Phenomena
We have seen that the Final Arguments principle will induce late closure of the final argument, but that what is taken as the final argument depends on the lexical form being considered. Let us now turn to the other contrasting pairs discussed above.

The Final Arguments principle can account for the preference to analyze (25a) as a relative clause structure, while the preferred analysis for (25b) is the complement structure.

(25)
a. $_1$The$_2$tourists$_3$objected$_4$to$_5$the$_6$guide$_7$that$_8$they$_9$couldn't$_{10}$hear$_{11}$.
b. $_1$The$_2$tourists$_3$signaled$_4$to$_5$the$_6$guide$_7$that$_8$they$_9$couldn't$_{10}$hear$_{11}$.

Assuming that the strongest form of *object* in a neutral context is *object* $\langle(\text{SUBJ}),(\text{TO OBJ})\rangle$, then the PP $_4$*to the guide*$_7$ in (25a) would be the final argument if it were attached into the partial VP constituent represented in (55). (The PCASE schema represents the fact that the PP can be a Prepositional Object. This PP possibility is thus coherent with the strongest lexical form of *object*, *object* ⟨(SUBJ),(TO OBJ)⟩. For a discussion of the PCASE schema, see chapter 4 of this volume.)

(55)

$$_3\text{VP} \rightarrow \text{V } e \ e \ _4\Bigg| \quad \underset{(\uparrow(\downarrow\text{PCASE}))=\downarrow}{\text{PP*}} \quad \underset{\downarrow\in(\uparrow\text{ADJ})}{\text{PP*}} \quad \left(\underset{(\uparrow\text{SCOMP})=\downarrow}{\text{S'}} \right)$$

The first *e* in (55) indicates that the alternative to the Object NP has been taken, while the second *e* indicates that the alternative to the PP Complement and the second Object NP has also been taken. Since the PP ₄*to the guide*₇ would be the final argument if it were attached into the partial VP constituent (55), the Final Arguments principle applies, giving low priority to the attachment of the PP into the VP. The option that is favored and therefore taken is the one that attaches the simple NP ₅*the guide*₇ as head of a partial complex NP constituent such as (56). (Again, the NP rule is simplified for expository purposes only.)

(56)

$$_5\text{NP} \rightarrow \ _5\Bigg| \quad \underset{(\uparrow\text{HEAD})=\downarrow}{\text{NP}} \quad \underset{\substack{(\uparrow\text{HEAD})=\Downarrow_{\text{NP}} \\ \uparrow=\downarrow}}{\text{S'}}$$

The NP ₅*the guide*₇ is attached under a complex NP node. As a result, a relative S' is hypothesized, and the relative clause ₇*that they couldn't hear*₁₁ is analyzed. The relative clause is attached as a sister to ₅*the guide*₇, completing the complex NP. This complex NP is then attached as the object of the preposition *to*, forming the PP ₄*to the guide that they couldn't hear*₁₁. This PP, if attached to the partial VP represented in (55), would be the final argument of the verb *object*. The attachment is therefore delayed by the Final Arguments principle, but none of the other options that arise at position 11 would lead to a successful analysis and so the PP would be attached to the VP. Eventually, the VP would be attached under the S node.

In contrast to sentence (25a), in sentence (25b) the Final Arguments principle would not delay the VP attachment of the PP ₄*to the guide*₇, since the PP would not be the final argument of the strongest lexical form of *signal*, which we assume to be *signal* ⟨(SUBJ),(TO OBJ),(SCOMP)⟩. The PP is therefore attached into a partial VP constituent like the one represented in (55). The attachment of the PP into this partial VP eventually leads to a Complement S' being proposed, and the Complement *that they couldn't hear* is then analyzed. This Complement, when attached into the VP, would be the final argument of the strongest form of *signal*. Its attachment is therefore delayed, but none of the options that are given priority would lead to a successful analysis. Thus, the Complement is attached into the VP and the VP is closed and attached under the S node.

It should be clear now how the analysis proceeds for the other contrasting pairs. We assume that the stronger form for *include* is *include* ⟨(SUBJ),(OBJ)⟩ and that the stronger form for *carry* is the benefactive *carry-for* ⟨(SUBJ),(OBJ),(FOR OBJ)⟩. Thus, in (26a), the VP attachment of the Object NP *the package* is delayed. It is attached under a complex NP node and the PP *for Susan* is attached as a sister to this simple NP. The complex NP is then attached into the VP. In (26b), on the other hand, the attachment of the Object NP *the package* into the VP is not delayed. It is attached into the VP by the default principle of Invoked Attachment. A Prepositional Object is then hypothesized and is eventually attached under the VP node.

(26)

a.   Joe included the package for Susan.

b.   Joe carried the package for Susan.

The closure phenomenon observed in (9) and (10) is accounted for in an equally straightforward way, if the lexical form *discuss-with* ⟨(SUBJ), (OBJ),(WITH OBJ)⟩ is stronger than the form *discuss* ⟨(SUBJ),(OBJ)⟩ and if the form *keep* ⟨(SUBJ),(OBJ),(PCOMP)⟩ is stronger than the form *keep* ⟨(SUBJ),(OBJ)⟩.

(9)

The women kept the dogs on the beach.

(10)

The women discussed the dogs with the policeman.

Examples (9) and (10) are analogous to (24b), (25b), and (26b), in that the VP attachment of the final argument of the strongest lexical form of the verb would be delayed, but later executed, since none of the options that are given priority would lead to a successful analysis.

Sentence (5) further illustrates the effects of the principle of Final Arguments. In contrast to the sentences already discussed, the effect of the Final Arguments principle does not interact with the Lexical Preference principle in this sentence.

(5)

$_1$Tom$_2$disputed$_3$Bill's$_4$dying$_5$at$_6$work$_7$.

The Final Arguments principle explains the preference to associate the PP *at work* with the lower verb *dying*. Once the verb *dying* has been analyzed, the partial VP constituent represented in (57) is obtained.

(57)

$$_4\text{VP} \rightarrow \text{V} \ _5\left|\begin{pmatrix} \text{NP} \\ (\uparrow\text{OBJ})=\downarrow \end{pmatrix}\right. \left(\left\{\begin{matrix} \text{NP} \\ (\uparrow\text{OBJ2})=\downarrow \\ \text{PP} \\ (\uparrow\text{PCOMP})=\downarrow \end{matrix}\right\}\right) \quad \begin{matrix} \text{PP*} \\ (\uparrow(\downarrow\text{PCASE}))=\downarrow \end{matrix} \quad \begin{matrix} \text{PP*} \\ \downarrow\in(\uparrow\text{ADJ}) \end{matrix}$$
$$\left(\begin{matrix} \text{S}' \\ (\uparrow\text{SCOMP})=\downarrow \end{matrix}\right)$$

Eventually, the partial constituent represented in (58) is obtained because the verb *dying* is not followed by an NP and does not take a Complement or a Prepositional Object. Note that each *e* extends from the position after the verb *dying* (that is, from position 5) to the position before the next word (that is, to position 5), but each *e* represents the alternative to a different category or set of categories.

(58)

$$_4\text{VP} \rightarrow \text{V} \ e \ e \ e \ _5\left| \begin{matrix} \text{PP*} \\ \downarrow\in(\uparrow\text{ADJ}) \end{matrix} \right. \left(\begin{matrix} \text{S}' \\ (\uparrow\text{SCOMP})=\downarrow \end{matrix}\right)$$

At this point in the analysis, a set of alternatives has been reached, namely, $\begin{smallmatrix} \text{PP*} \\ \downarrow\in(\uparrow\text{ADJ}) \end{smallmatrix}$ and *e*. Since the alternatives are not coherent with the strongest lexical form of *dying*, *dying* $\langle(\text{SUBJ})\rangle$, the Lexical Preference principle does not apply. The default principle of Syntactic Preference comes into effect, giving priority to the *e* hypothesis, since *e* is ranked higher than Prepositional Phrases (= P″) by either category or frequency level—it has no primes and is traversed every time an option in a rule is not taken or is not present in a string. Eventually, $_5e_5$ is found as an alternative to a PP Adjunct. But because $_5e_5$ is subsequent to the final argument of *dying*, the Final Arguments principle defers its attachment to the VP in favor of the other options that arise at its end position, that is, position 5. The hypothesis of a Prepositional Phrase at

5 therefore prevails. The PP ₅*at work*₇ can now be attached. There is
only one option for its attachment. It cannot be attached as a modifier
of *disputed,* because at this point the partial VP for *disputed* has been
analyzed only to position 3 and requires either an NP or *e* at 3. The PP
must be attached into the partial constituent represented in (58) as a
modifier of *dying.* Eventually, this lower VP is attached into a complex
NP, yielding [NP *Bill's dying at work*]. This NP is then attached into the
higher VP as a modifier of *disputed.* Eventually, the complex VP is
attached under the S node.

Thus, the preference will be to close the lower VP late. If the
modifier is rejected as incompatible with the lower verb, reanalysis will
take place. In an example like (21), the PP *on many occasions* is incompatible with *killing his very old father.*

(21)
Although the women talked about John's killing his very old father on
many occasions they repressed how much they disliked the old man.

Reanalysis proceeds by taking the previously deferred option to attach
e rather than the PP to the VP. The eventual result of this reanalysis is
to close the lower VP and attach the PP into the higher VP as a modifier
of *talked about.* This attachment results from the normal completion of
the recursive top-down analysis procedure, whereby the partial constituents hypothesized in order from the top down are completed in the
reverse order. Example (20) is another illustration of the effect of the
Final Arguments principle and reanalysis of an element.

(20)
Although an astronaut lectured on many renowned Russian space expeditions at our school the students weren't interested.

Notice that the bias for the simple sentence interpretation in (3) is
also explained simply.

(3)
The girl pushed through the door laughed.

In a rule-driven analysis, the partial S constituent (59) would be hypothesized at the outset of the sentence.

(59)

₁S → ₁| NP   VP
        (↑SUBJ)=↓

Since this partial constituent requires an NP at 1, partial NP constituents such as (60) and (61) would be hypothesized.

(60)

$_1$NP → $_1|$(DET)   ADJ*   N
$\quad\quad\quad\quad\quad\downarrow\in(\uparrow\text{MOD})$

(61)

$_1$NP → $_1|$ NP   VP
$\quad\quad\quad\quad(\uparrow\text{HEAD})=\downarrow$ $(\uparrow\text{HEAD})=(\downarrow\text{SUBJ})$
$\quad\quad\quad\quad\quad\quad\quad\quad\quad\uparrow=\downarrow$

A determiner and noun would then be found and an NP *the girl* would be analyzed. This NP must now be attached to something. There are two options for doing this. One is to attach the NP as Subject in the partial S constituent represented in (59), leading to the simple sentence interpretation. The other is to attach it as head of the partial complex NP constituent represented in (61). Since the NP would not be a final argument in either partial constituent, the Final Arguments principle would not come into effect. Instead, the default principle of Invoked Attachment applies, giving priority to the S attachment since it was this partial S constituent that caused an NP to be hypothesized. The simple NP $_1$*the girl*$_3$ is thus attached immediately under the S node as Subject.

Lexical Reanalysis and Garden Paths
In contrast to examples (24)–(26) and (9)–(10), the correct analysis for some sentences requires that a stronger lexical form be rejected in favor of a weaker form. This occurs when the weaker form is needed in order to satisfy the functional compatibility requirements of the grammar. Our theory of how lexical forms of verbs govern syntactic closure extends naturally to account for these cases.

An example of a sentence for which lexical reanalysis is required is (62), which is unambiguously a relative.

(62)
The tourists signaled to the guide that they didn't like.

In sentence (62), the strongest form of *signal, signal*⟨(SUBJ),(TO OBJ), (SCOMP)⟩, is inappropriate and must be rejected in favor of the weaker form, *signal*⟨(SUBJ),(TO OBJ)⟩. Our theory predicts that sentence (62) would be relatively easy to analyze, although there would be slight difficulty and a subsequent reanalysis of part of the sentence when the last word is encountered. Since the verb *like* must have an Object, the Complement analysis would fail. Thus, the Complement S' would not be closed and a complete functional structure for it would not be recovered. The parser would have to reconsider options that were not initially taken because alternative options were given higher priority. Thus, the parser would now take the option for attaching the simple NP $_5$*the guide*$_7$ into a partial complex NP constituent such as (63).

(63)

$$_5\text{NP} \rightarrow \ _5| \quad \underset{(\uparrow\text{HEAD})=\downarrow}{\text{NP}} \qquad \underset{\underset{\uparrow=\downarrow}{(\uparrow\text{HEAD})=\Downarrow_{\text{NP}}}}{\text{S}'}$$

A relative S' would then be hypothesized. The analysis of the relative clause is facilitated by the fact that all of its constituents except the relativized constituent (the "gap") have already been analyzed. Once the relative clause is analyzed, it is attached as a sister to the simple NP $_5$*the guide*$_7$, yielding a complex NP. This complex NP is now attached as a sister to the preposition *to,* forming a PP. This PP would then be attached into the VP and the VP would be attached under the S node. Because only a Subject and To Object have been found, the strongest lexical form of *signal, signal*⟨(SUBJ),(TO OBJ),(SCOMP)⟩, cannot be satisfied and the weaker lexical form, *signal*⟨(SUBJ),(TO OBJ)⟩, replaces it in the functional structure.

Lexical reanalysis might also take place when contextual factors favor one lexical form over another. In sentence (30a), for example, the context disfavors the stronger form of *carry,* the 3-place benefactive predicate "NP$_1$ carry NP$_2$ for NP$_3$," and favors the 2-place predicate "NP$_1$ carry NP$_2$."

(30)

a. When he arrived at our doorstep, I could see that Joe carried a package for Susan.

It is possible that the strongest lexical form of *carry* is rejected immediately on being retrieved from the lexicon (cf. Swinney 1979). However, the reaction time study of Holmes 1981 suggests that it may not be rejected until the functional structure with this form is constructed and then judged as implausible. A theory of sentence perception must explain both qualitative data arising from speakers' judgments and quantitative data derived from psycholinguistic experiments. In our future research, we plan to obtain measures of parsing complexity within sentences to test and develop our theory. But for a detailed interpretation of quantitative data, an explicit model of the processing sequences is required. Although the present study is based entirely on qualitative data, the computational interpretation given in appendix B lays the groundwork for future experimental investigations of the precise processes involved in sentence perception.

Since the parser is capable in principle of recovering all possible functional structures of a sentence, the question is raised of how garden paths that are difficult to recover from are explained. It is usually extremely difficult for people to find an acceptable analysis for the type of sentence we are referring to, even when they are assured that there is one. We propose a very simple hypothesis: once a functional structure for a complete constituent has been recovered, it is very difficult to give a new morphosyntactic analysis of a word within it. In sentence (3), for example, a functional structure for the simple sentence *The girl pushed through the door* is recovered based on the categorization of the verb *pushed* as an active intransitive tensed verb. In order to recover the required analysis, the verb would have to be recategorized as a passive participle based on the active transitive form of the verb. Since the initial categorization was successful in recovering the functional structure of a complete constituent, it may be difficult to recategorize the verb morphosyntactically. This hypothesis predicts correctly that sentence (64) would also be difficult to analyze successfully.

(64)
The boy got fat melted.

Initially, a complete and coherent functional structure for the simple sentence *The boy got fat* (i.e. *The boy became fat*) would be recovered. This functional structure is based on the categorization of *fat* as an adjective. However, in order to analyze the entire sentence to include the word *melted, fat* would have to be recategorized as a noun (i.e. *The boy got it (the fat) melted*). (Note that the Canonical Sentoid Strategy (section 11.2) does not explain this example.) In many cases where recategorization of a word within a completed functional structure is necessary, reassignment of one or more arguments is also required. This is true for both (3) and (64). The extent to which new assignments are required may also influence the difficulty of reanalysis.

Nondeterministic parsers have been criticized on the grounds that conscious garden paths are not experienced whenever backing up for reanalysis is required (Rich 1975, Marcus 1980). But it seems erroneous to assume that reanalysis of phrasal structure during backup must always cause conscious garden paths. As we have suggested, different types of reanalysis can occur. Reanalysis of phrasal structure without the need to recategorize a word may increase the complexity of local parsing decisions as measured by reaction times, but without the perception of a garden path (see Wanner, Kaplan, and Shiner 1975), while reanalysis which requires a new morphosyntactic analysis of a word within the functional structure of a completed constituent may cause a conscious garden path.

11.4 Consequences of the Theory

We have seen how our theory accounts for the full range of closure phenomena introduced in sections 11.1 and 11.2. In this section we demonstrate the explanatory power of our theory by showing that it leads to a number of surprising and interesting predictions in sentences more complex than those already discussed.

Late Closure Prevails in Complex Ambiguous Sentences

We have already seen that in simple sentences, a constituent that could be analyzed as an argument of the strongest lexical form of a verb *is* so analyzed. This is the case in sentence (65), for example.

(65)
Sue discussed her daughter's difficulties with the teachers.

In the preferred analysis of (65), *Sue* is analyzed as a Subject, *her daughter's difficulties* is analyzed as an Object, and *with the teachers* is analyzed as a With Object. Thus, the strongest lexical form of the verb, *discuss* ⟨(SUBJ),(OBJ),(WITH OBJ)⟩, is satisfied.

However, the theory predicts a different result for complex sentences where one VP is embedded in another. The theory predicts that a constituent following the final argument of the lower verb will be associated to the right, even though it could be analyzed as an argument of the strongest lexical form of the verb in the higher clause. Sentence (66) confirms this prediction.

(66)
$_1$Sue$_2$discussed$_3$the$_4$difficulties$_5$that$_6$her$_7$daughter$_8$was$_9$having$_{10}$with $_{11}$the$_{12}$teachers$_{13}$.

In sentence (66), the PP $_{10}$*with the teachers*$_{13}$ could be attached with the verb *discussed* or with the lower verb *having*. In the preferred analysis, it is associated with *having*, even though this eventually results in the strongest lexical form of *discuss* being rejected in favor of the weaker form *discuss*$\langle$(SUBJ),(OBJ)$\rangle$. Our theory predicts this preference. Once the gap in the relative has been found (*the difficulties that her daughter was having _____ with the teachers*), the NP denoting the gap (NP $\rightarrow$ e) could be attached as Object into the lower VP. However, it would be the final argument of the strongest lexical form of *have*, *have*$\langle$(SUBJ), (OBJ)$\rangle$. The Final Arguments principle therefore comes into effect, delaying the attachment of the NP into the VP. However, no other option will be successful since a gap NP cannot be modified, and so the NP is attached as Object into the VP, yielding the partial constituent represented in (67).

(67)

$$_8\text{VP} \rightarrow \text{AUX} \quad \text{V} \quad \underset{(\uparrow\text{OBJ})=\downarrow}{\text{NP}} \quad _{10}\left|\left(\left\{\begin{array}{c}\text{NP} \\ (\uparrow\text{OBJ2})=\downarrow \\ \text{PP} \\ (\uparrow\text{PCOMP})=\downarrow\end{array}\right\}\right)\right. \quad \underset{(\uparrow(\downarrow\text{PCASE}))=\downarrow}{\text{PP*}}$$

$$\underset{\downarrow\in(\uparrow\text{ADJ})}{\text{PP*}} \quad \left(\underset{(\uparrow\text{SCOMP})=\downarrow}{\text{S'}}\right)$$

A set of alternatives has now been reached in the expansion of the VP, namely, $\underset{(\uparrow\text{OBJ2})=\downarrow}{\text{NP}}$, $\underset{(\uparrow\text{PCOMP})=\downarrow}{\text{PP}}$, and e. Since none of the alternatives is coherent with the strongest lexical form of *have*, the Lexical Preference principle does not apply. Instead, the default principle of Syntactic Preference comes into effect, giving priority to the hypothesis e. An e is thus hypothesized. Subsequently, an e is analyzed, extending from the end of the NP gap (that is, from position 10) to the beginning of the next word (that is, to position 10). However, the alternative e is subsequent to the final argument of the verb *have*. Therefore, the Final Arguments principle comes into effect and defers the attachment of $_{10}e_{10}$ to the VP. The parser would then have to backtrack to options that arose at position 10 but were not taken. The option for hypothesizing $\underset{(\uparrow\text{OBJ2})=\downarrow}{\text{NP}}$ cannot lead to a successful analysis for sentence (66). The option for hypothesizing $\underset{(\uparrow\text{PCOMP})=\downarrow}{\text{PP}}$ would lead to the analysis of the PP *with the teachers*. However, *have* does not take a Prepositional

Complement. Thus, the option that was delayed by the Final Arguments principle would have to apply and $_{10}e_{10}$ would therefore be attached into the VP, yielding the partial VP constituent represented in (68).

(68)

$$_8\text{VP} \rightarrow \text{AUX} \quad \text{V} \quad \text{NP} \quad e \quad _{10}\Big| \quad \text{PP*} \qquad \text{PP*}$$
$$(\uparrow\text{OBJ})=\downarrow \qquad (\uparrow(\downarrow\text{PCASE}))=\downarrow \quad \downarrow\in(\uparrow\text{ADJ})$$
$$\begin{pmatrix} \text{S}' \\ (\uparrow\text{SCOMP})=\downarrow \end{pmatrix}$$

A new set of alternatives has now been reached in the VP rule, namely, $\dfrac{\text{PP}}{(\uparrow(\downarrow\text{PCASE}))=\downarrow}$ and e. Neither of the alternatives is coherent with the strongest lexical form of *have, have*⟨(SUBJ),(OBJ)⟩. Therefore, the principle of Lexical Preference does not apply. The default principle of Syntactic Preference comes into effect, giving priority to the hypothesis e over the alternative hypothesis PP. Again, an e extending from position 10 to position 10 will be analyzed, although this one is now taken as an alternative to $\dfrac{\text{PP}}{(\uparrow(\downarrow\text{PCASE}))=\downarrow}$. Once again, however, the principle of Final Arguments will come into effect because the e is subsequent to the final argument of the strongest lexical form of *have*. The VP attachment of $_{10}e_{10}$ as the alternative to $\dfrac{\text{PP}}{(\uparrow(\downarrow\text{PCASE}))=\downarrow}$ is therefore delayed in favor of options that arose at position 10. The PP hypothesis is thus favored. The PP *with the teachers* was analyzed previously as a possible Prepositional Complement but was rejected as a Complement of *have*. It is now attached into the lower VP, yielding [$_{VP}$ *was having ____ with the teachers*]. The PP is given the function of Prepositional Object and the strongest lexical form of *have, have*⟨(SUBJ),(OBJ)⟩, is rejected in favor of the weaker form *have*⟨(SUBJ), (OBJ),(WITH OBJ)⟩. The inclusion of the PP in the lower VP eventually leads to the rejection of the stronger form of *discuss, discuss*⟨(SUBJ), (OBJ),(WITH OBJ)⟩, in favor of the weaker form, *discuss*⟨(SUBJ),(OBJ)⟩.

Sentence (69) is another example in which late closure is preferred over early closure.

(69)
Joe carried the package that I included for Susan.

In the preferred analysis of (69), the PP *for Susan* is attached into the lower VP (*I included it (the package) for Susan*), even though this eventually results in the strongest lexical form of *carry, carry-for* ⟨(SUBJ),(OBJ),(FOR OBJ)⟩, being rejected in favor of the weaker form, *carry*⟨(SUBJ),(OBJ)⟩. Notice, too, that the strongest lexical form of *include, include*⟨(SUBJ),(OBJ)⟩, is rejected in favor of the weaker form, *include*⟨(SUBJ),(OBJ),(FOR OBJ)⟩, just as the stronger form of *have* is rejected in favor of the weaker form in sentence (66).

The question now arises, Exactly under what conditions can a stronger lexical form be rejected in favor of a weaker one? We have already seen that an unambiguous or contextually biased sentence can force the rejection of a stronger form in favor of a weaker one. But sentences (66) and (69) are ambiguous sentences and do not appear to be contextually biased one way or the other. In these sentences, the strongest form of *have* (for (66)) or *include* (for (69)) could have been incorporated into a well-formed analysis. Yet the strongest form is rejected after the application of the Final Arguments principle. Why could the strongest form be rejected in these cases? We tentatively hypothesize that only when the meaning of the weaker lexical form semantically includes (that is, entails) that of the stronger form can the weaker form override the stronger form in order to include another argument found through the application of the Final Arguments principle. Notice that *I included it for Susan* entails *I included it* and *Her daughter was having difficulties with the teachers* entails *Her daughter was having difficulties*. In contrast to the alternative lexical forms for *include* and *have*, the weaker lexical form of *want, want*⟨(SUBJ), (OBJ),(PCOMP)⟩, does *not* entail the stronger form ⟨(SUBJ),(OBJ)⟩. Note, for example, that *I wanted it on that rack* does not entail *I wanted it*. We would therefore predict that in an ambiguous sentence where a potential third argument of *want* is found through the application of the Final Arguments principle, the stronger form would not be rejected and early closure would result. Sentence (70) confirms this prediction.

(70)
The woman positioned the dress that I wanted on that rack.

In the preferred analysis of (70), the PP *on that rack* is attached as a Complement of the higher verb *positioned*. Sentence (71), given by Wales and Toner 1979, also bears out the prediction.

(71)
He seemed nice to her.

In the preferred analysis of (71) (see Wales and Toner and appendix A), the PP *to her* is attached as a To Object of the higher verb *seemed,* yielding the interpretation *He seemed to her to be a nice person,* although it could be attached to the adjective *nice,* yielding the interpretation *He seemed nice toward her.* The monadic form of *nice, nice⟨(SUBJ)⟩,* is *not* entailed by the dyadic form, *nice⟨(SUBJ),(TO OBJ)⟩;* note that *He is nice to her* does not entail that *He is nice.* We would therefore expect that the monadic form would not be overridden by the dyadic form. It does appear to be correct that the Final Arguments principle can force the rejection of the stronger lexical form in favor of a weaker form only when the weaker form bears a sufficiently close semantic relation to the stronger form.

Late Closure Occurs in Complex Unambiguous Sentences

A phenomenon that might seem rather puzzling has been noted by Fodor and Frazier 1980. Sentence (72), given by Fodor and Frazier, is unambiguous and has a perfectly acceptable analysis. However, on initial perception, it appears to be incomplete.

(72)
John put the book that Mary had been reading in the study.

Another instance of this phenomenon is given in (73).

(73)
The coach acquainted the athlete that we had seen with the teachers.

The verb *put* must take a PP. However, in (72), the PP *in the study* is initially associated with the lower VP (*Mary had been reading it (the book) in the study*). Similarly, in (73), the verb *acquainted* must take a With Object. However, the PP *with the teachers* is initially associated with the lower VP. The phenomenon is not puzzling—it is predicted by our theory of syntactic closure, since the principle of Final Arguments initially forces material into the lower VP, as shown in the preceding discussion of late closure in complex ambiguous sentences such as (66) and (69).

The Relative Complexity of Syntactic Binding Is a Function of the Strengths of the Lexical Forms of a Verb

It might be thought that the theory of syntactic closure is totally unrelated to locating gaps in sentences. Certainly, Frazier and Fodor 1978 treat syntactic closure independently from gap finding. However, the advantage of a competence-based performance theory is that it provides a coherent and unified approach to different phenomena: the one performance theory will make predictions throughout the grammar. Our theory of syntactic closure does have consequences for syntactic binding.

Fodor 1978 has noted that the difficulty of analyzing sentences containing a gap is a function of the strength of the different lexical forms of a verb. As Fodor observes, sentence (74), which requires the transitive form of *walk,* seems more difficult to analyze than sentence (75), which requires the intransitive form of the verb.

(74)
Which student$_i$ did the teacher walk ____$_i$ to the cafeteria?

(75)
Which student$_i$ did the teacher walk to the cafeteria with ____$_i$?

The verb *send* can be contrasted with the verb *walk*. Unlike *walk, send* usually takes a direct Object, although it can occur without one. Thus, sentence (76) seems easier to analyze than sentence (77).

(76)
Which student$_i$ did the teacher send ____$_i$ to the cafeteria?

(77)
Which student$_i$ did the teacher send to the cafeteria for ____$_i$?

Fodor observes that the data suggest that the parser expects to find certain constituents after a verb, depending on the constituents that the verb usually takes. So, for example, although the verb *walk* can take a direct Object, as in (74), it usually occurs without one, as in (75), and thus sentence (75) is easier to analyze than (74).

It is a consequence of our theory of syntactic closure that the relative complexity of syntactic binding is a function of the strength of lexical forms of a verb. Let us consider sentences (74) and (75). We assume, with Fodor, that the transitive form of *walk, walk*⟨(SUBJ),(OBJ), (TO OBJ)⟩, is weaker than the intransitive form *walk*⟨(SUBJ),(TO OBJ)⟩. After the verb *walk* in (74) and (75), a set of alternatives would be reached in the expansion of the VP, namely, $\underset{(\uparrow\text{OBJ})=\downarrow}{\text{NP}}$ and e. Since neither of these alternatives is coherent with the strongest lexical form of *walk, walk* $\langle(\text{SUBJ}),(\text{TO OBJ})\rangle$, the Lexical Preference principle does not apply. The default principle of Syntactic Preference comes into effect, giving priority to the e hypothesis, that there is not an Object NP. Hence, the parser would not analyze a gap (NP $\rightarrow e$), but would go on to the next set of alternatives in the expansion of the VP, namely, $\underset{(\uparrow\text{OBJ2})=\downarrow}{\text{NP}}$ $\underset{(\uparrow\text{PCOMP})=\downarrow}{\text{PP}}$, and e. This is a mistake for sentence (74), which does have a gap after *walk*. The need to recover from this error would increase the difficulty of processing this sentence, making it harder to analyze than sentence (75), which takes the strongest form of *walk*. In contrast to sentences (74) and (75), when the alternatives $\underset{(\uparrow\text{OBJ})=\downarrow}{\text{NP}}$ and e are reached in the expansion of the VP rule in sentences (76) and (77), the Lexical Preference principle would give priority to the $\underset{(\uparrow\text{OBJ})=\downarrow}{\text{NP}}$ since it is coherent with the strongest lexical form of *send, send* $\langle(\text{SUBJ}),(\text{OBJ}),(\text{TO OBJ})\rangle$. Partial NP constituents, including (78), would be hypothesized.

(78)

$$_7\text{NP} \rightarrow {}_7\Big|\quad e$$
$$\uparrow = \Uparrow_{\text{NP}}$$

A gap is therefore analyzed at position 7 in the sentences, making (77) more difficult to process than (76).

While the relative complexity of syntactic binding as a function of the strengths of lexical forms is a consequence of our theory of syntactic closure, it is unexplained by the Sausage Machine model. In the Sausage Machine model, closure effects are attributed to the architecture of the parser—the two stages and the narrow viewing window—which we have already seen to be inadequate, and Fodor's earlier insight is not drawn upon.

Locating Gaps in Ambiguous Sentences Is a Function of Lexical Preference

A further consequence of our theory of syntactic closure is that in ambiguous sentences where there is more than one possible location for a gap, the perceived location of the gap will depend on the strengths of the different lexical forms of a verb. Sentences (79) and (80) illustrate and confirm this prediction.

(79)
Those are the boys the police warned about fighting.

(80)
Those are the boys the police debated about fighting.

Sentences (79) and (80) are ambiguous between the analysis where a gap is located after the verb *warned* or *debated,* giving the interpretation *the police warned/debated THE BOYS about fighting,* and the analysis where the gap is located after *fighting,* yielding the interpretation *the police warned/debated about fighting THE BOYS.* While the preferred analysis for (79) is (81), the preferred analysis for (80) is (82).

(81)
Those are *the boys$_i$* the police warned ____$_i$ about fighting.

(82)
Those are *the boys$_i$* the police debated about fighting ____$_i$.

It immediately follows from our theory that in ambiguous sentences where there is more than one possible location for the gap, its perceived location will vary depending on the verb: that is, there will not be a consistent preference for one location across all verbs. For example, assuming that the lexical form *warn* ⟨(SUBJ),(OBJ),(ABOUT OBJ)⟩ is stronger than the form *warn* ⟨(SUBJ),(ABOUT OBJ)⟩, an NP will be hypothesized after *warned* and the possible gap there will be located. However, assuming that the lexical form *debate* ⟨(SUBJ),(ABOUT OBJ)⟩ is stronger than the form *debate* ⟨(SUBJ),(OBJ),(ABOUT OBJ)⟩, an NP will not be hypothesized after *debated* and the possible gap there will not be recognized.

11.5 Implications for Lexical Representation

The enormous complexity of syntactic closure phenomena could easily have led to the view that no simple theory could explain them. But the results of our study suggest that the complexity arises from the interactions of simple and independently constrained systems: first, a system of linguistically motivated syntactic rules and lexical representations, and second, a computationally simple system of memory structures and processes.

Our main goal here has been to construct and motivate a competence-based theory of syntactic closure which directly incorporates lexical-functional grammars as representations of linguistic knowledge. We have argued in general that a competence-based theory of sentence perception is simpler, stronger, and more explanatory than other approaches, in that it offers a coherent and unified approach to different phenomena. Thus, our theory of syntactic closure accounts for a variety of seemingly unrelated phenomena that had been observed in the literature—such as the lexical-expectation effect in gap-finding (Fodor 1978), garden paths (Bever 1970), "Minimal Attachment" (Frazier and Fodor 1978, Wanner 1980), and "Right Association" (Kimball 1973, Wanner 1980).

But a competence-based theory of sentence perception has the further advantage of opening new sources of evidence bearing on the nature of linguistic representation. Thus, we can now ask what properties of linguistic representation are implied by our performance theory. In particular, let us consider which properties of lexical representation are implied by the principles of lexically induced syntactic closure.

In lexical-functional theory, each lexical form of a lexical item specifies a functional context that must be satisfied in order to produce a well-formed sentence when the lexical item is inserted into a surface structure (see chapters 3 and 4 of this volume). In a simple sentence, an argument of the lexical form of a verb is satisfied by any surface category that has the function specified for that argument, regardless of the surface position of that category. Thus, with respect to the lexical form representation, the final argument of a verb is the argument that is the final *surface* argument in the sentence for that verb. The so-called "deep structure" order of constituents is not represented in the lexical form as it is in the strict subcategorization features of transformational theory.

The examples given in (83) show that the deep structure order of categories specified for a lexical item in transformational theory is *not* relevant to the Final Arguments principle.

(83)
a.   The teacher gave the boxes to the man in the office.
b.   The teacher gave to the man the boxes in the office.

In (83a) the To Object PP is the final argument of *give,* while in (83b) the direct Object NP is its final argument. In accordance with our theory of syntactic closure, there is a preference for late closure of the To Object PP in (83a) and for late closure of the direct Object NP in (83b). The deep structure order of the constituents, in which the direct Object NP precedes the To Object PP, is not important. Sentence (84) shows that it *is* grammatically possible for the direct Object NP in (83b) to be closed early, with the locative PP attaching upward.

(84)
The teacher gave to the man a word of wisdom in the office.

Next, recall that strict subcategorization features are *strictly local* in the deep structure constituent which they describe; thus, the subcategorization frame of a verb refers only to constituents of the VP that immediately dominates the verb. In contrast, lexical forms are local in the *functional structure* of the clause in which they appear (see again chapters 3 and 4). The functional structure of the verb, unlike a deep structure VP, includes the functional subject. Consequently, the lexical form representations predict that the final argument can be a subject (if it follows the other arguments in the sentence), but the strict subcategorization representations predict that the final argument cannot be a subject.

The examples given in (85) confirm the prediction of the lexical form representations.

(85)
a.　A library can be found in the barracks for the recruits.
b.　In the barracks can be found a library for the recruits.

For sentence (85a), there is a preference for late closure of the locative PP, while for (85b), where the locative PP is preposed and the subject is the final argument, it is the subject that closes late. Note that it is grammatically possible for the inverted subject to be closed early, with the following PP attaching upward.

(86)
In the barracks can be found a library, for the right people.

The examples in (87) also confirm the prediction of the lexical form representations.

(87)

a. The secretary placed the schedules in the packages for the participants.
b. In the packages were placed by the secretary the schedules for the participants.

For both (87a) and (87b) the preference is for late closure of the final argument of *placed*. The locative PP is closed late in (87a) and the subject is closed late in (87b). Sentence (88) shows that it *is* grammatically possible for the subject to close early, with the PP attaching upward.

(88)

In the packages were placed by the secretary the schedules, for the participants' sake.

Finally, while strict subcategorization features specify only "untransformed" structures, lexical forms can be created by lexical rules such as Passivization, *To* Dative, and *There* Insertion (see chapters 1, 2, and 3). Thus, the fact that the Final Arguments principle can apply to a passivized, inverted subject (as in (87b)) is just what the lexical form representations would lead us to predict. Similarly, the preference for late closure of the final arguments in each of the "transformed" structures in (89) is correctly predicted.

(89)

a. The gardener gave the bucket to the child near the shed.
b. The gardener gave the child the bucket near the shed.
c. The bucket was given by the gardener to the child near the shed.
d. The child was given by the gardener the bucket near the shed.
e. To the child was given by the gardener the bucket near the shed.
f. There was given to the child by the gardener a bucket near the shed.

Notice that in the favored readings of (89a) and (89c) the child is near the shed, while it is in the *disfavored* readings of the other examples that the child is near the shed. This difference exists even though the lexical content of all of the examples is virtually identical. Per-Kristian Halvorsen has observed that the sentences therefore provide evidence that syntactic bias effects cannot be explained solely in terms of contextual and semantic factors.

In conclusion, we see that our theory of syntactic closure requires a system of lexical representation in which the order of deep structure categories is not important, in which the subject is specified as an argument, and in which the arguments of "transformed" structures, including dative, passive, and *there*-insertion constructions, are lexically represented. All of these features of the lexical representations are independently motivated by the linguistic research in the theory of lexical forms in chapters 1–3. Thus, the choice of lexical forms over other lexical representations such as strict subcategorization features leads to a more explanatory theory of the mental representation of language.

Appendix A: Data for Subjects' Intuitions

11.A.1 Sentences Presented in the Text

In this section, each of the fully ambiguous sentences discussed in the study is given, together with possible interpretations for the sentence and the percentage of subjects preferring each interpretation.

Booklets containing the ambiguous sentences and their possible interpretations were given to the subjects, who were students and visitors at MIT and Harvard. The booklets were prepared so that any one booklet did not contain minimally contrasting sentences and so that there was an equal representation of sentences expected to show late closure and sentences expected to show early closure. The instructions given to the subjects were as follows:

In this study, we are attempting to see which meaning of different ambiguous sentences people get first. On every other page of the booklet you will be presented with an ambiguous sentence. You are to make up your mind which meaning of the sentence you got first (or which was the only one you got). Then, turn the page, where two possible interpretations for the sentence are given. Mark the one that matches the interpretation you got first. Repeat this procedure for all of the sentences. Don't dwell on possible interpretations. We want your first impression. So, as soon as you have one meaning for the sentence, turn the page and mark the interpretation that matches yours.

Twenty subjects responded to each sentence. Where indicated, one or two subjects did not give a preferred interpretation for a sentence. In this appendix, the interpretation resulting from late closure is given first wherever there is a choice between early and late closure. In the subjects' booklets, the ordering was random. The sentences have the same numbers that they are given in the body of the chapter.

(1)

Joe bought the book for Susan.

a.   Joe bought the book which was for Susan. (20%)

b.   Joe bought it (the book) for Susan. (80%)

(5)

Tom disputed Bill's dying at work.

a.   Tom disputed it (Bill's dying at work). (95%)

b.   Tom disputed it (Bill's dying) at work. (5%)

(7)

The women discussed the dogs on the beach.

a.   The women discussed the dogs which were on the beach. (90%)

b.   The women discussed them (the dogs) while on the beach. (10%)

(9)

The women kept the dogs on the beach.

a.   The women kept the dogs which were on the beach. (5%)

b.   The women kept them (the dogs) on the beach. (95%)

(10)

The women discussed the dogs with the policeman.

a.   The women discussed the dogs which were with the policeman.
     (0%)

b.   The women discussed them (the dogs) with the policeman. (100%)

(11)

Tom said that Bill had taken the cleaning out yesterday.

a.   That Bill had taken the cleaning out yesterday is what Tom said.
     (80%)

b.   Tom said it (that Bill had taken the cleaning out) yesterday. (20%)

(12)

Tom said Bill died yesterday.

a.   Bill died yesterday. (70%)

b.   Tom said it (that Bill died) yesterday. (30%)

(13)

Though Martha claimed that she will be the first woman president
yesterday she announced that she'd rather be an astronaut.

a.   Martha claimed it (that she will be the first woman president) yes-
     terday. (26%) $n=19$

b.   Yesterday she announced she'd rather be an astronaut. (74%)
     $n=19$

(14)

Joe took the book that I had wanted to include in my birthday gift for Susan.

a. I had wanted to include the book in my birthday gift to Susan. (80%)

b. I had wanted to include it (the book) for Susan. (20%)

(15)

Forgetting she shouldn't sometimes she ran.

a. Forgetting sometimes that she shouldn't she ran. (30%)

b. Forgetting she shouldn't she ran sometimes. (70%)

(16)

Joe included my gift for Susan.

a. Joe included my gift to Susan. (65%)

b. Joe included it (my gift) for Susan. (35%)

(20)

Although an astronaut lectured on many renowned Russian space expeditions at our school the students weren't interested.

a. At our school an astronaut lectured on many renowned Russian space expeditions. (80%)

b. An astronaut lectured somewhere, and the students at our school weren't interested. (20%)

(21)

Although the women talked about John's killing his very old father on many occasions they repressed how much they disliked the old man.

a. The women talked about it (John's killing his very old father) on many occasions. (70%)

b. On many occasions the women repressed how much they disliked the old man. (30%)

(22)

Joe arrived on the day that I had wanted to discuss my youngest daughter's difficulties with the teachers.

a. My youngest daughter's difficulties with the teachers were what I wanted to discuss. (30%)

b. I had wanted to discuss them (the difficulties) with the teachers. (70%)

(23)

Joe arrived on the day that I had wanted to discuss my youngest daughter's difficulties at the school.

a. My youngest daughter's difficulties at the school were what I wanted to discuss. (80%)

b. I had wanted to discuss them (the difficulties) at the school. (20%)

(24a)

The woman wanted the dress on that rack.

a. The woman wanted the dress which was on that rack. (90%)

b. The woman wanted it (the dress) on that rack. (10%)

(24b)

The woman positioned the dress on that rack.

a. The woman positioned the dress which was on that rack. (30%)

b. The woman positioned it (the dress) on that rack. (70%)

(25a)

The tourists objected to the guide that they couldn't hear.

a. The tourists objected to the guide who they couldn't hear. (55%)

b. The tourists objected to the guide about the fact that they couldn't hear. (45%)

(25b)

The tourists signaled to the guide that they couldn't hear.

a. The tourists signaled to the guide who they couldn't hear. (15%)

b. The tourists signaled to the guide the fact that they couldn't hear. (85%)

(26a)

Joe included the package for Susan.

a. Joe included the package which was for Susan. (65%)

b. Joe included it (the package) for Susan. (35%)

(26b)

Joe carried the package for Susan.

a. Joe carried the package which was for Susan. (10%)

b. Joe carried it (the package) for Susan. (90%)

(27a)

They wanted everything there.

a. They wanted everything which was there. (65%)

b. They wanted them (everything) there. (35%)

(27b)
They positioned everything there.
a.   They positioned everything which was there. (17%) $n=18$
b.   They positioned them (everything) there. (83%) $n=18$

(28a)
They objected to everyone that they couldn't hear.
a.   They objected to everyone who they couldn't hear. (55%)
b.   They objected to everyone about the fact that they couldn't hear.
     (45%)

(28b)
They signaled to everyone that they couldn't hear.
a.   They signaled to everyone who they couldn't hear. (10%)
b.   They signaled to everyone the fact that they couldn't hear. (90%)

(29a)
They included everything for them.
a.   They included everything which was for them. (65%)
b.   They included them (everything) for them. (35%)

(29b)
They carried everything for them.
a.   They carried everything which was for them. (30%)
b.   They carried them (everything) for them. (70%)

(30a)
When he arrived at our doorstep, I could see that Joe carried a package
for Susan.
a.   Joe carried a package which was for Susan. (75%)
b.   Joe carried it (a package) for Susan. (25%)

(30b)
Whenever she got tired, Joe carried a package for Susan.
a.   Joe carried a package which was for Susan. (5%)
b.   Joe carried it (a package) for Susan. (95%)

(32a)
The Boy Scout carried the package for his pet.
a.   The Boy Scout carried the package which was for his pet. (75%)
b.   The Boy Scout carried it (the package) for his pet. (25%)

(32b)

The Boy Scout carried the package for his aunt.

a.   The Boy Scout carried the package which was for his aunt. (10%)

b.   The Boy Scout carried it (the package) for his aunt. (90%)

(42)

We discussed running.

a.   We discussed the possibility of our running. (10%)

b.   We discussed the sport (running). (90%)

(65)

Sue discussed her daughter's difficulties with the teachers.

a.   Her daughter's difficulties with the teachers is what Sue discussed.
     (35%)

b.   Sue discussed them (the difficulties) with the teachers. (65%)

(66)

Sue discussed the difficulties that her daughter was having with the
teachers.

a.   Her daughter was having difficulties with the teachers. (60%)

b.   Sue discussed them (the difficulties) with the teachers. (40%)

(69)

Joe carried the package that I included for Susan.

a.   I included it (the package) for Susan. (70%)

b.   Joe carried it (the package) for Susan. (30%)

(70)

The woman positioned the dress that I wanted on that rack.

a.   I wanted it (the dress) on that rack. (25%)

b.   The woman positioned it (the dress) on that rack. (75%)

(71)

He seemed nice to her.

a.   He seemed nice towards her. (15%)

b.   He seemed to her to be a nice person. (85%)

(79)

Those are the boys the police warned about fighting.

a.   The police warned the boys about fighting. (89%) $n = 19$

b.   The police warned about fighting the boys. (11%) $n = 19$

(80)

Those are the boys the police debated about fighting.

a.   The police debated the boys about fighting. (45%)

b.   The police debated about fighting the boys. (55%)

(83a)

The teacher gave the boxes to the man in the office.

a.   The teacher gave the boxes to the man who was in the office. (100%)

b.   The teacher gave the boxes to the man, while they were in the office. (0%)

(83b)

The teacher gave to the man the boxes in the office.

a.   The teacher gave to the man the boxes which were in the office. (90%)

b.   The teacher gave to the man the boxes, while they were in the office. (10%)

(85a)

A library can be found in the barracks for the recruits.

a.   A library can be found in the barracks which are for the recruits. (60%)

b.   For the recruits, a library can be found in the barracks. (40%)

(85b)

In the barracks can be found a library for the recruits.

a.   In the barracks can be found a library which is for the recruits. (65%)

b.   For the recruits, a library can be found in the barracks. (35%)

(87a)

The secretary placed the schedules in the packages for the participants.

a.   The secretary placed the schedules in the packages which were for the participants. (60%)

b.   The secretary placed the schedules there (in the packages) for the participants. (40%)

(87b)

In the packages were placed by the secretary the schedules for the participants.

a.   In the packages were placed by the secretary the schedules which were for the participants. (100%)

b.   In the packages were placed by the secretary the schedules, for the participants' behalf. (0%)

(89a)

The gardener gave the bucket to the child near the shed.

a.   The gardener gave the bucket to the child who was near the shed. (80%)

b.   The gardener gave the bucket to the child, while they were near the shed. (20%)

(89b)

The gardener gave the child the bucket near the shed.

a.   The gardener gave the child the bucket which was near the shed. (75%)

b.   The gardener gave the child the bucket, while they were near the shed. (25%)

(89c)

The bucket was given by the gardener to the child near the shed.

a.   The bucket was given by the gardener to the child who was near the shed. (85%)

b.   The bucket was given by the gardener to the child, while they were near the shed. (15%)

(89d)

The child was given by the gardener the bucket near the shed.

a.   The child was given by the gardener the bucket which was near the shed. (95%)

b.   The child was given by the gardener the bucket, while they were near the shed. (5%)

(89e)

To the child was given by the gardener the bucket near the shed.

a.   To the child was given by the gardener the bucket which was near the shed. (100%) $n = 19$

b.   To the child was given by the gardener the bucket, while they were near the shed. (0%) $n = 19$

(89f)

There was given to the child by the gardener a bucket near the shed.

a. There was given to the child by the gardener a bucket which was near the shed. (85%)

b. There was given to the child by the gardener a bucket, while they were near the shed. (15%)

11.A.2 More Sentences

In the body of this chapter, we did not discuss all of the sentences for which we gathered data. Most of the sentences we did not present were similar to those in the text and showed the same effects. However, some sentences for which we collected data do require comment.

For sentences (90)–(92), the adverb can be associated with the higher or the lower VP. No consistent preference among subjects was found for either of the alternatives, as the data here show.

(90)

The men discussed John's killing himself last night.

a. John killed himself last night. (50%)

b. The men discussed it (John's killing himself) last night. (50%)

(91)

Tom discussed Bill's dying yesterday.

a. Bill died yesterday. (50%)

b. Tom discussed it (Bill's dying) yesterday. (50%)

(92)

The teachers discussed our selling the drugs yesterday.

a. The teachers discussed it (our selling the drugs yesterday). (50%)

b. The teachers discussed it (our selling the drugs) yesterday. (50%)

The results for sentences (90)–(92) thus differ from the results for sentences presented in this study. For example, for sentence (5), 95% of the subjects preferred the interpretation where the PP *at work* is associated with the lower VP.

(5)

Tom disputed Bill's dying at work.

Also, the preference for sentence (93), which is very similar to (92), is the same as that for (5).

(93)

The teachers discussed our selling the drugs during recess.

a.   The teachers discussed it (our selling the drugs during recess).
     (75%)

b.   The teachers discussed it (our selling the drugs) during recess.
     (25%)

We would like to suggest two possible reasons why there is no consistent preference for the interpretation of sentences such as (90)–(92). First, it may be that adverbs are not attached to a VP, but are instead attached to S and are free to be interpreted as modifying any verb in that S. Second, adverbs may be treated differently from other categories because they can occur in so many places within a structure. Thus, they may not be influenced by the Final Arguments principle.

For another group of sentences which did not show the same results as sentences presented in the study, it seemed that not enough care was taken in their construction. Sentence (94) is somewhat confusing because of the use of *tomorrow* and *yesterday* in the one sentence. It seems likely that there would be a tendency to put *tomorrow* in one clause and *yesterday* in the other. This tendency would favor the opposite result from what we were expecting.

(94)

Although Jane was worried about tomorrow's lecture yesterday Susan wasn't worried at all.

a.   Jane was worried yesterday. (42%) $n = 19$

b.   Yesterday Susan wasn't worried. (58%) $n = 19$

In sentence (95), the interpretation that our theory predicts would be preferred turns out to be a somewhat strange one, for it assumes that some hotels are restricted to men. This strangeness may have caused some subjects to reject that reading.

(95)

Rooms can be found in that hotel for men.

a.   Rooms can be found in that hotel which is for men. (40%)

b.   For men, rooms can be found in that hotel. (60%)

In sentence (96), the interpretation predicted by our theory as the preferred one seems to assume that there is only one shell on the beach. The strangeness of this may sometimes have led to the rejection of this interpretation.

(96)

An old man gave the child the shell on the beach.

a.   An old man gave the child the shell which was on the beach. (40%)

b.   An old man gave the child the shell, while they were on the beach. (60%)

In sentence (97), the phrase *her mother* produces a bias against the interpretation our theory would predict subjects to favor. The use of the phrase *her mother* assumes that the reader knows who *her* refers to or that the information will be specified. In the interpretation we were expecting to be the preferred one, *Mary* cannot be taken as the person to which *her* refers, while in the other interpretation *her* can refer to *Mary*.

(97)

Her mother placed a $20 bill in the book for Mary.

a.   Her mother placed a $20 bill in the book which was for Mary. (35%)

b.   Her mother placed a $20 bill there (in the book) for Mary. (65%)

The final sentence in the group which did not seem to be well constructed is (98). Neither interpretation of the sentence seems very sensible because of the vagueness of *someone*.

(98)

They signaled to someone that they couldn't hear.

a.   They signaled to someone who they couldn't hear. (50%)

b.   They signaled to someone the fact that they couldn't hear. (50%)

Sentences (99) and (100) also did not show the results we expected.

(99)

The police told the officer that was interviewing the boy that the woman had left.

a.   The officer was interviewing the boy that the woman had left. (10%)

b.   The police told him (the officer) that the woman had left. (90%)

(100)

The police signaled to the officer that was interviewing the boy that the woman had left.

a.   The officer was interviewing the boy that the woman had left. (20%)

b.   The police told him (the officer) that the woman had left. (80%)

It is possible that the interpretation of these sentences depends partly on a rule of Null Complement Anaphora (see Grimshaw 1979a). Null Complement Anaphora is exemplified in the sequence *The enemy is here. Will you tell/signal the officer?* The second sentence in this sequence is interpreted to mean *Will you tell/signal the officer that the enemy is here* even though the complement is not present. Sentence (101) shows the same effect as (99), but the opposite effect appears in sentence (102), in which *objected to* occurs instead of *told*. The dyadic form of *object, object* ⟨(SUBJ),(TO OBJ)⟩, is not subject to a rule of Null Complement Anaphora.

(101)
The man told the manager that was interviewing the woman that the salesman had cheated.
a. The manager was interviewing the woman that the salesman had cheated. (5%)
b. The man told him (the manager) that the salesman had cheated. (95%)

(102)
The man objected to the manager that was interviewing the woman that the salesman had cheated.
a. The manager was interviewing the woman that the salesman had cheated. (55%)
b. The man objected to him (the manager) that the salesman had cheated. (45%)

Finally, sentences (103) and (104) showed unexpected results.

(103)
They discussed our publishing the novel in a hasty manner.
a. They discussed it (our publishing the novel in a hasty manner). (30%)
b. They discussed it (our publishing the novel) in a hasty manner. (70%)

(104)
They discussed our publishing the novel hastily.
a. They discussed it (our publishing the novel hastily). (30%)
b. They discussed it (our publishing the novel) hastily. (70%)

More research is required to find out what particular aspect of these two sentences caused the results obtained.

Appendix B: A Computational Interpretation of the Theory

Here we present one computational interpretation of our theory of syntactic closure. It is based on Kaplan's 1981 General Syntactic Processor, which is extremely useful because it has the flexibility to allow different parsing strategies to be modeled and allows the use of a linguistically motivated competence grammar to recover the structures for a sentence.

The model that we suggest here is intended to show exactly how the sentence perception processes proposed in the theory might operate. The model takes lexical items as input and shows step by step how the constituent structure of the sentence is analyzed. Although the algorithm does not specify how the functional structure is built up, the functional structure can be constructed at the same time as the constituent structure by using the solution algorithm described in chapter 4. The model lays the groundwork for experimental investigations of the precise processes involved in sentence perception. These investigations will in turn lead to further development of the theory.

11.B.1 The Structure of the Computational Model
There are three major aspects of the computational model: working memory, a processor, and a set of nongrammatical scheduling principles.

Working Memory   There are two types of working memory in the model. First, there is a memory that keeps a *record of parsed structures* (called a *Chart* by Kaplan). At any moment in the analysis, the record of parsed structures specifies what has been discovered about the string up to that moment: all the paths that have been explored and the constituents that have been identified. Second, there is a memory for a *list of options* (called an *Agenda* by Kaplan). In this list, the options that could be taken at different positions in the string are specified. New options are added to the list as new possibilities emerge. The options are ordered from the "front" of the list to the "back" of the list.

The Processor   The processor is a device that is able to perform certain kinds of operations as described by the options that it finds on the options list. The processor takes one option at a time from the list and executes the appropriate operation for that option.

Scheduling Principles Scheduling principles determine the order in which the options are placed on the list and thereby affect the order in which the options are taken.

11.B.2 Options

Two types of options can arise during a parse. First, there are options for *hypothesizing* a particular category at a particular position in the string. The hypothesis of a category, C, at a position, p, is represented:

$[p, C]$

So, for example, the hypothesis of an NP at position 3 (that is, at the space before the third word in the string) would be represented:

$[3, NP]$

Second, there are options for *attaching* a complete constituent, once it is found, into a partial constituent. A complete constituent is one for which there are no more categories to be hypothesized as possible subconstituents. We will represent a complete constituent of category C using the position in the string at which that constituent begins, i, and the position at which it ends, n:

$_iC_n$

Thus, a complete PP extending from positions 6 to 9 in the string would be represented:

$_6PP_9$

Note that simple lexical items are treated as complete constituents. Thus, for example, a determiner extending from positions 1 to 2 in a sentence is represented:

$_1DET_2$

A partial constituent is one for which more categories can be hypothesized as possible subconstituents. A partial constituent is represented:

$$_iC \rightarrow C_1 \; C_2 \; ... \; C_r {}_j \,|\, A_1 \; A_2 \; ... \; A_s$$

where the string C_1 to C_r represents the subconstituents of C already analyzed and where the string A_1 to A_s represents the possible subconstituents of C to come. These possible subconstituents are given by the phrase structure rules of the grammar, which specify sets of alternatives. For example, an alternative might be a choice between a PP or *e*. The *j* subscript by the bar specifies the current position in the rule: it is the position at which the element to the right of the bar can be hypothesized. The subscript *i* represents the position in the string where the partial constituent C begins. Thus, a partial complex NP constituent for which an NP subconstituent extending from positions 3 to 6 in a string has been analyzed and for which either a PP or an S' can be hypothesized at 6 and attached, if found, is represented:

$$_3\text{NP} \rightarrow \quad \begin{matrix} \text{NP} \\ (\uparrow\text{HEAD})=\downarrow \end{matrix} \quad {}_6\Big| \left\{ \begin{matrix} \text{PP} \\ (\uparrow\text{HEAD})=(\downarrow\text{SUBJ}) \\ \uparrow=\downarrow \\ \text{S}' \\ (\uparrow\text{HEAD})=\Downarrow_{\text{NP}} \\ \uparrow=\downarrow \end{matrix} \right\}$$

The option for attaching a complete constituent, once it is found, into a partial constituent is represented:

$$[(_i\text{C} \rightarrow \text{C}_1\ \text{C}_2\ ...\ \text{C}_r\ _j\,|\,\text{A}_1\ \text{A}_2\ ...\ \text{A}_s)\ (_j\text{C}_n)]$$

where the category of the complete constituent $_j\text{C}_n$ is the same as one of the alternative categories of A_1. Thus, for example, the option for attaching the complete constituent

$$_6\text{PP}_9$$

into the partial constituent

$$_3\text{NP} \rightarrow \quad \begin{matrix} \text{NP} \\ (\uparrow\text{HEAD})=\downarrow \end{matrix} \quad {}_6\Big| \left\{ \begin{matrix} \text{PP} \\ (\uparrow\text{HEAD})=(\downarrow\text{SUBJ}) \\ \uparrow=\downarrow \\ \text{S}' \\ (\uparrow\text{HEAD})=\Downarrow_{\text{NP}} \\ \uparrow=\downarrow \end{matrix} \right\}$$

is represented:

$$[(_3\text{NP} \rightarrow \quad \begin{matrix} \text{NP} \\ (\uparrow\text{HEAD})=\downarrow \end{matrix} \quad {}_6\Big| \left\{ \begin{matrix} \text{PP} \\ (\uparrow\text{HEAD})=(\downarrow\text{SUBJ}) \\ \uparrow=\downarrow \\ \text{S}' \\ (\uparrow\text{HEAD})=\Downarrow_{\text{NP}} \\ \uparrow=\downarrow \end{matrix} \right\}\ )\ (_6\text{PP}_9)]$$

As soon as an option is removed from the list of options during the parse, the appropriate operation for that option is executed. To execute the appropriate operation for an option, a new partial or complete constituent as specified by the option is added to the record of parsed structures. The appropriate execution for the hypothesis option

$$[p, C]$$

is to add to the record of parsed structures the partial constituent

$$_pC \rightarrow {}_p | A_1 \ A_2 \ ... \ A_s$$

Thus, for example, the appropriate execution for the option [3, NP] would be to add to the record of parsed structures a partial NP constituent which lists all the possible subconstituents of an NP generated by the rules of the grammar. Using the grammar presented in section 11.3, the partial constituent added to the record of parsed structures for the hypothesis option [3, NP] would be:

$$
_3NP \rightarrow {}_3 | \left\{
\begin{array}{c}
\text{(DET)} \quad \text{ADJ*} \quad \text{N} \\
\downarrow \in (\uparrow \text{MOD}) \\[1em]
\begin{array}{cc}
\text{NP} & \left\{
\begin{array}{c}
\text{PP} \\
(\uparrow \text{HEAD}) = (\downarrow \text{SUBJ}) \\
\uparrow = \downarrow \\
\text{S}' \\
(\uparrow \text{HEAD}) = \Downarrow_{\text{NP}} \\
\uparrow = \downarrow
\end{array}
\right. \\
(\uparrow \text{HEAD}) = \downarrow &
\end{array} \\[2em]
\begin{array}{cc}
\text{NP's} & \text{VP} \\
(\uparrow \text{SUBJ}) = \downarrow &
\end{array} \\[1em]
e \\
\uparrow = \Uparrow_{\text{NP}}
\end{array}
\right\}
$$

The appropriate execution for the attachment option

$$[({}_iC \rightarrow C_1 \ C_2 \ ... \ C_r \ {}_j | A_1 \ A_2 \ ... \ A_s)({}_jC_n)]$$

is to add to the record of parsed structures the partial or complete constituent resulting from extending the partial constituent

$$_iC \rightarrow C_1 \ C_2 \ ... \ C_r \ {}_j | A_1 \ A_2 \ ... \ A_s$$

so that it includes the complete constituent

$$_jC_n$$

Consider, for example, the option for attaching a PP to a partial complex NP:

$$[(_3\text{NP} \rightarrow \quad \underset{(\uparrow\text{HEAD})=\downarrow}{\text{NP}} \quad _6 \left| \left\{ \begin{array}{c} \text{PP} \\ (\uparrow\text{HEAD})=(\downarrow\text{SUBJ}) \\ \uparrow=\downarrow \\ \text{S}' \\ (\uparrow\text{HEAD})=\Downarrow_{\text{NP}} \\ \uparrow=\downarrow \end{array} \right\} \right) \,(_6\text{PP}_9)]$$

The appropriate execution for this option would be to add to the record of parsed structures the *complete* constituent ($_3\text{NP}_9$), since once the PP is attached to the partial constituent, the complex NP would extend from positions 3 to 9 and there would be no more categories to be hypothesized as possible subconstituents of it. The appropriate execution for the option

$$[(_3\text{NP} \rightarrow \ _3\left| \ \underset{(\uparrow\text{HEAD})=\downarrow}{\text{NP}} \right. \quad \left\{ \begin{array}{c} \text{PP} \\ (\uparrow\text{HEAD})=(\downarrow\text{SUBJ}) \\ \uparrow=\downarrow \\ \text{S}' \\ (\uparrow\text{HEAD})=\Downarrow_{\text{NP}} \\ \uparrow=\downarrow \end{array} \right\} \right) \,(_3\text{NP}_6)]$$

would result in the addition of a *partial* constituent to the record of parsed structures: the appropriate execution would be to add to the record of parsed structures the partial constituent

$$_3\text{NP} \rightarrow \quad \underset{(\uparrow\text{HEAD})=\downarrow}{\text{NP}} \quad _6 \left| \left\{ \begin{array}{c} \text{PP} \\ (\uparrow\text{HEAD})-(\downarrow\text{SUBJ}) \\ \uparrow=\downarrow \\ \text{S}' \\ (\uparrow\text{HEAD})=\Downarrow_{\text{NP}} \\ \uparrow=\downarrow \end{array} \right\} \right.$$

11.B.3 Control Structure
We have now outlined the structure of the computational model and have given a general indication of how the different kinds of options are executed. We now define more explicitly the sequence of steps that the processor must take in order to guarantee that it will be able to find all

and only the constituent structures that the grammar assigns to a particular string. First, we define the special operations by which the analysis of a string is initiated. Second, we specify how the computation proceeds once it is started. Third, we define the conditions under which the processor halts with a grammatically correct analysis.

(a) Start   To the (empty) list of options, add the option for hypothesizing that a Sentence (S) begins at position 1 in the string.

(b) Continue   (i) Remove the option at the front of the list and execute the operation appropriate for that option.

(ii) Whenever a *partial* constituent $_iC \rightarrow C_1 C_2 \ldots C_{r\,j} | A_1 A_2 \ldots A_s$ is added to the record of parsed structures:

For each rule alternative in A_1, compare the category of the rule alternative with the category of every complete constituent, $_jC_n$, in the record of parsed structures.

—If there is a match between a rule alternative and a complete constituent, create the option for attaching the complete constituent into the partial constituent and place the option on the list of options.

—If there is not a match between a rule alternative and a complete constituent and if there is a rule for expanding the category of the rule alternative, create the option for hypothesizing that category and place the option on the list of options.

Whenever a *complete* constituent $_jC_n$ is added to the record of parsed stuctures:

For every partial constituent of the form $_iC \rightarrow C_1 C_2 \ldots C_{r\,j} | A_1 A_2 \ldots A_s$, compare the category of the complete constituent $_jC_n$ with the category of all the rule alternatives in A_1. For each instance where there is a match, create the option for attaching the complete constituent into the partial constituent and place the option on the list of options.

(c) Halt   The processor halts when the list of options is empty. When this happens, the string is a sentence if in the record of parsed structures there is at least one complete S constituent extending from position 1 in the sentence (that is, immediately before the first word) to position f (that is, immediately after the final word). When there is more than one complete constituent, $_1S_f$, the sentence is ambiguous, with each complete $_1S_f$ representing one reading of the sentence.

NOTE: There are various grammatical situations in which the steps outlined here will cause the processor to perform operations that have exactly the same effect as work that was performed earlier. For example, the processor could end up hypothesizing a given constituent several times at a particular string position. Each such hypothesis would be in response to the requirements of different higher-level constituent contexts. Since the constituent structure grammar is context free, the results of each such hypothesis will be indistinguishable from the results of any of the others. In the interest of avoiding needless, redundant computation, our processing model includes the following convention.

> *Avoid duplication*—never add to the record of parsed structures a partial or complete constituent that is already present.

11.B.4 Scheduling Principles
We now introduce the explicit scheduling rules that implement the theory of syntactic closure that we have presented. We begin with some preliminary notions in terms of which our scheduling principles are defined.

Preliminary Notes and Definitions
Coherency
   A rule alternative is coherent with a lexical form if the alternative bears a governable grammatical function which appears in the function-assignment list of the lexical form. In all other cases, the alternative is not coherent with the lexical form.
The Strongest Lexical Form
   Lexical forms are initially ranked according to their natural (that is, contextually neutral) strength, with the one on top being the strongest lexical form. If the naturally strongest lexical form is rejected during the analysis of a phrase, the next form in the rank becomes the strongest lexical form for that phrase.
Syntactic Priority
   Each syntactic category has a priority rating according to its strength.
The Final Argument
   The final argument of a lexical form of a given partial constituent is a subconstituent of that partial constituent which is coherent with the lexical form and which can be followed by no other subconstituent that is coherent with the form.

A Post-Final-Argument Element

Within a given partial constituent, any element occurring later in the string than the final argument of a lexical form is a post-final-argument element of that form.

The Creation of an Option at a Position n

An option is said to be created at a position n if, for an attachment option, the complete constituent ends at n

$$[(_iC \rightarrow C_1\ C_2\ ...\ C_r{}_j\,|\,A_1\ A_2\ ...\ A_s)(_jC_n)]$$

or if, for a hypothesis option, the category is hypothesized at n

$$[n,\ C]$$

Lexical and Syntactic Preference

For the options that are created when a *partial* constituent is added to the record of parsed structures:

—options for the rule alternatives that are coherent with the strongest lexical form of the predicate of the partial constituent are placed in front of options for the rule alternatives that are not coherent with this form.

—within this primary ordering, options for a rule alternative with stronger syntactic priority are placed in front of options for rule alternatives with weaker syntactic priority.

Final Arguments and Invoked Attachment

For the options that are created when a *complete* constituent $_jC_n$ is added to the record of parsed structures:

—options for attaching $_jC_n$ as the final argument or a post-final-argument element of the strongest lexical form of the predicate of the partial constituent are placed at the back of other options created at position n.

—within this primary ordering, options for attaching $_jC_n$ to the partial constituent that led to the creation of the hypothesis of C at j are placed in front of other attachment options for $_jC_n$.

General Scheduling Principles

Depth-first Processing

Unless specified otherwise, add new options to the front of the list of options.

Suspend on Success
    Suspend syntactic processing whenever a complete constituent $_1S_f$ is added to the record of parsed structures.

Notes

We would like to thank Jack Carroll, Ken Church, Janet Fodor, Merrill Garrett, Jane Grimshaw, Per-Kristian Halvorsen, Tom Roeper, Ed Walker, Tom Wasow, Ellen Woolford, and Annie Zaenen for valuable comments on an earlier draft of this chapter. We also wish to thank Ron Wilson for helping to collect the data. This material is based upon work supported by the National Science Foundation under Grant No. BNS 80–14730. It was also supported in part by a Sloan Postdoctoral Fellowship to the first author.

1. In our use, the terms *closed* and *closure* are purely descriptive, referring only to the position of the phrasal brackets.

2. It does not matter to our argument whether the clause-final S' restriction is a grammatical property of English or the result of some processing constraint on S's. Whichever is correct, the fact remains that the effect shown in sentences with S' Complements cannot be the outcome of the Sausage Machine architecture (the two-stage parser with a narrow viewing window), since the phenomenon is independent of length and does not appear in sentences without S' Complements.

3. Fodor and Frazier present other sentences besides (13) and (14) as evidence of a Local Association phenomenon, but (13) and (14) are of the type that they would agree provide the strongest motivation for the Sausage Machine. Arguments can easily be made against all of the other sentences given to motivate the model. Frazier and Fodor themselves point out objections to some of their examples. Other sentences clearly have nothing to do with the initial parsing of a sentence, but rather with how much "easier to recognize" some unpreferred structures are compared with others.

4. A very interesting computational motivation for the Final Arguments principle has been suggested by Ken Church (personal communication). The Final Arguments principle leads to right-branching structures at or after the final argument. Memory load can be computationally reduced for such structures through the elimination of right-branching recursion (see Church and Kaplan forthcoming). In contrast, memory for center-branching recursive structures cannot be eliminated in this way, thus suggesting that these structures are avoided because of the extra burden they impose on working memory.

5. Whenever an option for attaching an element into a particular structure is delayed because of the Final Arguments principle, and there are no more words after the element, the option will eventually have to be taken. Thus, the Final Arguments principle could be formulated so that it applies only when the relevant element is followed by more words. If this is done, it will be necessary to find the correct interpretation of "followed by more words." For example, it

may be that the Final Arguments principle should not apply when the relevant element is sentence-final, but perhaps it should also not apply when the element is, say, clause-final. It will also be necessary to consider how the perceptual mechanism "knows" whether the element is followed by more words, and, as Ken Church has pointed out to us, this is not at all a computationally trivial problem. Perhaps intonation or punctuation provides this perceptual information, but more research on this possibility is needed. Another possibility which we wish to consider in the future is whether the perceptual mechanism looks ahead a word or two in the string before making some decisions. This possibility could be motivated by the existence of lexically induced biases in constructions where the verb follows its arguments. A. Zaenen (personal communication) has hypothesized that this may be the case in Dutch.

Chapter 12

Sentence Planning Units: Marilyn Ford
Implications for the
Speaker's Representation
of Meaningful Relations
Underlying Sentences

Most psycholinguistic research into adult language behavior has been concerned with how speech is perceived and comprehended; a relatively small amount has been concerned with how speech is produced. Thus, it is usually admitted that little is known about the process of sentence production. However, one suggestion is commonly put forward as being virtually the only substantive proposal concerning production that can be made with some degree of certainty, namely, that the surface structure clause is the primary unit in which sentences are planned (see, for example, Bever, Carroll, and Hurtig 1976). Recently, however, even this proposal has been questioned. Ford and Holmes 1978 have obtained evidence indicating that the surface clause is not an important unit but, rather, that it is the so-called deep clause that is primary.

Surface structure clauses, which were first recognized as units in traditional grammar, are units of speech which contain one explicit finite (tensed) verb and which usually also contain a complete subject and predicate (see Roberts 1964, Gleason 1965). Examples of surface structure clauses are *John preferred to catch a taxi* and *although the sun was shining*. With the advent of transformational grammar, psycholinguists interested in perception began to consider the role of what they termed the "deep clause" or the "surface form of an underlying sentence". The rationale behind segmenting speech into deep clauses is that, since in transformational grammar all verbs indicate a deep sentoid in the deep representation of a sentence, every structural unit which contains or implies either a finite or a nonfinite verb and which would be regarded as the surface realization of a deep sentoid can be considered as a "clausal" or "sentential" unit. Deep and surface clauses may correspond, as is the case, for example, with the clause *although the sun was shining.* Alternatively, a number of deep clauses may comprise one surface clause; for example, in the surface clause *John preferred to catch a taxi,* there is a deep clause boundary between the segments *John preferred* and *to catch a taxi.* That is, in the surface clause, there are two underlying sentoids something like *John preferred it* and *John catch a taxi.*

The important point to consider here is that evidence has recently been obtained which indicates that a unit of speech corresponding to a deep clause is a major sentence planning unit. Using a "click" reaction time task, Ford and Holmes 1978 found that processing load during production was increased in the speech immediately prior to the boundary of a *deep* structure clause, regardless of whether or not the deep clause corresponded to a surface clause. No evidence could be found at all that the surface clause per se is important. Further, the results provided no evidence for the idea that a complete representation of a sentence is constructed before it is produced. Rather, they indicated that, in sentence production, each deep clause is successively planned and produced.

Results that have previously been taken as evidence that the surface clause is important come mainly from analyses of speech hesitations. In these studies, the deep clause unit has been ignored. For example, both Boomer 1965 and Hawkins 1971 found that hesitation pauses occur toward the beginning of surface structure clauses. However, as Ford and Holmes 1978 noted, since surface clause boundaries are always also deep clause boundaries, these findings could result from the importance of the deep clause. Further, since neither Boomer nor Hawkins made a distinction as to whether surface clause boundaries corresponded or did not correspond to a sentence boundary, it is even possible that the pauses occurred primarily at sentence boundaries and not at within-sentence clause boundaries.[1]

A study by Goldman-Eisler 1972 is another which could be taken as indicating that the surface clause is important. Unlike Boomer 1965 and Hawkins 1971, Goldman-Eisler did distinguish between sentence boundaries and within-sentence clause boundaries. While the results showed that sentences were preceded by a silent pause more often than were surface clauses within sentences and while the pauses before sentences were generally longer, it was also found that the frequency and length of pauses were greater before clauses than before within-clause words. Thus, it does seem that surface clauses are preceded by a pause significantly often. However, the crucial point still remains that pauses could be occurring at surface clause boundaries because these locations are also deep clause boundaries. Since previous studies of hesitations have ignored the deep clause, the present study was undertaken to determine whether speakers do pause within surface clauses at locations corresponding to deep clause boundaries and also to consider what implications these results, together with those of Ford and Holmes 1978, have for the sentence planning process.

It may seem strange that the deep clause unit has been virtually ignored in production studies and that the importance of the surface clause is so readily accepted. However, it could be that even to those who make use of concepts from transformational grammar when considering production, it is implausible that the deep clause rather than the surface clause could be a major planning unit. In any model of sentence production, planning for a sentence must include the construction of a representation of the underlying, or meaningful, relations of what is to be said and the mapping of this representation into a surface sequence. It follows that the way in which the underlying relations are represented will affect the way in which the planning process operates. However, when one considers how the underlying relations of a sentence are represented in a transformational grammar, it is apparent that sentence production could not proceed in successive phases during which a deep syntactic representation of one deep clause is first constructed and then mapped into a surface sequence. Rather, if the underlying representations of sentences as described in transformational grammar are relevant to sentence planning, it would be more likely that sentence production would proceed by the successive planning of each surface clause. To see that this is so, it is necessary to consider some aspects of the representation of sentences in a transformational grammar.

According to a transformational analysis of language, for a surface clause containing a number of deep clauses, it is not necessarily the case that all of the material in the surface form of a certain deep sentoid occurs in the deep representation of that sentoid; rather, some of the material may occur in the deep representation of some other, subordinate, sentoid. Consider, for example, sentence (1).

(1)

John appears ＿＿ to be liked by someone.

In a transformational grammar, there would be two deep sentoids in the representation of the relations underlying sentence (1). The main sentoid would be something like *it appears,* while the subordinate sentoid would be something like *someone to like John.* In the derivation of (1) in the grammar, the subordinate sentoid would be transformed into the passive sentoid *John to be liked by someone* and the subject *John* would be extracted from this sentoid and moved into the main sentoid, replacing *it,* or a dummy symbol, to generate the sequence *John appears.* There are many types of sentences with properties similar to (1), examples of which are given in (2)–(5). As for sentence (1), a transformational analysis would claim that the italicized material in each of these sentences had moved from the gap in the succeeding deep clause which is not tensed.

(2)
The food was believed _____ to be good.

(3)
The children seemed _____ happy enough.

(4)
I don't know *which book* John asked _____ to be banned.

(5)
Uli is difficult for most people to understand _____.

It is important to realize that in transformational grammar, while there are rules which extract material from a subordinate sentoid and insert it into a higher sentoid, there is a condition on this type of transformation: material cannot (except under special circumstances) be extracted from a finite sentoid. This condition is necessary because, in contrast to sentences like (1)–(3), sentences such as (6)–(8) are ungrammatical.

(6)
*John appears _____ is liked by someone.

(7)
*The food was believed _____ was good.

(8)
*The children seemed _____ were happy enough.

Sentence (9) is also ungrammatical, though in transformational grammar *Wh* Movement can extract material from a tensed sentoid under special circumstances.

(9)
*I don't know *which book* John asked if ____ could be banned.

Note, too, that an ungrammatical version of (5) is not given, since *is difficult* is never succeeded by a tensed clause.

It can be seen that according to a transformational analysis, *within* a surface structure clause the form of one deep clause may be dependent on the representation of the underlying relations of a following deep clause, but similar dependencies would not usually hold *between* surface structure clauses. Thus, if, in the process of planning sentences, underlying relations were represented as in transformational grammar, it would be impossible for sentence production to proceed by the successive planning of deep clauses in the left-to-right order in which they are spoken; it is not always possible to construct a representation of the underlying relations of one deep clause and to map this into a surface sequence without also having constructed a representation of the underlying relations of a following deep clause. Thus, for example, it would not be possible to plan and produce the clause *John appears* without having constructed the representation of the underlying relations of the succeeding deep clause on which it is dependent. It would be more likely that a sentence would be produced by constructing the representation of the underlying relations for an entire surface clause and then mapping this representation into a surface sequence.

The argument being made is not that because the order of elements in a deep syntactic representation is different from their surface order, it would be implausible for such a representation to be constructed and mapped into a surface sequence. There is no basis for such an argument. Rather, the argument is that if speakers constructed representations of meaningful relations as in transformational grammar, production could not proceed by the successive planning and uttering of each deep clause. Notice that the argument holds true regardless of precisely how the speaker is assumed to map the underlying relations into a surface form.

The question that arises from the preceding discussion is, What representation of meaningful relations would permit the successive planning of deep clauses in the order in which they are spoken? Of course, if speakers do not construct a representation equivalent to the deep syntactic structures of transformational grammar, then the units of speech which have been called the "deep" clause and the "surface" clause should probably be renamed, since those terms clearly reflect the theoretical framework of transformational grammar. Reasonably neutral terms are *basic clause,* for the so-called "deep" clause, and *full finite clause,* for the so-called "surface" clause. The term *full finite clause* is suggested here simply because the units of speech referred to have one finite verb and usually a complete subject and predicate. The term *basic clause* simply reflects the idea that a number of these units can comprise one full finite clause, though a full finite clause that does not contain a number of basic clauses is itself a basic clause. The relatively neutral terms suggested will be used for the present, and the question of what representation of meaningful relations might be developed in the planning of sentences will be discussed later in some detail. The issue that must be resolved first is whether more evidence for the importance of the basic clause unit can be provided by the technique of analyzing the occurrence of hesitations in speech—the technique on which most evidence for the primacy of the full finite clause is based.

Ford and Holmes 1978 have already noted that there are certain problems inherent in pause studies. First, while it is sometimes assumed that speakers *always* pause to plan (Goldman-Eisler 1968), there is no evidence for this view. In fact, the results obtained by Ford and Holmes show that speakers plan and talk at the same time; therefore, it cannot be expected that every planning unit will be preceded by a pause. Second, from the work of Goldman-Eisler 1972, it appears that both the frequency with which speakers do pause at a certain type of location and the length of time for which they pause there are not necessarily indicative of the difficulty of planning what is to be said. Thus, for example, when examining pausing before surface clauses, Goldman-Eisler 1972 observed that speakers paused less often and for shorter periods before subordinate clauses than before clauses that were merely conjoined with the preceding clause. Perhaps the frequency and length of pauses partly depend on the degree to which what has just been said is in some sense complete by itself. It may be that after units that are more complete, there is less need for the speaker to produce the following speech immediately, and also perhaps more chance to change what is to be said, if it has already been planned during the immediately preceding speech. It is also possible that the point of initiation of planning varies to some extent for different speech units.

While the interpretation of pause data is not straightforward, it seems necessary to examine the occurrence of hesitations in speech, since the evidence which is regarded as indicating that the full finite clause is important comes mainly from analyses of speech hesitations. The results of these studies may be misleading, since basic clause boundaries were ignored. If the *basic* clause is a major sentence planning unit, and if pauses do have some validity as an indicator of where planning takes place, then basic clause boundaries could be expected to be important locations for pausing, regardless of whether or not they correspond to the boundaries of full finite clauses. That is, it could be expected that pausing at basic clause boundaries within full finite clauses would be as frequent and long as pausing at the boundaries of full finite clauses. Despite the fact that the majority of studies on production rely on analyses of hesitations, it is still far from clear where speakers pause in the structure of sentences. Thus, apart from investigating the importance of the basic clause unit, a second objective of the present study was to provide a relatively clear picture of the occurrence of hesitations in speech.

12.1 Method

Procedure
The subjects were each interviewed individually by the experimenter in one half-hour session. Each subject spoke on five topics, the first of which was not used for data analysis, but merely to give the subject time to become relaxed in the interview situation. The initial topic for all subjects was Leisure Time Activities. The four test topics were Migrants, Family Life, Prevention and Punishment of Crime, and Attitudes to University Life. Four orderings of the test topics were used. When each new topic was introduced, subjects were asked three broad questions about it which were then repeated. Subjects talked for about five minutes on each topic. They were not told that the experiment was concerned with sentence production.

Data Analysis
The subjects' speech was transcribed verbatim by the experimenter, through repeated listening to tapes of the interviews. Once transcribed, the speech was segmented into sentences and into the units which are now being called basic and full finite clauses. The segmentation for the basic and full finite clauses was carried out in the same way as that for the deep and surface clauses, respectively, in the study by Ford and Holmes 1978.

Once the speech was transcribed and segmented, it was necessary to locate and measure the silent pauses. The tapes were played into a pen recorder with the paper running through at a speed of 50 millimeters per second. Thus, every half millimeter represented 10 milliseconds, while every centimeter represented 200. All silent pauses of 200 milliseconds or greater were located and measured to the nearest 10 milliseconds. Once all the measures were obtained, they were checked. The cutoff value of 200 milliseconds was equivalent to that used by Boomer 1965. Pauses below 200 milliseconds are not usually considered in pause studies, since they can occur as a normal part of the articulation of certain sounds. In the appendix, small samples of speech from six subjects are given, with the speech segmented into clauses and sentences and with the pauses marked.

Wherever possible, analyses were carried out on the proportionate frequencies of both silent pauses and filled pauses, such as "um" and "ah," and on the length of the silent hesitations. It is customary to apply an arcsin transformation to data consisting of proportions, since it is known that the variances and means are related in a specific way (Bartlett 1947). Thus, in the present study the observed proportionate frequencies for each subject were appropriately transformed. For the pause length data, the raw data were analyzed, but the logarithmic transformation suggested by Kirk 1968 and Winer 1970 for time scale data was also performed, in order to check whether the statistical decisions for the logarithmic data differed from those for the raw data. There were no instances where this happened. In one case the statistical decision for the raw proportion data differed from the decision for the arcsin data. This case is noted.

The data were analyzed using repeated measures analyses of variance, with orthogonal a priori comparisons between means being made where appropriate (Kirk 1968). Tukey 1953 HSD tests were also carried out where appropriate. Statistical decisions were based on a Type 1 error rate of $\alpha = 0.05$. It should be noted that the *min F'* statistic (Clark 1973) is not relevant to the obtained data. As Ford and Holmes 1978 argued in relation to the reaction time data of their study, since each subject produced a different number and a completely different set of speech "items," any significant findings could not result from any particular "item" or "items." Moreover, it would be impossible to calculate *min F'*.

Subjects
The subjects were 20 paid volunteers from the general student popula-
tion at the University of Melbourne. They were all native speakers of
English. Since two of the subjects stuttered, their speech was rejected.
The speech of a third subject was rejected because he had influenza.

12.2 Results

Sentences, Clauses, and Words
To see whether hesitations provide evidence that the basic clause is a
major sentence planning unit and to gain a clearer picture of the occurrence of hesitations in speech, pausing was first examined in four locations. These were the positions immediately preceding (a) sentences,
(b) full finite clauses that are not the first in a sentence, (c) basic clauses
that are not the first in a full finite clause, and (d) words that are not the
first in a clause. Notice that with this classification, the initial boundary
of a "lower order" unit is distinct from that of a "higher order" unit, so
that the results obtained are unambiguous with respect to the units of
interest.

In table 12.1 the mean data are shown for three measures of pausing.
These measures are the proportion of the different units preceded by a
silent pause, the length of the silent pauses, and the proportion of the
units preceded by a filled pause. In table 12.1, as in subsequent tables,
the figures in parentheses for the proportion data give the mean number
of items on which each individual subject's proportion was based,

Table 12.1
Mean data for pausing before sentences, full finite clauses, basic clauses,
and within-clause words

	Measure		
Unit	Proportion preceded by silent pause	Silent pause length	Proportion preceded by filled pause
Sentence	.659	1601	.262
	(198)	(130)	(198)
Full finite clause	.235	962	.043
	(154)	(36)	(154)
Basic clause	.206	1034	.032
	(115)	(23)	(115)
Within-clause word	.095	872	.020
	(1693)	(163)	(1693)

while the figures in parentheses for the pause length data give the mean number of pauses per subject. It should be noted here that in measuring pause lengths, when a specific unit was preceded by a redundant word or a speech disruption, such as a filled pause or an intruding sound, any silent pauses before or after these words or disruptions were totalled to give a measure of the silent pause length preceding the unit.

It can be seen from table 12.1 that the results for all three measures of pausing were essentially the same. Sentences were preceded by a silent pause far more often than were any other units, $F(1,48) = 1191.06$. Moreover, these silent pauses were longer than those before clauses and within-clause words, $F(1,48) = 150.50$. The difference between the proportionate frequency of filled pausing before sentences and other units was also significant, $F(1,48) = 480.07$. Clearly, the sentence is the most important location for pausing in speech. However, it is also clear that clause boundaries are important. Pauses were relatively more frequent and also longer before clauses than before within-clause words, the statistical results for the proportionate frequency of silent pausing, the length of silent pausing, and the proportionate frequency of filled pausing being $F(1,48) = 118.51$, $F(1,48) = 5.15$, and $F(1,48) = 7.32$, respectively. The most important finding was that there was no consistent difference between pausing at full finite clause boundaries and pausing at the boundary of a basic clause within a full finite clause. There was a tendency for a greater proportion of full finite than basic clauses to be preceded by a silence, with the difference for the transformed data just reaching significance, $F(1,48) = 4.05$. However, the difference for the raw data was not significant. Further, silent pause lengths tended to be longer before basic clauses than before full finite clauses, though the difference was not significant, $F(1,48) = 1.25$. The difference between the proportion of full finite and basic clauses preceded by a filled pause was also not significant, $F(1,48) = 3.25$. Thus, the results are in accord with the idea that it is the basic clause that is the important sentence planning unit—speakers pause comparatively often and for relatively long periods at full finite clause boundaries, which of course are also basic clause boundaries, but they also pause equally often and for equally long periods at basic clause boundaries that are within a full finite clause.

Conjunctions

So far, it has been shown that the locations immediately before sentences and clauses are important. An interesting finding by Boomer

1965 was that speakers often pause after the first word of a "phone-mic," or "surface," clause. As Fodor, Bever, and Garrett 1974 have suggested, the importance of this location could be attributed to the fact that it is often the position after a special word used in introducing a clause or connecting it with a preceding one. Examples of these conjunctions are *who, which, that, to, and, but, how, if, after, of (-ing), however,* and *subsequently.* Sometimes more than one word may intro-duce or connect a clause, for example, *that if* and *or which.* Pausing before words immediately following conjunctions was examined in the present study to determine whether or not these locations are impor-tant. If they are, then it would be worthwhile to ascertain whether the importance holds for sentences, for full finite clauses not at the initial boundary of a sentence, and for basic clauses not at the initial boundary of a full finite clause. Results would yield information concerning where speakers pause in the structure of sentences; they would also provide another test of the idea that it is the basic clause, and not the full finite clause, that is a major sentence planning unit, since pausing should be prominent after clause conjunctions for both full finite clauses and basic clauses within a full finite clause. Such a result would also show that the basic clause boundary is even more important as a location for hesitations than the results for pausing before the first word indicate on their own.

The first three analyses were intended to determine whether the postconjunction position is of any consequence for pausing. In these analyses, pausing before within-clause words was compared, as a function of whether the words immediately followed a conjunction or came later in a clause. The mean data for the three analyses, which were concerned with the three measures of pausing, are presented in table 12.2. It can be seen that for each measure, pausing was greater before the words immediately following conjunctions. Each of the dif-ferences was statistically significant, the results for the silent pause pro-portions, the silent pause lengths, and the filled pause proportions being $F(1,16) = 114.45$, $F(1,16) = 4.72$, and $F(1,16) = 43.37$, respectively.

Since the postconjunction positions are important for pausing, it is necessary to consider pausing in these locations with respect to the three units of interest. The mean data for the different measures of pausing are presented in table 12.3. Considering the mean pause lengths first, it was found that although the range in the means was quite large, the differences were not significant, $F(2,32) = 1.07$. It thus appears that these means may not be very reliable. The critical point, though, is that

Table 12.2
Mean data for pausing before within-clause words as a function of whether or not the words immediately follow a conjunction

Word position	Measure		
	Proportion preceded by silent pause	Silent pause length	Proportion preceded by filled pause
Immediately following a conjunction	.181 (207)	949 (37)	.046 (207)
Coming later in a sentence	.083 (1463)	847 (123)	.016 (1463)

Note: These results show that the values given in table 12.1 for pausing before within-clause words should be considered overestimates.

Table 12.3
Mean data for pausing after conjunctions as a function of whether the conjunction introduces a sentence, a full finite clause, or a basic clause

Conjunction type	Measure		
	Proportion followed by silent pause	Silent pause length	Proportion followed by filled pause
Sentence	.145 (32)	827 (4)	.013 (32)
Full finite clause	.165 (93)	974 (15)	.041 (93)
Basic clause	.211 (83)	953 (18)	.064 (83)

there is no evidence from the pause lengths to suggest that the importance of the postconjunction position does not hold for the basic clause as well as the full finite clause. The differences for the proportionate frequency of silent pausing were significant, $F(2,32) = 4.77$. However, it is obviously not for basic clauses that the position is least important, since the mean for these was the highest. In fact, a Tukey 1953 HSD test showed that the mean proportion for basic clauses was significantly greater than that for sentences. It should be noted here, though, that the proportionate frequency of silent pausing after a sentence conjunction (.145) was still high compared with the silent pausing elsewhere within a clause (.083, table 12.2). For filled pausing, the statistical results again showed that there were differences between the means, $F(2,32) = 9.41$. Once more, it is obvious that the postconjunction position in basic clauses is a relatively important one for pausing. An HSD test showed that for both full finite and basic clauses the proportion having a filled pause after the conjunction was greater than that for sentences. In fact, the proportionate frequency of filled pausing after sentence conjunctions (.013) is approximately equal to the frequency within a clause (.016, table 12.2).

The results of this study show clearly that regardless of whether or not basic clause boundaries correspond to full finite clause boundaries, the position immediately after the clause conjunction is an important location for pausing. The findings further support the notion that the basic clause is a major unit in sentence planning.

Full Finite Clauses

As yet, no distinction has been made between the boundaries of full finite clauses that correspond to a basic clause and the boundaries of those that contain more than one basic clause. Although the results so far indicate the primary importance of the basic clause as a major sentence planning unit, it could be that the full finite clause is also important—before each full finite clause containing a number of basic clauses, there may be some planning and integration of all of these clauses. In the study of Ford and Holmes 1978, no evidence could be found to suggest that this was true. To investigate the issue further, it was decided to compare pausing before full finite clauses as a function of the number of basic clauses contained, to determine whether pausing is relatively long and perhaps more frequent before full finite clauses that contain more than one basic clause. It has already been suggested that the length and frequency of pausing do not necessarily indicate the difficulty of planning what is to be said, but that they perhaps partly reflect the degree to which what has just been said is in some sense complete by itself. However, for different positions where it can be assumed that the latter factor would operate equally, differences in pausing might reflect variations in the effort required to plan what is to be said. Thus, it is interesting to compare pausing before the two different types of full finite clauses. If it is true that before a full finite clause containing a number of basic clauses, there is some planning and integration of all the clauses contained, then pausing might be longer and more frequent before these full finite clauses than before those made up of only one basic clause.

Separate analyses were performed for the initial or only full finite clause in a sentence and for subsequent clauses. (Discontinuous full finite clauses, having another clause embedded in the center, were omitted.) For the frequency of occurrence of silent pausing, two positions were examined: the locations before the first word of a clause and after a clause conjunction. Silent pause lengths and filled pausing before the first word of the clauses were also analyzed. Pause lengths after conjunctions were not examined, since when full finite clauses were separated into those corresponding and those not corresponding to a basic clause, for a number of subjects there were too few pauses to obtain reliable means for the two conditions. Filled pauses after conjunctions could not be analyzed either, since many subjects failed to produce instances in these locations for one or both of the conditions, especially in the initial clause analysis.

The mean data for the frequency of occurrence of silent pausing toward the beginning of the sentence-initial full finite clauses are given in table 12.4. There was a tendency for silent pausing to occur proportionately more often before the clauses which contained more than one basic clause. However, the difference failed to reach significance, $F(1,16) = 4.17$. Further, the interaction between pause location and type of full finite clause was also not significant, $F(1,16) = 1.57$. The main effect of pause location was significant, with proportionately more pauses occurring before the first word of the clause than after a conjunction, $F(1,16) = 381.29$.

The data for the pause lengths and the occurrence of filled pausing before the initial clauses are presented in table 12.5. The statistical results for pause lengths showed that there was a significant difference between the silent pause lengths before the clauses, $F(1,16) = 5.35$. However, the difference was not in the direction that could be explained by the suggestion that before full finite clauses containing more than one basic clause, planning and integration of all the basic clauses takes place; silent pauses were *shorter* before initial full finite clauses

Table 12.4
Mean proportion of initial full finite clauses preceded by a silent pause as a function of number of basic clauses and pause location

Number of basic clauses in full finite clause	Pause location	
	Before first word	After conjunction
One	.648	.129
	(147)	(23)
More than one	.671	.185
	(40)	(7)

with a number of basic clauses. The result could be considered positive evidence for the idea that before full finite clauses only the first basic clause is planned in any detail, since basic clauses that do not correspond to full finite clauses are on average shorter than those that do correspond. The data for the occurrence of filled pausing show the same direction of difference as the pause length data. However, the difference was not significant, $F < 1$.

The mean data for the frequency of occurrence of silent pausing toward the beginning of subsequent full finite clauses are presented in table 12.6. There was a tendency for silent pausing to occur more often before full finite clauses with more than one basic clause. However, neither the main effect of full finite clause type nor the interaction between this factor and pause location was significant, $F(1,16) = 1.09$ and $F < 1$, respectively. The main effect of pause location was significant, with pausing occurring proportionately more often before the first word of the clauses, $F(1,16) = 19.59$.

The mean data for the pause lengths and the occurrence of filled pausing before the subsequent clauses are presented in table 12.7. Silent pauses were slightly longer before full finite clauses containing

Table 12.5
Mean data for pausing before initial full finite clauses as a function of number of basic clauses

| Number of basic clauses in full finite clause | Measure | |
	Silent pause length	Proportion preceded by filled pause
One	1631 (95)	.256 (147)
More than one	1463 (27)	.249 (40)

Table 12.6
Mean proportion of subsequent full finite clauses preceded by a silent pause as a function of number of basic clauses and pause location

| Number of basic clauses in full finite clause | Pause location | |
	Before first word	After conjunction
One	.224 (116)	.151 (71)
More than one	.258 (33)	.173 (19)

Table 12.7
Mean data for pausing before subsequent full finite clauses as a function of number of basic clauses

Number of basic clauses in full finite clause	Measure	
	Silent pause length	Proportion preceded by filled pause
One	960	.043
	(26)	(116)
More than one	969	.041
	(8)	(33)

more than one basic clause. However, the difference was clearly not significant, $F < 1$. For the filled pausing data, the direction of the difference was opposite to that for silent pause lengths. Again, however, the difference did not approach significance, $F < 1$.

Overall, as in the study of Ford and Holmes 1978, no strong evidence could be found supporting the idea that before a full finite clause containing a number of basic clauses, planning and integration of all of the basic clauses takes place. It must be concluded that for the production of sentences, basic clauses are essentially planned and uttered one after the other.

12.3 Discussion

This study clearly shows that the results of previous investigations of speech hesitations have been misleading in their apparent support for the notion that the full finite ("surface") clause is a major sentence planning unit. These previous investigations ignored the basic ("deep") clause unit and thus failed to observe that the frequency and length of pausing are as great at basic clause boundaries within full finite clauses as they are at full finite clause boundaries. From the results presented here, it appears that the occurrence of hesitations in speech does support the conclusion suggested by the findings of Ford and Holmes 1978, that the basic clause is a major unit of sentence planning. The present results and those of Ford and Holmes must be considered together to see what implications they have for planning in sentence production.[2]

It will be useful to summarize briefly the results of the present study as well as those of the reaction time study of Ford and Holmes 1978. The results of the reaction time study indicated that during sentence production, processing load increases in the speech preceding a basic clause, regardless of whether or not the basic clause corresponds to a full finite clause. The present analysis of hesitations further showed that basic clause boundaries are the primary location of pausing within sentences, no matter whether the basic clause boundary is within a full finite clause or actually corresponds to a full finite clause boundary. No evidence could be found in either study to suggest that the full finite clause per se is important. Reaction times did not differ before full finite clauses as a function of the number of basic clauses contained, nor was pausing increased before full finite clauses containing more than one basic clause. In fact, for the sentence-initial full finite clauses, pause lengths were significantly shorter before those containing a number of basic clauses. This result could be taken as positive evidence that only the first basic clause is planned in any detail, since basic clauses within full finite clauses are on average shorter than basic clauses that correspond to a full finite clause. Another interesting result, obtained by Ford and Holmes, was that there were differences in processing load during the production of clauses of different syntactic types, such as relatives, complements, adverbials, and nonembedded clauses. However, it can also be seen from the reaction time data that processing load during basic clauses does *not* differ as a function of whether or not the clause corresponds to a full finite clause, again providing no support for the notion that basic clauses within a full finite clause are planned in any way different from those that correspond to a full finite clause. It seems that there is no evidence that before a full finite clause, planning and integration of all the basic clauses contained takes place. The results regarding sentences are also interesting. The present study showed that sentence boundaries are by far the most important location for pausing in speech. Also, Ford and Holmes found that processing load did not increase toward the end of the *last* basic clause of a sentence, suggesting that speakers do not initiate planning for one sentence during the end of the preceding sentence. The data clearly show that sentences are distinct units in speech. However, while this is so, it appears that they are planned essentially basic clause by basic clause. Not only is it true that processing load increases before basic clause boundaries within sentences and that when speakers pause they do so at basic clause boundaries, but also it is apparent from a detailed examination of the reaction time data of Ford and Holmes that there is no general decrease in processing load throughout a sentence.

The findings of the two studies provide a good basis for suggestions regarding planning in sentence production. The data suggest strongly that although a speaker may have a general idea of what is to be said in a sentence before it is produced, the detailed planning for the sentence proceeds in successive phases during each of which a representation of a unit corresponding to a basic clause is constructed and then mapped into a series of words to be uttered. It appears that this planning usually occurs in the speech immediately preceding the clause and may also occur in a pause before the clause. However, it appears that some decisions regarding a clause are also made during the production of that clause, leading to variations in production difficulty for clauses of different syntactic types.

This view of the production process obviously contradicts the idea discussed earlier, that the basic clause cannot be a sentence planning unit and that the full finite clause is much more likely to be primary. This idea is based on the belief that in sentence planning the representations of meaningful relations that are constructed and mapped into surface sequences are equivalent to those of transformational grammar. Fay 1977, 1979 makes an even stronger claim concerning the relevance of transformational grammar in a model of production. According to Fay, speakers perform operations analogous to the *rules* of transformational grammar—in particular, those of Chomsky's 1965 standard theory. The view presented here is, of course, also opposed to this strong claim.

Let us first consider whether it is unrealistic to claim that the basic clause, and not the full finite clause, is a sentence planning unit. It is true that, given the structure of language as described by transformational grammar, it is more likely that the full finite clause rather than the basic clause would be important. However, the production data suggest very strongly that the detailed planning for sentences occurs essentially basic clause by basic clause. The answer to the problem thus seems to be that the structure of language as described by transformational grammar is not relevant to the process of sentence production.

It is worthwhile to consider possible objections to this conclusion. First, it could be maintained that while the detailed planning for a sentence might usually proceed basic clause by basic clause, planning might proceed differently for any clause containing material which, in a transformational analysis, would be considered as having "moved" into this clause from some following clause. Specifically, it could be suggested that before a clause containing "moved" material, the speaker might plan both this clause and the clause on which it apparently depends. If this suggestion were correct, it would not be expected that speakers would pause between these clauses, since they would together form the planning unit. In fact, though, an analysis performed to test this prediction showed that speakers pause significantly often at the boundary between a clause containing "moved" material and the clause on which it apparently depends.

A second possible objection is that there might be some version of transformational grammar that does give a representation that allows sentences to be planned basic clause by basic clause. Some colleagues have claimed that trace theory (as presented in Chomsky 1976, 1977a, for example) gives the required representation. However, this claim is false. The underlying representation in trace theory is the same as that in any standard transformational grammar. Thus, this level of representation is not of the required type. The difficulty with the surface structure representation given in trace theory is that it does not encode the meaningful grammatical relations for the surface items in each basic clause. Thus, for example, the different semantic relations in sentences (10) and (11) are not represented in the surface structures (12) and (13) proposed by Chomsky 1977a:11. (Also see Chomsky 1976:336.)

(10)
The man promised Bill to leave.

(11)
The man persuaded Bill to leave.

(12)
$[_{S}[_{NP_1}$ the man$]$ $[_{VP}$ promised $[_{NP_2}$ Bill$]$ $[_{S'}$ COMP $[_{S}[_{NP_x}$ e$]$
    $[_{VP}$ to leave$]]]]]$

(13)
$[_{S}[_{NP_1}$ the man$]$ $[_{VP}$ persuaded $[_{NP_2}$ Bill$]$ $[_{S'}$ COMP $[_{S}[_{NP_x}$ e$]$
    $[_{VP}$ to leave$]]]]]$

It is intended that the meaningful grammatical relations be represented by logical form, which is derived from surface structure by means of interpretive rules. For example, a rule of control converts surface structure (12) into the (partially formed) logical form (14) and the surface structure (13) into the (partially formed) logical form (15).

(14)
$[_{S}[_{NP_1}$ the man$]$ $[_{VP}$ promised $[_{NP_2}$ Bill$]$ $[_{S'}$ COMP $[_{S}[_{NP_1}$ e$]$
    $[_{VP}$ to leave$]]]]]$

(15)

[$_S$[$_{NP_1}$ the man] [$_{VP}$ persuaded [$_{NP_2}$ Bill] [$_{S'}$ COMP [$_S$[$_{NP_2}$ e]
  [$_{VP}$ to leave]]]]]]

As Chomsky 1977a:11 notes, however, once the variable NP_x is fixed
by the rule of control as NP_1 or NP_2, the resulting category is indistinguishable from trace. This enables further rules and conditions of logical form to treat the two in the same way—a desirable result in the
theory. Consequently, the difference between the meaningful relations
in subject control and subject raising constructions is neutralized at the
level of logical form. For example, the difference in the relationship
between the surface subject and verb in sentences (16) and (17) is not
represented in the logical forms (18) and (19).

(16)
John expects to like Mary.

(17)
John seems to like Mary.

(18)
[$_S$[$_{NP_1}$ John] [$_{VP}$ expects [$_{S'}$ COMP [$_S$[$_{NP_1}$ e] [$_{VP}$ to like [$_{NP_2}$ Mary]]]]]]

(19)
[$_S$[$_{NP_1}$ John] [$_{VP}$ seems [$_{S'}$ COMP [$_S$[$_{NP_1}$ e] [$_{VP}$ to like [$_{NP_2}$ Mary]]]]]]

In trace theory, then, there is no level of representation of the type
required for planning to proceed basic clause by basic clause. That is,
there is no level at which, for each basic clause, there is a unit that
encodes the meaningful relations for the surface items in that clause. It
would be possible to encode the meaningful relations for surface subjects and verbs by adding lexical information to surface structures.
This, of course, would eliminate the need for transformational representations. In conclusion, then, transformational representations do
not appear to be relevant to sentence planning.

The question must now be asked, What representation of the meaningful relations underlying sentences would permit sentences to be
planned basic clause by basic clause? The answer is, One in which, for
each basic clause, there is a unit which encodes the meaningful grammatical relations for the surface items in that clause, such as the surface
subject, object, and verb. In fact, a very explicit theory that does give
the required type of representation is the lexical theory of syntax pre-

sented in this volume. Moreover, the lexical theory can be incorporated into realistic models of language use.

It is helpful to examine sentences (1)–(5) again, repeated here in (20)–(24). (The descriptions that follow are simplified for purposes of exposition.)

(20)
John appears to be liked by someone.

(21)
The food was believed to be good.

(22)
The children seemed happy enough.

(23)
I don't know which book John asked to be banned.

(24)
Uli is difficult for most people to understand.

In the lexical theory, all constructions, including those like (20)–(24), are base-generated, as opposed to being derived by transformational operations. Further, the theory provides an algorithm for constructing a representation of the underlying relations of a sentence in a single left-to-right traversal of the lexical sequence; thus, crucially, the form of any basic clause does not depend on the representation of the underlying relations in a succeeding clause. Take (20) as an example. In the representation of the underlying relations of this sentence, both basic clauses would have a functional structure of the type which Bresnan in chapter 5 terms a *clause nucleus*. A clause nucleus is a functional structure which has a subject and a lexical predicate which takes logical arguments. In the representation of *John appears*, it would be specified that *John* is the grammatical subject and that *appear* is a predicate which takes one argument and which occurs in the present tense in this particular sentence. The argument which *appear* takes is specified to be a Verb Complement. In the representation of *to be liked by someone*, *John* is designated to be the Subject. This is because the lexical component in the grammar specifies that the grammatical subject of the predicate *appear* must be the functional Subject of the Verb Complement of *appear*. In the functional structure, it is also specified that *like* takes two arguments and that, in this sentence, it occurs in the passive form with the infinitive *to be*. The arguments which *like* takes are specified to function as By-Object and Subject. The pronoun *someone* is designated as the By-Object. The most important point about the representation of the sentence in this lexically based syntax is that the surface subject *John* in the clause *John appears* does not depend on the succeeding Verb Complement (as it would in a transformational analysis); rather, the relations encoded in the functional representation of the Verb Complement depend partly on the verb *appear* and the Subject *John*.

The representation of the relations underlying sentences (21) and (22) can be constructed in a manner similar to the representation of (20). However, sentences (23) and (24) are quite different since, according to the theory, neither of these contains a complement. It is still true, though, that the representations given by the lexical theory are such that the form of one basic clause does not depend on the underlying relations of a succeeding clause. Sentence (23), for example, contains an embedded question. The theory explains the underlying relations in this sentence by syntactic binding and not by lexical encoding. The syntactic component of the grammar generates the phrase structure of the sentence with syntactic binding relations between *which book* and the node where the gap exists. Because of the syntactic binding, in the construction of the relations underlying the basic clause which contains the gap (that is, the clause *to be banned*), the features of *which book* are assigned to the grammatical function specified by the gap's phrase structure node—in this case, they are assigned to the function of Subject.

If the representation of meaningful relations as characterized in the lexical theory of syntax is assumed to be relevant to the planning process, then it would not be implausible for the basic clause to be a major sentence planning unit. However, it is necessary to consider the evidence which Fay 1977, 1979 claims to indicate that speakers actually construct deep syntactic representations as in transformational grammar and perform operations on them analogous to the rules of the grammar.

Fay bases his claim on a corpus of speech errors which he considers to be syntactic errors and which according to his argument appear to result from the malfunctioning of transformational rules. Examples of the errors are given in (25)–(30), together with what the speakers claimed they intended to say.

(25)
Intended: And when they chew coca, which they chew all day long,
          they . . .
Error: And when they chew coca, which they chew coca all day
          long, they . . .

(26)
Intended: Would you turn on the light?
Error: Would you turn on the light on?

(27)
Intended: What could I have done with the check?
Error: What could have I done with the check?

(28)
Intended: I know where a top for it is.
Error: I know where is a top for it.

(29)
Intended: I know where they all are.
Error: I know where they're all.

(30)
Intended: If that was done to me . . .
Error: If I was done that to . . .

According to Fay, the errors in (25) and (26) are similar, because in
both cases the elementary transformation of deletion has been omitted.
Fay claims that in (25) the noun phrase *coca* in the relative clause has
been copied at the front of the clause and transformed into a *wh*-word,
but that the original has not been deleted, leaving *coca* stranded in its
deep structure position. For (26), also, Fay claims that the copying
transformation has taken place, moving the particle to the right of the
noun phrase, while the deletion transformation has been omitted. (In
fact, if this were so, the speaker making the error should have reported
that the intended utterance was "Would you turn the light on?" Fay
could account for the error, though, as an accidental addition of the
copying transformation.) Fay explains the errors in (27) and (28) as
mistakes in applying the transformation of Subject–Auxiliary Inversion. According to Fay, in (27) Subject–Auxiliary Inversion has moved
too much material, while in (28) it has applied where it is not required.
For (29) Fay argues that the transformation of Auxiliary Shift has been
applied by mistake, moving the verb to the left of the quantifier. Fi-

nally, for (30) he claims that the deep structure has been misanalyzed and that the Passive transformation has therefore taken the object of a preposition and moved it into the subject position, instead of taking the direct object of the verb.

Since the errors Fay discusses can be described in terms of a malfunctioning of transformational operations, he claims that they provide evidence that speakers construct deep syntactic structures and perform transformational operations on them. In the model he proposes, speakers use transformations in precisely the form in which they are expressed in transformational grammar—in particular, in Chomsky's 1965 standard theory. Phrase structure rules and lexical insertion produce a deep structure, which thus corresponds to a psychological structure, and mental operations change this and intermediate structures in exactly the same way that transformational operations in a grammar convert the deep and intermediate structures into a surface structure. As Fay notes, his model predicts that a speaker must complete all of the syntactic planning of a sentence before the sentence is uttered. This is because, in a transformational grammar, transformations apply when the complete deep structure representation has been constructed; moreover, they apply to sentoids in the order from most deeply embedded to least deeply embedded, which does not correspond to the normal order of clauses in a sentence. Fay notes that the prediction may seem objectionable because of the intuition that speech is planned left-to-right. Certainly, Fay's model is opposed to the view of production which the data of the present study and that of Ford and Holmes 1978 suggest—that although a speaker may have a very general idea about most or all of a sentence before uttering it, a complete representation of the sentence is not worked out before its initiation and the detailed planning is carried out basic clause by basic clause as the sentence is produced. It will be argued, however, that there are difficulties in interpreting the evidence Fay presents.

While the errors which Fay 1977, 1979 discusses can be described in terms of a malfunctioning of transformational operations analogous to the operations of a transformational grammar, it is not at all clear that this shows that speakers perform the operations. After all, the fact that well-formed speech can be described in terms of transformational operations does not constitute evidence that speakers actually perform these operations. Fay seems to argue that support for his claim comes from the fact that, in the errors, material is misplaced only into positions where a transformational operation would place it or where it would be left if a transformation were omitted. Thus, for example, errors such as those shown in (31)–(36) presumably do not occur.

(31)
*And when they chew coca, which they chew all day coca long, they . . .

(32)
*Would you on turn the light?

(33)
*What could I done with have the check?

(34)
*I know where a is top for it.

(35)
*I know are where they all.

(36)
*If I done was that to . . .

However, there is a problem with Fay's argument. Since the errors Fay considers are so well-behaved with respect to where material is misplaced, any reasonable theory of language structure could describe them. Thus, for example, the errors could be described in terms of the lexical theory of syntax. Errors such as (25), (26), and (30) are particularly interesting types. According to the lexical theory, in relative clauses there are syntactic binding relations between the relative pronoun and the node where the gap exists. In the construction of a representation of the grammatical relations, features assigned to the relative pronoun are also assigned to the grammatical function specified by the node at the gap. Thus, the error in (25) can be described as the accidental expression of the features assigned to the grammatical function at the gap. As for the error in (26), in the lexical theory, verbs such as *turn on* would be marked in the lexicon as being able to occur in two ways: V *on* NP and V NP *on*. Thus, the error can be described as the accidental use of both ways of employing the verb *turn on*. The error in (30) involves an error in the passive construction. Passivization is formulated in the theory as a lexical rule operating on the lexical form of a verb. (The *lexical form* of a verb specifies what grammatical function must be performed by each of its arguments.) The rule of Passivization changes the lexical form of a verb by altering, in a regular way, the specification of what grammatical function the arguments must play.

Through Passivization, the argument assigned the function of Object for an active sentence is now assigned the function of Subject. The error in (30) can be regarded as resulting from the alteration of the grammatical function of the wrong argument in the lexical form. The specification of the argument assigned the function of To-Object for an active sentence has been altered to Subject. Thus, the lexical form of *do* used in constructing the sentence is incorrect and produces the error of (30). The errors in (28) and (29) can also be described in the lexical theory, by saying that the incorrect functional structure has been constructed, while the error in (27) could perhaps be considered as resulting from the blending of two functional structures. In short, because the errors Fay discusses are "well-behaved" with respect to syntactic structure, any reasonable theory of language structure will be able to give an account of them, and they thus provide no evidence that speakers perform transformational operations analogous to those of transformational grammar.

It has been argued so far that the data of the present study are opposed to the transformational model of production proposed by Fay 1977, 1979 and, moreover, that there is no evidence for Fay's model. It has also been argued that even if it is assumed that only the underlying representations of sentences as described by transformational grammar (and not necessarily the rules of grammar) are relevant to the planning of sentences, then it would not be expected that sentence planning would occur basic clause by basic clause. It would be expected that production would be more likely to occur by the successive planning of full finite clauses. Further, it has been shown that the representations of meaningful relations given by the lexical theory of syntax would permit sentence production to proceed by the successive planning of basic clauses in the order in which they are spoken. Moreover, an examination of the theory yields very interesting suggestions concerning the planning for each basic clause unit. (Again, in the discussion that follows, descriptions concerning the lexical theory are simplified for purposes of exposition.)

Since according to the theory each basic clause has a representation in which there is a subject and also a lexical predicate which takes logical arguments, then if the theory were incorporated into a model of production, planning for a basic clause would presumably include choosing the predicate, the subject, and the other required logical arguments, as well as sequencing all of the logical arguments in the way specified by the predicate's lexical form. Consider first sentence (37), which is very simple in that it consists of only one basic clause.

(37)
Fred handed the toys to a baby.

To produce this particular sentence, the speaker would presumably have decided that *Fred* was the agent of the action, that *the toys* were the theme, and that *a baby* was the goal or the recipient. The agent, theme, and goal are the logical arguments of the predicate *hand*. The speaker would also have retrieved the lexical form of *hand,* in order to know how to sequence the arguments. The ordinary lexical form of *hand,* which has had no lexical rule applied to it, specifies that the agent must be the Subject, the theme must be the Object, and the goal or recipient must be the To-Object. From knowing the arguments and the lexical form of *hand,* the speaker can sequence the words correctly and insert the preposition *to* before the To-Object. Other decisions for (37) would include choosing the correct tense for the predicate, the correct articles, and the correct singular and plural forms of the nouns.

Now consider sentences (38) and (39), which are more complex, each consisting of two basic clauses.

(38)
Susan strikes Fred as sure of herself.

(39)
Susan regards Fred as sure of himself.

The lexical forms of both *strike-as* and *regard-as* have three arguments. For *strike-as,* the argument that is the theme must function as the Subject, while the argument that is the experiencer must function as the Object. In contrast, for *regard-as,* the theme argument functions as the Object, while the experiencer argument functions as the Subject. For both *strike-as* and *regard-as,* the third argument functions as an Adjectival Complement, and it is specified in the lexical form of the predicates that the Complement has a certain functional subject. Thus, in both (38) and (39), the Adjectival Complement forms one basic clause, while the Subject, the verb, and the Object form another. Given the production data, it would be expected that most of the details of the two basic clauses in each sentence would be worked out in successive phases. For sentence (38), the speaker would decide that *Susan* is the theme and that *Fred* is the experiencer and would also retrieve the lexical form of *strike-as*. From knowing the theme and experiencer arguments and from knowing the lexical form of the predicate, the speaker knows that *Susan* must be the Subject and that *Fred* must be the Object and can thus successfully sequence the words in the first basic clause. For sentence (39), the speaker would decide that *Fred* is the theme and that *Susan* is the experiencer. On retrieving the lexical form of *regard-as,* the speaker would know that *Fred* must be the Object and that *Susan* must be the Subject. Again, this allows the speaker to correctly sequence the words in the first basic clause. The details of the second basic clause must then be planned. As for the first clause of both sentences, planning for the second will include choosing a predicate and retrieving its lexical form, deciding on the logical arguments, and sequencing the arguments in the way specified by the lexical form. For both (38) and (39), the speaker would retrieve the lexical form of *sure-of,* which takes two arguments. One of these arguments is specified as having the function of Subject, while the other is specified as having the function of an Of-Object. It has already been noted that for the lexical forms of *strike-as* and *regard-as,* the Adjectival Complement is marked as having a certain functional subject. It is specified that the functional subject of the Adjectival Complement of *strike-as* must be identical to the grammatical Subject of *strike-as*. Thus, for (38), the speaker will know that the argument of *sure-of* which has the function of subject must be identical to *Susan*. For the second argument of *sure-of,* the speaker must choose the correct reflexive form—that is, *herself*. In contrast to the predicate *strike-as,* it is specified that the functional subject of the Adjectival Complement of *regard-as* must be identical to the grammatical Object of *regard-as*. Thus, for (39), the speaker will know that the argument of *sure-of* which has the function of subject must be identical to *Fred*. Again, for the second argument of *sure-of,* the speaker must choose the correct reflexive form—that is, *himself*. The lexical forms of *strike-as* and *regard-as* also specify that for the Adjectival Complement, the clause must be introduced by the word *as*. Once the lexical form of the predicate *sure-of* has been retrieved and the correct logical arguments chosen, the words in the Adjectival Complement can be produced in their correct sequence; the logical argument that is the functional subject being suppressed, since it is identical to one of the arguments in the preceding clause.

From considering sentences (37)–(39) in relation to the lexical theory of grammatical representation, it is apparent that it could be fruitful to incorporate the theory into a model of production. The production data, together with the linguistic theory, suggest a model in which the detailed planning for a sentence proceeds in recurring phases, each of which consists of the planning of a basic clause unit. During each phase, a predicate is chosen and its lexical form retrieved, the logical arguments of the predicate decided upon, and the logical arguments sequenced in the way specified by the predicate's lexical form. Most of this planning would need to occur before the clause is produced. However, it is possible that the correct sequencing of the arguments may be worked out as the clause is being uttered, thus leading to differences in processing load during clauses of different types.

In chapter 11, Ford, Bresnan, and Kaplan incorporate the lexical theory of linguistic representation in a computational model of sentence perception. The linguistic theory could also be incorporated in a computational model of sentence production, leading to many interesting predictions. Factors influencing processing load may include the grammatical control of the subject of a clause, the application of lexical rules to the lexical form of a predicate, the number of arguments taken by the predicate, and syntactic binding relations.

The lexical theory of grammatical representation does not require that the basic clause be a major planning unit. However, the theory is consistent with that idea and suggests interesting possibilities regarding how each basic clause might be planned. It should be noted that neither the linguistic theory nor the production data imply that the basic clause is a major unit in sentence comprehension. It is apparent, though, that the basic clause is an important unit in production, with sentence production proceeding by the successive planning of basic clauses in the order in which they are spoken.

Appendix: The Segmentation of Speech Samples

Key
[ ]   sentence boundaries
( )   full finite clause boundaries
/   basic clause boundaries that are not full finite clause boundaries

Redundant words, repetitions, filled pauses, incomplete words, intruding sounds, and word choice mistakes are shown in italics. Silent pause lengths are marked in milliseconds.

...[(1230 I tend / to *just* go back there / an' 590 *an'* live in college / and not 460 live at University) (1610 which is 720 a pity *really*) (600 I suppose)]...

...[(I think) (they could provide better legal services for them) (500 *um* 860 *you know* 200 which entail *sort of* interpreter services / 'n' 540 *and* 550 banning 360 hire purchase for people) (who've been in Australia under three years)]...

...[(If 1380 there are some aspects of a 490 parent's personality) (2440 that 890 are very limiting) (the kid can get away from these / by associating with other adults / having other adults / to model on)]...

...[(*um* 2430 I came to University / 920 to make money mainly / 1050 *I mean* to 1600 have a key / to making money) (440 and also because there was no other 830 recourse open to me)]...

...[(1520 *but* I *th'* I think) (that 680 people should be allowed / to *live* 1260 *i'* go on / living in the society)] [(*an'* it should be) (that there is 1270 a reason / for them committing the crime) (1130 which can be 400 fixed up / 3390 through being 580 interviewed / 1220 *um* 230 through 230 some *sort of* guidance / 730 an' 260 hopefully through removing the cause of the problem)]...

...[(790 With the smaller family you're more likely / 510 to be able / to put the kids through to Matric) (if they want it)]...

Notes

I would like to thank Joan Bresnan for her encouragement and her valuable comments on an earlier draft of this chapter. I am also grateful to Bill Cooper, Merrill Garrett, and Bart Wright for their comments on this or related work. Part of the research reported here was carried out at the University of Melbourne while I was a graduate student with Virginia Holmes. I am very grateful for all of her help. My research was supported in part by a grant from the Australian Federation of University Women–Victorian Division and by NIH Grant 2–R01–HD05168–06AI awarded to Jerry Fodor.

1. It should perhaps be noted here that Boomer 1965 in fact examined what were termed "phonemic" clauses. However, these often correspond to surface clauses (Hawkins 1971, Fodor, Bever, and Garrett 1974). Although "phonemic" clauses are defined in terms of pitch and stress levels of speech, Lieberman 1965 has shown that there is often no physical basis to the levels of pitch and stress that linguists assign to speech when performing phonemic analyses. It seems that linguists often rely on their knowledge of grammatical structure to perform the analyses.

2. At this point some consideration should be given to possible objections to concluding that the pause data support the idea that the basic clause is a major planning unit. It could be argued that the pauses may have had nothing to do with planning units, but could have occurred merely for the intake of breath or perhaps to help the listener grasp the syntactic structure of the utterances. However, there are a number of points that must be made. First, the pattern of pausing was the same for both silent and filled pauses, such as "um" and "ah." Second, basic clause boundaries within a full finite clause are not positions where pausing is likely to aid the listener (Tanenhaus and Carroll 1975). Third, in a study by Fodor, Forster, Garrett, and Hakes 1974 it was noticed that readers did not breathe at basic clause boundaries within full finite clauses, even when attempts were made to induce them to do so. Finally, it must be remembered that the results of the pause study are not meant to be considered on their own, but must be considered in light of the reaction time study of Ford and Holmes 1978. A second possible objection is that it might be major phrases that are important, and not basic clauses. However, a control analysis was carried out to see if this was true. It was found that pausing at major phrase boundaries within clauses was equivalent to pausing before ordinary words within a clause; in fact, pausing was proportionately less frequent before predicate phrases than before the within-clause words.

References

Abbott, B. 1976. Right Node Raising as a test for constituenthood. *Linguistic Inquiry* 7, 639–642.

Ackermann, W. 1954. *Solvable cases of the decision problem*. Amsterdam: North Holland.

Aissen, J. 1975. Presentational There Insertion: A cyclic root transformation. In R. E. Grossman, L. J. San, and T. J. Vance, eds., *Papers from the Eleventh Regional Meeting of the Chicago Linguistic Society*. University of Chicago.

Akmajian, A., S. Steele, and T. Wasow. 1979. The category AUX in universal grammar. *Linguistic Inquiry* 10, 1–64.

Allen, C. L. 1975. Case-marking and the NP cycle in Old English. *Linguistic Analysis* 1, 389–401.

Allen, M. 1978. Morphological investigations. Doctoral dissertation, University of Connecticut.

Allwood, J. 1976. The Complex NP Constraint as a non-universal rule and some semantic factors influencing the acceptability of Swedish sentences which violate the CNPC. In J. Stillings, ed., *University of Massachusetts Occasional Papers in Linguistics*. Vol. 2. University of Massachusetts at Amherst.

Amritavalli, R. 1980. Expressing cross-categorial selectional correspondences: An alternative to the $\overline{\text{X}}$ syntax approach. *Linguistic Analysis* 6, 305–343.

Anderson, J. R. 1976. *Language, Memory, and Thought*. Hillsdale, N.J.: Lawrence Erlbaum.

Anderson, J. R. 1977. Induction of augmented transition networks. *Cognitive Science* 1, 125–157.

Anderson, J. R., and G. H. Bower. 1973. *Human Associative Memory*. Washington, D.C.: Winston & Sons.

Anderson, S. R. 1977. Comments on the paper by Wasow. In P. W. Culicover, T. Wasow, and A. Akmajian, eds., *Formal Syntax*. New York: Academic Press.

Andrews, A. D. 1971. Case agreement of predicate modifiers in Ancient Greek. *Linguistic Inquiry* 2, 127–151.

Andrews, A. D. 1973. Agreement and deletion. In C. Corum, T. Smith-Stark, and A. Weiser, eds., *Papers from the Ninth Regional Meeting of the Chicago Linguistic Society*. University of Chicago.

Andrews, A. D. 1976. The VP complement analysis in Modern Icelandic. In *Montreal Working Papers in Linguistics*. University of Montreal.

Andrews, A. D. 1979. A lexically based analysis of case-marking and the complement system in Icelandic. Paper presented at the Brown Workshop on Syntactic Theory, Brown University.

Andrews, A. D. 1981. The rudiments of coordinate structure in LFG. Ms., Department of Linguistics, Australian National University.

Andrews, A. D. To appear. Long distance agreement and functional interpretation. In P. Jacobson and G. K. Pullum, eds., *The Nature of Syntactic Representation*. Dordrecht: Reidel.

Aronoff, M. 1976. *Word Formation in Generative Grammar*. Linguistic Inquiry Monograph 1. Cambridge, Mass.: The MIT Press.

Babby, L. H. 1973a. A note on agreement in Russian. *Glossa* 7, 253–264.

Babby, L. H. 1973b. The deep structure of adjectives and participles in Russian. *Language* 49, 349–360.

Babby, L. H. 1975. *A Transformational Grammar of Russian Adjectives*. The Hague: Mouton.

Bach, E. 1977. Comments on the paper by Chomsky. In P. W. Culicover, T. Wasow, and A. Akmajian, eds., *Formal Syntax*. New York: Academic Press.

Bach, E. 1979. Control in Montague grammar. *Linguistic Inquiry* 10, 515–531.

Bach, E. 1980. In defense of passive. *Linguistics and Philosophy* 3, 297–341.

Baker, C. L. 1968. Indirect questions in English. Doctoral dissertation, University of Illinois.

Baker, C. L. 1977. Comments on the paper by Culicover and Wexler. In P. W. Culicover, T. Wasow, and A. Akmajian, eds., *Formal Syntax*. New York: Academic Press.

Baker, C. L. 1979. Syntactic theory and the projection problem. *Linguistic Inquiry* 10, 533–581.

Baker, C. L., and J. McCarthy, eds. In press. *The Logical Problem of Language Acquisition*. Cambridge, Mass.: The MIT Press.

Baker, M. 1982. Objects, themes, and lexical rules in Italian. Ms., Department of Linguistics and Philosophy, Massachusetts Institute of Technology. To appear in L. Levin, M. Rappaport, and A. Zaenen, eds., *Papers in LFG*. Bloomington, Ind.: Indiana University Linguistics Club.

Bartlett, M. S. 1947. The use of transformations. *Biometrics* 3, 39–52.

Bechhofer, R. 1976a. Reduced WH-questions. In J. Hankamer and J. Aissen, eds., *Harvard Studies in Syntax and Semantics*. Vol. 2. Harvard University.

Bechhofer, R. 1976b. Reduction in conjoined WH-questions. In J. Hankamer and J. Aissen, eds., *Harvard Studies in Syntax and Semantics*. Vol. 2. Harvard University.

Bell, S. 1980. Comparative restrictiveness of relational grammar and lexical syntax. Ms., Department of Linguistics, University of British Columbia, Vancouver.

Berwick, R. 1980. *Learning Structural Descriptions of Grammatical Rules from Examples*. Artificial Intelligence Technical Report TR–578. Artificial Intelligence Laboratory, Massachusetts Institute of Technology.

Berwick, R., and A. Weinberg. To appear. The role of grammars in models of language use. *Cognition*.

Bever, T. G. 1970. The cognitive basis for linguistic structures. In J. R. Hayes, ed., *Cognition and the Development of Language*. New York: Wiley.

Bever, T. G., J. M. Carroll, and R. Hurtig. 1976. Analogy *or* ungrammatical sequences that are utterable and comprehensible are the origins of new grammars in language acquisition and linguistic evolution. In T. G. Bever, J. J. Katz, and D. T. Langendoen, eds., *An Integrated Theory of Linguistic Ability*. Sussex: Harvester Press.

Biermann, A., and J. Feldman. 1972. A survey of results in grammatical inference. In S. Watanabe, ed., *Frontiers in Pattern Recognition*. New York: Academic Press.

Birnbaum, H. 1964. *Studies on Predication in Russian I: Predicative Case, Short Form Adjectives, and Predicatives*. Santa Monica, Calif.: The Rand Corporation.

Birnbaum, H. 1965. *Studies on Predication in Russian II: On the Predicative Use of the Russian Infinitive*. Santa Monica, Calif.: The Rand Corporation.

Bloomfield, L. 1933. *Language*. New York: Holt, Rinehart and Winston.

Boomer, D. S. 1965. Hesitation and grammatical encoding. *Language and Speech* 8, 148–158.

Bordelois, I. 1974. The grammar of Spanish causative complements. Doctoral dissertation, Massachusetts Institute of Technology.

Borer, H. 1978. Passive constructions in modern Hebrew. Ms., Department of Linguistics and Philosophy, Massachusetts Institute of Technology.

Borkin, A. 1974. Raising to object position: A study in the syntax and semantics of clause merging. Doctoral dissertation, University of Michigan. Also in *University of Michigan Papers in Linguistics* 2.1.

Borras, F. M., and R. F. Christian. 1971. *Russian Syntax. Aspects of Modern Russian Syntax and Vocabulary*. 2d ed. Oxford: Clarendon Press.

Bowerman, M. 1973. *Learning to Talk: A Cross-Sectional Study of Early Syntactic Development, with Special Reference to Finnish*. Cambridge: Cambridge University Press.

Bowerman, M. 1974. Learning the structure of causative verbs: A study in the relationship of cognitive, semantic, and syntactic development. *Papers and Reports on Child Language Development*, No. 8. Committee on Linguistics, Stanford University.

Bowerman, M. 1976. Semantic factors in the acquisition of rules for word use and sentence construction. In D. M. Morehead and A. E. Morehead, eds., *Normal and Deficient Child Language*. Baltimore: University Park Press.

Bowers, J. S. 1976. On surface structure grammatical relations, and the structure-preserving hypothesis. *Linguistic Analysis* 2, 225–242.

Braine, M. D. S. 1971. On two types of models of the internalization of grammars. In D. I. Slobin, ed., *The Ontogenesis of Grammar*. New York: Academic Press.

Braine, M. D. S. 1976. *Children's First Word Combinations*. Monographs of the Society for Research in Child Development 41, No. 164.

Brame, M. K. 1976. *Conjectures and Refutations in Syntax and Semantics*. New York: Elsevier North-Holland.

Brame, M. K. 1978. *Base-Generated Syntax*. Seattle, Wash.: Noit Amrofer.

Bresnan, J. 1972. Theory of complementation in English syntax. Doctoral dissertation, Massachusetts Institute of Technology. Published 1979 New York: Garland Press.

Bresnan, J. 1974. The position of certain clause-particles in phrase structure. *Linguistic Inquiry* 5, 614–619.

Bresnan, J. 1975. Transformations and categories in syntax. Paper presented at the Fifth International Congress of Logic, Methodology and Philosophy of Science, London, Ontario, Canada, 1975. [Published as Bresnan 1977.]

Bresnan, J. 1976a. Toward a realistic model of transformational grammar. Paper presented at the MIT-AT&T Convocation on Communications, "New Approaches to a Realistic Model of Language," Massachusetts Institute of Technology.

Bresnan, J. 1976b. On the form and functioning of transformations. *Linguistic Inquiry* 7, 3–40.

Bresnan, J. 1976c. Evidence for a theory of unbounded transformations. *Linguistic Analysis* 2, 353–393.

Bresnan, J. 1976d. Nonarguments for raising. *Linguistic Inquiry* 7, 485–501.

Bresnan, J. 1977. Transformations and categories in syntax. In R. E. Butts and J. Hintikka, eds., *Basic Problems in Methodology and Linguistics*. Dordrecht: Reidel.

Bresnan, J. 1978. A realistic transformational grammar. In M. Halle, J. Bresnan, and G. A. Miller, eds., *Linguistic Theory and Psychological Reality*. Cambridge, Mass.: The MIT Press.

Bresnan, J. 1979. A theory of grammatical representation. Duplicated lecture notes, Department of Linguistics and Philosophy, Massachusetts Institute of Technology.

Bresnan, J. 1979a. Bounded context parsability and learnability. Paper presented at the Workshop on Mathematics and Linguistics, Hampshire College, December 1979.

Bresnan, J. 1981. An approach to universal grammar and the mental representation of language. *Cognition* 10, 39–52.

Bresnan, J. 1982. On the nature of grammatical representation. Short-term Humanities Council Visiting Fellow Lecture, Princeton University, May 1982.

Bresnan, J. In preparation a. Instrumentalization.

Bresnan, J. In preparation b. Polyadicity, scope, and lexical rules.

Bresnan, J. To appear. *Grammatical Interpretation*.

Bresnan, J., and J. Grimshaw. 1978. The syntax of free relatives in English. *Linguistic Inquiry* 9, 331–391.

Bresnan, J., R. M. Kaplan, and A. Zaenen. Forthcoming. Cross-serial dependencies in Dutch. Published as J. Bresnan, R. M. Kaplan, S. Peters, and A. Zaenen. 1982. Cross-serial dependencies in Dutch. *Linguistic Inquiry* 13.4.

Brown, R. 1973. *A First Language: The Early Stages*. Cambridge, Mass.: Harvard University Press.

Brown, R. 1978. It may not be Phrygian, but it is not ergative, either. Ms., Harvard University.

Brown, R., and C. Hanlon. 1970. Derivational complexity and order of acquisition in child speech. In J. R. Hayes, ed., *Cognition and the Development of Language*. New York: Wiley.

Carey, S. 1978. The child as word learner. In M. Halle, J. Bresnan, and G. A. Miller, eds., *Linguistic Theory and Psychological Reality*. Cambridge, Mass.: The MIT Press.

Carnap, R. 1952. Meaning postulates. *Philosophical Studies* 3, 65–73. Reprinted in *Meaning and Necessity,* 2d ed., 1956. Chicago: University of Chicago Press.

Chomsky, C. 1969. *The Acquisition of Syntax in Children from 5 to 10.* Cambridge, Mass.: The MIT Press.

Chomsky, N. 1957. *Syntactic Structures.* The Hague: Mouton.

Chomsky, N. 1963. Formal properties of grammar. In R. D. Luce, R. Bush, and E. Galanter, eds., *Handbook of Mathematical Psychology.* Vol. 2. New York: Wiley.

Chomsky, N. 1964. *Current Issues in Linguistic Theory.* The Hague: Mouton.

Chomsky, N. 1965. *Aspects of the Theory of Syntax.* Cambridge, Mass.: The MIT Press.

Chomsky, N. 1969. Quine's empirical assumptions. In D. Davidson and J. Hintikka, eds., *Words and Objections: Essays on the Work of W. V. Quine.* New York: Humanities Press.

Chomsky, N. 1970. Remarks on nominalization. In R. A. Jacobs and P. S. Rosenbaum, eds., *Readings in English Transformational Grammar.* Waltham, Mass.: Ginn. Also in N. Chomsky. 1972. *Studies on Semantics in Generative Grammar.* The Hague: Mouton.

Chomsky, N. 1973. Conditions on transformations. In S. R. Anderson and P. Kiparsky, eds., *A Festschrift for Morris Halle.* New York: Holt, Rinehart and Winston.

Chomsky, N. 1976. Conditions on rules of grammar. *Linguistic Analysis* 2, 303–351.

Chomsky, N. 1977a. Introduction to *Essays on Form and Interpretation.* New York: Elsevier North-Holland.

Chomsky, N. 1977b. On *wh*-movement. In P. W. Culicover, T. Wasow, and A. Akmajian, eds., *Formal Syntax.* New York: Academic Press.

Chomsky, N. 1979a. Markedness and core grammar. Ms., Massachusetts Institute of Technology. Also in A. Belletti, L. Brandi, and L. Rizzi, eds. 1981. *Theory of Markedness in Generative Grammar.* Pisa: Scuola Normale Superiore.

Chomsky, N. 1979b. Pisa lectures. [Published as Chomsky 1981.]

Chomsky, N. 1980. On binding. *Linguistic Inquiry* 11, 1–46.

Chomsky, N. 1980a. On the representation of form and function. Paper presented at the CNRS Conference at Royaumont, France, June 1980.

Chomsky, N. 1980b. *Rules and Representations.* New York: Columbia University Press.

Chomsky, N. 1981. *Lectures on Government and Binding.* Dordrecht: Foris.

Chomsky, N., and M. Halle. 1968. *The Sound Pattern of English*. New York: Harper & Row.

Chomsky, N., and H. Lasnik. 1977. Filters and control. *Linguistic Inquiry* 8, 425–504.

Church, K. W. 1980. On memory limitations in natural language processing. Technical Report MIT/LCS/TR–245, Massachusetts Institute of Technology. Bloomington, Ind.: Indiana University Linguistics Club.

Church, K. W., and R. M. Kaplan. Forthcoming. Removing recursion from natural language processors based on phrase-structure grammars. Paper presented at the Modelling Human Parsing Strategies symposium, The Center for Cognitive Science, The University of Texas, Austin, March 1981.

Chvany, C. V. 1975. *On the Syntax of Be-Sentences in Russian*. Cambridge, Mass.: Slavica Publishers.

Clark, H. H. 1973. The language-as-fixed-effect fallacy: A critique of language statistics in psychological research. *Journal of Verbal Learning and Verbal Behavior* 12, 335–359.

Cole, P., W. Harbert, G. Hermon, and S. N. Sridhar. 1978. On the acquisition of subjecthood. *Studies in the Linguistic Sciences* 8, 44–71.

Cole, P., and J. Sadock, eds. 1977. *Grammatical Relations*. Syntax and Semantics, vol. 8. New York: Academic Press.

Comrie, B. 1974. The second dative: A transformational approach. In R. D. Brecht and C. V. Chvany, eds., *Slavic Transformational Syntax*. University of Michigan.

Comrie, B. 1976. The syntax of causative constructions: Cross-linguistic similarities and divergences. In M. Shibatani, ed., *The Grammar of Causative Constructions*. Syntax and Semantics, vol. 6. New York: Academic Press.

Comrie, B. 1977. In defense of spontaneous demotion: The impersonal passive. In P. Cole and J. Sadock, eds., *Grammatical Relations*. Syntax and Semantics, vol. 8. New York: Academic Press.

Craig, C. 1977. *The Structure of Jacaltec*. Austin: University of Texas Press.

Damourette, J., and E. Pichon. 1911–1940. *Des mots à la pensée; essai de grammaire de la langue française*. Collection des linguistes contemporains. Paris: Bibliothèque du "français moderne."

de Villiers, J. G. In press. The process of rule learning in child speech: A new look. In K. E. Nelson, ed., *Child Language*. Vol. 2. New York: Gardner Press.

de Villiers, J. G., H. T. Flusberg, and K. Hakuta. 1977. Deciding among theories of the development of coordination in child speech. Paper presented at the Stanford Child Language Research Forum, March 1977.

de Villiers, J. G., H. T. Flusberg, K. Hakuta, and M. Cohen. 1979. Children's comprehension of relative clauses. *Journal of Psycholinguistic Research* 8, 499–518.

Dixon, R. M. W. 1979. Ergativity. *Language* 55, 59–138.

Dowty, D. 1978. Governed transformations as lexical rules in a Montague grammar. *Linguistic Inquiry* 9, 393–426.

Dowty, D. To appear. Grammatical relations and relational grammar. In P. Jacobson and G. K. Pullum, eds., *The Nature of Syntactic Representation*. Dordrecht: Reidel.

Emonds, J. E. 1970. Root and structure-preserving transformations. Doctoral dissertation, Massachusetts Institute of Technology.

Emonds, J. E. 1975. A transformational analysis of French clitics without positive output constraints. *Linguistic Analysis* 1, 3–24.

Emonds, J. E. 1976. *A Transformational Approach to English Syntax*. New York: Academic Press.

Engdahl, E. 1980a. The syntax and semantics of questions in Swedish. Doctoral dissertation, University of Massachusetts at Amherst.

Engdahl, E. 1980b. Wh-constructions in Swedish and the relevance of subjacency. In J. T. Jensen, ed., *Proceedings of the Tenth Annual Meeting of NELS*. Department of Linguistics, University of Ottawa, Ontario.

Erreich, A., V. Valian, and J. Winzemer. 1980. Aspects of a theory of language acquisition. *Journal of Child Language* 7, 157–179.

Erteschik, N. 1973. On the nature of island constraints. Doctoral dissertation, Massachusetts Institute of Technology.

Evers, A. 1975. The transformational cycle in Dutch and German. Doctoral dissertation, Rijksuniversiteit, Utrecht.

Falk, Y. [Falk, E.] 1980. Word order and rules of syntax. Honors thesis, Brandeis University.

Falk, Y. 1980a. The English auxiliary system: A lexical-functional analysis. Ms., Department of Linguistics and Philosophy, Massachusetts Institute of Technology.

Farmer, A. 1980. On the interaction of morphology and syntax. Doctoral dissertation, Massachusetts Institute of Technology.

Fassi Fehri, A. 1981. Complémentation et anaphore en arabe moderne: Une approche lexicale fonctionnelle. Thèse de doctorat d'état, Université de Paris III.

Fauconnier, G. 1974. *La coréférence: syntaxe ou sémantique*. Paris: Seuil.

Fay, D. 1977. Transformational errors. Paper presented at the Twelfth International Congress of Linguists, Vienna.

Fay, D. 1979. Performing transformations. To appear in R. Cole, ed., *Perception and Production of Fluent Speech*. Hillsdale, N.J.: Lawrence Erlbaum.

Feldman, H., S. Goldin-Meadow, and L. Gleitman. 1977. Beyond Herodotus: The creation of language by linguistically deprived deaf children. In A. Lock, ed., *Action, Gesture, and Symbol: The Emergence of Language*. New York: Academic Press.

Fiengo, R. 1974. Semantic conditions on surface structure. Doctoral dissertation, Massachusetts Institute of Technology.

Fiengo, R. 1977. On trace theory. *Linguistic Inquiry* 8, 35–61.

Fodor, J. A., T. G. Bever, and M. F. Garrett. 1974. *The Psychology of Language: An Introduction to Psycholinguistics and Generative Grammar*. New York: McGraw-Hill.

Fodor, J. A., and J. D. Fodor. 1980. Functional structure, quantifiers, and meaning postulates. *Linguistic Inquiry* 11, 759–770.

Fodor, J. A., K. I. Forster, M. F. Garrett, and D. T. Hakes. 1974. A relation between syntax and respiration. Quarterly Progress Report No. 113. Research Laboratory of Electronics, Massachusetts Institute of Technology.

Fodor, J. D. 1978. Parsing strategies and constraints on transformations. *Linguistic Inquiry* 9, 427–473.

Fodor, J. D., and L. Frazier. 1980. Is the human sentence parsing mechanism an ATN? *Cognition* 8, 417–459.

Ford, M., and V. M. Holmes. 1978. Planning units and syntax in sentence production. *Cognition* 6, 35–53.

Fraser, B. 1974. *The Verb-Particle Construction in English*. New York: Academic Press.

Frazier, L., and J. D. Fodor. 1978. The sausage machine: A new two-stage parsing model. *Cognition* 6, 291–325.

Freidin, R. 1974. Transformations and interpretive semantics. In R. Shuy and N. Bailey, eds., *Towards Tomorrow's Linguistics*. Washington, D.C.: Georgetown University Press.

Freidin, R. 1975. The analysis of passives. *Language* 51, 384–405.

Friðjónsson, J. 1977. Um sagnfyllinga með nafnhætti. *Gripla* II.

Gazdar, G. To appear. Unbounded dependencies and coordinate structure. *Linguistic Inquiry* 12.2.

Gazdar, G. To appear b. Phrase structure grammar. In P. Jacobson and G. K. Pullum, eds., *The Nature of Syntactic Representation*. Dordrecht: Reidel.

Gleason, H. A. 1965. *Linguistics and English Grammar*. New York: Holt, Rinehart and Winston.

Godard, D. Forthcoming. Relative clauses in French. Doctoral dissertation, University of Pennsylvania.

Gold, E. M. 1967. Language identification in the limit. *Information and Control* 16, 447–474.

Goldman-Eisler, F. 1968. *Psycholinguistics: Experiments in Spontaneous Speech*. New York and London: Academic Press.

Goldman-Eisler, F. 1972. Pauses, clauses, sentences. *Language and Speech* 15, 103–113.

Greeno, J., M. Riley, and R. Gelman. To appear. Young children's counting and understanding of principles. *Cognitive Psychology*.

Grimshaw, J. 1979a. Complement selection and the lexicon. *Linguistic Inquiry* 10, 279–326.

Grimshaw, J. 1979b. The structure-preserving constraint: A review of *A Transformational Approach to English Syntax* by J. E. Emonds. *Linguistic Analysis* 5, 313–343.

Grimshaw, J. 1981. Subcategorization and grammatical relations. Paper presented at the Harvard Mini-Conference on the Representation of Grammatical Relations, Harvard University, 12 December 1981. Also in A. Zaenen, ed. 1982. *Subjects and Other Subjects: Proceedings of the Harvard Conference on the Representation of Grammatical Relations, December 1981*. Bloomington, Ind.: Indiana University Linguistics Club.

Grimshaw, J. In press. Form, function, and the language acquisition device. In C. L. Baker and J. McCarthy, eds., *The Logical Problem of Language Acquisition*. Cambridge, Mass.: The MIT Press.

Grimshaw, J. In preparation. Phrase structure and subcategorization.

Gross, M. 1968. *Grammaire transformationnelle du français. Syntaxe du verbe*. Paris: Larousse.

Gross, M. 1975. *Méthode en syntaxe*. Paris: Hermann.

Grosu, A., and S. Thompson. 1977. Constraints on the distribution of NP clauses. *Language* 53, 104–115.

Gruber, J. 1965. Studies in lexical relations. Doctoral dissertation, Massachusetts Institute of Technology.

Guéron, J. 1980. On the syntax and semantics of PP extraposition. *Linguistic Inquiry* 11, 637–678.

Hakuta, K. 1979. Comprehension and production of simple and complex sentences by Japanese children. Doctoral dissertation, Harvard University.

Hale, K. 1978. Obviation in modern Irish. Ms., Department of Linguistics and Philosophy, Massachusetts Institute of Technology.

Hale, K. 1979. On the position of Walbiri in a typology of the base. Blooming-ton, Ind.: Indiana University Linguistics Club.

Hale, K. To appear. Preliminary remarks on configurationality. In J. Pustejov-sky and P. Sells, eds., *Proceedings of the Twelfth Annual Meeting of NELS,* Graduate Linguistics Student Association, University of Massachusetts at Amherst.

Halle, M., J. Bresnan, and G. A. Miller, eds. 1978. *Linguistic Theory and Psychological Reality.* Cambridge, Mass.: The MIT Press.

Halliday, M. 1967. Notes on transitivity and theme. *Journal of Linguistics* 1, 37–81.

Halvorsen, P.-K. 1980. Modelling linguistic behavior: Notes on the computa-tional modelling of theories of syntactic and semantic processing. Paper pre-sented at the Symposia on Models in Linguistics, Oslo and Telemark, Norway.

Halvorsen, P.-K. 1982. Semantics for lexical-functional grammar. Ms., Center for Cognitive Science, Massachusetts Institute of Technology.

Halvorsen, P.-K. Forthcoming. An interpretation procedure for functional structures. Ms., Center for Cognitive Science, Massachusetts Institute of Technology.

Halvorsen, P.-K. In preparation. Formal and functional explanations in seman-tics. The theory of adverbs.

Hamburger, H., and K. Wexler. 1975. A mathematical theory of learning trans-formational grammar. *Journal of Mathematical Psychology* 12, 137–177.

Hankamer, J., and I. Sag. 1976. Deep and surface anaphora. *Linguistic Inquiry* 7, 391–428.

Hawkins, P. R. 1971. The syntactic location of hesitation pauses. *Language and Speech* 14, 277–288.

Hériau, M. 1976. Le verbe impersonnel en français moderne. Thèse de doc-torat d'état, Université de Haut-Bretagne, Rennes.

Hintikka, J. 1974. Quantifiers vs. quantification theory. *Linguistic Inquiry* 5, 153–177.

Hintikka, J. 1979. Quantifiers in natural languages. In E. Saarinen, ed., *Game Theoretical Semantics.* Dordrecht: Reidel.

Hintikka, J. 1980. On the *any*-thesis and the methodology of linguistics. *Lin-guistics and Philosophy* 4, 101–122.

Hoehle, T. 1978. *Lexikalistische Syntax: Die aktiv-passiv Relation und andere Infinitkonstruktionen im Deutschen.* Tübingen: Niemeyer.

Holmes, V. M. 1979. Some hypotheses about syntactic processing in sentence comprehension. In W. E. Cooper and E. C. T. Walker, eds., *Sentence Process-ing: Psycholinguistic Studies Presented to Merrill Garrett.* Hillsdale, N.J.: Law-rence Erlbaum.

Holmes, V. M. 1981. Processing surface structurally ambiguous sentences. Paper presented at the Eighth Experimental Psychology Conference, The University of Adelaide, May 1981.

Hopcroft, J., and J. Ullman. 1969. *Formal Languages and Their Relation to Automata*. Menlo Park, Calif.: Addison-Wesley.

Horning, J. 1969. A study of grammatical inference. Technical Report No. CS 139. Computer Science Department, Stanford University.

Hornstein, N. 1977. S and X' convention. *Linguistic Analysis* 3, 137–176.

Hornstein, N., and A. Weinberg. To appear. Case theory and preposition stranding. *Linguistic Inquiry* 12.1.

Huang, J. 1980. Topicalization and relativization in Chinese. Ms., Massachusetts Institute of Technology.

Hust, J. 1977. The syntax of the unpassive construction in English. *Linguistic Analysis* 3, 31–63.

Hust, J. 1978. Lexical redundancy rules and the unpassive construction. *Linguistic Analysis* 4, 61–89.

Huybregts, M. 1976. Overlapping dependencies in Dutch. In G. de Haan and W. Zonneveld, eds., *Utrecht Working Papers in Linguistics*. Instituut A. W. de Groot voor Algemene Taalwetenschap, Utrecht.

Jackendoff, R. 1972. *Semantic Interpretation in Generative Grammar*. Cambridge, Mass.: The MIT Press.

Jackendoff, R. 1975. Morphological and semantic regularities in the lexicon. *Language* 51, 639–671.

Jackendoff, R. 1976. Toward an explanatory semantic representation. *Linguistic Inquiry* 7, 89–150.

Jackendoff, R. 1977. $\overline{X}$ *Syntax: A Study of Phrase Structure*. Linguistic Inquiry Monograph 2. Cambridge, Mass.: The MIT Press.

Jakobson, R. 1932. Zur Struktur des Russischen Verbums. *Charisteria V. Mathesis oblata*, 74–83. Reprinted in E. P. Hamp, F. W. Householder, and R. Austerlitz, eds. 1966. *Readings in Linguistics II*. Chicago: University of Chicago Press.

Jakobson, R. 1936. Beitrag zur allgemeinen Kasuslehre. *Travaux du Cercle Linguistique de Prague* 1936, 240–299. Reprinted in E. P. Hamp, F. W. Householder, and R. Austerlitz, eds. 1966. *Readings in Linguistics II*. Chicago: University of Chicago Press.

Jakobson, R. 1963. Les embrayeurs, les catégories verbales et le verbe russe. *Essais de linguistique générale*. Paris: Editions de Minuit.

Jakobson, R. 1971. Morfologičeskie nabljudenija nad slavjanskim skloneniem. *American Contributions to the IVth International Congress of Slavists*. The Hague: Mouton.

Jenkins, L. 1972. Modality in English syntax. Doctoral dissertation, Massachusetts Institute of Technology.

Kajita, M. 1968. *A Generative-Transformational Study of Semi-Auxiliaries in Present-Day American English*. Tokyo: Sanseido.

Kaplan, R. M. 1972. Augmented transition networks as psychological models of sentence comprehension. *Artificial Intelligence* 3, 77–100.

Kaplan, R. M. 1973a. A general syntactic processor. In R. Rustin, ed., *Natural Language Processing*. New York: Algorithmics Press.

Kaplan, R. M. 1973b. A multi-processing approach to natural language. In *Proceedings of the 1973 National Computer Conference*. Montvale, N.Y.: AFIPS Press.

Kaplan, R. M. 1975. Transient processing load in relative clauses. Doctoral dissertation, Harvard University.

Kaplan, R. M. 1975b. On process models for sentence comprehension. In D. Norman and D. Rumelhart, eds., *Explorations in Cognition*. San Francisco: Freeman.

Kaplan, R. M. 1978. ATNs and what to do about them. Colloquium presented at Bolt, Beranek, and Newman, Cambridge, Mass.

Kaplan, R. M. 1980. Computational resources and linguistic theory. Paper presented at the Second Theoretical Issues in Natural Language Processing Conference, Urbana, Illinois, July 1978. Also in G. Lavendel, ed., *A Decade of Research*. New York: Bowker.

Kaplan, R. M. 1981. Active chart parsing. Technical Report, Xerox Palo Alto Research Center. Also presented at the Modelling Human Parsing Strategies symposium, The Center for Cognitive Science, The University of Texas, Austin, March 1981.

Kay, M. 1979. Functional grammar. In *Proceedings of the Fifth Annual Meeting of the Berkeley Linguistics Society*. University of California, Berkeley.

Kayne, R. S. 1975. *French Syntax*. Cambridge, Mass.: The MIT Press.

Kayne, R. S. 1979. Rightward NP movement in French and English. *Linguistic Inquiry* 10, 710–719.

Keenan, E. L. 1976. Towards a universal definition of subject. In C. N. Li, ed., *Subject and Topic*. New York: Academic Press.

Keenan, E. L. 1980. Passive is phrasal not (sentential or lexical). In T. Hoekstra, H. van der Hulst, and M. Moortgat, eds., *Lexical Grammar*. Dordrecht: Foris.

Kenny, A. 1963. *Action, Emotion, and Will*. London: Routledge and Kegan Paul.

Kimball, J. 1973. Seven principles of surface parsing in natural language. *Cognition* 2, 15–47.

Kiparsky, P. 1973. Elsewhere in phonology. In S. R. Anderson and P. Kiparsky, eds., *A Festschrift for Morris Halle*. New York: Holt, Rinehart and Winston.

Kiparsky, P. In preparation. Analogy. Ms., Department of Linguistics and Philosophy, Massachusetts Institute of Technology.

Kirby, K. M. 1979. Structural ambiguity and sentence processing. Master's thesis, The University of Melbourne.

Kirk, R. E. 1968. *Experimental Design: Procedures for the Behavioral Sciences*. Belmont, Calif.: Brooks/Cole.

Kisala, J. In preparation. Thematically-conditioned control phenomena in nominals. Ms., Department of Linguistics and Philosophy, Massachusetts Institute of Technology.

Klavans, J. 1982. Configuration in nonconfigurational languages. Paper presented at the First Annual West Coast Conference on Formal Linguistics, Stanford University, January 1982; to appear in the Proceedings.

Klenin, E. R. 1974. Russian reflexive pronouns and the semantic roles of noun phrases in sentences. Doctoral dissertation, Princeton University.

Kuno, S. 1973. Constraints on internal clauses and sentential subjects. *Linguistic Inquiry* 4, 363–386.

Lakoff, G. 1970. *Irregularity in Syntax*. New York: Holt, Rinehart and Winston.

Lapointe, S. G. 1978. A nontransformational approach to French clitics. In E. Battistella, ed., *Proceedings of the Ninth Annual Meeting of NELS. CUNY Forum Papers in Linguistics* 7–8, 33–44.

Lapointe, S. G. 1980. A theory of grammatical agreement. Doctoral dissertation, University of Massachusetts at Amherst.

Lehiste, I. 1970. *Suprasegmentals*. Cambridge, Mass.: The MIT Press.

Levelt, W. J. M. 1974. *Formal Grammars in Linguistics and Psycholinguistics*. 3 vols. The Hague: Mouton.

Levin, L., M. Rappaport, and A. Zaenen, eds. To appear. *Papers in LFG*. Bloomington, Ind.: Indiana University Linguistics Club.

Levin, L., and J. Simpson. 1981. Quirky case and lexical representations of Icelandic verbs. Paper presented at the Chicago Linguistic Society, 30 April 1981.

Lieber, R. 1978. Toward a theory of case. Ms., Massachusetts Institute of Technology.

Lieber, R. 1979. Inflection and the lexicon. Ms., Department of Linguistics and Philosophy, Massachusetts Institute of Technology.

References   843

Lieber, R. 1980. The organization of the lexicon. Doctoral dissertation, Massachusetts Institute of Technology.

Lieberman, P. 1965. On the acoustic basis of the perception of intonation by linguists. *Word* 21, 40–54.

McCloskey, J. 1979. *Transformational Syntax and Model Theoretic Semantics: A Case Study in Modern Irish.* Dordrecht: Reidel.

McCloskey, J. 1980. Is there raising in modern Irish? *Eriu* 31, 59–99.

McCloskey, J. 1981. Notes on case and control in modern Irish. Ms., Department of Irish, University College Dublin.

Macnamara, J. 1972. Cognitive basis for language learning in infants. *Psychological Review* 79, 1–13.

Maling, J. 1980. Transitive adjectives: A case of categorial reanalysis. Paper presented at the Fourth Groningen Round Table, "Problems in the Identification of Natural Categories," 4–8 July 1980. To appear in F. Heny, ed., *Linguistic Categories: Auxiliaries and Related Puzzles.* Dordrecht: Reidel.

Maling, J., and A. Zaenen. 1978. On the nonuniversality of a surface filter. *Linguistic Inquiry* 9, 475–497.

Maling, J., and A. Zaenen. 1979. Germanic word order and the format of surface filters. Revision of paper presented at the Amsterdam Colloquium on Local Constraints, April 1978. Published in F. Heny, ed. 1981. *Binding and Filtering.* London: Croom Helm.

Maling, J., and A. Zaenen. 1980. Notes on base-generation and unbounded dependencies. Paper presented at the Sloan Workshop on Alternatives to Transformational Grammar, Stanford University.

Maling, J., and A. Zaenen. To appear. A base-generated account of "extraction phenomena" in Scandinavian languages. In P. Jacobson and G. K. Pullum, eds., *The Nature of Syntactic Representation.* Dordrecht: Reidel.

Manzini, R. 1980. On control. Ms., Department of Linguistics and Philosophy, Massachusetts Institute of Technology.

Marantz, A. 1981. On the nature of grammatical relations. Doctoral dissertation, Massachusetts Institute of Technology.

Maratsos, M. 1978. New models in linguistics and language acquisition. In M. Halle, J. Bresnan, and G. A. Miller, eds., *Linguistic Theory and Psychological Reality.* Cambridge, Mass.: The MIT Press.

Maratsos, M., and M. A. Chalkley. In press. The internal language of children's syntax: The ontogenesis and representation of syntactic categories. In K. E. Nelson, ed., *Child Language.* Vol. 2. New York: Gardner Press.

Marcus, M. 1980. *A Theory of Syntactic Recognition for Natural Languages.* Cambridge, Mass.: The MIT Press.

Martin, R. 1970. La transformation impersonnelle. *Revue de Linguistique Romane* 34, 337–394.

Masica, C. P. 1976. *Defining a Linguistic Area: South East Asia.* Chicago: University of Chicago Press.

Matthews, R. 1979. Are the grammatical sentences of a language a recursive set? *Synthese* 40, 209–224.

Matthews, R. 1982. Knowledge of language in a theory of language processing. Paper presented at the conference on Constraints on Modelling Real-Time Processes, Marseilles, France, 21–26 June 1982, sponsored by the Max-Planck-Institute for Psycholinguistics, Nijmegen, and the Center for Psychosocial Research, Chicago.

Mickelson, L. R. 1968. Impersonal sentences in Russian. *American Contributions to the VIth International Congress of Slavists.* The Hague: Mouton.

Miller, G. A. 1962. Some psychological studies of grammar. *American Psychologist* 17, 748–762.

Miller, G. A. 1978. Semantic relations among words. In M. Halle, J. Bresnan, and G. A. Miller, eds., *Linguistic Theory and Psychological Reality.* Cambridge, Mass.: The MIT Press.

Miller, G. A., and P. Johnson-Laird. 1976. *Language and Perception.* Cambridge, Mass.: Harvard University Press.

Miller, G. A., and K. McKean. 1964. A chronometric study of some relations between sentences. *Quarterly Journal of Experimental Psychology* 16, 297–308.

Milsark, G. L. 1977. Toward an explanation of certain peculiarities of the existential construction in English. *Linguistic Analysis* 3, 1–29.

Mohanan, K. P. 1981a. Move NP or lexical rules: Evidence from Malayalam causativization. Ms., Department of Linguistics and Philosophy, Massachusetts Institute of Technology.

Mohanan, K. P. 1981b. Grammatical and anaphoric control. Ms., Department of Linguistics and Philosophy, Massachusetts Institute of Technology.

Mohanan, K. P. 1982. Lexical phonology. Doctoral dissertation, Massachusetts Institute of Technology.

Mohanan, K. P. To appear. Grammatical relations and anaphora in Malayalam. In A. Marantz and T. Stowell, eds., *MIT Working Papers in Syntax.* Department of Linguistics and Philosophy, Massachusetts Institute of Technology.

Mohanan, K. P. To appear a. Infinitival subjects, government, and abstract case. *Linguistic Inquiry* 13.2.

Montague, R. 1973. On the proper treatment of quantification in ordinary English. In J. Hintikka, J. Moravcsik, and P. Suppes, eds., *Approaches to Natural Language.* Dordrecht: Reidel.

Montalbetti, M. 1981. Consistency and clitics. Ms., Department of Linguistics and Philosophy, Massachusetts Institute of Technology.

Morgan, J. 1972. Verb agreement as a rule of English. In P. Peranteau, J. Levi, and G. Phares, eds., *Papers from the Eighth Regional Meeting of the Chicago Linguistic Society*. University of Chicago.

Morin, Y.-C. 1978. Interprétation des pronoms et des réfléchis en français. *Cahiers de Linguistique de L'UQUAM*, Montreal.

Napoli, D.J. 1973. The two *si*'s of Italian. Doctoral dissertation, Harvard University.

Nash, D. 1980. Topics in Walbiri grammar. Doctoral dissertation, Massachusetts Institute of Technology.

Neidle, C. In preparation. The role of case in Russian syntax. Doctoral dissertation, Massachusetts Institute of Technology.

Nelson, G., and D. Oppen. 1977. Fast decision procedures based on congruence closure. In *Proceedings of the 18th Annual Symposium on Foundations of Computer Science*, Providence, October 1977.

Oehrle, R. 1976. The grammatical status of the English dative alternation. Doctoral dissertation, Massachusetts Institute of Technology.

Olivier, D. 1968. Stochastic grammars and language acquisition mechanisms. Doctoral dissertation, Harvard University.

Ostler, N. P. M. 1976. Aspects of case-agreement in Ancient Greek. Ms., Massachusetts Institute of Technology.

Ostler, N. P. M. 1979. Case linking: A theory of case and verb diathesis. Doctoral dissertation, Massachusetts Institute of Technology.

Partee, B., ed. 1976. *Montague Grammar*. New York: Academic Press.

Perlmutter, D. 1971. *Deep and Surface Structure Constraints in Syntax*. New York: Holt, Rinehart and Winston.

Perlmutter, D., ed. In press. *Studies in Relational Grammar*. Chicago: University of Chicago Press.

Perlmutter, D., and P. Postal. 1977. Toward a universal characterization of passivization. In *Proceedings of the Third Annual Meeting of the Berkeley Linguistics Society*. University of California, Berkeley.

Peters, S. 1973. On restricting deletion transformations. In M. Gross, M. Halle, and M.-P. Schützenberger, eds., *The Formal Analysis of Natural Language*. The Hague: Mouton.

Peters, S., and R. Ritchie. 1973. On the generative power of transformational grammars. *Information Sciences* 6, 49–83.

Peterson, P. 1981a. Conjunction in LFG. Ms., Center for Cognitive Science, Massachusetts Institute of Technology.

Peterson, P. 1981b. The progressive construction in English: An analysis and its implications. Doctoral dissertation, University of Newcastle, New South Wales.

Pimenta-Bueno, M. 1976. A proposal for a unified treatment of reflexive, reciprocal, intrinsic and impersonal *se* in Portuguese. Ms., Stanford University.

Pinker, S. 1978. Mind and brain revisited: Forestalling the doom of cognitivism (Commentary on J. Haugeland's "The nature and plausibility of cognitivism"). *The Behavioral and Brain Sciences* 2, 244–245.

Pinker, S. 1979. Formal models of language learning. *Cognition* 7, 217–283.

Pinker, S. In press. Further thoughts on language learnability (Comments on the paper by Wexler). In C. L. Baker and J. McCarthy, eds., *The Logical Problem of Language Acquisition*. Cambridge, Mass.: The MIT Press.

Pinker, S., and D. Lebeaux. 1981. *Language Learnability and Language Development*. Forthcoming from Harvard University Press, Cambridge, Mass.

Pollock, J.-Y. 1978. Trace theory and French syntax. In S. J. Keyser, ed., *Recent Transformational Studies in European Languages*. Linguistic Inquiry Monograph 3. Cambridge, Mass.: The MIT Press.

Postal, P. 1964. *Constituent Structure*. Bloomington, Ind.: Indiana University Press.

Postal, P. 1971. *Cross-over Phenomena*. New York: Holt, Rinehart and Winston.

Postal, P. 1974. *On Raising: One Rule of English Grammar and Its Theoretical Implications*. Cambridge, Mass.: The MIT Press.

Postal, P. 1977. About a "nonargument" for raising. *Linguistic Inquiry* 8, 141–154.

Postal, P. 1979. Some arc pair grammar descriptions. To appear in P. Jacobson and G. K. Pullum, eds., *The Nature of Syntactic Representation*. Dordrecht: Reidel.

Pranka, P. 1979. *Se* constructions in Spanish. Ms., Massachusetts Institute of Technology.

Pul'kina, I., and E. Zakhava-Nekrasova. n.d. *Russian (A Practical Grammar with Exercises)*. Moscow: Progress Publishers.

Pullum, G. K. 1982. Free word order and phrase structure rules. In J. Pustejovsky and P. Sells, eds., *Proceedings of the Twelfth Annual Meeting of NELS*. Graduate Linguistics Student Association, University of Massachusetts at Amherst.

Pullum, G. K., and P. Postal. 1979. On an inadequate defense of "trace theory." *Linguistic Inquiry* 10, 689–706.

Putnam, H. 1961. Some issues in the theory of grammar. *Proceedings of Symposia on Applied Mathematics,* vol. 12. American Mathematical Society.

Quicoli, A. C. 1972a. Aspects of Portuguese complementation. Doctoral dissertation, State University of New York at Buffalo.

Quicoli, A. C. 1972b. Remarks on case agreement in ancient Greek. Ms., Massachusetts Institute of Technology.

Quine, W. V. O. 1960. *Word and Object*. Cambridge, Mass.: The MIT Press.

Rappaport, G. C. 1978. Two types of subject control in Russian. Paper presented at the Winter LSA Meeting, Boston, Mass.

Rappaport, G. C. 1979. Detachment and adverbial participle clauses in Russian. Doctoral dissertation, University of California, Los Angeles.

Rappaport, M. 1979. On the subject of "object" in modern Hebrew. Ms., Department of Linguistics and Philosophy, Massachusetts Institute of Technology.

Rappaport, M. 1980. On the derivation of derived nominals. Ms., Department of Linguistics and Philosophy, Massachusetts Institute of Technology. To appear in L. Levin, M. Rappaport, and A. Zaenen, eds., *Papers in LFG*. Bloomington, Ind.: Indiana University Linguistics Club.

Reinhart, T. 1976. The syntactic domain of anaphora. Doctoral dissertation, Massachusetts Institute of Technology.

Rich, C. 1975. On the psychological reality of Augmented Transition Network models of sentence comprehension. Ms., Massachusetts Institute of Technology.

Riemsdijk, H. van. 1978. *A Case Study in Syntactic Markedness*. Lisse: The Peter de Ridder Press.

Rivas, A. 1977. A theory of clitics. Doctoral dissertation, Massachusetts Institute of Technology.

Rizzi, L. 1976. La MONTEE DU SUJET, le *si* impersonnel et une règle de restructuration dans la syntaxe italienne. *Recherches Linguistiques* 4, 158–184.

Rizzi, L. 1978. A restructuring rule in Italian syntax. In S. J. Keyser, ed., *Recent Transformational Studies in European Languages*. Linguistic Inquiry Monograph 3. Cambridge, Mass.: The MIT Press.

Roberts, J. 1981. Toward a unified analysis of passive in Navajo. Ms., Department of Linguistics and Philosophy, Massachusetts Institute of Technology.

Roberts, P. 1964. *English Syntax: A Book of Programmed Lessons*. Alternate edition. New York: Harcourt, Brace and World.

Robertson, J. 1976. The structure of pronoun incorporation in the Mayan verbal complex. Doctoral dissertation, Harvard University. Published 1980 New York: Garland Press.

Rochester, S. R., and J. Gill. 1973. Production of complex sentences in monologues and dialogues. *Journal of Verbal Learning and Verbal Behavior* 12, 203–210.

Rochette, A. 1980. French infinitival complements. Syntax generals paper, Massachusetts Institute of Technology.

Roeper, T., J. Bing, S. Lapointe, and S. Tavakolian. 1979. A lexical approach to language acquisition. Ms., University of Massachusetts at Amherst.

Roeper, T., and M. E. A. Siegel. 1978. A lexical transformation for verbal compounds. *Linguistic Inquiry* 9, 199–260.

Rosen, C. 1976. Guess what about. In A. Ford, J. Reighard, and R. Singh, eds., *Proceedings of the Sixth Annual Meeting of NELS*. Department of Linguistics, University of Montreal.

Rosenbaum, P. S. 1967. *The grammar of English predicate complement constructions*. Cambridge, Mass.: The MIT Press.

Ross, J. R. 1967. Constraints on variables in syntax. Doctoral dissertation, Massachusetts Institute of Technology. Bloomington, Ind.: Indiana University Linguistics Club.

Ross, J. R. 1969. Guess who. In R. I. Binnick, A. Davison, G. Green, and J. Morgan, eds., *Papers from the Fifth Regional Meeting of the Chicago Linguistic Society*. University of Chicago.

Ross, J. R. 1969a. A proposed rule of tree-pruning. In D. Reibel and S. Schane, eds., *Modern Studies in English*. Englewood Cliffs, N.J.: Prentice-Hall.

Rothstein, S. 1981. On preposition stranding. Ms., Department of Linguistics and Philosophy, Massachusetts Institute of Technology.

Rouveret, A., and J.-R. Vergnaud. 1980. Specifying reference to the subject: French causatives and conditions on representations. *Linguistic Inquiry* 11, 97–202.

Ruwet, N. 1972. *Théorie syntaxique et syntaxe du français*. Paris: Seuil.

Selkirk, E. 1981. English word structure. Ms., University of Massachusetts at Amherst.

Sheldon, A. 1974. The role of parallel function in the acquisition of relative clauses in English. *Journal of Verbal Learning and Verbal Behavior* 13, 272–281.

Shopen, T. 1972. A generative theory of ellipsis: A consideration of the linguistic uses of silence. Doctoral dissertation, University of California, Los Angeles. Bloomington, Ind.: Indiana University Linguistics Club.

Siegel, D. 1973. Nonsources of unpassives. In J. Kimball, ed., *Syntax and Semantics*. Vol. 2. New York: Seminar Press.

Siegel, D. 1974. Topics in English morphology. Doctoral dissertation, Massachusetts Institute of Technology.

Simpson, J. 1980. Ngarluma as a W* language. Ms., Massachusetts Institute of Technology.

Simpson, J. In preparation. Control and predication in Warlpiri. Doctoral dissertation, Massachusetts Institute of Technology.

Simpson, J., and J. Bresnan. 1982. Control and obviation in Warlpiri. Paper presented at the First Annual West Coast Conference on Formal Linguistics, Stanford University, January 1982; to appear in the Proceedings.

Slobin, D. I. 1966. Grammatical transformations and sentence comprehension in children and adulthood. *Journal of Verbal Learning and Verbal Behavior* 5, 219–227.

Slobin, D. I. 1973. Cognitive prerequisites for the development of grammar. In C. Ferguson and D. I. Slobin, eds., *Studies in Child Language Development.* New York: Holt, Rinehart and Winston.

Slobin, D. I. 1979. The role of language in language acquisition. Invited address at the meeting of the Eastern Psychological Association, Philadelphia, April 1979.

Slobin, D. I. In press. Universal and particular in the acquisition of language. In L. Gleitman and E. Wanner, eds., *Language Acquisition: The State of the Art.* Cambridge: Cambridge University Press.

Smith, C. 1978. The syntax and interpretation of temporal expressions. *Linguistics and Philosophy* 2, 43–99.

Solan, L., and T. Roeper. 1978. Children's use of syntactic structure in interpreting relative clauses. In H. Goodluck and L. Solan, eds., *Papers in the Structure and Development of Child Language.* University of Massachusetts Occasional Papers in Linguistics, vol. 4. University of Massachusetts at Amherst.

Sorensen, H. C. 1957. *Studies on Case in Russian.* Copenhagen: Rosenkilde og Bagger.

Sridhar, S. 1979. New evidence for spontaneous demotion. *South Asian Languages Analysis* 1.

Stowell, T. 1978. What was there before there was there. In D. Farkas, W. M. Jacobsen, and K. W. Todrys, eds., *Papers from the Fourteenth Regional Meeting of the Chicago Linguistic Society.* University of Chicago.

Stowell, T. 1980. Subjects across categories. Ms., Massachusetts Institute of Technology.

Stowell, T. 1981. Origins of phrase structure. Doctoral dissertation, Massachusetts Institute of Technology.

Stump, G. 1981. The syntax and semantics of free adjuncts and absolutes. Doctoral dissertation, The Ohio State University.

Swinney, D. A. 1979. Lexical access during sentence comprehension: (Re)consideration of context effects. *Journal of Verbal Learning and Verbal Behavior* 18, 645–659.

Tanenhaus, M. K., and J. M. Carroll. 1975. The clausal processing hierarchy . . . and nouniness. In R. E. Grossman, L. J. San, and T. J. Vance, eds., *Papers from the Parasession on Functionalism. Chicago Linguistic Society.* Chicago: University of Chicago Press.

Thompson, S. 1973. On subjectless gerunds in English. *Foundations of Language* 9, 374–383.

Thráinsson, H. 1980. *On Complementation in Icelandic.* New York: Garland Press.

Tukey, J. W. 1953. The problem of multiple comparisons. Ms., Princeton University.

Valfells, S. 1970. Middle voice in Icelandic. In H. Benediktsson, ed., *The Nordic Languages and Modern Linguistics.* Reykjavík: Vísindaféleg Íslendinga.

Visser, F. Th. 1963–1973. *An Historical Syntax of the English Language.* Leiden: F. J. Brill.

Wales, R., and H. Toner. 1979. Intonation and ambiguity. In W. E. Cooper and E. C. T. Walker, eds., *Sentence Processing: Psycholinguistic Studies Presented to Merrill Garrett.* Hillsdale, N.J.: Lawrence Erlbaum.

Wanner, E. In press [1980]. The ATN and the sausage machine: Which one is baloney? *Cognition* 8, 209–225.

Wanner, E., and R. M. Kaplan. 1975. Syntactic processes in sentence comprehension. Ms., Harvard University.

Wanner, E., R. M. Kaplan, and S. Shiner. 1975. Garden paths in relative clauses. Ms., Harvard University.

Wanner, E., and M. Maratsos. 1978. An ATN approach to comprehension. In M. Halle, J. Bresnan, and G. A. Miller, eds., *Linguistic Theory and Psychological Reality.* Cambridge, Mass.: The MIT Press.

Wasow, T. 1977. Transformations and the lexicon. In P. W. Culicover, T. Wasow, and A. Akmajian, eds., *Formal Syntax.* New York: Academic Press.

Wasow, T. 1978. Remarks on processing, constraints, and the lexicon. In D. C. Waltz, ed., *Proceedings of the Second Theoretical Issues in Natural Language Processing Conference.* New York: Association for Computing Machinery.

Wasow, T. 1978b. On constraining the class of transformational languages. *Synthese* 39, 81–104.

Wasow, T. 1980. Major and minor rules in lexical grammar. In T. Hoekstra, H. van der Hulst, and M. Moortgat, eds., *Lexical Grammar.* Dordrecht: Foris.

Wasow, T. In press. Comments on the paper by Baker. In C. L. Baker and J. McCarthy, eds., *The Logical Problem of Language Acquisition.* Cambridge, Mass.: The MIT Press.

Wasow, T., and T. Roeper. 1972. On the subject of gerunds. *Foundations of Language* 8, 44–61.

Wehrli, E. 1978. Une analyse interprétative des clitiques. *Recherches Linguistiques à Montréal* 11, 205–225.

Wexler, K., and P. W. Culicover. 1980. *Formal Principles of Language Acquisition.* Cambridge, Mass.: The MIT Press.

Wharton, R. 1977. Grammar enumeration and inference. *Information and Control* 33, 253–272.

Williams, E. 1977. Discourse and logical form. *Linguistic Inquiry* 8, 101–139.

Williams, E. 1980. Passive. Ms., University of Massachusetts at Amherst.

Williams, E. 1980a. Predication. *Linguistic Inquiry* 11, 203–238.

Williams, E. 1982. Against small clauses. Ms., University of Massachusetts at Amherst.

Winer, B. J. 1970. *Statistical Principles in Experimental Design.* International student edition. London: McGraw-Hill.

Winograd, T. Forthcoming. *Language as a Cognitive Process.* Reading, Mass.: Addison-Wesley.

Wolff, J. 1977. The discovery of segments in natural language. *British Journal of Psychology* 68, 97–106.

Woods, W. 1970. Transition network grammars for natural language analysis. *Communications of the ACM* 13, 591–606.

Wright, W. 1971. *A Grammar of the Arabic Language.* Cambridge: Cambridge University Press.

Yokoyama, O. T. 1979. Studies in Russian functional syntax. Doctoral dissertation, Harvard University.

Zaenen, A. 1980. Extraction rules in Icelandic. Doctoral dissertation, Harvard University.

Zaenen, A. 1981. Characterizing syntactic binding domains. Occasional Paper No. 17. Center for Cognitive Science, Massachusetts Institute of Technology.

Zoega, G. T. 1951. *Íslenzk-Ensk Orðabók.* Reykjavík: Bókaverziun Sigurða Kristjánssonar.

List of Symbols

Angle bracket notation	$\langle\ \rangle$
	$\langle\ \rangle \ldots \langle\ \rangle$
Box notation	$\Box$
Brace notation	$\{\ \}$
Equations,	
constraining	$=_c$
defining	$=$
Kleene star notation	$*$
Linking schema	$\Uparrow\ =\ \Downarrow$
Metavariable,	
bounded domination	$\Uparrow\ ,\ \Downarrow$
immediate domination	$\uparrow\ ,\ \downarrow$
Metavariable category subscript notation	$\Downarrow_x\ ,\ \Uparrow_x$
Parenthesis notation	(x)
	$((x\ y)\ z)$
	$\begin{matrix}(x)\\y\end{matrix}$
Root node category superscript notation	$\Downarrow^x$

Set value notation $\in$

Square bracket notation $[\ ]$

Superscript notation $^i[\ ]$

Name Index

Subject Index